JAPAN & BELGIUM

JAPAN & BELGIUM

An Itinerary of Mutual Inspiration

W.F. Vande Walle editor
David De Cooman assistant editor

LANNOO

FOREWORD

The year 2016 marks the 150th anniversary of friendship between Japan and Belgium and I cannot think of a better way to conclude this year than with the publication of this magnificent book.

The diplomatic relations between our two countries started in 1866, at the very end of the Edo period, during which Japan's interaction with the outside world was quite limited. This was a mere twelve years after the Tokugawa Government first concluded diplomatic ties with the USA in 1854. Belgium became Japan's ninth international partner. Ever since then our bilateral relations have always been marked by mutual trust, friendship in times of need, and solidarity.

In the process of its modernization, Japan learned a lot from Belgium. It was from Belgium that Japan took the model for its central bank. The Japanese glass industry adopted techniques to make flat glass from Belgium, and now one of the leading Japanese glass companies has a large investment in Belgium. Since the Great East Japan Earthquake in 2011, thanks to the goodwill of Belgian and Japanese volunteers, the Fukko (Reconstruction) Concert has been organized on 11 March each year. When Prime Minster Abe visited Belgium this year, he went directly from the airport to the Maelbeek metro station, to lay a wreath on the site where innocent civilians had lost their lives in the 22 March terrorist attacks.

The highlight of this memorable year was the state visit of their Majesties King Philippe and Queen Mathilde to Japan in October. Having followed their majesties' delegation, I was once again extremely impressed by the warm and close relationship existing at the top level of our two countries. At the same time, the friendship between our two countries is embedded in exchanges from people to people. Almost all varieties of the martial arts of Japan (*budō*) enjoy a high level of popularity in Belgium, while at present seven Japanese cities host Belgian Beer weekends.

In view of all these bonds, I have no doubt that our friendship will last for many more centuries to come, and that it will continue to be characterized by mutual trust, friendship in times of need, and solidarity. In order to ensure this, it is always useful to learn from past history. For that purpose, the reader now has the best material in his or her hand. Please do enjoy reading this work so that you may become another engine for strengthening our friendship. Welcome to the club!

Masafumi Ishii
Ambassador of Japan to the Kingdom of Belgium

< Porcelain baluster-shaped flower vase, decorated with peonies and birds in cobalt blue under the glaze, bearing the seal of Seifū Yohei III (1851-1914) on the bottom. The vase, roughly a half meter high, was exhibited at the Paris World Exposition of 1900, and subsequently entered the Imperial Household. After Crown Prince Hirohito's visit to Belgium in 1921 he donated it to the University of Louvain/Leuven. It was shipped to Belgium together with a collection of Japanese books for the university library in 1925.

FOREWORD

A hundred and fifty years ago, Belgium signed a treaty of friendship and trade with Japan. At the time, Belgium was a young, dynamic and progressive country, which around the turn of the century would become one of the biggest industrial economies in the world. In those days, Japan was a new country on the international scene, carrying a great history, tradition and knowledge, and eventually to become one of the largest economies in the world. Both countries knew that forging an international friendship would form the basis for understanding, cooperation and development.

A hundred and fifty years of mutual inspiration have created a common development in our societies. The Asian and Western cultures in Japan and Belgium might be very diverse in many ways, but through respect and cooperation we can call ourselves likeminded countries to whom Freedom, Democracy, Peace and Development are ideas which are not only shared and pursued together on the bilateral field, but also on the multilateral field.

And also today, both countries cherish these significant ideas and pursue these worthy goals.

The commemoration of the 150th anniversary of friendship between our two countries in 2016 has been living proof of this very notion. After 150 years our relations are strong, diversified and forward-looking.

In Japan and in Belgium many festivities took place in all the different facets of our societies. These activities were organized and supported by officials, businesses, academics and artists alike. The highlight of this Year of Commemoration was naturally the royal visit to Japan of King Philippe and Queen Mathilde of the Belgians.

This book provides an excellent contribution to the marking of our 150th year of friendship. The work draws on a remarkable overview of fields of reciprocal collaboration and motivation – at times amazing, unexpected and surprising, but always demonstrating how we have learnt from each other and that we are building upon each other's knowledge and experience.

I would like to express my sincere thanks to Professor Vande Walle for his painstaking efforts in bringing this information together and for having inspired the many authors who have contributed to the engaging result. I wish the readers many cheerful moments in discovering what has grown between our two countries and invite them to invest further in what is yet to come in the relationship between Japan and Belgium.

Gunther Sleeuwagen
Ambassador of Belgium to Japan

CONTENTS

> The room housing the Japanese book donation to the University of Louvain/
Leuven in the university's Central Library.
Picture postcard dating from before the Second World War.
Photograph by Digitaal Labo KU Leuven. Standing on top of the shelves in the background
is the vase donated by Crown Prince Hirohito.

INTRODUCTION

W.F. Vande Walle

When plans were made to celebrate the 150th anniversary of the Treaty of Amity, Commerce and Navigation concluded between Japan and Belgium in 1866, the Celebration Committee set up for the purpose of planning and managing the various celebration events, put forward the idea of publishing a book on the history of Japanese-Belgian relations.

Eleven years earlier, I had edited a book on the same subject, titled *Japan & Belgium: Four Centuries of Exchange*, which was published to mark Belgium's participation in the 2005 Aichi World's Fair. In order to mark Belgium's participation with something "more durable," Robert Gillet, commissioner-general of the Belgian pavilion in that fair, who in a former life had been an editor of art books, had espoused the idea, launched by the Belgian diplomat François Delahaut, to publish a book about the history of Belgian-Japanese relations. I was entrusted with its editorship, and thanks to the contribution of many, and the support of among others the Japan Foundation and the Belgian Ministry of Economic Affairs, the book saw the light of day as a superbly illustrated tome, which had the looks of an art book but dealt with history, admittedly also including art history. It garnered considerable success and turned out to be a long-seller, if not a bestseller, and is now out of print.

It was with this background in mind that I was entrusted with the editorship of the present book. One of the motivations to take on the job was the ambition to do justice in this sequel to various topics which had been left out or had insufficiently been dealt with in the first book. Although we have yet again not been able to include all relevant topics pertaining to the historical relationship between the two countries, we have in some cases ventured outside the glamorous bounds of international diplomacy and high culture, and shed light on a few topics which may at first sight be unexpected, unprepossessing or pedestrian, but are of vital importance to society. Perhaps to the surprise of some readers you will find contributions on the penal system as well as transfer of know-how in the field of agriculture and livestock.

Since the treaty belongs to the history of Belgium as an independent kingdom, the time frame within which we would select our topics automatically narrowed itself down to the nineteenth and twentieth centuries, in contrast to the first book, which had covered the entire span of the history of the Low Countries, the Spanish Netherlands, the Austrian Netherlands and Belgium. The title of the present book, *Japan & Belgium: An Itinerary of Mutual Inspiration*, echoes the title of the former book, and indicates the connection between the two publications.

This book is divided into six parts, which deal respectively with contacts and exchanges in the diplomatic field (first part), Belgian sources for some cases of institutional modernization in Japan (second part), Belgium's image and perception in Japan and the Belgian presence in that country (third part), influences and inspiration in the field of literature (fourth part), and in the fields of applied and decorative arts (fifth part), and finally, the transfer of know-how, including trade and investment in the post-war era (sixth part).

The book includes eighteen contributions of varying length by thirteen authors from Belgium or Japan. The direct occasion being the 150th anniversary of the bilateral treaty, it was only natural that the first part would open with a sizable article on this very topic. By pure coincidence the author, Dirk De Ruyver, happens to live in the Yokohama-Tokyo area, within a stone's throw of the spot in Yokohama where the Belgian legation was located in the 1885-1893 period, and walking distance from the place where Commodore Matthew Perry went ashore to sign the first US treaty with Japan in 1854. In his article, the longest in the book, the author clarifies the circumstances in which the treaty between Belgium and Japan came about, paying particular attention to the conditions prevailing in Yokohama at the time the foreign representatives came knocking at Japan's door pressing for treaty negotiations. The historical scene De Ruyver portrays is not unlike a play unfolding in Yokohama. It had been going on for a while when the Belgian envoy Auguste t' Kint de Roodenbeek entered the scene. The author describes what preceded t' Kint's arrival on the stage, and how the other actors in the play reacted when t' Kint suddenly made his appearance. Moreover, although the players on the scene did have some measure of freedom, there were others behind the scenes who had written the script. Who were they and why did they write the parts as they did? These last two questions were certainly important for Belgium and to some extent also for the four Great Powers that had already concluded treaties with Japan and were now dominating the diplomatic scene. The Belgian-Japanese treaty was the ninth treaty of amity signed by Japan. Had the conclusion of treaties by now become routine for the shogunate or not? How did the negotiations for the Belgian-Japanese treaty compare to the previous treaties entered into by Japan? In order to answer these questions it was crucial for the author to clarify the circumstances in which the treaties of amity had come about, from the first one down to 1866. While previous studies on the first diplomatic contacts between Japan and Belgium were written from a Belgian perspective, De Ruyver's contribution attempts to give more scope to the Japanese perspective, as well as including the reactions of other foreign representatives in Japan, thus giving an international perspective on the Belgian-Japanese treaty of 1866 in the small international cosmos which Yokohama was then.

Yutaka Yabuta's article analyzes the way Belgium was perceived by the first Japanese envoys and students to visit the country in the wake of the Meiji Restoration, notably as they recorded their impressions and reflections in their reports. He makes an assessment of the official record of the Iwakura Mission (1871-1873), singling out Belgium, one of the countries toured by the mission, with a view to shedding light on the concept of the "small nation" as articulated in the early Meiji period. He compares the notion as it is framed in the Iwakura Mission's account with Sufu Kōhei's study of Belgium. Japan, unable to modernize at a single stroke to stand alongside "great powers" on the scale of France or Great Britain, needed to have a "model nation" for a gradualist modernization. In this sense, the "small nation" of Belgium was recognized as being one such "model nation" for Far Eastern, and similarly small, Japan. Belgium was indeed one of the leading nations in the fields of industry and commerce, and at the cutting edge of technological innovation. For countries embarking upon modernization and industrialization, Belgium could constitute an inspiring example. One would expect then that Japan, in the process of acquiring Western know-how, would turn to Belgium. One of the objectives of the articles contained in this book was therefore to explore the Belgian contributions to the modernization of Japan. In spite of the many interesting cases we have identified, we must also admit to a relative lack of Belgian interest in Japan in those days. There was clearly a lack of grasp of the real Japan. The image Belgians had of Japan did not correspond to contemporary economic or social reality. For example, Belgium was not sufficiently informed about the fast progress Japan was making in its modernization efforts. We may ask whether there were enough people with

vision to see the tremendous future potential. Chances are that the Belgians tended to look at Japan as a developing country, just like any other of its kind, purveyor of artisanal and folkloristic items for the curio cabinets of the enlightened European bourgeoisie. Even Belgian diplomatic and consular circles could not always collect all relevant and necessary information. *Japon et Belgique: Revue publiée par La Société d'Etudes Belgo-Japonaise* (1906-1914) did offer interesting and useful information but its readership was too limited and its lifespan too short to foster a real Belgian expertise on Japan.

The first part concludes with an essay by David De Cooman on the Belgian leg of Crown Prince Hirohito's European tour of 1921. In order to appreciate the tour's significance against its historical background, he has not only drawn on official records by first-hand witnesses, but also tapped into sources and recorded observations discussing the deeper issues that were at stake in Japan's domestic politics.

The second part consists of an article on Leuven Central Prison as a model for the modern penal system in Meiji Japan by Keiji Shibai and Dimitri Vanoverbeke, and an article on the influence of the Belgian constitution on the Meiji constitution, by the latter author. In the early Meiji period several Japanese experts from the Ministry of Justice toured Europe to study penitentiary systems. They were especially impressed by the French and Belgian systems. Leuven Prison would eventually serve as the model for Miyagi Prison, the construction of which in 1879 marked a turning point in the history of penal institutions and policy in modern Japan. One of the experts from the Ministry of Justice was Inoue Kowashi, who would later become one of the architects of the Meiji constitution. In his article Dimitri Vanoverbeke explores the early stages of constitutionalism in Japan, making ample reference to the writings of various authors, including the aforementioned Sufu Kōhei and Inoue Kowashi. He clarifies the extent and depth to which the Belgian constitution was a source of inspiration for the Japanese constitution.

The third part of the book is devoted to Japanese perceptions of Belgium and Belgians living in Japan, who helped to shape and influence some of those perceptions. The first article, by myself, is an exploration of some Belgian pictorial sources in the above-mentioned official report of the Iwakura Mission.

From Fumitaka Kurosawa's article on Japanese perceptions of Belgium in the Meiji and Taishō periods it becomes clear that with Japan's victory in the Sino-Japanese War and Russo-Japanese War, Japan attained a ranking on a par with the European and North American great powers. At that point the paradigm of the small state, mentioned above, lost much of its attraction, and there was a marked decrease in the number of authors who refer to Belgium in the early twentieth century.

In his article Ryōju Sakurai deals with several topics: the location of the Belgian legation and consulates; the number of Belgians in Japan, where they lived and what they did; and the relative importance of the bilateral trade between the two countries. The figures adduced in this article seem to bear out a decrease in the relative importance of the mutual trade relations in the period from 1876 to 1938, thus confirming the view that Belgium underachieved in its commercial ties with Japan.

The last article in this part is my study on the linguistic and ethnographic contributions by the scholar-missionary Willem A. Grootaers. He was only one of many scholar-missionaries active in Japan, but his career is remarkable and exceptional in that his scholarship covered both linguistics and ethnography and that he spent major parts of his life respectively in pre-Communist China and in post-war Japan.

The fourth part opens with a translation of the first Japanese critical essay on Belgian literature (1895), written by Ueda Bin, setting the scene for the two following contributions. Sadafumi Muramatsu's study of the way Georges Rodenbach's *Bruges-la-Morte* was transfused in Nagai Kafū's *The River Sumida* is the digest of a book-length in-depth study the author has published on the topic, while in my own study on the reception in Japan of Maeterlinck's *The Blue Bird* I have attempted to explain the enduring popularity of this philosophical fairy tale.

In the fifth part, two authors highlight the cross-cultural dimension of Art Nouveau. Yōko Takagi contributes an original study on how *katagami* (Japanese stencils) opened new avenues of creation to some Belgian artists, while Nathalie Vandeperre contributes an enlightening study on King Leopold II's orientalist architectural projects and the collections of Far Eastern art that were assembled as a complement to this orientalist dream. If the preceding chapters mainly deal with various aspects of high culture, Kazuko Iwamoto's Japanese perspective on Tintin takes us into the field of popular culture.

Further down the road of the popular, the sixth part invites the reader to explore two cases of exchange in lesser-known areas: the transfer of know-how in the fields of flax growing and chicken breeding, both studies by myself. In the final chapter Henri Delanghe analyses the characteristics of post-war trade and investment relations.

The history of Belgian-Japanese relations may be subdivided into several phases: the first from 1850 to 1895, which is the period of laying solid foundations. The next phase runs from 1895 to 1905, between the year of the victory in the Sino-Japanese War and the year of the victory in the Russo-Japanese War. In 1896 a new commercial treaty between Japan and Belgium was signed and a direct shipping line was opened between the two countries. Although victory in the Sino-Japanese War had boosted Japan's standing, it was nevertheless forced to bow to the Triple Intervention. The Japanese victory in the Russo-Japanese War (1905) marked a real watershed. The Japanese participation in the Liège World Exposition of 1905 bespoke the newly won self-confidence.

The relations between Japan and Belgium generally continued amicably throughout the remainder of the Meiji period (1868-1912) and the Taishō period (1912-1926). The Shōwa era (1926-1989) was much more turbulent and eventful. Emperor Hirohito reigned from Christmas Day 1926, when he ascended the throne at the age of twenty-five, until his demise on 7 January 1989. This makes his reign one of the longest in human history, encompassing as it did both the pre-war and post-war periods. With the exception of the first few years, the first two decades of the Shōwa era were marked by conflict and strife, increasingly isolating Japan from the rest of the world. The Manchurian Incident in September 1931 triggered a chain of events which dragged Japan into the quagmire of a desperate war. These events did not fail to affect the relations between Japan and Belgium, although Belgian diplomacy did take a remarkably conciliatory stance in the controversies surrounding Japan's actions on the international scene. The absolute low point in Belgian-Japanese relations was the Pacific War (1941-1945), a time when Japan and Belgium found themselves in opposite camps. The upshot was the rupture of diplomatic and, to all intents and purposes, pretty much all relations between the two countries, which were only gradually restored after the surrender of Japan in August 1945.

Japan's remarkable recovery and emergence as an economic power in the post-war period naturally led to the full restoration of bilateral relations and their further development to an unprecedented level in many fields. In the background of this intensified relationship was Belgium's status as a host country for many international organizations, most notably the European institutions and NATO. While Belgium enjoyed brisk economic growth and prosperity as a founding member of what was to become the European Union, Japan's spectacular growth catapulted the country to the status of economic world power, a development accompanied by commercial frictions with some major competitors in the international market. Belgium was one of the first European countries to benefit from direct Japanese investment. Notable in this respect is Honda Motor Corporation's investment in a production plant in Aalst as early as 1962, the first Japanese investment in Europe by any of Japan's major industrial companies. The post-war period is a long and peaceful one, but when studied in detail, may obviously be further subdivided in several phases.

The reader may notice that among the eighteen contributions there is a strong chronological bias towards the second half of the nineteenth century and the early part of the twentieth. There are good reasons for this because this time-bracket constitutes a seminal phase in the history both of Belgium and Japan. Japan began to reap the fruits of its modernization in the last quarter of the nineteenth century. The industrial take-off of the country can be situated in the 1890s. This is the time when the railway network was fully developed, the first successes in exports were recorded, and an efficient banking system was established. Also the protectionist policies which Japan would be criticized for in subsequent years date from this period. In the field of legislation we must mention the first constitution of 1889 and the first civil code of 1896. In the area of politics the cabinet system was adopted in 1885, and the first party cabinet was formed in 1898. In the field of international politics, the rise to regional power status was symbolically confirmed by the abolition of extraterritoriality for foreigners and the opening of the whole country in 1899, the treaty of alliance with Britain in 1902, and the annexations of Formosa (1895) and Korea (1910).

In European and Belgian history too this period is very important. The foundations of our present society were laid then, a society based on the use of petrol, electricity and chemical industry. Never before had daily life and the outlook of the earth been changed so dramatically as in the period 1880-1914. The 1880s saw the advent of the automobile, built by Siegfried Markus and Karl Benz. In 1884 the International Meridian Conference held in Washington, D.C., selected the Greenwich Meridian as an international standard for zero degrees longitude, forming the basis for the introduction of Standard Time in all developed countries. International standards were adopted and introduced in many areas. Inventions and innovations

followed one after another at unprecedented speed, while the psychoanalysis of Sigmund Freud (1856-1939), the scientific management of Frederick Taylor (1856-1915), the phenomenology of Edmund Husserl (1859-1938), the relativity theory (1905 and 1915) of Albert Einstein (1879-1955) and the quantum physics of Max Planck (1858-1947) and Niels Bohr (1885-1962) shaped a new way of viewing man and reality. These innovations had a profound impact on people's lifestyles, including the many ailments we nowadays associate with modern living.

In the political and social fields too, new times were afoot: the establishment of trade unions and socialist parties, the first social legislation, universal suffrage and in some countries even suffrage for women (New Zealand as the first in 1893; Finland in 1906). The elites failed to see the writing on the wall, however. The bourgeoisie was enjoying unprecedented prosperity and Europe's hegemony in the world was unchallenged. Western values seemed to have universal validity. The old monarchies of Germany, Austria-Hungary and Russia were still in power, the belief in a promising future was unquestioned. It was not until 1918 that Oswald Spengler's *Der Untergang des Abendlandes* declared the demise of the Eurocentric view of history, and opened the eyes of his readers to a fundamentally different concept of modernity. Only after the First World War would the clamour for emancipation of labourers, women and colonial peoples grow insistent.

These observations invite the historian to test concepts from the history of mentality like Eurocentrism or optimism about progress on the specific case of contemporary Belgian representations of Japan. Did the self-confident bourgeois consider this far-off land worthy of serious attention? In his self-complacency, did he consider Western culture as the one and only truth, and its adoption by all peoples as the necessary prerequisite for civilization and progress? Or were there already at that time, even before the First World War, signs of cultural relativism and recognition of Oriental civilizations as valuable in their own right? Was European world hegemony really believed to be unassailable, or were there already far-sighted minds who realized that this blind self-confidence was no longer justified? In order to pursue these questions and verify the existence of these notions Japan would quite naturally be a most adequate touchstone, since that country offers the experience of an attempt at alternative modernization.

Bilateral relations cannot be subsumed in the diplomatic and economic dimension. They were far from limited to a one-directional exchange of Western goods, technology and capital from West to East. Japan made an impressive contribution in the area of artistic influence. The advent of abstract art would revolutionize the fine arts in the twentieth century, but the groundwork for this revolution was laid in the works of Symbolists and Art Nouveau artists, while the designs of Henry Van de Velde, Otto Wagner or Frank Lloyd Wright constituted one of the bases for *Bauhaus* and *Neue Sachlichkeit*, trends which fundamentally shaped the outlook of the entire twentieth century. Japanese influences were at work in the articulation of all these innovating trends. Japan has indeed often worked as a source of inspiration, today as in the past.

Acknowledgements

This book could not have come into being without the collaboration of a great number of people. It was HE Luc Liebaut, Belgian ambassador in Japan from 2011 to 2015, who first contacted the editor to discuss the possible publication of a book on the history of Belgian-Japanese relations as a way to mark the 150th anniversary of the signature of the Treaty of Amity, Commerce and Navigation between the two countries. While stationed in Japan, he continued to follow up the project and managed to secure support from the Belgian Ministry of Foreign Affairs. In Belgium the members of the *Celebration Committee for the 150 Years of Friendship between Japan and Belgium*, chaired by HE Masafumi Ishii, Ambassador of Japan to the Kingdom of Belgium, encouraged the editor throughout the process of writing and editing, and secured most of the financing for the production and publication of the book. The Celebration Committee grew out of the synergy between the Japanese Embassy's Cultural and Information Centre, the Nihonjinkai a.s.b.l. (The Japanese Association in Belgium), the Belgium-Japan Association & Chamber of Commerce (BJA), presided over by Prof. Gilbert Declerck, and Friends of Japan, chaired by the editor, who wishes to express his gratitude to Ms Etsuko Kurihara, first secretary and Director of the Japan Information and Cultural Centre of the Embassy of Japan in Belgium, and Ms Anja Oto-Kellens, Executive Director of the Belgium-Japan Association & Chamber of Commerce, for their involvement in the many events programmed by the Celebration Committee, including this book project.

Many other people extended their help at various stages in the writing, editorial and production process. The editors are most grateful to Prof. Paul Arblaster, who has proven to be an excellent copy editor; to Mr Geert Benoit of Yamagata Europe, Ghent, for liaising with the owners of valuable documents and photographs related to Jun'ichi Hobo and Constant Huybrecht; to Mr Philippe Haeyaert, local historian in Wevelgem, for sending his articles on Constant Huybrecht and graciously supplying copies of photographs related to that topic. Ms Yashiro was very helpful in securing permission for reproducing documents held by Jidō bunka kenkyū sentā (Centre for research on children's culture) of Shirayuri University, Tokyo. Gratitude is also due to Mr Koichi Hobo, grandson of Jun'ichi Hobo, for giving permission to reproduce some of the photographs featuring his grandfather, and to Mr Hein Vandewalle for sending photographs featuring his father and giving permission to reproduce them here. The editors owe a special debt of gratitude to Prof. Fumio Inoue, emeritus professor of Meikai University, Chiba Prefecture, Japan, for donating three dialect-geographical maps of Japan and generously supplying a wealth of photographs on Willem Grootaers.

Mr Bruno Vandermeulen of the IT Services of the Faculty of Arts at the University of Leuven and his collaborators, in particular Ms Erika Scheltens, and Mr Frederic Van Cutsem from UBD Digitalisering Leuven (Digitaal Labo KU Leuven), graciously processed all requests for high resolution scanning or photographing of a great number of illustrations reproduced here. Mr Hiroyuki Yamamoto, Inspiration Publishing, Brussels, and Mr Maxime Darge from the Cultural and Information Centre of the Japanese Embassy in Brussels, equally provided us with some of the photographs reproduced here.

A number of institutions have graciously provided photographs and other illustrative materials for inclusion in this book. Their names are included in the relevant credits that accompany the many reproductions in this book, but special mention has to made here of the Cultural and Information Centre of the Japanese Embassy in Brussels, the Diplomatic Archives of the Ministry of Foreign Affairs of Japan (Gaikō shiryōkan, Tokyo), the Yokohama Archives of History, the Jidō bunka kenkyū sentā (Centre for research on children's culture) of Shirayuri University (Tokyo), Tamagawa Gakuen (Tokyo), the Sapporo City Board of Education, the Design Museum Gent (Ghent), The Royal Military Museum (Het Koninklijk Museum van het Leger en de Krijgsgeschiedenis / Musée Royal de l'Armée et d'Histoire Militaire, Brussels), The Archives of the Royal Palace (Archief van het Koninklijk Paleis/ Archives du Palais royal, Brussels), in particular its former director Prof. Gustaaf Janssens (honorary archivist), the libraries of the Université catholique de Louvain and Honda Motor Europe Logistics NV (Ghent), for supplying photographic material and/or giving permission to include it as illustrations in the book.

Some of the contributions included in this book were the result of research that was funded by the FWO (Fonds voor Wetenschappelijk Onderzoek Vlaanderen) and the Japan Society for the Promotion of Science. A great debt of gratitude is owed to these two organizations for providing the means to pursue this venture.

The editors and authors owe a great debt of gratitude to Mr Niels Famaey, Publisher Arts & Style at Lannoo Publishing, Ms Sarah Theerlynck, Arts editor at Lannoo Publishing, and Ms Leen Depooter, graphic designer, who gave the book an elegant and attractive design and layout.

Last but not least special thanks are due to Hilde De Meulenaere for her encouragement and support throughout the project.

Note on spelling, romanization and the use of Chinese characters and the Japanese syllabary (hiragana and katakana).

Belgium is a union of two main linguistic communities (besides a small German-speaking community), so as a rule federal institutions have an official Dutch and French name. However, in recent years they have also adopted an official English name, which we have generally used for the sake of convenience.

Names of Japanese persons are arranged in the order used in Japan, i.e. the family name precedes the given name. There are two exceptions to this rule: the names of Japanese authors of books or articles written in a Western language and the names of the Japanese contributors to this book are given in the "reversed order", with the personal name preceding the family name. Sometimes this leads to slight anomalies, such as when the name of a Japanese contributor of one article is mentioned in the text of another contribution. People unfamiliar with Japanese names are often at a loss as to which is the personal name and which the family name, and tend to pick the wrong one. My own feeling, in which I am not alone, is that it would be much wiser to follow the Japanese order consistently, but that means going against the tendency among many Japanese to subvert the order of their name in compliance with Western practice whenever they transcribe it into roman letters. The upshot of this tendency of compliance has at any rate been that we now come across both styles, and have to live with the ensuing confusion.

Japanese words are romanized in what is commonly called the modified Hepburn system, as used for example in the successive editions of *Kenkyūsha's Japanese English Dictionary*. For the benefit of readers who are less familiar with this system, we may add that, roughly speaking, vowels are pronounced as in Italian, and consonants as in English. When a word is represented in another romanization system, we have added the Hepburn transcription between brackets. Common Japanese words that have entered the English lexicon are not italicized. Chinese words are transliterated in *Hanyu pinyin*, reflecting present-day standard pronunciation, except in quotations, where the original transcription is respected, and except for those words that have an accepted spelling in the English language.

In most of the contributed articles one will come across Chinese characters inserted in the running text. We hope that the readers who are not familiar with these graphs (kanji), do not experience their presence as an unnecessary impediment to the smooth reading of the text. We have notably included them following the names of Japanese persons, lesser-known place names, titles of Japanese books, institutions, important concepts and notions, or typically Japanese phenomena. All graphs that are included in the list of the *Jōyō kanji* are consistently given in their simplified form. It is common practice in the field of Japanese studies to reproduce the kanji, and since this book is also intended as a work of reference, we assume that both the students of Japanese studies, and Japanese readers, would appreciate the original renderings of the aforesaid word categories.

> Mural in the "salon japonais" in the Chinese Pavilion, Laeken. Japanese embroidery, featuring two flying *apsaras* (celestial maidens), from the late Meiji period (early twentieth century), ordered by Alexandre Marcel, architect of the Japanese Tower in Laeken, from a Japanese workshop.

FIRST
PART

DIPLOMATIC
CONTACTS
AND
EXCHANGES

THE FIRST TREATY BETWEEN BELGIUM AND JAPAN (1866)

Dirk De Ruyver

JAPAN & BELGIUM
An Itinerary of Mutual Inspiration

Commodore Matthew Calbraith Perry, USN (*c.*1856–1858).
Photograph by Mathew Brady (1823–1896).
The Metropolitan Museum of Art, New York, USA

THE FIRST TREATY BETWEEN BELGIUM AND JAPAN (1866)

The Treaty of Kanagawa (1854)

On 31 March 1854, Japan and the United States signed a treaty.[1] This treaty ended an era of over 200 years during which Japan had banned all foreigners from its soil, with the exception of the Chinese and the Dutch, who were limited to the City of Nagasaki. The Dutch found themselves on a fan-shaped islet in the Bay of Nagasaki, called Deshima, bound by rules that were mostly imposed upon them unilaterally by the Japanese authorities.[2]

The Americans deplored the way the Japanese treated the Dutch. They considered Deshima to be a mere prison. The American envoy negotiating the treaty with Japan, Commodore Matthew Calbraith Perry, was expected to deliver a better deal for his country.[3]

The United States had several reasons to press Japan for a treaty. By the 1850s, the US had expanded its economic development from the Atlantic to the Pacific Ocean.[4] A major driving force in this movement of expansion was the steam engine. It had given birth to railways, an ideal means of transport in a vast country like the US. It also gave rise to steamships, which enabled the Americans to explore the Pacific. Whaling was bringing more and more American vessels into the vicinity of Japan.[5] However, shipwrecked Americans found themselves badly treated in Japan, where foreigners were forbidden.[6] The American press had published appalling stories from shipwrecked American sailors who had succeeded in returning to the US after having endured hardship and harsh treatment in Japan. There was pressure on the US government to do something about this.[7]

In 1844 the United States had concluded a treaty with China that focused on trade between the two countries and introduced foreign settlements in five Chinese cities.[8] Ships leaving from America for China passed Japan without being able to provision themselves there. For European countries, Japan was at the far end of the Asian continent, but for the Americans, Japan was the first country met when sailing into Asia. If the United States wanted its trade with China to blossom, Japan had to open up. Perry's primary goal was to open Japan, not so much in the first instance for its internal market or for free trade as such, but for the supplies Japan could provide to American vessels passing by, including daily necessities, coal, wood, and so forth.[9]

The 1854 treaty between the US and Japan secured just that. The ports of Shimoda and Hakodate were opened, enabling American whaling ships and trading vessels to take on supplies. Shipwrecked Americans were ensured humane treatment while awaiting repatriation. Instead of rules unilaterally imposed by the Japanese authorities, as in Deshima, the American treaty secured important rights for American citizens, which could not be unilaterally altered by the Japanese. Great Britain succeeded in concluding a similar treaty on 14 October 1855.[10]

On 22 October 1854, the governor of Nagasaki handed a dispatch to the Dutch at Deshima, in which the Japanese authorities confirmed that the Treaty of Kanagawa was also applicable to them. Henceforth, Dutch vessels were allowed to receive supplies or repairs at Shimoda and Hakodate.[11]

The Dutch, who had tried in vain to induce Japan to negotiate a treaty with them in 1844,[12] reached a temporary agreement with the Japanese government on 9 November 1855.[13] This agreement was transformed into a formal treaty on 30 January 1856.[14] It contained 28 articles, considerably more than the treaties with the Americans (12 articles) or the British (7). That the 1856 treaty with the Dutch contained far more practical stipulations was a natural outcome of the 250 years of contact between the Dutch and the Japanese. Article 2 ensured the right of extraterritoriality for Dutch citizens in Japan.[15]

Russia concluded a treaty with Japan on 7 February 1856.[16] It contained the basic elements of extraterritoriality for both Russian nationals in Japan and Japanese nationals in Russia, stating in article 8:

> Both a Russian in Japan and a Japanese in Russia are always free and will not be submitted to any oppression. Whoever commits a crime, can be arrested, but will be judged only in accordance with the laws of his own country.[17]

The Harris Treaty of 1858

As a consequence of the Kanagawa Treaty of 1854, the US appointed Townsend Harris[18] as consul to Japan, based in Shimoda. Having arrived there on 21 August 1856, together with his Dutch secretary Henry Heusken,[19] he came under the impression that the Japanese authorities interpreted the Kanagawa Treaty rather restrictively.[20] When the first American merchants and their families appeared in Shimoda and Hakodate to establish them-selves as traders between the American sailors and the Japanese suppliers, they were refused permanent resi-dence by the Japanese authorities.[21] At best, they were allowed to stay a few months to take in supplies, but had to leave once this was done. Harris negotiated an additional convention with Japan, signed in Shimoda on 17 June 1857, ensuring permanent residence for American nationals in the business of supplying Ameri-can vessels.[22] Though still very restricted when compared with the Chinese open ports, this provision gave the Americans the right to establish foreign settlements in the open ports of Japan. It was strengthened by a provi-sion granting extraterritoriality to the Americans in Japan.

The Netherlands and Russia each signed a supplementary treaty with Japan, on 16 and 24 October 1857 respectively, both in Nagasaki.[23] Since the Dutch already enjoyed the right to trade with Japan, they were provided with provisions that defined this right in greater detail. The Additional Articles secured by Russia included rights of trade that went considerably further than those obtained by the American consul Harris. The Russian Convention contained more detailed descriptions of these rights, in a similar way to those the Dutch had received. It was also explicitly mentioned that Russians residing constantly or permanently in Japan had the right to bring their wives and families to live with them.[24]

On 29 July 1858, after months of patient negotiations by Townsend Harris, Japan and the United States signed a treaty of amity and commerce in Edo (modern-day Tokyo).[25] This treaty not only contained commercial rights for individual citizens, but elevated the relations between the two countries to a political level, introducing friendly diplomatic relations. This treaty was quickly followed by similar treaties concluded between Japan and the Netherlands, Russia, Great Britain and France.[26] As a consequence, the ports of Kanagawa,[27] Nagasaki and

Hakodate were opened in July 1859 for these five countries.[28]

Belgian Initiatives

In the Belgian Ministry of Foreign Affairs, the news of the treaties with Japan came trickling in. Eight days after the signing of the first treaty between Japan and the US, on 8 April 1854, the Belgian consul in Canton (Guangzhou), William Walkingshaw, proposed in a letter to the Belgian Ministry that he should be assigned full powers to negotiate a treaty with Japan. This suggestion received a positive welcome in Brussels from both Henri de Brouckère, minister of foreign affairs, and King Leopold I. However, on 14 February 1857, Walkingshaw reported from Hong Kong that few benefits had been obtained from the treaties that other nations had already concluded with Japan. Subsequently, the new Belgian minister of foreign affairs, Viscount C. Vilain XIIII, shelved the project for treaty negotiations with Japan.[29]

On 23 February 1858, the Belgian consul in the Dutch town of Flushing (Vlissingen), P. E. Bourceret informed the Belgian Ministry of Foreign Affairs that the Dutch public gazette, the *Staatscourant*, had published a report concerning the Additional Articles signed by the Dutch and Japanese on 16 October 1857. On 11 March 1858, he sent a French translation of this report to the ministry in Brussels.[30]

Townsend Harris. Painting by James Bogle (1855).
City College of New York.

BARON ADOLPHE DE VRIÈRE.

On 30 June 1858, J.-B. d'Egremont, Belgian consul general in Singapore, dispatched two proposals to start treaty negotiations with Japan to the Belgian minister of foreign affairs. The foreign minister, Baron Adolphe de Vrière, rejected them both. He preferred to wait, since a treaty with Japan was not considered urgent.[31] However, in December 1858, the minister changed course: he sent for additional information from the Belgian representative in The Hague, and his ministry prepared a proposal for a mission to the Far East.[32] On 24 December 1858, the Belgian Senate approved a budget for a commercial mission to China and Japan, after an active intervention by the duke of Brabant, the future King Leopold II.

From the debate in the Senate it is clear what had changed the mind of the Belgian government:[33] the treaties of Tianjin between China and respectively Great Britain (26 June 1858) and France (27 June 1858) on the

one hand, and the treaties of Edo between Japan and the United States, Great Britain, the Netherlands and Russia, signed in July and August 1858, on the other.[34] Incidentally, on the same day as the debate in the Belgian Senate, a cabinet decree was promulgated in The Hague, ratifying the treaty between the Netherlands and Japan signed at Edo on 18 August 1858.[35]

After the Senate had passed the budget for a mission to the Far East, the Ministry of Foreign Affairs started to look for practical information for its organization. On 31 December 1858 it provided the Belgian diplomatic agents in London, Paris, Saint Petersburg, and Lisbon with a list of questions on this topic. The same day, the Ministry sent a similar list of questions concerning a mission to Japan to its legation in The Hague.[36]

The decision of the Belgian Senate to provide funds for a mission to the Far East generated a large influx of information, proposals and advice in the first half of 1859.[37] The Ministry of Foreign Affairs translated the information obtained into a new, detailed financial plan for the project.[38] Nevertheless, the Ministry also met with some critical notes and negative opinions from within its own ranks.

From the Belgian legation in The Hague, Baron du Jardin expressed his doubts about the success of a mission to Japan.[39] According to his information, Belgium could not supply many products of any interest for the Japanese market; nor would it find in Japan many goods meeting its own needs. Du Jardin was joined in his remarks by Director de Varlet of the Department of Foreign Trade of the Ministry.[40] August Moxhet, former Belgian consul at Singapore, and Sylvain Van de Weyer, Belgian minister at London, also made critical remarks.[41] In their view, to make sufficient impression on a country like China, the Belgian government would have to send at least one war vessel. Van de Weyer feared that the plans for the Belgian mission were insufficient in this regard.

On top of that, in early April 1859, the Belgian Ministry of Foreign Affairs received information that a Danish merchant ship had been refused access to Japan, because Denmark and Japan had not concluded a commercial treaty.[42] It was a clear indication that without a treaty, any Belgian commercial mission would end in failure on the shores of Japan.

By the end of May 1859, Minister de Vrière had decided to put an end to the project and leave the initiative for a mission to the private sector.[43] The former

Baron Adolphe De Vrière. Date unknown.

Belgian consul in Brazil, Captain Charles Sheridan, was planning an expedition to the Far East at that time. When confronted with the decision of the Belgian Senate to provide funds for an official mission, he complained about unfair state competition luring his own customers away. In its edition of 2 April 1859, the *Journal de Gand* broke this story, waging war against a government initiative it considered to be killing private initiative.[44]

Another initiative came from the Belgian consul in Amsterdam, J. N. W. C. Sieburgh. In a letter of 21 July 1859, Sieburgh launched the idea of loading a Dutch ship exclusively with Belgian products and sending it to Japan.[45] Because of the flag of the ship, the Belgian load would fall under the treaty between Japan and the Netherlands, and would be allowed into Japan. Making use of the services of a Dutch trading house in Kanagawa, he believed such an undertaking was worth trying. The Belgian Ministry of Foreign Affairs supported Sieburgh and organized a tour for him around the main industrial centres of Belgium from 4 to 13 August 1859.[46] After that, Sieburgh appointed a commercial agent in his own name to continue the search for Belgian industrialists interested in the Japanese market.[47] On 29 September 1859, Sieburgh informed Baron de Vrière that his agent had visited some sixty Belgian manufacturing companies, and had discovered nearly everywhere a great reluctance to ship by consignment.[48] It is unclear whether Sieburgh's initiative ever came to anything.[49]

Japanese Promise to Belgium

Baron de Vrière decided to change course. Instead of focusing on a mission, his new strategy was aimed at establishing a consulate general in China and Japan, for which he would request a budget from Parliament at the end of 1859. The new consul general would then be charged with concluding a treaty with both countries. The Belgian minister was informed that Portugal had requested the Dutch commissioner at Deshima to investigate whether the Japanese government would be susceptible to treaty negotiations. Portugal received a positive reply. Hence, on 17 June 1859, de Vrière dispatched a letter to Van de Weyer, the Belgian minister at London, explaining the new plans and requesting him to investigate whether the British authorities would be willing to ask the same question to the Japanese government on behalf of Belgium.[50]

On 13 July 1859, Van de Weyer sent a positive reply to de Vrière. The British government agreed to instruct its diplomatic agent in Japan to investigate whether Japan would be willing to conclude a commercial treaty with Belgium. The Belgian government was required to file an official request. Six days later, the Belgian Ministry of Foreign Affairs instructed Van de Weyer to send such an official request to the British government.[51] This was consequently done on 9 August 1859. The official letter from Van de Weyer to the British foreign secretary, John Russell, reiterated the message from Brussels:[52]

> The Belgian government aims to send a special envoy to Japan to negotiate a treaty of commerce. This mission will not be surrounded with the splendour customary in those parts, and will probably not even be presented under the Belgian flag. The Belgian government is therefore anxious to learn in advance the reception that the Japanese government would extend to the Belgian proposal of concluding a treaty of commerce between the two countries.

Van de Weyer mentioned that he had been requested to contact John Russell to find out whether the British government, in these circumstances, would lend Belgium a helping hand by instructing its agent in Japan to enquire whether the Japanese government would be willing to treat with the Belgian government. Van de Weyer added that Portugal had used a similar path: the Dutch commissioner at Deshima had acted as go-between and obtained a favourable reply. He rounded off his letter with the assurance that the aim of the Belgian government was not to demand special favours from Japan, but only to obtain treatment for Belgium on the same footing as the most favoured nations.

By a dispatch of 13 August 1859, Russell forwarded the Belgian request to Rutherford Alcock, the British representative at Edo, and instructed him to take the necessary steps with the Japanese authorities.[53] Maurice Delfour of the Belgian legation in London informed Baron de Vrière in Brussels on 17 August 1859 of the British foreign secretary's positive attitude towards the Belgian request.[54]

Meanwhile, in Japan, the ports of Yokohama (Kanagawa), Hakodate and Nagasaki had been opened to foreigners since early July 1859. Rutherford Alcock represented Great Britain at the court of the shogun at Edo from the beginning.[55] The shogun was assisted by a

board of chief councillors and councillors (*tairō* 大老 and *rōjū* 老中). The practical implementation of government policies was in the hands of commissioners (the *bugyō* 奉行). From day one, the foreign representatives were confronted with numerous problems and malfunctions of the 1858 treaties.[56]

After having received the dispatch from the Foreign Office with the Belgian request, Alcock started investigating the chances for a Belgian treaty with Japan. On 23 November 1859, he sent a first report to the British foreign secretary, John Russell, which arrived at the Foreign Office on 29 January 1860.[57] The report was not very promising. In an informal meeting with one of the councillors in charge of foreign affairs, Alcock had cautiously introduced the Belgian request. The reaction of the councillor was so peculiar that Alcock described it in graphic detail in his dispatch to Russell:

> On my referring to Belgium therefore, the governor [i.e. councillor] who spoke, counted the existing Treaty Powers on his fingers, — and added — with

these five we find dearness and scarcity already resulting from foreign trade, with daily increasing difficulties, what then is to become of us, if new Countries are to be added to the list?

Alcock added in his dispatch to Russell that the Japanese government looked upon all foreign treaties, international trade and relations, as so many unmitigated evils. According to him, the ruling classes in Japan showed a manifest repugnance to all intercourse with foreigners. Nevertheless, on 7 December 1859, Alcock brought the Belgian request up again during an audience with the councillors in charge of foreign affairs. He confirmed the request in writing on 12 December 1859 "to ascertain if any impediment existed to the favourable reception of (a) Diplomatic Agent duly accredited (*for*) the purpose of concluding a Treaty demanding no special advantage but simply the equal participation in that already conceded to other nations."[58] During the same meeting of 7 December 1859, Alcock had also given an overview of the main violations of the treaty between Great Britain and Japan by the Japanese. He demanded improvement, adding that "normal relations between countries are maintained by treaties and diplomacy, but if this is not possible, sometimes by war."[59] Clearly, the introduction of the Belgian request for a treaty with Japan had not come at the most favourable time.

During the meeting of 7 December 1859, Alcock was assisted by the interpreter of the French consulate general at Edo, the French missionary Girard. On 10 December 1859, the French consul general at Edo, Duchesne de Bellecourt, sent a dispatch to the French Ministry of Foreign Affairs, including the minutes of the meeting, drafted by Girard and approved by Alcock.[60] In this letter, de Bellecourt mentioned that Alcock's meeting with the councillors had taken four hours. He confirmed the dire situation of the open port of Yokohama as a result of the unfaithful implementation of the treaties by the Japanese authorities. He also mentioned the Belgian request for a treaty with Japan, as follows:[61]

> Her Britannic Majesty's Representative announced to the ministers [i.e. councillors] the arrival of a mission sent by H.M. the King of the Belgians with the object of negotiating the conclusion of a commercial treaty. Mr Alcock requested, in the name of the family ties which join the sovereigns of England and Belgium, the acceptance by the Japanese government of the Belgian negotiators, who are to present themselves at Edo under the

Sir Rutherford Alcock in 1864. Engraving after a photograph by Felice Beato, published in *The Illustrated London News*, 23 July 1864, page 97. See also e.g. The New York Public Library – Digital Collection *The Illustrated London News*, 23 July 1864, p. 97.

British flag. The ministers [i.e. councillors] have replied with words that bespeak little eagerness to negotiate with other Powers — "We will reply to this a little later!"

On 18 December 1859, the councillors in charge of foreign affairs, Manabe Akikatsu 間部詮勝 and Wakisaka Yasuori 脇坂安宅, gave a formal answer in writing to Alcock's dispatch of 12 December.[62] They replied that the opening of the ports had resulted in a lot of inconveniences – so many that, at present, the councillors did not wish to conclude a treaty with Belgium. They first wanted their people to get used to foreign trade, understand the advantages of it, and see these advantages increase.

Alcock had another meeting with Councillor Wakisaka Yasuori on 13 January 1860.[63] Not only Belgium, but also Switzerland had requested treaty negotiations with Japan. Furthermore, Alcock informed the councillors that he had knowledge of other countries sending or preparing missions to Japan: Prussia, Norway and Sweden, Denmark, and Austria. He advised that the board of councillors (the rōjū 老中) should decide the course to adopt with all these other European countries, before giving a definitive answer to either Belgium or Switzerland. He warned the councillors that it was difficult in the current circumstances for any nation to isolate itself entirely, or to refuse intercourse with some,

and enter into relations with others. He made his Japanese counterparts imagine how foreign delegations would feel if, after having travelled halfway round the world and arriving in Japan, they were sent away empty-handed.

Alcock acknowledged that the treaties had generated difficulties, and that it was likely that problems would be inherent to new treaties too. He understood that Japan wanted to gain more experience with international trade and relations before allowing treaties with other countries. He interpreted the position of the Japanese government as not refusing treaties as such, but as demanding sufficient time for Japan to adapt to the requirements of international trade and other consequences of the treaties. He argued that such a delay could be achieved by postponing the date a treaty would come into effect, rather than refusing to treat. While the latter option would offend countries that had made the effort of sending missions to Japan, the former would avoid this. Furthermore, nations seeking treaty negotiations with Japan would see sufficient reason in the current circumstances in Japan for not insisting upon treaties coming into immediate operation.

Concerning Belgium and Switzerland, Alcock pointed out that these two countries had only asked to inquire if the Japanese government would be disposed to receive their properly accredited agents for the purpose of negotiating treaties at some future date. Therefore, even

Dutch dispatch no. 25 from Wakisaka Nakatsukasa no Tajū (Wakisaka Yasuori) and Andō Tsushima no Kami (Andō Nobumasa, 1820-1871) to Rutherford Alcock (19 February 1860 (28th day of the 1st month of the 7th year of Ansei). University of Tokyo Volume VII 1967, F.O. 262 (462), pp. 32-33 (YAH microfilm outprint no. Ca4/01.20/679, pp. 32-33).

should the councillor reply affirmatively, it would not entail any immediate action.

Interestingly, in a dispatch of 20 January 1860 the French Consul General de Bellecourt informed his ministry in Paris that the Swiss delegation leader Rudolph Lindau had obtained the promise from the Japanese government that it would not treat with any other nation without conceding the same advantages to the Swiss Confederation.[64] According to Swiss sources, Japan gave this promise on 13 January 1860.[65]

In a letter dated 19 February 1860, the Councillors Wakisaka Yasuori and Andō Nobumasa 安藤信正 took up the topics that Alcock had introduced during their meeting on 13 January 1860, and which Alcock had put into a dispatch the day after.[66] They declared that they did not endorse immediate treaty negotiations with Belgium and Switzerland, because Japan was not yet familiar enough with international trade. Andō and Wakisaka recalled Alcock's warning that other countries would also send missions to Japan for treaty negotiations. They referred to his advice to conclude treaties whose date of execution would be sufficiently postponed. The refusal to treat, which they had already announced to the Swiss mission, was not permanent. Once the circumstances in Japan allowed new treaties to be concluded with other countries, this prerogative would also be extended to Belgium. The next day, Alcock sent this promise from the Japanese government to the British foreign secretary, John Russell, and included in his dispatch an overview of all his efforts to obtain this result.[67]

In London, the Belgian legation was informed, and Minister Sylvain Van de Weyer gave the foreign minister in Brussels, Baron de Vrière, a short briefing about the result in a letter dated 5 May 1860.[68] He emphasized that Alcock had been able to avoid a flat refusal from the Japanese government of a treaty with Belgium, even though the Japanese authorities manifested a profound aversion to enter into normal and continued relations with foreigners. Van de Weyer referred to Lord Howard de Walden, the English Representative in Brussels, for more details. The latter sent a longer dispatch to de Vrière on 7 May 1860. He described Alcock's efforts, and reiterated the promise of the Japanese government that in due time, when Japan had reached a certain level of commerce and prosperity, new treaties might be concluded with other countries. And once this was the case, then it was understood that Japan would grant the same privilege to Belgium.[69]

In his letter of thanks,[70] the Belgian minister of foreign affairs wrote to Lord Howard de Walden that King Leopold I of Belgium had seen his report of 7 May 1860. De Vrière acknowledged that the British consul general in Edo, Alcock, had obtained the best result possible in the current situation: a formal promise from Japan to enter into treaty negotiations with Belgium if any other nation would treat with Japan. He hoped that Alcock would remind the Japanese government of its promise in due time. The British Foreign Office transmitted this message to Alcock on 15 June 1860.[71]

The Treaty with Portugal of 1860

In view of Japan's promise, any new treaty would entitle Belgium to its own treaty negotiations with Japan. In fact, Foreign Minister de Vrière was convinced that Belgium would not have to wait long.[72] Prussia had already dispatched a delegation to China and Japan, and de Vrière expected the Prussian envoy, Count Eulenburg, to succeed in obtaining a treaty with Japan.

In fact, the first treaty to be concluded was not with Prussia, but with Portugal. In an appendix to the additional articles concluded between Japan and the Netherlands on 16 October 1857 at Nagasaki, the Japanese government had stated that it had no objections to a similar treaty with the Kingdom of Portugal, should that country so desire. In early March 1858, the Dutch Cabinet decided to notify the Portuguese government of the Japanese decision.[73]

Also in the framework of the additional articles concluded between Japan and the Netherlands in 1857, the Japanese government had conceded in writing that it was willing to conclude similar treaties with all other nations, and that it had no objections to this statement being communicated to other countries.[74] On 9 July 1860, the Dutch Commissioner Donker Curtius paid an official visit to Councillor Andō Nobumasa (Andō Tsushima no Kami) in Edo. Curtius reminded the Japanese government of its 1857 promise to him, and of the communications made by the Dutch government to several countries about this opportunity. He then asked whether Japan would conclude a treaty with Portugal, Belgium and Prussia. The Japanese government replied that it would conclude a treaty with Portugal as promised to the Dutch. In the case of Belgium, it would only conclude a treaty if the internal circumstances of Japan

would allow it, and it added that the English minister was aware of this precondition. All other countries should be informed that Japan was currently not in a position to make good on its promise to conclude treaties. It assured the Dutch commissioner that this position also applied to the Prussian mission that was on its way to Japan.[75]

Three days later, on 12 July 1860, Isidoro Francisco Guimarães, governor of Macao and Portuguese plenipotentiary, arrived in the Bay of Edo on board the Portuguese corvette *Dom João I*.[76] He took up residence with the British minister at Edo, Rutherford Alcock, who was an old acquaintance.[77] It took the Portuguese envoy only 3 weeks to conclude a treaty with Japan, which was signed at Edo on 3 August 1860.[78]

The Japanese government was keen to emphasize that the treaty with the Portuguese was the result of the promise made to the Dutch in 1857, and did not constitute a precedent for treaties with other countries.[79]

In Brussels, Belgian Foreign Minister de Vrière got wind of the conclusion of a treaty between Portugal and Japan through an article in *The Times* of 22 October 1860. He reacted promptly: on 25 October he sent a dispatch to Baron Solvyns, the Belgian Representative in Lisbon, asking whether he could confirm this news. He clearly indicated what was at stake: if Portugal had signed a treaty with Japan, Belgium was entitled to a similar treaty.[80]

In his reply of 21 November 1860, Solvyns confirmed the news and gave a detailed overview of the proceedings

(Utagawa) Gountei Sadahide (歌川) 五雲亭貞秀 (1807-1879). General view of Yokohama 1860 (4th month) 横浜本町並びに港崎町細見全図. Triptych print in *ōban* format, published by Yamamoto Heikichi 山本平吉.
Collection of Yokohama Archives of History 横浜開港資料館, Yokohama prints 横浜絵, p. 16. The licensed quarters are at bottom left; the Foreign Settlement and its harbour fills the bottom right, stretching away beyond it is the Japanese town.

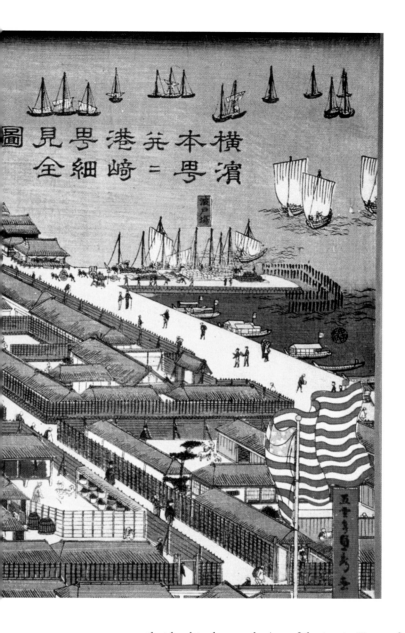

The Treaty with Prussia of 1861

In the meantime, in early June 1860, Townsend Harris, the American representative at Edo, had received a dispatch from the American secretary of state, officially requesting him to assist a Prussian mission heading for Japan under the leadership of Count Friedrich Albrecht zu Eulenburg.[83] Harris accepted the request, but referred to the refusal of Japan to treat with Belgium and Switzerland earlier in 1860.[84] He expected that the Japanese government might take a similar stance with Prussia.

The Prussian mission, on board the two war vessels SMS Arcona and SMS Thesis, arrived in Edo Bay on 4 September 1860.[85] Two weeks earlier, on 22 August 1860, Harris had pleaded again with Councillors Andō and Wakisaka in favour of a treaty with Prussia, but to no avail. In a letter of 2 September, the officials explained their position: since the opening of the ports and due to foreign trade, the products on which Japanese people depended for their survival had become gradually scarce and expensive. This had caused turmoil among the Japanese officials and citizens, particularly among those who had seen their trade negatively affected. An additional treaty, for example with Prussia, would only add to the distress and disorder in the country.[86]

Eulenburg and his delegation took up residence in Akabane, Edo, on 8 September 1860.[87] On 5 September,[88] the Prussian envoy had entered into communication with the Japanese authorities, but by the end of November 1860, the Japanese had finally refused to enter into treaty negotiations with Prussia.[89] However, Townsend Harris enabled a breakthrough by combining negotiations for a Prussian treaty with the Japanese desire to postpone the opening of the cities of Osaka and Edo, and the ports of Hyōgo and Niigata.[90] He proposed to limit the ports open to Prussia to Nagasaki, Yokohama and Hakodate, and not to mention the opening of Osaka, Edo, Hyōgo and Niigata. In a letter to Harris dated 13 December 1860, the councillor in charge of foreign affairs, Andō Nobumasa (Andō Tsushima no Kami), consented to Harris's proposal, and had already appointed commissioners to negotiate with the Prussian envoy.[91]

Through a letter of 21 December 1860, Honda Tadamoto 本多忠民, Andō Nobumasa 安藤信正, Naitō Nobuchika 内藤信親, and Kuze Hirochika 久世広周, all councillors (rōjū) of the shogun in Edo, informed Sakai Tadaaki 酒井忠義 [the Kyoto shoshidai] in Kyoto about

that lead to the conclusion of the treaty. He emphasized that the British minister at Edo had lent a helpful hand, but that also the Russian government had instructed its representation in Japan to assist the Portuguese envoy. The treaty with Portugal was based on the one signed between Great Britain and Japan in 1858.[81] One week later, Solvyns transmitted a French translation of the Japanese-Portuguese Treaty and its additional articles, which arrived at the Foreign Ministry in Brussels on 10 December 1860.[82] This confirmation does not seem to have led to any follow-up action from the Belgian Foreign Ministry.

Mitglieder der Preussischen Expedition nach Ostasien.
(Nach einer in Tientsin aufgenommenen Photographie.)

1. Dr. Lucius, Arzt der Gesandtschaft. 2. Lieutenant Graf zu Eulenburg, Attaché. 3. Dr. Th. von Bunsen, Attaché. 4. Maler Wilhelm Heine. 5. Lieutenant von Brandt, Attaché. 6. Graf zu Eulenburg, Chef der Gesandtschaft, Gesandter und ausserordentl. bevollmächtigter Minister. 7. Der Verfasser. 8. Maler August Berg.

Spiess, Japan-Expedition.   Leipzig, Verlag von Otto Spamer.

the proposal. They added that, due to prior promises, a treaty with Prussia also implied the conclusion of treaties with Switzerland and Belgium. In the case of Belgium, they referred to the family links between the Queen of England and the King of Belgium to explain the promise given to the English minister Alcock. In his function of *shoshidai* 所司代 it was Sakai's duty to inform the Imperial Palace. Sakai himself was against the proposal and on 8 January 1861 petitioned the emperor to repudiate the whole scheme.[92]

The Imperial Palace was genuinely upset by the proposal. To show its discontent, the Palace cancelled the project of a marriage between the emperor's younger sister, Princess Kazu no Miya, and the shogun.[93] After some days of consultation between Sakai and the Imperial Palace, the two sides came to an agreement on 21 January 1861: the communication between Sakai and the Palace about the Prussian, Swiss and Belgian treaties was withdrawn, and the date of the wedding between Princess Kazu no Miya and the shogun was to be postponed.[94]

In Edo, the negotiations between Japan and Prussia led to an agreement, and a treaty was signed on 24 January 1861.[95] It had taken three months and three weeks since the arrival of the Eulenburg mission in Edo.[96] The treaty obtained was only partially satisfactory to Count Eulenburg.[97] He had been mandated to negotiate a treaty not only for Prussia, but also for the states belonging to the Zollverein, the Mecklenburg Grand Duchies and the Hanseatic Cities. Once he had understood how many states and cities this implied, Councillor Andō Nobumasa resolutely refused to include them in the negotiations.[98] Therefore, the treaty obtained applied only to Prussia. Since the other German states had entrusted the defence of their rights to the Prussian expedition, they might feel that their interests had not been properly looked after.[99]

Compared with the treaties of 1858, the treaty with Prussia secured the opening of the ports of Kanagawa, Nagasaki and Hakodate, but did not mention anything about the ports of Hyōgo and Niigata, nor about opening up the cities of Osaka and Edo.[100] This fact allowed the government of the shogun to claim to have obtained an important concession, since it gave the impression to its opponents that the Foreign Powers were willing to concede to the Japanese demand to postpone, or even forego the opening of these four places. In fact, Andō Nobumasa was so satisfied with this format that he proposed to the British minister Alcock to use it for a treaty with Belgium.[101] Alcock did not foresee any problem in that case.[102] Similarly, this idea was sent to the Dutch consul general, De Wit, for a treaty with Switzerland.[103]

Japan Closes the Door

In Brussels, the Ministry of Foreign Affairs had been informed about the departure of the Prussian mission to the Far East,[104] but the conclusion of a treaty between Prussia and Japan on 24 January 1860 seemed to have gone unnoticed.[105]

The idea of sending a mission or a diplomatic agent to Japan had given way to plans in China. On 1 July 1861, Baron de Vrière appointed Louis Bols as consul general to China. On 26 October 1861, de Vrière was succeeded as foreign minister by Charles Rogier, who continued his predecessor's policy. Rogier gave Bols detailed instructions on 20 December 1861. While Bols was to

Gustav Spiess. *Die Preussische Expedition nach Ostasien während der Jahre 1860-1862*. Berlin and Leipzig: Verlag von Otto Spamer, 1864.

engage actively in treaty negotiations with China, his only orders regarding Japan were to gather information from his office in Shanghai.[106]

Belgium's inactivity towards Japan might also be explained by an article that had appeared in the German business magazine *Preussisches Handelsarchiv* on 1 November 1861. It stated plainly that the Austrian Ministry of Foreign Affairs had, through the intermediation of the American minister resident in Japan, received a circular note from the Japanese government, dated 1 May 1861, announcing that Japan would not conclude any more treaties. The Belgian Ministry of Foreign Affairs translated the article into French for inclusion in the Belgian public gazette *Le Moniteur Belge*.[107]

The note had been sent to Austria by Townsend Harris, American minister at Edo, at the request of the Japanese government. It was part of a new foreign policy of the shogun's councillors, which came into force on 1 May 1861. The Japanese government had decided that its own interests were best served by postponing the opening of the ports of Hyōgo and Niigata and the cities of Edo and Osaka to the Treaty Powers. And that beyond those already in existence no further treaties would be signed with foreign countries.

In pursuance of the first objective, the Japanese government wrote to the Treaty Powers, referring to the Prussian envoy's decision to waive the opening of those four places in his Treaty, having taken note of the internal state of affairs in Japan.[108]

As to the second part of the government's decision, Councillors Kuze Hirochika and Andō Nobumasa contacted Townsend Harris, and requested him to send a circular letter from the Japanese government to the governments of the "Principal Powers in the world". Their request ran as follows[109] (translated from the Dutch):

> Concerning the state of affairs in our country, we are sending a written announcement to your Excellency, which shall be published, and we wish you to inform your Government of this.
> According to our laws, we are not permitted to write letters to foreign governments except for those with whom we have concluded treaties. As such, we request that, through the friendly mediation of your Excellency, certified translations of the aforementioned announcement will be sent to each Government of the Powers of the World, except for Belgium and Switzerland.

Dutch letter from Kuze Yamato no Kami (Kuze Hirochika) and Ando Tsushima no Kami (Andō Nobumasa) to Townsend Harris, 1 May 1861 (22nd day of the 3rd month of Bunkyū 1). University of Tokyo Volume IX and Volume X 1968 Legation in Japan. U.S. National Archives, RG 84, N.A. T400 (7) Vol. 5 (1 January – 22 December 1861). (YAH microfilm outprint no. Ca4/01.14/7, pp. 33-34, p. 38).

神奈川横濱華郭之光景

(Utagawa) Gountei Sadahide (歌川)五雲亭貞秀 (1807-1879). View of the licensed quarters of Yokohama, in Kanagawa 神奈川横浜華郭之光景. Triptych print in ōban format (36 × 69 cm), published by Yamaguchiya Tōbē 山口屋 藤兵衛, dated second month of Man'en 1 万延元年2月 (March 1860).

Collection of Yokohama Archives of History 横浜開港資料館, Yokohama prints 横浜絵, p. 12. The licensed quarters of Yokohama (in the foreground) were built on reclaimed bogland and opened in the 11th month of 1859, a few months after the opening of the port. In the background the Foreign Settlement, indicated by the national flags, and to its left the native town.

At the American legation at Edo, the Dutch letter was translated into French and English, but in these versions, the clause "except for Belgium and Switzerland" was deleted.[110] The circular letter itself gave an overview of the recent relations of Japan with foreign countries and of the drawbacks resulting from them. It ended with Japan's decision not to conclude any more treaties for the time being:[111]

Circular.

During a period of nearly three hundred years our Empire had no intercourse with foreign Powers. Our Country produced all that was necessary in sufficient abundance; the prices of articles of consumption were reasonable and scarcely subject to any fluctuation; peace and quietness prevailed everywhere.

Upon the recommendation however of His Majesty the President of the United States, the law excluding foreigners was modified and a Treaty concluded with His Excellency Commodore Perry, Envoy Extraordinary of the United States on the 3rd day of the 3rd month of the 1st year of Ansei (31 March 1854), whereby it was agreed that ships of the United States should be furnished with wood, water and provisions in the ports of Simoda and Hakodadi.

Since then, another Treaty was concluded on the 19th day of the 6th month of the 5th year of Ansei (29 July 1858) with His Excellency Townsend Harris, minister plenipotentiary of the United States, granting freedom of trade; similar Treaties were subsequently concluded with five other Powers, all of which are now in force.

The result, however, anticipated from the opening of the ports to foreign Commerce has not been realized; the rich experience no advantage, nor the poor derive any benefit therefrom.

The prices of the necessaries of life are daily advancing, owing to steadily increasing exportation, and the humbler classes not being able to supply their wants as heretofore and often exposed to hunger and cold, attribute this to foreign trade and to the acts of their Government. The higher and also the wealthier classes are also opposed to foreign trade, because they do not perceive the benefit thereof.

The policy of exclusion of foreigners having been in force during so long a period had become like an established custom with our people; it is evident therefore, even if the difficulty already mentioned, did not exist, that it is next to impossible to change or cause to modify public opinion and to allay the uneasiness entertained concerning foreign trade. There is no doubt however that in course of time our people will acknowledge that benefit is to be derived from foreign trade; but in the present state of public opinion to conclude Treaties with other Powers would lead to complications and perhaps even to insurrection. And whereas, under the present circumstances, it has been deemed necessary to propose the postponement of the opening of the ports of Hiogo and Niigata and of the admittance for trade in the Cities of Edo and Osacca, as stated in the Treaties, we have to state in consequence, that we cannot enter into new Treaties with other Powers; our object with this Circular being to furnish information respecting the present state of affairs in our Country, and to prevent the sending of diplomatic Agents to Japan for the purpose of establishing relations with our Government, which, to our regret, we would have to decline for the present.

It is the desire of our Government that the foregoing be brought to the knowledge of the several Governments of the Principal Powers of the World.

Stated with respect and courtesy.

Harris sent a French and an English translation of this circular and the letter of the councillors in charge of foreign affairs to the ministers of foreign affairs of Austria, Spain, Sardinia, Denmark, Sweden and Norway, and Brazil.[112] Through the Foreign Ministry of Austria, the message was published in the *Preussisches Handelsarchiv* of 1 November 1861, but the fact that Belgium and Switzerland were exempted from this new rule was not mentioned. Since the Belgian Ministry of Foreign Affairs had prepared a French translation of this news article for inclusion in the *Moniteur Belge*, it is possible that the Ministry had come to believe that Japan's doors were closed for a treaty with Belgium.

The Swiss Treaty of 1864

In the meantime, Switzerland was on a different path. In a letter dated 10 January 1861 to the Dutch consul general J. K. de Wit, Councillors Andō and Kuze were contemplating the idea of concluding a treaty with the Swiss Confederation along the same lines as the then draft treaty between Prussia and Japan. They asked for De Wit's thoughts on this suggestion.[113] The Dutch transferred this suggestion to Bern, where the Japanese proposal was warmly welcomed by the Swiss Federal Council. The Belgian representative at Bern, Bourguignon, informed the Belgian foreign minister, then still Baron de Vrière, in a dispatch dated 10 May 1861.[114] He added that Switzerland had received the proposal through the intermediation of the Dutch consular agent in Japan.[115] For more than a year, the Belgian legation at Bern would continue to keep de Vrière informed about the Swiss response to the Japanese proposal.[116]

When in July 1861 the Legislative Councils of the Swiss Confederation approved a budget for a mission to Japan in 1862,[117] de Vrière was puzzled. In his dispatch of 14 August 1861 to the Belgian chargé d'affaires in Bern, Helman de Grimberghe, he wanted to know how the Swiss government had succeeded in getting the Japanese to propose treaty negotiations to them, while this had been denied to other countries, and what kind of assurances they had received from the Japanese government. In addition, he asked for details of the budget and the composition of the mission to be sent to Japan.[118] Apparently, at that point in time, the Belgian Ministry of Foreign Affairs still had some interest in a mission to Japan.

Helman de Grimberghe provided the Belgian foreign minister with some answers in his dispatch of 19 August 1861: it was through the Dutch government that the Swiss Federal Council had learnt of Japan's readiness to conclude a treaty with Switzerland, but the Council was unaware of how this willingness had been secured. On the composition of the Swiss mission to the Far East nothing had been decided, but Aimé Humbert, president of the "Union horlogère", was mentioned as delegation leader. The budget of 100,000 francs, approved by the Confederal Legislative Councils, was considered to be insufficient, but the Swiss government was counting on some financial support from industry.[119]

Two days later, Helman de Grimberghe was able to inform de Vrière that he had met with Humbert.[120] In fact, through de Grimberghe, de Vrière had been in contact with Aimé Humbert since May 1859.[121]

Some of Helman de Grimberghe's dispatches were summarized in a report that was published in the *Moniteur Belge* in September 1861,[122] the foreign minister apparently being eager to inform the Belgian business world.

The frustration of de Vrière was understandable: while both Belgium and Switzerland had been promised treaty negotiations by the Japanese at a similar time and under similar conditions, it seemed as though the government in Edo had preferred to start negotiations with the Swiss Confederation. As mentioned above, this situation was the result of the different response from the British and the Dutch Representatives in Japan. While Rutherford Alcock had understood that the suggestion from the councillors on 10 January 1861 was merely an idea, and had therefore only given his own opinion, J. K. de Wit had taken the suggestion as a request for advice

Aimé Humbert. Photograph by Victoire & Arambourg (Lyon), 1888. Bibliothèque nationale de France.

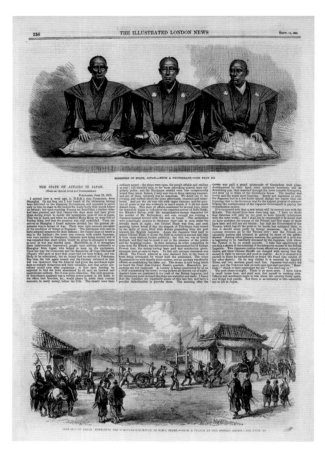

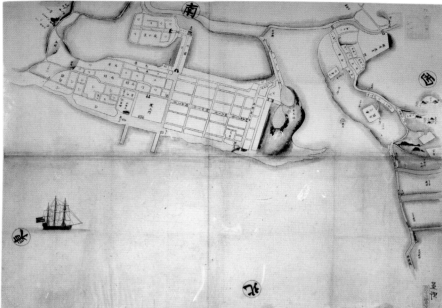

and transmitted it to Europe. There, it took the form of a formal proposal for treaty negotiations from the Japanese government.

On 31 January 1862, Helman de Grimberghe informed de Vrière that the Swiss mission to Japan had been adjourned indefinitely due to recent developments in Japan and after consultation with the Dutch government.[123] No further details were given about these "recent developments". It might have been related to the dispatch from Townsend Harris, with the Japanese circular letter of 1 May 1861 attached, reaching Europe. Since this dispatch had not mentioned the exemption for Switzerland and Belgium, the Swiss government might have concluded that it, too, had been banned from treaty negotiations like the governments of all other countries.

In Japan, meanwhile, the Dutch consul general J. K. de Wit sent a dispatch to the councillors in charge of foreign affairs on 18 December 1861, transmitting a message from the Swiss government. In their reply of 22 February 1862, Andō and Kuze confirmed the commitment to a treaty with Switzerland, referring to their letter to De Wit

of 10 January 1861. They concluded from De Wit's letter that neither in Japan nor Switzerland were there any objections to a treaty between the two countries.[124] In fact, in an earlier dispatch of 25 August 1861 to De Wit, they had already confirmed their commitment, both to Switzerland and to Belgium.[125]

Not surprisingly, the Belgian chargé d'affaires at Bern, Helman de Grimberghe, could announce in his dispatch of 12 May 1862 to the Foreign Ministry in Brussels that the Swiss Confederation was again considering sending a mission to Japan.[126] And when Aimé Humbert, the future delegation leader, visited the Netherlands early in July 1862, Helman de Grimberghe informed the new Belgian foreign minister, Charles Rogier, that Humbert might pass through Brussels for consultation on the Swiss projects in the Far East and on the Belgian position on trade with Japan.[127]

On 20 January 1863, Dutch consul general De Wit at Deshima informed the councillors in charge of foreign affairs at Edo in writing that a Swiss mission was to be expected in Nagasaki, probably in March 1863. He stated that the object of the mission was to obtain a treaty with Japan.[128] However, the situation in Japan had changed. There had been an attempt on the life of councillor Andō Nobumasa in February 1862, and though not killed, he had been severely wounded. In May 1862, both Andō and Kuze were replaced as councillors in charge of foreign affairs,[129] and the new councillors, Mizuno

Mizuno Izumi no Kami (Tadakiyo), Itakura Suō no Kami (Katsukiyo) and Ogasawara Zusho no Kami (Nagamichi). Engraving after photographs made by Mr. Saunders, residing in Shanghai. Ogasawara is on the left; Itakura probably in the middle; Mizuno probably at the right. *The Illustrated London News*, volume 43 (July–December 1863), 12 September 1863, p. 256.

横浜港写図 Hand drawn and coloured map of the Yokohama Foreign Settlement (52 × 68 cm). Early 1860.

Collection of Yokohama Archives of History, collection of maps, no. 五味 2-72. Originally in the possession of the Shogunal magistrate Hoshino Kingo, bearing the rank *Kanagawa bugyō shihai kumigashira* 神奈川奉行支配組頭星野金吾

Tadakiyo 水野忠精, Itakura Katsukiyo 板倉勝静 and Ogasawara Nagamichi 小笠原長行, turned out to be far more cautious. They countered De Wit's dispatch with a request for a postponement of the journey of the Swiss delegation from Nagasaki to Edo, though they confirmed that there was no objection to a treaty with Switzerland.[130] According to the councillors, the postponement was needed because the shogun would not be in Edo in the spring of 1863, and "national feelings" were still in disarray. De Wit expressed surprise upon reading the Japanese request for a postponement. Though protesting against it, he did develop a scheme for the Swiss delegation to arrive in Edo only around 15 May 1863, a timing he considered acceptable to both the Japanese and the Swiss.[131]

The Swiss delegation, under the leadership of Aimé Humbert, arrived at Nagasaki on 9 April 1863. In accordance with the wishes of the Japanese government, Humbert announced that he would spend some time in Nagasaki, but that the chancellor-secretary of the Swiss legation, Brennwald, and two attachés would leave for Kanagawa earlier, to prepare for the establishment of the delegation in Edo and for the treaty negotiations.[132]

In the meantime, De Wit had sent his Chancellor, J. P. Metman, to Yokohama to prepare for the arrival of the Swiss delegation and to assist with the treaty negotiations. Metman announced his arrival in

Yokohama to the Japanese authorities on 12 April 1863.[133] The news of the arrival of the Swiss mission at Nagasaki must have spread like wildfire among the foreign community in Yokohama. Already on 16 April 1863, the American Minister Robert Pruyn sent a letter about the Swiss mission to the councillors in charge of foreign affairs. The letter was dispatched from the US legation in Edo. In it, he expressed support for treaty negotiations with Switzerland. He also warned the councillors that concluding a treaty with the Swiss Confederation might spark treaty requests from other countries, since it would run counter to the circular letter that the American legation in Edo had transmitted on behalf of Japan to six countries in May 1861.[134]

At the time the American minister was involved in negotiations with the government at Edo to renew the 1858 treaty between the US and Japan. This renewal was one of the conditions which the US government had attached to its acceding to the postponed opening of Hyōgo, Niigata, Edo and Osaka. The negotiations had started in December 1862 and had resulted in an agreement. However, on 17 April 1863, the Japanese government requested the postponement of the signing of the new treaty.[135] Though not at all satisfied, Pruyn agreed to postpone signing for two to three months, provided that the Japanese officials would address a letter to him promising to conclude no commercial

---

Chōōji temple in Edo (probably 1863).
Photograph Nederlands Scheepvaartmuseum S.3628(03)

Dirk de Graeff van Polsbroek (1813-1916).
Photograph Nederlands Scheepvaartmuseum S.3628(03)

treaty, or grant any commercial concessions whatsoever, until 30 days after the signature of his treaty.[136] The Japanese government agreed to this condition.

On 19 April 1863, C. Brennwald, chancellor-secretary of the legation of the Swiss Confederation, arrived in Yokohama to start the preparations for the arrival of his legation.[137] The Dutch had agreed to host the Swiss legation in their consular residence in Benten, Yokohama, and in their own legation buildings in the Chōōji temple in Edo.[138] One week later, on 26 April 1863, Aimé Humbert and the rest of the Swiss delegation arrived in Yokohama. Until the end of 1863, Humbert, supported by the Dutch consul, later consul general, Dirk de Graeff van Polsbroek, would insist on initiating treaty negotiations but to no avail due to the delaying tactics of the Japanese authorities.[139] Without the consent of the Japanese authorities, Humbert even moved his delegation from Yokohama to the Chōōji temple in Edo on 28 May 1863,[140] only to be escorted back to Yokohama on a Japanese naval ship eleven days later, on 8 June 1863.[141]

On 24 June 1863, the Japanese government announced a major shift in its foreign policy. It had decided to close all open ports and to expel the foreigners. All foreign legations were furnished with a dispatch from Councillor Ogasawara to that effect,[142] stating:

> I have the honour to inform YE [*Your Excellency*] that I received full Powers to act as herein stated. I received orders from HM the Taicoon,[143] now residing at Kioto, and who received orders from the Mikado[144] to cause the opened ports to be closed and to remove the foreigner subjects of the Treaty Powers, as our people will have no intercourse with them—hence negociations on this subject will afterwards take place with YE.
> Stated with respect and Esteem.

All foreign representatives rejected the decision in the strongest terms, and refused to carry it out.[145]

Unsurprisingly, this shift in policy had repercussions for the promise made by Japan to Switzerland and Belgium. In a dispatch of 2 September 1863, the Japanese government at Edo explained to the American minister, Robert Pruyn, that even though the former councillor Andō Nobumasa had made an exception for Belgium and Switzerland when announcing that Japan would not conclude any new treaties, the current circumstances were such that it was not appropriate to conclude treaties even with those two countries.[146]

On 26 October 1863, another twist in Japan's foreign policy was announced. During a joint meeting with the councillors of the shogun at Edo, the American minister Pruyn and the Dutch consul general De Graeff van Polsbroek were informed that the Ogasawara letter of 24 June 1863 would be retracted, and that among the open ports, only Yokohama would have to be closed for foreigners.[147] The decision was again rejected by all

Residence of de Graeff van Polsbroek at Benten (Yokohama) in 1863. Engraving in Aimé Humbert, *Le Japon Illustré*. vol I. Paris: Librairie de L. Hachette et Cie., 1870.

Chōōji temple entrance in Edo in 1863 (with Swiss and Dutch flags). Engraving in Aimé Humbert, *Le Japon Illustré*. vol I. Paris: Librairie de L. Hachette et Cie., 1870.

foreign representatives. In early November 1863, all foreign legations received a request from the Japanese government to return the Ogasawara letter.[148]

The year 1863 was drawing to an end, and despite the support of the Dutch consul general De Graeff van Polsbroek, the Swiss envoy Aimé Humbert had not even obtained a meeting with the councillors in charge of foreign affairs at Edo. Already considering leaving without a treaty, Humbert turned to the American Minister Robert Pruyn in a letter dated 7 December 1863.[149] Humbert had been informed about the dispatch that Pruyn had sent to the Japanese government on the arrival of the mission from Switzerland.[150] According to Humbert, that communication must have had such an effect upon the Japanese government that it included Switzerland among the countries barred from treaty negotiations.

On 12 December 1863, Pruyn reacted in a long letter to Humbert.[151] He denied that his communication with the councillors had been the cause of Humbert's failure. He attributed the lack of results to the attitude of the Japanese government and the current situation in Japan. He referred to his own failure in getting the revision of the treaty with the US signed. In doing so, he mentioned that he had only agreed to a postponement of the signing ceremony, after the Japanese government had submitted a written promise that it would not sign any other treaty before the revision had been signed. Pruyn concluded his letter by offering Humbert any assistance in his power, even to the extent of uniting with the other Treaty Powers.

While Humbert was not completely convinced by Pruyn's explanation, he preferred to question the promise Pruyn had received from the Japanese government, since he considered this a possible obstacle for his own negotiations. In no uncertain terms, he demanded the waiving of this clause in the case of the conclusion of a treaty between Switzerland and Japan.[152] Pruyn defended his actions again in another long letter, but concluded by stating:

> If the Japanese government regard the engagement entered into with myself as the obstacle to the conclusion of a treaty with Switzerland, and if I shall receive a letter from Your Excellency, informing me that the Japanese government has made a declaration to that effect, I will waive so much of this stipulation as required my treaty to be signed before the conclusion of a treaty with the Swiss Confederation.[153]

Having obtained what he wanted, Humbert wrote an unctuous letter to Pruyn to wrap up all discussions and smooth over any hard feelings.[154]

While Humbert was taking on the American minister[155] to dispose of a potential obstacle to the Swiss treaty negotiations, the Dutch consul general De Graeff van Polsbroek launched a new offensive towards the councillors. In an extensive dispatch to them, dated 14 December 1863, he mentioned that the Swiss envoy would agree not to list the names of the open ports in the treaty, instead just carrying an article allowing Swiss nationals to trade in all ports open to the other treaty countries, and under the same rights. This clause would still not prejudice the Japanese policy of closing Yokohama, and transferring all foreign trade to the two remaining ports, Hakodate and Nagasaki. Van Polsbroek also mentioned that the negotiations could take place in Yokohama, as long as the exchange ceremony would take place in Edo. His proposal took into account the Japanese government's preference to keep foreign representatives out of Edo.[156]

His initiative resulted in a meeting with two Japanese commissioners of foreign affairs on 20 December 1863.[157] Finally, after another letter on 2 January 1864, Van Polsbroek received a positive reply from the councillors in charge of foreign affairs, dated 16 January 1864, stating their intention shortly to appoint plenipotentiaries for the negotiations with the Swiss envoy at Yokohama.[158] These plenipotentiaries, the commissioners of foreign affairs (*gaikoku bugyō* 外国奉行) Takemoto Masatsune 竹本正雅, Kikuchi Takayoshi 菊池隆吉, and Hoshino Kazuyuki 星野千之, were scheduled to have their first meeting with Humbert in the Dutch consulate general at Benten, Yokohama, on 26 January 1864.[159]

The negotiations went so smoothly that already on 30 January 1864, the councillors invited Aimé Humbert and his delegation to a signing ceremony, to take place in the Dutch legation at Chōōji temple in Edo at 10 a.m. on 6 February 1864. Humbert gladly accepted, and planned to go by Dutch vessel from Yokohama to Edo, and to return the same day.[160] Ten months had elapsed since Humbert's arrival at Nagasaki on 9 April 1863.

On 4 February, Humbert also sent a (customs) tariff agreement to the three Japanese plenipotentiaries, as the final piece of their negotiations.[161] This agreement became the object of a circular letter of the Japanese authorities. The new tariffs were implemented at

Yokohama on 8 February 1864, and at Nagasaki and Hakodate on 8 March 1864.[162]

The same timing was used for the new tariff convention between the United States and Japan, finally concluded nine days before the treaty with Switzerland, on 28 January 1864, by Robert H. Pruyn, US minister resident, and Shibata Sadatarō 柴田貞太郎, commissioner of foreign affairs.[163] It had taken Pruyn thirteen months since the beginning of the negotiations in December 1862. The US-Japan Convention provided for a reduction of a number of customs tariffs. Since the treaty between Switzerland and Japan included a most-favoured-nation clause,[164] these tariff reductions also applied to businesses from Switzerland, as to other countries that had obtained the same clause.[165] It was therefore not abnormal that the Convention with the US should precede the Swiss treaty.

On 20 February 1864, not long after the treaty between the Swiss Confederation and Japan had been signed, the exchange of the ratifications of the treaty of 24 January 1861 between Prussia and Japan took place in Edo.[166] The Prussian envoy, Guido von Rehfues, had arrived at Yokohama in mid-August 1863 with the treaty ratified by the King of Prussia.[167] It had taken him half a year to induce the Japanese government to accept the exchange of the ratifications. As a result, the government of the shogun was involved in signing or exchanging three bilateral agreements in less than one month, which indicated a softening of its foreign policy by early 1864.

The Japanese-Swiss treaty itself stood out because of its article 3, opening: "From the day this treaty enters into force, the cities and ports open to foreign trade, will be open to Swiss citizens and businesses."[168] It seems that this clause, first mentioned in Van Polsbroek's dispatch of 14 December 1863, was important in bringing about the conclusion of this treaty. To make sure that there was no misunderstanding, Humbert had to submit an additional notification to the Japanese commissioners, stating:

> that he understands article 3 of this treaty in the following sense: that where the cities and ports are open (or) will be opened to the citizens and the trade of Switzerland it should be understood, that, if the other contracting Nations agree to leave the port of Kanagawa, the Swiss Federal Council will not object to the fact that Swiss citizens leave this port in a similar way as the nationals of the other Nations.[169]

The Belgian legation in Bern delivered a copy of the Treaty between Japan and the Swiss Confederation to the Belgian Ministry of Foreign Affairs in Brussels on 11 and 25 May 1864.[170]

While the Swiss government had sent an embassy to Japan, and obtained a treaty with that country, the Belgian government had concentrated its efforts on China. Consul General Louis Bols had arrived at Shanghai in April 1862. By early August 1862 he was in a position to present a treaty with China to Charles Rogier in Brussels. However, the Belgian foreign minister was not satisfied, and refused to accept the terms proposed. With regard to Japan, Bols advised total inactivity, because of the unstable internal situation there. The Belgian Ministry seems to have followed that advice faithfully. On 25 November 1863, Bols was recalled to Brussels.[171] In early 1864, after considerable efforts, Switzerland had its treaty with Japan. Belgium, on the other hand, did not have a treaty either with China or with Japan. Belgium was however not the only one. Siam[172] (now Thailand), the Sandwich Islands[173] (Hawaii), and Denmark[174] had all tried in vain to start treaty negotiations with Japan.

Charles Rogier, c.1855. Author unknown.

The Appointment of Auguste t'Kint

In March 1864, Louis Bols arrived in Brussels, and was discharged of his duties as consul general to China the following month. The Belgian Ministry of Foreign Affairs started looking for a replacement. In a letter to Louis Bols, dated 7 September 1864, Foreign Minister Charles Rogier mentioned that the choice of the new consul general had been decided.[175] It was to be Auguste t'Kint (de Roodenbeek),[176] who was informed about the decision around 20 September 1864.[177] On 1 November 1864 a Royal Decree appointed him consul general to China.[178]

Auguste had been born in Antwerp on 22 November 1816. His father, Pierre-Joseph t'Kint, was a broker on the Antwerp stock exchange. His mother was Anne Waumans. From 1832 till 1840, Auguste t'Kint worked for several trading companies in Antwerp and Brussels.[179] In October 1840, he joined the civil service as an official of the Belgian Interior Ministry (Home Office).[180] On 20 October 1841, a Royal Decree appointed him one of the three government commissioners tasked with a fact-finding mission to Verapaz in Guatemala.[181] The mission was to be organized by the Belgian Company for Colonization (*Compagnie belge de colonisation*). In the event, he was the only government commissioner to arrive in Guatemala on 12 February 1842. He stayed ten days, then left for Belgium again, submitting his report on 23 May 1842.[182]

In 1843, t'Kint was back in Guatemala as a special commissioner for the Belgian Company for Colonization. By 14 October 1843, he had negotiated a favourable deal for the company. He stayed in Central America until July 1844, after which he returned to Belgium. He arrived in Brussels in August 1844. He was involved in treaty negotiations between Nicaragua and the Belgian Company for Colonization, aimed at constructing a canal in Nicaragua. The treaty was signed in Paris on 2 December 1844. By the end of 1845 t'Kint would again leave for Guatemala. Early in 1847, he was joined there by his two brothers with the aim of establishing a trading company. One of the brothers, Florent t'Kint, would stay on; the other would return to Belgium. On 10 May 1847, Auguste announced his departure for Brussels, leaving his brother Florent in charge in Guatemala. While in Brussels, Auguste t'Kint wrote a report about his work in Guatemala dated 23 September 1847. On 11 May 1848, he returned to the capital of Guatemala.[183]

On 12 July 1855, Auguste t'Kint was appointed Belgian consul general in Guatemala, with a remit in seven Central American republics. He undertook a study tour of Belgian industry before taking up his post. In 1858, he was appointed plenipotentiary for Central America by King Leopold I. In that capacity, he concluded treaties with five Central American republics. On 30 November 1859, he was appointed Belgian chargé d'affaires for Mexico, and on 7 December 1859 plenipotentiary for the same country. On 20 July 1861, he concluded a treaty with Mexico on behalf of Belgium.[184]

In total, t'Kint stayed some 18 months in Mexico as Belgian chargé d'affaires.[185] In the aftermath of a French military intervention in Mexico, he thought it was wise to leave the country for Europe on 6 October 1862.[186] The Ministry of Foreign Affairs in Brussels looked upon some of t'Kint's actions in Mexico with a baleful eye, and started an investigation, but t'Kint was ultimately cleared of any wrongdoing.[187]

On 14 April 1863, Auguste t'Kint informed the Belgian Foreign Minister Charles Rogier that the Belgian representative in Paris had arranged a meeting for him with the French Foreign Minister Édouard Drouyn de Lhuys. The French minister consulted him extensively on the situation in Mexico, and according to t'Kint, asked him to stay for a few more days in Paris for further consultation. Two days later, t'Kint had an audience with Emperor Napoleon III on the same topic. Over the next three weeks, the French foreign minister regularly consulted t'Kint. On 4 May 1863, he had another audience with Napoleon III. On 10 May 1863, two days before leaving Paris for Brussels, he had an audience with the French empress and a final meeting with Drouyn de Lhuys. The main topic of all these meetings, again, was the situation there. T'Kint informed Charles Rogier in Brussels about the content of his talks with the French emperor.[188]

Back in Brussels, t'Kint received an urgent telegram from the Austrian Archduke Ferdinand Maximilian. In a dispatch dated 20 May 1863 t'Kint informed Rogier, asking him for his permission to travel to the archduke's castle, Miramare.[189] Since France had made plans for Ferdinand Maximilian to be enthroned as emperor of Mexico, it is likely that the archduke wished to consult t'Kint on the state of affairs there.[190] Two days later, Rogier gave his permission, adding that t'Kint was officially on furlough, and that he could use his time as he thought fit, as long as his activities had a purely unofficial character. Rogier was not entirely satisfied with the way t'Kint handled affairs. He deplored t'Kint's stay in Paris, and his experiences in Mexico had been widely published in the press, and he warned t'Kint that journalists should not be involved in the projects undertaken by the Ministry. On 26 April 1863, t'Kint had received the French title and honour of Officer in the Legion of Honour. On that occasion, he was referred to as the chargé d'affaires of Belgium in Mexico. Rogier reminded t'Kint that he had lost this title when he left Mexico, and that his current title was consul general. Clearly, Minister Rogier's patience with Auguste t'Kint was reaching its limits.[191]

It took t'Kint only one day to reply to Rogier. He reassured him that he would only go to Miramare in an unofficial capacity, and that he had done nothing to elicit the telegram from Archduke Ferdinand Maximilian. He also assured the Belgian minister that he had not communicated with any French or Belgian journalist about his stay in Paris. Concerning the title of chargé d'affaires, he had considered that he could continue to use it, since he was on leave and had not been recalled. However, in view of Rogier's stance, he promised to make sure that this title would not be used any longer.[192]

T'Kint was received several times in Miramare by Archduke Ferdinand Maximilian and his wife, Archduchess Charlotte, who was a daughter of the Belgian King Leopold I. He also attended a gala dinner thrown for the future emperor and empress of Mexico by Napoleon III in March 1864.[193]

On 22 March 1864, Charles Rogier sent a proposal to the minister of the royal household containing the new letters of accreditation for t'Kint as chargé d'affaires in Mexico.[194] A week later, Charles Rogier informed t'Kint that the Belgian government had decided to send him to Mexico again in the same capacity as in 1861 and 1862, that of chargé d'affaires. T'Kint argued that it was not in the country's interest to be represented at the court of the emperor of Mexico in a quality lower than the other powers. However, Rogier insisted that t'Kint should accept the title the king would accord him. As a result, on 12 April 1864, t'Kint received his appointment as Belgian chargé d'affaires to Mexico, and two days later his instructions. Rogier ordered him to take up his post in Mexico as soon as possible.[195]

Still, the struggle to make t'Kint minister plenipotentiary instead of chargé d'affaires continued to be waged

for several days. An unsigned note, afterwards dated "20 April 1864", mentioned that the Mexican emperor and empress had told the author of the note that they would really appreciate having a Belgian minister plenipotentiary at their court as soon as possible. Things became somewhat urgent since the emperor and empress would arrive in Mexico City on 12 June 1864. In the publication *Mémorial Diplomatique* of 24 April 1864, the following notice appeared (my English translation of the French text):[196]

> Mr t'Kint, who until now had the title of minister resident of Belgium in Mexico, will be elevated to the rank of envoy extraordinary and minister plenipotentiary. This distinguished diplomat, who, since the rupture between France and the government of Juarez [*the republican government of Mexico*], had been able to render the most signal services to the French residents, also took an active part in the preliminary negotiations which led to the convention between France and Emperor Maximilian...[197]

Things took a surprisingly different turn. Around 20 September 1864, Charles Rogier informed t'Kint that his destination was not going to be Mexico, but China and Japan. Though t'Kint replied that he was willing to go wherever the king wanted him to go, he must have been devastated. His whole career had been built in Central America and his family business was located there. His knowledge of Mexico had opened doors to the palaces of the French Emperor Napoleon III and the Mexican Emperor Maximillian. On 15 October 1864, he lodged an urgent appeal to King Leopold I to reconsider the decision, arguing that his experience would be more useful to the nation in Latin America.[198] This was in vain. On 1 November 1864, the king signed a Royal Decree appointing Auguste t'Kint consul general for China.

By selecting t'Kint, the Belgian government had opted for a diplomat with ample experience in treaty negotiations. However, this may not have been the only reason. As we have seen, t'Kint was at loggerheads with the Foreign Ministry about his title as Belgian representative in Mexico. He definitely wanted to be elevated to the rank of minister, and had made his point to Charles Rogier, waving letters from the Mexican emperor demanding a Belgian minister at his court.[199] T'Kint may have overplayed his hand. On 2 August, Jules Devaux[200] had sent a hand-written note to "Sire". The note described how Baron de Malaret[201] had come to warn Devaux. T'Kint had just left de Malaret's office, mentioning that he would go to Paris to request the emperor to pressure Leopold I to appoint him minister. Devaux advised "Sire" to warn t'Kint urgently and not to send him to Mexico without giving him his terms... In his note, Devaux quoted de Malaret as describing t'Kint as "cet intriguer" (*this intriguer*).[202] It is not impossible that someone in the Royal Palace wanted to teach t'Kint a lesson by sending him to the Far East.

T'Kint and the Treaty with China

Having selected the new consul general for China, the Belgian Ministry of Foreign Affairs had to decide on the process of securing a treaty with that country. Since Belgium had rejected the treaty negotiated by Louis Bols, relations with China were stalled. The new consul general had to get things back on track by concluding a new treaty. On 15 October 1863, the Danish diplomat Waldemar von Raasløff had already suggested to the Belgian Ministry of Foreign Affairs that they request the assistance of the British Foreign Office. Raasløff himself had successfully secured a treaty between Denmark and China with British support in 1863.[203]

The idea was kept in mind. Almost a year later, on 13 October 1864, the Belgian Foreign Minister Charles Rogier informed S. Van de Weyer, Belgian minister in London, that t'Kint would become the new consul general in China. He asked Van de Weyer to approach the British government for support for t'Kint from Thomas Francis Wade.[204] Rogier believed that Wade was to leave for Beijing in December 1864. The letter from Charles Rogier mentioned that Wade had been instrumental in the treaty negotiations between Denmark and China.[205] Maurice Delfosse at the Belgian legation in London dispatched a message on 18 October 1864, informing Rogier that Wade had already left for Beijing, and that he had sent a request to Lord Russell to obtain the support of the British Representative in Beijing.[206]

Great Britain was not the only government willing to support the mission of the new Belgian consul general in China. The Dutch Navy Minister Willem J. C. van Kattendijke, who had lived in Japan himself for three years, also offered support in both China and Japan.[207]

On 9 December 1864, Rogier gave instructions to t'Kint on his mission to China. The new consul general, who was to be posted in Shanghai, should reorganize the consulates in China, study the market, and conclude a treaty with China. Three days later, t'Kint pointed out that he did not need a permanent residence in Shanghai since he had to travel extensively in the region. The Ministry, however, insisted on a permanent residence in Shanghai in accordance with the standing of a consul general. Establishing the permanent residence could, however, be deferred until after his trip to Tianjin and Beijing.[208]

On the same date the Belgian minister informed the presidents of twelve chambers of commerce in Belgium about the appointment of Auguste t'Kint. He requested a meeting for t'Kint to get acquainted with the local industry, since the new consul general had to pay special attention to the development of trade with the Far East. T'Kint would report on his visits on 21 January 1865.[209]

On 12 December 1864, the Belgian foreign minister stepped up his efforts to gather support for t'Kint. He sent a dispatch to the Belgian legation in Turin, asking them to intervene with the Italian government for support from its representatives in the Far East. The Belgian legation in London was requested to obtain letters of recommendation for t'Kint from trading companies in London to English enterprises in China. At the same time, the legation was asked to inquire about the possibility of t'Kint receiving a British passport to facilitate his travel from Shanghai to Beijing. Both requests came from t'Kint himself.[210] On 21 December 1864, Henry Solvyns, Belgian Representative in Turin, informed Charles Rogier that the Italian government had agreed to recommend t'Kint to its agents in Bombay, Point de Galle [Galle in Sri Lanka], Penang, Hong Kong and Shanghai.[211]

T'Kint had received his instructions for China on 9 November 1864. Although the Belgian Foreign Ministry was mainly focusing on the mission to China, Japan was not forgotten. On 21 December 1864, Charles Rogier requested the Belgian legation in Bern to send an additional copy of the Japanese-Swiss treaty of 6 February 1864. The Belgian Representative to the Swiss Confederation, Grenval, dispatched it two days later.[212] On 31 January 1865, it was given to t'Kint as a point of reference for a treaty with Japan, together with the treaty between Japan and Prussia of 24 January 1861, and the Convention of Paris, an additional convention between Japan and France of 20 June 1864.[213]

Support also came from the Belgian business world. Victor Lynen, one of the businessmen of Antwerp, whose company t'Kint had visited, sent letters of recommendation addressed to the Brothers Gütschow. The Gütschows had been living in China and Japan for four years, and had established companies in Shanghai and Yokohama.[214] Charles Rogier also provided him with instructions for Japan. He informed t'Kint that the communications between Shanghai and Japan were frequent and speedy, giving him all facilities for undertaking an excursion to Japan when he considered it appropriate. He was requested to look out for favourable circumstances in Japan that might enable him to conclude a commercial treaty there. Rogier considered it useful to give t'Kint full powers before his departure. He wanted the outcome of any treaty negotiations with Japan to be on the same footing as the treaties concluded by the other nations. On 4 February 1865, Rogier made it clear that t'Kint should strive for a treaty of amity, commerce and navigation with both China and Japan, and not merely a commercial treaty.[215] And finally, before leaving Brussels, t'Kint was promoted from Knight to Officer in the Order of Leopold.[216]

From Hong Kong, t'Kint dispatched a report to Charles Rogier on 26 June 1865. He described his visits to Hong Kong, Canton and Macao. At these places, he received valuable information from British and Dutch diplomats on treaty negotiations with China.[217] While staying in Hong Kong, Auguste t'Kint also received information on the internal situation in China and Japan, which he compiled into a report to Rogier.[218] Shortly afterwards, on 7 July 1865, he left Hong Kong, to arrive at Shanghai three days later.[219]

On 10 June 1865, a Japanese mission led by Shibata Takenaka 柴田剛中 (also called Shibata Sadatarō 柴田貞太郎), lord of Hyūga 日向 and commissioner of foreign affairs, arrived in Hong Kong. The mission had been dispatched to England and France by the shogunate. On 13 June 1865, in Hong Kong, Shibata met a German national called Millasson who had accompanied Commodore Perry to Japan (1853-1854), and on account of this old connection had called on Shibata in his hotel. From him, Shibata learned that Belgium had sent a plenipotentiary to Japan and China. Millasson showed him a business card of the envoy. It named Auguste t'Kint de Roodenbeek. According to Millasson's information, the Belgian envoy had left Hong Kong for Beijing one week before.[220] Shibata believed that

t'Kint would soon arrive in Japan, and informed the commissioners of foreign affairs (*gaikoku bugyō* 外国奉行) in Edo. They transmitted this message to the councillors (*rōjū* 老中). Since the shogun had gone to Osaka, the message was also sent to the councillors who had accompanied him there. It is therefore likely that the councillors of the shogun were aware that a Belgian envoy was on his way to Japan.[221]

The normal route for a foreign diplomat dispatched to negotiate a treaty with China would lead to Tianjin. In that city the imperial court had installed an official to handle foreign affairs. Auguste t'Kint decided to follow the same strategy as the Danish diplomat Raasløff, ignoring the Tianjin administration and heading directly for Beijing.[222] Having arrived in Beijing, he reported back to Rogier on 8 August 1865: he had made contact with the British, French and Russian legations there. At the British legation, Thomas Francis Wade had been informed about t'Kint's mission a few months before.[223]

Around the time of t'Kint's arrival in Beijing, the duke of Brabant (Belgian Crown Prince Leopold) delivered two letters to the Belgian Ministry of Foreign Affairs. One requested the support of Rutherford Alcock, the newly

Shibata Sadatarō (Takenaka) in Holland, 1862. From left: Fukuda Sakutarō, Ōta Genzaburō, Fukuzawa Yukichi, Shibata Sadatarō.
Taken in Holland in 1862 (Bunkyū 2).

appointed British plenipotentiary for China and an acquaintance of the duke, for t'Kint's mission. On 6 May 1865 the duke had returned from an Asian trip that had taken him as far as China.[224] He was aware that the Chinese government had plans to establish railways, and that Japanese feudal lords were ordering machines and steamships through the British legation. He therefore requested Alcock to look after the Belgian commercial interests in China and Japan. The Belgian Foreign Ministry dispatched the letters on 7 August 1865 to its legation in London with the request to have them delivered to Alcock through the British Foreign Secretary, Lord Russell. On 19 August, the legation in London confirmed that the letters had been delivered. Rogier dispatched a letter to t'Kint informing him. In the same dispatch, he requested t'Kint to thank the Dutch vice consul in Shanghai, Mr Kroes. The latter had made preparations for a visit by the duke of Brabant to Shanghai, but the Belgian Crown Prince had not got that far.[225]

In Beijing, on 7 September 1865, Chinese plenipotentiaries were appointed to negotiate a treaty with Belgium. T'Kint regularly informed Rogier of the progress of the talks. Throughout the whole negotiation process and the preceding preparations, the Belgian diplomat would depend heavily on the support of the British legation. Finally, on 2 November 1865, he was able to sign the Belgian-Chinese Treaty of Amity, Commerce and Navigation in Beijing.[226]

Having signed the treaty, Auguste t'Kint moved back to Shanghai, where he arrived on 24 November 1865. The next day, he sent the signed copies of the treaty to Brussels.[227] The Belgian Chamber of Representatives approved the treaty on 23 February 1866, the Senate on 6 March. The ratified copies were exchanged in Shanghai on 26 October 1866.[228]

T'Kint Moves to Japan

While the Belgian consul general was making his way from Beijing to Shanghai in mid-November 1865, a large fleet of foreign war vessels had gathered in the Port of Hyōgo, Japan, at the request of the foreign representatives in Japan. The aim of this show of military power was to obtain the emperor's sanction to the foreign treaties.

Originally, the Foreign Powers believed that the shogun in Edo had the authority to conclude treaties.

Much was derived from information obtained through the Dutch factory in Deshima, explaining that Japan had two emperors: the spiritual emperor in Kyoto (called mikado, later emperor, by the foreign representatives) and the secular or temporal emperor in Edo (called tycoon, later shogun, by the foreigners). During their long, exclusive experience in Japan, the Dutch had only entertained relations with the temporal emperor in Edo, and none with the spiritual emperor in Kyoto. They therefore presumed that the shogun was the authority to deal with when it came to government affairs, such as negotiating treaties.[229]

When in 1844 the Dutch King William II wrote a letter advising Japan to open its borders, the letter was addressed to "the Great Mighty Ruler of the Great Empire of Japan, keeping residence in the Imperial Palace in Edo". In the letter, even the term "Great Mighty Emperor" was used in reference to the shogun.[230]

When Commodore Perry negotiated the first US-Japan Treaty in 1853-1854, the Americans were aware of the system of "two emperors". Unquestioningly they had assumed that talks were to be held with the administration of the shogun in Edo. The letters from the American President Millard Fillmore and from Commodore Perry were addressed to "His Imperial Majesty, the Emperor of Japan", meaning the shogun in Edo, rather than the emperor in Kyoto.[231] The British and the French missions, sent to conclude the 1858 treaties with Japan, similarly operated on the assumption of the "two emperors" system.[232]

Townsend Harris was probably the first diplomat to discover that the emperor in Kyoto did have some authority in secular matters. On 18 February 1858, a letter from the councillor in charge of foreign affairs Hotta Masayoshi 堀田正睦 to Harris confirmed that the negotiations for a new treaty between the US and Japan had come to an agreement, and that the treaty text was ready for signing. However, the councillor announced that the signing would have to wait until the return of an embassy sent by the shogun to Kyoto, to present the treaty "respectfully to the knowledge of His Majesty the Spiritual Emperor".[233] The councillors then explained to Harris that the "Spiritual Emperor" did not exercise any political power, but that his opinion was the "voice of Heaven", and would be implicitly obeyed by all classes. Harris asked them, what they would do, if the emperor in Kyoto refused his assent. The councillors promptly replied that the government had determined not to receive any objections from Kyoto. They also promised that the delay would not take longer than 60 days.[234]

However, on 14 April 1858, the councillor in charge of foreign affairs Hotta Masayoshi dispatched from Kyoto a Dutch letter to Harris, informing him that the talks in Kyoto were taking more time than expected. The reason given was that "...not only the conversations held from the beginning, between you and the Commissioners, but even all circumstances relating there unto are to be punctually presented to the notice of His Majesty the Spiritual Emperor..."[235]

Hotta returned from Kyoto to Edo on 1 June 1858. During a meeting with Harris he gave a full oral and written account of the background of the decision to delay the signing of the treaty. He said that in Kyoto he found a very alarming excitement among the people. The emperor had received letters from some of the most powerful feudal lords, remonstrating against the treaty and warning the emperor in Kyoto that great evils would ensue if he gave his assent to it. The emperor was much alarmed. He did not refuse his assent to the treaty, but told the envoy of the shogun that more time was needed, in order to seek reconciliation with the dissenting feudal lords. Once that had happened, the emperor would give his assent. The next day, 2 June 1858, the councillors declared to Harris that the government of the shogun would need until 4 September 1858 to bring about the reconciliation requested.[236] In the end, Harris would sign his treaty on 29 July 1858.

However, five years later, on 24 June 1863, the foreign legations received the news that by order of the emperor in Kyoto the shogun was forced to close the open ports and to expel the foreigners from Japan.[237] Although this order never came into effect, it did show that the emperor had more political power than the foreign representatives had originally thought.

Some two years later, on 30 October 1865, the representatives of Great Britain, France, the Netherlands and the United States of America had come to the conclusion that the foreign treaties would only be faithfully maintained by Japan if the emperor in Kyoto gave consent to them. A consensus had developed among the foreign representatives that a fleet of war vessels should be sent to Hyōgo, the port closest to Kyoto, where both the emperor and the shogun were then residing. Objectives of this display of military power were to obtain the consent of the emperor for the treaties; the opening of the ports of Hyōgo and Osaka; and a new

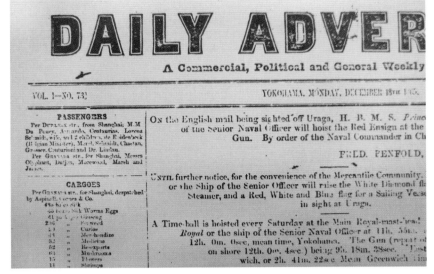

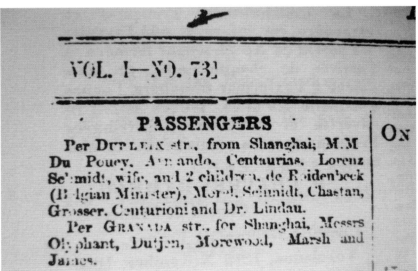

general customs tariff of five per cent.[238] The foreign representatives fully succeeded by 24 November 1865. The consent of the emperor was announced to the feudal lords on 1 December 1865.[239]

In Shanghai, Auguste t'Kint learnt about the results of the negotiations in Hyōgo through the local newspapers. He discussed this new political fact with Charles Alexander Winchester, the British consul at Shanghai. Winchester had lived in Japan for three and a half years, and had only left Yokohama four months earlier. He interpreted the results obtained in Hyōgo as favourable for Belgian treaty negotiations with Japan. He also remarked, though, that negotiations in Japan demanded a lot of patience. As a result, t'Kint decided to leave for Yokohama as soon as possible. On 8 December 1865, he

Arrival of t'Kint de Roidenbeck [*sic*] in Yokohama on 16 December 1865. *Japan Times' Daily Advertiser* 1:73 (Mon 18 Dec 1865), front page.

Arrival of t'Kint de Roidenbeck [*sic*] in Yokohama on 16 December 1865. *Japan Times' Daily Advertiser* 1:73 (Mon 18 Dec 1865), front page (detail).

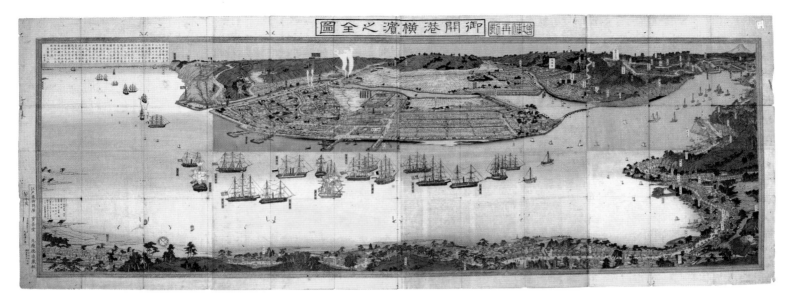

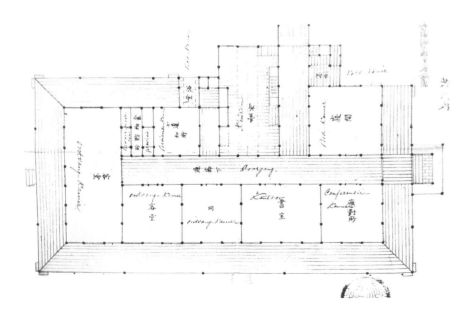

Gyokuransai Hashimoto Yuzuru 玉蘭斎橋本謙, alias Utagawa Sadahide. 増補再刻御開港横浜の全図. Revised complete map of the open port of Yokohama (70 × 186 cm), printed from woodblocks owned by Hōzendō Maruya Tokuzō 宝善堂丸屋徳造. Published in early 1866. First edition published in 1860.

Collection of Yokohama Archives of History 横浜開港資料館, collection of maps, no. 60. The map gives an indication of the building at lot no. 82 at the left.

Panorama of Yokohama from the Bluff, photograph by Felice Beato (1833-1907). June 1864.

Collection of Yokohama Archives of History 横浜開港資料館, F. ベアト写真集 1 幕末日本の風景と人びと, pp. 13-14.

Floor plan of Van Polsbroek's residence at Benten, Yokohama (June 1864). Attachment to a Dutch "rechtstitel" (title of rights) from Komai Sagami no kami 駒井相模守, Governor of Kanagawa, dated 5th month of the 1st year of Genji.

Tokyo University Historiograpical Institute, Microfilm Hdup 6951-1: Legatie Japan, Edo Tokio no. 13, L.J. no. 36. This is the floor plan of the official residence of the Dutch Consul General in Japan.

wrote a report to Belgian Foreign Minister Charles Rogier about his decision, referring to the full powers he had received from Rogier for treaty negotiations in Japan on 31 January 1865. He also estimated the additional budget needed for this journey, and he mentioned that he probably would have to rent a house in Yokohama.[240] His decision was so sudden that he did not have the time to establish the Belgian Consulate General in Shanghai as requested by Rogier.[241]

On 12 December 1865, Auguste t'Kint boarded the 970-ton heavy French steamer Dupleix commanded by Captain Melizan. One of his fellow passengers was Dr Rudolph Lindau, the Swiss envoy who in 1860 had obtained a promise from the Japanese government for a treaty with Switzerland. Dupleix and its passengers arrived in Yokohama on Saturday 16 December 1865, and were greeted by fair weather and a high temperature of 50 degrees Fahrenheit (10 degrees Celsius) and a low temperature of 40 degrees Fahrenheit (4 degrees Celsius). The arrival of "de Roidenbeek (Belgian minister)" was published in *The Japan Times* of 18 December 1865. The same newspaper carried announcements by British minister Harry Parkes, French minister Léon Roches and Dutch consul general Dirk de Graeff van Polsbroek, each in his own national language, about the results obtained at Hyōgo.[242]

When treaties were signed in Edo by the plenipotentiaries of the US, the Netherlands, Russia, Great Britain, and France in 1858, of Portugal in 1860,[243] of Prussia in 1861 and of Switzerland in 1864, the diplomats were accompanied by a military or civilian mission. When t'Kint set foot on land in Yokohama, he was by no means accompanied by a large mission. He had simply brought his personal "maître d'hôtel", a butler in charge of his personal belongings and household affairs whose family name was Vandevelde. This was a young man, whom t'Kint had employed since his departure from Brussels. He also acted as copyist or scribe, in view of his very good handwriting. T'Kint discharged him in November 1866.[244] The Dutch political agent and consul general in Japan, Dirk de Graeff van Polsbroek, mentioned in a letter of 6 January 1866 both his own secretary and the secretary of the Belgian envoy.[245]

Having arrived in Yokohama, t'Kint found temporary lodging at Benten, Yokohama, where the Dutch consulate general and consular residence of Van Polsbroek was located.[246] Not for long, however. By 12 January 1866, t'Kint had rented a house in Yokohama.[247] This house was located in the Foreign Settlement of Yokohama, at no. 82. Within the next days, he would furnish it with furniture for a drawing room, dining room, bedrooms, and an office, and with a collection of fine curios, crystal, glassware and crockery, saddlery, wines, arms, books and other paraphernalia.[248]

British or Dutch?

On 21 December 1865, Auguste t'Kint (de Roodenbeek) wrote from Yokohama a letter in French to the councillors of foreign affairs in Edo. In that letter, he mentioned that the Belgian king had been informed that, through the mediation of friendly nations, the shogun of Japan had in the past promised to conclude a treaty of amity, commerce and navigation with Belgium. He introduced himself as the plenipotentiary and envoy of the king to Japan, and informed the councillors of his arrival in Yokohama. He informed them furthermore about his upcoming visit to Edo to present himself and his letters of credence to the government of the shogun. Finally, he declared that the main object of his mission was to conclude a treaty with Japan and to cultivate friendly relations between Japan and Belgium.[249]

As a result, a Japanese commissioner of foreign affairs came to visit t'Kint in the residence of Van Polsbroek at Yokohama on 27 December 1865. The conversation mainly focused on Belgium and its future relationship with Japan. T'Kint noticed that a Japanese translator interpreted from Dutch to Japanese, and vice versa, and remarked that in this way, he himself was refamiliarized with the Dutch language. The next day, the governor of Yokohama, Kanagawa *gaikoku bugyō* 神奈川外国奉行, paid him a visit, and when given the choice between conversing in Dutch or in English, t'Kint opted for Dutch, reasoning that the Japanese were more familiar with this language. The Belgian envoy experienced these two meetings as very friendly.[250] Probably as a result of these meetings, Kikuchi Takayoshi, Hoshino Kazuyuki, Ezure Akinori 江連堯則 and Kurimoto Joun 栗本鋤雲, all commissioners of foreign affairs, wrote a report on t'Kint's arrival in which they mentioned the shogunal government's promise to former British Minister Alcock to conclude a treaty with Belgium.[251]

Van Polsbroek and Commander J. Van der Meersch of the Dutch warship Zoutman proposed to take t'Kint from Yokohama to Edo on board the Zoutman. The trip went ahead on 31 December 1865, the Zoutman flying the Belgian flag.[252] The Japanese batteries in Kanagawa fired fifteen salutes;[253] the Zoutman, in its turn, fired fifteen salutes when t'Kint and Van Polsbroek disembarked at Edo. Escorted by Japanese officers and soldiers, they both entered the Dutch legation in Edo. Guards remained in the surroundings of the legation, and accompanied the foreign representatives wherever they went.[254]

The next day, 1 January 1866, a commissioner of foreign affairs visited t'Kint, to compliment him upon his arrival at Edo. During the meeting, he mentioned that only one of the five councillors (*rōjū*) was currently in Edo, the other four being in Osaka with the shogun. For that reason, the commissioner considered a meeting with the councillor impossible for the time being. T'Kint experienced the meeting as far more reserved than the two that had taken place in Yokohama.[255]

The commissioner also expressed surprise that the Belgian envoy was residing with the Dutch political agent. Since in 1860 it had been the British minister who had obtained the Japanese promise of a treaty with Belgium, the commissioner thought it more natural that the British minister would be involved. Van Polsbroek explained that t'Kint had obtained letters of recommendation from some of his friends and acquaintances, and therefore, he had invited the Belgian envoy to stay with him in Yokohama, and to make use of the Dutch legation buildings in Edo. In a letter written the same day, Van Polsbroek also commented that the commissioner's message about the inability of the councillor to receive the Belgian envoy without delay ran counter to the politeness due to an envoy of a friendly power. He insisted that t'Kint should be received as soon as possible by the councillor.[256]

Auguste t'Kint did indeed bring some letters for Van Polsbroek.[257] One of them was a letter of recommendation from the Dutch consul in Shanghai.[258] This was probably P. T. Kroes, Dutch vice consul in Shanghai. At the request of the duke of Brabant, the Belgian foreign minister had ordered t'Kint to make contact with Kroes to convey the duke's gratitude.[259]

Still, it is difficult to imagine that t'Kint had not received a letter of recommendation from Charles Alexander Winchester, the British consul he had met just before leaving Shanghai for Yokohama. Winchester had been the British chargé d'affaires in Japan after Minister Rutherford Alcock had left, and until Harry Parkes took over as minister on 8 July 1865.[260] He would surely have

been in a position to recommend t'Kint to Parkes. In the first two days after his arrival in Yokohama, t'Kint had at least inquired about Parkes. By 18 December 1865, he knew Parkes was absent.[261] Harry Parkes had gone to Shanghai to fetch his family. He would return to Yokohama on the evening of 25 December 1865 with his wife and two children.[262] He was aware of t'Kint's arrival in Yokohama by 29 December 1865 at the latest.[263]

T'Kint also had a letter of recommendation from the French minister of foreign affairs, Édouard Drouyn de Lhuys. He had received it while passing through Paris on his way to the Far East. Within two days after his arrival in Yokohama, he had visited the French minister to Japan, Léon Roches. In his first dispatch from Japan to the Belgian Foreign Minister Rogier, t'Kint mentioned that both Van Polsbroek and Roches spontaneously gave their support to his mission. Both declared that the circumstances for treaty negotiations were no less unfavourable than previously, but that patience would be needed. To his disappointment, t'Kint observed that Roches was opposed to private businessmen becoming consuls. Besides, Roches thought that the shogun might possibly not want to conclude another treaty so soon after his struggle to obtain the emperor's ratification of the current foreign treaties, even though he had obtained a complete victory. T'Kint, on the other hand, wanted to initiate the negotiations as soon as possible.[264] Roches's hesitant attitude may have convinced the Belgian envoy to side with Van Polsbroek. Moreover, Roches had been struggling with his health, and may not have made a very active impression on t'Kint.[265]

The choice of Van Polsbroek also had practical consequences. Since the communication with Japanese officials had to be conducted in Dutch, being supported by the Dutch meant that additional translations from Dutch into French or English would be unnecessary. Although t'Kint was most likely educated in French, being born and raised in Antwerp should have given him at least a passive knowledge of Dutch.[266]

The Dutch could pride themselves on an impressive record of successful treaty negotiations, based on their extensive knowledge of Japan. Through patient negotiations from 1855 to 1858, they had contributed to the opening of Japan to other nations. To prevent other Western Powers complaining that the Netherlands was keeping Japan to itself, the Dutch government had pursued an active policy to open up Japan.[267] The intervention of the Dutch Commissioner Donker

Curtius, for example, had resulted in a Japanese promise of a treaty with Portugal. This had enabled the Portuguese to conclude a treaty with Japan in merely three weeks in 1860. Dirk de Graeff van Polsbroek himself was intensively involved in the Swiss treaty negotiations with Japan, and enabled a breakthrough in these negotiations at the end of 1863.[268]

Since the opening of the ports in 1859, the influence of the Dutch in Japan had declined, relatively speaking. Since 1864, both France and Britain had a considerable number of troops stationed in Yokohama, while the Dutch had none.[269] An active policy of helping out foreign envoys seeking a treaty with Japan could at least prop up the influence of the Dutch with the Japanese government. Van Polsbroek explicitly referred to this policy in his letter to the councillor.[270]

The Japanese officials did not object to the assistance given by Van Polsbroek to t'Kint. However, to be sure that there were no British objections, they did inform the British legation about the arrival of the Belgian envoy on 5 January 1866. In their letter, reference was made to the Japanese promise given to former British Minister Rutherford Alcock concerning treaty negotiations with Belgium.[271]

Yokohama versus Edo

T'Kint would acknowledge another merit of working together with Van Polsbroek. All eight treaties signed by Japan with foreign countries since 1858 contained an article allowing these countries to have a diplomatic agent residing in Edo, and consuls or consular agents in each open port.[272] However, by mid-1863, all consuls and consular agents at Kanagawa, and all diplomatic agents at Edo, found themselves based in Yokohama, due to the deteriorating safety of foreigners. The last diplomat to move from Edo to Yokohama was the American Minister Pruyn on 31 May 1863.[273] The situation implied that the diplomatic agents had to maintain two locations: a residence in Yokohama where they spent most of their time; and the official legation in Edo only used when personal meetings with the government of the shogun necessitated a presence in his capital.[274] The difference between these two locations could not be greater. The residence in Yokohama was built in western style, and based in a port through which all necessities for westerners came in. The legation building in Edo was based in a Buddhist temple, some quarters of which where transformed into rooms acceptable for westerners. Due to the unsafe situation, the temples were surrounded by Japanese guards, sometimes, depending on the country, supplemented with foreign troops. Most necessities had to be brought from Yokohama to these temple-legations, in which living was lonely and separated from all western luxury and culture.[275] In contrast to this, foreigners in Yokohama could enjoy balls,[276] theatres and brass bands,[277] skating,[278] regattas, racing, club life,[279] and other social activities.[280]

By mid-1865, only one diplomat had moved back into the official legation of his country in Edo: the American chargé d'affaires ad interim A. L. C. Portman. On 1 June 1865, he wrote to US Secretary of State William H. Seward: "I have now been residing for some time in the Capital [Edo], even though the legation building is not yet finished."[281] The American legation building at Zenpukuji temple 善福寺, where Portman was residing, had suffered extensive fire damage in 1863. The Japanese government had ordered its reconstruction in 1864.[282]

The British legation had been established in the Tōzenji temple 東禅寺 in Edo since 1859, but this location was abandoned for Yokohama after two assaults on the legation in July 1861 and June 1862.[283] When British Minister Harry Parkes arrived in Japan in July 1865 to take up his post, one of the first things he did was to select a temple in Edo that could host a new temporary English legation.[284] By early September 1865, he temporarily accepted lodging in the Daichūji temple 大中寺[285] while a new legation was being on the grounds of the Sengakuji temple 泉岳寺 in Takanawa, Edo.[286] The British legation would finally move from Yokohama to Takanawa during the first half of November 1866, although part of the legation staff would still remain at Yokohama.[287]

In 1865, the following temples in Edo had been placed at the disposal of the other foreign representatives living in Yokohama: Saikaiji temple 済海寺 for France; Kōgaku-in 広岳院 for Prussia,[288] but from March 1866 onwards Shuntōin 春桃院 in Azabu;[289] Shōsenji 正泉寺 (located between the French and the Dutch legations in Edo) for Switzerland.[290] From 1859 onwards, the Russians had the Tengyōin temple 天暁院 at their disposal, but since their main base in Japan was at Hakodate, they hardly used the Edo temple.[291]

The assistance of the Dutch political agent and consul general Van Polsbroek enabled t'Kint to use the Dutch official legation, located in the Chōōji temple 長応寺 in Edo. It saved him the trouble of obtaining and maintaining his own legation building in Edo.[292] In this t'Kint was following the same path as the Swiss envoy, who had also resided at the Dutch official legation in the Chōōji temple during his short stay in Edo in 1863. At Yokohama, the Swiss envoy made extensive use of Van Polsbroek's residence at Benten.[293]

In fact, the Chōōji became a tool in Van Polsbroek's policy of ensuring and maintaining Dutch influence with the Japanese government. He not only opened up the Dutch legation building in Edo for visiting foreign envoys seeking a treaty with Japan, such as the Swiss Aimé Humbert or the Belgian Auguste t'Kint, but also placed it at the disposal of envoys of countries that had already concluded a treaty with Japan but preferred not to maintain a legation at Edo, or whose legation was not habitable for some time.

In early March 1865, British chargé d'affaires Charles Winchester took up residence with Van Polsbroek in the Chōōji temple, since the British legation in Edo had not yet been furnished.[294] Later the same month, the Russian consul, based in Hakodate, came to visit Edo. At the invitation of Van Polsbroek, he likewise stayed at the Dutch legation.[295] In early May 1865, Van Polsbroek invited a Russian admiral visiting Edo to take up residence at the Chōōji temple. The Japanese government refused permission, however, and requested the admiral to postpone his journey to Edo because of largescale popular festivities taking place in Edo around that time.[296] During his first visit to Edo from 20 to 24 July 1865, the English minister Harrry Parkes found the British legation at the Tōzenji completely uninhabitable. He, too, found lodging at the Dutch legation in Edo.[297] And the Portuguese consul at Kanagawa, N. P. Kingdon, was granted the use of the Dutch legation in Edo for a couple of days from 18 January 1866 onwards.[298]

Although the dilapidated Dutch legation buildings in Edo were sufficient for short stays, they were not equipped for a long-term residence. By the end of September 1865, Van Polsbroek requested the Japanese government to repair and extend the buildings, since he intended to make Edo his first place of residence, just like Portman had done and Parkes was planning to do.[299] After some additional negotiations,[300] the construction of a new wing was completed by early October 1866.[301]

First Meeting with the Japanese Government

On 3 January 1866, Councillor Mizuno Tadakiyo agreed to meet with t'Kint for an initial exchange of information.[302] The previous day Mizuno had sent a dispatch to two councillors, Itakura Katsukiyo and Ogasawara Nagamichi, who were in attendance on the shogun in Osaka. All three officials – Mizuno, Itakura, and Ogasawara – had been involved with the Swiss mission in 1863.[303]

Mizuno's dispatch contained the reports of t'Kint's first meetings with the commissioners of foreign affairs (*gaikoku bugyō* 外国奉行). Mizuno inquired whether the shogun would give permission for a treaty with Belgium to be concluded.[304]

T'Kint and Van Polsbroek were informed on 6 January 1866 that the date for the first meeting with the councillors in Edo had been fixed for 10 January 1866. T'Kint had hoped for an immediate visit to the councillors. He did not understand why he had to wait ten days for what was basically a courtesy call.[305] Apparently, Van Polsbroek had not foreseen such a waiting period either. He informed the Japanese government that he would return with t'Kint to Yokohama on 7 January 1866 to pick up some materials there, leaving their staff at the Dutch legation in Edo. He planned to be back on 8 or 9 January.[306]

The meeting on 10 January 1866 took place in the afternoon.[307] t'Kint was accompanied by the Dutch political agent Van Polsbroek.[308] They were received in the palace of Matsudaira Yasuhide 松平康英, one of the two councillors of the shogun attending the meeting, the other being Mizuno Tadakiyo.[309] Two commissioners of foreign affairs were also present. The councillors acknowledged Auguste t'Kint in his capacity of envoy and plenipotentiary from Belgium.[310] t'Kint informed the councillors about the object of his mission. They replied that since the shogun was absent from Edo, they first had to ask for orders from him concerning the treaty negotiations with Belgium. They would communicate with t'Kint in Yokohama on this subject later.

On the one hand, t'Kint was pleased that this first meeting had taken place relatively quickly. In the past, some envoys had been kept waiting for months before being received by the councillors for the first time. But on the other hand, he had experienced the attitude of the councillors as very cold and reserved, similar to the three meetings he had had with the commissioners of foreign affairs in Edo. Van Polsbroek and t'Kint thought that the appointment of Matsudaira Yasuhide as one of the councillors in charge of foreign affairs might have been one of the reasons. Matsudaira was considered to be less friendly to foreigners than his predecessor.[311] The English minister Harry Parkes had had a meeting with the same two councillors the same day, and according to t'Kint had been received in a similarly cold manner.[312]

Parkes had arrived in Edo on 9 January 1866, and had his meeting with the councillors (*rōjū* 老中) at 11 the next morning, before t'Kint and Van Polsbroek's meeting. It was Parkes's first visit to the councillors of the shogun since the emperor had ratified the foreign treaties at the end of November 1865.[313] The meeting was therefore important, all the more so because the *Japan Times* in Yokohama had cast some doubts on the genuineness of the ratifications by the emperor in Kyoto. According to this local English newspaper, the ratifications were a fraud, committed by the administration of the shogun simply to get rid of the foreign fleet that had anchored at Hyōgo in November 1865 to pressure Japan for imperial ratification.[314] It was therefore crucial for Parkes to obtain reassurances from the shogun's councillors.

On 10 January 1866, Parkes noticed that Sakai Hida no Kami 酒井飛騨守,[315] a junior councillor who had taken a leading part in and a friendly attitude to the relations with the foreign representatives in 1864-1865, had been removed. Parkes was introduced to the new councillor Matsudaira Yasuhide, whom he had never previously met, and to the two "junior councillors" (called "governors" by t'Kint) who were also new to him. Just like the Belgian envoy, Parkes experienced the meeting as far more formal than usual. He attributed this to the fact that it was the initial meeting with most of the top officials present, and that his visit took place in the presence of a considerable number of Japanese commissioners of foreign affairs and other subordinate officials. According to Parkes, the Belgian envoy Auguste t'Kint had met with the same Japanese officials immediately after his own audience. T'Kint had noticed a similar degree of reserve, and made an unfavourable comparison with the reception of foreign dignitaries in Beijing.[316]

During the meeting on 10 January 1865, Parkes raised the treaty negotiations between Belgium and Japan as the first topic. He referred to the services rendered by his predecessor Rutherford Alcock and mentioned that the Dutch would now assist Belgium in a similar manner. He assumed and hoped that no difficulty would impede these treaty negotiations, and assured the councillors that all the foreign representatives in Japan heartily wished the Belgian envoy much success. The councillors replied that satisfactory results might be hoped for after due discussion. The point was made, and the meeting moved on to other topics.[317]

Harry Parkes sent a special dispatch to the Foreign Office concerning the 10 January meeting between t'Kint and the councillors in Edo. He had received information, probably from t'Kint or Van Polsbroek, that the councillors had deferred treaty negotiations until the shogun's return to Edo. Parkes expected that this might take another one or two months. According to Parkes, t'Kint was in no hurry and would take up residence in Yokohama in the meantime.[318] On the instructions of the British Foreign Office, the British minister in Brussels would transmit the content of this dispatch to the Belgian foreign minister on 23 March 1866.[319] The first meeting between t'Kint and the Japanese officials would be finalized by a communication between Van Polsbroek and the Japanese government, sent by the former to t'Kint on 14 January 1866.[320]

T'Kint and the Press in Yokohama

After the meeting with the councillors on 10 January 1866, t'Kint returned to Yokohama within two days.[321] By the end of the month, no progress seemed to have been made with the treaty negotiations. T'Kint probably kept himself busy with furnishing his house in Yokohama. On 24 January 1866, he and Van Polsbroek visited the French frigate *Guerrière*, which had arrived in port.[322]

On 20 January 1866, the local newspaper *Japan Herald* published an article that the Belgian envoy did not appreciate.[323] According to t'Kint, the aim of the article was indirectly to encourage the Japanese government not to conclude any further foreign treaties. The article referred to the meeting of t'Kint in Edo (on 10 January 1866). During the talks, the councillors had allegedly expressed the wish that, for commercial affairs, the Belgians seek the protection of nations who had already signed a treaty with Japan. They expected the same attitude from any other non-treaty country. The Japanese government would not be prepared to conclude new "alliances". The newspaper remarked that Denmark and Italy were equally poised to send missions to

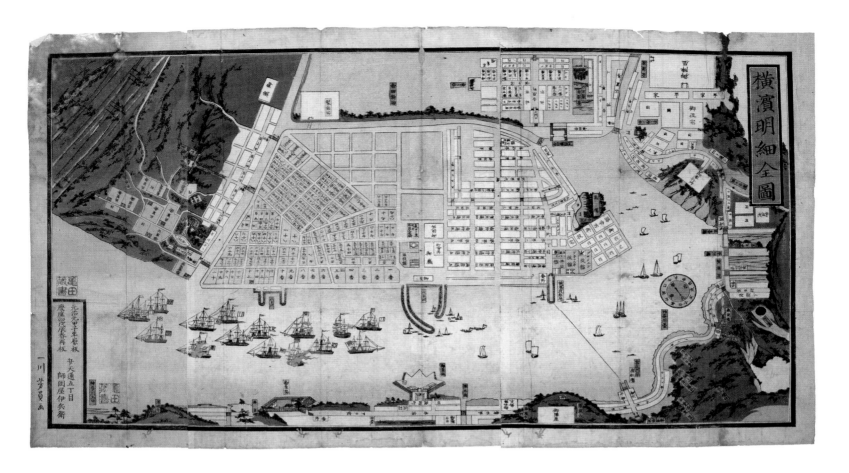

conduct treaty negotiations with Japan, and added: "At present, we do not call to mind more than one Belgian subject belonging to this port (besides His Excellency the Belgian minister), and that one has lately left for a visit to his country".

T'Kint addressed a rectification to the editor of the *Japan Herald*. By doing so, he hoped to minimize the negative effect of the publication, which he considered a danger to his mission. His reply was published in the *Japan Herald* of 23 January 1866. t'Kint denied that the councillors had expressed the wish that Belgium should rely on countries that already had a treaty with Japan, and added "...and as contrary to this, the Gorodjo [*sc. Gorōjū*, the councillors of the shogun] has given to me, the most satisfactory assurances..." [for the conclusion of a treaty with Belgium]. The editor was forced to admit that the councillors had not expressed this wish during the meeting with t'Kint, but insisted that they had done so on another occasion. He denied that the object of the article, either directly or indirectly, was to discourage the Japanese government from concluding a treaty with Belgium. He added that when England, America and

France concluded treaties with Japan, none of these countries had subjects in Japan either. According to the editor, the statement that only one Belgian was currently established in Yokohama went to show the need for a treaty with Belgium in order to raise the number of its nationals in Japan. T'Kint was satisfied with the editor's reply.

The *Japan Times* picked up the story, however, as it was a good occasion to scold its competitor, the *Japan Herald*. In its edition of 26 January 1866, the *Japan Times* stated in its overview of "The Week":

> We are glad to hear that the Belgian Minister H. E. M. Augt. Kint de Roodenbeck, has advanced fairly on his way towards achieving the purpose for which he came to Japan. We had not intended taking any notice of his proceedings until success had crowned his efforts to obtain a treaty for his country – a country so purely commercial and so able to exchange benefits with Japan as is Belgium. But our contemporary, the *Japan Herald*, having neglected the excellent opportunity of silence which presented itself on this subject, we do not

Utagawa Issen Yoshikazu 歌川一川芳員 (active between 1848 and 1870). Detailed map of Yokohama 横浜明細全図 (50 × 90 cm), published by Kinkōdō 錦港堂. Original edition 1864, reprinted in the spring of 1868. Collection of Yokohama Archives of History 横浜開港資料館, Collection of maps, no. 66.

commit an indiscretion in speaking now to record a success, which, now partial, will soon we trust become complete.[324]

T'Kint's suspicion that the article in the *Japan Herald* might have a negative influence on Japanese officials was not without foundation. On 20 January 1866, the Japanese handwritten newspaper *Nippon Shinbun* translated and published part of the article that had appeared in the *Japan Herald* the same day. It clearly mentioned the Japanese government's supposed suggestion to the Belgian envoy that nationals from non-treaty countries should seek protection from treaty powers for their businesses in Japan. It did not mention the fact that only one Belgian was currently established in Yokohama.[325] On 27 January 1866, the *Nippon Shinbun* published a Japanese translation of the rectification sent in by t'Kint to the *Japan Herald*. The comments of the editor in response to t'Kint's rectification were not included.[326]

In his dispatch of 31 January 1866 to the Belgian Foreign Minister Charles Rogier, t'Kint described the whole affair with the local press. He concluded that he had the support of all his colleagues, the foreign representatives in Japan. He added, however, that just as he had experienced in China, the representatives who were relatively well established in Japan had no desire for a new envoy to succeed in his negotiations quickly. He did not mention any names.[327]

Death of a King

On 6 February 1866, the British steamer *Granada* arrived at Yokohama with the latest mail.[328] The mail contained a dispatch from the Belgian foreign minister to Auguste t'Kint announcing the death of Leopold I. The first king of the Belgians had passed away on 10 December 1865, after a long illness. In fact, the local English newspapers had recently given some coverage to the Belgian king's illness.

On 23 January 1866, the American corvette Fujiyama had brought telegraphic news to Yokohama, including a telegraph message dated London, 6 December 1865 with news that Queen Victoria had sent her personal physician to Brussels to attend to the health of the Belgian king, who was in a critical condition. Leopold I was Victoria's uncle. This message appeared in the *Japan*

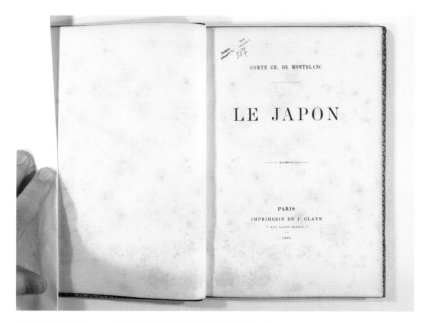

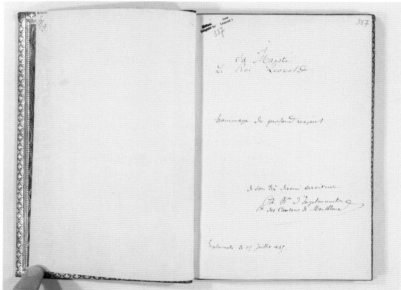

Times Daily Advertiser (Second Edition) on 24 January 1866.[329] It was translated into Japanese and published by the *Nippon shinbun* on 26 January 1866.[330]

On 7 February 1866, t'Kint informed the councillors and the foreign diplomats.[331] Messages of sympathy came pouring in[332] and t'Kint devoted a dispatch on them to Rogier. He particularly mentioned the condolences from the ministers of France and Britain, the Japanese councillors, and the governor of Kanagawa.[333] The local newspapers in Yokohama swiftly followed. The *Japan Times* of 9 February 1866 eulogized the deceased king.[334]

Title page of *Le Japon*, by Comte Charles de Montblanc (1865).
Archives of the Royal Palace, Brussels.

Dedication by Montblanc to King Leopold I on flyleaf of *Le Japon*, signed and dated 25 July 1865.
Archives of the Royal Palace, Brussels. Photograph by Hans Coppens.

The news also appeared in Japanese in the *Nippon shinbun* of the same day.[335] On 17 February 1866, the *Japan Times* published a report from its correspondent in Paris about the death of Leopold I both in French and in English.[336]

A Japanese Visit to Brussels

T'Kint not only received a dispatch from Rogier about the death of the Belgian king. Probably with the same steamer Granada, a letter from Rogier arrived about the visit of a Japanese delegation in Brussels.[337] The dispatch was dated Brussels, 1 December 1865. At that point the Belgian foreign minister was still ignorant of the treaty that t'Kint had concluded with China, and unaware that t'Kint had moved to Japan. The content of the letter went as follows (English translation of a part of the French text):

> Four persons from Japan arrived not long ago in Belgium. They had been sent by the Prince of Satsuma, king of the Lew-Chew Islands [i.e. Ryūkyū], to study the political and industrial organization of the most important countries in Europe. They visited our most important manufacturing centres, accompanied by Count de Montblanc d'Ingelmunster, who has already visited Japan and has maintained connections there. Their mission did not have an official character, but they have let on that after their return [to Japan], it is likely that a new Japanese Embassy will be sent to Europe to conclude treaties with several Powers, invested with (full) powers from the mikado [i.e. the emperor in Kyoto]. They have, as it happens, shown Belgium the most favourable disposition. Not only would Belgium be one of the first states with whom the said Embassy would negotiate, but we could also hope to obtain certain special advantages relating to supplies from the Japanese government.

The draft of this letter contained a phrase that had been struck through: "These overtures have been confirmed to us by Count de MontBlanc". The minister believed that Belgium should await the results of these overtures before t'Kint made any move to the government of the shogun for the conclusion of a treaty. He hoped that t'Kint would agree with this view. The minister promised to keep t'Kint informed of developments.

The Satsuma mission to Europe had first arrived in England on 21 June 1865. Belgium was the second country the delegation visited. After their arrival on Belgian soil, they were accompanied by the "Comte des Cantons Charles Montblanc d'Ingelmunster", who had indeed visited Japan.[338]

On 10 October 1865, a dispatch was sent from the Belgian foreign minister to the minister of the royal household.[339] The draft text, here translated from French to English (with deleted words struck through and marginal annotations given in italics) ran thus:

> The Prince of Satsuma is one of the great feudal lords of the Empire of Japan. He is, furthermore, King of Lew-Chew, neighbouring the Island of Formosa and, in that latter quality, it seems he is independent.
>
> He has sent a mission to Europe for a kind of exploration, charged with studying different European nations from a political, commercial and industrial viewpoint. The mission is composed of four persons, of whom one speaks French fairly well and another English.
>
> Having visited France,[340] the envoys of the Japanese Prince have just arrived in Brussels. They have been presented to me by Count de Montblanc d'Ingelmunster, who has travelled to Japan and who has extensive notions on the organization of the country. I was very much interested by their conversation, and I expect to be able to facilitate their access to our principal industrial and commercial centres.
>
> It will not be without importance for the future development of our relations with Japan if the representatives of one of the most powerful princes of that faraway country carry away a favourable idea of Belgium and its resources of all kinds.
>
> Perhaps the King and H.R.H. the Duke of Brabant will consider it fit to receive these Envoys *and the Count de Montblanc*. It goes without saying that the reception of these strangers will have a purely ~~official~~ unofficial character. Their mission In fact, *they are not charged with any official mission towards the Government. Their role is to observe, and to prepare to a certain extent the ground for sending a far more considerable mission that will be invested (undoubtedly) with an official character.*
>
> I would be much obliged to you, Sir, if you could

inform me about the intentions of H.M. and H.R.H. in this regard.

The Envoys will await the reply, which I shall transmit to them, to organize their itinerary in Belgium.

Since the draft text was addressed to the minister of the royal household, a high-level official in the Foreign Ministry must have been the author, and must have met with the Satsuma delegation. In fact, according to the diary of one of the delegates, Godai Tomoatsu 五代友厚, the mission met with the Belgian minister of foreign affairs in Brussels at 2 p.m., most likely on 9 October 1865.[341] According to the diary, the Japanese delegates conversed with Charles Rogier for several hours about topics that included visits to a number of factories in the country. This coincides with the contents of the text of 10 October 1865 drafted by the Ministry of Foreign Affairs. Two days later, the Satsuma delegates were visited by the deputy minister of foreign affairs. They discussed a variety of matters and had dinner together.[342]

On 13 October 1865, the Foreign Ministry dispatched an urgent letter to de Montblanc, who was lodged in the Hôtel de l'Europe in Brussels. The duke of Brabant (the later King Leopold II) had agreed to meet the Satsuma envoys and de Montblanc on Sunday 15 October 1865 at 4 p.m.[343] Next day, the Belgian Foreign Ministry sent dispatches to the governors of the provinces of Liège, East Flanders and Namur, informing them about the Satsuma mission touring the country, accompanied by Count de Montblanc. The Ministry requested the governors to show hospitality to the mission and to facilitate the access of the delegates to those establishments they wished to visit. The presidents of the chambers of commerce of Verviers and Charleroi also received such messages. Letters of recommendation to the governors and the chamber presidents had to be sent to de Montblanc, but only after the signature of Mr Van Praet, minister of the royal household[344] had been received.[345]

Around that time, Godai noted in his diary that his delegation wanted to conclude a treaty of friendship with the Belgian government. As a starting point, the Satsuma delegation signed a commercial contract with Count de Montblanc on 15 October 1865.[346] Interestingly, two representatives from the Belgian government attended the signing as witnesses. One of them was Edouard Degrelle.[347] He was a nephew of Charles Rogier, and was employed at the Belgian Ministry of Foreign Affairs.[348] The other has not been identified.

At 4 p.m. on the same day, 15 October 1865, the Satsuma delegation was received in audience by the duke of Brabant. Godai describes the event as follows in his diary:[349]

Sunday. Today is a holiday. At 4 p.m. visit to the 'Duc de Brabant', (Crown) Prince of the currently reigning King. This man is personally gifted with a brilliant mind, able to hold responsibility for state affairs, and welcoming us, gave (us) a friendly treatment and was cordial.

On 18 October 1865, another letter left the Ministry of Foreign Affairs. This time, the addressee was the Belgian minister of defence. The minister was requested to provide authorization for the Satsuma mission to visit the fortifications of Antwerp. The chief cabinet of the minister of war ad interim gave his consent in a letter of 21 October 1865.[350] After visiting Cologne, Berlin and Amsterdam, the Satsuma delegation returned to Belgium. Together with de Montblanc, they visited Antwerp. After that, they returned to Brussels, visited Namur and arrived in Paris on 12 or 13 November 1865, in the company of de Montblanc.[351]

The Satsuma mission and de Montblanc's journey through Belgium had a profound effect on the policy of the Belgian government towards Japan. Until then, the government had relied entirely on Auguste t'Kint, who had received full powers to conclude a treaty with Japan. The letter from Rogier to t'Kint of 1 December 1865 clearly showed that the Belgian government now seriously believed that a high level mission empowered by the emperor in Kyoto would be sent to Europe to conclude treaties with several countries. As a result, the full powers of t'Kint were put on hold.

The influence of the Satsuma mission and of Count de Montblanc on the duke of Brabant and the Belgian Ministry of Foreign Affairs is perfectly depicted in a note written by Edouard Degrelle to the Belgian foreign minister (his uncle), shortly after the Satsuma envoys had left Brussels.[352] Degrelle praised all de Montblanc's efforts to connect the industrial and commercial circles of Belgium with markets in Japan. He referred to the duke of Brabant's high regard for de Montblanc's publications concerning the Far East, and he concluded by proposing to bestow a Belgian decoration, the Cross of the Knight of the Order of Leopold, on Count de Montblanc d'Ingelmunster.[353]

It is striking that the Belgian government did not request any advice from its diplomatic agents in London, Paris or The Hague, concerning the Satsuma mission. The presence of Count de Montblanc may have given the Foreign Ministry sufficient confidence in the Satsuma connection. In his dispatch of 1 December 1865 to t'Kint,[354] Rogier explained that Belgium could expect some special advantages and would be among the first countries to negotiate with the future Imperial Mission to Europe. Edouard Degrelle, in his note of 21 November 1865 to Rogier, mentioned that there was talk of a commercial enterprise between Japan and the European countries, in which Belgium — thanks to Count de Montblanc being the negotiator — would have a major stake, finding new and immense markets for the export of Belgian products.[355] By not including its foreign network in the discussion, the Belgian Foreign Ministry may have wanted to avoid other European nations getting wind of the lucrative deals that Belgium was hoping to harvest from its relations with Satsuma.[356]

In his dispatch of 8 December 1865, t'Kint had asked the Belgian foreign minister for a budget to cover the costs of his mission to Japan. When this request arrived in Brussels,[357] the administration concentrated mainly on checking t'Kint's financial logic. Still, an internal note of 1 February 1866 referred to Rogier's dispatch of 1 December 1865 sent to t'Kint requesting the latter not to leave for Japan. The note concluded that t'Kint probably had not received the dispatch in time.[358] There is no evidence that the mission of t'Kint to Japan had upset the Ministry. It therefore looks like the Belgian government had softened its new Japan policy based on the talks with Satsuma and de Montblanc in October 1865.

Due to the death of Leopold I, Auguste t'Kint needed new credentials from the new monarch, Leopold II. Having received the dispatch of 1 December 1865 from Foreign Minister Rogier, t'Kint concluded that he would not receive these letters of credence. In a long dispatch, dated 14 February 1866, he disputed the new policy of Brussels,[359] arguing firstly that Minister Rogier himself mentioned in his dispatch that the Satsuma mission had no official character, and had neither the right nor the authority to negotiate new treaties. Building a policy on the ideas of such a mission, would be deplorable.

Secondly, t'Kint had heard different persons and different opinions in Japan, but he could not consider it likely that the emperor in Kyoto would send an Embassy to Europe to conclude bilateral treaties. The idea of such an imperial mission might have resulted from the rivalry between the prince of Satsuma and the current shogun. The members of the commission, sent to Europe by this prince, might have hoped that the intrigues of the shogun's enemies would induce the emperor to disavow the shogun for having continued relations with the foreigners against his imperial will. Consequently, the prince of Satsuma would then be appointed as shogun, and would send an embassy to Europe to negotiate new treaties with the consent of the emperor. But t'Kint argued that in contrast to all this, the emperor had ratified the treaties concluded by the current shogun, and had not sent an Embassy to Europe.

Thirdly, t'Kint was very critical towards the so-called special advantages that might accrue to Belgium from the relationship with Satsuma. All the countries that had concluded treaties with Japan would naturally oppose such a privileged treatment of Belgian trade. Since the beginning of their relations with Japan and with China, all these countries had adhered to the principle of a uniform treatment for all nations. This liberal principle had been established by the Great Powers, whose arms had opened the Far East for world trade. The nations that came later had followed this rule as a matter of course, and had limited themselves to demanding the same advantages as those granted to all other countries.

If the members of the Satsuma mission had mentioned special advantages granted to Belgium only for Japanese government procurement, t'Kint remarked that until then the Japanese government had purchased mainly from England, the Netherlands, France and the United States. T'Kint thought that the Japanese government would not limit its purchases to one country (Belgium), but would continue to buy from several countries taking into account the best conditions available. Belgium should aim to get the highest share possible of such government procurement. T'Kint admitted that Japanese visits to the industrial and commercial centres of Belgium was a way towards that goal. But he also added that a treaty of amity and commerce between Belgium and Japan would be the best foundation for a convention on special advantages for Belgium in the field of government procurement. A treaty would enable Belgian traders to organize their operations in the open ports of Japan without delay. They would enjoy the same privileges and advantages alongside traders from other treaty countries.

As already explained in his dispatch of 8 December 1865 sent from Shanghai, t'Kint pointed out that there was a certain urgency to concluding a treaty with Japan, since the Port of Hyōgo and the City of Osaka, two major commercial centres, would open for foreign trade on 1 January 1868. On 14 February 1866, he conveyed his hopes to the Belgian minister that the ministry would soon send him new full powers for concluding a treaty with Japan. He pointed out that the request for treaty negotiations had been initiated already. In view of the slow pace of negotiations in Japan, t'Kint defended his arrival in Japan as just on time. Once a treaty had been concluded with Japan and the ratifications exchanged, he believed there would be still sufficient time left for Belgian traders to organize their activities in Japan and to take full advantage of the opening of Osaka and Hyōgo.

Apparently, in Brussels, the Foreign Ministry had come to a similar conclusion. On 27 February 1866, even before the dispatch with t'Kint's arguments had arrived, a letter had been drafted to the Royal Palace containing a proposal for new credentials for t'Kint, as Leopold II's special envoy to Japan.[360] In the meantime, the ministry had received t'Kint's dispatch of 18 December 1865, announcing his arrival in Yokohama.[361]

On 5 March 1866, the foreign minister in Brussels dispatched a letter to t'Kint announcing a complete U-turn.[362] First, the letter referred to the instructions of 1 December 1865 given to t'Kint not to initiate treaty negotiations with Japan. The minister also referred to the dispatch from t'Kint of 18 December 1865 sent from Yokohama. This dispatch had announced the arrival of t'Kint in Japan, and the ratification of the foreign treaties by the emperor in Kyoto as a reason for t'Kint proceeding to Japan. As a consequence of this, the minister approved t'Kint's move to initiate treaty negotiations with the government at Edo. He added that t'Kint should consider the instructions of 1 December 1865 as non-existent. To this dispatch the letter of credence was attached, signed by Leopold II and empowering the Belgian envoy to conclude a treaty with Japan. The effects of the Satsuma visit had been completely wiped out.

Auguste t'Kint was not the only diplomat in Yokohama to be confronted with the aftermath of the Satsuma mission in Belgium. The French representative in Japan, Léon Roches, received a letter from the French foreign minister dispatched on 9 November 1865. Through the French vice consul in the Belgian city of Liège, the minister had been informed that the Japanese government had ordered 12 cannons at the *Fonderie nationale* in Liège and the corresponding projectiles from Frederix, an industrialist based in the same city.[363] Roches contacted the Japanese government in Edo, but they denied having bought any such material in Belgium. Roches therefore suggested that the procurement could have been done by one of the powerful and rich feudal lords.[364] In view of the timing, it is clear that the French vice consul in Liège was being faced with the aftermath of the Satsuma mission in Belgium.

Japanese Commissioners Appointed

Having been received by the Japanese government on 10 January 1866, t'Kint's mission seemed to have stalled. No Japanese councillors had been appointed in the meantime. T'Kint attributed this to the absence of the shogun from his capital Edo and to the systematically slow pace of diplomatic affairs in Japan, in particular when it came to concluding a new treaty. In early February 1866, t'Kint was considering a new approach to the Japanese government when he was informed of the death of Leopold I. Understanding that his full powers as envoy of Leopold I had come to an end, he decided to renounce any further initiative for a treaty with Japan until he had obtained new full powers.[365]

On 27 January 1866, the British minister Harry Parkes received a dispatch from the Foreign Office in London announcing that Denmark would send a mission to Japan for treaty negotiations in the spring of 1866. By chance, the same day, Parkes had a meeting with Councillors Mizuno Tadakiyo and Matsudaira Yasuhide. He confronted them with this message and on the basis of the remarks made by the councillors, Parkes concluded that the Japanese government was currently not willing to extend its relations with other European countries. The councillors gave as reason that it was inconvenient and not appropriate to have treaty negotiations when the shogun was absent from Edo. In his reply to the Foreign Office, dated 14 February 1866, Parkes added that the Belgian minister (Auguste t'Kint) had made little progress since his arrival two months before. According to Mizuno and Matsudaira, they were still awaiting instructions on how to deal with the Belgian request for treaty negotiations.[366]

These instructions had in the meantime been sent from Osaka in a letter dated 9 February 1866. It was signed by three of the shogun's councillors (*rōjū* 老中): Ogasawara Nagamichi, Matsudaira Munehide 松平宗秀 and Itakura Katsukiyo. It was addressed to one of the shogun's councillors in Edo, Mizuno Tadakiyo. The three councillors informed Mizuno that a treaty with Belgium should be based on the treaty that Japan had concluded with Prussia.[367] Four days later, on 13 February 1866, Mizuno received the dispatch and acknowledged the content.[368] One day later, on 14 February, he sent a letter to his three colleagues in Osaka, reminding them that the current position of the government was that treaty negotiations could not be held without the presence of the shogun in Edo. The dispatch from Osaka of 9 February changed that position, and Mizuno wanted to make sure that his colleagues were aware of this.[369] He repeated his request for more details and consultation in a letter dated 17 February 1866.[370]

The reply came in the format of a formal note from the shogun appointing Kikuchi Takayoshi and Hoshino Kazuyuki, commissioners of foreign affairs, and Ōkubo Chikugo no Kami 大久保筑後守, *metsuke* 目付, as plenipotentiaries empowered to conclude a treaty with Belgium. An additional document dated 25 February 1866 confirmed these appointments.[371] Kikuchi and Hoshino were among the Japanese officials who negotiated the treaty with the Swiss Confederation in 1864.[372]

Mizuno Tadakiyo and Matsudaira Yasuhide informed t'Kint of these appointments on 28 February. They added that the plenipotentiaries would visit t'Kint in Yokohama to discuss the upcoming negotiations.[373] In a reply to the Japanese commissioners of 3 March 1865, the Belgian envoy welcomed the appointments. He added that he was looking forward to meeting the three negotiators.[374]

T'Kint now found himself in an awkward position. Japanese plenipotentiaries had been chosen, but t'Kint himself did not have the full powers needed to start negotiations. Worse still, the latest instructions that he had received from Brussels had ordered him not to initiate treaty negotiations with Japan. He considered refusing to negotiate, but in the end decided to start the negotiations on his own responsibility, strongly believing that the full powers needed from Brussels would arrive later.[375]

In fact, t'Kint had discussed the matter of a possible imperial mission from Japan to Europe with his diplomatic colleagues from England, France, the US and the Netherlands in Yokohama. All confirmed that there

was no chance of such a mission materializing. Léon Roches, the French Representative, even made an extensive report on Japan's foreign policy in the period 1858-1864 available to t'Kint.

The Belgian envoy concluded that the emperor in Kyoto had only ratified the treaties because of the presence of the shogun and his army at Osaka and Kyoto, and because of the presence of the foreign representatives and the foreign fleet in Hyōgo. He considered the emperor still to be very anti-foreign, and sending an imperial mission to strengthen relations with European powers did not fit this picture.

On the basis of this analysis, t'Kint decided to enter into negotiations with the Japanese commissioners. After all, he had already presented himself as the Belgian plenipotentiary to the Japanese government on 10 January 1866. Otherwise, he thought Belgium would lose valuable time in getting its products on to the promising Japanese market. Around 10 March 1866, t'Kint had his first meeting with the Japanese plenipotentiaries at his residence in Yokohama. By 14 March 1866, the Japanese commissioners had returned to Edo, but t'Kint believed they would return to Yokohama shortly. The first meeting mainly touched upon the general dispositions of a treaty. T'Kint did not expect any serious obstacle against a treaty based on the same principles as the other treaties in force in Japan.

In his communication to the Foreign Ministry in Brussels, t'Kint did not elaborate on these general dispositions of a treaty with Japan. The English minister Harry Parkes, on the other hand, gave more details in his dispatch of 16 March 1866 to the Foreign Office in London. According to Parkes, the Japanese government recognized its promise of a treaty with Belgium. However, the Japanese negotiators had informed t'Kint that the basis for such a treaty could only be the treaty between Prussia and Japan. This treaty contained no stipulation relative to the opening of Hyōgo, Niigata, Osaka and Edo. Such a fundamental tenet would run counter to the consent obtained from the emperor on 24 November 1865, which explicitly included the opening of these two cities and two ports. Parkes was much alarmed and was determined to request a clarification from the Japanese government.[376]

Furthermore, the Japanese government asked Parkes to use his influence to prevent Denmark from sending a mission to Japan. According to Councillors Mizuno Tadakiyo and Matsudaira Yasuhide, Japan did not produce enough to provide for both domestic consumption and export. Hence, foreign trade had led to instability in Japan. The two councillors referred to the communication of the former American Minister Townsend Harris in 1861 to a number of countries, announcing that Japan would no longer allow any new treaty negotiations. An exception was made for those countries already in treaty relations with Japan, and for Switzerland and Belgium to whom such relations had been promised. Since Denmark was one of the recipients of this communication, the Danish government ought to be aware of this situation. The two councillors added that this policy would remain in place until Japan became more used to international trade, and until the general public learned to appreciate the advantages of foreign relations.[377] The Dutch political agent and consul general Dirk de Graeff van Polsbroek received a similar reply when inquiring about a possible Japanese treaty with Denmark or with the Free Hanseatic Cities.[378]

While t'Kint had initiated treaty negotiations with the councillors, the *Japan Times* ran an editorial on 16 March 1866 pleading for the conclusion of treaties with a confederation of feudal lords of Japan (*daimyō* 大名), sanctioned by the emperor in Kyoto, rather than treaties with the shogun alone. According to the *Japan Times*, the feudal lords were only bound to recognize the existence of the treaties with the shogun, but the treaties as they stood in March 1866, were not applicable to them. This became clear when a vessel belonging to the Lord of Satsuma arrived in Yokohama and the captain proposed to sell certain Japanese produce to the European merchants. The local authorities refused permission for the Satsuma officers and crew to land, and the trade was forbidden. The *Japan Times* believed that a treaty concluded directly with the emperor in Kyoto would not be a good idea, because the emperor would not be able to enforce such a treaty. Therefore, it preferred a treaty with a confederation of feudal lords, sanctioned by the emperor in Kyoto. The newspaper believed that there was still enough time before the opening of Hyōgo to conclude such a treaty with the feudal lords. It feared that in the absence of such a treaty, the opening of Hyōgo would be accompanied by bloodshed.[379]

The Belgian envoy, too, noticed that doubts were raised about the ratification of the foreign treaties by the emperor in Kyoto.[380] The government of the shogun had continuously argued that the hostile attitude towards the foreigners of a number of feudal lords and part of the population was preventing them from extending foreign relations.[381] On the other hand, those same feudal lords explained that they were favourable towards foreign relations and that they were willing to open the ports under their control. However, they were opposed to the foreign trade monopoly of the shogun. The foreign representatives were not sure what to believe, and therefore continued their policy of relying on the shogun for the implementation of the foreign treaties.

On 19 March 1866, Auguste t'Kint informed Councillors Kikuchi, Hoshino and Ōkubo, that he was ready to hold the next meeting related to the treaty negotiations.[382] It took another four weeks, on 16 April 1866, before t'Kint met with Hoshino in Yokohama, Kikuchi apparently being "indisposed".[383] The meeting took a little less than three hours.[384] According to t'Kint, the Japanese negotiators relentlessly confronted him with the state of affairs in Japan and the opinion of the people, neither of which allowed any extension of foreign relations. Still, t'Kint did not believe that the negotiators were aiming at terminating the talks. The negotiations had progressed, and some stipulations had been agreed upon, among others the right to open Belgian consulates in Japan.

The Belgian envoy had understood that an indirect approach towards the Japanese government was to be preferred. He therefore heavily relied on the foreign representatives in Yokohama, such as the Dutch political agent Dirk de Graeff van Polsbroek, and increasingly on Harry Parkes, the English minister, and Léon Roches, the French minister. T'Kint observed that the latter two had the most influence with the Japanese government in Edo.

Still, frustrated with the slow pace of the negotiations in Yokohama, t'Kint went to stay a few days in Edo during the week of 3 May 1866, probably to put some pressure on the Japanese government. There he met with one of the Japanese negotiators. At Edo he also discussed the slowness of the treaty negotiations with the French Minister Léon Roches. T'Kint received information that the councillors in Edo had sent a high government official to Osaka to consult the shogun on the question of new foreign treaties. This official was expected to return to Edo within a week, and t'Kint decided not to undertake further action in the meantime.[385] At the same time, the Japanese government seemed to have approached the English minister Parkes for assistance in dealing with the Belgian treaty request, simultaneously informing him that a Danish treaty on the same basis as the English or French treaties would be difficult.[386]

Having returned to Yokohama, Auguste t'Kint met with Jules Adrian on 9 May 1866.[387] Adrian was General Manager of the Maison Adrian et Cie in Nagasaki.[388] While on a business trip in Europe, he had visited the Belgian Ministry of Foreign Affairs in Brussels, probably late November 1865, to put forward his candidacy for the post of Belgian consul in Nagasaki.[389] On 10 March 1866, the Belgian Foreign Ministry entrusted a dispatch for t'Kint to Adrian. This contained, among other things, the ratifications of the Belgian-Chinese Treaty, the official announcement of the death of King Leopold I and the enthronement of King Leopold II, and the new credentials from King Leopold II mandating t'Kint to conclude a treaty of amity, commerce and navigation with Japan.[390] Adrian embarked from Marseille on 16 March 1866.[391] He reached Yokohama on 8 May 1866 on board the Dupleix, a steamer belonging to the French shipping company Messageries Impériales.[392] The arrival of the full powers for t'Kint put an end to the uncertainty about his mandate.

On 16 May 1866, t'Kint informed the councillors in charge of foreign affairs in Edo that he had received a message from Leopold II addressed to the shogun.[393] Consequently, t'Kint received a call from a commissioner of foreign affairs (*kaigai bugyō* 海外奉行), Ishino Noritsune 石野則常. t'Kint informed the commissioner that he had received a letter from the king of the Belgians addressed to the shogun, announcing the death of Leopold I and the accession to the throne of Leopold II. T'Kint explained to Ishino that protocol required the envoy of the king to place such a royal letter into the hands of the sovereign to whom it was addressed. The shogun being in Osaka, t'Kint proposed to present the letter to the councillors in charge of foreign affairs and to request them to deliver it in person to the shogun in Osaka. To Ishino, t'Kint requested a conference with the councillors for this purpose.[394]

On 24 May 1866, Commissioner Ishino replied in writing to t'Kint's request. Ishino had informed the councillors (*rōjū* 老中), but being occupied with an important matter of state, they had replied that they were for the time being unable to commit to a date for a meeting with t'Kint. A colleague of Ishino would soon be dispatched to Yokohama to give more details to the Belgian envoy.[395]

T'Kint was much taken aback by this negative reply. He probably consulted the French minister Léon Roches,

and perhaps also the British minister Parkes,[396] before reacting in two ways. On 31 May 1866, he wrote to the three Japanese negotiators Kikuchi, Hoshino and Ōkubo, stating that their last meeting had been 40 days ago. He requested a new meeting.[397] The same day, he addressed a dispatch to the councillors in charge of foreign affairs. T'Kint thought it likely that the negative reply was the result of a misunderstanding, and asked the councillors to deprecate the letter from Commissioner Ishino. However, should this not be the case, then the Belgian envoy was perfectly willing to travel to Osaka himself to present the letter from Leopold II to the shogun in person.[398] The draft versions of the two letters bore the dates 29 May 1866 and 30 May 1866 respectively, showing that t'Kint took his time over sending his official reaction. At the same time, the two letters are proof that t'Kint had scaled back his indirect approach through other foreign representatives, and now seemed to favour a more direct style of negotiation.[399]

Two dispatches dated 11 June 1866 show t'Kint's dissatisfaction with the course events had taken.[400] T'Kint recalled that a high official of the Japanese government in Edo had travelled to Osaka and returned to Edo with the shogun's consent to continuing the policy of refusing any additional foreign treaties. Hence, the English minister Harry Parkes again received a negative reply when requesting treaty negotiations for Denmark around 8 June 1866. T'Kint mentioned that he would safeguard the ongoing treaty negotiations with Belgium, and that he was confident that these negotiations would lead to a treaty.

In a confidential dispatch of 11 June 1866 to Charles Rogier in Brussels, t'Kint described his growing doubts concerning the interventions of the French Minister Léon Roches with the Japanese government in Edo. Roches would have advised the councillors to refuse all requests for new treaty negotiations, and to promulgate a decree opening up navigation and trade with Japan to all nations in the open ports. Furthermore, all foreigners would be allowed to call upon the consulates of the countries holding treaties with Japan to defend their interests. After consultation with the shogun in Osaka, the councillors rejected Roches's proposal.

T'Kint had always believed that Roches looked favourably on a Belgian treaty with Japan. He had therefore followed Roches's advice to abandon all attempts at treaty negotiations with Japan until the councillors in Edo had received instructions from the shogun at Osaka. It had meant a period of inactivity of some three to four weeks. The Belgian envoy considered a treaty binding the treaty parties a better option than a revocable decree promulgated by one party, Japan. He could not understand the new position that Roches had taken. He had come to the conclusion that he could only count on his own efforts to secure a treaty, hence his letters of 31 May 1866 to the Japanese ministers and the Japanese plenipotentiaries for the treaty negotiations with Belgium.

Already on 3 June 1866, the councillors replied that their busy schedule did not permit a meeting with t'Kint. They did promise, however, to propose a date for such a meeting once the current press of business had passed.[401] Two days later, the councillors in charge of foreign affairs sent a reply to t'Kint's second letter, the one addressed to the Japanese plenipotentiaries responsible for the Belgian treaty negotiations. Although the councillors stated their intentions to conclude "friendship" between both countries, they admitted that the negotiations had not yet resulted in a conclusion. A few articles still needed to be agreed, so negotiations with t'Kint were postponed. In view of t'Kint's proposal on 31 May 1866 that talks be resumed, the councillors promised to deliberate again among themselves, and once they had reached a decision they would give the Belgian envoy a date for the next meeting.[402]

In light of these replies and his doubts about Roches, t'Kint turned to the English minister Parkes. On 8 June 1866, he had a meeting with Parkes about the negotiations for a Belgian treaty, followed by a confidential letter two days later.[403] In this, t'Kint described how, on the advice of the French Minister Roches, he had waited for the Japanese commissioners in Edo to receive instructions from the shogun in Osaka on the conclusion of new foreign treaties. As a result, the last meeting that t'Kint had had with any of the Japanese negotiators, namely with Hoshino Kazuyuki, had taken place some two months before. Then he had been informed that the other negotiator, Kikuchi Takayoshi, was indisposed. Since then, t'Kint had been waiting in vain for a new meeting with all negotiators. Finally, on 31 May 1866, he had addressed them a letter requesting a new meeting. T'Kint now asked Parkes to intervene in Edo in favour of his request for such a meeting. He gave Parkes *carte blanche* in his talks with the Japanese government, regarding the clause on which ports and cities would be open to Belgian nationals.

Harry Parkes had a meeting with one of the Japanese plenipotentiaries for the Belgian treaty negotiations.[404] The Japanese official did his utmost to avoid the topic of the Belgian Treaty.[405] Still, t'Kint travelled from Yokohama to Edo, where he stayed at the Dutch legation. It is likely that the Dutch representative, Polsbroek, accompanied him.[406] On 20 June 1866, he invited the plenipotentiaries appointed by the shogun for the Belgian treaty negotiations to a meeting at the Dutch legation.[407] The plenipotentiary with whom Parkes had met, visited t'Kint the next morning.[408] The Belgian envoy received a promise from the Japanese representative that negotiations for a treaty with Belgium would be resumed in Yokohama once the Japanese side had held another meeting with Parkes first. T'Kint hoped that negotiations could be picked up in Yokohama on Monday 25 June 1866.

The meeting did not materialize as t'Kint had hoped. He made no mention of it in his dispatch to Charles Rogier dated 27 June 1866. On the contrary, he mentioned that the Japanese side had used every means to postpone negotiations for a treaty they did not want. T'Kint had to remind the Japanese authorities that the whole world was watching how these negotiations would end, and that the good name of the shogun was in danger if the appointment of the three Japanese plenipotentiaries were seen as an "illusory measure". Nevertheless, t'Kint believed that the Japanese government would finally bring the negotiations to a good end.[409] On 28 June 1866, he sent a dispatch to the councillors of foreign affairs in Edo asking them to send the commissioners of foreign affairs and the plenipotentiaries for the treaty with Belgium to Yokohama, at latest on 30 June 1866, since he wanted to give them an important message which could not be delayed.[410] The treaty negotiations would finally be resumed on 2 July 1866 in Yokohama.[411]

A Convention with Priority

After t'Kint presented his credentials to the Japanese government on 10 January 1866, it had taken about two months before the Japanese plenipotentiaries were appointed on 2 March 1866 to negotiate the treaty with Belgium. Except for a preliminary meeting shortly after that, it took another four months before in-depth negotiations could start on 2 July 1866. Contemporary sources give several reasons for this slow pace.

The French Minister Léon Roches believed that under the pressure of the foreign fleet in Hyōgo in November 1865, the shogun had been forced to twist the emperor's arm too far. Having obtained the ratification of the foreign treaties by the emperor, the opening of Hyōgo, Osaka, Edo and Niigata at latest on 1 January 1868, and negotiations for new customs regulations and a new tariff, the shogun had hardly any political space left to manoeuvre for additional concessions, such as additional foreign treaties.[412] On top of that, judging from t'Kint's dispatches, the foreign representatives in Yokohama believed that the emperor was still very much against foreign relations.[413] Some of them started doubting the emperor's commitment to opening Hyōgo and Osaka, both located in the neighbourhood of Kyoto.[414]

Some believed that the shogun would first have to reaffirm his authority before he would be able to sign new treaties. Political instability had forced him to leave his capital (Edo) for Osaka.[415] The presence of the shogun and of his troops close to Kyoto was apparently necessary to keep the situation under control. The feudal lord of Chōshū 長州 had been the most vocal among the opponents of the shogun, and by mid-1866, the foreign community in Japan was expecting a military clash between the two.[416] The *Japan Times* doubted the shogun's ability to exert his authority on the unruly feudal lords. It openly argued for new treaties with the latter, rather than with the shogun.[417]

In the midst of the shogun's military campaign against Chōshū, senior councillors in Edo agreed that until Chōshū had been defeated and peace restored to Japan it was better not to make new foreign treaties.[418] Even before the military campaign, they continuously stressed that the situation in Japan did not allow treaties with additional countries. They cited political reasons by referring to the negative influence of some feudal lords, such as Chōshū. They also observed that foreign trade had led to adverse economic effects, stirring up aversion among the general public, with people fearing for their livelihood. When the Dutch representative De Graeff van Polsbroek remarked that the emperor's sanctioning of the existing foreign treaties meant a firm base for the conclusion of treaties with additional countries, the councillors in Edo firmly disagreed, pointing to the current unfavourable situation of the country at large.[419]

The Japanese government in Edo also regularly replied that urgent state affairs prevented them from starting the negotiations for a treaty with Belgium. The implementation of the agreement reached in Hyōgo on 24 November 1865 between emperor, shogun and foreign representatives was indeed a huge operation.

As part of this process, the Japanese government on 27 May 1866 lifted the ban on travel abroad for any Japanese national.[420] The decision to break with this legislation of two centuries' standing must have involved considerable consultation among the Japanese government officials. No wonder that the councillors in Edo had replied to t'Kint on 24 May 1866 that they were occupied with an important matter of state and did not have the time for a meeting with him, even though it would only involve the receipt of a letter to the shogun from the Belgian King Leopold II.[421] Similarly, when Hoshino Kazuyuki met with t'Kint on 16 April 1866 to inform him that his colleague Kikuchi Takayoshi was "indisposed", several foreign representatives mentioned on the very same day the results of extensive negotiations with the Japanese government. Among the results obtained was freedom of trade for all Japanese nationals in the open ports of Japan.[422]

When the negotiations for a treaty between Belgium and Japan restarted early in July 1866, Chōshū had not submitted, the shogun had not yet returned to Edo, and the general public was not yet appeased. In fact, on 10 July 1866, rice riots had broken out in Edo,[423] as they would again at the end of October.[424] The only element that had changed was the signing of a convention on 25 June 1866, introducing new customs regulations, including a general tariff of five per cent, and additionally, bonded warehouse regulations. With the additional regulations, this convention was by far the largest that Japan had thus far concluded with foreign powers.[425] Negotiations had begun on 5 February 1866 and kept the Japanese and foreign representatives busy till 25 June 1866.[426] Because of the intensity of the daily consultations, the American chargé d'affaires, A. L. C. Portman, temporarily moved from Edo to Yokohama, where the talks were being held.[427] One of the Japanese negotiators was Kikuchi Takayoshi, who had been appointed to that position in early February 1866.[428] Small wonder that he hardly had any time when he was appointed plenipotentiary for the treaty negotiations with Belgium in early March 1866. The conclusion of the Convention on 25 June 1866 freed these Japanese officials for other matters. They could now devote themselves to carrying out the promise that the Japanese government had made to Belgium in February 1860 for a treaty of amity, commerce and navigation.

As early as 16 April 1866, Auguste t'Kint acknowledged the efforts demanded from the foreign and Japanese government officials during the negotiations for the new Tariff Convention.[429] He also recognized the importance of this convention for the content of the Treaty between Belgium and Japan. The Belgian envoy had been promised by the Japanese government that the negotiations on the Belgian-Japanese Treaty would resume once the new tariff convention had been signed by England, the United States, France and the Netherlands. Since this was accomplished on 25 June 1866, t'Kint expected the Japanese plenipotentiaries to arrive in Yokohama very soon after.[430] T'Kint explained to the English minister Parkes that he did not consider the slow pace of his negotiations as lost time, since the delay had allowed the Tariff Convention of 25 June 1866 to be concluded. T'Kint was well aware that he would never have received a similar low tariff for Belgium if it were not for the new Tariff Convention negotiated by the four powers.[431]

The Treaty of 1 August 1866

Before Auguste t'Kint and the Japanese plenipotentiaries gathered again on 2 July 1866, the starting point of their negotiations had not yet been decided. The Japanese government had proposed the January 1861 Treaty with Prussia as the basis for negotiation. T'Kint was aware that this Treaty did not mention the opening of Osaka, Hyōgo, Edo and Niigata, and ran counter to the promises obtained from the emperor on 24 November 1865. T'Kint remarked that many alterations had been made in the meantime, particularly to the commercial body of the treaty, and that the text had to be adjusted accordingly. He mentioned in particular the opening of the four places aforementioned. The Japanese representatives took their time in studying t'Kint's proposal, but finally rejected it, sticking to their plan to use the text of the Prussian Treaty unchanged. At that point, the talks had stalled.[432]

The meeting of 2 July 1866 therefore started without a common base for the negotiations. Nevertheless, t'Kint could report that the meeting with the Japanese plenipotentiaries resulted in a more or less final agreement. Still, the Japanese negotiators wanted to return to Edo to consult the senior councillors of the shogun on certain points, promising to return to

Yokohama within two or three days. They did not keep their promise. The Japanese plenipotentiaries had just left for Edo when the Italian frigate, the Magenta, arrived in Yokohama with the aim of concluding a treaty between Italy and Japan. T'Kint suspected that the Japanese government feared any further negotiations with Belgium at a moment they would have to refuse negotiations with the Italian mission.[433] While Belgium had been promised a treaty by Japan in February 1860,[434] Italy had been included in the list of countries that had received a communication from the American Representative Townsend Harris in May 1861.[435] That communication mentioned that Japan was not willing to enter into treaty relations with any country, except for those with whom it had already treaties, and with whom it had promised to treat.

According to t'Kint, the Japanese negotiators would use any means to avoid the opening of Hyōgo, Osaka and Edo to foreign trade. It was apparent that the importance of the results obtained by the foreign powers in Hyōgo in November 1865 had been much overrated. However, t'Kint did admit that the Japanese government had shown its good will by accepting that the Convention of 25 June 1866 and the new tariff for the three open ports be included in the Belgian Treaty.[436] T'Kint was aware that this convention did not mention the opening of Osaka, Hyōgo, Edo and Niigata either, but only contained the general term "the cities to be opened".[437]

Apparently, news had got out that a Belgian treaty was imminent. On 14 July 1886 the Japanese hand-written newspaper *Nippon shinbun gaihen* noted that a treaty with Belgium might be concluded within the next couple of days.[438]

On 8 July, t'Kint had written to Edo reminding the three Japanese plenipotentiaries of their promise to return to Yokohama for further negotiations.[439] The plenipotentiaries replied on 11 July, promising that they would come to t'Kint's residence the next morning.[440] It would prove to be a crucial meeting. After four hours of discussions, the negotiators came to an agreement on all stipulations of the treaty between Belgium and Japan. The negotiations were conducted in Dutch, and t'Kint still had to make the necessary translations and copies.[441] On 13 July 1866, the Japanese plenipotentiaries wrote an internal note on the languages to be used for the treaty text and on the procedure for the treaty exchange.[442]

T'Kint's final problems were the dates that ratifications would be exchanged and that the treaty

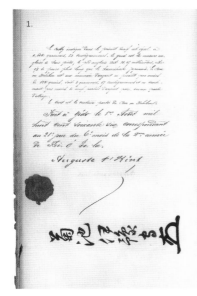
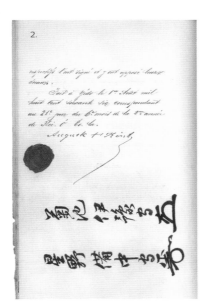
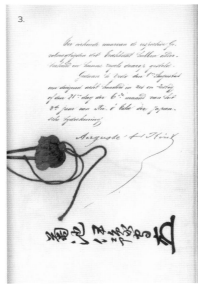
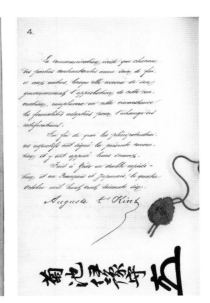

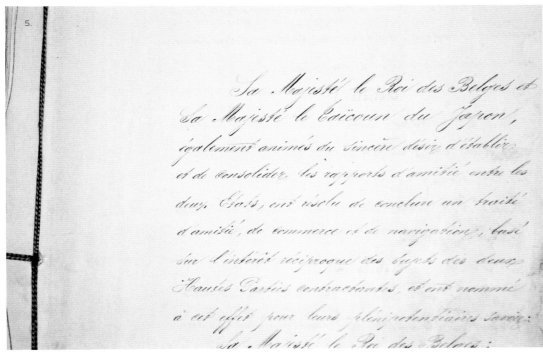

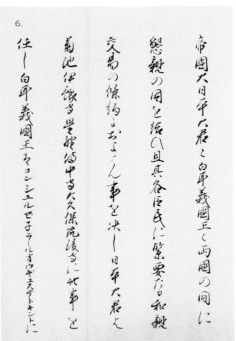

The Treaty between Belgium and Japan of 1866 (1>3). The convention was signed by t'Kint, Kikuchi, Hoshino and Ōkubo (whose signature is not visible here). Signatures under the French and Dutch versions.

Archives of the Belgian Ministry for Foreign Affairs, Brussels. Photographs courtesy of Hiroyuki Yamamoto, Inspiration Publishing, Brussels.

Additional Convention between Belgium and Japan of 1866 (4). The convention was signed by t'Kint, Kikuchi and Hoshino (whose signature is not visible here) on 4 October 1866.

Archives of the Belgian Ministry for Foreign Affairs, Brussels. Photograph courtesy of Hiroyuki Yamamoto, Inspiration Publishing, Brussels.

Opening lines of the French version of the treaty of 1 August 1866 (5).

Archives of the Belgian Ministry for Foreign Affairs, Brussels. Photograph courtesy of Hiroyuki Yamamoto, Inspiration Publishing, Brussels.

Opening lines of the Japanese version of the treaty of 1 August 1866 (6).

Archives of the Belgian Ministry for Foreign Affairs, Brussels. Photograph courtesy of Hiroyuki Yamamoto, Inspiration Publishing, Brussels.

would come into effect. Like the Prussian Treaty, the Belgian Treaty did not give a time frame for the exchange of ratifications. The implementation date of the Prussian Treaty was fixed at two years after the signing of the Treaty. Despite Japanese pressure to accept similar conditions for the Belgian Treaty, t'Kint obtained 1 January 1867 as the day that the treaty would come into force. Since the Japanese plenipotentiaries claimed that it would be difficult for the shogun to ratify the Treaty before his return to Edo, and since this return was uncertain, it was important to keep the date for implementation of the Treaty independent from the exchange of the ratifications. This would prevent the treaty from becoming a dead letter. Also, in view of the possibility that Osaka, Hyōgo and Edo would join the open ports and cities in Japan on 1 January 1868, an early implementation date was considered advantageous for Belgian trade with Japan. T'Kint had also obtained a most favoured nation clause without having to concede any compensation in return.

On 17 July 1866, the Japanese plenipotentiaries Kikuchi Takayoshi and Hoshino Kazuyuki filed a report, probably to the councillor in charge of foreign affairs, about the results of their negotiations with t'Kint. They first stressed that the treaty with Belgium was based on the Prussian Treaty, and that it had to be announced at the next New Year. They recalled that the first proposal of the Belgian envoy was based on the existing treaties and contained considerable inconveniences for Japan. During preliminary talks in Yokohama, Hoshino had succeeded in getting rid of these inconvenient parts, such as the opening of the ports of Hyōgo and Niigata and the cities of Osaka and Edo. The two councillors now considered the treaty text to be fit for signing.[443]

On 21 July 1866, the Belgian envoy informed the councillors about the agreement reached with the shogun's plenipotentiaries.[444] The same day, the French minister Léon Roches informed the French Foreign Ministry in Paris that the Belgian envoy had obtained an agreement on a treaty with Japan.[445] Two days later, t'Kint solicited a date to sign the treaty in Edo, favouring one not later than 27 July 1866. That day, an English mail steamer would leave Yokohama and t'Kint wanted to dispatch the treaty with this ship.[446] However, when the Japanese government approached one of its official translators for the Dutch language, Nishi Kichijūrō 西吉十郎, it turned out that it was highly questionable whether the necessary translation and editing for the

Treaty would be finished by 27 July.[447] T'Kint again suspected that this delay was due to the arrival of the Italian mission. He thought that the Japanese government would be embarrassed to sign a treaty with Belgium while at the same time having to refuse treaty negotiations with Italy.[448]

On 26 July 1866, Kikuchi and Hoshino finally agreed that the Treaty between Belgium and Japan would be signed at 9 in the morning on 1 August 1866 (21st day of the 6th month of Keiō 2).[449] The Chōōji temple at Edo, home of the Dutch legation, was designated as the place for the ceremony. T'Kint was invited to travel to Edo one day before, on 31 July 1866, in order to compare and finalize the translations of the treaty text.[450]

On 1 August 1866, the Treaty of Amity, Commerce and Navigation between the shogun of Japan and the king of Belgium was signed at Edo by Kikuchi Takayoshi, Hoshino Kazuyuki and Ōkubo Chikugo no Kami for Japan, and by Auguste t'Kint for Belgium.[451] The Dutch consul general and political agent, Dirk de Graeff van Polsbroek, attended the ceremony.[452] The official copies of the treaty, addressed to the Belgian Foreign Ministry, were included in the diplomatic bag of the British legation and sent to London around mid-August 1866.[453]

After the signing, gifts were exchanged. The Japanese presented the Belgian envoy and his legation secretary with seven scrolls of Japanese brocade, called *Yamato-nishiki*. They also had the provisions necessary for a large feast delivered to t'Kint: 10 ducks, 10 chickens, and a basket of vegetables, a basket of fruits, and a small box of sweets. The secretary was further provided with two rolls of damask.[454]

T'Kint presented various rifles, shotguns, revolvers and a sabre to be delivered to the shogun, rifles to the three senior councillors of the shogun, shotguns to the plenipotentiaries Kikuchi and Hoshino, a revolver to Ōkubo, and furthermore, revolvers to one of the Japanese vice councillors in charge of foreign affairs, to the governor of Kanagawa, and to the translator and secretaries.[455]

On 7 August 1866, Auguste t'Kint wrote a long dispatch[456] to Belgian Foreign Minister Charles Rogier, which he sent together with the text of the Belgian-Japanese Treaty.[457] In his letter, he described the details of the treaty.

T'Kint had used the text of the treaties already concluded between Japan and other countries as a guideline, in particular the treaties with Prussia and the Swiss Confederation, copies of which he had received from the

Belgian Foreign Ministry. The Treaty between Japan and Belgium therefore provided for such rights, among others, as access to the open ports of Japan, the appointment of a diplomatic agent and consuls, freedom of religious practice for the Belgians, extraterritoriality, freedom of trade and navigation in the open ports, and the status of most favoured nation. It also stated that the official language to be used by the Belgian diplomatic and consular agents in communicating with the Japanese authorities would be French, but during the first five years, a Dutch or Japanese translation had to be added. The Treaty itself was drawn up in French, Japanese and Dutch and had four copies in each language. The Dutch version served as original in case of doubt.

The Belgian Treaty differed only slightly from the Prussian and the Swiss treaties. A Japanese national wanting to file a complaint against a Prussian or a Swiss national had to do so with the Japanese authorities. To make a complaint against a Belgian, a Japanese national would have to approach the Belgian consul. Only if the latter was unable to mediate a friendly solution could the Japanese authorities be invited to help out. Here the Belgian Treaty followed the provisions of the 1858 Treaty between Japan and England.[458] Kikuchi and Hoshino pointed out these provisions in their report of 17 July 1866, and advised that the Japanese authorities involved, such as the commissioners of Kanagawa (*Kanagawa bugyō* 神奈川奉行), should be well informed about these differences.[459] One day later, the relevant officials were informed.[460]

In the Treaty between Switzerland and Japan, the names of the open ports (Yokohama, Nagasaki, and Hakodate) were not added, in contrast to the Prussian and Belgian treaties. At the time of the treaty negotiations with the Swiss Confederation, in early 1864, the Japanese government was still considering closing the Port of Yokohama. By mid-1866 this option was no longer taken into account, so the names of the three open ports reappeared in the Treaty with Belgium.[461] On the other hand, none of the three treaties mentioned the opening of Hyōgo, Osaka, Edo or Niigata. The Belgian Treaty ensured that Belgian trade was permitted in all Japanese ports open for foreign trade without exception. The right to use any port to be opened in the future was also cemented into the Belgian Treaty through the most favoured nation clause.[462] While the Prussian Treaty provided for a period of nearly two years before implementation, the Swiss Treaty had come into effect

immediately. The Belgian Treaty gave its date of implementation as 1 January 1867, five months after the signing ceremony.[463] Of course, it had taken the Swiss envoy 10 months from his arrival in Japan in 1863 to obtain a treaty with Japan, compared with 7 months and 2 weeks for t'Kint in 1866, and 3 months and 3 weeks for the Prussian envoy in 1861.

The treaties were followed by a set of commercial rules for foreign trade in the open ports. These formed an integral part of the treaty. While there was a proviso in the Prussian and Swiss commercial rules that enabled the Japanese authorities to seize any suspect cargo, t'Kint had avoided this clause, seeing it as a danger to the free movement of goods.[464] The new tariff, obtained by the Representatives of Great Britain, France, the Netherlands and the United States on 25 June 1866, had been included in these commercial rules negotiated by t'Kint.[465]

The Italian Treaty of 1866

On 5 July 1866, while t'Kint and the Japanese plenipotentiaries were still negotiating the Treaty between Belgium and Japan, the Italian corvette Magenta arrived in Yokohama on 5 July 1866.[466] Its commander, Captain V. F. Arminjon, had been appointed Italian plenipotentiary to conclude a treaty with Japan and China. Arriving in Yokohama, Arminjon in the first instance looked to the French Minister Léon Roches. The Italian mission had received the explicit backing of the French government, which had promised the assistance of its minister in Japan.[467] Being told that Roches was detoxing in the hot spring resort of Atami, Arminjon steered the Magenta to Ajiro, a village close to Atami where Roches had moved into a villa.[468]

Roches pledged his support to Arminjon but warned that the current timing was not good for treaty negotiations. In his view, the Edo government was showing a strong aversion to the opening of Osaka and Hyōgo to foreigners. He mentioned that the opening of these places had not been included in the Convention of 25 June 1866, and attributed this ultimately to the strong opposition from the emperor in Kyoto and some of the Japanese feudal lords.[469] Still, Roches was sufficiently confident that a treaty with Japan could be concluded.[470]

The French legation dispatched a message to the councillors announcing the arrival of the Italian mission and the purpose of its visit. The Japanese government in Edo reacted quickly. On 11 July 1866, the French legation received their reply. Without the consent of the shogun, currently not in Edo, the councillors were not entitled to start any treaty negotiations. Furthermore, Japan had no desire to conclude treaties with additional countries, because of strong opposition from powerful groups in its society. If Italy really wanted a treaty with Japan, the councillors urged them to renounce the opening of Hyōgo, Osaka, Edo and Niigata. Basically, the Italians were requested to accept the Prussian Treaty of 1861 as the basis for their own. In the meantime, Arminjon had visited all foreign representatives then present in Yokohama, including Auguste t'Kint. The Italian envoy had heard their opinions, and was therefore able to take up a position rather quickly. He decided to accept the "Prussian solution", rather than risk ending up with no treaty. Since the opening of Osaka, Hyōgo, Edo and Niigata was guaranteed in Japan's treaties with America, Britain, the Netherlands, Russia, France and Portugal, Arminjon hoped that this provision would be included in the Treaty between Italy and Japan at the time of the opening, provided for 1 January 1868.[471]

The Italian envoy delivered his reply in an official dispatch to the councillors, dated 12 July 1866.[472] He moved the Magenta to Edo on 14 July 1866. The following day, the Italian corvette was visited by Ezure Akinori, commissioner of foreign affairs (*kaigai bugyō* 海外奉行). Ezure repeated the content of the reply given by the Japanese government in its dispatch of 11 July 1866, and asked the Italian envoy to return to Yokohama. Arminjon refused, and insisted on an audience with the councillors to present his credentials. On 16 July 1866, Mermet de Cachon of the French legation, who assisted Arminjon, received an informal communication that the presence of the Magenta in Edo was fuelling opposition to an Italian treaty, and that it would be better if the corvette could move to Yokohama. In order to break the deadlock, Roches proposed to Arminjon to travel on board the Magenta to Nagasaki, but the Italian envoy preferred to wait at Edo for a reply from the shogun.[473] Roches left for the south of Japan without Arminjon, announcing his departure from Yokohama to the Japanese senior councillors in Edo on 22 July.[474] He arrived in Nagasaki on 28 July 1866.[475]

On 25 July 1866, the Italian mission received a letter from the councillors, confirming that its request would be sent to the shogun, who was at that time engaged in military manoeuvres against the feudal lord of Chōshū.[476] The letter was brought to the Magenta by Kikuchi Takayoshi, commissioner of foreign affairs (and also Japanese plenipotentiary for the Belgian treaty negotiations). Arminjon provided him with a copy of his letter of credentials. Three days later, the councillors in Edo informed the Italian mission that it had received a reply from Osaka: due to the war with Chōshū, the shogun did not have the time for treaty negotiations.[477]

Auguste t'Kint, extremely anxious about any adverse effect the Italian mission might have on his own treaty negotiations, was rather critical of Arminjon's handling of the situation. According to him, the continuous presence of the Magenta in the port of Edo, engaging in fire drills with its cannons, irritated rather than intimidated the Japanese authorities. By 27 July 1866, he also perceived that the French Minister Roches had put considerable pressure on the Japanese government to conclude a treaty with Italy.[478]

On 5 August 1866, four days after the Belgian Treaty had been signed, Councillors Inoue Masanao 井上正直 and Matsudaira Yasuhide informed Arminjon that the shogun had appointed three plenipotentiaries to negotiate a treaty with Italy: two commissioners of foreign affairs, Shibata Sadatarō 柴田貞太郎 (also called Shibata Takenaka 柴田剛中, bearing the title of Hyūga no Kami 日向守) and Asahina Masahiro 朝比奈昌広 (bearing the title of Kai no Kami 甲斐守), and Ushigome Chūzaemon 牛込忠左衛門 as *metsuke*. The Japanese government assigned the Daichūji temple in Mita Koyama at Edo 三田小山大中寺 as the location for the negotiations. The Italian envoy confirmed his agreement by a dispatch dated 7 August 1866. Accompanied by 150 marines from the Magenta, the Italian mission entered the Daichūji on 12 August 1866 for the first negotiations. Agreement was reached the next day. On 25 August 1866, the signing ceremony took place in Edo, and on 1 September 1866, the Italian mission left Yokohama for Shanghai on board the Magenta.[479]

Opinions of the Foreign Representatives

The conclusion of the treaties with Belgium and Italy, both in August 1866, drew the attention of the foreign representatives in Yokohama.

On 13 August 1866, the British minister Harry Parkes informed the Foreign Office in London of the conclusion of the Treaty between Belgium and Japan.[480] He drew special attention to three elements:

1) With regards to jurisdiction, the Belgian envoy had opted for the definition used in the English Treaty of 1858, rather than the Prussian Treaty of 1861. Should a Japanese national want to file a complaint against a Belgian, the Japanese national had to approach the Belgian consul. Only if the latter was unable to find a friendly solution could the Japanese authorities be invited to assist.

2) The Belgian Treaty did not mention the opening of Osaka, Hyōgo, and Edo, following the Prussian Treaty.

3) The Customs Tariff was based on the Convention of 25 June 1866. The Japanese government was reluctant to sign the same Convention with the Belgian envoy, but agreed to communicate it to him through an official dispatch.

On 2 September 1866, Parkes informed the Foreign Office in London about the conclusion of a treaty between Japan and Italy. He believed that this treaty was almost a transcript of that concluded with Belgium. Parkes remarked that, again, the opening of Osaka, Hyōgo, Edo and Niigata went unmentioned. He seemed increasingly worried by the Japanese government's persistence in this matter. Parkes had hoped that the confirmation of the foreign treaties of 1858 by the emperor in Kyoto would have removed the old objections. But now, he had to conclude that the Japanese government had not yet surmounted all problems.[481]

On 12 September 1866, Parkes dispatched the texts of the Belgian and Italian treaties, respectively in Dutch and French, to the Foreign Office in London. He commented that the Convention of 25 June 1866 had been incorporated in the Italian Treaty in its entirety, in contrast to the Belgian Treaty.[482] The Foreign Office sent the treaties to the Board of Trade for revision. The Board remarked that article XV of both treaties contained the old system of exchange of Japanese and foreign coins weight for weight, while article VI of the Convention of 25 June 1866 provided for an exchange on the intrinsic value of the coins. Apparently, the Belgian and Italian treaties had not taken these recent modifications into account. The Foreign Office informed Parkes of this inconsistency.[483] Parkes confronted the Japanese government with this fact, and the senior councillors agreed that this old article had slipped into the Belgian and Italian treaties by mistake.[484]

The Swiss consul C. Brennwald informed the Swiss Federal Council (*Bundesrat*) about the Italian Treaty.[485] The Dutch political agent Dirk de Graeff van Polsbroek sent a report to the Dutch foreign minister, indicating the assistance he had given to t'Kint.[486]

Several diplomats commented on the rapidity with which the Italian envoy had obtained a treaty. Seven weeks had elapsed between his arrival on 5 July 1866 and the signing of the treaty on 25 August. Arminjon attributed the quick result to his firm stance towards the Japanese government. Not only had he posted his corvette in the harbour of Edo, he had also threatened the Japanese negotiators that if a treaty were not concluded quickly, another Italian envoy would come to request a treaty including the opening of Edo, Osaka and Hyōgo. At least, this is how Arminjon explained his success to the British minister Parkes.[487]

The Belgian envoy, Auguste t'Kint, mentioned that he had regular contact with the Italian plenipotentiary. To facilitate Arminjon's task, t'Kint transmitted the translations of the Tariff Convention and the text of the Treaty between Japan and Belgium. T'Kint also advised the Italian mission on how to negotiate a treaty with China.[488]

The French minister Léon Roches, who returned to Yokohama from a trip to the south of Japan on 13 August 1866, the day the Japanese and Italian plenipotentiaries reached an agreement, attributed the speedy conclusion of the Italian Treaty to his legation's intervention. During the negotiations, the Italians had been assisted by the French legation secretary, Mermet de Cachon.[489] The Italian government would recognize Roches's efforts by bestowing on him the title of Grand Officer of the Order of Saints Maurice and Lazarus.[490] On the other hand, a few months before the Italian Treaty was concluded, Roches had admitted that even his own interventions in favour of a Belgian treaty had yielded no result.[491]

Still, Henri de Bellonet, chargé d'affaires of France in Beijing, recalled that while the treaty negotiations between Italy and Japan were steaming ahead, the signing of the Treaty between Belgium and Japan seemed not to materialize. Fearing that the Italian Treaty might be signed earlier than the Belgian one, t'Kint would have asked the intervention of Léon Roches to arrange an early date for the signing ceremony of the Belgian Treaty. De Bellonet referred to a conversation with Arminjon as his source of information. In general, de Bellonet was rather critical of the Belgian envoy's negotiating skills. In his view, this was proved by the nine months needed to arrange the Belgian Treaty compared to the few weeks for the Italian Treaty.[492]

In the treaty negotiations between Belgium and Japan, t'Kint had reached an agreement with the Japanese plenipotentiaries on 12 July 1866.[493] At that point in time, the negotiations between Japan and Italy had not even started. The councillors in Edo had not yet received a mandate from the shogun in Osaka for negotiations with Italy. These negotiations would only start after the Treaty with Belgium was signed.[494] It is not impossible that Léon Roches intervened with the Japanese government in Edo to accelerate the signing of the Belgian Treaty before he left for Nagasaki around 22 July 1866. He might have done this to clear the way for the start of the Italian treaty negotiations. However, neither the Japanese nor the French archives contain material proof of any such intervention.[495]

The Japanese government itself explained its willingness to conclude a treaty with Italy by referring to the declaration of war by Italy in the military conflict between Prussia and Austria. In a letter to the American minister Van Valkenburgh, the councillors mentioned:[496]

> However, the reason that the (Italian)[497] Ambassador gave, was, not only for the benefit of commerce, but was this; that, when Italian men of war, which are in the Eastern seas maybe in peril, they could have no port in which to take refuge, unless the treaty was made, and Italy was now engaged in war with Austria. This reason, made it unavoidable for us to consent, and in compassion, we could not refuse…

The government of the shogun was a military government. In their view, military and political matters had far greater importance than commercial affairs.[498] Within the social structure of Japanese society during the Edo period, traders and commercial agents had the lowest status, samurai the highest.[499] On top of that, in

August 1866 the Edo government was fighting its own war against Chōshū.

The Edo government had been informed in detail about the development of the war in Europe through regular dispatches from the Dutch political agent Van Polsbroek. The first such dispatch was sent on 2 August 1866, 3 days before the appointment of the Japanese plenipotentiaries for the treaty negotiations with Italy. It announced the declaration of war between Prussia and Italy on the one hand, and Austria on the other hand.[500]

The conclusion of treaties with Belgium and with Italy precipitated further approaches to the Japanese government for additional treaties. As early as 10 August 1866, the Dutch political agent Van Polsbroek filed such a request in favour of a treaty between Japan and the Free Hanseatic Cities. In his dispatch, Van Polsbroek argued that the conclusion of a treaty with Belgium was proof of the increasing authority of the shogun after the ratification of the treaties by the emperor. He dismissed the viewpoint of the senior councillors that the shogun was not able to conclude more treaties in view of strong internal opposition.[501] Five days later, Van Polsbroek notified the Japanese government that he had received a proxy from the government of Denmark to conclude a treaty with Japan.[502] In a second letter that same day, he mentioned that the Italian envoy had informed him that the Japanese government had appointed plenipotentiaries to negotiate a treaty with Italy. Van Polsbroek was not pleased. He recalled the efforts made by his predecessor in 1861 and 1862, and by Van Polsbroek himself to obtain a treaty for Denmark. Each time, the Japanese government had argued that the circumstances did not allow the conclusion of any more treaties with Western countries. The appointment of Japanese plenipotentiaries for treaty negotiations with Italy showed that these circumstances had changed. Van Polsbroek expected that the Japanese government would therefore immediately appoint councillors for the negotiation of a treaty with Denmark.[503]

When the American Minister Van Valkenburgh discovered that Italy had concluded a treaty with Japan, he reminded the councillors on 14 September 1866 that his predecessor, Townsend Harris, had notified Austria, Brazil, Denmark, Italy, Spain and Sweden about the unwillingness of Japan to make any more treaties. Van Valkenburgh added that this notification had been made at the explicit request of the Japanese government. He suggested that Japan should officially inform him of the treaty concluded with Italy, and request the US government to notify the other five countries that Japan was now prepared to enter into treaty relations with them. One of the councillors in charge of foreign affairs immediately contacted Van Valkenburgh. He explained that Japan was willing to make treaties with these countries, whenever envoys should arrive properly accredited for that purpose. However, since the shogun was at war with Chōshū, his government currently preferred to defer treaty negotiations until peace was restored in the country. At his request, Van Valkenburgh on 27 September 1866 received a dispatch from the Japanese government, dated 14 September 1866, confirming this commitment.[504] This communication was a first sign of a new policy of the councillors towards additional foreign treaties. It coincided with the death of Shogun Tokugawa Iemochi at the end of August 1866, and the appointment of Hitotsubashi (Tokugawa Keiki) as his successor.[505]

Finally, a claim has been made in Dutch sources that the Treaty between Belgium and Japan had been negotiated by the Dutch political agent Dirk de Graeff van Polsbroek rather than by t'Kint.[506] The Belgian envoy was said to have left Japan for family reasons before a treaty was concluded. Our analysis of each stage of the negotiations should make it sufficiently clear that independent sources demonstrate that the negotiations with the Japanese government were conducted by Auguste t'Kint. Van Polsbroek mainly provided logistical support and advice. He should also be credited for arranging the first meeting between the Belgian envoy and the Japanese government on 10 January 1866. T'Kint proposed that the Cross of Officer in the Order of Leopold be awarded Van Polsbroek for the services he had rendered Belgium.[507] The Belgian government agreed, and promulgated a Royal Decree to that effect, signed by King Leopold II on 13 November 1866.[508]

Leaving Japan

When Auguste t'Kint learned that the Italian envoy Arminjon and the Japanese plenipotentiaries would sign the Convention of 25 June 1866, containing the new Customs Tariff, as a separate document, he was not amused. When he had requested the same favour, it had been refused. He had agreed to an official letter from the Japanese government confirming that the provisions of

the Convention also applied to Belgium, on condition that no country beyond the four initial signatories would be allowed to sign the Convention or add it to a new treaty with Japan.[509]

Furthermore, on 10 August 1866, the new Portuguese governor of Macao and Portuguese minister plenipotentiary to Japan, José Rodrigues Coelho do Amaral, arrived in Yokohama. He took up residence at Van Polsbroek's, both in Edo and Yokohama. The aim of his visit was to present his credentials to the court of the shogun, but also to sign the Convention of 25 June 1866.[510] The councillors invited him to a meeting in Edo on 29 August 1866, four days after the Italian Treaty had been concluded.[511] Having signed the Convention of 25 June 1866, Amaral left Japan from Yokohama shortly after 6 September 1866.[512] In April 1867, the Portuguese version of the Convention would be used as starting point for a version to be signed by Japan and the Swiss Confederation.[513]

On 15 September 1866, Auguste t'Kint had a meeting with Hoshino Kazuyuki, Japanese commissioner of foreign affairs and one of the plenipotentiaries for the Treaty with Belgium. The topic of the meeting was the signing of the Convention of 25 June 1866. It would then be added to the Treaty between Belgium and Japan as an addendum.[514] Two weeks later, t'Kint sent a proposal to the councillors in charge of foreign affairs to adapt the text of the Convention to better align it with the Treaty. On 2 October 1866, the two sides agreed on the adapted text, and on 4 October 1866, Auguste t'Kint, Kikuchi Takayoshi and Hoshino Kazuyuki signed the Additional Convention to the Treaty between Belgium and Japan of 1 August 1866. Three days later, t'Kint sent a dispatch to Rogier, informing him of the conclusion of this Additional Convention.[515]

The Additional Convention between Belgium and Japan contained the same stipulations as the Convention of 25 June 1866. It only differed on those points that were particular to the four original Western signatories. For all other matters, the Japanese government preferred that the text remain the same. As a result, the Belgian Convention also stated that the approbation by the two governments through an official communication would replace the normal formalities for the exchange of ratifications.

In his dispatch of 7 August 1866 to Rogier, t'Kint explained that the Convention contained several positive elements for international trade. He mentioned the

Panorama de Benten, partie de la ville de Yokohama. — Dessin de Thérond d'après une photographie.

establishment of bonded warehouses, the repositioning of the Japanese currency to its intrinsic value, freedom of trade with foreigners by all classes of Japanese society including feudal lords, freedom of direct trade with foreign countries, abolition of the old law prohibiting any Japanese to travel abroad, and so forth. T'Kint considered this Convention the most extensive and most liberal of all conventions thus far concluded by Japan. Technically, it was not necessary for Belgium to sign it, because it was referred to in the Treaty of 1 August 1866. However, by becoming one of the signatories, Belgium would have to agree to any future adjustment of the Convention, and would therefore participate in full in the negotiations for any modification. For this reason, t'Kint thought it wise to assure the convention rights for Belgium through a bilateral agreement between Belgium and Japan.[516]

With the signing of the Additional Convention, t'Kint's assignment to Japan came to an end. The Belgian envoy started preparing for his departure by putting his furniture and other household items to public auction in Yokohama. On 1 October 1866, a preliminary notice appeared in the Yokohama local press announcing that the auction would take place on 8 October in the residence of t'Kint at Yokohama Foreign Settlement no. 82. The auctioneer in charge was to be Messrs. Hansard & Co.[517] On 8 and 9 October, a final notice appeared, stating that the auction was to take place a day later than originally announced, at 10 a.m. on 9 October 1866.[518]

On 13 October 1866, a Japanese newspaper announced the imminent departure of the Belgian envoy.[519] Finally, on 17 October 1866, t'Kint boarded the Labourdonnais, a Messageries Impériales steamer, bound for Shanghai. He arrived there 4 days later. Also on board were Mermet de Cachon, secretary of the French legation in Yokohama, and General Guy, commander of British forces in China and Hong Kong.[520]

View of Benten – Yokohama (1863?). Illustration from Aimé Humbert, "Le Japon 1863-1864," in *Le Tour du Monde, Nouveau Journal des Voyages, 1866 deuxième semestre*, ed. Édouard Charton (Paris/London/Leipzig: L. Hachette et Cie, 1866), p. 5.

Chinese Interlude

On 9 May 1866, while in Yokohama, t'Kint had received the ratifications of the Treaty between China and Belgium by way of Jules Adrian, general manager of the *Maison Adrian et Cie* in Nagasaki. The Chinese government had informed t'Kint that it would exchange ratifications in Shanghai.[521] At the end of July 1866 and through the intermediation of the British legation in Beijing, t'Kint had received a note from the Chinese government dated 12 June 1866 with more details on the exchange of the ratifications.[522] The exchange took place in Shanghai on 27 October 1866.[523]

In Brussels, King Leopold II was informed of an article in the *China Mail* mocking his efforts to acquire Formosa (Taiwan). In an internal note, dated 1 December 1866, the Belgian king demanded that t'Kint should rectify the article concerned. He also highlighted his vision on how to conquer the markets of China and Japan, where he saw major investments happening every day. He made a case for the establishment of a Belgian trading house, and requested t'Kint to explore the commercial possibilities for such a company in China and Japan. His staff was ordered to inform Auguste, Baron Lambermont, secretary general of the Belgian Ministry of Foreign Affairs.[524]

The king's démarche led to a letter from Lambermont to t'Kint on 4 December 1866. Having received it in Shanghai, t'Kint in vain looked through several months' issues of the *China Mail*. In Shanghai, no one seemed to have noticed such an article. The Belgian envoy advised that this newspaper, to which he ascribed a questionable reputation, was beneath the king's notice.[525] In accordance with Leopold II's wishes, t'Kint did undertake a long journey throughout China to map out the commercial possibilities for Belgian industry. Leaving Shanghai on 2 March 1867, he visited Foochow (Fuzhou), Amoy (Xiamen), Formosa (Taiwan), and Hong Kong, before returning to Shanghai around 4 June 1867.[526]

While Auguste t'Kint was spending his time in China, the Belgian government took care of the legalization and ratification of the Belgian-Japanese Treaty of 1 August 1866. The Foreign Ministry in Brussels had received t'Kint's dispatch about the Treaty with Japan on 26 October 1866. One day later, the Ministry had ordered the public gazette, the *Moniteur Belge*, to publish its content.[527] On 24 November 1866, the Belgian Foreign Ministry confirmed that it had received the French,

Dutch and Japanese versions of the Treaty, and that the legislative process could start.[528] On 8 November 1866, the Foreign Ministry sent a proposal for a Royal Decree to King Leopold II, including an extensive motivation. The Belgian king signed the decree four days later.[529] The Treaty was also sent to the Belgian Parliament, followed on 7 December 1866 by the Additional Convention signed by t'Kint in Edo on 4 October 1866.[530] On 22 December 1866, the President of the Senate informed Charles Rogier that Parliament had adopted both the Treaty and the Additional Convention.[531] Promulgation took place on 27 December 1866, after King Leopold II, the Foreign Minister Charles Rogier and the Minister for Justice Jules Bara had ratified the Treaty and Convention.[532] The *Moniteur Belge* published the ratification two days later.[533] Auguste t'Kint was informed of the ratification through a dispatch of 25 January 1867, which he received two months later in Shanghai.[534]

The promulgation came just in time. The Treaty had come into effect on 1 January 1867, and Belgium wanted to take advantage of it as quickly as possible. Auguste t'Kint thought that establishing a Belgian trading company ("Comptoir Belge") in Yokohama would be the best way of implementing the treaty's commercial side. However, given the time it would take to get such an establishment started, he would prefer to install a

Auguste, Baron Lambermont (1819-1905). Portrait in oils (1903) by Emile Wauters (1846-1933).
Royal Museums of Fine Arts of Belgium.

Belgian vice consul in Yokohama already, in order to support businesses from Belgium. Two days before he left Yokohama for Shanghai, t'Kint proposed a candidate for this position: Maurice Lejeune.

Maurice Lejeune had been born in Amsterdam. He headed the trading company Hecht, Lilienthal & Cie at Yokohama. According to t'Kint's dispatch of 15 October 1866, this trading house was one of the most respectable in Yokohama, and could be compared with well-established companies like Mess. de Rothschild frères in Paris or M. Lambert in Brussels.[535] It was located in the Foreign Settlement of Yokohama at lot no. 164a.[536]

Of Lejeune himself, t'Kint wrote that he was a member of the local chamber of commerce and one of the most intelligent traders in Yokohama. He had been educated in Belgium, at the Athenée in Antwerp and at the University of Liège, and accordingly was intimately familiar with Belgium and its commercial possibilities. T'Kint explained to Lejeune that the post of Belgian consul would be reserved for the head of a Belgian trading house to be established. In the meantime, Lejeune would be vice consul, administering the Consulate. Lejeune accepted these conditions. T'Kint concluded that the appointment of Lejeune would have a positive influence on the future relations between Japan and Belgium. He therefore proposed Lejeune be given the title of vice consul but the authority of a consul.[537]

Maurice Lejeune had been in Japan for some time. The Dutch political agent Dirk de Graeff van Polsbroek mentioned him as a resident of Yokohama in June 1863.[538] Lejeune was also mentioned in a list of "Dutch Residents and Officials" in Yokohama, published in the *Chronicle and Directory for China, Japan & The Philippines* for the year 1864. In the same publication's Yokohama Directory for the year 1865, published on 12 January 1865, Maurice Lejeune headed a list of three foreigners enrolled under the company "Hecht, Lilienthal and Co." The other two foreigners were C. Ravel and E. A. Daniels (listed in that order). The 1866 edition mentioned two foreigners at "Hecht, Lilienthal & Co., merchants", Maurice Lejeune and E. A. Daniels. The 1867 edition, which appeared on 6 February 1867, put Maurice Lejeune at the head of a list of six foreigners working at the same company. The five others were P. Brunat, J. Bernhard, J. Wolfs, J. B. Cazet, and F. W. Poortenaar.[539] In June 1865, Lejeune became one of 26 members of the newly established Municipal Council in

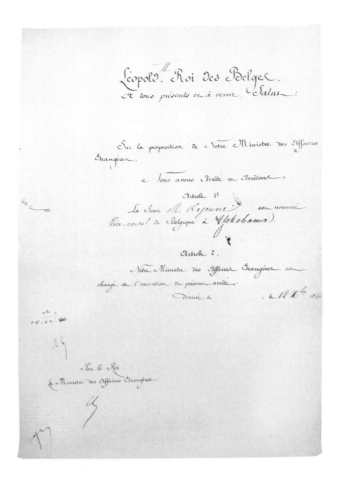

Yokohama.[540] He was re-elected in May 1866.[541] Within the new Council, he became responsible for the Police Committee.[542]

On 1 December 1866, the Foreign Ministry in Brussels proposed Maurice Lejeune's candidacy as vice consul to King Leopold II. Two weeks later, the Ministry sent a reminder to the Royal Palace. Lejeune was appointed Belgian vice consul at Yokohama by a Royal Decree of 18 December 1866.[543] The same day, the Ministry of Foreign Affairs proposed Jules Adrian as Belgian consul at Nagasaki. Adrian had already shown interest in this position at the end of 1865. His appointment was formalized by a Royal Decree of 21 December 1866.[544] His candidacy was also supported by Auguste t'Kint.[545] For the position in Yokohama, two other candidates had called on the Belgian Foreign Ministry. These were Rodolphe Lindau, who had headed the first Swiss mission to Japan in 1859 and who was a former consul for Switzerland at Yokohama,[546] and Joseph Keymeulen, a Belgian who had worked at Shanghai and was now based in Yokohama. He had regularly sent his observations on China and Japan to Leopold II.[547] The Belgian Foreign Ministry did not take up these candidacies.[548]

Draft decree appointing Maurice Lejeune as Belgian Vice Consul in Yokohama (18 December 1866). MOFA Belgium 883. Brussels, 25 January 1867. Minute Indicateur B no. 476 (no order number), containing a draft dispatch from the Belgian Ministry of Foreign Affairs in Brussels to Maurice Lejeune in Yokohama, with several annexes, among which the decree appointing him Belgian Vice Consul at Yokohama (decree dated 18 December 1866).
Archives of the Belgian Ministry for Foreign Affairs, Brussels.
Photograph by Dirk De Ruyver.

On 25 January 1867, the Foreign Ministry in Brussels dispatched an original of the Royal Decree and a brevet containing the appointment as Belgian vice consul to Maurice Lejeune in Yokohama.[549] Upon receiving these, Maurice Lejeune, as a Dutch national, requested approval from the Dutch political agent Dirk de Graeff van Polsbroek. This was standard procedure for consular agents with a different nationality than the country appointing them.[550] Van Polsbroek officially informed the Japanese government about this appointment on 28 March 1867. The Edo government recognized Lejeune as Belgian consul on 6 April 1867.[551] Lejeune sent his oath of office to Belgium on 10 April 1867.[552] The local satirical magazine, the *Japan Punch*, published a cartoon about the Belgian Vice Consulate at Yokohama in its edition of October 1867. Vice Consul Maurice Lejeune is likely to be depicted in this cartoon.[553]

Auguste t'Kint did not wait for the official appointments of his consuls before putting them to work. From Shanghai on 7 December 1866, he sent an extensive report on the commercial possibilities in Japan. This report was partly based on information that he had requested from Maurice Lejeune in Yokohama. On 4 February 1867, the Foreign Ministry in Brussels ordered the publication of t'Kint's report in the *Moniteur Belge*. The information from Lejeune, dated Yokohama 30 October 1866, was to be included in the "Recueil Consulaire". [554]

In January 1867, while in Shanghai, t'Kint made a short visit to Nagasaki in Japan, to meet the future Belgian consul, Jules Adrian. He requested a report from Adrian on commercial opportunities in Nagasaki for Belgian companies. While in Nagasaki, t'Kint also met Alfred Howell, an English trader and consul for Portugal in Hakodate. Howell had lived in Belgium for a number of years. With the support of the British Vice Admiral King, Howell applied for the post of Belgian consul at Hakodate. T'Kint requested him to compile a report on commercial possibilities in Hakodate. On the basis of that work, he would consider Howell's candidacy.[555] Belgium, however, was never to open a consulate at Hakodate.[556]

Before leaving Belgium for China in January 1865, Auguste t'Kint had visited the main industrial and commercial centers of Belgium. One of his conclusions from these visits was that Belgium needed trade companies in China and Japan, what he called "comptoirs belges".[557] In a dispatch dated Shanghai,

24 November 1866, t'Kint informed the Foreign Ministry in Brussels that Belgium was entitled to receive from Japan a piece of land in the centre of Yokohama Foreign Settlement and close to the port for the construction of Belgian consular premises. Such consular lots were given in return for a small rent to be paid to the Japanese authorities in Yokohama. According to t'Kint, it would be very advantageous for a Belgian trading house or "comptoir belge" to be established on this consular land in Yokohama, and its director appointed consul of Belgium.[558]

On 18 December 1866, the Antwerp Chamber of Commerce dispatched a letter to the Belgian Ministry of Foreign Affairs, inquiring about the establishment of a "comptoir belge" in Yokohama. On 31 December, the Belgian Foreign Minister Charles Rogier replied that the government did not have the means to establish such a venture, but that it was willing to subsidize the costs involved to a certain extent, if a private company would take on this challenge. After having received t'Kint's dispatch of 24 November 1866, the minister again inquired on 21 January 1867 whether the Chamber in Antwerp saw any private sector interest in a trading affiliate in Yokohama. On 29 January, the Chamber replied that it saw little chance of any Belgian company opening a branch in Japan.[559]

On 14 February 1867, Charles Rogier sent a dispatch to Auguste t'Kint, informing him that the Belgian government was currently not able to take a definite decision on a concession for consular land in Yokohama. The minister cited financial reasons, but also remarked that the private sector was reluctant to establish a trading company in Yokohama. He concluded by asking t'Kint to ask the Japanese government for a postponement of the decision, adding that Belgium would apply for a concession in due time.[560] After returning to Yokohama in June 1867, t'Kint came to an agreement with the Japanese authorities. A decision on a Belgian consular lot in Yokohama was suspended until the Belgian government would apply for a concession.[561]

Return to Yokohama

Towards the end of his trip through China, t'Kint had arrived in Hong Kong by 27 May 1867. Originally, he had not planned to return to Yokohama. In early March 1867, probably before 2 March, when he had set off on his trip

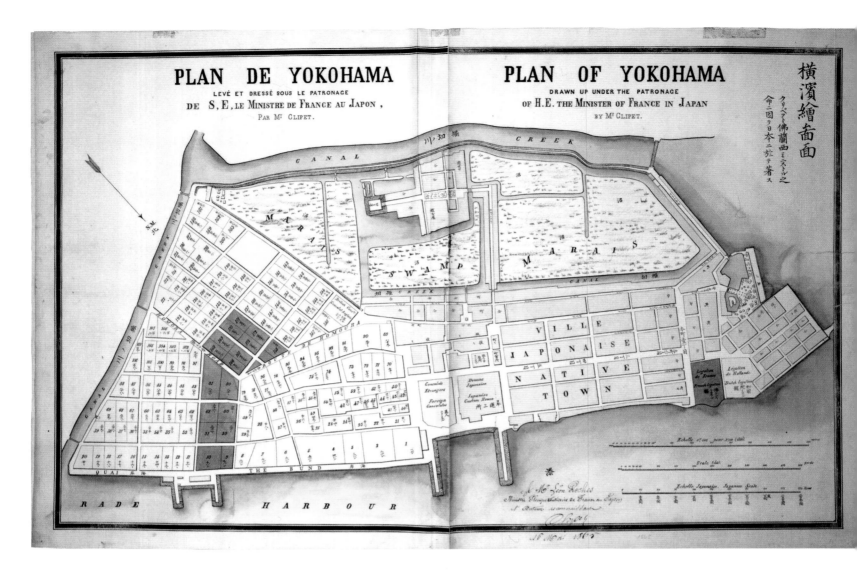

PLAN DE YOKOHAMA

LEVÉ ET DRESSÉ SOUS LE PATRONAGE
DE S. E, LE MINISTRE DE FRANCE AU JAPON,
PAR Mᵣ CLIPET.

PLAN OF YOKOHAMA

DRAWN UP UNDER THE PATRONAGE
OF H. E. THE MINISTER OF FRANCE IN JAPAN
BY Mᵣ CLIPET.

横濱繪面面

クリペ卜佛蘭曲ミニストル之
令二図ラ日本二於テ著ス

through Taiwan and the Chinese mainland, he seems to have requested the Dutch political agent in Japan, Dirk de Graeff van Polsbroek, to exchange the ratifications of the Treaty between Belgium and Japan and to request a piece of land from the Edo government for a Belgian consular building in Yokohama. Van Polsbroek informed the Japanese government of these two requests, mentioning that the Belgian envoy had to return to Europe due to family reasons. The Japanese ministers promised to provide a plot of land for a Belgian consular building, once it had been notified of the appointment of a Belgian consul in Yokohama.[562] It is likely that in early March 1867 Auguste t'Kint had also informed the Belgian Foreign Ministry about a possible return to Europe for family reasons. Even though he had not formally requested leave, the Ministry awarded him home leave on 13 May 1867.[563]

When t'Kint arrived in Hong Kong at the end of May 1867, he received a dispatch from the Belgian Foreign Office about the exchange of the ratifications in Japan,

and consequently, he must have changed plans.[564] In reply to the Ministry, t'Kint mentioned that he had requested the Belgian vice consul Lejeune to look for an appropriate residence in Yokohama for him. In accordance with the conversations he had had in Brussels before his departure to China early in 1865, t'Kint thought that he was to travel to Siam (Thailand) for treaty negotiations, once the treaties with China and Japan had been concluded. Thinking he would not return to Japan, he had sold his furniture in Yokohama, which he now regretted. According to t'Kint, prices had gone up considerably for household items. In view of his deteriorating health, t'Kint would now prefer to stay in Yokohama for a longer period, ascribing the city a more suitable climate for his recovery than Hong Kong or Shanghai.[565]

There remained only one problem: by 30 May 1867, the Belgian ratifications of the Treaty with Japan had not arrived in Hong Kong, where t'Kint had expected to receive them. The Belgian envoy decided not to wait, and

Map of Yokohama, showing the Dutch legation on the right, and lot no. 82 on the left.
Collection of Yokohama Archives of History, collection of maps. Collection BLUM Q-II-137, made and signed by the French minister Clipet in May 1865.

to leave for Yokohama while passing through Shanghai. To his surprise, the ratifications were delivered to him at his address in Shanghai.[566]

On 5 June 1867, t'Kint left Shanghai on board the Messageries Impérales steamer Phasé. Also on board was the Italian Count de la Tour, bearing the ratifications of the Treaty between Japan and Italy. T'Kint and de la Tour arrived in Yokohama on 9 June 1867. The local newspapers in Yokohama recorded their arrival.[567] The British and French ministers in Edo saw the arrival of the Italian plenipotentiary as worth a dispatch to their respective foreign ministers. The American minister also mentioned the arrival of the Belgian envoy.[568]

Though Auguste t'Kint had left Yokohama only some eight months before, the town had changed markedly. On 26 November 1866, a huge blaze had reduced large parts of the Japanese town and the foreign settlement to ashes. A number of consulates had gone up in flames.[569] On his arrival in Yokohama, t'Kint could witness the ongoing reconstruction of the foreign settlement.[570]

Change came not only in mortar and bricks. On 5 October 1866, 12 days before t'Kint had left Japan, the foreign representatives were officially informed about the death of Shogun Iemochi and the appointment of Hitotsubashi as his successor.[571] Under the new shogun, relations with the foreign representatives became more cordial.[572] Much to his own surprise,[573] the Dutch representative Van Polsbroek succeeded in concluding a Treaty between Denmark and Japan.[574] The Japanese plenipotentiaries were appointed on 29 December 1866, and after very short negotiations the Treaty was signed on 12 January 1867 at the Dutch legation in Edo.[575] The Dutch and English Representatives had been requesting such a treaty as early as 1861.[576] On 17 June 1867, outline agreement was reached for a treaty between Japan and the Sandwich Islands (Hawaii).[577] The first attempt for such a treaty dated back to 1861.[578]

On 9 February 1867, the Japanese government sent a written announcement of the death of Emperor Kōmei to the diplomatic corps in Japan.[579] According to the English minister Parkes, this communication was made in an unusually open way.[580] The foreign community regarded Emperor Kōmei as an ardent opponent of the foreign treaties.[581]

The diplomatic agents of Britain, France, the United States and the Netherlands were invited to a joint audience with the shogun in Osaka, an event that took place on 29 April 1867. A few days later, the same foreign representatives were individually received by the shogun.[582] This was the first time that any of these foreign diplomats had been received in audience since the former shogun had gone to Osaka in July 1865.[583] On 25 April 1867, after some days of negotiations in Osaka, Minister of Foreign Affairs Itakura Katsukiyo officially announced that the cities of Osaka and Edo, the port of Hyōgo and a port on the West Coast of Japan would be opened as planned on 1 January 1868.[584] From Osaka, the Dutch political agent Van Polsbroek informed Belgian vice consul Lejeune in Yokohama of this provision, mentioning that it also applied to Belgian nationals. The Japanese government confirmed this orally to Lejeune on 15 May 1867. Lejeune informed the Foreign Ministry in Brussels. On 6 July 1867, the Ministry requested the *Moniteur Belge* to publish Lejeune's dispatch.[585]

Exchange of the Ratifications

On 10 June 1867, one day after his arrival in Yokohama, Auguste t'Kint received a visit from Asahina Masahiro 朝比奈 昌広, Japanese commissioner of foreign affairs. - T'Kint requested the commissioner to inform the Japanese councillors that he had brought the Belgian ratifications, signed by King Leopold II. The Belgian envoy also had meetings with the French minister Léon Roches and the Prussian chargé d'affaires, von Brandt, both of whom were residing in Yokohama. The Representatives of the Netherlands, Britain and the United States, on the other hand, had opted to move their residence to Edo.[586]

Two days after the meeting with the commissioner, on 12 June 1867, the Belgian envoy wrote to the councillors, confirming the content of the meeting he had had with Asahina. T'Kint added that he had also been assigned the duty of investigating how Belgium and Japan could increase their friendly relations. He requested another meeting with the commissioner to discuss this matter and to prepare the exchange of ratifications. T'Kint also politely declined the offer of the Japanese government to provide a house for him in Edo, since t'Kint had the opportunity to stay at the legation of a friendly nation. On the other hand, the Belgian envoy mentioned that he was having trouble finding a suitable residence in Yokohama and that he felt the need to discuss this with the commissioner.[587]

On 28 June 1867, the councillor in charge of foreign affairs, Inoue Masanao, replied to t'Kint inviting him to a meeting at his residence at 10 a.m. on 30 June 1867. The letter mentioned that Japanese plenipotentiaries would be appointed for the exchange of the ratifications, and that t'Kint would be shown around several buildings that might serve as his residence.[588]

Two days earlier, on 26 June 1867, Councillor Inoue had sent a letter to t'Kint informing him about the provisions that had been agreed with the representatives of the Netherlands, England, France and the United States concerning the opening of Osaka and Hyōgo on 1 January 1868. On 12 July 1867, the councillor informed the Belgian envoy that the planned opening of Osaka, Hyōgo, Edo and a port on the West Coast had been publicly announced.[589] For t'Kint, these announcements were important. In mid-December 1865, he had rushed to Japan to conclude a treaty, because he was aware of the commercial opportunities that the opening of these additional cities and ports could yield to the Belgian economy.

In a dispatch of 11 July 1867, t'Kint informed his foreign minister about the meeting with the Japanese councillor in charge of foreign affairs in Edo. Both had agreed to speed up the preparation for the exchange of the ratifications. However, after his visit to Edo, t'Kint fell ill in Yokohama, and had to stay at home for 15 days. In the meantime, the Japanese government had provided t'Kint with a temple as his residence in Edo: the Kōrinji temple 光林寺 in Azubu. It was located a mile from the other legations. After his health had been restored, t'Kint moved to this new dwelling in Edo. The move was completed before 5 August 1867.[590]

The Belgian envoy also came to an agreement with the Japanese authorities to suspend the allocation of a consular plot of land in Yokohama until the Belgian government had reached a decision on such a concession. In order to facilitate the decision, he sent Rogier detailed information on the construction costs of a consulate or a Belgian trading post ("comptoir belge") at Yokohama in a dispatch of 11 July 1867. During the same period, he received permission from Brussels to take home leave. T'Kint planned to leave Japan no earlier than October 1867, when the climate would become better for travelling. Aware of the slow pace of things in Japan, he hoped that the ratifications would have been exchanged by then.[591]

On 16 July 1867, the councillor in charge of foreign affairs, Ogasawara Nagamichi, informed t'Kint that one

of the commissioners of foreign affairs, Ishino Noritsune, had been ordered to take care of the exchange of the ratifications with Belgium, and that all discussions should be held with him.[592] T'Kint had met with Ishino already in 1866. At the same time, the Japanese newspaper *Bankoku shinbunshi* 萬国新聞紙 made reference to the conclusion of the Treaty with Belgium.[593] Around that time, on 19 July 1867, the Dutch political agent Dirk de Graeff van Polsbroek informed the Japanese government that the arrival of the Danish ratifications was expected on 25 July, and he requested a date for their exchange. Van Polsbroek had been appointed as plenipotentiary for this exchange by the Danish government.[594] On 22 July 1867, Ogasawara informed t'Kint that Hirayama Toshochō, deputy commissioner of foreign affairs (*wakadoshiyori narabini gaikokusōbugyō* 若年寄並外国惣奉行), would also serve as his contact person.[595]

By 5 August 1867, t'Kint had had one meeting with Ishino, who promised to speed up ratification of the Belgian-Japanese Treaty by the shogun, who was still in Osaka. T'Kint expected that the Japanese ratifications would arrive in Edo from Osaka in the first half of September 1867. To maintain pressure he dispatched a letter to Ishino on 12 August 1867, asking how long it would be before the exchange could take place. According to t'Kint, the Italian envoy had not made any better progress with the exchange of his ratifications.[596] On 15 August 1867, the Japanese government appointed Koide Hozumi 小出秀実, one of the commissioners of

Kōrinji temple at Minami-Azabu, Tokyo.
Photograph by Dirk De Ruyver, 20 November 2015.

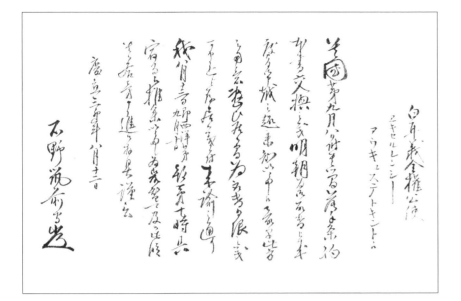

foreign affairs, as plenipotentiary for the exchange of the ratifications of the Treaty with Denmark. On 28 August 1867, he was replaced by Ishikawa Toshimasa 石川利正.[597]

Leopold II had ordered t'Kint to convey in person the king's best wishes to the new shogun for a long and prosperous reign, and to communicate the king's desire to expand the friendly relations between both courts and countries. Shortly after his arrival in Japan, t'Kint had informed the councillor in charge of foreign affairs of his intention to travel to Osaka for an audience with the shogun. The councillor had objected to this plan because of the dangers of such an overland journey. As an alternative, t'Kint sent his photograph to Ogasawara Nagamichi, the new councillor in charge of foreign affairs, on 12 August 1867, with a request to dispatch it with the best wishes of the Belgian king to the shogun in Osaka.[598] It took Ogasawara until 4 October 1867 before replying to t'Kint that his portrait and the message of best wishes of Leopold II would be sent to the shogun.[599] Later, Ogasawara informed t'Kint that the shogun had been pleased with the friendly feelings shown by the Belgian king.[600]

By the end of August, t'Kint had had two more meetings with Ishino, and during the second of these, on the morning of 29 August, Ishino mentioned that the treaty copies to be ratified by the shogun had arrived in Osaka. He then discussed the details of the exchange ceremony that should take place in the residence of t'Kint in Edo.[601] As a result of the meeting, t'Kint sent the Dutch translation of the official statement describing the proceedings of the exchange ceremony to Ishino the next day.[602] The same 30 August 1867, Ishino sent a letter to

the Italian legation about the preparations for the exchange of the treaty ratifications between Japan and Italy.[603]

On 8 September 1867, t'Kint wrote an extensive report on commercial prospects in the two ports and two cities to be opened on 1 January 1868, and dispatched it to Rogier advising that it be published.[604] On the same day, in a dispatch to Ishino, Auguste t'Kint inquired whether the exchange of the ratifications could take place two days later, on 10 September. On 9 September, Ishino accepted the proposal, mentioning that ratification on the Japanese side had been completed, and that he had himself been about to suggest the exchange. Consequently, as proposed by t'Kint, Ishino visited the Belgian legation at the Kōrinji in Edo to exchange the ratifications, according to the Japanese calendar at 7 in the morning on the 13th day of the 8th month of Keiō 3, or according to the Western calendar at 10 a.m. on 10 September 1867.[605]

In a dispatch of 10 September 1867, t'Kint described the event as follows:[606]

> On 10 September 1867, the Japanese commissioner came with a commissioner of foreign affairs and several other officials and employees. After the exchange, a light repast was offered to them, during which the best atmosphere prevailed. Having toasted the Tycoon (*shogun*) and the development of the relations between Belgium and Japan, the Japanese Commissioner Ishino Chikuzen no Kami (*Ishino Noritsune*) rose and in a few words mentioned that the Japanese government desired that the relations between Japan and Belgium, that started so happily, might be fertile for the government and for the commerce of both countries, and he finished by proposing a toast to the king of Belgium.

The *Japan Herald* published an article about the exchange in its edition of 1 October 1867.[607] That same day, the Dutch political agent Dirk de Graeff van Polsbroek, in his capacity of Danish plenipotentiary, exchanged the ratifications of the Treaty between Denmark and Japan with Ishikawa Toshimasa, commissioner of foreign affairs and Japanese plenipotentiary, in the Dutch legation (Chōōji temple) in Edo.[608] On 9 October 1867, the Japanese government publicly announced for the first time that it had concluded treaties with Portugal, Prussia, Switzerland, Belgium, Italy and Denmark.[609]

Letter from Ishino to t'Kint agreeing on the exchange of the ratified treaties on 10 September 1867. MOFA Belgium 2098. 9 September 1867 (12th day of the 8th month of Keiō 3). Japanese original of a letter from Ishino Chikuzen no Kami (Ishino Noritsune) to Auguste t'Kint.
Archives of the Belgian Ministry for Foreign Affairs, Brussels.

In its edition of 12 October 1867, the Japanese newspaper *Chūgai shinbunshi* published an article about the treaties concluded and exchanged by the Japanese government with Belgium and Denmark. The newspaper expressed the hope that both countries would contribute to the commercial development of Japan.[610] Harry Parkes, the British minister in Japan, informed his government about the exchange of the ratifications between Japan and Belgium in a dispatch dated 11 September 1867.[611]

Two weeks after the exchange of the ratifications, on 24 September 1867, Auguste t'Kint informed the councillor in charge of foreign affairs, Ogasawara Nagamichi, that he had received a declaration from King Leopold II approving the Additional Convention concluded between Japan and Belgium on 4 October 1866 in Edo. Sending a copy of this declaration in French, and a Dutch translation, t'Kint requested a similar declaration from the Japanese government.[612] His request triggered a written advice from the junior councillors and commissioners in charge of foreign affairs to Ogasawara.[613] T'Kint repeated his request on 12 October 1867.[614] Four days later, Ogasawara sent the requested declaration in which the shogun gave his consent to the Additional Convention of 4 October 1866.[615] In a dispatch dated 24 October 1867, t'Kint informed Foreign Minister Rogier of the exchange of these declarations. He attributed the long time it had taken for this exchange to materialize to Councillor Ogasawara Nagamichi being unavailable due to illness.[616]

While t'Kint had pressed ahead with the exchange of the Belgian ratifications, the Italian plenipotentiary, Count de la Tour, was having difficulty in proceeding. According to t'Kint, de la Tour had also to carry out a special mission to Beijing, and wanted to proceed quickly with the exchange of ratifications in Japan.[617] However, the Japanese government had difficulties in providing the Italian mission with a legation building. It had first proposed the Kōrinji in Edo, but the Italian plenipotentiary did not accept it. The temple was then given to t'Kint.[618] The Italian mission had a larger composition than the Belgian one. Count de la Tour was at least accompanied by his wife and by the legation secretary, Count Arese.[619] T'Kint, on the other hand, was unmarried and, at that stage, was likely to travel without a legation secretary.[620]

On 10 September 1867, the day of the exchange of the ratifications between Belgium and Japan, the Italian secretary, Count Arese, informed Ishino Noritsune that Count de la Tour would leave Yokohama for Edo on 18 September with the aim of exchanging the Italian ratifications.[621] Five days later, Ishino dispatched some more details about the preparation of the exchange of the treaty ratifications between Japan and Italy, in addition to his letter of 30 August 1867.[622]

Count de la Tour did go to Edo, but since no agreement had been reached on his residence in this city, it is unclear where he was lodging. The most likely possibility was the American legation in Edo, since the American minister Van Valkenburgh had offered his services.[623] On 26 September 1867, the Italian legation informed the Japanese government that Count de la Tour would wait another five days in Edo to exchange the ratifications.[624] But, two days later, Ishino Noritsune replied to de la Tour that the Japanese government would not be able to exchange the ratifications by 30 September 1867. He proposed going to Yokohama on 2 or 3 October to perform the exchange.[625] Finally, on 3 October 1867, the ratifications of the Italian-Japanese Treaty were exchanged.[626] The location of the Italian legation, however, remained a problem.[627] By the end of 1867, Count de la Tour had taken up residence at Benten, Yokohama, in a number of rooms in the house of the Dutch political agent Van Polsbroek.[628]

Final Chapter

T'Kint had already alluded to his departure for Belgium in a dispatch of 8 October 1867.[629] He requested a meeting with the Japanese councillor in charge of foreign affairs, Ogasawara Nagamichi, whom he had not yet met, or with a representative should the councillor be unavailable. Though the date of his departure was not yet fixed, t'Kint expected to move from Edo to Yokohama around 22 October 1867 and to depart from there on one of the mail steamers. He hoped to meet Ogasawara before leaving. He further requested that any communication after his departure should be addressed to the (vice) consul in Yokohama. T'Kint also promised to send some publications on machine building to the Japanese government once back in Belgium. The idea had come from a visit to the Sawayama book shop, which specialized in western books (*seiyō shosekirui Sawayama* 西洋書籍類澤山).

Besides the shogun's consent to the Additional Convention of 4 October 1866, t'Kint tried to obtain one further favour from the Japanese government. He requested that Kōrinji temple in Edo would be reserved as a residence for the next Belgian diplomatic representative. The Japanese government turned the request down around 20 October 1867, arguing that the Kōrinji served as a temporary residence for any foreign diplomat arriving unexpectedly, as had been the case with t'Kint.[630]

On 19 October 1867, the Belgian envoy received a farewell visit from Inaba Masakuni 稲葉正邦, the shogun's chief councillor, accompanied by Ishino Noritsune, the plenipotentiary responsible for the exchange of the ratifications with t'Kint. The visit unfolded in a long conversation about how to nurture the relations between Belgium and Japan, with particular attention to trade between the two countries. Five days later, on 24 October, Ishino paid another visit to say his personal farewell to t'Kint.[631] Since the councillor in charge of foreign affairs, Ogasawara Nagamichi, was ill, t'Kint was not able to meet him. T'Kint sent him a letter on 21 October 1867, announcing the end of his mission to Japan. Ogasawara replied 6 days later, wishing t'Kint a safe return home.[632]

Auguste t'Kint probably moved from Edo to Yokohama on 26 October 1867. He had received one last request from Ishino. Ishino wanted to have t'Kint's advice on exchange rate fluctuations between the Japanese and the foreign currencies. From Yokohama, t'Kint dispatched an essay on this topic on 29 October 1867. Probably two days later, on 31 October, t'Kint left Yokohama for Hong Kong.[633]

T'Kint arrived in Brussels by 23 March 1868 at the latest.[634] He made use of his home leave to improve his health at the German spa resort of Kaiserbad in Aachen, and to renew his connections with the industrial and commercial centres of Belgium.[635]

In the meantime, from July 1868 onwards, the Belgian Ministry of Foreign Affairs began preparing for the establishment of a permanent diplomatic post in the Far East. On 31 December 1868, it drafted a Royal Decree for that purpose. The Belgian Lower House (Chamber) approved this initiative on 20 April, the Senate on 29 April 1869. The Ministry proposed that King Leopold II appoint Auguste t'Kint as extraordinary envoy and minister plenipotentiary for China and Japan on 4 May 1869. A week later, t'Kint was informed about his appointment and the king's approval. The relevant Royal Decree appeared in the *Moniteur Belge* on 13 May 1869.[636]

On 5 July 1869, the foreign ministry prepared t'Kint's Letters of Credence, which were sent to the Royal Palace for the king's signature. These were dispatched to t'Kint on 16 July, together with his instructions from the minister of foreign affairs. T'Kint also received a budget for an exploratory tour of the most important industrial and commercial centres in Belgium, before leaving for the Far East.[637]

By 14 November 1869, t'Kint had arrived in Hong Kong. From there, he was planning to visit Canton (Guangzhou), Macao and the Philippines, before travelling to Japan to present his credentials in Edo.[638] During his visit to the Philippines, t'Kint fell ill and was confined to his bed for several weeks. After that, he changed his itinerary. He returned to Hong Kong, then moved on to Shanghai and Beijing. From Beijing, he dispatched a letter to the Belgian Foreign Ministry, dated 11 August 1870. He now expected to arrive in Japan by early October 1870. At the same time, he asked the ministry for further home leave due to the weakened condition of his health. The ministry refused, however, hoping that his health would improve in Japan.[639]

Auguste t'Kint returned to Yokohama on 9 November 1870, after having visited Nagasaki, Hyōgo and Osaka.[640]

Viscount Inaba Masakuni, Superintendent of the Shintoist Jingū Sect. *Taiyō* 太陽 (Hakubunkan 博文館) 4:16 (5 Aug 1898), frontispiece.

Japan had changed tremendously. The shogunate had been replaced by an imperial government, with direct rule by Emperor Meiji.[641] The presence of Belgian officials had been increased: besides the vice consulate in Yokohama and the consulate in Nagasaki, a consulate had been established in Edo, headed by Louis Strauss. A Royal Decree, signed by Leopold II on 19 January 1871, would also create a consulate in Osaka, headed by the American Franklin Blake.[642] During his second tenure in Japan, t'Kint was depicted twice in the satirical periodical the *Japan Punch*.[643]

In a dispatch of 19 January 1871, t'Kint again applied for home leave on health grounds. This time, the application was granted. T'Kint left Yokohama probably on 13 September 1871 for Hyōgo, Osaka and Nagasaki.[644] From Hyōgo, he sent a dispatch to the Japanese government in Edo on 8 October.[645] By 17 November, t'Kint was in Shanghai, whence he departed to Hong Kong on 30 November. He arrived in that city before 6 December. One week later, t'Kint was travelling to Canton and Macao. Back in Hong Kong by the end of the month, he planned to leave for Europe in January 1872. By 21 February 1872, he was in Naples (Italy).[646]

During his home leave, t'Kint would remain at the disposal of the Foreign Ministry in Brussels until he was granted unlimited leave due to ill health on 21 May 1873. He died unmarried in Brussels on 20 March 1878 at the age of 61. He was buried in the family tomb at the cemetery of Laken.[647] By 1965, this tomb was abandoned.[648]

Conclusion

In 1859, the Belgian Foreign Minister, Baron de Vrière, decided to request the Foreign Office in London to investigate through the English legation in Edo whether Japan would be willing to conclude a treaty with Belgium. As a result, in 1860 Belgium received a promise from Japan: if Japan were to conclude a treaty with any other country, it would also treat with Belgium.

This was to be a decisive element in the process leading to the Treaty of 1 August 1866. In the eyes of the Japanese administration, Belgium was one of only three nations to which such a promise had been made, the two others being Portugal and Switzerland. From 1 May 1861 onwards, Japan firmly closed the door to all other countries demanding a treaty, until it changed course again at the end of August 1866, with the conclusion of the Italian Treaty.

The promise that the Swiss Confederation received from the Japanese government early in 1860 came at the expense of a costly semi-official trade mission by the Swiss Confederation. Belgium and Portugal had obtained the same promise in a much more economical way, through the good offices of, respectively, the English and the Dutch representatives in Japan.

Due to the proximity of its trade colony in Macao, the Portuguese were the first to make use of the promise. In a mere three weeks, they obtained their treaty with Japan on 3 August 1860. The Swiss delegation sent to hold treaty negotiations arrived in Yokohama in April 1863, at a moment that the Japanese authorities had decided to close all open ports and expel the foreigners. It took the Swiss ten months to convince the Japanese authorities to honour their commitment. The Swiss-Japanese Treaty was signed on 6 February 1864.

Belgium waited till the end of 1864 to appoint a plenipotentiary for treaty negotiations with Japan. Having concluded a treaty with China on 2 November 1865, Auguste t'Kint believed the time had come to move to Japan, when he heard about the endorsement of the foreign treaties by the emperor in Kyoto. Arriving in Yokohama on 16 December 1865, it took the Belgian envoy seven and a half months to obtain a treaty with Japan. During that time, he had to surmount several difficulties, among them a complete change of strategy at the Foreign Ministry in Brussels and the death of his sovereign Leopold I. In contrast to all other foreign plenipotentiaries who had come to negotiate a treaty with Japan, t'Kint was not accompanied by a large military or civilian delegation to make an impression on the Japanese government. He brought only one secretary and his extensive experience as a treaty negotiator in Latin America.

Though t'Kint had rightly understood the importance of the ratification by the Japanese emperor, he had underestimated the length of the process to implement the concessions obtained. The negotiations for the Convention of 25 June 1866, for example, started on 5 February 1866. They involved a large number of Japanese officials at a time that the shogun's administration was physically split between Osaka and Edo, and kept the foreign diplomats and the Japanese officials going for more than 4 months. One week after the Convention was signed, the treaty negotiations between Belgium and Japan started in earnest.

Treaties with Japan in the last ten years of the shogunate tended to be concluded during certain limited periods when a window of opportunity had opened, soon to be firmly closed again by the Japanese authorities. The first five treaties were signed in 1858 in a period of two and a half months. The Portuguese

Fearful Encounter

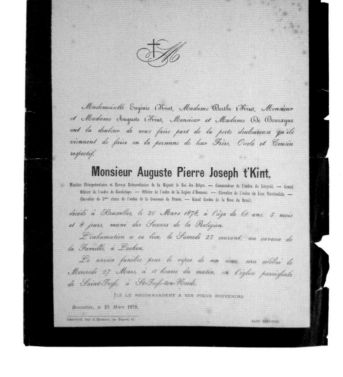

Auguste t'Kint and Louis Strauss in *The Japan Punch* (November 1870).
Collection of Yokohama Archives of History. Louis Strauss was the first Belgian Consul in Tokyo.

Auguste t'Kint and Louis Strauss in *The Japan Punch* (February 1871).
T'Kint is the second person from left; Strauss the third person (in battle position).
Collection of Yokohama Archives of History. The cartoon depicts a disagreement between Belgian Vice Consul Fritz Geisenheimer and Belgian Consul Louis Strauss.

Announcement of the death of Auguste t'Kint (Brussels, 23 March 1878).
MOFA Belgium 316. Brussels, 23 March 1878.
Archives of the Belgian Ministry for Foreign Affairs, Brussels.

Treaty, concluded considerably later, on 3 August 1860, had a similar content as the treaties of 1858. The only reason for the conclusion of this Treaty was the Japanese promise of October 1857.

The Prussian Treaty of 24 January 1861 clearly differed from the six earlier treaties. It only came into existence once the provision of opening Osaka, Hyōgo, Edo and Niigata had been dropped. This format became the blueprint for any new treaty with the shogunate.

On 28 January 1864, the Americans signed a new tariff convention with Japan, preceding the conclusion of the Swiss Treaty by nine days and the exchange of the Prussian Ratifications by 23 days. Since all treaties had the clause of most favoured nation, the new convention between the USA and Japan had consequences for all other treaty nations, including Switzerland. It is therefore not abnormal that this Convention preceded the Swiss Treaty and the exchange of the Prussian Ratifications. Similarly, the Belgian Treaty had to wait until the Convention of 25 June 1866 was finalized. And the Italian treaty negotiations only started after the Belgian Treaty was signed. This sequential approach might also have been forced upon the Japanese government due to a shortage of appropriate government officials in Edo, as a result of the shogun's administration being effectively split between Edo and Osaka.

The Belgian Treaty was the first to be concluded after the emperor had ratified the foreign treaties. It was the ninth treaty of amity, commerce and navigation signed by Japan. It came into existence two and a half years after the eighth, the Swiss Treaty. It signified the start of a new era of openness, which delivered treaties for Belgium, Italy and Denmark, and a first agreement on a treaty with Hawaii. While the origin of the Belgian Treaty lay in a promise made by Japan in 1860, the Italian Treaty made an effective end to a five-year Japanese policy of refusing any treaties with countries to which no treaty had previously been promised.

The Belgian negotiations only began after a clear decision by the shogun, then residing in Osaka, to allow them. This overturned the far more cautious approach of the two councillors of the shogun remaining in Edo. Though the emperor had endorsed the foreign treaties of 1858, including the opening of Osaka, Hyōgo, Edo and Niigata, the shogun ordered the use of the Prussian model, excluding any mention of the opening of these four places. Confronted with this fact, the diplomatic corps in Yokohama started doubting whether the endorsement by the emperor would be fully implemented. For that reason, the Belgian treaty negotiations were the first litmus test for the earnestness of emperor and shogun towards the opening of the additional four foreign settlements.

Generally speaking, the conclusion of these new treaties from August 1866 onwards was part of a process that had started with the emperor's ratification of the treaties in November 1865, and that would lead to the public announcement of the opening of the cities of Osaka and Hyōgo by mid-1867. During that process, long-standing policies of the Japanese government were reversed, such as the prohibition for Japanese citizens to travel abroad or to trade directly with foreigners. It shows that the government of the shogun had taken a path to open up Japan completely instead of containing foreign relations to a few open ports. It had taken a new shogun and a new emperor to declare Osaka and Hyōgo open and to speed up that process. For the foreign representatives in Japan, including t'Kint, the slowness of that process made them doubt the sincerity of the concessions obtained from emperor and shogun in Hyōgo in November 1865.

In his quest for a treaty with Japan, t'Kint was supported by some of the other foreign representatives. The Dutch political agent Dirk de Graeff van Polsbroek

38 柴田貞太郎

provided considerable logistic support. Particularly in the beginning of his stay, t'Kint actively sought his advice and support. While time was passing and t'Kint's frustration growing, he increasingly sought the advice of the French minister Léon Roches and the English minister Harry Parkes. In the final stages of his mission, t'Kint took more and more distance from the position of Roches, and seems to have favoured the interventions of Parkes. The Japanese also consulted Parkes on the treaty negotiations with Belgium.

The archives do not confirm the claims in some Dutch and French sources that the treaty between Belgium and Japan was to an important extent negotiated by their diplomats, rather than by t'Kint. All documents clearly indicate that t'Kint was in charge of these negotiations. They also indicate that he was not afraid of taking his own line, as long as this advanced the Belgian case. Throughout his career, he had learned to interpret the instructions from Brussels in a pragmatic way. This pragmatism served him well in the negotiations between Belgium and Japan.

Shibata Sadatarō in Paris.
Picture from album by Nadar (Gaspard-Felix Tournachon)

JAPANSCHE GEZANTEN.

REFERENCES

Adams 1874
Francis Ottiwell Adams. *The History of Japan from the Earliest Period to the Present Time*. Vol. 1. London: Henry S. King & Co., 1874.

Adams 1875
Francis Ottiwell Adams. *The History of Japan from the Earliest Period to the Present Time*. Vol. 2. London: Henry S. King & Co., 1875.

Alcock 1863
Rutherford Alcock. *The Capital of the Tycoon: A Narrative of a Three Years' Residence in Japan*. Vol. 1. London: Longman, 1863.

Arminjon 1869
F.V. Arminjon. *Il Giapppone e il Viaggio della Corvetta Magenta Nel 1866*. Genova: Co' tipi del R.I. dei Sordo-Muti, 1869.

Arminjon 1987
F.V. Arminjon and Ōkubo Teruo 大久保昭男. *Itaria Shisetsu no Bakumatsu Kenbunki* イタリア使節の幕末見聞記. Tokyo: Shinjinbutsu Ōraisha 新人物往来社, 1987.

Bertelli 2011
Giulio Antonio Bertelli. "The Rise of the Meiji Government and the Activity of Italian Diplomats Centering on Official Italian Primary Sources 明治政府の樹立と駐日イタリア公使・領事の外交活動について〜イタリア側公文書を中心に〜". In *ICIS The International Academic Forum for the Next Generation Series Vol.3 Creations as a Milestone in Cultural Interaction – Historical and Contemporary Perspectives –*. Osaka: Institute for Cultural Interaction Studies, Kansai University, 2011.

Black 1880
John R. Black. *Young Japan. Yokohama and Yedo. A Narrative of the Settlement and the City from the Signing of the Treaties in 1858 to the Close of the Year 1879. With a Glance of the Progress of Japan during a Period of Twenty-One Years*. Vol. 1. London: Trubner & Co. Yokohama: Kelly & Co., 1880.

Black 1881
John R. Black. *Young Japan. Yokohama and Yedo. A Narrative of the Settlement and the City from the Signing of the Treaties in 1858 to the Close of the Year 1879. With a Glance of the Progress of Japan during a Period of Twenty-One Years*. Vol. 2. London: Trubner & Co. Yokohama: Kelly & Co., 1881.

Shibata Takeuchi in Holland (1862), Engraving from the *Nederlandsch Magazijn* 1862. The illustration depicts three members of the Japanese delegation visiting the Netherlands in 1862 (from left to right: Matsudaira Yasunao, Shibata Sadatarō, Takeuchi Yasunori).

Cosenza 1959
Maria Emilio Cosenza. *The Complete Journal of Townsend Harris – First American Consul and Minister to Japan.* Rutland, Vermont, and Tokyo: Charles E. Tuttle Company, second edition (revised), 1959.

De Chassiron 1861
Ch. De Chassiron. *Notes sur le Japon, La Chine et L'Inde, 1858 –1859 – 1860.* Paris: Ch. Reinwald, 1861.

***Die Preussische Expedition* 1864**
Die Preussische Expedition nach Ost-Asien nach amtlichen Quellen. Erster Band. Berlin: Verlag der königlichen geheimen Oberhofbuchdruckerei, 1864.

***Die Preussische Expedition* 1866**
Die Preussische Expedition nach Ost-Asien nach amtlichen Quellen. Zweiter Band. Berlin: Verlag der königlichen geheimen Oberhofbuchdruckerei, 1866.

***Directory China* 1865**
The Chronicle and Directory for China, Japan and the Philippines for 1865. Hong Kong: Daily Press, s.a.

Duchesne 1966
Albert Duchesne. "T'Kint (Auguste-Pierre-Joseph)". In *Biographie Belge d'Outre-Mer*, vol. 6, col. 1017, 15 March 1966. Brussels: Académie Royale des Sciences d'Outre-Mer, 1968.

Fabri 1965
Jos. Fabri S.J. "Auguste t'Kint (1816-1878), Commissaire spécial de la Compagnie belge de colonisation". In *Expansion belge – Belgische Expansie 1831-1865.* Brussels: Académie Royale des Sciences d'Outre-Mer / Koninklijke Academie voor Overzeese Wetenschappen, 1965.

Griffis 1895
William Elliot Griffis. *Townsend Harris – First American Envoy in Japan.* Boston and New York: Houghton, Mifflin and Company. Cambridge: The Riverside Press, 1895.

Hawks 1856
Francis L. Hawks. *Narrative of the Expedition of an American Squadron to the China Seas and Japan 1852, 1853 and 1854, under the Command of Commodore M.C. Perry, by Order of the Government of the United States.* Washington: Beverley Tucker, 1856.

Humbert 1870
Aimé Humbert. *Le Japon Illustré.* Tome Premier. Paris: Librarie de L. Hachette et Cie., 1870.

Isomi et al. 1989
Isomi Tatsunori 磯見辰典, Kurosawa Fumikata 黒沢文貴 and Sakurai Ryōju 桜井良樹. *Nihon Berugī Kankei-shi* 日本ベルギー関係史. Tokyo: Hakusuisha 白水社, 1989.

***Japan Directory* 1864**
"The Japan Directory". In *The Chronicle & Directory for China, Japan & the Philippines for the year 1864.* Hong Kong: Daily Press, s.a.

Katō 2001
Katō Hideaki 加藤英明. "Tokugawa Bakufu Gaikokukata: Kindaiteki Taigai Jimu Tantoshō no Senku – sono Kikō to Hito" 徳川幕府外国方：近代的対外事務担当省の先駆—その機構と人. In *Bakumatsu Ishin to Gaikō* 幕末維新と外交, ed. Yokoyama Yoshinori 横山伊徳. Tokyo: Yoshikawa Kōunkan 吉川弘文館, 2001.

Kawasaki 1988
Kawasaki Seirō 川崎晴朗. *Bakumatsu Chūnichi Gaikōkan*・Ryōjikan 幕末の駐日外交官・領事官. Tokyo: Yūshōdō Shuppan 雄松堂出版, 1998.

Kitane 1987 (volume 7)
Kitane Yutaka 北根豊, ed. *Nihon Shoki Shinbun Zenshū 7 Keiō gannen jūichigatsu – Keio ninen ichigatsu.*日本初期新聞全集 7 慶応元年十一月 — 慶応二年一月. Tokyo: Perikansha ペリカン社, 1987.

Kitane 1987 (volume 9)
Kitane Yutaka 北根豊, ed. *Nihon Shoki Shinbun Zenshū 9 Keiō ninen hachigatsu – jūichigatsu.*日本初期新聞全集 9 慶応に年八月 — 十一月. Tokyo: Perikansha ペリカン社, 1987.

Klatt 2009
Norbert Klatt, Johannes Rösing and Clara von Ammon. *Briefe aus der Verlobungszeit 1863 über Köln, Bremen und die erste internationale Postkonferenz in Paris.* Göttingen: Norbert Klatt Verlag, 2009.

Leenders 2012
Gertjan Leenders. *Een adellijk bastion? Adellijke vertegenwoordiging in de Belgische diplomatie 1840-2000.* Unpublished M.A. dissertation, Ghent University, 2012.

List of Foreign Residents 1868
"The List of Foreign Residents in China, Japan, The Philippines and Siam for 1868 and The Yokohama Directory". In *The Chronicle & Directory for China, Japan & the Philippines for the year 1868.* Hong Kong: Daily Press, 13 January 1868.

Machida 2001
Machida Toshiaki 町田俊昭. *Kaikoku Kanimoji Bunsho Ronkō* 開国蟹文字文書論考. Tokyo: Ogawa Tosho 小川図書, 2001.

Minato City Local History Museum 2005
Minato City Local History Museum 港区立港郷土資料館. *Foreign Legations in Edo. Materials compiled to commemorate the 150th anniversary of the opening of Japan.* 江戸の外国公使館. 開国150周年記念史料集. Tokyo: Kōsaidō 廣済堂, 2005.

Ministry of Foreign Affairs of Japan 1874
Ministry of Foreign Affairs of Japan 外務所. *Treaties and Conventions concluded between Empire of Japan and Foreign Nations, together with Regulations and Communications 1854-1874* 締盟各国条約類纂. 自嘉永7年至明治7年. Tokyo: Nisshūsha Printing Office 行印社日就社, 1874.

Moeshart 1987
Herman J. Moeshart. *Journaal van Jonkheer Dirk De Graeff van Polsbroek 1857-1870. Belevenissen van een Nederlands diplomaat in het negentiende eeuwse Japan.* Assen and Maastricht: Van Gorcum, 1987.

MOFA Belgium 316
Archives of the Belgian Ministry of Foreign Affairs, Brussels. *File Pers 316 Auguste t'Kint de Roodenbeek (1842-1878).*

MOFA Belgium 883
Archives of the Belgian Ministry of Foreign Affairs, Brussels. *File Pers 883 Consulat Yokohama. Indicateur La B no. 476 Vice Consulat Yokohama – Personnel.*

MOFA Belgium 1890
Archives of the Belgian Ministry of Foreign Affairs, Brussels. *Arrêtes Royaux (Royal Decrees) 1890, 26e Année du Règne de S.M. Léopold II, Roi des Belges.*

MOFA Belgium 2016 I.A.
Archives of Belgian Ministry of Foreign Affairs, Brussels. *No. 2016 Mission Extraordinaire au Japon. Dossier no. 2016 I.A.: E. Mouttet 1846 (Missions et Explorations).*

MOFA Belgium 2016 I.B.
Archives of Belgian Ministry of Foreign Affairs, Brussels. *No. 2016 Mission Extraordinaire au Japon, file no. 2016 I.B.: Japon – Missions et Explorations. Aug. t'Kint de Roodenbeek.*

MOFA Belgium 2016 I.C.
Archives of Belgian Ministry of Foreign Affairs, Brussels. *No. 2016 I.C.: Mission Extraordinaire au Japon (Aug. t'Kind de Roodenbeek). Documents japonais. Correspondances des consuls avec les autorités japonaises, etc.*

MOFA Belgium 2098
Archives of the Ministry of Foreign Affairs of Belgium, Brussels. *No. 2098 (file 139 – Japon), Litta B no. 2483: Traité de Commerce (et de Navigation) avec le Japon. Projet Renseignement.*

MOFA Belgium 2704 III
Archives of the Belgian Ministry of Foreign Affairs. *No. 2704 III. Litt.a B no. 1746: Traité de commerce et de navigation conclu le 2 9bre 1865 entre la Belgique et la Chine / Correspondances du 1864 au 1867 III.*

MOFA Belgium 2864 XI
Archives of the Belgian Ministry of Foreign Affairs, Brussels. *No. 2864 XI: Japon, Usines, Sociétés, Entreprises diverses, Intérêts Belges. Indicateur La B no. 2483/2668 du 1866: Comptoir belge au Japon.*

MOFA Belgium 2865 IV
Archives of the Belgian Ministry of Foreign Affairs, Brussels. *No. 2865 IV. Japon. Légation à Yokohama 1866-1892. Rapports Yokohama 1866-1869.*

MOFA Belgium 10819/15
Archives of the Belgian Ministry of Foreign Affairs, Brussels. *No. 10819/15 Japon. Voyages en Belgique de Princes Japonais 1865-1910. File « 1865. Envoyés Japonais à Belgique (Pièces restitués par Nr. 1881). (Prince de Satsuma) ».*

MOFA Belgium – Japon Politique
Archives of the Belgian Ministry of Foreign Affairs. *Correspondance Politique Légations – Japon 1 (1866-1890).*

MOFA Belgium – Lambermont
Archives of the Belgian Ministry of Foreign Affairs. *Film P328-Df387: Papiers Lambermont 1851 – juil 1876.*

MOFA Belgium – Mexique 1
Archives of the Belgian Ministry of Foreign Affairs. *Correspondance Politique – Légations. Mexique 1: 1861-1867.*

NAB Rogier 2300
National Archives of Belgium, Brussels. *Archives Charles Rogier (Microfilm 2300), no. I 124 – 115 (Lettres des différents fonctionnaires du ministère des Affaires étrangères 1862-1867; Lettres de Ed. Degrelle, 1865-1867).*

NAB Rogier 2301
National Archives of Belgium, Brussels. *Archives Charles Rogier (Microfilm 2301), no. I 124 – 156.*

Nakai 1968
Nakai Akio 中井晶夫. "Puroisen kantai no Higashi Ajia ensei (1860-1862)" プロ
イセン艦隊の東アジア遠征 (一八六〇ー六二). In *Jōchi Shigaku* 上智史學 13
(1968), pp. 112-135.

Nakatake 1999
Nakatake Kanami 中武香奈美. "Furansu kaigun to chūnichi kōshi Rosshu no
tainichi seisaku" フランス海軍と中日公使ロッシュの対日政策. In *Yokohama
Eifutsu chūtongun to gaikokujin kyoryūchi* 横浜英仏駐屯軍と外国人居留地, ed.
Taigaikankei-shi Kenkyūkai 対外関係史研究会 and Yokohama Kaikō Shiryōkan
横浜開港資料館. Tokyo: Tōkyōdō Shuppan 東京堂出版, 1999.

NAN Scheepsjournalen
Nationaal Archief Nederland – National Archives of the Netherlands,
Ministerie van Marine. *Scheepsjournalen 1813-1985.*

Nihon Keieishi Kenkyūjo 1974
Nihon Keieishi Kenkyūjo 日本経営史研究所, ed. *Tomoatsu Godai Denki Shiryō
Daiyonkan* 五代友厚伝記史料第四巻. Tokyo: Tōyō Keizai Shinpōsha 東洋経済
新報社, 1974.

Nitta 1975 [2]
Nitta Mitsuo 新田満夫. *The Japan Punch [2]*. Tokyo: Yūshōdō Shoten 雄松堂書
店, 1975.

Nitta 1975 [3]
Nitta Mitsuo 新田満夫. *The Japan Punch [3]*. Tokyo: Yūshōdō Shoten 雄松堂書
店, 1975.

Oliphant 1859
Laurence Oliphant. *Narrative of the Earl of Elgin's Mission to China and Japan
in the Years 1857, '58 and '59*. Vol. 2. Edinburgh and London: William
Blackwood and Sons, 1859.

Ōyama 1999
Ōyama Mizuyo 大山瑞代. "Yokohama Chūtonchi no Eikoku rikugun" 横浜駐屯
地の英国陸軍. In *Yokohama Eifutsu chūtongun to gaikokujin kyoryūchi* 横浜英
仏駐屯軍と外国人居留地, Taigaikankei-shi Kenkyūkai 対外関係史研究会 and
Yokohama Kaikō Shiryōkan 横浜開港資料館. Tokyo: Tōkyōdō Shuppan 東京堂
出版, 1999.

Pereira 1863
Feliciano Antonio Marques Pereira. *Viagem da Corveta Dom João I á Capital do
Japão no anno de 1860*. Lisboa: Imprensa Nacional, 1863.

Royal Palace Belgium 176/134
Archives of the Belgian Royal Palace, Brussels. *Archives of Cabinet Leopold I, no.
176/134. M. T'Kint, III B k 1.*

Royal Palace Belgium – Duke of Brabant
Archives of the Belgian Royal Palace, Brussels. *Archives of the Duke of Brabant.
Travel Notes. China 6 documents.*

Satow 2006
Ernest Satow. *A Diplomat in Japan*. Berkeley, CA: Stone Bridge Press, 2006.
Reproduction of the first edition, published in London by Seeley, Service & Co.,
Ltd., 1921.

Schodt 2003
Frederik L. Schodt. *Native American in the Land of the Shogun: Ranald
MacDonald and the Opening of Japan*. Berkeley, CA.: Stone Bridge Press, 2003.

Société du Grand Armorial de France 1948
Société du Grand Armorial de France, ed. *Grand Armorial de France. Catalogue
Général des Armoiries des Familles nobles de France*. Vol. 5. Paris: Société du
Grand Armorial de France, 1948.

Tanaka 1998
Tanaka Masahiro 田中正弘, ed. *Kindai Nihon to Bakumatsu Gaikō Monjo
Hensan no Kenkyū* 近代日本と幕末外交文書編纂の研究. Kyoto: Shibunkaku
Shuppan 思文閣出版, 1998.

Truong 1957
Truong-Bun-Lim. *Les Débuts des Relations entre la Belgique et le Japon (1854-
1896)*. Leuven: Université Catholique de Louvain, 1957.

TUHI 1054.01/1
Tokyo University. Historigraphical Institute. *Archives of the Japanese Ministry
of Foreign Affairs. Diplomatic Correspondence (received) 1054.01 England
Volume I (1859-1860)*. 東京大学史料編纂所 / 外務省・引継資料1054.01 英国 第
一巻 (1859-1860).

TUHI 1054.01/3
Tokyo University. Historiographical Institute. *Archives Japanese Ministry of
Foreign Affairs. Diplomatic Correspondence (received) 1054.01 England, Volume
III (1865)*. 東京大学史料編纂所 / 外務省・引継資料1054.01 英国、第三巻
(1865).

TUHI 1054.01/4
Tokyo University. Historiographical Institute. *Archives Japanese Ministry of
Foreign Affairs. Diplomatic Correspondence (received) 1054.01 England, Volume
IV (1866)*. 東京大学史料編纂所/ 外務省・引継資料1054.01 英国、第四巻
(1866).

TUHI 1054.02/1
Tokyo University. Historigraphical Institute. *Archives Japanese Ministry of
Foreign Affairs. Diplomatic Correspondence (received) 1054.02 America, Volume I
(1859-1863)*. 東京大学史料編纂所 / 外務省・引継資料1054.02 米国 第一巻
(1859-1863).

TUHI 1054.02/3
Tokyo University. Historiographical Institute. *Archives Japanese Ministry of
Foreign Affairs. Diplomatic Correspondence (received) 1054.02 America, Volume 3
(1867-1869)*. 東京大学史料編纂所 / 外務省・引継資料1054.02 米国 第三巻
(1867-1869).

TUHI 1054.03/2
Tokyo University. Historiographical Institute. *Archives Japanese Ministry of
Foreign Affairs. Diplomatic Correspondence (received) 1054. (0)3 France, Volume
II (1863-1869)*. 東京大学史料編纂所 / 外務省・引継資料1054.3 仏国、第二巻
(1863-1869).

TUHI 1054.04/1
Tokyo University. Historiographical Institute. *Archives Japanese Ministry of
Foreign Affairs. Diplomatic Correspondence (received) 1054.04 The Netherlands
Volume I (1844-1863)*. 東京大学史料編纂所/ 外務省・引継資料1054.04 蘭国 第
一巻 (1844-1863).

TUHI 1054.04/2
Tokyo University. Historiographical Institute. *Archives Japanese Ministry of
Foreign Affairs. Diplomatic Correspondence (received) 1054.04 The Netherlands,
Volume II (1864-1865)*. 東京大学史料編纂所 / 外務省・引継資料1054.04 蘭国、
第二巻 (1864-1865).

TUHI 1054.04/3
Tokyo University. Historiographical Institute. *Archives Japanese Ministry of
Foreign Affairs. Diplomatic Correspondence (received) 1054.04 The Netherlands,
Volume III (1866-1867)*. 東京大学史料編纂所/ 外務省・引継資料1054.04 蘭国、
第三巻 (1866-1867).

TUHI 1054.05
Tokyo University. Historiographical Institute. *Archives Japanese Ministry of
Foreign Affairs. Diplomatic Correspondence (received) 1054.05 Prussia, Germany
(1861-1868)*. 東京大学史料編纂所/ 外務省・引継資料1054.05 独国 (1861-1868).

TUHI 1054.07/1
Tokyo University. Historiographical Institute. *Archives Japanese Ministry of
Foreign Affairs. Diplomatic Correspondence (received) 1054.07 Italy, volume I
(1866-1874)*. 東京大学史料編纂所 / 外務省・引継資料1054.07 伊国 第一巻
(1866-1874).

TUHI 1054.08
Tokyo University. Historiographical Institute. *Archives Japanese Ministry of
Foreign Affairs. Diplomatic Correspondence (received) 1054.(0)8 Belgium.* 東京大
学史料編纂所 / 外務省・引継資料1054.8 白国

TUHI 1054.09/1
Tokyo University. Historiographical Institute. *Archives Japanese Ministry of
Foreign Affairs. Diplomatic Correspondence (received) 1054.09 Denmark, volume
I (1861-1881)*. 東京大学史料編纂所/ 外務省・引継資料 1054.09 丁国 第一巻
(1861-1881).

TUHI 1054.10/1
Tokyo University. Historiographical Institute. *Archives Japanese Ministry of
Foreign Affairs. Diplomatic Correspondence (received) 1054.10 Switzerland
Volume I (1863-1875)*. 東京大学史料編纂所/ 外務省・引継資料1054.10瑞国 第
一巻 (1863-1875).

TUHI 1054.11
Tokyo University. Historiographical Institute. *Archives Japanese Ministry of
Foreign Affairs. Diplomatic Correspondence (received) 1054.11 Portugal (1859-
1881)*. 東京大学史料編纂所/ 外務省・引継資料1054.11葡国 (1859-1881).

TUHI 1055.1/1
Tokyo University. Historiographical Institute. *Archives Japanese Ministry of
Foreign Affairs. Diplomatic Correspondence (sent) 1055.1 England Volume I (1859-1860)*. 東
京大学史料編纂所 / 外務省・引継資料1055.1 英国 第一巻 (1859-1860).

TUHI 1055.1/4
Tokyo University. Historiographical Institute. *Archives Japanese Ministry of
Foreign Affairs. Diplomatic Correspondence (sent) 1055.1 England Volume IV
(1865-1867)*. 東京大学史料編纂所 / 外務省・引継資料1055.1 英国 第四巻 (1865-
1867).

TUHI 1055.2/1
Tokyo University. Historiographical Institute. *Archives Japanese Ministry of
Foreign Affairs Diplomatic Correspondence (sent) 1055.2 America, Volume I
(1859-1862)*. 東京大学史料編纂所 / 外務省・引継資料1055.2 米国 第一巻 (1859-
1862).

TUHI 1055.2/3
Tokyo University. Historiographical Institute. *Archives Japanese Ministry of
Foreign Affairs. Diplomatic Correspondence (sent) 1055.2 U.S.A., Volume 3 (1866-
1867)*. 東京大学史料編纂所 / 外務省・引継資料1055.2 米国 第三巻
(1866-1867).

TUHI 1055.4/1
Tokyo University. Historiographical Institute. *Archives Japanese Ministry of Foreign Affairs. Diplomatic Correspondence (sent) 1055.4 The Netherlands Volume I (1860-1863).* 東京大学史料編纂所/ 外務省・引継資料1055.4 蘭国 第一巻 (1860-1863).

TUHI 1055.4/2
Tokyo University. Historiographical Institute. *Archives Japanese Ministry of Foreign Affairs. Diplomatic Correspondence (sent) 1055.4 The Netherlands, Volume II (1864-1865).* 東京大学史料編纂所/ 外務省・引継資料 1055.4 蘭国、第二巻 (1864-1865).

TUHI 1055.4/3
Tokyo University. Historiographical Institute. *Archives Japanese Ministry of Foreign Affairs. Diplomatic Correspondence (sent) 1055.4 The Netherlands, Volume III (1866-1867).* 東京大学史料編纂所/ 外務省・引継資料 1055.4 蘭国、第三巻 (1866-1867).

TUHI 1055.5/1
Tokyo University. Historiographical Institute. *Archives Japanese Ministry of Foreign Affairs. Diplomatic Correspondence (sent) 1055.5 Prussia Volume 1 (1860-1864).* 東京大学史料編纂所/ 外務省・引継資料1055.5 独国 第一巻 (1860-1864).

TUHI 1055.5/2
Tokyo University. Historiographical Institute. *Archives Japanese Ministry of Foreign Affairs. Diplomatic Correspondence (sent) 1055.5 Prussia Volume II (1865-1867).* 東京大学史料編纂所/ 外務省・引継資料1055.5 独国 第二巻 (1865-1867).

TUHI 1055.6/1
Tokyo University. Historiographical Institute. *Archives Japanese Ministry of Foreign Affairs. Diplomatic Correspondence (sent) 1055.6 Switzerland Volume I (1863-1867).* 東京大学史料編纂所 / 外務省・引継資料 1055.6 瑞国 第一巻 (1863-1867).

TUHI 1055.7
Tokyo University. Historiographical Institute. *Archives Japanese Ministry of Foreign Affairs. Diplomatic Correspondence (sent) 1055.7 Portugal (1860-1867).* 東京大学史料編纂所 / 外務省・引継資料 1055.7 葡国 (1860-1867).

TUHI 1055.8/1 Belgium
Tokyo University. Historiographical Institute. *Archives Japanese Ministry of Foreign Affairs. Diplomatic Correspondence (sent) 1055.8 Belgium etc. Volume I (1859-1867).* 東京大学史料編纂所 / 外務省・引継資料1055.8 白国など 第一巻 (1859-1867).

TUHI 1055.8/1 Denmark
Tokyo University. Historiographical Institute. *Archives Japanese Ministry of Foreign Affairs. Diplomatic Correspondence (sent) 1055.8 Denmark etc. Volume I (1859-1867)* 東京大学史料編纂所 / 外務省・引継資料 丁国など 第一巻 (1859-1867).

TUHI 1055.8/1 Italy
Tokyo University. Historiographical Institute. *Archives Japanese Ministry of Foreign Affairs. Diplomatic Correspondence (sent) 1055.8 Italy etc. Volume I (1859-1867).* 東京大学史料編纂所 / 外務省・引継資料1055.8 伊国など 第一巻 (1859-1867).

TUHI. Dutch Consulate General 1864-1866
Tokyo University. Historiographical Institute. *Het Archief van het Consulaat Generaal te Yokohama (1860-1870). Correspondentie met het Departement van Buitenlandse Zaken 1864-1866.*

TUHI. Dutch Consulate General 1867-1870
Tokyo University. Historiographical Institute. *Het Archief van het Consulaat Generaal te Yokohama (1860-1870). Correspondentie met het Departement van Buitenlandse Zaken 1867-1870.*

TUHI Ishin 3
Tokyo University. Historiographical Institute. *Ishin Shiryō Kōyō, Volume 3* 維新史料綱要3巻. *Dainippon Ishin Shiryō Kōhon*大日本維新史料稿本 (abbreviated to D.I.S.K.).

TUHI Ishin 6
Tokyo University. Historiographical Institute. Ishin Shiryō Kōyō, Volume 6 維新史料綱要6巻. Dainippon Ishin Shiryō Kōhon大日本維新史料稿本 (abbreviated to D.I.S.K.).

TUHI Ishin 7
Tokyo University. Historiographical Institute. *Ishin Shiryō Kōyō, Volume 7* 維新史料綱要7巻. *Dainippon Ishin Shiryō Kōhon*大日本維新史料稿本 (abbreviated to D.I.S.K.).

TUHI. LJ29.
Tokyo University. Historiographical Institute. *Algemeen Rijksarchief, The Hague – Netherlands. Legatie Japan, Edo (Tokio), no. 12, L.J. no. 29. Microfilm HdUp 6951-1.12.*

TUHI. LJ36.
Tokyo University. Historiographical Institute. *Algemeen Rijksarchief, The Hague, Netherlands. Legatie Japan, Edo Tokyo. Microfilm Hdup 6951-1 no. 13 / L.J. no. 36. Eigendommen en meubelen van het (Nederlandse) government in Japan 1859, 1861, 1862, 1863, 1867, 1870, 1872, 1873, 1874, 1875.*

TUHI. LJ37.
Tokyo University. Historiographical Institute. *Algemeen Rijksarchief, The Hague, Netherlands. Legatie Japan, Edo Tokyo. Microfilm Hdup 6951-1 no. 13 / L.J. no. 37.*

TUHI. MOFA Netherlands 1865
Tokyo University. Historiographical Institute. *Het Archief van het Ministerie van Buitenlandse Zaken (1813-1870). Japanse Aangelegenheden 1852-1870. BUZA 3145(7) 1865. Original Reference: Het Ministerie van Buitenlandse Zaken Consulaire Afdeling. Fonds Ministerie van Buitenlandse Zaken, 2e supplement. Inventory no. 2.05.01. Series (B-Dossier). Archive no. 3145.*

TUHI. MOFA Netherlands 1867
Tokyo University. Historiographical Institute. *Het Archief van het Ministerie van Buitenlandse Zaken 1813-1870. Japanse Aangelegenheden 1852-1870.* オランダ外務省本省文書・対日通商条約締結関係等往復文書*Bu.Za 3146(5)-1867. Original Reference: Het Ministerie van Buitenlandse Zaken, Consulaire Afdeling. Fonds: Ministerie van Buitenlandse Zaken, 2e Supplement. Inventory no. 2.05.01. Series (B-dossier). Archive no. 3146.*

University of Tokyo Volume VI 1966
University of Tokyo. *Historical documents relating to Japan in foreign countries: An inventory of microfilm acquisitions in the Library of the Historiographical Institute (Shiryō Hensan-jo), The University of Tokyo, Volume VI. The United Kingdom Part I. Tokyo,* 1966. (General) Japan Correspondence, 1856-1868. (Consulted in the Yokohama Archives for History 横浜開港資料館).

University of Tokyo Volume VII 1967
University of Tokyo. *Historical documents relating to Japan in foreign countries: An inventory of microfilm acquisitions in the Library of the Historiographical Institute (Shiryō Hensan-jo), The University of Tokyo, Volume VII. The United Kingdom Part II. Tokyo,* 1967. Embassy and Consular Archives, Japan (1859-1879). Correspondence Japan. (Consulted in the Yokohama Archives for History 横浜開港資料館).

University of Tokyo Volume IX and Volume X 1968 Diplomatic
University of Tokyo. *Historical documents relating to Japan in foreign countries: An inventory of microfilm acquisitions in the Library of the Historiographical Institute (Shiryō Hensan-jo), The University of Tokyo, Volume IX and Volume X. The United States. Tokyo,* 1968. U.S. Department of State. Diplomatic instructions from the Department of State 1801-1906, Japan. (Consulted in the Yokohama Archives for History 横浜開港資料館).

University of Tokyo Volume IX and Volume X 1968 Japan
University of Tokyo. *Historical documents relating to Japan in foreign countries: An inventory of microfilm acquisitions in the Library of the Historiographical Institute (Shiryō Hensan-jo), The University of Tokyo, Volume IX and Volume X. The United States. Tokyo,* 1968. U.S. Department of State. Notes from the Japanese Foreign Office. (Consulted in the Yokohama Archives for History 横浜開港資料館).

University of Tokyo Volume IX and Volume X 1968 Legation
University of Tokyo. *Historical documents relating to Japan in foreign countries: An inventory of microfilm acquisitions in the Library of the Historiographical Institute (Shiryō Hensan-jo), The University of Tokyo, Volume IX and Volume X. The United States. Tokyo,* 1968. U.S. Department of State. Records of the U.S. Legation in Japan, 1855-1912. (Consulted in the Yokohama Archives for History 横浜開港資料館).

University of Tokyo Volume IX and Volume X 1968 Ministers
University of Tokyo. *Historical documents relating to Japan in foreign countries: An inventory of microfilm acquisitions in the Library of the Historiographical Institute (Shiryō Hensan-jo), The University of Tokyo, Volume IX and Volume X. The United States. Tokyo,* 1968. U.S. Department of State. Despatches from U.S. Ministers to Japan 1855-1906. (Consulted in the Yokohama Archives for History 横浜開港資料館).

University of Tokyo Volume XI Switzerland 2-1
University of Tokyo. *Historical documents relating to Japan in foreign countries: An inventory of microfilm acquisitions in the Library of the Historiographical Institute (Shiryō Hensan-jo), The University of Tokyo, Volume XI. Switzerland, German Democratic Republic, Federal Republic of Germany, Sweden. Tokyo,* 1968. Bundesarchiv Bern. 6951-35-2-1. Freundschafts- und Handelsvertrag mit dem Taikun von Japan 1.8.1862-1868.

University of Tokyo Volume XI Switzerland 5-1
University of Tokyo. *Historical documents relating to Japan in foreign countries: An inventory of microfilm acquisitions in the Library of the Historiographical Institute (Shiryō Hensan-jo), The University of Tokyo, Volume XI. Switzerland, German Democratic Republic, Federal Republic of Germany, Sweden. Tokyo,* 1968. Bundesarchiv Bern. 6951-35-5-1. Eidgenössisches politische Departement. Dokumente des Konsulardienst in Yokohama, Bd 1, Allgemeines 1864-1867.

University of Tokyo Volume XI Switzerland 5-2
University of Tokyo. *Historical documents relating to Japan in foreign countries: An inventory of microfilm acquisitions in the Library of the Historiographical Institute (Shiryō Hensan-jo), The University of Tokyo, Volume XI. Switzerland, German Democratic Republic, Federal Republic of Germany, Sweden.* Tokyo, 1968. Bundesarchiv Bern. 6951-35-5-2. Dokumente des Kunsulardienste in Yokohama, Bd 2 Politische and Jahresberichte 1865/1900. Protocol de l'année 1866.

University of Tokyo Volume XIII 1965 Consulaire
University of Tokyo. *Historical documents relating to Japan in foreign countries: An inventory of microfilm acquisitions in the Library of the Historiographical Institute (Shiryō Hensan-jo), The University of Tokyo, Volume XIII. France.* Tokyo, 1965. Correspondance Consulaire et Commerciale, Yedo 1859-1877. (Consulted in the Yokohama Archives for History 横浜開港資料館).

University of Tokyo Volume XIII 1965 Politique
University of Tokyo. *Historical documents relating to Japan in foreign countries: An inventory of microfilm acquisitions in the Library of the Historiographical Institute (Shiryō Hensan-jo), The University of Tokyo, Volume XIII. France.* Tokyo, 1965. Correspondance Politique, Japon 1854-1896. (Consulted in the Yokohama Archives for History 横浜開港資料館).

University of Tokyo Volume XIV 1966
University of Tokyo. *Historical documents relating to Japan in foreign countries: An inventory of microfilm acquisitions in the Library of the Historiographical Institute (Shiryō Hensan-jo), The University of Tokyo, Volume XIV. France.* Tokyo, 1966. (Consulted in the Yokohama Archives for History 横浜開港資料館).

Van der Chijs 1867
J.A. van der Chijs. *Neêrlands streven tot openstelling van Japan voor den wereldhandel – uit officiële, grotendeels onuitgegeven bescheiden toegelicht.* Amsterdam: Frederik Muller, 1867.

Vande Walle 1996
W.F. Vande Walle. "Count de Montblanc and the 1865 Satsuma Mission to Europe". *Orientalia Louvaniensia Periodica* 27 (1996), pp. 151-176.

Vande Walle 2003
W.F. Vande Walle. "Belgian Treaties with China and Japan under King Leopold I". In *The History of the Relations between the Low Countries and China in the Qing Era (1644-1911)*, ed. W.F. Vande Walle and Noël Golvers, pp. 419-437. Leuven: Leuven University Press, 2003.

Vande Walle 2005
W.F. Vande Walle. "An Extraordinary Destiny: Count de Montblanc (1833-1894)". In *Japan & Belgium. Four Centuries of Exchange*, ed. W.F. Vande Walle, pp. 140-157. The Commissioners-General of the Belgian Government at the Universal Exhibition of Aichi, Japan, 2005.

YAH
Yokohama Archives of History 横浜開港資料館 www.kaikou.city.yokohama.jp.

Yokohama Directory 1865
"The Yokohama Directory". In *The Chronicle & Directory for China, Japan & the Philippines for the year 1865*. Hong Kong: Daily Press, 12 January 1865.

Yokohama Directory 1866
"The Yokohama Directory". In *The Chronicle & Directory for China, Japan & the Philippines for the year 1866*. Hong Kong: Daily Press, 24 February 1866.

Yokohama Directory 1867
"The Yokohama Directory". In *The Chronicle & Directory for China, Japan & the Philippines for the year 1867*. Hong Kong: Daily Press, 6 February 1867.

Yokoyama 1993
Yokoyama Yoshinori. "Dutch-Japanese Relations during the Bakumatsu Period". *Journal of the Japan-Netherlands Institute* 5 (1993).

NOTES

1 Ministry of Foreign Affairs of Japan 1874, p. 1.

2 See e.g., Hawks 1856, p. 19 and pp. 27-34; Oliphant 1859, vol. II, pp. 10-12.

3 Hawks 1856, pp. 381-382.

4 Hawks 1856, p. 75, and Machida 2001, pp. 73-74.

5 These elements were even mentioned in the formal letter from President Millard Fillmore to the shogun, dated Washington 13 November 1852, as reasons for the US to request treaty negotiations with Japan. See Hawks 1856, pp. 256-257. They were also brought up during the treaty negotiations in 1854. See Hawks 1856, p. 350.

6 This element was mentioned in a formal letter from Commodore Perry to the shogun, dated from the US frigate *Susquehanna* off the coast of Japan, 7 July 1853. See Hawks 1856, pp. 258-259.

7 Schodt 2003, p. 319.

8 Hawks 1856, p. 382, and Machida 2001, pp. 73-74.

9 Hawks 1856, p. 323 and pp. 382-383, and Machida 2001, pp. 77-78.

10 Ministry of Foreign Affairs of Japan 1874, p. 6. The ports opened by the British treaty were Nagasaki and Hakodate. As a consequence of article IX of the Perry Treaty (the most favoured nation clause), American citizens automatically gained the right to make use of the port of Nagasaki.

11 Van der Chijs 1867, pp. 115-117.

12 Machida 2001, pp. 7-35 and pp. 39-45.

13 Van der Chijs 1867, pp. 185-192.

14 Van der Chijs 1867, p. 205.

15 Ministry of Foreign Affairs of Japan 1874, p. 15.

16 Ministry of Foreign Affairs of Japan 1874, p. 9. The ports opened by the Russian Treaty were Shimoda, Nagasaki and Hakodate.

17 English translation of the original Dutch version of the treaty. Since only Dutch and Chinese nationals were allowed to enter Japan, Dutch and Chinese had become the official languages of the Japanese government for communication with the outside world. See e.g. Machida 2001, pp. 1-2.

18 Townsend Harris (1804-1878). Encyclopædia Britannica Online, s.v. "Townsend Harris," (accessed 5 Dec 2015): https://www.britannica.com/biography/Townsend-Harris.

19 Griffis 1895, pp. 33-34, and Cosenza 1959, pp. 199-200.

20 Griffis 1895, pp. 133-134, and Cosenza 1959, pp. 327-329.

21 Hawks 1856, pp. 390-392. This concerned a number of American families on the American schooner C.E. Foote, arriving in Shimoda in March 1855 and Hakodate in June 1855.

22 Ministry of Foreign Affairs of Japan 1874, p. 23, particularly article II; Griffis 1895, pp. 159-160; Cosenza 1959, pp. 373-374.

23 Ministry of Foreign Affairs of Japan 1874, pp. 26 and 43.

24 Ministry of Foreign Affairs of Japan 1874, p. 50, Article XXVII of the Supplementary Treaty between Russia and Japan.

25 For the treaty, see Ministry of Foreign Affairs of Japan 1874, p. 52. For the negotiations, see Griffis 1895, pp. 237-321, and Cosenza 1959, pp. 484-561.

26 Ministry of Foreign Affairs of Japan 1874, p. 71: the treaty between the Netherlands and Japan signed at Edo, 18 August 1858; p. 90: between Russia and Japan at Edo, 7 August 1858; p. 111: between Great Britain and Japan at Edo, 26 August 1858; and p. 130: between France and Japan at Edo, 9 October 1858.

27 The port of Kanagawa was established in a small fishing village, called Yokohama. See Black 1880, pp. 26-29, and Adams 1874, pp. 117-118.

28 Article III of the Harris Treaty of 1858 provided that the port of Shimoda would be closed six months after Kanagawa was opened. The same clause also provided for the gradual opening of the ports of Niigata (or another port on the West Coast of Japan) and Hyōgo, and the cities of Edo and Osaka. See Ministry of Foreign Affairs of Japan 1874, p. 54.

29 Truong 1957, pp. 49-59. According to Truong, Walkingshaw became Belgian consul at Canton in 1851.

30 MOFA Belgium 2098. Flessingue (Eng. Flushing; Du. Vlissingen), 23 February 1858, Bourceret to M. Delambermont (Directeur de consulats, Bruxelles); also Flessingue, 11 March 1858, dispatch no. 119 from Bourceret to Belgian Ministry of Foreign Affairs.

31 MOFA Belgium 2098. Brussels, 23 August 1858, Minute Indicateur B no. 2483, order no. 96, Belgian Ministry of Foreign Affairs, 30 June 1858. De Vrière's position towards a treaty with China was different. From his letters to d'Egremont of 16 March and 23 August 1858, it is clear that he was actively seeking such a treaty. See Vande Walle 2003, p. 425.

32 MOFA Belgium 2098. Brussels, 18 December 1858, Belgian Ministry of Foreign Affairs, Minute B 2383, No. d'ordre 401, containing a draft letter to Baron du Jardin at The Hague; and: Belgian Legation at The Hague, 20 December 1858, dispatch no. 742/407 from du Jardin to de Vrière.

33 MOFA Belgium 2016 I.B. Extract of the *Moniteur Belge* with a report on the session in the Belgian Senate of 24 Dec 1858, pp. 59-61.

34 Truong too mentions that the Belgian minister of foreign affairs, de Vrière, changed course because he was informed about the treaties signed between Japan and five Western Powers in 1858. See Truong 1957, p. 62. Truong does not mention his source for this statement. The Archives of the Belgian Ministry on Japan do not seem to contain any information that would explain the change of heart in December 1858. However, during the debate of 24 December 1858 in the Belgian Senate, the duke of Brabant explicitly mentions the treaties of Tianjin ("Tiensjing") and Edo ("Jeddo").

35 Van der Chijs, p. 386.

36 MOFA Belgium 2016 I.B. Brussels, 31 Dec 1858. Minute Indicateur B no. 1746, Belgian Ministry of Foreign Affairs to its representatives in London (Van De Weyer), Paris (Rogier), Saint Petersburg (vicomte de Jonghe) and Lisbon (Carolus). Also MOFA Belgium 2098. Brussels, 31 December 1858, Minute of the Belgian Ministry of Foreign Affairs, Indicateur B no. 2483, order no. 413, containing a draft to Baron du Jardin in The Hague.

37 The related correspondence is held at the Archives of the Belgian Ministry of Foreign Affairs, Brussels, no. 2098 (file 139 – Japon), Litta B no. 2483: Traité de Commerce (et de Navigation) avec le Japon. Projet Renseignement.

38 Truong 1957, pp. 68-71.

39 MOFA Belgium 2098. The Hague, 1 February 1859, Belgian Legation no. 67/36 from Baron du Jardin to Baron de Vrière; also The Hague, 4 April 1859, Belgian Legation no. 196/111 from Baron du Jardin to Baron de Vrière.

40 Truong 1957, p. 72. A draft of a confidential note from de Varlet is kept at MOFA Belgium 2016 I.B. Brussels, 24 February 1859, Belgian Ministry of Foreign Affairs, unnumbered but with the title "Expedition au Japon – Note pour Monsieur le Ministre".

41 Vande Walle 2003, p. 428.

42 MOFA Belgium 2098. Antwerp, 31 March 1859, President and Secretary of the Antwerp Chamber of Commerce and Industry to the Belgian Minister of Foreign Affairs in Brussels. This dispatch contained a copy of a letter and two newspapers from Wm. Grancit in Hong Kong with news on Japan. The letter from Grancit was dated Hong Kong 29 January 1859.

43 MOFA Belgium 2016 I.B. Brussels, 30 May 1859. Minute Indicateur B no. 1746, no. ordre 36, Belgian Ministry of Foreign Affairs to de Grimberghen in Bern. This position was reiterated on 29 July 1859 in a letter from Baron de Vrière to the Belgian consul in Amsterdam, J.N.W.C. Sieburgh. See MOFA Belgium 2098. Brussels, 29 July 1859, Minute, Indicateur B no. 2483, order no. 209, from the Belgian Ministry of Foreign Affairs to Sieburgh, Amsterdam.

44 Vande Walle 2003, p. 428.

45 MOFA Belgium 2098. Amsterdam, 21 July 1859, Belgian consulate in Amsterdam, no. 866/281, stamped in Brussels on 23 July (1859), B no. 1796, J.N.W.C. Sieburgh to Baron A. de Vrière, Brussels; also Brussels, 5 August 1859, Hôtel de Flandre, J.N.W.C. Sieburgh to A. Lambermont, Director of the Consular Department at the Belgian Ministry of Foreign Affairs.

46 MOFA Belgium 2098. Brussels, 5 August 1859, Hôtel de Flandre, Belgian consul J.N.W.C. Sieburgh to Lambermont, informing him of his arrival in Brussels on 4 August 1859 evening; and: Antwerp, 13 August 1859, letter from Belgian consul J.N.W.C. Sieburgh to Lambermont, informing him of his departure for Amsterdam.

47 MOFA Belgium 2098. Antwerp, 13 August 1859, letter from Belgian consul J.N.W.C. Sieburgh to Lambermont.

48 MOFA Belgium 2098. Amsterdam, 29 September 1859, Belgian Consulate in Amsterdam, no. 878/286, stamped in Brussels on 1 October (1859), B 2482, no. 13016, letter from Belgian consul J.N.W.C. Sieburgh to Baron A. de Vrière.

49 The last initiative taken by Sieburgh in this regard was a circular letter to all Chambers of Commerce in Belgium, dated Amsterdam, 21 December 1859. See Truong 1957, p. 106.

50 MOFA Belgium 2098. Brussels 17 June 1859, Minute Indicateur B no. 2483, order no. 166, Belgian Ministry of Foreign Affairs to Van de Weyer, London.

51 MOFA Belgium 2098. London, 13 July 1859, dispatch no. 343 from Sylvain Van de Weyer to Baron de Vrière; also Brussels 19 July 1859, Minute B no. 2483, order no. 200, Belgian Ministry of Foreign Affairs to Van de Weyer, London.

52 University of Tokyo Volume VII 1967, F.O. 262 (2), no. 6951-4-1-1, pp. 22-23 (YAH microfilm outprint no. Ca4/01.20/2, pp. 26-27). London (50 Portland Place), 9 August 1959, copy of a letter in French from Sylvain Van de Weyer to J. Russell (foreign secretary, London).

53 University of Tokyo Volume VII 1967, F.O. 262 (2), no. 6951-4-1-1, pp. 21-23 (YAH microfilm outprint no. Ca4/01.20/2, pp. 25-27), F.O., 13 August 1859, orig-

inal dispatch no. 22 from Russell to Alcock. A draft version of this letter is preserved at University of Tokyo Volume VI 1966, F.O. 46 (6), no. 6951-3-1-2, pp. 61-63 (YAH microfilm outprint no. Ca4/01.9/6, pp. 71-73).

54 MOFA Belgium 2098. London 17 August 1859, Maurice Delfour to de Vrière.

55 At the time of the opening of the ports, foreigners used the term "tycoon" instead of "shogun".

56 See e.g. Alcock 1863, pp. 136-151.

57 University of Tokyo Volume VI 1966, F.O. 46 (10), pp. 216-219. (YAH microfilm outprint no. Ca4/01.9/10, pp. 62-65). British Consulate General at Edo, 23 November 1859, dispatch no. 39 from Alcock to Foreign Office. For a draft, see University of Tokyo Volume VII 1967, F.O. 262 (4), pp. 193-196 (YAH microfilm outprint no. Ca4/01.20/4, pp. 91-95). For a printed version, see University of Tokyo Volume VII 1967, F.O. 262 (3), pp. 87-88 (YAH microfilm outprint no. Ca4/01.20/3, pp. 47-50).

58 TUHI 1054.01/1, p. 383. 12 December 1859, English letter no. 91 (*number written in pencil*) from R. Alcock to the Japanese councillors in charge of foreign affairs. – Draft letter: University of Tokyo Volume VII 1967, F.O. 262 (458-459), p. 137. (YAH microfilm outprint no. Ca4/01.20/677).

59 TUHI 1054.01/1, p. 391. 14 December 1859, English letter no. 93 (*number written in pencil*) from R. Alcock to the Japanese councillors in charge of foreign affairs.

60 University of Tokyo Volume XIII 1965 Consulaire, Volume 1, pp. 138-144 (YAH microfilm outprint no. Ca4/01.31/2, pp. 1-7). Also University of Tokyo Volume XIII 1965 Politique, pp. 294-301 (YAH microfilm outprint no. Ca4/01.36/2, pp. 108-115). Edo, 9 December 1859, de Bellecourt to (Count Colonna) Walewski (French minister of foreign affairs). The archives of the *Correspondance Consulaire* do not contain the minutes of the meeting as noted by Girard. The archives of the *Correspondance Politique* only have a small part of it.

61 English translation of the French original by the author of this article.

62 University of Tokyo Volume VII 1967, F.O. 262 (457), pp. 159-160 (YAH microfilm outprint no. Ca4/01.20/676, pp. 163-164). 18 December 1859 (25th day of the 11th month of Ansei 6), original letter in Dutch from Manabe Shimōsa no Kami 間部下総守 (Manabe Akikatsu, 1804-1884) and Wakisaka Nakatsukasa no Tayū 脇坂中務大輔 (Wakisaka Yasuori, 1809-1874) to Rutherford Alcock, British plenipotentiary and consul general at Edo. A copy of the letter is available at: TUHI 1055.1/1. 18 December 1859 (25th day of the 11th month of Ansei 6).

63 TUHI 1054.01/1, pp. 441-447. A draft is kept at University of Tokyo Volume VII 1967, F.O. 262 (462), pp. 15-17 (YAH microfilm outprint no. Ca4/01.20/680, pp. 15-17). British Consulate General, Edo, 14 January 1860, English letter no. 8 (*number written in pencil*) from R. Alcock probably to the Japanese councillors in charge of foreign affairs. A Japanese report of the meeting can be found at TUHI Ishin 3, p. 249. D.I.S.K. 1082, pp. 1-17. Microfilm reproduction REEL no. Ansei 安政 – 166, pictures 006.tiff – 023.tiff. Japanese report about a meeting between Alcock and Wakisaka on 13 January 1860 (21st day of the 12th month of Ansei 6).

64 University of Tokyo Volume XIII 1965 Politique, volume 2 (1860), pp. 22-23 (YAH microfilm outprint no. Ca4/01.36/3, pp. 21-22). Consulate General of France at Edo, 20 January 1860, de Bellecourt to Walewski.

65 University of Tokyo Volume IX and Volume X 1968 Ministers. U.S. National Archives, RG 59, M133, N.A. 133 (21) Vol. 5-1 (4 January -12 February 1864). (YAH microfilm outprint no. Ca4/01.4/21, pp. 46-48). Benten, Kanagawa, 15 December 1863, English translation of a dispatch from Aimé Humbert, Envoy Extraordinary of the Swiss Confederation in Japan, to General Pruyn, minister resident of the United States in Japan.

66 University of Tokyo Volume VII 1967, F.O. 262 (462), pp. 32-33 (YAH microfilm outprint no. Ca4/01.20/679, pp. 32-33). 19 February 1860 (28th day of the 1st month of Ansei 7), Dutch dispatch no. 25 from Wakisaka Nakatsukasa no Tayū (Wakisaka Yasuori) and Andō Tsushima no Kami 安藤対島守 (Andō Nobumasa, 1820-1871) to Rutherford Alcock.

67 University of Tokyo Volume VII 1967, F.O. 262 (15), pp. 39-42 (YAH microfilm outprint no. Ca4/01.20/20, pp. 18-22). 20 February 1860, draft dispatch no. 11 from Rutherford Alcock to John Russell.

68 MOFA Belgium 2098. London, 5 May 1860, stamped in Brussels on 12 May 1860, and mentioning "revenue du Palais le 12 Mai", 7329, B 2483, dispatch no. 206 from Van de Weyer to de Vrière.

69 MOFA Belgium 2098. Brussels, 7 May 1860, British Legation, mentioning "revenue du Palais le 14 Mai 1860", stamped by Belgian MOFA on 19 May, no. 7660 B 2483, baron (Howard de Walden) to de Vrière.

70 MOFA Belgium 2098. Brussels, 6 June 1860, Minute Indicateur B no. 2483, containing a draft letter in French from the Belgian Ministry of Foreign Affairs to Lord Howard de Walden, British Legation at Brussels.

71 University of Tokyo Volume VII 1967, F.O. 262 (13), p. 36 (YAH microfilm outprint no. Ca4/01.20/18, pp. 40-41). F.O., 15 June 1860, dispatch no. 55 from John Russell to Rutherford Alcock. – Draft of this dispatch at: University of Tokyo Volume VI 1966, F.O. 46 (16), p. 125 (YAH microfilm outprint no. Ca4/01.9/16, p. 12).

72 MOFA Belgium 2098. Brussels, 6 June 1860, Minute Indicateur B no. 2483, containing a draft letter in French from the Belgian Ministry of Foreign Affairs to Lord Howard de Walden, British Legation in Brussels.

73 Van der Chijs 1867, respectively p. 280 en p. 291.

74 Van der Chijs 1867, respectively p. 280 and p. 284.

75 TUHI Ishin 3, p. 318. D.I.S.K. 1116, pp. 32-34. Microfilm reproduction REEL no. Man'en 万延 – 009, pictures 976-978.tiff. Japanese report of a meeting between Andō Tsushima no Kami (Andō Nobumasa) and Donker Curtius on 9 July 1860 (21st day of the 5th month of Man'en 1). See also University of Tokyo Volume XIII 1965 Politique, volume 2 (1860), pp. 225-230 (YAH microfilm outprint no. Ca4/01.36/4, pp. 86-92). Consulate General of France at Edo, 4 August 1860, dispatch no. 39 from de Bellecourt to Thouvenel.

76 TUHI 1054.11. Edo Bay, Aboard H.M.S. *Dom João I*, 12 July 1860, copy of a letter in Dutch from Isidoro Guimarães, Portuguese plenipotentiary, to the Japanese councillors in charge of foreign affairs at Edo. The journey of the *Dom João* to Edo is described in Pereira 1863.

77 University of Tokyo Volume XIII 1965 Politique, volume 2 (1860), pp. 204-206 (YAH microfilm outprint no. Ca4/01.36/4, pp. 74-76). Consulate General of France at Edo, 25 June 1860, dispatch no. 38 from de Bellecourt to (Edouard) Thouvenel (French minister of foreign affairs). Also MOFA Belgium 2098. 21 November 1860, Solvyns to de Vrière.

78 TUHI 1054.11. British Legation at Edo, 4 August 1860, copy of a letter in Dutch and English from Isidoro Guimarães, Portuguese plenipotentiary, to the Japanese councillors in charge of foreign affairs. Also University of Tokyo Volume IX and Volume X 1968 Ministers. U.S. National Archives, RG 59, M133, N.A. 133 (10) Vol. 3-1 (2 January – 1 October 1860). (YAH microfilm outprint no. Ca4/01.4/10, pp. 98-99). Legation of the United States at Edo, 4 August 1860, dispatch no. 28 from Townsend Harris, US consul general in Japan, to Lewis Cass, secretary of state at Washington. Furthermore, University of Tokyo Volume XIII 1965 Politique, volume 2 (1860), pp. 225-230 (YAH microfilm outprint no. Ca4/01.36/4, pp. 86-92). Consulate General of France at Edo, 4 August 1860, dispatch no. 39 from de Bellecourt to Thouvenel.

79 TUHI 1055.1/1. 20 July 1860 (3rd day of the 6th month of Man'en 1), letter in Dutch from Wakisaka Nakatsukasa no Tayū 脇坂中務大輔 and Andō Tsushima no Kami 安藤対馬守 (Andō Nobumasa) to Rutherford Alcock, envoy extraordinary and minister plenipotentiary of Great Britain.

80 MOFA Belgium 2098. Brussels, 25 October 1860, Minute Indicateur B, no. 2483, order no. 44, draft letter from the Belgian Ministry of Foreign Affairs to Mr Solvyns at Lisbon. For Baron Ignace Henri Stanislas Solvyns (1817-1895), see Leenders 2012, p. 115.

81 MOFA Belgium 2098. 21 November 1860, Solvyns to de Vrière.

82 MOFA Belgium 2098. Lisbon, 28 November 1860, Solvyns to de Vrière, registered in Brussels on 10 December 1860, no. 17155, B 2483.

83 University of Tokyo Volume IX and Volume X 1968 Ministers. US National Archives, RG 59, M133, N.A. 133 (10) Vol. 3-1 (2 January – 1 October 1860). (YAH microfilm outprint no. Ca4/01.4/10, pp. 66-68). Legation of the United States in Edo, 7 June 1860, dispatch no. 17 from Townsend Harris, US consul general in Japan, to Lewis Cass, secretary of state at Washington.

84 Harris had already communicated about the Japanese refusal to treat with Belgium and Switzerland, and its background on 15 May 1860. See University of Tokyo Volume IX and Volume X 1968 Ministers. US National Archives, RG 59, M133, N.A. 133 (10) Vol. 3-1 (2 January – 1 October 1860). (YAH microfilm outprint no. Ca4/01.4/10, pp. 66-68). Legation of the United States in Edo, 15 May 1860, dispatch no. 16 from Townsend Harris, US consul general in Japan, to Lewis Cass, secretary of state at Washington.

85 *Die Preussische Expedition* 1864, pp. 255-256.

86 University of Tokyo Volume IX and Volume X 1968 Legation. US National Archives, RG 84, T400, N.A. T400 (5) Vol. 4 (5 August – 30 December 1860). (YAH microfilm outprint no. Ca4/01.14/5, pp. 30-34). 2 September 1860 (17th day of the 7th month of Man'en 1), Japanese letter, with Dutch and English translations, from Wakisaka Nakatsukasa no Tayū (Wakisaka Yasuori) and Andō Tsushima no Kami (Andō Nobumasa) to Townsend Harris, minister plenipotentiary of the US of America.

87 *Die Preussische Expedition* 1864, p. 261 and p. 264.

88 TUHI 1055.5/1. 6 September 1860 (2nd day of the 7th month of Man'en 1), (copy of a) letter in Dutch from Wakisaka Nakatsukasa no Tayū (Wakisaka Yasuori) and Andō Tsushima no Kami (Andō Nobumasa) to Eulenburg.

89 For the Prussian account of the negotiations, see *Die Preussische Expedition* 1864, pp. 261-352, and *Die Preussische Expedition* 1866, pp. 1-110. According to this account, the Japanese refusal was received during a conference between Townsend Harris and Andō Tsushima no Kami (Andō Nobumasa) on 24 November 1860 (pp. 107-108). Townsend Harris, however, mentioned 1 December 1860. See University of Tokyo Volume IX and Volume X 1968 Ministers. US National Archives, RG 59, M133, N.A. 133 (11) Vol. 3-2 (2 October 1860 – 1 February 1861). (YAH microfilm outprint no. Ca4/01.4/11, pp. 93-97). Legation of the United States at Edo, 26 January 1861, dispatch no. 6 from Townsend Harris to Lewis Cass, US secretary of state.

90 *Die Preussische Expedition* 1866, pp. 107-109. Andō had already hinted at that combination in a meeting with Rutherford Alcock in October 1860. See *Die Preussische Expedition* 1866, pp. 57-59. Also Nakai 1968, pp. 123-124.

91 University of Tokyo Volume IX and Volume X 1968. Legation. US National Archives, RG 84, N.A. T400 (5) Vol. 4 (5 August – 30 December 1860). (YAH microfilm outprint no. Ca4/01.14/5, pp. 80-82). 13 December 1860 (21st day of the 11th month of Man'en 1), Japanese letter, with Dutch and English translations, from Andō Tsushima no Kami (Andō Nobumasa) to Townsend Harris, plenipotentiary & minister of the United States of America.

92 TUHI Ishin 3, p. 372. D.I.S.K. 115(?)4, pp 21-29. Microfilm reproduction REEL no. Man'en 万延, pictures 368.tiff – 376.tiff. Copy of a dispatch from Sakai Wakasa no Kami dated 8 January 1861 (28th day of the 11th month of Man'en 1) and of a dispatch dated 21 December 1860 (10th day of the 11th month of Man'en 1) from Honda Mino no Kami 本多美濃守 (Honda Tadamoto 1817-1883), Andō Tsushima no Kami (Andō Nobumasa), Naitō Kii no Kami 内藤紀伊守 (Naitō Nobuchika 1813-1874) and Kuze Yamato no Kami 久世大和守 (Kuze Hirochika 1819-1864) to Sakai Wakasa no Kami 酒井若狭守 (Sakai Tadaaki 1813-1873).

93 TUHI Ishin 3, p. 374. Copy of a dispatch from the Imperial Palace to Sakai Wakasa no Kami (Sakai Tadaaki), dated 11 January 1861 (1st day of the 12th month of Man'en 1).

94 TUHI Ishin 3, p. 376. Copy of a dispatch from Sakai Wakasa no Kami (Sakai Tadaaki) to the Imperial Palace, dated 17 January 1861 (7th day of the 12th month of Man'en 1), followed by additional communication on 19 and 21 January 1861 (the 9th and 11th day of the 12th month of Man'en 1). – The wedding took place, anyhow, in Edo on 11 March 1862 (11th day of the 2nd month of Bunkyū 2).

95 University of Tokyo Volume IX and Volume X 1968 Ministers. US National Archives, RG 59, M133, N.A. 133 (11) Vol. 3-2 (2 October 1860 – 1 February 1861). (YAH microfilm outprint no. Ca4/01.4/11, pp. 95-97. Legation of Prussia, Edo, 25 January 1861, copy of a letter in French (and its English translation by A.L.C. Portman) from Count Eulenburg to Townsend Harris.

96 The negotiations are described in: *Die Preussische Expedition* 1866, pp. 116-179.

97 *Die Preussische Expedition* 1866, pp. 162-164.

98 TUHI 1055.5/1. 11 January 1861 (1st day of the 12th month of Man'en 1), (copy of a) letter in Dutch from Andō Tsushima no Kami (Andō Nobumasa) to Count Eulenburg, extraordinary envoy and minister plenipotentiary of Prussia. See also *Die Preussische Expedition* 1866, pp. 125-135 and pp. 144-145.

99 Nakai 1968, pp. 114-115, p. 120 and p. 126.

100 Ministry of Foreign Affairs of Japan 1874, pp. 186-206, in particular article 3 of the treaty. Eulenburg also had to concede to a relatively long period before the treaty would enter into force. Article 23 provided for 1 January 1863 as starting date for execution.

101 TUHI 1055.1/1. 10 January 1861 (30th day of the 11th month of Man'en 1), Andō Tsushima no Kami (Andō Nobumasa) to Rutherford Alcock. Also University of Tokyo Volume VII 1967, F.O. 463, Vol. 681 pp. 8-9 (YAH microfilm outprint no. Ca4/01.20/681, pp. 86-87). Copy of the Japanese letter from Andō: TUHI Ishin 3, p. 373. D.I.S.K. 115(?)4, pp. 126-127. Microfilm reproduction REEL no. Man'en 万延 – 018, pictures 540.tiff – 544.tiff.

102 University of Tokyo Volume VII 1967, F.O. 262, Vol. 465, pp. 10-11 (YAH microfilm outprint no. Ca4/01.20/682, pp. 116-117).

103 TUHI 1055.4/1. 10 January 1861 (30th day of the 11th month of Bunn Ku (*sic: Man'en*) 1. letter in Dutch from Kuze Yamato no Kami (Kuze Hirochika) and Andō Tsushima no Kami (Andō Nobumasa) to J. K. de Wit, Dutch consul general. See also: 22 February 1862 (24th day of the 1st month of Bunkyū 1). Letter in Dutch from Kuze Yamato no Kami and Andō Tsushima no Kami (Andō Nobumasa) to J.K. de Wit. – Copy of the Japanese letter from Andō: TUHI Ishin 3, p. 373. D.I.S.K. 115(?)4, p. 128. Microfilm reproduction REEL no. Man'en 万延 – 018, pictures 544.tiff – 546.tiff. Jan Karel de Wit (born in Utrecht, the Netherlands, in 1819). See Yokoyama 1993, pp. 11-18.

104 MOFA Belgium 2016 I.B. Berlin, 8 August 1859, copy of dispatch no. 357 (in French) from Nothomb to Baron de Vrière. Also MOFA Belgium 2098. Brussels, 6 June 1860, Belgian Ministry of Foreign Affairs, Minute Indicateur B no. 2483, containing a draft letter in French to Lord Howard de Walden, British Legation in Brussels. In this letter, the Belgian Ministry mentions the departure of the Eulenburg mission to Japan.

105 Truong 1857 does not mention the Eulenburg Treaty, nor have I found any influence of this treaty on the policy of the Belgian government towards Japan.

106 Truong 1957, pp. 119-120, and Vande Walle 2003, p. 431.

107 MOFA Belgium 2098. Draft for the *Moniteur Belge* entitled "Refus de la part du Japon de conclure de nouveaux traités de commerce". At the bottom: "Handelsarchiv de Berlin du 1 Novembre 1861". See also Truong 1957, pp. 120-121.

108 As an example of such a letter, see University of Tokyo Volume IX and Volume X 1968 Legation. US National Archives, RG 84, N.A. T400 (7) Vol. 5 (1 January – 22 December 1861). (YAH microfilm outprint no. Ca4/01.14/7, pp. 17-32). 2 May 1861 (23rd day of the 3rd month of Bunkyū 1), Japanese letter, with Dutch and English translations, from Kuze Yamato no Kami (Kuze Hirochika) and Andō Tsushima no Kami (Andō Nobumasa) to the US secretary (of state).

109 TUHI 1055.2/1. 1 May 1861, (22nd day of the 3rd month of Bunkyū 1), copy of a letter in Dutch from the (*Japanese*) governors (*sic: councillors*) to Townsend Harris.

110 University of Tokyo Volume IX and Volume X 1968 Legation in Japan. US National Archives, RG 84, N.A. T400 (7) Vol. 5 (1 January – 22 December 1861). (YAH microfilm outprint no. Ca4/01.14/7, pp. 33-34, p. 38). 1 May 1861 (22nd day of the 3rd month of Bunkyū 1), letter in Dutch, with draft French and draft English translations, from Kuze Yamato no Kami (Kuze Hirochika) and Andō Tsushima no Kami (Andō Nobumasa) to Townsend Harris. The final English version can be found at University of Tokyo Volume IX and Volume X 1968 Ministers. US National Archives, RG 59, M133, N.A. 133 (12) Vol. 3-3 (13 February – 20 June 1861), p. 95. (YAH microfilm outprint no. Ca4/01.4/12). The omission of the phrase "except for Belgium and Switzerland" resulted in April 1863 in a diplomatic incident between the US Minister Pruyn and the Japanese councillors in charge of foreign affairs, on the occasion of the arrival of the Swiss embassy in Japan. See University of Tokyo Volume IX and Volume X 1968 Ministers. US National Archives, RG 59, M133, N.A. 133 (18) Vol. 4-4 (5 May – 27 June 1863). (YAH microfilm outprint no. Ca4/01.4/18, pp. 51-55). U.S. Legation, Edo, 16 April 1863, English dispatch no. 43 from Pruyn to Matsudaira Bōzu no Kami (most likely Matsudaira Buzen no Kami 松平豊前守) and Inoue Kawachi no Kami 井上河内守 (Inoue Masanao), councillors in charge of foreign affairs at Edo.

111 English translation of the Dutch version of this circular letter, as made by A.L.C. Portman of the US Legation at Edo on 1 May or 2 May 1861. Copies of it are preserved at: University of Tokyo Volume IX and Volume X 1968 Ministers. US National Archives, RG 59, M133, N.A. 133 (12) Vol. 3-3 (13 February – 20 June 1861). (YAH microfilm outprint no. Ca4/01.4/12, pp. 96-98). – A copy of the Dutch original and the French translation can be found at: University of Tokyo Volume IX and X 1968 Legation. U.S. National Archives, RG 84, N.A. T400 (7) Vol. 5 (1 January – 22 December 1861). – (YAH microfilm outprint no. Ca4/01.14/7, pp. 34-37).

112 University of Tokyo Volume IX and Volume X 1968 Ministers. US National Archives, RG 59, M133, N.A. 133 (12) Vol. 3-3 (13 February – 20 June 1861). (YAH microfilm outprint no. Ca4/01.4/12, pp. 93-100). Legation of the United States at Edo, 4 May 1861, dispatch no. 19 from Townsend Harris to Lewis Cass, US secretary of state.

113 TUHI 1055.4/1. 10 January 1861 (30th day of the 11th month of Bunn Ku (*sic: Man'en* 1). letter in Dutch from Kuze Yamato no Kami (Kuze Hirochika) and Andō Tsushima no Kami (Andō Nobumasa) to J. K. de Wit, Dutch consul general.

114 MOFA Belgium 2098. Bern, 10 May 1861, Belgian Legation to the Swiss Confederation, dispatch no. 59 from Bourguignon to de Vrière.

115 MOFA Belgium 2098. Bern, 11 May 1861, Belgian Legation to the Swiss Confederation, dispatch no. 61 from Bourguignon to de Vrière.

116 MOFA Belgium 2098. Dispatches of Bourguignon dated 10, 11, 18, 20 and 27 May 1861. Dispatches from Helman de Grimberghe, Belgian chargé d'affaires in Bern, dated 14, 19, 21 and 24 August, 9 September and 3 October 1861, 31 January, 12 May and 7 July 1862.

117 MOFA Belgium 2098. Simple note mentioning "Moniteur belge du 10 Juillet 1861. Suisse – Berne, 3 Juillet" (1861). It stated that the Swiss "Conseil des États" had approved a budget of 100,000 francs for an expedition to Japan to conclude a commercial treaty enabling Swiss citizens to reside in Japan.

118 MOFA Belgium 2098. Brussels 14 August 1861, Minute Indicateur B no. 2483, order no. 60, draft letter from the Belgian Ministry of Foreign Affairs to Helman de Grimberghe at Bern. For Viscount Roger Helman de Grimberghe (1830-1879), see Leenders 2012, p. 112.

119 MOFA Belgium 2098. Bern, 19 August 1861, Belgian Legation to the Swiss Confederation, no. 104, Grimberghe to de Vrière.

120 MOFA Belgium 2098. Bern, 21 August 1861, Belgian Legation to the Swiss Confederation, dispatch no. 105, Helman de Grimberghe to de Vrière.

121 MOFA Belgium 2016 I.B. Brussels, 30 May 1859, Minute Indicateur B no. 1746, order no. 36, draft letter from the Belgian Ministry of Foreign Affairs to "de Grimberghen" in Bern.

122 MOFA Belgium 2098. Brussels, 6 September 1861, Minute Indicateur B no. 2483, order no. 67, draft letter from the Belgian Ministry of Foreign Affairs to Helman de Grimberghe in Bern.

123 MOFA Belgium 2098. Bern, 31 January 1862, Belgian Legation to the Swiss Confederation, dispatch no. 14 from Helman de Grimberghe to de Vrière. This dispatch mentions "revenue du Palais le 18 février" and is stamped in Brussels "19 Feb. no. 2549, B 2483". Apparently, it was (first) sent to the Royal Palace before it was registered at the Ministry of Foreign Affairs in Brussels.

124 TUHI 1055.4/1. 22 February 1862 (24th day of the 1st month of Bunkyū 1), letter in Dutch from Kuze Yamato no Kami (Kuze Hirochika) and Andō Tsushima no Kami (Andō Nobumasa) to J. K. de Wit, Dutch consul general. The letter from De Wit dated 18 December 1861 has not been found in the archives yet, but its content is partly mentioned in the letter from Kuze and Andō to De Wit, dated 22 February 1862.

125 TUHI 1055.4/1. 25 August 1861 (20th day of the 7th month of Bunkyū 1), letter in Dutch from Kuze Yamato no Kami (Kuze Hirochika) and Andō Tsushima no Kami (Andō Nobumasa) to J. K. de Wit, Dutch consul general. Copy of the Japanese version in TUHI Ishin 3, p. 476. D.I.S.K. 1237, pp. 53-61. Microfilm reproduction REEL no. Bunkyū 文久 – 017, pictures 342.tiff – 354.tiff.

126 MOFA Belgium 2098. Bern, 12 May 1862, Belgian Legation to the Swiss Confederation, dispatch no. 46 from Helman de Grimberghe to de Vrière.

127 MOFA Belgium 2098. Bern, 7 July 1861, Belgian Legation to the Swiss Confederation, dispatch no. 64, Helman de Grimberghe to Rogier.

128 TUHI 1054.04/1, pp. 319-320. Consulate General of the Netherlands in Japan, Deshima, 20 January 1863, letter in Dutch from J. K. de Wit to the councillors in charge of foreign affairs of the tycoon of Japan (*now called the shogun*).

129 Adams 1874, pp. 146-148.

130 TUHI 1055.4/1. 22 February 1863, letter in Dutch from Mizuno Izumi no Kami 水野和泉守 (Mizuno Tadakiyo 1833 – 1884), Itakura Suō no Kami 板倉周防守 (Itakura Katsukiyo 1823-1889), and Ogasawara Zusho no Kami 小笠原図頭 (Ogasawara Nagamichi 1822-1891) to J. K. de Wit, Dutch consul general.

131 TUHI 1054.04/1, pp. 347-350. Consulate General of the Netherlands in Japan, Deshima, 9 March 1863, letter in Dutch no. 85 from J. K. de Wit to the councillors in charge of foreign affairs of the tycoon (shogun) of Japan; pp. 363-364. Consulate General of the Netherlands in Japan, Deshima, 24 March 1863, letter in Dutch no. 110 from J. K. de Wit to the councillors in charge of foreign affairs of the tycoon (shogun) of Japan.

132 TUHI 1054.10/1. Deshima, Dutch Consulate General in Japan, 10 April 1863, copy of a letter in French from Aimé Humbert to the Japanese councillors in charge of foreign affairs of the tycoon (shogun) at Edo.

133 TUHI 1054.04/1, pp. 371-372. Yokohama, 12 April 1863, letter in Dutch from J.P. Metman, chancellor of the Dutch consul general in Japan, to the Japanese commissioners of foreign affairs at Edo. – For Johannes Petrus Metman (1835-1897), see Yokohama 1993, p. 69, footnote 14.

134 University of Tokyo Volume IX and Volume X 1968 Ministers. US National Archives, RG 59, M133, N.A. 133 (18) Vol. 4-4 (5 May – 27 June 1863) (YAH microfilm outprint no. Ca4/01.4/18, pp. 51-55). US Legation, Edo, 16 April 1863, English dispatch no. 43 from Pruyn to Matsudaira Buzen no Kami 松平豊前守 and Inoue Kawachi no Kami (Inoue Masanao), councillors in charge of foreign affairs at Edo. – See also: University of Tokyo Volume IX and Volume X 1968 Ministers. US National Archives, RG 59, M133, N.A. 133 (18) Vol. 4-4 (5 May – 27 June 1863). (YAH microfilm outprint no. Ca4/01.4/18, pp. 48-55). US Legation in Japan, Yokohama, 15 June 1863, dispatch no. 33 from Robert H. Pruyn to William H. Seward, US secretary of state at Washington, received there on 27 August 1863.

135 University of Tokyo Volume IX and Volume X 1968 Legation. US National Archives, RG 84, N.A. T400 (11) Vol. 8 (1 January – 4 June 1863). (YAH microfilm outprint no. Ca4/01.14/11, pp. 105-106). 17 April 1863 (30th day of the 5th (*sic: 2nd*) month of Bunkyū 3), draft English translation of a letter from Matsudaira Buzen no Kami 松平豊前守 and Inoue Kawachi no Kami (Inoue Masanao) to Robert H. Pruyn, minister resident of the United States of America.

136 TUHI 1054.02/1, pp. 707-720. Legation of the United States in Japan, Edo, 18 April 1863, English dispatch no. 46 from Pruyn to Matsudaira Buzen no Kami and Inoue Kawachi no Kami (Inoue Masanao), councillors in charge of foreign affairs at Edo.

137 TUHI 1054.10/1. Yokohama, 20 April 1863, (copy of a) letter in French from C. Brennwald, chancellor-secretary of the legation of the Swiss Confederation, to the Japanese commissioners of foreign affairs in Edo.

138 TUHI 1054.04/1, pp. 382-383. Dutch Consulate, Kanagawa, 20 April 1863, Dutch dispatch no. 86 from Dirk de Graeff van Polsbroek (Dutch consul) to the Japanese commissioners of foreign affairs at Edo.

139 TUHI 1054.04/1, pp. 479-487. Dutch Consulate General, Kanagawa, 7 September 1863, dispatch no. 63/335 from De Graeff van Polsbroek to the Japanese councillors in charge of foreign affairs at Edo. Copies of the correspondence between the Swiss mission and the Japanese government at Edo can be found at TUHI 1055.6/1.

140 TUHI 1054.10/1. Edo, 29 May 1863, (copy of a) letter in French from Aimé Humbert to the Japanese councillors in charge of foreign affairs in Edo.

141 TUHI 1054.04/1, pp. 479-487. Dutch Consulate General, Kanagawa, 7 September 1863, dispatch no. 63/335 from De Graeff van Polsbroek to the Japanese councillors in charge of foreign affairs at Edo.

142 A copy of the Japanese letter from Ogasawara, and its Dutch and English translations, can be found at: University of Tokyo Volume IX and Volume X 1968 Legation. US National Archives, RG 84, N.A. T400 (11) Vol. 8 (1 January – 4 June 1863). (YAH microfilm outprint no. Ca4/01.14/11, pp. 52-55). 24 June 1863 (9th day of the 5th month of Bunkyū 3), Japanese letter, with Dutch and English translations, from Ogasawara Zusho no Kami (Ogasawara Nagamichi) to Robert H. Pruyn, minister resident of the United States of America.

143 Taicoon or tycoon refers to the shogun.

144 Mikado refers to the emperor in Kyoto.

145 The British chargé d'affaires, Edward St. John Neale, for example, replied to Ogasawara that this decision was in fact a declaration of war from the Japanese side. He requested Ogasawara to inform the tycoon (shogun) and the mikado (emperor) of this. See Adams 1874, pp. 278-279.

146 University of Tokyo Volume IX and Volume X 1968 Legation. US National Archives, RG 84, N.A. T400 (12) Vol. 9 (4 July – 26 December 1863). (YAH microfilm outprint no. Ca4/01.14/12, pp. 47-52). 2 September 1863 (20th day of the 7th month of Bunkyū 3. Draft English translation mentions 3 September 1863). Japanese letter, with Dutch and draft English translation, from Matsudaira Buzen no Kami, Mizuno Izumi no Kami (Mizuno Tadakiyo), Itakura Suō no Kami (Itakura Katsukiyo), Inoue Kawachi no Kami (Inoue Masanao), Arima Tōtōmi no Kami to Robert H. Pruyn, minister resident of the United States of America.

147 TUHI 1054.04/1, pp. 509-511. Dutch Consulate General, Kanagawa, 28 October 1863, dispatch no. 96/394 from De Graeff van Polsbroek to the Japanese councillors in charge of foreign affairs at Edo. Also TUHI 1054.02/1, pp. 829-831. US Legation, Yokohama, 28 October 1863, English dispatch no. 118 from Pruyn to the *rōjū* 老中 (board of senior councillors of the shogun).

148 Adams 1874, pp. 132-134.

149 University of Tokyo Volume IX and Volume X 1968 Ministers. US National Archives, RG 59, M133, N.A. 133 (21) Vol. 5-1 (4 January – 12 February 1864). (YAH microfilm outprint no. Ca4/01.4/21, pp. 39-40). Benten, Kanagawa, 11 December 1863, English translation of a dispatch from Aimé Humbert, Envoy Extraordinary of the Swiss Confederation in Japan, to General Pruyn, minister resident of the United States of America in Japan.

150 Though Humbert did not mention the precise date of the communication by Pruyn to the Japanese government, he was probably referring to Pruyn's dispatches of 16 and 18 April 1863.

151 University of Tokyo Volume IX and Volume X 1968 Ministers. US National Archives, RG 59, M133, N.A. 133 (21) Vol. 5-1 (4 January – 12 February 1864). (YAH microfilm outprint no. Ca4/01.4/21, pp. 41-45). Legation of the United States in Japan, Kanagawa, 12 December 1863. English dispatch no. 132 from Robert Pruyn to Aimé Humbert.

152 University of Tokyo Volume IX and Volume X 1968 Ministers. US National Archives, RG 59, M133, N.A. 133 (21) Vol. 5-1 (4 January – 12 February 1864). (YAH microfilm outprint no. Ca4/01.4/21, pp. 46-48). Benten, Kanagawa, 15 December 1863, English translation of a dispatch from Aimé Humbert to General Pruyn.

153 University of Tokyo Volume IX and Volume X 1968 Ministers. US National Archives, RG 59, M133, N.A. 133 (21) Vol. 5-1 (4 January – 12 February 1864). (YAH microfilm outprint no. Ca4/01.4/21, pp. 49-53). Legation of the United States in Japan, Kanagawa, 16 December 1863, English dispatch no. 135 from Robert Pruyn to Aimé Humbert.

154 University of Tokyo Volume IX and Volume X 1968 Ministers. US National Archives, RG 59, M133, N.A. 133 (21) Vol. 5-1 (4 January – 12 February 1864). (YAH microfilm outprint no. Ca4/01.4/21, pp. 54-56). Yokohama, 19 December 1863, English translation of a dispatch from Aimé Humbert to General Pruyn.

155 Pruyn informed the US State Department about the discussions he had had with Humbert. See University of Tokyo Volume IX and Volume X 1968 Ministers. US National Archives, RG 59, M133, N.A. 133 (21) Vol. 5-1 (4 January – 12 February 1864). (YAH microfilm outprint no. Ca4/01.4/21, pp. 37-38). Legation of the United States in Japan, Kanagawa, 7 January 1864, dispatch no. 8 from Robert Pruyn to William Lewis, US secretary of state in Washington, received there on 14 March (1864).

156 TUHI 1054.04/1, pp. 541-549. Dutch Consulate General, Kanagawa, 14 December 1863, dispatch no. 142/475 from De Graeff van Polsbroek to the Japanese councillors in charge of foreign affairs at Edo.

157 TUHI 1054.04/1, pp. 550-551. Dutch Legation, Kanagawa, 20 December 1863, dispatch no. 152/485 from De Graeff van Polsbroek to Takemoto Kai no Kami 竹本甲斐守 (Takemoto Masatsune) and Ikeda Chikugo no Kami 池田筑後守, Japanese commissioners of foreign affairs at Edo. Also see pp. 561-562. Dutch Legation, Kanagawa, 23 December 1863, urgent dispatch no. 153/500 from De Graeff van Polsbroek to the Japanese councillors in charge of foreign affairs at Edo.

158 TUHI 1055.4/1. 16 January 1864 (8th day of the 12th month of Bunkyū 3), letter in Dutch from Mizuno Izumi no Kami (Mizuno Tadakiyo), Itakura Suō no Kami (Itakura Katsukiyo), Inoue Kawachi no Kami (Inoue Masanao) and Arima Tōtōmi no Kami (Arima Michizumi) to D. de Graeff van Polsbroek.

159 University of Tokyo Volume IX and Volume X 1968 Ministers. US National Archives, RG 59, M133, N.A. 133 (21) Vol. 5-1 (4 January – 12 February 1864). (YAH microfilm outprint no. Ca4/01.4/21, pp. 73-74). Benten (Yokohama), 24 January 1864, English translation of a dispatch from Aimé Humbert to General Pruyn.

160 TUHI 1055.6/1. 30 January 1864 (22nd day of the 12th month of Bunkyū 3), (copy of a) letter in Dutch from Takemoto Kai no Kami 竹本甲斐守 (Takemoto Masatsune 1825 – 1868), Kikuchi Iyo no Kami 菊池伊予守 (Kikuchi Takayoshi 1812 – ?) and Hoshino Kingo 星野金吾 (probably Hoshino Kazuyuki) to Aimé Humbert. Also TUHI 1054.10/1. Yokohama, 1 February 1864, (copy of a) French letter from Aimé Humbert to the Japanese Commissioners Takemoto Kai no Kami (Takemoto Masatsune), Kikuchi Iyo no Kami (Kikuchi Takayoshi) and Hoshino Kingo (Hoshino Kazuyuki 星野千之) at Edo.

161 TUHI 1054.10/1. Yokohama, 4 February 1864, (copy of a) letter in French from Aimé Humbert to the Japanese Commissioners Takemoto Kai no Kami (Takemoto Masatsune), Kikuchi Iyo no Kami (Kikuchi Takayoshi) and Hoshino Kingo no Kami (Hoshino Kazuyuki).

162 TUHI 1054.10/1. Yokohama, 11 February 1864, (copy of a) letter in French from Aimé Humbert to the Japanese councillors in charge of foreign affairs at Edo.

163 University of Tokyo Volume IX and Volume X 1968 Ministers. US National Archives, RG 59, M133, N.A. 133 (21) Vol. 5-1 (4 January – 12 February 1864). (YAH microfilm outprint no. Ca4/01.4/21, pp. 77-79). Edo, 28 January 1864 (20th day of the 12th month of Bunkyū 3), Convention between the United States and Japan.

164 Ministry of Foreign Affairs of Japan 1874, p. 214, article XVI.

165 In a letter to the British chargé d'affaires in Japan, Pruyn explained the effect of the US-Japan Convention on the customs tariffs for Great Britain and France. See University of Tokyo Volume IX and Volume X 1968 Ministers. U.S. National Archives, RG 59, M133, N.A. 133 (21) Vol. 5-1 (4 January – 12 February 1864). (YAH microfilm outprint no. Ca4/01.4/21, pp. 116-120). Legation of the United States in Japan, Kanagawa, 12 February 1864, dispatch no. 27 from Robert H. Pruyn, minister resident of the United States in Japan, to Col. E. St. John Neale, HBM chargé d'affaires in Japan.

166 TUHI 1055.5/1. 19 February 1864 (12th day of the 1st month of Bunkyū 4), (copy of a) letter in Dutch from Takemoto Hayato 竹本隼人 (正) no Kami, Takemoto Kai no Kami (Takemoto Masatsune), Ogasawara Settsu no Kami 小笠原摂津守, Tamura Higo no Kami 田村肥後守 and Shibata Hyūga no Kami 柴田日向守 (Shibata Sadatarō, also called Shibata Takenaka) to Maximilian von Brandt, consul of Prussia.

167 TUHI 1054.05, p. 87. Yokohama, 15 August 1863, copy of a German letter from Guido von Rehfues to the Japanese councillors in charge of foreign affairs at Edo, mentioning that he arrived on board of the Prussian naval ship The Gazelle, carrying the ratified treaty of 24 January 1861 signed at Edo. For Guido von Rehfues (1818-1894), see Klatt 2009, pp. 36-37 and p. 206.

168 Ministry of Foreign Affairs of Japan 1874, pp. 207-222, my English translation of the French version.

169 TUHI 1054.10/1. Yokohama, 28 January 1864, (copy of a) letter from Aimé Humbert to the Japanese commissioners for the treaty negotiations; a letter translated into Dutch by Y.P. Metman, Chancellor of the Dutch Consulate General, attached to the Swiss Legation.

170 MOFA Belgium 2098. Brussels, 21 December 1864, Minute, Indicateur Be no. 2483, order no. 77, from the Belgian Ministry of Foreign Affairs to J. Greindl in Bern.

171 Vande Walle 2003, p. 431, and Truong 1957, pp. 133-138, p. 142 and p. 127.

172 The request from Siam to Japan was done through the Dutch vice consul in Yokohama, Dirk de Graeff van Polsbroek, on 1 April 1861 and Japan refused the offer on 20 April 1861. See TUHI 1054.04/1, pp. 36-40. Yokohama, 1 April 1861, dispatch from Polsbroek, Vice Consul of the Netherlands, to the Japanese councillors in charge of foreign affairs; TUHI 1055.4/1. 20 April 1861 (11th day of the 3rd month of Bunkyū 1), letter in Dutch from the "Governors" to Polsbroek, Dutch vice consul.

173 The request from the Sandwich Islands (Hawaii) went through the US Minister Townsend Harris, and was refused by Japan on 18 June 1861. See University of Tokyo Volume IX and Volume X 1968 Legation. US National Archives, RG 84, N.A. T400 (8) Vol. 5 (1 January – 22 December 1861). (YAH microfilm outprint no. Ca4/01.14/8, pp. 2-3 and p. 5). 18 June 1861, (11th day of the 5th month of Bunkyū 1), letter in Dutch from Kuze Yamato no Kami (Kuze Hirochika) and Andō Tsushima no Kami (Andō Nobumasa), with English translation, to Townsend Harris, minister and plenipotentiary of the US of America.

174 The Dutch consul general J. K. de Wit introduced a Danish treaty request on 23 March 1861. Japan refused this offer on 17 May 1861. However, De Wit would continue to insist till 20 March 1862, in vain. See TUHI 1055.4/1. 17 May 1861 (8th day of the 4th month of Bunkyū 1), letter in Dutch from Kuze Yamato no Kami (Kuze Hirochika) and Andō Tsushima no Kami (Andō Nobumasa) to J. K. de Wit, Dutch Consul General; TUHI 1054.09/1, and: TUHI 1054.04/1. Dispatches from De Wit to the Japanese councillors in charge of foreign affairs, dated Yokohama 17 July 1861, Yokohama 18 August 1861, Yokohama 29 August 1861, Yokohama 2 October 1861, Yokohama 20 March 1862.

175 Truong 1957, p. 142. Truong refers to a letter in French from Charles Rogier to Louis Bols dated Brussels 7 September 1864, mentioning that the new consul general had been decided (Archives of the Belgian Ministry of Foreign Affairs, no. 2833).

176 Jos. Fabri remarks that neither the birth certificate of Auguste t'Kint nor the death certificate of his father Pierre-Joseph (deceased in Antwerp on 20 August 1827) carries the suffix "de Roodenbeek" following the family name t'Kint. In the early stages of the career of Auguste t'Kint, and in official publications (such as the Royal Decree of 1 November 1864), the name is written without "de Roodenbeek". However, in his own communications, Auguste t'Kint adds "de Roodenbeek" to his signature. – According to a private communication from Thierry t'Kint de Roodenbeke dated 7 September 2014, the name "t'Kint de Roodenbeek" was given to Corneille t'Kint de Roodenbeke (1720-1785), from whom Auguste did not descend. Hence, the suffix "de Roodenbeek" was inappropriately added to the name of Auguste t'Kint.

177 Royal Palace Belgium 176/134, Brussels, 15 October 1864, Aug^te t'Kint de Roodenbeek to "Sire" (Belgian King Leopold I).

178 MOFA Belgium 2704 III. Royal Decree dated 1 November 1864 from Leopold I, appointing Auguste J. T'Kint to consul general in China; Brussels, 9 December 1864, Minutes containing draft letter from Belgian MOFA to Consul General Aug. t'Kint in Brussels.

179 Fabri 1865, pp. 216-217.

180 MOFA Belgium 316. An undated overview of t'Kint's career in his handwriting, probably connected with his appointment as envoy extraordinary and minister plenipotentiary to China and Japan in May 1869, mentions 14 October 1840. Jos. Fabri mentions 10 October 1840, but does not refer to any specific source (Fabri 1865, p. 217).

181 MOFA Belgium 316. An undated overview of t'Kint's career; and Fabri 1865, pp. 217-218.

182 Fabri 1865, pp. 220-222.

183 Fabri 1965, pp. 226-244.

184 MOFA Belgium 316. An undated overview of t'Kint's career; and Fabri 1865, pp. 224-246.

185 MOFA Belgium – Mexique 1. File no. 51: Brussels, 23 May 1863, dispatch without order number from Aug. t'Kint de Roodenbeek to Charles Rogier, stamped in Brussels on 26 May 1863, 8786 and A3690.

186 MOFA Belgium – Mexique 1. File no. 36, Belgian Mission, Mexico, 5 October 1862, dispatch without order number from Aug. t'Kint de Roodenbeek to Charles Rogier, stamped in Brussels on 8 December 1862, A3690. – See also: File no. 52: Brussels, 23 May 1863, dispatch without order number from Aug. t'Kint de Roodenbeek to Charles Rogier, stamped in Brussels on 26 May 1863, 8843, A3690.

187 MOFA Belgium – Mexique 1. Files no. 38-41: internal investigation of the conduct of t'Kint in Mexico by the Belgian Ministry of Foreign Affairs. Main file is no. 39, dated 16 November 1862. – Duchesne 1866 mentions that t'Kint had practically completely broken off the relations with Mexico without backing from the Belgian Ministry of Foreign Affairs.

188 MOFA Belgium – Mexique 1. File no. 44: Paris, 14 April 1863, dispatch without order number from Aug. t'Kint de Roodenbeek to Charles Rogier. File no. 45: Paris, 17 April 1863, dispatch with order no. 2 from Aug. t'Kint de Roodenbeek to Charles Rogier, stamped in Brussels on 24 April 1863, A3690; File no. 47: Paris, 5 May 1863, dispatch without order number from Aug. t'Kint de Roodenbeek to Charles Rogier, stamped in Brussels on 12 May 1863, A3690; File no. 48: Paris, 11 May 1863, dispatch without order number from Aug. t'Kint de Roodenbeek to Charles Rogier, stamped in Brussels on 13 May 1863, A 3690.

189 MOFA Belgium – Mexique 1. File no. 49: Brussels, 20 May 1863, dispatch without order number from Aug. t'Kint de Roodenbeek to Charles Rogier, stamped in Brussels on 9 June 1863, A3690. Miramare Castle is a 19th-century castle near Trieste, northeastern Italy.

190 Duchesne 1966 states that in 1863, King Leopold I had selected t'Kint to conduct a thorough examination of the true state of affairs in Mexico, based on a list of 300 questions. This research was to assist the decision as to whether or not to install the Austrian Archduke Ferdinand as emperor in Mexico. Ferdinand was married to Princess Charlotte, King Leopold's daughter. In his writings and actions of that time, t'Kint was in favour of a monarchy in Mexico.

191 MOFA Belgium – Mexique 1. File no. 50: Brussels, 22 May 1863, Belgian Ministry of Foreign Affairs, Minutes, Indicateur A no. 3690, order no. 1 with 2 annexes, containing a letter in French to t'Kint, Belgian consul general, at that moment in Brussels.

192 MOFA Belgium – Mexique 1. File no. 51: Brussels, 23 May 1863, dispatch without order number from Aug. t'Kint de Roodenbeek to Charles Rogier, stamped in Brussels on 26 May (1863), 8786 and A3690.

193 Duchesne 1966.

194 MOFA Belgium – Mexique 1. File no. 58: Brussels, 22 March 1864, Belgian Ministry of Foreign Affairs, Minutes, Indicateur A no. 3690 with an annex containing credential letters, to the minister of the royal household.

195 This account is given by Auguste t'Kint himself. See Royal Palace Belgium 176/134. Brussels, 15 October 1864, Aug^te t'Kint de Roodenbeek to "Sire" (Belgian King Leopold I). – See also MOFA Belgium – Mexique 1. File without number: Brussels, 12 April 1864, Charles Rogier to the minister of foreign affairs of Mexico; File no. 59: Brussels, 14 April 1864, Minute A 3690 order number 9 with 2 annexes, draft dispatch from the Belgian Foreign Ministry to t'Kint, Belgian consul general. Duchesne 1966 states that the Belgian officials refused to propose t'Kint as minister of the king of the Belgians to the Mexican court, because of the unorthodox way in which t'Kint had ruptured the relations with Mexico in 1862.

196 MOFA Belgium – Mexique 1. File 60: unsigned note, afterwards marked "No. 73 du 20 Avril 1864"; File no. 61: French note written by hand, being an "Extrait de mémorial diplomatique. 24 Avril 1864 – no. 17 – page 263"; File no. 63: Belgian Consulate, Mexico 28 June 1864, French dispatch with order no. 14 from D. Graue to Charles Rogier, stamped in Brussels on 8 August (1864), 12075 and A3690, informing Rogier that the Mexican emperor and empress have arrived in the capital of Mexico on 12 June 1864.

197 This probably concerned a convention about the support from the French Emperor Napoleon III to Archduke Maximilian in his new capacity as emperor of Mexico.

198 Royal Palace Belgium 176/134. Brussels, 15 October 1864, Aug^te t'Kint de Roodenbeek to "Sire" (Belgian King Leopold I).

199 Royal Palace Belgium 176/134. Brussels, 15 October 1864, Aug^te t'Kint de Roodenbeek to "Sire" (Belgian King Leopold I).

200 Jules Devaux (1828-1886) became secretary to the Belgian Crown Prince Leopold (later King Leopold II) on 1 October 1858, and would become his Cabinet Chief in 1866.

201 It probably refers to Paul de Martin d'Ayguesvives, Baron de Malaret, a French diplomat who had served in Brussels as minister in 1862-1863. See Liste chronologique des ambassadeurs de France en Belgique, published on the website of the French Embassy in Brussels, consulted on 21 August 2015: http://www.ambafrance-be.org/Liste-chronologique-des; also Société du Grand Armorial de France 1948, p. 2, "Martin Ayguesvives".

202 Royal Palace Belgium 176/134. 2 August, hand-written note from Jules Devaux to "Sire". No year is mentioned, but it is likely to be 1864. On top of this note, in pencil, is written: "Il faut renommer t'Kint Chargé d'Affaires comme il l'était" (t'Kint has to be reappointed as chargé d'affaires as he was (before)).

203 Vande Walle 2003, p. 432, referring to a letter from Raasløff to Lambermont, London, 15 October 1863 (Archives of the Belgian Ministry of Foreign Affairs, no 2833, I).

204 This refers to Thomas Francis Wade (1818 – 1895), who had taken up the post of British chargé d'affaires at Beijing since 23 June 1864. See Vande Walle 2003, p. 433.

205 MOFA Belgium 2704 III. Brussels, 13 October 1864, letter of the Belgian MOFA to S. Van de Weyer, Belgian minister in London.

206 MOFA Belgium 2704 III. London 18 October 1864, letter from Maurice Delfosse to Ch. Rogier.

Lord John Russell was British foreign secretary from 1859 till 1866.

207 MOFA Belgium 2704 III. Hand-written note of 30 October (1864) with the following text in French: "Mr. de Kattendijk, Ministre de la marine en hollande, qui a rendu 3 ans au Japon, a fait son offre de service personnel pour notre consul en Chine et a promis de mettre les agents (et influencer) de la hollande au Japon à la disposition de la Belgique, si nous en avions besoin".

208 MOFA Belgium 2704 III. Brussels, 9 December 1864, minutes containing draft letter from the Belgian foreign minister to Consul General Aug. t'Kint; Brussels, 12 December 1864, letter from Aug. t'Kint de Roodenbeek to Charles Rogier; Brussels, 6 January 1865, Minutes containing draft letter from the Belgian foreign minister to Consul General t'Kint.

209 MOFA Belgium 2704 III. Brussels, 9 December 184, minutes with draft letter from Belgian MOFA to the Presidents of 12 Chambers of Commerce; Brussels, 21 January 1865, letter from t'Kint to Rogier.

210 MOFA Belgium 2704 III. Brussels, 12 December 1864, Minutes containing a draft letter from the Belgian foreign minister to Mr Solvyns in Turin; Minutes containing draft letter from the Belgian foreign minister to Mr Delfosse in London.

211 MOFA Belgium 2704 III. Turin, 21 December 1864, letter from Henry Solvyns to Charles Rogier.

212 MOFA Belgium 2098. Brussels, 21 December 1864, Minutes, Indicateur Be no. 2483, order no. 77, from the Belgian foreign minister to J. Greindl in Bern; Bern, 23 December 1864, Belgian Legation to the Swiss Confederation, no. 136, Grenval to Rogier.

213 MOFA Belgium 2098. Brussels, 31 January 1865, draft letter Indicateur no. 2483, order no. E, from the Belgian minister of foreign affairs to A. t'Kint, consul general of Belgium in Brussels. The Convention of Paris of 25 June 1864 was concluded between the French minister of foreign affairs, Drouyn de Lhuys and the Japanese embassy visiting Paris, represented by Ikeda Chikugo no Kami 池田筑後守, Kawatsu Izu no Kami 河津伊豆守 and Kawada Sagami no Kami 河田相模守 (See Ministry of Foreign Affairs of Japan 1874, pp. 227-229). The shogun refused to ratify the convention and the members of the Japanese Embassy were disgraced. See e.g. University of Tokyo Volume IX and Volume X 1968 Ministers. US National Archives, RG 59, M133, N.A. 133 (23) Vol. 5-3 (11 June – 29 August 1864) (YAH microfilm outprint no. Ca4/01.4/23, p. 97). US Legation in Japan, Kanagawa, 2 September 1864, dispatch no. 55 being a telegram from Robert H. Pruyn, minister resident in Japan, to William H. Seward, secretary of state in Washington.

214 MOFA Belgium 2704 III. Antwerp, 19 January 1865, letter from Victor Lynen to the Belgian foreign minister. For Victor Lynen (1834-1894), see the website of the *Genootschap voor Antwerpse Geschiedenis*, "Victor Lynen, Antwerpse gastheer van Franz List" (accessed 12 Dec 2015), www.gvag.be/lezingen/2012-2/victor-lynen-antwerpse-gastheer-van-franz-liszt. Charles Gütshow was a merchant in Shanghai, while P. Gütshow managed Gütshow and Co. in Yokohama. See too Directory China 1865, p. 67, p. 202 and p. 238.

215 MOFA Belgium 2098, and MOFA Belgium 2704 III. Brussels, 4 February 1865, draft letter Indicateur B no. 1746, order no. F from the Belgian minister of foreign affairs to t'Kint, consul general in Brussels.

216 MOFA Belgium 316. An undated overview of t'Kint's career in his handwriting. Auguste t'Kint was accorded the title of Knight in the Order of Leopold on 28 March 1859, and of Officer on 30 January 1865.

217 MOFA Belgium 2704 III. Hong Kong, 26 June 1865, Auguste t'Kint to Charles Rogier.

218 MOFA Belgium 2704 III. Hong Kong, 5 July 1865, t'Kint to Rogier.

219 MOFA Belgium 2704 III. Shanghai, 15 July 1865, t'Kint to Rogier.

220 This account of the departure date of t'Kint from Hong Kong does not correspond with the information t'Kint communicated to Rogier. T'Kint may have left Hong Kong several times to visit Canton or Macao, before definitively leaving on 7 July 1865 for Shanghai – hence the confusion.

221 TUHI Ishin 6, p. 256. D.I.S.K. 2408 (2415), pp. 32-35. Microfilm reproduction REEL no. Keiō 慶応 – 036, pictures 944.tiff – 950.tiff. This Japanese text gives the name of the German national as ミラソン (Millasson, Milason, Millason, Milasson, Milathon, Millathon, Millerthon, maybe even Wilson?). Isomi et al. 1989, pp. 37-38, and pp. 43-44, endnotes nos. 11 and 12, give Lason as name for the German. Vande Walle 2003, p. 436, reproduces the name of Lason from Isomi. Shogun Tokugawa Iemochi 徳川家茂 had left Edo on 9 June 1865. He would die in Osaka on 28 August 1866. See e.g. TUHI 1055.7. 8 June 1865 (15th day of the 5th month of Keiō 1), (copy of a) letter in Dutch from the "Governors" to N.P. Kingdon. Also Adams 1875, volume II, book III, Chapter VI 1866, p. 37.

222 Vande Walle 2003, p. 433.

223 MOFA Belgium 2704 III. Peking (Beijing), 8 August 1865, t'Kint to Rogier.

224 Royal Palace Belgium – Duke of Brabant. "Voyage de S.M.R. Monseigneur Le Duc de Brabant en 1864-1865".

225 MOFA Belgium 2704 III. Hand-written note dated "Jeudi Soir", arriving at Belgian Ministry of Foreign Affairs on 4 August 1865, accompanied by two letters from the duke of Brabant; Brussels, 7 Augustus 1865, Minute containing draft letter from Belgian foreign minister to Bartholeyns in London; London, 19 August 1865, Montmoyen de Toncleer (Tongres?) to Charles Rogier ; Undated draft letter from Belgian Ministry of Foreign Affairs to Consul General t'Kint in Shanghai, informing him about the duke of Brabant's letters to Alcock. Directory China 1865, p. 191, mentions P.T. Kroes as acting vice consul for the Netherlands in Shanghai.

226 Vande Walle 2003, pp. 433-435. MOFA Belgium 2704 III. Three dispatches from t'Kint to Rogier, sent from Peking (Beijing) on 1 October, 18 October and 4 November 1865.

227 MOFA Belgium 2704 III. Shanghai, 25 November 1865, dispatch from t'Kint to Rogier; Yokohama, 14 February 1866, dispatch Litt A no. 3, No ordre 34, from t'Kint to Rogier, stamped in Brussels on 10 April, 6898, B1746/2483.

228 Vande Walle 2003, p. 435.

229 Hawks 1856, Introduction pp. 4-5. Also Machida 2011, p. 18.

230 Machida 2001, pp. 29-35. Also Van der Chijs 1867, pp. 47-52. Own translation of: "Grootmachtigen Beheerscher van het groote rijk Japan, die zijnen zetel houdt in het Keizerlijke Paleis in Jedo" and "Grootmachtig Keizer".

231 Hawks 1856, pp. 11-19: Introduction. Section III Government. Examples of such communication: Hawks 1856, pp. 244-245 and pp. 256-261.

232 For the English mission, see Oliphant 1859, pp. 36-38. For the French mission: De Chassiron 1861, p. 70.

233 University of Tokyo Volume IX and Volume X 1968 Ministers. US National Archives, RG 59, M133, N.A. 133 (6) Vol. 1-4 (10 December 1857 – 29 June 1858). (YAH microfilm outprint no. Ca4/01.4/6, pp. 69-70). 18 February 1858, copy of a letter in Dutch (and its English translation) from Hotta Bitchū no Kami 堀田備中守 (Hotta Masayoshi) and Moriyama Takichirō 森山多吉郎 to Townsend Harris.

234 University of Tokyo Volume IX and Volume X 1968 Ministers. US National Archives, RG 59, M133, N.A. 133 (6) Vol. 1-4 (10 December 1857 – 29 June 1858). (YAH microfilm outprint no. Ca4/01.4/6, pp. 58-71). US Consulate General, Edo, 4 March 1858, dispatch no. 6 from Townsend Harris, US consul to Japan, to Lewis Cass, secretary of state at Washington.

235 University of Tokyo Volume IX and Volume X 1968 Ministers. US National Archives, RG 59, M133, N.A. 133 (7) Vol. 2-1 (1 July – 26 August 1858). (YAH microfilm outprint no. Ca4/01.4/7, pp. 18-19). 14 April 1858 (1st day of the 3rd month of Ansei 5), letter in Dutch (and its English translation) from Hotta Bitchū no Kami (Hotta Masayoshi) and Moriyama Takichirō to Townsend Harris.

236 University of Tokyo Volume IX and Volume X 1968 Ministers. US National Archives, RG 59, M133, N.A. 133 (7) Vol. 2-1 (1 July – 26 August 1858). (YAH microfilm outprint no. Ca4/01.4/7, pp. 11-24). Consulate General at Shimoda, 8 July 1858, dispatch no. 19 from Townsend Harris to probably Lewis Cass, secretary of state at Washington. Also University of Tokyo Volume IX and Volume X 1968 Legation. US National Archives, RG 84, N.A. T400 (1) Vol. 1 (3 December 1856 – 21 December 1858). (YAH microfilm outprint no. Ca4/01.14/1, pp. 75-100 and pp. 103-104). Undated Japanese and Dutch texts, followed by an English translation, and according to the English translation received by the US Legation in Japan on 5 June 1858.

237 A copy of the Japanese letter from Ogasawara, and its Dutch and English translations, can be found at: University of Tokyo Volume IX and Volume X 1968 Legation. US National Archives, RG 84, N.A. T400 (11) Vol. 8 (1 January – 4 June 1863). (YAH microfilm outprint no. Ca4/01.14/11, pp. 52-55). 24 June 1863 (9th day of the 5th month of Bunkyū 3), Japanese letter, with Dutch and English translations, from Ogasawara Zusho no Kami (Ogasawara Nagamichi) to Robert H. Pruyn, minister resident of the United States of America.

238 University of Tokyo Volume XIII 1965 Politique, volume 13, Année 1865 (Léon Roches), pp. 263-282. (YAH microfilm outprint no. Ca4/01.36/34). Yokohama, 31 October 1865, dispatch no. 48 from Léon Roches to Drouyn de Lhuys (French foreign minister at Paris), including a Memorandum in French concluded between the four Powers. Also Adams 1875, Book II, Chapter IV 1865, pp. 16-17; and TUHI. Dutch Consulate General 1864-1866. Anno 1865 (3), no. 75-104. Microfilm 6951-2-8-3; microfilm outprint no. 7551-48-7.Kanagawa, 30 October 1865, letter in Dutch no. 70/82 from the Dutch political agent (Van Polsbroek) and consul general to the Dutch minister of foreign affairs at The Hague.

239 University of Tokyo Volume VI 1966, vol. 58, FO46 (166), p. 120. (YAH microfilm outprint Ca4/01.9/166). 24 November 1865, copy of a dispatch from the mikado (emperor) to the tycoon (shogun), giving his consent to the foreign treaties. Also Adams 1875, Book II, Chapter IV 1865, pp. 16-30.

240 MOFA Belgium 2098. Shanghai, 8 December 1865, Indicateur A no. 2, Order no. 23, and Indicateur A no. 3, order no. 25 from t'Kint de Roodenbeek to the Belgian Minister of Foreign Affairs Charles Rogier in Brussels.

241 MOFA Belgium 2704 III. Yokohama, 11 July 1866, letter from Aug. t'Kint de Roodenbeek to Charles Rogier in Brussels, Litt. C(?) no. 7, order no. 51, stamped in Brussels on 6 September 1866, B 1746/1996 no. 15377. For Charles Alexander Winchester (? – 1883), See the website of *Hong Kong's First*, "Dr. Charles Alexander Winchester" (accessed 12 Dec 2015), http://hongkongsfirst.blogspot.jp/2013/01/dr-charles-alexander-winchester.html.

242 MOFA Belgium 2098. Yokohama, 18 December 1865. Indicateur A no. 3, order no. 26 from t'Kint de Roodenbeek to Charles Rogier in Brussels. Also Kitane 1987 (volume 7), pp. 1-2. *Japan Times' Daily Advertiser* 1:73 (Yokohama, Monday 18 Dec 1865), front page and p. 190; p. 17. *Japan Herald* 4:200 (Yokohama, Saturday 23 Dec 1865), front page; p. 19. Japan Herald 4:200 (Yokohama, Saturday 23 Dec 1865), p. 777. "Meteorological Table from 16th to 22nd December, 1865".

243 The Portuguese plenipotentiary was accompanied by several officers. On 14 July 1860, British Vice Consul R. Eusden requested Japanese currency from the Japanese authorities for the officers of the Portuguese mission, who wanted to buy souvenirs to take home to Portugal. He received a reply from the Japanese authorities on 24 July 1860. See TUHI 1054.01/1, p. 677. Edo, 14 July 1860, letter no. 70 from R.E(usden) to the Japanese commissioners of foreign affairs. Also TUHI 1055.1/1. 24 July 1860 (7th day of the 6th month of Man'en 1), (Japanese) Commissioners to R. Eusden, British vice consul.

244 MOFA Belgium 2865 IV. Edo, 29 August 1867, Extraordinary Mission of Belgium, Litt C no. 4, order no. 114, letter from Aug. t'Kint de Roodenbeek to Charles Rogier in Brussels, stamped in Brussels 25 October 1867 (B 2483 no. 17260). T'Kint cited as reasons for the dismissal of Sr. Vandevelde his repeated insubordination, and his temper being completely incompatible with the difficulties and dangers of faraway journeys.

245 TUHI 1054.04/3, pp. 21-22. Edo, 6 January 1866, (copy of a) letter in Dutch no. 4/10 from D. de Graeff van Polsbroek (political agent and consul general of the Netherlands in Japan) to the Japanese commissioners of foreign affairs in Edo.

246 MOFA Belgium 2098. Yokohama, 18 December 1865. Indicateur A no. 3, Order no. 26 from t'Kint de Roodenbeek to Charles Rogier in Brussels. Also TUHI. Dutch Consulate General 1864-1866. Anno 1865 (3), No. 75-104. Microfilm 6951-2-8-3; microfilm outprint no. 7551-48-7, pp. 90-91. Kanagawa, 18 December 1865, letter in Dutch no. 84/102 from the Dutch Political Agent and Consul General (Van Polsbroek) to the Dutch minister of foreign affairs at The Hague. On the Dutch Consulate General located at Benten, see also TUHI 1054.04/2. Kanagawa, 27 October 1865, Dutch dispatch no. 123/269 from Polsbroek to the Japanese commissioners of foreign affairs.

247 MOFA Belgium 2098. Yokohama, 12 January 1866. Indicateur a no. 3, order no. 30 from t'Kint de Roodenbeek to Charles Rogier in Brussels.

248 Kitane 1987 (volume 9), p. 37, *The Daily Japan Herald* 2:908, p. 1870. Yokohama, Japan, Monday 8 October 1866. Also Kitane 1987 (volume 9), p. 42, *Daily Japan Herald* 2:909, p. 1874. Yokohama, Japan, Tuesday 9 October 1866. Allotment no. 82 did not only contain the house rented by t'Kint. The trading company McKechnie & Co. had a store at no. 82, boarding the Main Street of Yokohama Foreign Settlement. See Kitane 1987 (volume 9), p. 14. *Daily Japan Herald* 2:903 (Yokohama, Japan, Tuesday 2 Oct 1866), p. 1852; p. 15. *Daily Japan Herald* 2:904 (Yokohama, Japan, Wednesday 3 Oct 1866), front page; p. 23. *Daily Japan Herald* 2:905 (Yokohama, Japan, Thursday 4 Oct 1866), front page; p. 27. *Daily Japan Herald* 2:907 (Yokohama, Japan, Saturday 6 Oct 1866), front page.

249 TUHI 1054.08, pp. 1-2. Yokohama, 21 December 1865, letter in French from August t'Kint de Roodenbeek to the Japanese councillors in charge of foreign affairs in Edo. Also MOFA Belgium 2098. Yokohama, 21 December 1865, no. 1, A. no. 9 (possible n. 3), draft letter probably from t'Kint de Roodenbeek to the Japanese commissioners of foreign affairs in Edo. The translation of this letter into Japanese, made by the Japanese administration, is published in Isomi et al. 1989, p. 39. The original is kept at: TUHI Ishin 6, p. 256. D.I.S.K. 2408 (2415), pp. 8-9. Microfilm reproduction REEL no. Keiō 慶応 – 036, pictures 905.tiff – 907.tiff.

250 MOFA Belgium 2098. Yokohama, 12 January 1866. Indicateur A no. 3, Order no. 30, letter from t'Kint de Roodenbeek to Charles Rogier in Brussels.

251 TUHI Ishin 6, p. 256. D.I.S.K. 2408 (2415), pp. 16-17. Microfilm reproduction REEL no. Keiō 慶応 – 036, pictures 918.tiff – 920.tiff. Japanese report by Kikuchi Iyo no Kami (Kikuchi Takayoshi), Hoshino Bitchū no Kami 星野備中守 (Hoshino Kazuyuki), Ezure Kaga no Kami 江連加賀守 (Ezure Akinori) and Kurimoto Aki no Kami 栗本安芸守 (Kurimoto Joun), all commissioners of foreign affairs, dated 31 December 1865 (14th day of the 11th month of Keiō 1). See the website of *Mfj*, "星野氏 - 星野氏の歴史" (accessed 6 Dec 2015), http://mfj.co.jp/hoshinoshinorekishi. According to Katō 2001, p. 11, Ezure was commissioner of foreign affairs (*gaikoku bugyō* 外国奉行) from 10 October 1864 till 26 May 1868.

252 According to the logbook of the *Zoutman*, the ship weighed anchor at Yokohama Port at 9 a.m. and arrived at Edo at 11 a.m. See NAN Scheepsjournalen, Inv. nr. 5290, Scheepsjournaal Schroefstoomschip 2de klas Zoutman, folio 197, 31 December 1865.

253 The salutes by the Japanese batteries at Kanagawa were a topic of discussion between Van Polsbroek and the Japanese. See TUHI 1054.02/2, pp. 449-450. Kanagawa, 28 December 1865, (copy of a) letter in Dutch no. 152/326 from D. de Graeff van Polsbroek to the Japanese commissioners of foreign affairs in Edo. The same letter can be found at MOFA Belgium 2098, and a Japanese translation at TUHI Ishin 6, p. 256. D.I.S.K. 2408 (2415), pp. 14-15. Microfilm reproduction REEL no. Keiō 慶応 – 036, pictures 915.tiff – 917.tiff. Also TUHI 1055.4/2. 29 December 1865 (12th day of the 11th month of Keiō 1), Mizuno Izumi no Kami (Mizuno Tadakiyo) to D. de Graeff van Polsbroek. The same letter can be found at MOFA Belgium 2098, and a copy of the Japanese version at TUHI Ishin 6, p. 256. D.I.S.K. 2408 (2415), pp. 12-13. Microfilm reproduction REEL no. Keiō 慶応 – 036, pictures 912.tiff – 914.tiff. MOFA Belgium 2098. 29 December 1865 (12th day of the 11th month of Keiō 1), copy of a letter in Dutch from Ezure Kaga no Kami (Ezure Akinori) to D. de Graeff van Polsbroek, with a copy of the Japanese version at TUHI Ishin 6, p. 256. D.I.S.K. 2408 (2415), p. 11. Microfilm reproduction REEL no. Keiō 慶応 – 036, pictures 910.tiff – 911.tiff.

254 MOFA Belgium 2098. Yokohama, 12 January 1866. Indicateur A no. 3, order no. 30, letter from t'Kint de Roodenbeek to Charles Rogier in Brussels; and: Yokohama, 8 January 1866, no. 5, A. no. 3, draft letter probably from t'Kint de Roodenbeek to D. de Graeff van Polsbroek.

255 MOFA Belgium 2098. Yokohama, 12 January 1866. Indicateur A no. 3, Order no. 30, letter from t'Kint de Roodenbeek to Charles Rogier in Brussels.

256 TUHI 1054.04/3, pp. 1-5. 1 January 1866, Edo, copy of a letter in Dutch from D. de Graeff van Polsbroek to the (Japanese) commissioners of foreign affairs in Edo. The same letter can be found at: MOFA Belgium 2098. A Japanese translation is kept at: TUHI Ishin 6, p. 256. D.I.S.K. 2408 (2415), pp. 21-23. Microfilm reproduction REEL no. Keiō 慶応 – 036, pictures 926.tiff – 928.tiff. This translation was partly published in Isomi et al. 1989, p. 44, endnote 16.

257 MOFA Belgium 2098. Yokohama, 18 December 1865. Indicateur a no. 3, order no. 26, letter from t'Kint de Roodenbeek to Charles Rogier in Brussels.

258 TUHI. Dutch Consulate General 1864-1866. Anno 1865 (3), no. 75-104. Microfilm 6951-2-8-3; microfilm outprint no. 7551-48-7, pp. 90-91. Kanagawa, 18 December 1865, letter in Dutch no. 84/102 from the Dutch Political Agent and Consul General (Van Polsbroek) to the Dutch minister of foreign affairs at The Hague.

259 MOFA Belgium 2704 III. Draft letter from Belgian Ministry of Foreign Affairs to Consul General t'Kint in Shanghai (no date, but probably August 1865). Directory China 1865, p. 191, mentions P.T. Kroes as acting vice consul for the Netherlands in Shanghai.

260 Satow 2006, pp. 143-145. Also TUHI 1054.01/3, pp. 230-238. Yokohama, 18 July 1865, English letter (no. 3) from English minister Harry Parkes to the Japanese commissioners of foreign affairs.

261 MOFA Belgium 2098. Yokohama, 18 December 1865. Indicateur A no. 3, order no. 26, letter from t'Kint de Roodenbeek to Charles Rogier in Brussels.

262 TUHI 1054.01/3, pp. 399-402, British Legation, 26 December 1865, English letter from Harry Parkes, English minister to Japan, to Mizuno Izumi no Kami (Mizuno Tadakiyo), councillor of the shogun's cabinet at Edo. Also Kitane 1987 (volume 7), p. 29. *Japan Times' Daily Advertiser* 1:79 (Yokohama, 27 Dec 1865), front page. Parkes's family was among the passengers of the British steamer *Cadiz*.

263 University of Tokyo Volume VI 1966, vol. 58, FO46 (167), pp. 186-187. (YAH microfilm outprint Ca4/01.9/167, pp. 63-64). Yokohama, 29 December 1865, dispatch no. 78, Parkes to Russell. A draft version of this dispatch can be found at: University of Tokyo Volume VII 1967, despatches from Parkes, October – December 1865), vol. 92, FO262 (112), p. 103. (YAH microfilm outprint no. Ca4/01.20/112, p. 107).

264 MOFA Belgium 2098. Yokohama, 18 December 1865. Indicateur A no. 3, order no. 26, letter from t'Kint de Roodenbeek to Charles Rogier in Brussels. On 25 January 1866, Roches would reply to Drouyn de Lhuys, referring to the letter of recommendation. In his reply, he mentioned that Van Polsbroek was taking care of the mission of t'Kint, but that he himself had invited the Japanese councillors to adopt a favourable attitude to the treaty request from Belgium. Roches believed that t'Kint would not meet any major obstacles in obtaining the objectives of his mission. See University of Tokyo Volume XIII 1965 Consulaire, volume 4, pp. 168-169 (YAH microfilm outprint no. Ca4/01.31/13, pp. 23-24). Yokohama, 25 January 1865, Roches to Drouyn de Lhuys.

265 Due to his illness, Roches was not able to attend the festivities for the French National Day in Yokohama on 15 August 1865. He spent the month of August 1865 at the hot water spa of Atami. When Councillor (*rōjū* 老中) Matsudaira Hōki no Kami 松平伯耆守 (Matsudaira Munehide) visited Roches in Yokohama around 10 January 1866, Roches was only able to receive the Japanese councillor at his bedside. See University of Tokyo Volume XIII 1965 Politique (YAH microfilm outprint no. Ca4/01.36/33, pp. 230-233). Atami, 21 Augustus 1865, dispatch no. 43 from Roches to Drouyn de Lhuys, (French minister of foreign affairs). Also University of Tokyo Volume XIV 1966 Politique, Japon 1854-1896 (YAH microfilm outprint no. Ca4/01.36/35, pp. 3-19).

266 Fabri 1965, pp. 216-217.

267 Van der Chijs 1867. This publication is completely devoted to revealing the Dutch policy of opening up Japan to the world. See in particular for this policy in the period 1855-1857: pp. 197-198, pp. 211-217, pp. 227-235.

268 For the Portuguese and Swiss treaty negotiations, see the relevant paragraphs above.

269 The British Army was stationed in Yokohama from January 1864 until March 1875, with at its peak more than 1,500 men. The French army was stationed in Yokohama from June 1863 until March 1875, with about 300 men at its peak. See Ōyama 1999, p. 80, respectively Nakatake 1999, pp. 360-361.

270 TUHI 1054.04/3, pp. 1-5. 1 January 1866, Edo, copy of a letter in Dutch from D. de Graeff van Polsbroek to the (Japanese) councillors in charge of foreign affairs in Edo. The same letter can be found at MOFA Belgium 2098.

271 TUHI 1055.1/4. 5 January 1866 (19th day of the 11th month of Keiō 1), letter in Dutch from Kikuchi Iyo no Kami (Kikuchi Takayoshi), Hoshino Bitchū no Kami (Hoshino Kazuyuki), Ezure Kaga no Kami (Ezure Akinori) and Kurimoto Aki no Kami (Kurimoto Joun) to R. Eusden, secretary of the British legation. Text of the original Japanese letter at TUHI Ishin 6, p. 256. D.I.S.K. 2408 (2415), p. 31. Microfilm reproduction REEL no. Keiō 慶応 – 036, pictures 942.tiff – 943.tiff. Text of the letter in Dutch to Eusden can be found at University of Tokyo Volume VII 1967, Japan Correspondence (September 1865 – January 1866), vol. 484, FO262 (695) (YAH microfilm outprint no. Ca4/01.20/695, pp. 87-88). The English translation made at the British Legation can be found at University of Tokyo Volume VII 1967, Japan Correspondence (September 1865 – January 1866), vol. 486, FO262 (697) (YAH microfilm outprint no. Ca4/01.20/697, pp. 2-3). No British objection has been found in the archives.

272 Ministry of Foreign Affairs of Japan 1874, p. 53 (US), p. 72 (the Netherlands), pp. 91-92 (Russia), p. 112 (Great Britain), p. 131 (France), p. 152 (Portugal), p. 187 (Prussia) and p. 208 (Switzerland).

273 University of Tokyo Volume IX and Volume X 1968 Ministers. US National Archives, RG 59, M133, N.A. 133 (18) Vol. 4-4 (5 May – 27 June 1863). (YAH microfilm outprint no. Ca4/01.4/18, pp. 35-41). US Legation in Japan, Yokohama, 12 June 1863, dispatch no. 31 from Robert H. Pruyn to William H. Seward, US secretary of state in Washington, received there on 27 August 1863.

274 The system of maintaining a residence in Yokohama and a residence in Edo is clearly explained in a dispatch from English minister Harry Parkes to the Foreign Office: University of Tokyo Volume VI 1966, vol. 79, FO46 (125) and FO46(216), pp. 79-88. (YAH microfilm outprints Ca4/01.9/215 and Ca4/01.9/216). Edo, 16 March 1867, dispatch no. 40, Parkes to Stanley. On 5 April 1865, the representatives of France, Britain, the Netherlands and the United States signed a memorandum addressed to the Japanese government, defending their right to keep an official legation at Edo, even if they currently all resided at Yokohama. See TUHI 1054.03/2, pp. 372-375. Residence of Léon Roches (French minister to Japan) at Yokohama, 5 April 1865, memorandum. See also Adams 1874, pp. 162-163 about the system of "Edo-Yokohama" in 1862.

275 MOFA Belgium 2098. Yokohama, 12 January 1866, Indicateur A no. 3, Order no. 30 from t'Kint de Roodenbeek to Charles Rogier in Brussels, last page. Also University of Tokyo Volume VI 1966, vol. 72, FO46 (200), pp. 9-12 (YAH microfilm outprint no. Ca4/01.9/200, pp. 9-12). Edo, 15 November 1866, dispatch no. 185 from Parkes to Stanley; University of Tokyo Volume VI 1966, vol. 79, FO46 (216), pp. 84-88 (YAH microfilm outprint no. Ca4/01.9/216). Edo, 16 March 1867, dispatch no. 40 from Parkes to Stanley.

276 Kitane 1987 (volume 7), p. 88. *Japan Times' Daily Advertiser* 1:91 (Yokohama, Monday 11 Jan 1866), p. 262.

277 Kitane 1987 (volume 7), p. 82. *Japan Times' Daily Advertiser*. Second Edition (Yokohama, 9 Jan 1866).

278 Kitane 1987 (volume 7), p. 98. *Japan Times* 1:19 (Yokohama, Friday 12 Jan 1866), p. 118.

279 Kitane 1987 (volume 7), p. 65. *Japan Times* 1:18 (Yokohama, Friday 5 Jan 1866), p. 109.

280 A fairly good description of life in Yokohama in 1866 is given in the dairy of the Italian Envoy V.F. Arminjon. See Arminjon 1869 and Arminjon 1987, pp. 49-65.

281 University of Tokyo Volume IX and Volume X 1968 Ministers. US National Archives, RG 59, M133, N.A. 133 (26) Vol. 6-2 (7 March – 21 July 1865). (YAH microfilm outprint no. Ca4/01.4/26, p. 60). US Legation in Japan, Edo, 1 June 1865, dispatch no. 29 from Portman, chargé d'affaires ad interim, to William H. Seward, secretary of state at Washington. Anton L.C. Portman served as translator, and later as secretary at the American legation to Japan during the Bakumatsu period from 1861 onwards. See Kawasaki 1988, p. 115, p. 120, p. 124, p. 126, p. 131, p. 135, p. 140.

282 Minato City Local History Museum 2005, pp. 34-43.

283 Adams 1874, pp. 132-137 and pp. 155-163.

284 The search started not later than two weeks after Parkes had arrived in Japan on 8 July 1865. See TUHI 1054.01/3, pp. 239-242. Edo, 23 July 1865, English letter from English minister Harry Parkes to the Japanese commissioners of foreign affairs. This search is also described in University of Tokyo Volume VI 1966, vol. 87, FO46 (243) (YAH microfilm outprint no. Ca4/01.9/243, pp. 153-197). Yokohama, 10 August 1865, dispatch no. 21 from Parkes to Russell; and pp. 198-204: Yokohama, 25 August 1885, dispatch no. 34 from Parkes to Russell.

285 TUHI 1054.01/3. Yokohama, 4 September 1865, English letter from English minister Harry Parkes to the Japanese commissioners of foreign affairs.

286 Richard Eusden mentioned in a letter of 21 November 1865 that the British legation was based at Daichūji, and William Willis, Eusden's colleague at the British legation, sent a letter from the Daichūji temple on 26 November 1865. See TUHI 1054.01/3, pp. 385-386. Yokohama, 21 November 1865, letter from Richard Eusden, English chargé d'affaires, to the Japanese commissioners of foreign affairs; pp. 393-396. Daichūji, 26 November 1865, letter written by Willis (British legation).

287 University of Tokyo Volume VI 1966, vol. 72, FO46 (200), pp. 9-12 (YAH microfilm outprint no. Ca4/01.9/200, pp. 9-12). Edo, 15 November 1866, dispatch no. 185 from Parkes to Stanley. See also pp. 67-74: Edo, 16 November 1866, dispatch no. 190 from Parkes to Stanley.

288 TUHI 1055.5/2. 27 April 1865 (3rd day of the 4th month of Genji 2), (copy of a) letter in Dutch from the "commissioners" to Van Brandt, consul of Prussia. – See also: Minato City Local History Museum 2005, pp. 68-69.

289 TUHI 1054.05, pp. 369-371. Kanagawa, 5 June 1866, first letter from the Dutch Political Agent and Consul General De Graeff van Polsbroek as acting consul for Prussia to the commissioners of foreign affairs at Edo. See also Minato City Local History Museum 2005, pp. 68-69.

290 TUHI 1054.10/1. Swiss Consulate General at Kanagawa, 12 January 1865, (copy of a) letter in Dutch from Lindau, Swiss consul, to the Japanese commissioners of foreign affairs at Edo; Sôsenji, 22 February 1865, 8 p.m. (copy of a) letter in Dutch from Ed. Schnell, Swiss Chancellor, to the Japanese commissioners of foreign affairs at Edo. See also: Minato City Local History Museum 2005, pp. 68-69.

291 Minato City Local History Museum 2005, pp. 60-63.

292 MOFA Belgium 2098. Yokohama, 7 August 1866, Indicateur A no. 3, order no. 56 from t'Kint de Roodenbeek to the Belgian minister of Foreign Affairs Charles Rogier, registered in Brussels on 26 October 1866.

293 Aimé Humbert gave a detailed description of Van Polsbroek's residence at Benten. See Humbert 1870, pp. 52-75.

294 TUHI. MOFA Netherlands 1865. Microfilm 6951-54-7/8; microfilm outprint no. 7551-56-53, pp. 17-64. Kanagawa, 17 March 1865, dispatch no. 13/18 from Van Polsbroek to the Dutch Ministry of Foreign Affairs, registered there on 22 May 1865.

295 TUHI. MOFA Netherlands 1865. Microfilm 6951-54-7/8; microfilm outprint no. 7551-56-54, pp. 2-3. Kanagawa, 31 March 1865, dispatch no. 19/26 from Van Polsbroek to the Dutch Ministry of Foreign Affairs, registered there on 2 June 1865. – Also: TUHI. Dutch Consulate General 1864-1866. Anno 1865 (1), No. 1-36. Original Reference: Het Nationaal Archief, Het Ministerie van Buitenlandse Zaken. Inventory no. 2.05.15. Consulate Yokohama, Archives no. 16. Microfilm 6951-2-8-3; microfilm outprint no. 7551-48-5, pp. 91-92. – Kanagawa, 31 March 1865, draft despatch no. 19/26 from Van Polsbroek to the Dutch minister of foreign affairs in The Hague.

296 TUHI. LJ36. "Stukken over de Legatie te Yedo". 5 May 1865, exhibit no. 129, letter in French from Robert Lundh, Commander of *Le Varaique* (?) to Van Polsbroek, dated Yokohama, Corvette "Le Varaique"(?), 5 April 1865; Yokohama, 5 April 1865, letter no. 129 from the Commander of the Russian warship *Varaigne* (?).

297 University of Tokyo Volume VI 1966, vol. 87, FO46 (243) (YAH microfilm outprint no. Ca4/01.9/243, pp. 124-152). Yokohama, 26 July 1865, dispatch no. 15 from Parkes to Russell. Also, Japan Correspondence vol. 87, FO46 (244) (YAH microfilm outprint no. Ca4/01.9/244, pp. 256-306). Edo, 16 March 1867, copy of dispatch no. 41(?) from Parkes to Stanley.

298 TUHI 1054.04/3, p. 29. Kanagawa, 16 January 1866, no. 8/24, (copy of a) letter in Dutch from L. Tkleintjes, Chancellor at the Dutch legation in Japan, to the commissioners of foreign affairs in Edo. Same letter at: TUHI. LJ36. "Stukken over de Legatie te Yedo". – N.P. Kingdon took up the post of Portuguese consul at Kanagawa in 1864, and was replaced by Edward Loureiro in January 1868. See Kawasaki 1988, p. 184, pp. 186-187, pp. 189-190, p. 192 and p. 194.

299 TUHI. LJ36. "Stukken over de Legatie te Yedo". Edo, 22 September 1865, draft dispatch no. 52/62 in Dutch from Van Polsbroek to the Dutch minister of foreign affairs at The Hague; 24 September 1865, dispatch no. 110/238 to the Dutch minister of foreign affairs at The Hague; 9 January 1866, exhibit no. 12, letter from the "Assistant" (?) of the Dutch legation to Tamoe (?) To Hiojo no Kami, commissioner of foreign affairs, dated Edo, 24 September 1865.

300 See for example: TUHI. LJ36. "Stukken over de Legatie te Yedo". Kanagawa, 20 February 1866, draft letter no. 31/81 from Polsbroek to the Japanese commissioners of foreign affairs.

301 TUHI. LJ36. "Stukken over de Legatie te Yedo". Edo, 8 October 1866, draft dispatch no. 146/325 from Van Polsbroek to the Japanese commissioners of foreign affairs at Edo.

302 TUHI 1055.8/1 Belgium, 1st letter. 3 January 1866 (17th day of 11th month of Keiô 1), copy of letter in Dutch from Mizuno Izumi no Kami (Mizuno Tadakiyo) to Augustus t'Kint van Roodenbeek. – The Japanese text of this letter was published in Isomi et al. 1989, p. 40. Copy of the Japanese text is also kept at: TUHI Ishin 6, p. 256. D.I.S.K. 2408 (2415), p. 20. Microfilm reproduction REEL no. Keiô 慶応 – 036, pictures 924.tiff – 925.tiff.

303 In 1863, Itakura Katsuyo bore the title of Suô no Kami 周防守, while in 1866 his title was Iga no Kami 伊賀守. Ogasawara Nagamichi bore in 1863 the title of Zusho no Kami 図書頭 while in 1866 he was addressed with the title Iki no Kami 壱岐守.

304 TUHI Ishin 6, p. 256. D.I.S.K. 2408 (2415), p. 7 and pp. 18-19. Microfilm reproduction REEL no. Keiô 慶応 – 036, picture 903.tiff and 921.tiff – 923.tiff. Japanese dispatch from Mizuno Izumi no Kami (Mizuno Tadakiyo) to Itakura Iga no Kami (Itakura Katsukiyo) and Ogasawara Iki no Kami (Ogasawara Nagamichi) in Osaka, dated 2 January 1866 (16th day of the 11th month of Keiô 1).

305 MOFA Belgium 2098. Yokohama, 12 January 1866. Indicateur A no. 3, Order no. 30 from t'Kint de Roodenbeek to Charles Rogier in Brussels. According to a letter from Polsbroek to the Japanese councillor of foreign affairs, the date for the meeting was set as the 24th day of the 10th (sic: 11th) month (of Keiô 1), corresponding with 11 January 1866. See TUHI 1054.04/3, pp. 21-22. Edo, 6 January 1866, no. 4/10 (copy of a) letter in Dutch from D. de Graeff van Polsbroek to the Japanese councillor in charge of foreign affairs in Edo. The meeting took place on 10 January 1866.

306 TUHI 1054.04/3, pp. 21-22. Edo, 6 January 1866, no. 4/10 (copy of a) letter in Dutch from D. de Graeff van Polsbroek to the Japanese councillors in charge of foreign affairs in Edo. Japanese translation in TUHI Ishin 6, p. 256. D.I.S.K. 2408 (2415), pp. 24-25. Microfilm reproduction REEL no. Keiô 慶応 – 036, pictures 929.tiff – 931.tiff. Since the Dutch steamship *Zoutman* was anchored in Yokohama, the journey back and forth cannot have been on board this ship. While the *Zoutman* was anchored at Yokohama on 8 January 1866, it gave 11 salutes in recognition of the salutes fired by the French station ship for the Dutch consul general. This would signify that Van Polsbroek was at least in Yokohama on that day. See NAN Scheepsjournalen, Inv. nr. 5290, Scheepsjournaal Schroefstoomschip 2de klas *Zoutman*, folio 200, 8 January 1866.

307 University of Tokyo Volume VI 1966, vol. 87, FO46 (179) (YAH microfilm outprint no. Ca4/01.9/179, pp. 7-32). Yokohama, 16 January 1866, dispatch no. 2 from Parkes to Clarendon, in particular the 3rd page of the meeting minutes (marked p. 15), made by Dr. Willis, of a meeting between Parkes and the Japanese commissioners on 10 January 1866. This meeting started at 11 a.m. and took 3 hours. The meeting between t'Kint and Van Polsbroek on the one hand and the same Japanese commissioners on the other hand can therefore only have started at 2 p.m. at the earliest on the same day.

308 MOFA Belgium 2098. Yokohama, 12 January 1866. Indicateur A no. 3, Order no. 30 from t'Kint de Roodenbeek to Charles Rogier in Brussels.

309 University of Tokyo Volume VI 1966, vol. 87, FO46 (179) (YAH microfilm outprint no. Ca4/01.9/179, pp. 7-32). Yokohama, 16 January 1866, dispatch no. 2 from Parkes to Clarendon. According to Parkes, also "second councils" (wakadoshiyori 若年寄) Inaba Hyōbu Masami 稲葉兵部正巳 and Matsudaira Nui no Kami 松平縫守 participated to the meeting on 10 January 1866. According to a note in a Japanese diary, dated 10 January 1866 (24th day of the 11th month of Keiō 1) at least Mizuno, Matsudaira Yasuhide and Inaba participated to the meeting with the Dutch and Belgian envoys. See TUHI Ishin 6, p. 256. D.I.S.K. 2408 (2415), p. 30. Microfilm reproduction REEL no. Keiō 慶応 – 036, pictures 939.tiff – 940.tiff. – Matsudaira Yasuhide was mentioned with the title of Suō no Kami 周防守.

310 A Japanese note dated 14 January 1866 (28th day of the 11th month of Keiō 1) from Hirayama Kenjirō, commissioner of foreign affairs, indicates that during this meeting on 10 January 1866, t'Kint presented his credentials. A Japanese version of the Letter of Credence of 14 December 1864, with 10 January 1866 (24th day of the 11th month of Keiō 1) added, is attached to this note, and kept at: TUHI Ishin 6, p. 256. D.I.S.K. 2408 (2415), pp. 27-29. Microfilm reproduction REEL no. Keiō 慶応 – 036, pictures 934.tiff – 939.tiff. See also Isomi et al. 1989, p. 40.

311 Matsudaira replaced Sakai Tadashige 酒井忠績 who was great elder (tairō 大老) of the shogun, and who was dismissed on 29 December 1865.

312 MOFA Belgium 2098. Yokohama, 12 January 1866. Indicateur A no. 3, Order no. 30 from t'Kint de Roodenbeek to Charles Rogier in Brussels.

313 University of Tokyo Volume VI 1966, vol. 87, FO46 (179) (YAH microfilm outprint no. Ca4/01.9/179, pp. 7-32). Yokohama, 16 January 1866, dispatch no. 2 from Parkes to Clarendon, in particular the first two pages (pp. 7-8).

314 Kitane 1987 (volume 7), p. 37. Japan Times 1:17 (Yokohama, 29 Dec 1865), p. 102.

315 This probably refers to Sakai Tadamasu 酒井忠毗 (1815-1876) who served as a junior councillor (wakadoshiyori 若年寄) of foreign affairs in the Bakumatsu period.

316 University of Tokyo Volume VI 1966, vol. 87, FO46 (179) (YAH microfilm outprint no. Ca4/01.9/179, pp. 7-32). Yokohama, 16 January 1866, dispatch no. 2 from Parkes to Clarendon, in particular the 3rd, 4th and 5th pages (marked pp. 8-9).

317 University of Tokyo Volume VI 1966, vol. 87, FO46 (179) (YAH microfilm outprint no. Ca4/01.9/179, pp. 7-32). Yokohama, 16 January 1866, dispatch no. 2 from Parkes to Clarendon, in particular the 3rd and 4th pages of the meeting minutes (marked pp. 15-16), made by Dr. Willis.

318 University of Tokyo Volume VI 1966, vol. 65, FO46 (179) (YAH microfilm outprint no. Ca4/01.9/179, pp. 101-102). Yokohama, 17 January 1866, dispatch no. 11 from Parkes to Clarendon. A draft version of this dispatch can be found at: University of Tokyo Volume VII 1967, Japan Correspondence (despatches from Parkes to F.O. 1866), vol. 107, FO262 (131) (YAH microfilm outprint no. Ca4/01.20/131, pp. 21-22).

319 MOFA Belgium 2098. Brussels, 23 March 1866, English letter from Howard de Walden et Seaford to Belgian minister of Foreign Affairs Charles Rogier, stamped in Brussels on 26 March 1866, B no. 2483 and 6017.

320 MOFA Belgium 2098. Kanagawa, 14 Jan 1866, no. 5/21, letter in French from D. de Graeff van Polsbroek to Auguste t'Kint de Roodenbeek. The archives have only preserved the cover letter of Van Polsbroek's dispatch to t'Kint. The attachment with the communication between Van Polsbroek and the Japanese government is missing. It is therefore not absolutely sure that the communication referred to the meeting of 10 January 1866, since it is not mentioned in the cover letter, but this is very likely.

321 T'Kint sent his dispatch no. 30 (about his meeting with the Japanese councillors) on 12 January 1866 from Yokohama. See MOFA Belgium 2098. Yokohama, 12 January 1866. Indicateur A no. 3, Order no. 30 from t'Kint de Roodenbeek to Charles Rogier in Brussels.

322 NAN Scheepsjournalen. Zoutman scheepsjournaal inv. nr. 5291, Folio 7, "Woensdag 24 januari 1866". The Dutch war vessel Zoutman fired 11 salvoes in recognition of the salute given to the Dutch political agent Van Polsbroek by the Guerrière. The Zoutman also saluted the French Rear Admiral and the Belgian minister (t'Kint).

323 MOFA Belgium 2098. Yokohama, 31 January 1866. Indicateur A no. 3, order no. 32 from t'Kint de Roodenbeek to Charles Rogier in Brussels.

324 Kitane 1987, vol. 7, p. 150. Japan Times 1:21 (26 Jan 1866), p. 132.

325 Kitane 1987, vol. 7, p. 127. Nippon Shinbun 204 (20 Jan 1864 [sic; should be 1866] – [Keiō 1] 12th month 4th day).

326 Kitane 1987, vol. 7, pp. 161-162. Nippon Shinbun 205 (27 Jan 1866 – [Keiō 1] 12th month 11th day).

327 MOFA Belgium 2098. Yokohama, 31 January 1866. Indicateur A no. 3, order no. 32 from t'Kint de Roodenbeek to Charles Rogier in Brussels.

328 Kitane 1987, vol. 7, p. 204. Japan Times 1:23 (9 Feb 1866), p. 149, under "The Week". The arrival of the Granada in Yokohama is mentioned in the same newspaper on the front page.

329 Kitane 1987, vol. 7, p. 143. Japan Times' Daily Advertiser. Second Edition (Yokohama, 24 Jan 1866). The telegrams arrived in Bombay and were then brought by ship to Yokohama. The article mentions "Thacken (?)" instead of Laken or Laeken, the location of the palace that served as the residence of Leopold I.

330 Kitane 1987, vol. 7, p. 156. Nippon Shinbun 21 (26 Jan 1866 – (Keiō) gannen 12th month 10th day).

331 Examples of this communication can be found in following archives: To the Japanese councillors in charge of foreign affairs: TUHI 1054.08. Yokohama, 7 February 1866, letter in Dutch from Aug. t'Kint de Roodenbeek to the Japanese commissioners of foreign affairs in Edo. To the British minister: University of Tokyo Volume VII 1967, Correspondence from various persons to Parkes, 1866, vol. 119, FO262 (148), pp. 66-67 (YAH microfilm outprint no. Ca4/01.20/148, pp. 70-71). Mission Extraordinaire de Belgique, Yokohama, 7 February 1866, French dispatch from t'Kint de Roodenbeek to Parkes. Copy: University of Tokyo Volume VI 1966, vol. 65, FO46 (180), pp. 194-195. (YAH microfilm outprint Ca4/01.9/180, pp. 63-64). To the American chargé d'affaires: University of Tokyo Volume IX and Volume X 1968 Legation in Japan. US National Archives, RG 84, T400. N.A. T400 (87) Vol. 44(1) (20 December 1865 – 26 April 1866). (YAH microfilm outprint no. Ca4/01.14/87, p. 39). Mission Extraordinaire de Belgique, Yokohama, 7 February 1866, French dispatch from t'Kint de Roodenbeek to Portman. – To the Swiss consul: University of Tokyo Volume XI Switzerland 5-2. Actes reçus. 7 February 1866, acte no. 24, from the minister of Belgium.

332 Examples of these communications can be found at following archives. From the Japanese commissioners: TUHI 1055.8/1 Belgium, 2nd letter. 8 February 1866 (23rd day of the 12th month of Keiō 1), (copy of) a letter in Dutch from Mizuno Izumi no Kami (Mizuno Tadakiyo) and Matsudaira Suō no Kami (Matsudaira Yasuhide) to t'Kint de Roodenbeek. From the British minister: University of Tokyo Volume VII 1967, Correspondence from Parkes to various persons, 1866 – drafts, vol. 121, FO262 (153), pp. 28-29 (YAH microfilm outprint no. Ca4/01.20/153, pp. 28-29). British Legation, Yokohama, 7 February 1866, draft dispatch no. 14 from Parkes to t'Kint. From the Swiss consul: University of Tokyo Volume XI Switzerland 5-2. Actes expédiés. 7 February 1866, acte no. 17, to "t'Kint, Ministre Belge".

333 MOFA Belgium – Japon Politique. Yokohama, 14 February 1866, Mission Extraordinaire de Belgique, Litta C No. 1 – No. d'ordre 33. Dispatch from Auguste t'Kint to Charles Rogier.

334 Kitane 1987, vol. 7, p. 204. Japan Times 1:23 (9 Feb 1866), p. 149, under "The week" and under "Miscellaneous".

335 Kitane 1987, vol. 7, p. 181. Nippon Shinbun 23 (9 Feb 1866 – (Keiō) gannen 12th month 24th day).

336 Kitane 1987, vol. 7, pp. 228-229. The Japan Times 1:24 (17 Feb 1866), pp. 158-159.

337 MOFA Belgium 2704 III. Brussels, 1 December 1865, Minute containing draft letter from the Belgian minister of foreign affairs to t'Kint, consul general in Shanghai, China, Indicateur B no. 1746/2483, order no. 89. Also at: MOFA Belgium 2098.

338 For the visit of the Satsuma mission to Belgium and the involvement of Charles, Count de Montblanc d'Ingelmunster (1833-1894), see Vande Walle 1996, pp. 151-176 and Vande Walle 2005, pp. 140-157.

339 MOFA Belgium 10819/15. Brussels, 10 October 1865, Minute Indicateur A. No. 4332, containing a draft letter from the Belgian Ministry of Foreign Affairs to the minister of the royal household.

340 This is not correct. The Satsuma mission came from England first to Belgium, and went later to France. See Vande Walle 1996, p. 170.

341 Nihon Keieishi Kenkyūjo 1974, p. 30. According to Vande Walle 1996, p. 168, the most likely date for this meeting was 9 October 1865. This is one day before the date of the draft letter to the minister of the royal household. For Godai Tomoatsu 五代友厚 (1836-1885), see the website of bakusin, "Godai" (accessed 19 Dec 2015), http://www.bakusin.com/godai.html.

342 Nihon Keieishi Kenkyūjo 1974, p. 30.

343 MOFA Belgium 10819/15. Brussels, 13 October 1865, Minute Indicateur A. No. 4332, with draft urgent letter from the Belgian Ministry of Foreign Affairs to Count de Montblanc, Hôtel de l'Europe, Brussels.

344 See Wikipedia, s.v. "Jules Van Praet" (accessed 12 Sep 2015), https://nl.wikipedia.org/wiki/Jules_Van_Praet.

345 MOFA Belgium 2098. Brussels, 14 October 1865. Minutes of Belgian Ministry of Foreign Affairs containing a draft letter to the governors of the provinces of Liège, Ghent and Namur, Indicateur B no. 2483 (no order number).

346 *Nihon Keieishi Kenkyūjo* 1974, p. 30. An English translation of this note can be found in Vande Walle 1996, p. 169; a Japanese version at TUHI Ishin 6, p. 192. D.I.S.K. 2366, pp. 31-49. Microfilm reproduction REEL no. Keiō 慶応 – 027, pictures 313.tiff – 335.tiff.

347 *Nihon Keieishi Kenkyūjo* 1974, pp. 50-51. The names of the two witnesses according to the Japanese text of the contract are Yudowardo Denreru ユドワルド・デンレル and Aruzoru Renīsu アルゾル・レニース. The first name is likely to be Edouard Degrelle. The second name has not yet been identified (Arthur Denijs ?). A short description of the contract in English is given by Vande Walle 1996, p. 169.

348 NAB Rogier 2301. Brussels, 11 December 1863, letter from the Italian minister, comte de Montalto, to Charles Rogier, sending the decoration and diploma of Knight in the Order of Saints Maurice and Lazarus, bestowed by Prince Amadeo of Savoy to Edouard de Grelle, followed by an undated draft reply, (probably) from Charles Rogier, mentioning three times that Edouard Degrelle is his nephew ("mon neveu"), and describing himself as Degrelle's uncle ("l'oncle"). Furthermore, the same Archives of Charles Rogier contain correspondence with several officials of the Belgian Foreign Ministry, among whom Edouard Degrelle. See file no. I.124-115 (Microfilm 2300).

349 *Nihon Keieishi Kenkyūjo* 1974, p. 30. Own English translation of Godai's note.

350 MOFA Belgium 10819/15, Brussels, 18 October 1865, Minute Indicateur A. no. 4332, containing a draft letter from the Belgian Ministry of Foreign Affairs to the Belgian minister of the army and war in Brussels; 21 October 1865, 21/8re, 16094, A 4332, letter from the Belgium Ministry of War (Ministère de la Guerre – Cabinet) to the Belgian minister of foreign affairs in Brussels.

351 *Nihon Keieishi Kenkyūjo* 1974, pp. 31-34, and Vande Walle 1996, pp. 169-170.

352 NAB Rogier 2300. A note for the foreign minister, dated 21 November 1865, made by Edouard Degrelle. The note bears the date of 21 November 1865, but it looks like this date was added afterwards.

353 Eventually de Montblanc did not receive this decoration in 1865 or 1866. However, the title of Knight in the Order of Leopold was bestowed upon him by a Royal Decree of 11 August 1890. See MOFA Belgium 1890, volume 3, p. 84, no. 9808.

354 MOFA Belgium 2704 III. Brussels, 1 December 1865, Minute containing draft letter from the Belgian Ministry of Foreign Affairs to t'Kint, consul general in Shanghai, China, Indicateur B no. 1746/2483, order no. 89.

355 NAB Rogier 2300. A note for the foreign minister, dated 21 November 1865, made by Edouard Degrelle.

356 It must be said that this is only a hypothesis. No tangible evidence has been found in the archives that the Ministry was deliberately excluding its diplomats abroad from the discussion.

357 This dispatch was registered in the Belgian Ministry in Brussels as incoming mail on 1 February 1866. See MOFA Belgium 2098. Shanghai, 8 December 1865, Indicateur A no. 2, dispatch order no. 23 from t'Kint de Roodenbeek to Charles Rogier in Brussels.

358 MOFA Belgium 2098. Brussels, 1 February 1866, internal note Indicateur no. 2483.

359 MOFA Belgium 2704 III. Yokohama, 14 February 1866, dispatch from t'Kint to Belgian MOFA minister Charles Rogier, Litt A no. 3, No. ordre 34, registered in Brussels on 10 April, 6898, B1746/2483. Also at MOFA Belgium 2098.

360 MOFA Belgium 2098. Brussels, 27 Feb 1866. Minute of the Belgian Ministry of Foreign Affairs. Indicateur no. 2483, no. 19, with 1 annex.

361 The Ministry registered this dispatch as incoming mail on 9 February 1866. See MOFA Belgium 2098. Yokohama, 18 December 1865. Indicateur A no. 3, dispatch with order no. 26 from t'Kint de Roodenbeek to Charles Rogier in Brussels.

362 MOFA Belgium 2098. Brussels, 5 March 1866, Minute, Indicateur B no. 2483, containing the draft dispatch order no. 93 from the Belgian Foreign Ministry to Mr t'Kint in Yokohama, at Mr D. de Graeff van Polsbroek, consul general of the Netherlands in Japan.

363 University of Tokyo Volume XIII 1965 Consulaire, volume 4, pp. 126-127 (YAH microfilm outprint no. Ca4/01.31/12, pp. 137-138). 9 November 1865, draft dispatch from the French Foreign Ministry to Léon Roches in Edo.

364 University of Tokyo Volume XIII 1965 Consulaire, volume 4, pp. 165-166 (YAH microfilm outprint no. Ca4/01.31/13, pp. 20-21). Consulate General of France in Japan, Yokohama, 26 January 1866, dispatch no. 52 (Directions des Consulats) from Léon Roches to Drouyn de Lhuys (French foreign minister) in Paris, stamped there on 26 March 1866, no. 2859.

365 MOFA Belgium 2704 III. Yokohama, 14 February 1866, Litt A no. 3, dispatch with order no. 34 from Auguste t'Kint to Charles Rogier, stamped in Brussels on 10 April, 6898, B1746/2483. See also MOFA Belgium 2098.

366 University of Tokyo Volume VI 1966, vol. 65, FO46 (180), pp. 199-203. (YAH microfilm outprint Ca4/01.9/180, pp. 56-60). Yokohama, 14 February 1866, dispatch no. 24 from Parkes to Clarendon. – A draft version of this dispatch can be found at: University of Tokyo Volume VII 1967, despatches from Parkes to F.O. 1866), vol. 107, FO262 (131), pp. 61-62 (YAH microfilm outprint no. Ca4/01.20/131, pp. 61-62). Parkes mentioned in his dispatch that he had met two Japanese commissioners at Edo, Mizuno Iyo no Kami and Matsudaira *Hōki* no Kami. The latter name is probably a mistake. Matsudaira Hōki no Kami (Matsudaira Munehide) was in Osaka at the time. Parkes probably met his colleague Matsudaira *Suō* no Kami (Matsudaira Yasuhide), who was then based in Edo.

367 TUHI Ishin 6, p. 277. D.I.S.K. 2424 (2433), pp. 12-14. Microfilm reproduction REEL no. Keiō 慶応 – 040, pictures 0023.tiff – 0026.tiff. 9 February 1866 (24th day of the 12th month of Keiō 1), dispatch from Ogasawara Iki no Kami (Ogasawara Nagamichi), Matsudaira Hōki no Kami 松平伯耆守 (Matsudaira Munehide 1809-1873) and Itakura Iga no Kami (Itakura Katsukiyo) to Mizuno Izumi no Kami (Mizuno Tadakiyo).

368 TUHI Ishin 6, p. 277. D.I.S.K. 2424 (2433), pp. 17-18. Microfilm reproduction REEL no. Keiō 慶応 – 040, pictures 0030.tiff – 0031.tiff. 14 February 1866 (29th day of the 12th month of Keiō 1), dispatch from Mizuno Izumi no Kami (Mizuno Tadakiyo) to Ogasawara Iki no Kami (Ogasawara Nagamichi), Matsudaira Hōki no Kami (Matsudaira Munehide) and Itakura Iga no Kami (Itakura Katsukiyo).

369 TUHI Ishin 6, p. 277. D.I.S.K. 2424 (2433), pp. 15-16. Microfilm reproduction REEL no. Keiō 慶応 – 040, pictures 0027.tiff – 0029.tiff. 13 February 1866 (28th day of the 12th month of Keiō 1), dispatch from Mizuno Izumi no Kami (Mizuno Tadakiyo) to Ogasawara Iki no Kami (Ogasawara Nagamichi), Matsudaira Hōki no Kami (Matsudaira Munehide) and Itakura Iga no Kami (Itakura Katsukiyo).

370 TUHI Ishin 6, p. 277. D.I.S.K. 2424 (2433), pp. 19-21. Microfilm reproduction REEL no. Keiō 慶応 – 040, pictures 0032.tiff – 0037.tiff. 17 February 1866 [3rd day of the 1st month (shōgatsu) (of Keiō 2)], dispatch from Mizuno Izumi no Kami (Mizuno Tadakiyo) to Ogasawara Iki no Kami (Ogasawara Nagamichi), Matsudaira Hōki no Kami (Matsudaira Munehide) and Itakura Iga no Kami (Itakura Katsukiyo). See also: TUHI Ishin 6, p. 300. D.I.S.K. 2438 (2449), p. 38 and p. 41. Microfilm reproduction REEL no. Keiō 慶応 – 042, pictures 0833.tiff – 0834.tiff and 0840.tiff – 0842.tiff.

371 TUHI Ishin 6, p. 300. D.I.S.K. 2438 (2449), p. 37, pp. 39-40 and pp. 45-47. Microfilm reproduction REEL no. Keiō 慶応 – 042, pictures 0832.tiff, 0836.tiff – 0838.tiff and 0849.tiff – 0851.tiff. Ōkubo Chikugo no Kami 大久保筑後守 might refer to Ōkubo Tadatsune 大久保忠恒 who was the last one to hold both the title of Chikugo no Kami and of *metsuke* before the Meiji Restoration in 1868. See the Japanese website "中村藩十代藩主相馬樹" (accessed 19 Dec 2015), http://members.jcom.home.ne.jp/bamen1/hanshu33.htm.

372 University of Tokyo Volume IX and Volume X 1968 Ministers. US National Archives, RG 59, M133, N.A. 133 (21) Vol. 5-1 (4 January – 12 February 1864). (YAH microfilm outprint no. Ca4/01.4/21, pp. 73-74). Benten (Yokohama), 24 January 1864, English translation of a dispatch from Aimé Humbert to General Pruyn.

373 TUHI Ishin 6, p. 300. D.I.S.K. 2438 (2449), p. 43. Microfilm reproduction REEL no. Keiō 慶応 – 042, pictures 0845.tiff – 0846.tiff. 28 February 1866 [14th day of the 1st month (shōgatsu) (of Keiō 2)] Japanese version of a dispatch from Mizuno Izumi no Kami (Mizuno Tadakiyo) and Matsudaira Suō no Kami (Matsudaira Yasuhide) to Auguste t'Kint de Roodenbeek. Dutch translation at TUHI 1055.8/1 Belgium, 3rd letter. (Copy of) an undated letter in Dutch to Augustus t'Kint van Roodenbeek.

374 TUHI 1054.08, pp. 23-24. Yokohama, 3 March 1866, letter in Dutch from Aug. t'Kint de Roodenbeek to the Japanese commissioners of foreign affairs in Edo. Japanese translation at TUHI Ishin 6, p. 300. D.I.S.K. 2438 (2449), p. 44 and p. 48. Microfilm reproduction REEL no. Keiō 慶応 – 042, pictures 0847.tiff – 0848.tiff and 0853.tiff – 0854.tiff.

375 MOFA Belgium 2098. Yokohama, 14 March 1866. Indicateur A no. 3, dispatch with order no. 36 from t'Kint de Roodenbeek to Charles Rogier, stamped in Brussels on 12 May 1866.

376 University of Tokyo Volume VI 1966, vol. 67, FO46 (185), Despatches from Harry S. Parkes to Foreign Office February-April 1866, pp. 216-219. (YAH microfilm outprint Ca4/01.9/185, pp. 56-60). Yokohama, 16 March 1866, dispatch no. 53 from Parkes to Clarendon. A draft version of this dispatch can be found at University of Tokyo Volume VII 1967, despatches from Parkes to F.O., 1866, vol. 107, FO262 (131), pp. 127-129 (YAH microfilm outprint no. Ca4/01.20/131, pp. 129-131).

377 University of Tokyo Volume VI 1966, vol. 67, FO46 (185), Despatches from Harry S. Parkes to Foreign Office February-April 1866, pp. 220-225. (YAH microfilm outprint Ca4/01.9/185, pp. 104-109). 15 March 1866, English translation of a dispatch from Mizuno Izumi no Kami (Mizuno Tadakiyo) and Matsudaira Suō no Kami (Matsudaira Yasuhide) to Harry Parkes. A draft translation can be found at University of Tokyo Volume VII 1967, Japan Correspondence (January-December 1866: English version of communication from Japan to the British Legation), vol. 486, FO262 (697), pp. 13-15 (YAH microfilm outprint no. Ca4/01.20/697, pp. 16-18).

378 TUHI 1055.4/3. 28 March 1866 (12th day of the 2nd month of Keiō 2), Mizuno Izumi no Kami (Mizuno Tadakiyo) and Matsudaira Suō no Kami (Matsudaira Yasuhide) to D. de Graeff van Polsbroek.

379 Kitane 1987, vol. 7, pp. 329-330. *Japan Times* 1:28 (16 Mar 1866), pp. 186-187. – On 27 April 1866, the *Japan Times* renewed its call for treaty negotiations with a confederation of feudal lords. See Kitane 1987, vol. 8, p. 94. *Japan Times* 1:33 (28 [*sic*: should be 27] Apr 1866), p. 223, under "The Week". This opinion was also published in the hand-written Japanese newspaper *Nippon Shinbun*. See Kitane 1987, vol. 8, p. 100. *Nippon Shinbun* 33 (27 Apr 1866 [13th day of 3rd month of Keiō 2]).

380 MOFA Belgium 2098. Yokohama, 16 April 1866. Indicateur A no. 3, duplicate and original of dispatch order no. 38 from t'Kint de Roodenbeek to Charles Rogier, registered in Brussels on 9 June 1866.

381 For example, in its communication with the Dutch representative De Graeff van Polsbroek concerning a request for treaty negotiations with Denmark, the government of the shogun argued on 26 April 1866 that, even though the emperor had ratified the foreign treaties, the situation of Japan did not allow the conclusion of any additional treaties. See TUHI 1054.04/3, pp. 179-183. Kanagawa, 10 August 1866, (copy of) a Dutch dispatch no. 104/259 from D. de Graeff van Polsbroek to the Japanese commissioners of foreign affairs at Edo, referring to a dispatch of the Japanese commissioners of the 12th day of the 3rd month (of Keiō 2), being 26 April 1866.

382 TUHI 1054.08, p. 25. Yokohama, 19 March 1866, letter in Dutch from Auguste t'Kint to Kikuchi Iyo no Kami (Kikuchi Takayoshi), Hoshino Bitchū no Kami (Hoshino Kazuyuki) and Ōkubo Chikugo no Kami. – A Japanese translation can be found at: TUHI Ishin 6, p. 326. D.I.S.K. 2459 (2472), pp. 38-40. Microfilm reproduction REEL no. Keiō 慶応 – 046, pictures 0944.tiff – 0947.tiff.

383 TUHI 1054.08, pp. 31-32 (French), p. 37 (Dutch). Yokohama, 31 May 1866, letter in French and Dutch from Auguste t'Kint to Kikuchi Iyo no Kami (Kikuchi Takayoshi), Hoshino Bitchū no Kami (Hoshino Kazuyuki) and Ōkubo Chikugo no Kami, plenipotentiaries of the shogun. Also MOFA Belgium 2098. Yokohama, 29 May 1866, Mission Extraordinaire de Belgique, draft dispatch from t'Kint de Roodenbeek to Kikuchi Iyo no Kami (Kikuchi Takayoshi), Hoshino Bitchū no Kami (Hoshino Kazuyuki) and Ōkubo Chikugo no Kami, plenipotentiaries of the shogun in Edo. – Japanese version can be found at: TUHI Ishin 6, p. 426. D.I.S.K. 2539 (2554), pp. 119-121. Microfilm reproduction REEL no. Keiō 慶応 – 061, pictures 1056.tiff and 1057.tiff – 1058.tiff.

384 MOFA Belgium 2098. Yokohama, 16 April 1866. Indicateur A no. 3, duplicate and original of dispatch order no. 38 from t'Kint de Roodenbeek to Charles Rogier, registered in Brussels on 9 June 1866.

385 MOFA Belgium 2098. Yokohama, 10 May 1866. Indicateur A no. 3, duplicate of the dispatch with order no. 42 from t'Kint de Roodenbeek to Charles Rogier, registered in Brussels on 12 July 1866.

386 TUHI Ishin 6, p. 426. D.I.S.K. 2539 (2554), p. 123. Microfilm reproduction REEL no. Keiō 慶応 – 061, pictures 1061.tiff – 1062.tiff. 4 May 1866 [20th day of the 3rd month (of Keiō 2)]. A draft note in Japanese addressed to the English minister (*Eikoku kōshi* 英国公使). We did not find any trace of this note in the archives of the English legation in Tokyo.

387 MOFA Belgium 2704 III. Yokohama, 10 May 1866, Litt. A no. 1, dispatch with order no. 41 from Aug. t'Kint de Roodenbeek to Charles Rogier, registered in Brussels on 12 July 1866, B 1746 no. 12380.

388 MOFA Belgium 2704 III. Brussels, 10 March 1866. Ind. B no. 1746. Minute containing draft letter with order no. 96 from the Belgian Ministry of Foreign Affairs to Aug. t'Kint in Shanghai, China. For more information on the activities of Jules Adrian in Nagasaki, see the website of *Nagasaki Foreign Settlement*, "Nagasaki. People, Places and Scenes of the Nagasaki Foreign Settlement 1859-1941," (accessed 19 Dec 2015), http://www.nfs.nias.ac.jp/page030.html.

389 MOFA Belgium 2704 III. Brussels, 1 December 1865, Indicateur B no. 1746/2483. Minute containing draft letter with order no. 89 from the Belgian Ministry of Foreign Affairs to t'Kint, consul general in Shanghai.

390 MOFA Belgium 2704 III. Brussels, 10 March 1866. Indicateur B no. 1746. Minute containing a draft letter from the Belgian Ministry of Foreign Affairs to J. Adrian in Paris.

391 MOFA Belgium 2704 III. Brussels, 10 March 1866. Ind. B no. 1746. Minute containing a draft letter with order no. 96 from the Belgian Ministry of Foreign Affairs to Aug. t'Kint in Shanghai, China. – Also: MOFA Belgium 2704 III. A small undated note (probably written mid-May 1866) within minute ordre no. 96 of 10 March 1866, bearing number B2483.

392 Kitane 1987, vol. 8, p. 133 and p. 140. *Japan Times* 1:35 (Yokohama, Friday, 11 May 1866), respectively front page and page 242.

393 TUHI 1054.08, p. 26. Yokohama, 16 May 1866, (copy of a) letter in Dutch from Auguste t'Kint de Roodenbeek to the Japanese commissioners of foreign affairs in Edo. – A Japanese translation can be found at: TUHI Ishin 6, p. 418. D.I.S.K. 2531 (2548), pp. 60-61. Microfilm reproduction REEL no. Keiō 慶応 – 060, pictures 0504.tiff – 0506.tiff.

394 TUHI 1054.08, pp. 27-30 (Dutch); pp. 33-35 (French). Yokohama, 31 May 1866, letter in Dutch and French from Aug. t'Kint de Rk. to the Japanese commissioners of foreign affairs in Edo. Also MOFA Belgium 2098. Yokohama, 30 May 1866, Mission Extraordinaire de Belgique, draft dispatch from t'Kint de Roodenbeek to the Japanese commissioners of foreign affairs in Edo; Japanese version at TUHI Ishin 6, p. 426. D.I.S.K. 2539 (2554), pp. 119-121. Microfilm reproduction REEL no. Keiō 慶応常 – 061, pictures 1055.tiff and 1057.tiff – 1058.tiff. Ishino Noritsune 石野則常, referred to with his title Chikuzen no Kami 筑前守, was commissioner of foreign affairs from 21 February 1866 (7th day of the 1st month of Keiō 2) till 1 November 1867 (6th day of the 10th month of Keiō 3). See Katō 2001, p. 12.

395 TUHI 1055.8/1 Belgium, 4th letter. 24 May 1866 (10th day of the 4th month of Keiō 2), (copy of) a letter in Dutch from Ishino Chikuzen no Kami (Ishino Noritsune) to Auguste t'Kint. The Japanese version can be found at TUHI Ishin 6, p. 418. D.I.S.K. 2531 (2548), p. 62. Microfilm reproduction REEL no. Keiō 慶応 – 060, pictures 0507.tiff – 0509.tiff.

396 University of Tokyo Volume XIII 1965 Politique, vol. 14, pp. 157-164 (YAH microfilm outprint no. Ca4/01.36/36, pp. 1-8. Yokohama, 27 May 1866, dispatch no. 63 from L. Roches to Drouyn de Lhuys (French minister of foreign affairs). On page 160, Roches wrote: "Malgré mes efforts et ceux de mon collègue d'Angleterre, l'Envoyé de Belgique n'a pu surmonter encore les difficultés opposées à l'accomplissement de sa mission" (Despite my efforts and those of my colleague from England, the Envoy of Belgium has not yet overcome the difficulties opposed to the accomplishment of his mission).

397 TUHI 1054.08, pp. 31-32 (French), p. 37 (Dutch). Yokohama, 31 May 1866, letter in French and Dutch from Auguste t'Kint to Kikuchi Iyo no Kami (Kikuchi Takayoshi), Hoshino Bitchū no Kami (Hoshino Kazuyuki) and Ōkubo Chikugo no Kami, plenipotentiaries of the shogun. Also MOFA Belgium 2098. Yokohama, 29 May 1866, Mission Extraordinaire de Belgique, draft dispatch from t'Kint de Roodenbeek to Kikuchi Iyo no Kami (Kikuchi Takayoshi), Hoshino Bitchū no Kami (Hoshino Kazuyuki) and Ōkubo Chikugo no Kami, plenipotentiaries of the shogun in Edo. A Japanese version can be found at: TUHI Ishin 6, p. 426. D.I.S.K. 2539 (2554), pp. 119-121. Microfilm reproduction REEL no. Keiō 慶応 – 061, pictures 1055.tiff and 1057.tiff – 1058.tiff.

398 TUHI 1054.08, pp. 27-30 (Dutch); pp. 33-35 (French). Yokohama, 31 May 1866, letter in Dutch and French from Aug. t'Kint de Rk. to the Japanese councillors in charge of foreign affairs in Edo. Also MOFA Belgium 2098. Yokohama, 30 May 1866, Mission Extraordinaire de Belgique, draft dispatch from t'Kint de Roodenbeek to the Japanese councillors in charge of foreign affairs in Edo. A Japanese translation can be found at: TUHI Ishin 6, p. 418. D.I.S.K. 2531 (2548), pp. 64-66. Microfilm reproduction REEL no. Keiō 慶応 – 060, pictures 0512.tiff – 0514.tiff. Also Isomi et al. 1989, p. 40.

399 The Japanese commissioners would finally propose receiving the letter from Leopold II during a meeting with t'Kint on 29 August 1866 at Edo. Due to bad weather, the meeting could not proceed, and t'Kint proposed rescheduling the meeting to around 10 September 1866. The Leopold's letter was finally presented to the shogun shortly before his death. See TUHI 1055.8/1 Belgium, 11th letter. 25 August 1866 (16th day of the 7th month of Keiō 2), (copy of a) letter in Dutch from the (Japanese) commissioners to "August de Kint"; 16th letter, not mentioned date in 1866 (...th day of the ...th month of Keiō 2), (copy of a) letter in Dutch from Inoue Kawachi no Kami (Inoue Masanao), Inaba Mino no Kami (Inaba Masakuni), Matsudaira Suō no Kami (Matsudaira Yasuhide) to the minister of foreign affairs of Belgium. Also TUHI 1054.08, pp. 59-61. Yokohama, 28 August 1866, letter in Dutch from Auguste t'Kint to the Japanese commissioners of foreign affairs in Edo; MOFA Belgium 2098. Yokohama, 26 August 1866, Buitengewone Zending van België, letter in Dutch (probably from t'Kint) to the Japanese commissioners of foreign affairs.

400 This refers to MOFA Belgium 2098. 11 June 1866: Yokohama, Indicateur A no. 3, duplicate of order no. 43 from t'Kint de Roodenbeek to Charles Rogier, registered in Brussels on 11 August 1866; Mission extraordinaire de Belgique, Litt. A no. 3, order no. 44, being a confidential letter from t'Kint de Roodenbeek to Charles Rogier, registered in Brussels on 11 August 1866. It is likely that both dispatches were taken on board the Messageries Impériales steamer Dupleix, which received cargo up till noon on 11 June 1866, and left Yokohama on 12 June 1866. See Kitane 1987, vol. 8, p. 230. *Daily Advertiser* 1:209 (9 Jun 1866), p. 805.

401 TUHI 1055.8/1 Belgium, 5th letter. 3 June 1866 (20th day of the 4th month of Keiō 2), (copy of a) letter in Dutch from Mizuno Izumi no Kami (Mizuno Tadakiyo) and Matsudaira Suō no Kami (Matsudaira Yasuhide) to August t'Kint. Japanese version can be found at: TUHI Ishin 6, p. 418. D.I.S.K. 2531 (2548), pp. 67-68. Microfilm reproduction REEL no. Keiō 慶応 – 060, pictures 0516.tiff – 0517.tiff.

402 TUHI 1055.8/1 Belgium, 6th letter. 5 June 1866 (22nd day of the 4th month of Keiō 2), (copy of a) letter in Dutch from the commissioners (of foreign affairs) to Auguste t'Kint; Japanese version at TUHI Ishin 6, p. 426. D.I.S.K. 2539 (2554), p. 122. Microfilm reproduction REEL no. Keiō 慶応 – 061, pictures 1056.tiff and 1059.tiff – 1061.tiff. Kikuchi Iyo no Kami (Kikuchi Takayoshi), Hoshino Bitchū no Kami (Hoshino Kazuyuki) and Ōkubo Chikugo no Kami to Auguste t'Kint.

403 University of Tokyo Volume VII 1967, Correspondence from various persons to Parkes, 1866, vol. 119, FO262 (149), pp. 239-240 (YAH microfilm outprint no. Ca4/01.20/149, pp. 86-88). Mission Extraordinaire de Belgique, Yokohama, 10 June 1866, original letter in French from t'Kint to Parkes. Copy of this French dispatch in University of Tokyo Volume VI 1966, vol. 69, FO46 (192), pp. 276-281. (YAH microfilm outprint no. Ca4/01.9/192, pp. 16-21).

404 University of Tokyo Volume VII 1967, Correspondence from various persons to Parkes, 1866, vol. 119, FO262 (149), pp. 251-253 (YAH microfilm outprint no. Ca4/01.20/149, pp. 101-103). Mission Extraordinaire de Belgique, Yokohama, 22 June 1866, original letter in French from t'Kint to Parkes. – Copy of this French dispatch: University of Tokyo Volume VI 1966, vol. 69, FO46 (192), pp. 276-281. (YAH microfilm outprint no. Ca4/01.9/192, pp. 16-21).

405 MOFA Belgium 2098. Yokohama, 27 June 1866. Indicateur A no. 3, duplicate of dispatch with order no. 45 from t'Kint de Roodenbeek to Charles Rogier, registered in Brussels on 27 August 1866.

406 Van Polsbroek sent the dispatch from Edo on 21 June 1866. See TUHI 1054.04/3, pp. 139-140. Edo, 21 June 1866, dispatch no. 80/202 from Polsbroek to the Japanese commissioners of foreign affairs at Edo. – t'Kint also mentioned that he received information from Van Polsbroek about the whereabouts of Harry Parkes while being in Edo. See University of Tokyo Volume VII 1967, Correspondence from various persons to Parkes, 1866, vol. 119, FO262 (149), pp. 251-253 (YAH microfilm outprint no. Ca4/01.20/149, pp. 101-103). Mission Extraordinaire de Belgique, Yokohama, 22 June 1866, original letter in French from t'Kint to Parkes. There is a copy of this French dispatch in University of Tokyo Volume VI 1966, vol. 69, FO46 (192), pp. 276-281. (YAH microfilm outprint no. Ca4/01.9/192, pp. 16-21).

407 TUHI 1054.08, p. 41. Edo, 20 June 1866, (copy of a) letter in Dutch from Auguste t'Kint to the plenipotentiaries of the shogun; Japanese version at TUHI Ishin 6, p. 461. D.I.S.K. 2564 (2586), p. 53. Microfilm reproduction REEL no. Keiô 慶応 – 066, pictures 0327.tiff – 0329.tiff.

408 University of Tokyo Volume VII 1967, Correspondence from various persons to Parkes, 1866), vol. 119, FO262 (149), pp. 251-253 (YAH microfilm outprint no. Ca4/01.20/149, pp. 101-103). Mission Extraordinaire de Belgique, Yokohama, 22 June 1866, original letter in French from t'Kint to Parkes; copy of this French dispatch in University of Tokyo Volume VI 1966, vol. 69, FO46 (192), pp. 276-281. (YAH microfilm outprint no. Ca4/01.9/192, pp. 16-21).

409 MOFA Belgium 2098. Yokohama, 27 June 1866. Indicateur A no. 3, duplicate of a dispatch with order no. 45 from t'Kint de Roodenbeek to Charles Rogier, registered in Brussels on 27 August 1866.

410 TUHI 1054.08, p. 42. Yokohama, 28 June 1866, (copy of a) letter in Dutch from Auguste t'Kint de Rk. to the Japanese commissioners of foreign affairs in Edo; Japanese version at TUHI Ishin 6, p. 461. D.I.S.K. 2564 (2586), p. 54. Microfilm reproduction REEL no. Keiô 慶応 – 066, pictures 0329.tiff – 0331.tiff.

411 MOFA Belgium 2098. Yokohama, 11 July 1866. Indicateur A no. 3, duplicate and original of a dispatch with order no. 52 from t'Kint de Roodenbeek to Charles Rogier, registered in Brussels on 7 September 1866. – Also: University of Tokyo Volume VI 1966, vol. 69, FO46 (192), pp. 272-275. (YAH microfilm outprint no. Ca4/01.9/192, pp. 12-15). Nagasaki, 25 July 1866, dispatch no. 120 from Parkes to Clarendon. – Draft of this dispatch: University of Tokyo Volume VII 1967, despatches from Parkes to F.O. 1866, vol. 108, FO262 (132), pp. 124-125. (YAH microfilm outprint no. Ca4/01.20/132, pp. 128-129).

412 MOFA Belgium 2098. Yokohama, 18 December 1865. Indicateur A no. 3, Order no. 26, letter from t'Kint de Roodenbeek to Charles Rogier in Brussels; Yokohama, 10 May 1866. Indicateur A no. 3, duplicate of dispatch with order no. 42 from t'Kint de Roodenbeek to Charles Rogier, registered in Brussels on 12 July 1866.

413 See e.g. MOFA Belgium 2098. Yokohama, 11 June 1866. Indicateur A no. 3, duplicate of a dispatch with order no. 43 from t'Kint de Roodenbeek to Charles Rogier, registered in Brussels on 11 August 1866.

414 See for example: University of Tokyo Volume VII 1967, Correspondence from various persons to Parkes, 1866, vol. 119, FO262 (149), pp. 251-253 (YAH microfilm outprint no. Ca4/01.20/149, pp. 101-103). Mission Extraordinaire de Belgique, Yokohama, 22 June 1866, original letter in French from t'Kint to Parkes; copy of French dispatch in University of Tokyo Volume VI 1966, vol. 69, FO46 (192), pp. 276-281. (YAH microfilm outprint no. Ca4/01.9/192, pp. 16-21).

415 See e.g. MOFA Belgium 2704 III. Hong Kong, 5 July 1865, Auguste t'Kint to Charles Rogier.

416 Kitane 1987, vol. 8, p. 94. *Japan Times* 1:33 (29 [sic: should be 27] Apr 1866), p. 223, under "The Week"; Kitane 1987, vol. 8, p. 284. *Japan Times* 1:42 (30 Jun 1866), p. 291, under "News from the Inland Sea". Also MOFA Belgium 2098. Yokohama, 11 June 1866. Indicateur A no. 3, duplicate of a dispatch with order no. 43 from t'Kint de Roodenbeek to the Charles Rogier, registered in Brussels on 11 August 1866.

417 Kitane 1987, vol. 8, p. 152. *The Japan Times* 1:36 (19 May 1866), p. 244.

418 University of Tokyo Volume IX and Volume X 1968 Ministers. US National Archives, RG 59, M133, N.A. 133 (32) Vol. 7-4 (21 September – 31 December 1866). (YAH microfilm outprint no. Ca4/01.4/32, pp. 10-11). 14 September 1866 (6th day of the 8th month of Keiô 2), English translation and copy of a communication from Inoue Kawachi no Kami (Inoue Masanao), Matsudaira Suô no Kami (Matsudaira Yasuhide), Matsudaira Nui no Kami to R.B. Van Valkenburgh, minister resident of the United States of America. Also University of Tokyo Volume XIII 1965 Politique, volume 14, pp. 157-164 (YAH microfilm outprint no. Ca4/01.36/36, pp. 1-8). Yokohama, 27 May 1866, dispatch no. 63 from L. Roches to Drouyn de Lhuys (French minister of foreign affairs).

419 TUHI 1054.04/3, pp. 179-183. Kanagawa, 10 August 1866, (copy of a) letter in Dutch no. 104/259 from D. de Graeff van Polsbroek to the Japanese senior councillors in charge of foreign affairs in Edo.

420 See for example: University of Tokyo Volume IX and Volume X 1968 Ministers. U.S. National Archives, RG 59, M133, N.A. 133 (31) Vol. 7-3 (21 April – 7 August 1866). (YAH microfilm outprint no. Ca4/01.4/31, pp. 63-66). US Legation in Japan, Edo, 1 June 1866, dispatch no. 28 from Portman to W.H. Seward, secretary of state at Washington, informing the latter about the receipt of a letter form the Japanese senior councillors in charge of foreign affairs, dated 27 May 1866, announcing that Japanese nationals of all classes are free to travel abroad.

421 TUHI 1055.8/1 Belgium, 4th letter. 24 May 1866 (10th day of the 4th month of Keiô 2), (copy of) a letter in Dutch from Ishino Chikuzen no Kami (Ishino Noritsune) to Auguste t'Kint.

422 University of Tokyo Volume XIII 1965 Politique, volume 14. Année 1866 (Léon Roches), pp. 120-130 (YAH microfilm outprint no. Ca4/01.36/35, pp. 120-130). Yokohama, 16 April 1866, dispatch no. 61 from L. Roches to Drouyn de Lhuys at Paris, registered there on 5 June 1866. Also MOFA Belgium 2098. Yokohama, 16 April 1866. Indicateur A no. 3, duplicate and original of dispatch with order no. 38 from t'Kint de Roodenbeek to Charles Rogier, registered in Brussels on 9 June 1866.

423 Kitane 1987, vol. 8, p. 302. *Nippon Shinbun* (hand-written Japanese newspaper) 45 (21 Jul 1866 [19th day of the 6th month of Keiô 2]).

424 TUHI. MOFA Netherlands 1867. Microfilm 6951-54-8/9; microfilm outprint no. 7551-56-61, pp. 79-80. Edo, 30 October 1866, Dutch dispatch no. 77/94 from Van Polsbroek to the Dutch minister of foreign affairs in The Hague, registered there on 20 December 1866 and marked with no. 11580. Van Polsbroek mentions that new rice riots occurred in Edo, and that as a result, the number of guards at the foreign legations in Edo had been doubled. Also TUHI 1054.01/4, pp. 271-278. Yokohama, 5 November 1866, English dispatch from Harry Parkes, English minister to Japan, to the Japanese councillors in charge of foreign affairs.

425 Ministry of Foreign Affairs of Japan 1874, pp. 249-296.

426 University of Tokyo Volume VI 1966, vol. 68, FO46 (191), Despatches from Harry S. Parkes to the Foreign Office. (YAH microfilm outprint no. Ca4/01.9/191, pp. 23-45). Nagasaki, 16 July 1866, dispatch no. 105 from Parkes to Clarendon. Even t'Kint was involved in some of these discussions, such as on 12 May 1866 (see pp. 29-30).

427 University of Tokyo Volume IX and Volume X 1968 Ministers. US National Archives, RG 59, M133, N.A. 133 (30) Vol. 7-2 (8 February – 11 April 1866). (YAH microfilm outprint no. Ca4/01.4/30, p. 43). US Legation in Japan, Yokohama, 20 March 1866, dispatch no. 10 from Portman to W.H. Seward, secretary of state at Washington.

428 Tanaka 1998, p. 88. Kikuchi is mentioned with his first name Takayoshi 隆吉 rather than with his title of Iyo no Kami 伊予守.

429 MOFA Belgium 2098. Yokohama, 16 April 1866. Indicateur A no. 3, duplicate and original of dispatch with order no. 38 from t'Kint de Roodenbeek to Charles Rogier, registered in Brussels on 9 June 1866.

430 MOFA Belgium 2098. Yokohama, 27 June 1866. Indicateur A no. 3, duplicate of a dispatch with order no. 45 from t'Kint de Roodenbeek to Charles Rogier, registered in Brussels on 27 August 1866. – The Japanese government sent the text of the Convention to t'Kint on 16 August 1866. See TUHI Ishin 6, p. 519. D.I.S.K. 2612 (2643), pp. 112-123. Microfilm reproduction REEL no. Keiô 慶応 – 072, pictures 0960.tiff – 0974.tiff. 16 August 1866 [7th day of the 7th month (of Keiô 2)], dispatch from Inoue Kawauchi no Kami (Inoue Masanao), Matsudaira Suô no Kami (Matsudaira Yasuhide), Matsudaira Nui Donoryô to Auguste t'Kint, and dispatch from Kikuchi Iyo no Kami (Kikuchi Takayoshi) and Hoshino Bitchû no Kami (Hoshino Kazuyuki) to Auguste t'Kint.

431 University of Tokyo Volume VI 1966, vol. 69, FO46 (192), pp. 272-275. (YAH microfilm outprint no. Ca4/01.9/192, pp. 12-15). Nagasaki, 25 July 1866, dispatch no. 120 from Parkes to Clarendon.

432 University of Tokyo Volume VII 1967, Correspondence from various persons to Parkes, 1866, vol. 119, FO262 (149), pp. 251-253 (YAH microfilm outprint no. Ca4/01.20/149, pp. 101-103). Mission Extraordinaire de Belgique, Yokohama, 22 June 1866, original letter in French from t'Kint to Parkes. – Copy of this French dispatch: University of Tokyo Volume VI 1966, vol. 69, FO46 (192), pp. 276-281. (YAH microfilm outprint no. Ca4/01.9/192, pp. 16-21).

433 MOFA Belgium 2098. Yokohama, 11 July 1866. Indicateur A no. 3, duplicate and original of dispatch with order no. 52 from t'Kint de Roodenbeek to Charles Rogier, registered in Brussels on 7 September 1866.

434 University of Tokyo Volume VII 1967, F.O. 262 (462), pp. 32-33 (YAH microfilm outprint no. Ca4/01.20/679, pp. 32-33). 19 February 1860 (28th day of the 1st month of Ansei 7), Dutch dispatch no. 25 from Wakisaka Nakatsukasa no Tayū (Wakisaka Yasuori) and Andō Tsushima no Kami (Andō Nobumasa) to Rutherford Alcock.

435 University of Tokyo Volume IX and Volume X 1968 Ministers. US National Archives, RG 59, M133, N.A. 133 (12) Vol. 3-3 (13 February – 20 June 1861). (YAH microfilm outprint no. Ca4/01.4/12, pp. 93-100). Legation of the United States at Edo, 4 May 1861, dispatch no. 19 from Townsend Harris to Lewis Cass, US secretary of state. Technically speaking, Harris had sent his communication to the court of Sardinia.

436 MOFA Belgium 2098. Yokohama, 11 July 1866. Indicateur A no. 3, duplicate and original of dispatch with order no. 52 from t'Kint de Roodenbeek to Charles Rogier, registered in Brussels on 7 September 1866.

437 University of Tokyo Volume VII 1967, Correspondence from various persons to Parkes, 1866, vol. 119, FO262 (149), pp. 251-253 (YAH microfilm outprint no. Ca4/01.20/149, pp. 101-103). Mission Extraordinaire de Belgique, Yokohama, 22 June 1866, original letter in French from t'Kint to Parkes. – Copy of this French dispatch: University of Tokyo Volume VI 1966, vol. 69, FO46 (192), pp. 276-281. (YAH microfilm outprint no. Ca4/01.9/192, pp. 16-21). In fact, the final version of the Convention of 25 June 1866 uses the term "Ports open to foreign trade". See Ministry of Foreign Affairs of Japan 1874, pp. 249-257.

438 Kitane 1987, vol. 8, p. 299. Hand-written Japanese newspaper *Nippon Shinbun Gaihen* 日本新聞外篇, part no. 13. 14 July 1866 (3rd day of the 6th month of Keiō 2).

439 TUHI 1054.08, p. 43. Yokohama, 8 July 1866, letter in Dutch from Auguste t'Kint to the Plenipotentiaries Kikuchi Iyo no Kami (Kikuchi Takayoshi), Hoshino Bitchū no Kami (Hoshino Kazuyuki) and Ōkubo Chikugo no Kami; Japanese version at TUHI Ishin 6, p. 461. D.I.S.K. 2564 (2586), pp. 51-52. Microfilm reproduction REEL no. Keiō 慶応 – 066, pictures 0324.tiff – 0327.tiff.

440 MOFA Belgium 2098. Yokohama, 11 July 1866. Indicateur A no. 3, duplicate and original of a dispatch with order no. 52 from t'Kint de Roodenbeek to the Charles Rogier, registered in Brussels on 7 September 1866.

441 MOFA Belgium 2098. Yokohama, 12 July 1866. Indicateur A no. 3, duplicate and original of the dispatch with order no. 53 from t'Kint de Roodenbeek to Charles Rogier, registered in Brussels on 26 September 1866.

442 TUHI Ishin 6, p. 496. D.I.S.K. 2596 (2627), pp. 17-18. Microfilm reproduction REEL no. Keiō 慶応 – 072, pictures 0032.tiff – 0035.tiff. 13 July 1866 [2nd day of the 6th month (of Keiō 2)], internal note in Japanese from Kikuchi Iyo no Kami (Kikuchi Takayoshi), Hoshino Bitchū no Kami (Hoshino Kazuyuki) and Ōkubo Chikugo no Kami.

443 TUHI Ishin 6, p. 496. D.I.S.K. 2596 (2627), pp. 19-21. Microfilm reproduction REEL no. Keiō 慶応 – 072, pictures 0035.tiff – 0038.tiff. 17 July 1866 [6th day of the 6th month (of Keiō 2)], report in Japanese from Kikuchi Iyo no Kami (Kikuchi Takayoshi) and Hoshino Bitchū no Kami (Hoshino Kazuyuki).

444 TUHI 1054.08, pp. 44-45. Yokohama, 21 July 1866, (copy of a) letter in Dutch from Auguste t'Kint de Rk. to the Japanese senior councillors of foreign affairs in Edo. – Japanese translation can be found at: TUHI Ishin 6, p. 496. D.I.S.K. 2596 (2627), p. 21. Microfilm reproduction REEL no. Keiō 慶応 – 072, pictures 0039.tiff – 0040.tiff.

445 University of Tokyo Volume XIII 1965, Politique, volume 14, pp. 220-222 (YAH microfilm outprint no. Ca4/01.36/36). Yokohama, 21 July 1866, dispatch no. 68 from L. Roches to Drouyn de Lhuys (French minister of foreign affairs) in Paris, registered there on 29 September 1866, p. 222: "L'envoyé Belge est enfin parvenu à s'entendre avec les Ministres du Taikoun (*shogun*) et son traité sera signé dans quelques jours". (The Belgian envoy has finally reached agreement with the ministers of the taikoun [*shogun*] and his treaty will be signed in a few days).

446 TUHI 1054.08, pp. 47-48. Yokohama, 23 July 1866, (copy of a) letter in Dutch from Auguste t'Kint to the Japanese senior councillors of foreign affairs in Edo. See also MOFA Belgium 2098. Yokohama, 23 July 1866, Mission Extraordinaire de Belgique, (copy of a) letter in Dutch probably from t'Kint de Roodenbeek to the Japanese senior councillors of foreign affairs at Edo. A Japanese translation can be found at TUHI Ishin 6, p. 496. D.I.S.K. 2596 (2627), p. 22. Microfilm reproduction REEL no. Keiō 慶応 – 072, pictures 0040.tiff – 0042.tiff.

447 TUHI Ishin 6, p. 496. D.I.S.K. 2596 (2627), pp. 22-24. Microfilm reproduction REEL no. Keiō 慶応 – 072, pictures 0042.tiff – 0044.tiff. 24 July 1866 [13th day of the 6th month (of Keiō 2)], Japanese verbal note (author unknown).

448 MOFA Belgium 2098. Yokohama, 27 July 1866. Indicateur A no. 3, dispatch with order no. 55 from t'Kint de Roodenbeek to Charles Rogier in Brussels.

449 Conversion from the old Japanese calendar (*wareki* 和暦) to the modern Western calendar (*seireki* 西暦) using http://keisan.casio.jp/exec/system/1239884730.

450 TUHI 1055.8/1 Belgium, 7th letter. 26 July 1866 (15th day of the 6th month of Keiō 2), (copy of a) letter in Dutch from the commissioners (of foreign affairs) to Aug. t'Kint. Also MOFA Belgium 2098. 26 July 1866 (15th day of the 6th month of Keiō 2), Dutch version of a letter from Kikuchi Iyo no Kami (Kikuchi Takayoshi) and Hoshino Bitchū no Kami (Hoshino Kazuyuki) to Auguste t'Kint. A Japanese version can be found at TUHI Ishin 6, p. 496. D.I.S.K. 2596 (2627), p. 25. Microfilm reproduction REEL no. Keiō 慶応 – 072, pictures 0044.tiff – 0047.tiff. 26 July 1866 [15th day of the 6th month (of Keiō 2)].

451 MOFA Belgium, original French and Dutch versions of the Treaty between Belgium and Japan of 1 August 1866.

452 MOFA Belgium 2098. Yokohama, 7 August 1866. Indicateur A no. 3, original and copy of dispatch with order no. 56 from t'Kint de Roodenbeek to Charles Rogier, registered in Brussels on 26 October 1866.

453 University of Tokyo Volume VI 1966, vol. 69, FO46 (192), pp. 339-341. (YAH microfilm outprint no. Ca4/01.9/192, pp. 79-81). Yokohama, 13 August 1866, dispatch no. 125 from Parkes to Clarendon. – Also: MOFA Belgium 2098. Yokohama, 7 August 1866. Indicateur A no. 3, original and copy of dispatch with order no. 56 from t'Kint de Roodenbeek to Charles Rogier, registered in Brussels on 26 October 1866, footnote; Japanese version of the text of the Treaty between Japan and Belgium at TUHI Ishin 6, p. 496. D.I.S.K. 2596 (2627), pp. 26-39. Microfilm reproduction REEL no. Keiō 慶応 – 072, pictures 0047.tiff – 0062.tiff. 6th month of the 2nd year of Keiō (no day given).

454 TUHI Ishin 6, p. 496. D.I.S.K. 2596 (2627), pp. 40-42. Microfilm reproduction REEL no. Keiō 慶応 – 072, pictures 0062.tiff – 0066.tiff. 1 August 1866 [21st day of the 6th month (of Keiō 2)].

455 MOFA Belgium 2098. Yokohama, 7 August 1866. Indicateur A no. 3, original and copy of order no. 57 from t'Kint de Roodenbeek to Charles Rogier, registered in Brussels on 26 October 1866. Also TUHI Ishin 6, p. 496. D.I.S.K. 2596 (2627), pp. 42-44. Microfilm reproduction REEL no. Keiō 慶応 – 072, pictures 0067.tiff – 0070.tiff. 1 August 1866 [21st day of the 6th month (of Keiō 2)], Japanese translations of two letters from Auguste t'Kint to the Japanese senior councillors in charge of foreign affairs.

456 MOFA Belgium 2098. Yokohama, 7 August 1866. Indicateur A no. 3, original and copy of a dispatch with order no. 56 from t'Kint de Roodenbeek to Charles Rogier, registered in Brussels on 26 October 1866.

457 T'Kint would send a package with official versions of the treaty to Brussels on 12 January 1866. See MOFA Belgium 2098. Mission extraordinaire de Belgique, Yokohama, 12 August 1866. Litt. A no. 3, dispatch with order no. 60 from t'Kint de Roodenbeek to Charles Rogier, registered in Brussels on 6 October 1866.

458 Ministry of Foreign Affairs of Japan 1874, article V in the Prussian, Swiss and Belgian Treaties, respectively p. 190, p. 210 and p. 300.

459 TUHI Ishin 6, p. 496. D.I.S.K. 2596 (2627), pp. 19-21. Microfilm reproduction REEL no. Keiō 慶応 – 072, pictures 0035.tiff – 0038.tiff. 17 July 1866 [6th day of the 6th month (of Keiō 2)], report in Japanese from Kikuchi Iyo no Kami (Kikuchi Takayoshi) and Hoshino Bitchū no Kami (Hoshino Kazuyuki).

460 TUHI Ishin 6, p. 496. D.I.S.K. 2596 (2627), pp. 45-47. Microfilm reproduction REEL no. Keiō 慶応 – 072, pictures 0072.tiff – 0076.tiff. 18 July 1866 [7th day of the 6th month (of Keiō 2)].

461 Ministry of Foreign Affairs of Japan 1874, article III in the Prussian, Swiss and Belgian Treaties, respectively p. 188, p. 208 and p. 299.

462 MOFA Belgium 2098. Yokohama, 7 August 1866. Indicateur A no. 3, original and copy of a dispatch with order no. 56 from t'Kint de Roodenbeek to Charles Rogier, registered in Brussels on 26 October 1866.

463 Ministry of Foreign Affairs of Japan 1874, last article in the Prussian, Swiss and Belgian Treaties, respectively p. 196, p. 215 and p. 307.

464 MOFA Belgium 2098. Yokohama, 7 August 1866. Indicateur A no. 3, original and copy of a dispatch with order no. 56 from t'Kint de Roodenbeek to Charles Rogier, registered in Brussels on 26 October 1866.

465 Ministry of Foreign Affairs of Japan 1874, p. 310. This was done in a simple manner, by adding just one sentence: "The Tariff for in and outgoing goods is in accordance with the Convention of 25 June 1866." (*English translation from the Dutch*).

466 Arminjon 1987, pp. 32-34. The arrival of the *Magenta* in Yokohama was subject of some reports by the foreign representatives and the local press there. See e.g. MOFA Belgium 2098. Yokohama, 11 July 1866. Indicateur A no. 3, duplicate and original of order no. 52 from t'Kint de Roodenbeek to the Belgian minister of Foreign Affairs Charles Rogier, registered in Brussels on 7 September 1866; University of Tokyo Volume XI Switzerland 2-1. Swiss Consulate General at Yokohama, 13 July 1866, German dispatch no. 13/53 (3/105) from C. Brennwald to Handels und Zoll Dept. Bern; Kitane 1987 (volume 8), p. 299. *Nippon Shinbun Gaihen* 日本新聞外篇 part no. 13 (14 Jul 1866 [3rd day of the 6th month of Keiō 2]).

467 This is mentioned by t'Kint in a report to the Belgian Foreign Ministry. See MOFA Belgium 2098. Shanghai, 12 December 1866, Extraordinary Mission of Belgium, Litta A No. 1, dispatch with order no. 85 from t'Kint de Roodenbeek to Charles Rogier in Brussels. The American government had also ordered its minister resident in Japan, Van Valkenburgh, to assist the Italian mission. The dispatch concerned arrived in Yokohama after the treaty between Italy and Japan was concluded. See University of Tokyo Volume IX and Volume X 1968 Diplomatic. U.S. National Archives, RG 59, M77. Roll 104, Vol. 1 (1) (12 September 1855 – 30 March 1868), pp. 187-188. (YAH microfilm outprint no. Ca4/01.8/2, pp. 96-97). U.S. Department of State at Washington, 24 July 1866, (copy of) dispatch no. 4 from William H. Seward to R.B. Van Valkenburgh at Edo. – Vittorio Arminjon (1830-1897). Bertelli 2011, p. 94.

468 Arminjon 1987, pp. 35-37. The Japanese characters for Ajiro are 網代.

469 Arminjon 1987, pp. 42-43.

470 University of Tokyo Volume XIII 1965 Politique, volume 14, pp. 220-222 (YAH microfilm outprint no. Ca4/01.36/36). Yokohama, 21 July 1866, dispatch no. 68 from L. Roches to Drouyn de Lhuys (French minister of foreign affairs) in Paris, registered there on 29 September 1866, p. 222.

471 Arminjon 1981, pp. 68-71.472 TUHI 1055.8/1 Italy, 1st letter. 25 July 1866 (14th day of the 6th month of Keiō 2), letter in Dutch from Mizuno Izumi no Kami (Mizuno Tadakiyo), Inoue Kawachi no Kami (Inoue Masanao) and Matsudaira Suō no Kami (Matsudaira Yasuhide) to V.F. Arminjon, confirming the receipt of Arminjon's letter of 12 July (1866). The Japanese government in Edo received the letter on 14 July 1866 (3rd day of the 6th month of Keiō 2). A Japanese translation of Aminjon's letter is kept at: TUHI Ishin 6, p. 471. D.I.S.K. 2569, p. 12. Microfilm reproduction REEL no. Keiō 慶応 – 067, pictures 229.tiff – 233.tiff.

473 Arminjon 1987, pp. 76-83. Mermet de Cachon's real name was Eugène-Emmanuel Mermet-Cachon (1828-1889).

474 TUHI Ishin 6, p. 479. D.I.S.K. 2575, p. 32. Microfilm reproduction REEL no. Keiō 慶応 – 068, picture 495.tiff. Japanese translation of a dispatch from Léon Roches to the Japanese government in Edo (bakufu 幕府), dated 22 July 1866 (11th day of the 6th month of Keiō 2), announcing his departure to Nagasaki on the French warship Laplace, leaving de Cachon in charge of the French legation.

475 University of Tokyo Volume XIII 1965 Politique, volume 14, pp. 230-243 (YAH microfilm outprint no. Ca4/01.36/36, pp. 70-83). Yokohama, 27 August 1866, dispatch no. 69 from L. Roches to Drouyn de Lhuys in Paris.

476 TUHI 1055.8/1 Italy, 1st letter. 25 July 1866 (14th day of the 6th month of Keiō 2), letter in Dutch from Mizuno Izumi no Kami (Mizuno Tadakiyo), Inoue Kawachi no Kami (Inoue Masanao) and Matsudaira Suō no Kami (Matsudaira Yasuhide) to V.F. Arminjon.

477 Arminjon 1987, pp. 105-108.

478 MOFA Belgium 2098. Yokohama, 27 July 1866, Indicateur A no. 3, dispatch with order no. 55 from t'Kint de Roodenbeek to the Belgian minister of Foreign Affairs Charles Rogier in Brussels; Extraordinary Mission of Belgium, Shanghai, 12 December 1866. Litta A No. 1, dispatch with order no. 85, t'Kint de Roodenbeek to Charles Rogier in Brussels. It should be noted, however, that Roches was absent from Edo/Yokohama probably from 22 July onwards, but at latest from 24 July, returning on 13 August 1866. See TUHI Ishin 6, p. 479. D.I.S.K. 2575, p. 32. Microfilm reproduction REEL no. Keiō 慶応 – 068, picture 495.tiff. Japanese translation of a dispatch from Léon Roches to the Japanese government in Edo (bakufu 幕府), dated 22 July 1866 (11th day of the 6th month of Keiō 2), announcing his departure to Nagasaki on the French warship Laplace. Also University of Tokyo Volume XIII 1965 Politique, volume 14, pp. 230-243 (YAH microfilm outprint no. Ca4/01.36/36): Yokohama, 27 August 1866, dispatch no. 69 from L. Roches to Drouyn de Lhuys in Paris; and Arminjon 1987, p. 104, mentioning that Roches had already left Yokohama on 24 July 1866. On pp. 125-128, Arminjon writes that Roches arrived back in Yokohama on 4 August 1866 and the British minister, Parkes, on 5 August 1866. However, above dispatch no. 69 from Roches mentions clearly that they returned on the same day, 13 August 1866. This corresponds with the timeframe for Parkes given by Black 1881, p. 7.

479 TUHI 1055.8/1 Italy, 3rd letter. 5 August 1866 (the letter itself does not mention any date, but according to a note of the Historiographical Institute, the date was the 25th day of the 6th month of Keiō 2), (copy of an) English letter from Inoue Kawachi no Kami (Inoue Masanao) and Matsudaira Suō no Kami (Matsudaira Yasuhide) to V.F. Arminjon. Also TUHI 1054.07/1, pp. 1-4. Yokohama, on board the corvette Magenta, 7 August 1866, copy of an Italian letter and its French translation from Arminjon to the Japanese senior councillors of foreign affairs; and pp. 9-12. Yokohama, 30 August 1866, copy of an Italian letter and its French translation from Arminjon to the Japanese senior councillors of foreign affairs. Also Arminjon 1987, pp. 116-123, 142-156. For Shibata Sadatarō 柴田貞太郎, see above. Asahina Masahiro 朝比奈昌広 was commissioner of foreign affairs from 1 November 1865 (13th day of the 9th month of Keiō 1) till 29 July 1867 (28th day of the 6th month of Keiō 3). See Katō 2001, p. 11.

480 University of Tokyo Volume VI 1966, vol. 69, FO46 (192), pp. 339-341. (YAH microfilm outprint no. Ca4/01.9/192, pp. 79-81). Yokohama, 13 August 1866, dispatch no. 125 from Parkes to Clarendon. Draft of this dispatch in University of Tokyo Volume VII 1967, despatches from Parkes to F.O., 1866, vol. 108, FO262 (132), pp. 142-143. (YAH microfilm outprint no. Ca4/01.20/132, pp. 146-147).

481 University of Tokyo Volume VI 1966, vol. 70, FO46 (194), pp. 227-230. (YAH microfilm outprint no. Ca4/01.9/194, pp. 107-110). Yokohama, 2 September 1866, dispatch no. 140 from Parkes to Stanley.

482 University of Tokyo Volume VI 1966, vol. 69, FO46 (192). (YAH microfilm outprint no. Ca4/01.9/192, pp. 57-92). Yokohama, 12 September 1866, dispatch no. 156 from Parkes to Stanley. Draft of this dispatch in University of Tokyo Volume VII 1967, despatches from Parkes to F.O. 1866), vol. 109, FO262 (133), pp. 55-56. (YAH microfilm outprint no. Ca4/01.20/133, pp. 55-56).

483 University of Tokyo Volume VI 1966, vol. 75, FO46 (207), p. 178 (YAH microfilm outprint no. Ca4/01.9/207, p. 64). 13 November 1866, draft dispatch from the Foreign Office to the Board of Trade; pp. 213-215 (YAH microfilm outprint no. Ca4/01.9/207, pp. 110-112), Whitehall, 1 December 1866, dispatch from the Office of the Committee of the Privy Council for Trade to the Undersecretary of State, Foreign Office. Also University of Tokyo Volume VI 1966, vol. 106, FO262 (207), pp. 214-216 (YAH microfilm outprint no. Ca4/01.20/130, pp. 91-93). 6 December 1866, copy of dispatch no. 58 from the Foreign Office to Harry Parkes. Draft of this dispatch: University of Tokyo Volume VI 1966, vol. 64, FO46 (178), pp. 200-201 (YAH microfilm outprint no. Ca4/01.9/178).

484 University of Tokyo Volume VI 1966, vol. 79, FO46 (218), pp. 369-371 (YAH microfilm outprint no. Ca4/01.9/218, pp. 84-86). Edo, 13 April 1867, dispatch no. 67 from Parkes to Stanley.

485 University of Tokyo Volume XI Switzerland 5-1. 12 September 1866, dispatch no. 11/130 from C. Brennwald to the Swiss Federal Council "Bundesrath", p. 5. This refers to Casper Brennwald, who served as chancellor-secretary of the Swiss legation visiting Japan in 1863. See earlier.

486 The original dispatch from Van Polsbroek, dated 12 August 1866 and bearing no. 55/66, has not yet been found. Therefore, the precise content of this dispatch is not known. However, the reply from the Dutch foreign minister has been preserved. See TUHI. LJ36. "B. Benten (Jan. 1862 – June 1877): stukken betrekking hebbende op het lot "Benten". The Hague, 20 October 1866, copy of Dutch dispatch no. 9279/80/29 from the Dutch Ministry of Foreign Affairs to Van Polsbroek, mentioning that it was a pleasure to learn from Van Polsbroek's dispatch no. 56/66 dated 12 August (1866), that the efforts of Van Polsbroek to assist the Belgian envoy in his mission had been crowned with success.

487 University of Tokyo Volume VI 1966, vol. 70, FO46 (194), pp. 227-230. (YAH microfilm outprint no. Ca4/01.9/194, pp. 107-110). Yokohama, 2 September 1866, dispatch no. 140 from Parkes to Stanley.

488 MOFA Belgium 2098. Extraordinary Mission of Belgium, Shanghai, 12 December 1866. Litta A No. 1, dispatch with order no. 85 from t'Kint de Roodenbeek to Charles Rogier in Brussels.

489 University of Tokyo Volume XIII 1965 Politique, volume 14, pp. 230-243 (YAH microfilm outprint no. Ca4/01.36/36, pp. 70-83). Yokohama, 27 August 1866, dispatch no. 69 from L. Roches to Drouyn de Lhuys in Paris.

490 University of Tokyo Volume XIII 1965 Politique, volume 15 (1867, Mr. Roches), pp. 85-93 (YAH microfilm outprint no. Ca4/01.36/37, pp. 87-95). Mission de France au Japon, Yokohama, 26 June 1867, dispatch no. 85 from Roches to Moustier, p. 87.

491 University of Tokyo Volume XIII 1965 Politique, vol. 14 (1866 – Leon Roches), pp. 157-164 (YAH microfilm outprint no. Ca4/01.36/36, pp. 1-8. Yokohama, 27 May 1866, dispatch no. 63 from L. Roches to Drouyn de Lhuys, p. 160.

492 MOFA Belgium 2704 III. Peking (Beijing), 12 December 1866, difficult to read, small letter of 6 pages, written by Henri de Bellonet. The same letter shows that de Bellonet was at loggerheads with t'Kint about the appointment of a Belgian consul in Shanghai. According to de Bellonet, t'Kint had appointed a French national without the consent of the French legation.

493 MOFA Belgium 2098. Yokohama, 12 July 1866. Indicateur A no. 3, duplicate and original of the dispatch with order no. 53 from t'Kint de Roodenbeek to Charles Rogier, registered in Brussels on 26 September 1866.

494 Arminjon 1987, pp. 105-108.

495 Relevant French archives in University of Tokyo Volume XIII 1965 and University of Tokyo Volume XIV 1966. The Japanese archives concerned: Tokyo University. Historiographical Institute. Ishin shiryō kōyō 維新史料綱要 Dainippon Ishin shiryō kōhon 大日本維新史料稿本 On-line microfilm reproduction, researched for the word ロッシュ (Roches): wwwap.hi.u-tokyo.ac.jp/ships/db.html (accessed 24 October 2015); and TUHI 1054.03/2.

496 University of Tokyo Volume IX and Volume X 1968 Ministers. US National Archives, RG 59, M133, N.A. 133 (32) Vol. 7-4 (21 September – 31 December 1866). (YAH microfilm outprint no. Ca4/01.4/32, pp. 10-11). 14 September 1866 (6th day of the 8th month of Keiō 2), English translation and copy of a communication from Inoue Kawachi no Kami (Inoue Masanao), Matsudaira Suō no Kami (Matsudaira Yasuhide), Matsudaira Nui no Kami to R.B. Van Valkenburgh. The quotation is taken from the English translation as preserved in the Archives of the US Department of State.

497 Italicized words added.

498 The shogun's interest in military matters even showed in small details. When the American minister Van Valkenburgh sent a photograph of a war scene to the Japanese senior councillors, they came back to him on 15 January 1867 asking for more such photographs since the shogun was greatly interested in such material. See University of Tokyo Volume IX and Volume X 1968 Japan. US National Archives, RG 84, N.A. T400 (16) Vol. 12 (1 January – 28 September 1867). (YAH microfilm outprint no. Ca4/01.14/16, pp. 15-17). 15 January 1867 (10th day of the 12th month of Keiō 2), Dutch dispatch no. 4 of 1867 from Inoue Kawachi no Kami (Inoue Masanao), Inaba Mino no Kami (Inaba Masakuni) and Matsudaira Suō no Kami (Matsudaira Yasuhide) to Van Valkenburgh.

499 Immediately after the opening of the Port of Yokohama in July 1859, the Dutch vice consul Dirk de Graeff van Polsbroek was confronted with Japanese government officials who were unable to understand why foreign traders did not bow to them, did not take off their hats to greet them, and why they even walked and talked with vice consul Van Polsbroek as if they were his equal. Van Polsbroek remarked that in Japan, businessmen were of the lowest social rank, even lower than farmers. See Moeshart 1987, p. 53.

500 TUHI 1054.04/3, pp. 153-156. Kanagawa, 2 August 1866, dispatch no. 93/240 from Van Polsbroek to the Japanese senior councillors in charge of foreign affairs at Edo. Other dispatches from Van Polsbroek to the Japanese senior councillors in charge of foreign affairs at Edo on the same subject: pp. 175-177 (Kanagawa, 10 August 1866, dispatch no. 103/257), 187-191 (Kanagawa, 13 August 1866, dispatch no. 106/261), 213-214 (Kanagawa, 24 August 1866, dispatch no. 114/273), 223-225 (Kanagawa, 29 August 1866, dispatch no. 119/279).

501 TUHI 1054.04/3, pp. 179-183. Kanagawa, 10 August 1866, no. 104/259, (copy of a) letter in Dutch from D. de Graeff van Polsbroek to the Japanese senior councillors in charge of foreign affairs in Edo.

502 TUHI 1054.04/3, pp. 193-194. Kanagawa, 15 August 1866, no. 110/266, (copy of a) letter in Dutch from D. de Graeff van Polsbroek to the Japanese senior councillors in charge of foreign affairs in Edo. Also: TUHI 1054.09/1, 9th letter.

503 TUHI 1054.04/3, pp. 196-205. Kanagawa, 15 August 1866, no. 111/267, (copy of a) letter in Dutch from D. de Graeff van Polsbroek to the Japanese senior councillors in charge of foreign affairs at Edo. Also: TUHI 1054.09/1, 10th letter.

504 University of Tokyo Volume IX and Volume X 1968 Ministers. US National Archives, RG 59, M133, N.A. 133 (32) Vol. 7-4 (21 September – 31 December 1866). YAH microfilm outprint no. Ca4/01.4/32, pp. 10-11. 14 September 1866 (6th day of the 8th month of Keiō 2), English translation and copy of a communication from Inoue Kawachi no Kami (Inoue Masanao), Matsudaira Suō no Kami (Matsudaira Yasuhide), Matsudaira Nui no Kami to R.B. Van Valkenburgh. YAH microfilm outprint no. Ca4/01.4/32, pp. 5-11. US Legation in Japan, Edo, 28 September 1866, R.B. Van Valkenburgh, minister resident of the United States in Japan, to William H. Seward, secretary of state at Washington, registered there on 9 January 1867. Also TUHI 1055.2/3. Probably 14 September 1866 (…th day of the 8th month of Keiō 2), letter in Dutch from Inoue Kawachi no Kami (Inoue Masanao), Matsudaira Suō no Kami (Matsudaira Yasuhide), and Matsudaira Nui no Kami to R. Van Valkenburgh.

505 MOFA Belgium – Japon Politique. Yokohama, 12 September 1866. Mission Extraordinaire de Belgique, Litta A No. 2 – Attachment to ordre no. 65. Auguste t'Kint to Charles Rogier in Brussels. Also MOFA Belgium 2098. Yokohama, 12 September 1866, dispatch with order no. 65, Auguste t'Kint de Roodenbeek to Charles Rogier, registered in Brussels on 24 November 1866. And TUHI 1054.08, pp. 63-64. Yokohama, 19 September 1866, letter in Dutch from Auguste t'Kint de Roodenbeek to the Japanese senior councillors in charge of foreign affairs in Edo. Also TUHI 1055.8/1 Belgium, 12th letter. 17 September 1866 (9th day of the 8th month of Keiō 2), (copy of a) letter in Dutch from Inoue Kawachi no Kami (Inoue Masanao), Matsudaira Suō no Kami (Matsudaira Yasuhide), Matsudaira Nui no Kami to August t'Kint; 15th letter. 5 October 1866 (27th day of the 8th month of Keiō 2), (copy of a) letter in Dutch from Inoue Kawachi no Kami (Inoue Masanao), Matsudaira Suō no Kami (Matsudaira Yasuhide) and Matsudaira Nui no Kami to Auguste t'Kint.

506 Moeshart 1987, p. 23: "Op 31 december ging De Graeff met de Belgische Gezant 't Kint van Roodenbeek in de Zoutman naar Edo, om te trachten ook voor België een tractaat te sluiten. De Belgische Gezant moest echter wegens familieomstandigheden voortijdig zijn bezoek aan Japan afbreken, en Dirk de Graeff voltooide de onderhandelingen voor België alleen."

507 MOFA Belgium 2098. Yokohama, 7 August 1866. Indicateur A no. 3, dispatch with order no. 56 from t'Kint de Roodenbeek to Charles Rogier, registered in Brussels on 26 October 1866.

508 MOFA Belgium 2098. Brussels, 24 November 1866, Belgian Ministry of Foreign Affairs. Indicateur B no. 2483. Minute with order no. 111, containing the draft reply to A. t'Kint, consul general in Shanghai to his letter of 7 August 1866 (order no. 56).

509 TUHI 1054.08, pp. 55-57. Yokohama, 27 August 1866, (probably 17 August 1866) letter in Dutch from Auguste t'Kint de Roodenbeek to the Japanese senior councillors in charge of foreign affairs in Edo. Also MOFA Belgium 2098. Yokohama 17 August 1866, Buitengewone Zending van België, letter in Dutch to the Japanese senior councillors in charge of foreign affairs. A Japanese version of this dispatch can be found at TUHI Ishin 6, p. 519. D.I.S.K. 2612 (2643), pp. 124-126. Microfilm reproduction REEL no. Keiō 慶応 – 072, pictures 0975.tiff – 0978.tiff. 27 August 1866 (probably 17 August 1866), registered by the Japanese administration on 19 August 1866 [10th day of the 7th month (of Keiō 2)].

510 TUHI 1054.11. Portuguese Consulate at Kanagawa, 11 August 1866, (copy of a) letter in Portuguese, with Dutch translation, from José Rodrigues Coelho do Amaral to the Japanese senior councillors in charge of foreign affairs in Edo; 13 August 1866, (copy of a) letter in English from Edward Clarke, Portuguese consul at Kanagawa, to the Japanese commissioners of foreign affairs in Edo.

511 TUHI 1055.7. 26 August 1866 (17th day of the 7th month of Keiō 2), (copy of a) letter in Dutch from Inoue Kawachi no Kami (Inoue Masanao), Matsudaira Suō no Kami (Matsudaira Yasuhide), Matsudaira Nui no Kami to José Rodrigues Coelho do Amaral.

512 TUHI 1054.11. Portuguese legation at Edo, 5 September 1866, (copy of a) letter in Portuguese, with Dutch translation, from José Rodrigues Coelho do Amaral to the Japanese senior councillors in charge of foreign affairs.

513 TUHI 1054.10/1. Edo, 6 April 1867, letter in Dutch without number from C. Brennwald to the Japanese senior councillors in Edo; Edo, 11 April 1867, dispatch no. 33 from Brennwald to Ezure Kaga no Kami (Ezure Akinori), Japanese commissioner in Edo.

514 TUHI 1054.08, pp. 67-68. Yokohama, 19 September 1866, letter in Dutch from Auguste t'Kint de Roodenbeek to the Japanese senior councillors in charge of foreign affairs in Edo. Draft of this dispatch at: MOFA Belgium 2098.

515 TUHI 1054.08, pp. 69-75. Yokohama, 29 September 1866, letter in Dutch from Auguste t'Kint to the Japanese commissioners of foreign affairs in Edo, Kikuchi Iyo no Kami (Kikuchi Takayoshi) and Hoshino Bitchū no Kami (Hoshino Kazuyuki). – Also TUHI 1055.8/1 Belgium, 13th letter. 2 October 1866 (24th day of the 8th month of Keiō 2), (copy of a) letter in Dutch from the (Japanese) commissioners to Auguste t'Kint; MOFA Belgium 2098. Extraordinary Mission of Belgium, Yokohama, 7 October 1866, draft and original of a dispatch with order no. 67 from Aug. t'Kint de Roodenbeek to Charles Rogier in Brussels.

516 MOFA Belgium 2098. Extraordinary Mission of Belgium, Yokohama, 7 October 1866, draft and original of a dispatch with order no. 67 from Aug. t'Kint de Roodenbeek to Charles Rogier in Brussels.

517 Kitane 1987, vol. 9, p. 8: *Daily Japan Herald* 2:902, Yokohama, Japan, Monday 1 Oct 1866, p. 1846. – The same preliminary notice would also appear on 2, 3 and 6 October 1866. See Kitane 1987, vol. 9, pp. 12 (*Daily Japan Herald* 2:903 (Yokohama, Japan, Tuesday 2 Oct 1866), p. 1850), 16 (*Daily Japan Herald* 2:904, Yokohama, Japan, Wednesday 3 Oct 1866, p. 1854), 28 (*Daily Japan Herald* 2:907, Yokohama, Japan, Saturday 6 Oct 1866, p. 1866).

518 Kitane 1987, vol. 9, pp. 37 (*Daily Japan Herald* 2:908, Yokohama, Japan, Monday 8 Oct 1866, p. 1870), 42 (*Daily Japan Herald* 2:909, Yokohama, Japan, Tuesday 9 Oct 1866, p. 1874. Under "Appointments this day").

519 Kitane 1987, vol. 9, p. 53. *Nippon Shinbun Gaihen* 日本新聞外編 21 (13 Oct 1866 [5th day of the 9th month of Keiō 2].

520 MOFA Belgium 2704 III. Shanghai, 22 October 1866. Litt. A no. 1, dispatch with order no. 70 from Aug. t'Kint de Roodenbeek to Charles Rogier, registered in Brussels on 8 December 1866, B 1746 no. 20577. Also Kitane 1987, vol. 9, p. 65. *Daily Japan Herald* 2:916 (Yokohama, Japan, Wednesday 17 Oct 1866), p. 1902. The full name of General Guy was Philip Melmoth Nelson Guy KCB (1804-1878).

521 MOFA Belgium 2704 III. Yokohama, 10 May 1866, Litt. A no. 1, dispatch with order no. 41 from Aug. t'Kint de Roodenbeek to Charles Rogier, registered in Brussels on 12 July 1866, B 1746 no. 12380.

522 MOFA Belgium 2704 III. Yokohama, 27 July 1866, Litt. A no. 1, dispatch with order no. 54 from Aug. t'Kint de Roodenbeek to Charles Rogier, registered in Brussels on 9 October 1866, B 1746 no. 17259.

523 MOFA Belgium 2704 III. Shanghai, 29 October 1866. Litt A no. 1, dispatch with order no. 74 from Aug. t'Kint de Roodenbeek to Charles Rogier, registered in Brussels on 3 January 1867, B 1746 no. 123.

524 Royal Palace Belgium – Duke of Brabant, note from Leopold II of 1 December 1866 to "Cher Comte".

525 MOFA Belgium – Lambermont. Shanghai, 22 February 1867, no. 132, letter from t'Kint to Lambermont.

526 The dispatches of t'Kint concerning his journey in China in April and May 1867 are as follows. MOFA Belgium 2098. Shanghai, 18 February 1867, Duplicata, Litta A No. 4, dispatch with order no. 91 from t'Kint de Roodenbeek to Charles Rogier, registered in Brussels on 8 May 1867; Shanghai, 21 March 1867, Extraordinary Mission of Belgium, Litta A No. 4, dispatch with order no. 96 from t'Kint de Roodenbeek to Charles Rogier, registered in Brussels on 8 May 1867 and 15 June 1866; Shanghai, 4 June 1867, Extraordinary Mission of Belgium, t'Kint de Roodenbeek to Charles Rogier, registered in Brussels on 31 July 1867. Also MOFA Belgium – Lambermont. Shanghai, 22 February 1867, no. 132, letter from t'Kint to Lambermont. And MOFA Belgium 2704 III. Shanghai, 2 March 1867. Litt. A. no. 4, dispatch with order no. 92 from Aug. t'Kint de Roodenbeek to Charles Rogier, registered in Brussels on 4 May 1867 (B 1746 no. 7560); Shanghai, 19 March 1867, (probably copy of a) dispatch no. 93 from Aug. t'Kint de Roodenbeek to "Mr. Le Ministre", registered in Brussels on 10 May 1867 (4336, B 1746, no. 7920); Shanghai, 19 March 1867. Indicateur A no. 2, dispatch with order no. 94 from Aug. t'Kint de Roodenbeek to Charles Rogier, registered in Brussels on 13 May 1867 (B 1746 no. 8062); Foochow (Fuzhou), 24 April 1867. Litt A no. 4, dispatch no. 98 from Aug. t'Kint de Roodenbeek to Charles Rogier, registered in Brussels on 22 June 1867 (B 1746, no. 10309).

527 MOFA Belgium 2098. Brussels, 27 October 1866, Belgian Ministry of Foreign Affairs, Minute, Indicateur B no. 2483, draft letter in the name of the secretary general to the *Moniteur Belge*, partie non officielle, Premier Bruxelles.

528 MOFA Belgium 2098. Brussels, 24 November 1866, Belgian Ministry of Foreign Affairs, Minute, Indicateur B no. 2483, order no. 111, containing a draft reply to A. t'Kint, consul general in Shanghai, to his dispatch no. 56 of 7 August 1866.

529 MOFA Belgium 2098. Brussels, 8 November 1866, Belgian Ministry of Foreign Affairs, Minute, Indicateur B no. 2483, draft letter in French with two annexes, addressed to the king of the Belgians (Leopold II).

530 MOFA Belgium 2098. Brussels, 7 December 1866, Belgian Ministry of Foreign Affairs, B no. 2483, copy of a letter in French from Charles Rogier to the President of the Central Section in charge of examining the treaty concluded between Belgium and Japan on 1 August 1866.

531 MOFA Belgium 2098. Brussels, 22 December 1866, Belgian Senate, President and Secretaries of the Belgian Senate to the Belgian minister of foreign affairs, registered there on 24 December 1866.

532 MOFA Belgium 2098. Brussels, 24 December 1866, Belgian Ministry of Foreign Affairs, Minute, Indicateur B no. 2483, containing a draft letter to the minister for the royal court (*Ministre de la Maison du Roi*) in Brussels; Brussels, 24 December 1866, Belgian Ministry of Foreign Affairs, Minute, Indicateur B no. 2483, containing a draft letter to the *Moniteur Belge* – partie officielle.

533 MOFA Belgium 2098. Brussels, 5 January 1867, Belgian Ministry of Foreign Affairs, Indicateur B no. 2483, including one annex, being a minute containing a draft letter to the Belgian king.

534 MOFA Belgium 2098. Shanghai, 21 March 1867, Extraordinary Mission of Belgium, Litta A No. 4, dispatch with order no. 96 from t'Kint de Roodenbeek to Charles Rogier, registered in Brussels on 8 May 1867 and 15 June 1867.

535 MOFA Belgium 883. Yokohama, 15 October 1866, Extraordinary Mission of Belgium, Litta no. 1, duplicate of a dispatch with order no. 69 from Aug. t'Kint de Roodenbeek to Charles Rogier, registered in Brussels on 3 January 1867, B476 no. 122.

536 The List of Foreign Residents in China, Japan, The Philippines and Siam for 1868 and The Yokohama Directory in: The Chronicle & Directory for China, Japan & the Philippines for the year 1868. Hong Kong: Daily Press, 13 January 1868, respectively p. 91 and p. 246.

537 MOFA Belgium 883. Yokohama, 15 October 1866, Extraordinary Mission of Belgium, Litta no. 1, duplicate of a dispatch with order no. 69 from Aug. t'Kint de Roodenbeek to Charles Rogier, registered in Brussels on 3 January 1867, B476 no. 122.

538 TUHI. LJ37. Kanagawa, 5 January 1864, draft dispatch no. 5/7 from Polsbroek to the Japanese councillors in charge of foreign affairs. In this dispatch, Van Polsbroek mentioned that American citizen Brown received a piece of land in Yokohama, while 12 Dutch nationals who had arrived earlier, had not yet received any land. Van Polsbroek added a list of 12 names, of which the last one was: "LEJEUNE ? – JUNY 1863" [sic]. Interestingly enough, Maurice Lejeune is not included in a list of Dutch residents living at Kanagawa (including Yokohama), compiled by Van Polsbroek in February 1866. See TUHI. LJ29. 12 February 1866, circular note no. 20/68 from Van Polsbroek.

539 *Japan Directory* 1864, p. 300; *Yokohama Directory* 1865, p. 238; *Yokohama Directory* 1866, p. 235; *Yokohama Directory* 1867, p. 251.

540 Black 1880, p. 366. Interestingly, Lejeune was categorized among the four members representing the French nationals. As council member, Lejeune regularly appeared in council reports published in the local newspapers. For, e.g., the Council meeting of 8 January 1866, see Kitane 1987 (volume 7), pp. 84 (*Japan Times' Daily Advertiser* 1:90 (Yokohama: Mon 10 Jan 1866), p. 258, 88 (*Japan Times' Daily Advertiser* 1:91 (Yokohama: Thu 11 Jan 1866), p. 262, 98 (*Japan Times* 1:19 (Yokohama: Fri 12 Jan 1866), p. 118. For the council meeting of 23 February 1866, Kitane 1987 (volume 7), p. 274 (*Japan Times* 1:26 (2 Mar 1866), p. 124. Under "Local". For the council meeting of 7 March 1866, Kitane 1987 (volume 7), pp. 299 (*Daily Advertiser* [1]:137 (9 Mar 1866), p. 418, 303. *Japan Times* [1]:27 (9 Mar 1866), p. 181. For the council meeting of 6 April 1866, Kitane 1987 (volume 8), p. 39 (*Japan Times*. [1]:30 (6 Apr 1866), p. 203. Under "Local"). For the council meeting of 7 May 1866, Kitane 1987 (volume 8), pp. 124 (*Daily Advertiser* 1:183 (9 May 1866), p. 701 sc. 704?), 128 (*Japan Times' Daily Advertiser and Yokohama "Bell"* 1:182 (Yokohama: Tue 8 May 1866), front page, 138 (*Japan Times* [1]:35 (11 May 1866), p. 240). For the council meeting of 23 May 1866, Kitane 1987 (volume 8), p. 188 (*Japan Times* [1]:37 (26 May 1866), p. 255. Under "Local").

541 Kitane 1987 (volume 8), p. 188. *Japan Times* [1]:37 (26 May 1866), p. 255. Under "Local" (continued). Again, he was registered among the four council members representing the French nationals.

542 University of Tokyo Volume XI Switzerland 5-2. Actes reçus. 14 June 1866, acte no. 113, from "'Comité de Police du Conseil Municipal M. Lejeune"; Actes expédiés. 20 June 1866, acte no. 89, to "M. Lejeune, Comité de Police du Conseil Municipal".

543 MOFA Belgium 883. Brussels, 1 December 1866, Minute B 476 (no order number) containing a draft letter from the Belgian Ministry of Foreign Affairs to the Belgian king; Correspondence (Overview): 15 December 1866, overview no. 3, report (from the Belgian Ministry of Foreign Affairs) to the Belgian King Leopold II; Brussels, 18 December 1866, draft royal decree to be signed by Leopold II, and draft brevet to be signed by the minister of Foreign Affairs Charles Rogier.

544 MOFA Belgium 2704 III. Brussels, 1 December 1865. Indicateur B no. 1746/2483. Minute containing draft letter with order no. 89 from the Belgian Foreign Ministry to t'Kint, consul general in Shanghai. Also MOFA Belgium 2098. Brussels, 24 November 1866, Minute, Indicateur B no. 2483, containing a draft dispatch with order no. 111 from the Belgian Ministry of Foreign Affairs to A. t'Kint, consul general in Shanghai; MOFA Belgium 2865 IV. Brussels, 25 January 1867, Indicateur B No. 2483 (476 et 475). Minute containing a draft letter with order no. 2 from the Belgian Foreign Ministry to t'Kint in Shanghai, with an attachment. See too Truong 1957, p. 174.

545 MOFA Belgium 2865 IV. Shanghai, 7 December 1866, Extraordinary Mission of Belgium, Litta B no. 3, order no. 82, Aug. t'Kint de Roodenbeek to Charles Rogier, registered in Brussels on 31 January (1867), B 2483 no. 1873. See also Truong 1957, p. 172.

546 MOFA Belgium 883. Yokohama, 10 November 1866, Rodolphe Lindau to Belgian minister of foreign affairs, registered in Brussels at 19 January 1867, B476 no. 1292.

547 Keymeulen applied two times for the position in Yokohama, on 17 January 1865 and on 7 July 1866: MOFA Belgium 2098. Litta B no. 2483: Procedure à charge du sieur Keymeulen. Yokohama, 17 January 1865, J. Keymeulen to Ch. Rogier, registered in Brussels on 21 March (1865), B 1746 no. 4577; Brussels (Boulevard d'Anvers no. 12), 7 July 1866, Joseph Keymeulen to Charles Rogier, registered in Brussels on 11 July (1866), B. 1746 no. 12299.

548 Keymeulen never received a reply from the Foreign Ministry. Lindau was sent a formal refusal on 31 January 1867. See MOFA Belgium 883. Brussels, 31 January 1867, Minute Indicateur B no. 476 (no order number), containing a draft dispatch from Belgian Ministry of Foreign Affairs in Brussels to Rodolphe Lindau in Yokohama.

549 MOFA Belgium 883. Brussels, 25 January 1867, Minute Indicateur B no. 476 (no order number), containing a draft dispatch from Belgian Ministry of Foreign Affairs in Brussels to Maurice Lejeune in Yokohama, with several annexes.

550 MOFA Belgium 2016 I.C. Edo, 27 March 1867: letter in Dutch no. 61/114 from D. de Graeff van Polsbroek (political agent and consul general of the Netherlands in Japan) to Maurice Lejeune, appointed consul of H.M. the king of the Belgians at Kanagawa. Polsbroek acknowledged the receipt of this dispatch ("Missive no. 1"), dated 23 March 1867, from Lejeune and authorized Lejeune to fulfil the function of Belgian consul at Kanagawa until the Dutch king himself granted the permission. For that purpose, Van Polsbroek sent a dispatch to the Dutch government on 29 March 1867. See TUHI. Dutch Consulate General 1867-1870. Archief no. 17, Anno 1867 (1), No. 1-38. Microfilm 6951-2-8-4; microfilm outprint no. 7551-48-8, p. 78. Edo, 29 March 1867, letter in Dutch no. 30/30 from Van Polsbroek to the Dutch Ministry of Foreign Affairs.

551 TUHI 1054.08, pp. 105-106. Edo, 28 March 1867, letter in Dutch from D. de Graeff van Polsbroek to the Japanese councillors in charge of foreign affairs in Edo. Also TUHI 1054.04/3, pp. 510-511. Edo, 28 March 1867, no. 62/116, (copy of a) letter in Dutch from D. de Graeff van Polsbroek to the Japanese councillors in charge of foreign affairs; TUHI 1055.4/3. 6 April 1867 (1st day of the 3rd month of Keiō 3), letter from Inoue Kawachi no Kami (Inoue Masanao), Matsudaira Suō no Kami (Matsudaira Yasuhide) and Ogasawara Iki no Kami (Ogasawara Nagamichi) to D. de Graeff van Polsbroek. Japanese versions of these dispatches can be found at TUHI Ishin 7, p. 56. D.I.S.K. 2836 (2858), pp. 96-98. Microfilm reproduction REEL no. Keiō 慶応 – 117, pictures 0431.tiff – 0434.tiff.

552 MOFA Belgium 883. Yokohama, 10 April 1867, Belgian Vice Consulate no. 4, dispatch from Maurice Lejeune to the Belgian minister of foreign affairs, registered in Brussels on 11 June 1867, B476 no. 9604.

553 Nitta 1975 [2], p. 65 (Japan Punch of October 1867).

554 MOFA Belgium 2865 IV. Shanghai, 7 December 1866, Extraordinary Mission of Belgium, Litta B no. 3, order no. 82, Aug. t'Kint de Roodenbeek to Charles Rogier, registered in Brussels on 31 January (1867), B 2483, no. 1873; Brussels, 4 February 1867, Minute containing a draft letter from the secretary general of the Belgian Foreign Ministry, Direction B no. 2483, order no. (not mentioned), 1 annex, to the Moniteur Belge – partie non-officielle. Truong 1957 mentions on p. 175 that both were published on 21 February 1867.

555 MOFA Belgium 2098. Nagasaki, 21 January 1867, Extraordinary Mission of Belgium, Litta A No. 1, order no. 89, t'Kint de Roodenbeek to Charles Rogier in Brussels.

556 Truong 1957, p. 173.

557 MOFA Belgium 2704 III. Indicateur B no. 1746, Brussels, 21 January 1865, dispatch from t'Kint to Charles Rogier.

558 MOFA Belgium 2864 XI. Shanghai, 24 November 1866, Extraordinary Mission of Belgium, Litta B No. 1, dispatch with order no. 77 from Aug. t'Kint de Roodenbeek to Charles Rogier, registered in Brussels on 16 January 1867, no. 1021.

559 MOFA Belgium 2864 XI. Brussels, 31 December 1866, Belgian Ministry of Foreign Affairs, E. 7770, copy of a letter from Ch. Rogier to the Chamber of Commerce in Antwerp, replying to the Chamber's letter of 18 December 1866; Brussels, 21 January 1867. Indicateur B no. 2483 (no order no.), Minute containing a draft letter from Belgian Ministry of Foreign Affairs to the Chamber of Commerce in Antwerp; Antwerp, 29 January 1867, Chamber of Commerce and Fabrics of Antwerp to the Belgian foreign minister, registered in Brussels on 31 January 1867, no. 1881.

560 MOFA Belgium 2098. Brussels, 14 February 1867, Belgian Ministry of Foreign Affairs. Indicateur B no. 2483, dispatch with order no. 4 from Charles Rogier to t'Kint de Roodenbeek in Shanghai.

561 MOFA Belgium 2864 XI. Yokohama, 11 July 1867, Extraordinary Mission of Belgium, Litta B no. 3, dispatch with order no. 107 from Aug. t'Kint de Roodenbeek to Charles Rogier, registered in Brussels on 13 September 1867, no. 15016.

562 No such request from t'Kint has been found in the archives, but several dispatches of Van Polsbroek and the Japanese councillors do mention the request. See TUHI 1054.08, pp. 97-98. Edo, 7 March 1867, two letters in Dutch no. 48/96and 49/97 from D. de Graeff van Polsbroek to the Japanese councillors in charge of foreign affairs in Edo, about the ratifications and t'Kint returning to Europe, and about the consular land respectively. Copies of these two letters can also be found at TUHI 1054.04/3, pp. 484-487. A copy of dispatch no. 49/97 (consular land) can also be found at: TUHI. LJ37. Also TUHI 1055.4/3. Two letters dated 8 March 1867 (3rd day of the 2nd month of Keiō 3) from Inoue Kawachi no Kami (Inoue Masanao), Matsudaira Suō no Kami (Matsudaira Yasuhide) and Ogasawara Iki no Kami (Ogasawara Nagamichi) to D. de Graeff van Polsbroek, two about the ratification and one about the consular land. Japanese versions of this correspondence can be found at TUHI Ishin 7, p. 36. D.I.S.K. 2822 (2845), pp. 180-187. Microfilm reproduction REEL no. Keiō 慶応 – 114, pictures 0436.tiff – 0447.tiff. 7 and 8 March 1867 [2nd and 3rd day of the 2nd month (of Keiō 3)].

563 An internal note from the Belgian Foreign Ministry mentioned that a request from t'Kint for home leave had been introduced to Foreign minister Charles Rogier on 4 or 5 May 1867. Since dispatches from Shanghai took about two months to reach Brussels, it is likely that t'Kint dispatched the message about his planned return to Europe before he left on a trip into Mainland China on 2 March 1867. See MOFA Belgium 2098. 8 May 1867, internal note of the Belgian Ministry of Foreign Affairs. For the Ministry's approval of home leave, MOFA Belgium 2704 III. Brussels, 13 May 1867, Minute containing a draft letter from the Belgian Foreign Ministry to t'Kint, consul general of Belgium in Shanghai.

564 MOFA Belgium 2098. Brussels, 23 March 1867, Belgian Ministry of Foreign Affairs, Indicateur B no. 2483, order no. 9, minute containing a draft letter to t'Kint in Shanghai, with one annex.

565 MOFA Belgium 2098. Hong Kong, 27 May 1867, Hong Kong, Mission of Belgium. Litta A No. 3, dispatch with order no. 101 from t'Kint de Roodenbeek to Charles Rogier, registered in Brussels on 22 July 1867. Also, MOFA Belgium 2704 III. Hong Kong, 27 May 1867. Litt. A no 1/3, dispatch with order no. 102 from Aug. t'Kint de Roodenbeek to Charles Rogier, registered in Brussels on 26 July 1867, B 1746 no. 12360. Draft of this dispatch at MOFA Belgium 2098.

566 MOFA Belgium 2098. Hong Kong, 30 May 1867, Extraordinary Mission of Belgium, Litta A No. 3, dispatch with order no. 104 from t'Kint de Roodenbeek to Charles Rogier, registered in Brussels on 26 July 1867; Shanghai, 4 June 1867, Extraordinary Mission of Belgium, dispatch from t'Kint de Roodenbeek to Charles Rogier, registered in Brussels on 21 July 1867. T'Kint's dispatches concerning the location of the Belgian ratification led to an extensive correspondence between the Belgian Foreign Ministry and the Belgian Consulates in Marseille and Shanghai. This correspondence is not discussed in this study, but can be consulted at MOFA Belgium 2098.

567 Kitane 1988 (volume 11), p. 250. Daily Japan Herald 2:1,116, front page and p. 2,700. Yokohama, Japan, Monday 10 June 1867. "Yokohama Shipping Intelligence – Arrivals / Passengers". For Count Vittorio Sallier de la Tour (1827-1904), see Bertelli 2011, p. 96.

568 University of Tokyo Volume XIII 1965 Politique, vol. 15 (1867, Mr. Roches), p. 87 (YAH microfilm outprint no. Ca4/01.36/37, p. 89). Mission de France au Japon, Yokohama, 26 June 1867, dispatch no. 85 from Roches to Moustier. Also, University of Tokyo Volume VI 1966, vol. 81, FO46 (223), pp. 132-133 (YAH microfilm outprint no. Ca4/01.9/223). Edo, 27 June 1867, dispatch no. 114 from Parkes to Stanley; University of Tokyo Volume IX and Volume X 1968 Ministers. U.S. National Archives, RG 59, M133, N.A. 133 (34) Vol. 8-2 (18 May – 20 October 1867). (YAH microfilm outprint no. Ca4/01.4/34, pp. 90-92). U.S. Legation in Japan, Edo, 22 August 1867, dispatch no. 43 from R. B. Van Valkenburgh, minister resident of the United States in Japan, to William H. Seward, secretary of state at Washington.

569 Though t'Kint was not in Yokohama at that time, he reported on the disaster from Shanghai. See MOFA Belgium 2865 IV. Shanghai, 8 December 1866, Extraordinary Mission of Belgium, Letter Litt. B no. 2 / Order no. 83, letter sent by Aug. t'Kint de Roodenbeek to Charles Rogier, Belgian foreign minister, and registered in Brussels on 4 February (1867), A/B 2483 no 2238. A map with the damaged parts of Yokohama was published by the Japan Herald. See Kitane 1988 (volume 12), p. 300-304 + map p. 308. Japan Herald Mail Summary, Market Report and Price Current. New Series 1:16 (Yokohama: 1 Dec 1866), pp. 1-5. An extensive report about the blaze is provided by Black 1881 pp. 17-26.

570 MOFA Belgium 2098. Yokohama, 11 June 1867, Extraordinary Mission of Belgium, Ind. A no. 3, dispatch with order no. 106 from t'Kint de Roodenbeek to Charles Rogier, registered in Brussels on 12 August 1867.

571 The announcement to t'Kint, for example, can be found at TUHI 1055.8/1 Belgium, 15th letter. 5 October 1866 (27th day of the 8th month of Keiō 2), (copy of a) letter in Dutch from Inoue Kawachi no Kami (Inoue Masanao), Matsudaira Suō no Kami (Matsudaira Yasuhide) and Matsudaira Nui no Kami to August t'Kint.

572 Adams 1875, pp. 47-48.

573 The English minister Harry Parkes described the surprise of Van Polsbroek who suddenly learned from the Japanese government that it was willing to conclude a treaty with Denmark, after the Dutch political agent had for months tried in vain just to draw the attention of Japanese councillors to this subject. Parkes also mentioned that the Danish treaty was based on the Belgian and Italian treaties. See University of Tokyo Volume VI 1966, vol. 78, FO46 (212), pp. 22-24 (YAH microfilm outprint no. Ca4/01.9/212, pp. 22-24). Edo, 16 January 1867, dispatch no. 2 from Parkes to Stanley.

574 TUHI. Dutch Consulate General 1867-1870. Archief no. 17, Anno 1867 (1), No. 1-38. Microfilm 6951-2-8-4; microfilm outprint no. 7551-48-8, pp. 3-5: Edo, 15 January 1867, letter in Dutch no. 1/1 from the political agent and consul general (Van Polsbroek) to the Dutch Ministry of Foreign Affairs at The Hague; pp. 6-7: Edo, 16 January 1867, letter in Dutch no. 2/2 from the political agent and consul general (Van Polsbroek) to the Dutch Ministry of Foreign Affairs at The Hague.

575 For the correspondence between Van Polsbroek and the Japanese government on the negotiations for Danish Treaty, see TUHI 1054.09/1. 16th letter: Edo, 27 December 1866, (copy of a) letter in Dutch no. 209/448 from D. de Graeff van Polsbroek to the Japanese councillors in charge of foreign affairs in Edo; 17th letter. Edo, 29 December 1866, (copy of a) letter in Dutch no. 211/453 from D. de Graeff van Polsbroek to the Japanese councillors in charge of foreign affairs in Edo; 18th letter. Edo, 31 December 1866, no. 215/457 "SPOED" (urgent), (copy of a) letter in Dutch no. 215/457 from D. de Graeff van Polsbroek to Shibata Hyūga no Kami (Shibata Sadatarō, also called Shibata Takenaka), Kurimoto Aki no Kami (Kurimoto Joun) and Ōkubo Tatemaki. Also TUHI 1054.04/3, p. 390: Edo, 29 December 1866, (copy of a) letter in Dutch no. 211/453 from D. de Graeff van Polsbroek to the Japanese councillors in charge of foreign affairs in Edo; p. 396: Edo, 31 December 1866, no. 215/457, (copy of a) letter in Dutch no. 215/457 from D. de Graeff van Polsbroek (political agent and consul general of the Netherlands in Japan) to the Japanese Commissioners.

576 TUHI 1055.4/1. 17 May 1861 (8th day of the 4th month of Bunkyū 1), letter in Dutch from Kuze Yamato no Kami (Kuze Hirochika) and Andō Tsushima no Kami (Andō Nobumasa) to J.K. De Wit, Dutch consul general, acknowledging the receipt of De Wit's letters no. 98 and no. 99 of 23 March (1861). In these letters De Wit announced his appointment as plenipotentiary to negotiate a treaty for Denmark with Japan.

577 University of Tokyo Volume IX and Volume X 1968. Legation. U.S. National Archives, RG 84, N.A. T400 (94) Vol. 46 (19 June – 26 December 1867). (YAH microfilm outprint no. Ca4/01.14/94, p. 6). Kanagawa, 17 June 1867, Eugène M. Van Reed, HHM Commissioner, to General Van Valkenburgh, American minister at Edo. The Hawaiian-Japanese treaty text obtained under the Tokugawa shogunate would not be signed. The Hawaiian government appointed Mr Van Reed, a trader living in Yokohama, as its minister plenipotentiary to sign the treaty. The Japanese government, however, considered the post of minister plenipotentiary too high to be filled by a commercially active person, and refused the appointment of Mr Van Reed on 20 October 1867. Before the matter had been resolved, the Tokugawa shogunate had perished. See University of Tokyo Volume IX and Volume X 1968 Ministers. U.S. National Archives, RG 59, M133, N.A. 133 (35) Vol. 8-3 (3 October – 2 December 1867). (YAH microfilm outprint no. Ca4/01.4/35, pp. 68-70). 20 October 1867 (23rd day of the 9th month of Keiō 3), English dispatch from Ogasawara Iki no Kami (Ogasawara Nagamichi) to R.B. Van Valkenburgh, minister resident of the United States. Last communication about the Hawaiian Treaty with the Tokugawa shogunate dated from 22 February 1868. See TUHI 1054.02/3, pp. 309-310. Yokohama, Legation of the United States in Japan, 22 February 1868, English dispatch no. 20 from A.L.C. Portman to the Japanese ministers at Edo.

578 University of Tokyo Volume IX and Volume X 1968 Legation. U.S. National Archives, RG 84, T400, N.A. T400 (8) Vol. 5 (1 January – 22 December 1861). (YAH microfilm outprint no. Ca4/01.14/8, pp. 2-3 and p. 5). 18 June 1861, (11th day of the 5th month of Bunkyū 1), letter in Dutch from Kuze Yamato no Kami (Kuze Hirochika) and Andō Tsushima no Kami (Andō Nobumasa), with English translation, to Townsend Harris, minister and plenipotentiary of the US of America, sending a negative reply to the request of the king of the Sandwich Islands (Hawaii) for a treaty.

579 See e.g. TUHI. MOFA Netherlands 1867. Microfilm 6951-54-8/9; microfilm outprint no. 7551-56-63. pp. 4-6. Edo, 14 February 1867, letter in Dutch no. 16/16 from the political agent and consul general (Van Polsbroek) to the Dutch minister of foreign affairs at The Hague, registered there on 6 April 1867. Attached to this dispatch is letter no. 2770 from the Japanese senior councillors (rōjū) to Van Polsbroek, dated 5th day of the 1st month of Keiō 3 (being 9 February 1867), mentioning that the mikado (emperor) died on the 29th day of the 12th month (of Keiō 2, being 3 February 1867).

580 University of Tokyo Volume VI 1966, vol. 78, FO46 (214), pp. 235-238 (YAH microfilm outprint no. Ca4/01.9/214). Edo, 14 February 1867, dispatch no. 25 from Parkes to Stanley.

581 See e.g. Adams 1875, p. 46, or Black 1881, p. 37.

582 Adams 1875, pp. 57-60.

583 Except for French minister Léon Roches, who had been received separately by the shogun in March 1867. See Adams 1875, p. 51.

584 See e.g. the extensive report of the British minister Harry Parkes on the negotiations in Osaka and the result obtained: University of Tokyo Volume VI 1966, vol. 80, FO46 (219), pp. 61-85 (YAH microfilm outprint no. Ca4/01.9/219). Osaka, 26 April 1867, dispatch no. 74 from Parkes to Stanley.

585 MOFA Belgium 2098. Yokohama, 29 April 1867, Vice Consulate of Belgium, dispatch no. 7 from Maurice Lejeune to the Belgian minister of foreign affairs, registered in Brussels on 3 July 1867; Yokohama, 15 May 1867, Vice Consulate of Belgium at Yokohama, Japan. Indicateur no. 10, dispatch no. 5 from Maurice Lejeune to the Belgian minister of foreign affairs, registered in Brussels on 22 July 1867. – Also MOFA Belgium 2865 IV. Brussels, 6 July 1867, Belgian Ministry of Foreign Affairs, Indicateur B no. 2483/476, Minute with a draft letter to the *Moniteur Belge*, partie non-officielle, including a translation in annex.

586 MOFA Belgium 2098. Yokohama, 11 June 1867, Extraordinary Mission of Belgium, Ind. A no. 3, dispatch with order no. 106 from t'Kint de Roodenbeek to Charles Rogier, registered in Brussels on 12 August 1867.

587 TUHI 1054.08, pp. 109-111, Yokohama, 12 June 1867, letter in Dutch from Aug. t'Kint de Roodenberk [sic], plenipotentiary envoy of Belgium, to the Japanese councillors in charge of foreign affairs in Edo.

Draft version of this dispatch in MOFA Belgium 2098. Yokohama, 12 June 1867, Extraordinary Mission of Belgium, (no. 20 added in different writing style).

588 MOFA Belgium 2098. 28 June 1867 (26th day of the 5th month of Keiō 3), Japanese letter and its Dutch translation from Inoue Kawachi no Kami (Inoue Masanao) to Auguste t'Kint. – Dutch translation can also be found at: TUHI 1055.8/1 Belgium, 22nd letter. The Okuyū Hitsuhichō 奥右筆秘帳 contains an entry on this meeting, dated 30 June 1867 [28th day of the 5th month (of Keiō 3)]. See TUHI Ishin 7, p. 142. D.I.S.K. 2892 (2906), pp. 121-122. Microfilm reproduction REEL no. Keiō 慶応 – 129, pictures 762.tiff – 0764.tiff.

589 MOFA Belgium 2098. 26 June 1867 (24th day of the 5th month of Keiō 3), Japanese letter and its Dutch translation from Inoue Kawachi no Kami (Inoue Masanao) to Auguste t'Kint, with the plans and rules for the settlements in Osaka and Hyōgo attached; 12 July 1867 (11th day of the 6th month of Keiō 3), Japanese letter and its Dutch translation from Ogasawara Iki no Kami (Ogasawara Nagamichi) to Auguste t'Kint. Dutch translations also at TUHI 1055.8/1 Belgium, 21st letter (although this copy gives 27 June 1867 – the 25th day of the 5th month of Keiō 3 – as the date of the letter); 24th letter of 12 July 1867 (11th day of the 6th month of Keiō 3).

590 MOFA Belgium 2098. Yokohama, 11 July 1867, Extraordinary Mission of Belgium, Ind. A no. 3, dispatch with order no. 109 from t'Kint de Roodenbeek to Charles Rogier, registered in Brussels on 13 September 1867; Edo, 5 August 1867, Mission extraordinaire de Belgique, Litt. A no. 3, draft dispatch with order no. 111, probably from Auguste t'Kint to Charles Rogier in Brussels.

591 MOFA Belgium 2704 III. Yokohama, 11 July 1867, Litt. C. no. 7, dispatch with order no. 110 from Aug. t'Kint de Roodenbeek to Charles Rogier, registered in Brussels on 13 September 1867, B 1746 no. 15019, confirming the receipt of dispatch B 1746 order no. 12 and dated 13 May 1867 from Rogier, awarding t'Kint a home leave in Belgium. Also MOFA Belgium 2864 XI. Yokohama, 11 July 1867, Extraordinary Mission of Belgium, Litta B no. 3, dispatch with order no. 107 from Aug. t'Kint de Roodenbeek to Charles Rogier, registered in Brussels on 13 September 1867, no. 15016.

592 MOFA Belgium 2098. 16 July 1867 (15th day of the 6th month of Keiō 3), Japanese letter and its Dutch translation from Ogasawara Iki no Kami (Ogasawara Nagamichi) to Auguste t'Kint. Dutch translation at TUHI 1055.8/1 Belgium, 25th letter. Japanese version at TUHI Ishin 7, p. 183. D.I.S.K. 2914 (2927), p. 86. Microfilm reproduction REEL no. Keiō 慶応 – 129, pictures 0957.tiff – 0958.tiff.

593 Kitane 1988 (volume 12), p. 71. *Bankoku Shinbunshi* 萬国新聞紙 mid July 1867 (mid of the 6th month of Keiō 3), under "カラ" (kara): 政府「ベルジャム」と条約を結いたり。(Government concluding a treaty with Belgium).

594 TUHI 1054.09/1, 20th letter. Edo, 19 July 1867, no. 1/4, (copy of a) letter in Dutch from D. de Graeff van Polsbroek (plenipotentiary of the king of Denmark) to the Japanese councillors in charge of foreign affairs at Edo.

Also TUHI 1054.04/3, p. 631. Edo, 19 July 1867, no. 1/4, (copy of a) letter in Dutch from D. de Graeff van Polsbroek (political agent and consul general of the Netherlands in Japan) to the Japanese councillors in charge of foreign affairs.

595 TUHI Ishin 7, p. 183. D.I.S.K. 2914 (2927), pp. 87-88. Microfilm reproduction REEL no. Keiō 慶応 – 134, pictures 959.tiff – 0960.tiff.

596 MOFA Belgium 2098. Edo, 5 August 1867, Mission extraordinaire de Belgique, Litt. A no. 3, draft dispatch with order no. 111 probably from Auguste t'Kint to Charles Rogier in Brussels. Also TUHI 1054.08, pp. 113-116. Edo, 12 August 1867, letter in Dutch from Aug. t'Kint de Roodenberk [sic] to Ishino Chikuzen no Kami (Ishino Noritsune), commissioner of foreign affairs in Edo. Japanese translation at TUHI Ishin 7, p. 183. D.I.S.K. 2914 (2927), pp. 80-85. Microfilm reproduction REEL no. Keiō 慶応 – 134, pictures 947.tiff – 0956.tiff.

597 TUHI 1055.4/3. 15 August 1867 (1st day of the 3rd month of Keiō 3), dispatch from Ogasawara Iki no Kami (Ogasawara Nagamichi) to D. de Graeff van Polsbroek. Also TUHI 1055.8/1 Denmark, 5th letter. 28 August 1867 (29th day of the 7th month of Keiō 3), letter in Dutch from Ogasawara Iki no Kami (Ogasawara Nagamichi) to D. de Graeff van Polsbroek.

598 TUHI 1054.08, pp. 113-116 (Dutch version), and pp. 119-121 (French version). Edo, 12 August 1867, letter in French and Dutch from Aug. t'Kint de Roodenberk [sic] (in Dutch version) or Auguste t'Kint (in French version) to Ogasawara Iki no Kami (Ogasawara Nagamichi), Japanese councillor in charge of foreign affairs in Edo.

599 TUHI 1055.8/1 Belgium, 38th letter. 4 October 1867 (7th day of the 9th month of Keiō 3), letter in Dutch from Ogasawara Iki no Kami (Ogasawara Nagamichi) to August t'Kint.

600 TUHI 1055.8/1 Belgium, 28th letter. (Copy of a) letter in Dutch from Ogasawara Iki no Kami (Ogasawara Nagamichi) to Auguste t'Kint. This copy mentions the 3rd day of the 7th month of Keiō 3, which is 2 August 1867, as date. It is more likely that the correct date was 3rd day of the 10th month, which corresponds to 29 October 1867. This would be more in line with the letter from t'Kint to Ogasawara, dated 12 August 1867, and from Ogasawara to t'Kint, dated 4 October 1867.

601 MOFA Belgium 2098. Edo, 29 August 1867, Mission de Belgique, Litt. A no. 3, draft dispatch with order no. 115, probably from August t'Kint de Roodenbeek to Charles Rogier in Brussels.

602 TUHI 1054.08, p. 123. Edo, 30 August 1867, copy of a letter in Dutch from Aug. t'Kint de Roodenberk [sic] to Ishino Chikuzen no Kami (Ishino Noritsune), commissioner of foreign affairs in Edo. – See also TUHI Ishin 7, p. 214. D.I.S.K. 2930 (2946), p. 69. Microfilm reproduction REEL no. Keiō 慶応 – 138, pictures 0308.tiff – 0309.tiff.

603 TUHI 1055.8/1 Italy, 23rd letter. 30 August 1867 (2nd day of the 8th month of Keiō 3), English letter from Ishino Chikuzen no Kami (Ishino Noritsune) to Count Arese, secretary of the Italian legation.

604 MOFA Belgium 2864 XI. Edo, 8 September 1867, Mission extraordinaire de Belgique, Litta B no. 3, order no. 116, with 3 annexes, to Charles Rogier, registered in Brussels on 12 November 1867, no. 18166.

605 TUHI 1054.08, p. 125. Edo, 8 September 1867, letter in Dutch from Auguste t'Kint to Ishino Chikuzen no Kami (Ishino Noritsune), commissioner of foreign affairs in Edo. Also TUHI 1055.8/1 Belgium, 33ʳᵈ letter. Probably 9 September 1867 (instead of 10 September) (13ᵗʰ (probably 12ᵗʰ) day of the 8ᵗʰ month of Keiō 3), letter in Dutch from Ishino Chikuzen no Kami (Ishino Noritsune) to August t'Kint. Original letter from Ishino in MOFA Belgium 2098. 9 September 1867 (12ᵗʰ day of the 8ᵗʰ month of Keiō 3), Japanese original and Dutch translation of a letter from Ishino Chikuzen no Kami (Ishino Noritsune) to Auguste t'Kint. Japanese versions of these dispatches at TUHI Ishin 7, p. 214. D.I.S.K. 2930 (2946), p. 66 and pp. 70-73. Microfilm reproduction REEL no. Keiō 慶応 – 138, picture 0304.tiff and pictures 0310.tiff – 0317.tiff.

606 MOFA Belgium 2098. Edo, 10 September 1867, A no. 3, draft letter with order no. 119 from t'Kint to Charles Rogier, containing two annexes.

607 MOFA Belgium 2016 I.A. Article from *Japan Herald – Mail Summary, Market Report and Price Current*, Yokohama, 1 October 1867.

608 TUHI Ishin 7, p. 234. D.I.S.K. 2945, pp. 145-147. Microfilm reproduction REEL no. Keiō 慶応 – 140, pictures 1008.tiff – 1012.tiff. 2 October 1867 (5ᵗʰ day of the 9ᵗʰ month of Keiō 3), report of Ishikawa Kawachi (Ishikawa Toshimasa) about the exchange of the Portuguese and Japanese ratifications on the 4ᵗʰ day (1 October).

609 TUHI Ishin 7, p. 239. D.I.S.K. 2946 (2968), pp. 86-89. Microfilm reproduction REEL no. Keiō 慶応 – 141, pictures 0842.tiff – 0848.tiff. Japanese announcement of 9 October 1867 [12ᵗʰ day of the 9ᵗʰ month (of Keiō 3)].

610 Kitane 1988 (volume 12), p. 228. *Chūgai Shinbunshi* 中外新聞紙 7 (12 October 1867 [15ᵗʰ day of the 9ᵗʰ month of Keiō 3]), p. 289.

611 University of Tokyo Volume VI 1966, vol. 81, FO46 (225), pp. 453-454 (YAH microfilm outprint no. Ca4/01.9/225, pp. 73-74). Edo, 11 September 1867, dispatch no. 153 from Parkes to Stanley.

612 TUHI 1054.08, pp. 127-129. Edo, 24 September 1867, letter in Dutch from Auguste t'Kint to Ogasawara Iki no Kami (Ogasawara Nagamichi), Japanese councillor in charge of foreign affairs in Edo, followed by the Dutch translation of the declaration of Leopold II in attachment. Draft of the Dutch version of the dispatch in MOFA Belgium 2098. Edo, 24 September 1867, Mission of Belgium, Litt. A no. 3 (no order number), draft of a letter in Dutch from Auguste t'Kint to Ogasawara Iki no Kami (Ogasawara Nagamichi), Japanese councillor in charge of foreign affairs in Edo. Japanese version at TUHI Ishin 7, p. 214. D.I.S.K. 2930 (2946), p. 74. Microfilm reproduction REEL no. Keiō 慶応 – 138, pictures 0318.tiff – 0320.tiff.

613 TUHI Ishin 7, p. 214. D.I.S.K. 2930 (2946), pp. 76-77. Microfilm reproduction REEL no. Keiō 慶応 – 138, pictures 0322.tiff – 0324.tiff.

614 TUHI 1054.08, p. 137. Edo, 12 October 1867, Auguste t'Kint to Ogasawara Iki no Kami (Ogasawara Nagamichi), Japanese councillor in charge of foreign affairs in Edo. Draft of this dispatch in MOFA Belgium 2098. Edo, 11 October 1867, Belgian Mission, Litt. A no. 3 (no order number), draft of a letter in Dutch from t'Kint to "Ogawara" [sic] Iki no Kami, Japanese councillor in charge of foreign affairs in Edo. The draft was apparently made one day before the final letter. Japanese version at TUHI Ishin 7, p. 214. D.I.S.K. 2930 (2946), p. 75. Microfilm reproduction REEL no. Keiō 慶応 – 138, pictures 0320.tiff – 0321.tiff.

615 MOFA Belgium 2098. 16 October 1867 (19ᵗʰ day of the 9ᵗʰ month of Keiō 3), original Japanese letter and its Dutch translation from Ogasawara Iki no Kami (Ogasawara Nagamichi) to August t'Kint with the approval of the shogun attached (Japanese original and Dutch translation). Copy of this dispatch and its Dutch enclosure at TUHI 1055.8/1 Belgium, 36ᵗʰ letter. This copy mentions as date the 19ᵗʰ day of the 8ᵗʰ month of Keiō 3. It is likely that the copyist made a mistake, writing the 8ᵗʰ instead of the 9ᵗʰ month, the latter corresponding to 16 October 1867. Japanese version at TUHI Ishin 7, p. 214. D.I.S.K. 2930 (2946), pp. 78-79. Microfilm reproduction REEL no. Keiō 慶応 – 138, pictures 0325.tiff – 0326.tiff.

616 MOFA Belgium 2098. Edo, 24 October 1867, Belgian Mission, Litt. A no. 3, draft of a French dispatch with order no. 122 from Auguste t'Kint to Charles Rogier.

617 MOFA Belgium 2098. Edo, 5 August 1867, Mission extraordinaire de Belgique, Litt. A no. 3, draft letter in French with order no. 111, probably from August t'Kint de Roodenbeek to Charles Rogier in Brussels.

618 TUHI 1055.8/1 Italy, 34ᵗʰ letter. English letter from Ishino Chikuzen no Kami (Ishino Noritsune) to Count Arese, secretary of the Italian legation, dated 9ᵗʰ month of Keiō 3, without mentioning the day. On the basis of the communication between the Italian mission and the Japanese government, this letter should have been written after 4 October and before 27 October 1867.

619 Kitane 1988 (volume 11), p. 250. *Daily Japan Herald* 2:1,116 (Yokohama, Japan: Mon 10 Jun 1867), front page and p. 2,700. Yokohama Shipping Intelligence – Arrivals / Passengers.

620 On 11 October 1867, the Japanese commissioners sent a dispatch to the "Secretary of the Belgian Legation" about the appointment of a new vice commissioner. Embarrassed because of not knowing the name of the secretary, they requested the Belgian Legation to inform him about it. If not, they would send their dispatches to the Belgian minister (Auguste t'Kint). No reply has been found in the Belgian or Japanese archives. Since t'Kint had arrived in Japan on 9 June 1867, it is highly unlikely that he would not have revealed the name of the secretary by 11 October 1867, if there had been one. See TUHI 1055.8/1 Belgium, 39ᵗʰ letter. 11 October 1867 (14ᵗʰ day of the 9ᵗʰ month of Keiō 3), letter in Dutch from the (Japanese) commissioners to the secretary of the Belgian legation.

621 TUHI 1054.07/1, pp. 27-29. Yokohama, 10 September 1867, copy of a letter in French from Count Arese, secretary of the Italian legation, to Ishino Chikuzen no Kami (Ishino Noritsune), commissioner of foreign affairs at Edo.

622 TUHI 1055.8/1 Italy, 28ᵗʰ letter. 15 September 1867 (18ᵗʰ day of the 8ᵗʰ month of Keiō 3), English letter from Ishino Chikuzen no Kami (Ishino Noritsune) to Count Arese.

623 University of Tokyo Volume IX and Volume X 1968 Ministers. U.S. National Archives, RG 59, M133, N.A. 133 (34) Vol. 8-2 (18 May – 20 October 1867). Microfilm outprint no. Ca4/01.4/34, pp. 82-84. U.S. Legation in Japan, Edo, 18 August 1867, dispatch no. 40 from R.B. Van Valkenburgh, minister resident of the United States in Japan, to William H. Seward, secretary of state at Washington, in particular page 83.

624 TUHI 1054.07/1, p. 30. Edo, 26 September 1867, anonymous English message mentioning that the Italian minister will wait 5 days to exchange the treaty.

625 TUHI 1055.8/1 Italy, 30ᵗʰ letter. 28 September 1867 (1ˢᵗ day of the 9ᵗʰ month of Keiō 3), English letter from Ishino Chikuzen no Kami (Ishino Noritsune) to Count de la Tour.

626 TUHI Ishin 7, p. 235. D.I.S.K. 2943, pp. 112-113. Microfilm reproduction REEL no. Keiō 慶応 – 141, pictures 165.tiff – 168.tiff. Japanese report from Ishino Chikuzen no Kami (Ishino Noritsune) dated 5 October 1867 (8ᵗʰ day of the 9ᵗʰ month of Keiō 3) about the exchange of the ratifications of the Treaty between Italy and Japan on 3 October 1867 (6ᵗʰ day of the 9ᵗʰ month of Keiō 3).

627 Further communication about this problem can be found in following dispatches: TUHI 1055.8/1 Italy, 30ᵗʰ letter. 28 September 1867 (1ˢᵗ day of the 9ᵗʰ month of Keiō 3), English letter from Ishino Chikuzen no Kami (Ishino Noritsune) to Count de la Tour; 34ᵗʰ letter. English letter from Ishino Chikuzen no Kami (Ishino Noritsune) to Count Arese, dated 9ᵗʰ month of Keiō 3, without mentioning the day. On the basis of the communication between the Italian mission and the Japanese government, this letter should have been written after 4 October and before 27 October 1867. Also TUHI 1054.07/1, pp. 31-33: Edo, Italian Legation, 30 September 1867, copy of an English letter from Count de la Tour probably to Ishino Chikuzen no Kami (Ishino Noritsune); pp. 34-36: Yokohama, 4 October 1867, copy of an English letter from Count Arese, secretary of the Italian legation, to Ishino Chikuzen no Kami (Ishino Noritsune).

628 TUHI. LJ36. "B. Benten (Jan. 1862- June 1877): stukken betrekking hebbende op het lot "Benten". 23 December 1867, draft dispatch no. 240/454 from Van Polsbroek to the commissioner of Kanagawa; 16 January 1868, exhibit no. 20 or 207, being a dispatch from Mizuno Wakasa no Kami 水野若狭守 and Yoda Ise no Kami 依田伊勢守 (commissioners of Kanagawa) to Van Polsbroek, acknowledging the receipt of Polsbroek's dispatch no. 240/454, dated 23 December 1867, and communicating the agreement of the Japanese authorities with this arrangement.

629 TUHI Ishin 7, p. 214. D.I.S.K. 2930 (2946), pp. 82-84. Microfilm reproduction REEL no. Keiō 慶応 – 138, pictures 0330.tiff – 0333.tiff. Japanese translation of a dispatch probably from t'Kint to the Japanese commissioners of foreign affairs, registered by the Japanese administration on 8 October 1867 [11ᵗʰ day of the 9ᵗʰ month (of Keiō 3)].

630 TUHI 1055.8/1 Belgium, 41ˢᵗ letter. 19 October 1867 (22ⁿᵈ day of the 9ᵗʰ month of Keiō 3), letter in Dutch from Ezure Kaga no Kami (Ezure Akinori), Ishino Chikuzen no Kami (Ishino Noritsune), Kawakatsu Ōmi no Kami, Ishikawa Kawachi no Kami (Ishikawa Toshimasa), Kikuchi Iyo no Kami (Kikuchi Takayoshi), Kasuya Chikugo no Kami, Sakae Tsushima no Kami and Kaji Seizaburō to Auguste t'Kint. A Japanese version can be found at TUHI Ishin 7, p. 214. D.I.S.K. 2930 (2946), pp. 85-86. Microfilm reproduction REEL no. Keiō 慶応 – 138, pictures 0334.tiff – 0336.tiff. The Japanese version is dated 20 October 1867 [23ʳᵈ day of the 9ᵗʰ month (of Keiō 3)].

631 MOFA Belgium 2098. Edo, 24 October 1867, Belgian Mission, Litt. A no. 3, order no. 122, draft of a dispatch with order no. 122 from Auguste t'Kint to Charles Rogier.

632 TUHI 1054.08, pp. 139-141. Edo, 21 October 1867, letter in French from Auguste t'Kint to Ogasawara Iki no Kami (Ogasawara Nagamichi), Japanese councillor in charge of foreign affairs at Edo. Also TUHI 1055.8/1 Belgium, 44ᵗʰ letter. 27 October 1867 (1ˢᵗ day of the 10ᵗʰ month of Keiō 3), letter in Dutch from Ogasawara Iki no Kami (Ogasawara Nagamichi) to Auguste t'Kint. Japanese versions of these dispatches at TUHI Ishin 7, p. 214. D.I.S.K. 2930 (2946), pp. 67-68, pp. 80-81, pp. 87-88. Microfilm reproduction REEL no. Keiō 慶応 – 138, pictures 0305.tiff – 0307.tiff, pictures 0328.tiff – 0329.tiff and pictures 0337.tiff – 0339.tiff.

633 MOFA Belgium 2098. Edo, 24 October 1867, Belgian Mission, Litt. A no. 3, order no. 122, draft of a dispatch with order no. 122 from Auguste t'Kint to Charles Rogier. Also TUHI 1054.08, pp. 143-146. Yokohama, 29 October 1867, letter in Dutch from Auguste t'Kint to Ishino Chikuzen no Kami (Ishino Noritsune), Japanese commissioner of foreign affairs in Edo. A Japanese version of the dispatch of 29 October 1867 can be found at TUHI Ishin 7, p. 266. D.I.S.K. 2961 (2986), pp. 80-84. Microfilm reproduction REEL no. Keiō 慶応 – 144, pictures 0885.tiff – 0861.tiff.

634 MOFA Belgium – Japon Politique, no. 6, Brussels, 23 March 1868, dispatch from Auguste t'Kint to Jules Vander Stichelen, Belgian foreign minister, registered in Brussels on 3 April 1868.

635 See e.g. MOFA Belgium 2704 III. Paris, 1 September 1868, letter from t'Kint de Roodenbeek to baron (probably Baron Auguste Lambermont, secretary general of the Belgian Ministry of Foreign Affairs); MOFA Belgium 2864 XI. Kaiserbad, Aix-la-Chapelle (Aachen), 10 September 1868, B2483, no. 1480, Aug. t'Kint de Roodenbeek to "Mon cher baron" (probably Baron Auguste Lambermont).

636 Truong 1857, pp. 211-217. Also MOFA Belgium 316. Brussels, 4 May 1869, Indicateur A. no. 4639, Minute containing a draft letter from the Belgian Ministry of Foreign Affairs to the Belgian king; Brussels, 11 May 1869, Indicateur A. no. 4639, Minute containing a draft letter form the Belgian Ministry of Foreign Affairs to Auguste t'Kint in Brussels.

637 MOFA Belgium 316. Brussels, 5 July 1869, Indicateur A. no. 4639, Minute containing a draft letter from the Belgian Ministry of Foreign Affairs to the minister for the royal household; Brussels, 16 July 1869, Indicateur A. no. 4639, Minute containing a draft letter from the Belgian Ministry of Foreign Affairs to Auguste t'Kint in Brussels; Laeken, 30 July 1869, copy of Royal Decree no. 46.

638 MOFA Belgium 316. Hong Kong, 14 November 1869, Belgian Legation, dispatch with order no. 1 from Auguste t'Kint to Jules Vander Stichelen, Belgian foreign minister, registered in Brussels on 1 March 1870, A4369 no. 3473. Truong 1957, p. 216, mistakenly gives 14 October 1869 as the date of this letter.

639 MOFA Belgium 316. Internal note entitled "Note relative à une demande de congé faite par M. Auguste t'Kint, envoyé extraordinaire du Roi en Chine et au Japon". In the margins of the text, the date 24 November 1870 is mentioned; Peking (Beijing), 11 August 1870, Belgian Legation, dispatch with order no. 29 from Auguste t'Kint to Jules Vander Stichelen, Belgian foreign minister, registered in Brussels on 18 October 1870, B 1746 no. 14936; Brussels, 4 November 1870, Direction A 4369, Minute containing draft dispatch with order no. 16 from the Belgian Foreign Ministry to t'Kint in Japan.

640 MOFA Belgium 883. Yokohama, 12 November 1870, Belgian Legation, dispatch with order no. 39 from Auguste t'Kint to Baron d'Anethan, Belgian foreign minister in Brussels.

641 The Belgian authorities, represented in Japan by Vice Consul Maurice Lejeune, were officially informed of the change of government on 12 May 1868. See MOFA Belgium 883. Yokohama, 13 May 1868, Belgian Vice Consulate no. 22, dispatch from Lejeune to the Belgian minister of foreign affairs, registered in Brussels on 31 July 1868, B 476 no. 12242.

642 Truong 1957, pp. 217-225 (Consulate in Edo) and p. 231 (Consulate in Osaka).

643 Nitta 1975 [3], p. 94 (*Japan Punch* of November 1870) and p. 120 (*Japan Punch* of February 1871).

644 MOFA Belgium 316. Yokohama, 19 January 1871, Belgian Legation, dispatch with order no. 48 from Auguste t'Kint to Baron d'Anethan, Belgian foreign minister in Brussels; Brussels, 7 April 1871, Direction A 4369, Minute containing a draft letter with order no. 9 from the Belgian Ministry of Foreign Affairs to t'Kint; Edo, 8 September 1871, Belgian Legation, Litt. C no. 11, dispatch with order no. 87 from Auguste t'Kint de Roodenbeek to Baron d'Anethan, registered in Brussels on 4 November 1871, A 4369 no. 15849.

645 TUHI 1054.08, pp. 413-415. Hyōgo, 8 October 1871, letter in French from Auguste t'Kint to the Japanese councillors in charge of foreign affairs at Edo.

646 MOFA Belgium 316. Hong Kong, 6 December 1871, Belgian Legation, Litt. C no. 1, dispatch with order no. 94 from Auguste t'Kint de Roodenbeek to Baron d'Anethan, Belgian foreign minister, registered in Brussels on 22 January 1872, A 4369; Hong Kong, 13 December 1871, copy of a part of dispatch no. 7 from Belgian consul Nicaise to the Belgian minister of foreign affairs; Hong Kong, 28 December 1871, Belgian Legation, Litt. C no. 11, dispatch with order no. 98 from Auguste t'Kint de Roodenbeek to Baron d'Anethan, Belgian foreign minister, registered in Brussels on 13(?) February 1872, A 4369; Naples, 21 February 1872, Belgian Legation in China and Japan, dispatch without order no. from Auguste t'Kint de Roodenbeek to Count d'Aspremont-Lynden, Belgian foreign minister, registered in Brussels on 4 March 1872, A 4369 no. 3914. In Naples, t'Kint assisted his sister Sidonie, who had fallen ill, till her death on 13 March 1872. He then took care of the process to get the body of his sister to Belgium for burial. See Rome, 19 March 1872, letter from Auguste t'Kint de Roodenbeek to Count d'Aspremont-Lynden, registered in Brussels on 30 March 1872, A 4369.

647 MOFA Belgium 316. Brusssels, 27 May 1873, Minute, Direction A no. 4369 (no order number) containing a draft letter from the Belgian Ministry of Foreign Affairs to A. t'Kint, including a copy of a Royal Decree dated 21 May 1873; Brussels, 23 March 1878, death notice of Auguste Pierre Joseph t'Kint.

648 Fabri 1965, p. 247, note [2] identifies the grave where Auguste t'Kint was buried as the family grave t'Kint-Waumans (Auguste's parents) in Laeken Cemetery, tomb 301. In 1965, this tomb was abandoned. During a visit to the cemetery on 5 February 2015, the author was not able to locate tomb 301.

A TRUE ACCOUNT OF A JOURNEY OF OBSERVATION THROUGH THE UNITED STATES OF AMERICA AND EUROPE AND AN ACCOUNT OF THE STATE OF BELGIUM: RESONANCES OF THE SMALL NATION CONCEPT

Yutaka Yabuta

Studio photograph of the Iwakura Mission.
Sitting in the middle in traditional Japanese dress, but wearing Western shoes
and holding a top hat in his left hand, is Iwakura Tomomi.
In Western dress from left to right: the deputy ambassadors Kido Takayoshi,
Yamaguchi Naoyoshi, Itō Hirobumi and Ōkubo Toshimichi.

A TRUE ACCOUNT OF A JOURNEY OF OBSERVATION THROUGH THE UNITED STATES OF AMERICA AND EUROPE AND AN ACCOUNT OF THE STATE OF BELGIUM: RESONANCES OF THE SMALL NATION CONCEPT

Introduction

From a corner of the outer garden of the Meiji jingū shrine in Tokyo, the silhouette of the Seitoku Kinen Kaigakan 聖徳記念絵画館 (Meiji Memorial Picture Gallery) with its characteristic circular dome is visible through the alley of ginkgo trees, marking one of the scenic spots of the capital. The building was completed in October 1926 (Taishō 15) and designated a national important cultural asset in 2011. As suggested by its name, it is an institution glorifying the achievements of the reign of the Meiji emperor in eighty mural paintings, forty of which are painted in Japanese style and forty in Western style. The murals are large, 3 metres high by 2.5 metres wide. The series begins with *The Restoration of the Imperial Rule*, followed by *The Surrender of Edo-jō Castle*, while the third is *The Dispatch of the Iwakura Embassy to Europe and the U.S.*, painted by the Japanese-style painter Yamaguchi Hōshun 山口蓬春 (1893-1971). The series was completed in April 1936 (Shōwa 11), that is to say sixty-five years after the dispatch of the embassy headed by Iwakura Tomomi 岩倉具視 in 1871 (Meiji 4).

The inclusion of this historic event shows the perceived importance of the embassy dispatched by the new government on an eighteen-month mission to twelve Western countries. However, the "reading" of this historic event does not stop here. Appraisal and discussion of its significance is possible and has been conducted from various angles, which include the political historical assessment of the Coup of 1873 in the wake of the embassy's return to Japan, as well as its significance in the biographies of the embassy's leader Iwakura Tomomi and his entourage, and the dispatch of female students abroad, such as Tsuda Umeko 津田梅子. In particular, the compilation and publication of the voluminous official record titled *A True Account of the Ambassador Extraordinary & Plenipotentiary's Journey of Observation through the United States of America and Europe (Tokumei zenken taishi Bei-Ō kairan jikki 特命全権大使米欧回覧実記)* (henceforth: *A True Account*)[1] has supplied a solid basis for any such attempt at appraisal. In that sense, the value of *A True Account* as a text is infinitely great.

A True Account, published in October 1878 and featuring a preface with explanatory notes dated January 1876 (Meiji 9), was written in a mixture of *kanji* and *katakana*, following standard practice of government publications of that time. Those features have been preserved in the five-volume Iwanami Bunko version (1977), which is today generally used as the sole text. Its style, moreover, which reflects the schooling of its author, the mission's official secretary Kume Kunitake 久米邦武, is redolent of that of Classical Chinese studies.[2] The compilation reflects to a high degree both in content and in form the contemporary situation of the early years of the Meiji period. Thus far, many assessments of the Iwakura mission have been conducted on the aforementioned premises, and recently an English-language five-volume translation of the book has been published.[3] Accordingly, the assessment inevitably assumes an international dimension.

The present essay is likewise an attempt at assessment, singling out Belgium, one of the countries toured by the mission. Belgium is singled out to shed light on the concept of the "small nation" in the early Meiji period. Several studies have thus far been devoted to the "small nation" concept during this period, notably Tanaka Akira's 田中彰 pioneering work *Shōkokushugi: Nihon no kindai o yominaosu 小国主義 - 日本の近代をよみなおす*.[4] In this short article, I will attempt a new assessment of this notion by comparing it with, among others, Sufu Kōhei's 周布公平 *Berugī-koku shi 白耳義国志*, which appeared in 1877 (Meiji 10), around the time of *A True Account*.

The Concept of a Small Nation in *A True Account of a Journey of Observation through the United States of America and Europe*

In an expository comment in the first volume of the Iwanami edition of *A True Account*, Tanaka Akira points out that:

> The countries the Iwakura mission was most interested in were the United States and the United Kingdom, followed by Germany and France, admittedly followed by Italy and Russia. Although some were more advanced than others, all were "great powers" of the time. The "lesser countries", by contrast, were Belgium, the Netherlands, Switzerland, Sweden, and Denmark. The number of fascicles devoted to them amounts to a total of 12 [out of 100] vols. So one can say that the degree of interest in small countries as a whole was not low at all.[5]

Tanaka's judgement was based on the proportion of text within the total volume, and when reading the actual text of *A True Account*, there are indeed many passages that testify to the mission's keen interest in small nations:

> * No paper currency is issued in Sweden, Denmark, Belgium, or Switzerland. The fiscal affairs in these small independent countries are managed with meticulous care, and great attention is paid to financial regulations.[6]
> * Meanwhile, smaller powers like Belgium, Holland, Denmark and Switzerland fortify their defences like hedgehogs with their spines bristling on their backs.[7]
> * [...] and now, [as a result of the passage of time], they stand amid the great powers and preserve their independence, although they are numerically inferior even to the inhabitants of Paris in France. All this is due to their character, which is solid, industrious, patriotic and unwavering.[8]

Of course, this reflects the reality that Japan's fourteen Western treaty partners (including Spain and Portugal which could not be toured[9]) found themselves in the situation that "[peoples] from the great powers inevitably take pride in their strength and look down on those from small countries."[10]

There is no doubt that the scenes the members of the mission saw right in front of their eyes surpassed their book knowledge and made a deep impression on them. Reading the following passage with this in mind, one senses an unusual degree of excitement in the mission's view of "small nations". Kume writes:

> [...] let us present a profile of two small countries, namely, Belgium and Holland. In terms of size and population, they may both be compared with the island of Tsukushi [Kyushu]. Their territories consist of unproductive wetlands, yet squeezed as they are among larger powers they manage to preserve their independent spirit, and, if anything, their commercial power is actually superior, for they not only hold interests in Europe but exert an influence on world trade as well. This is due to the diligence and co-operative nature of the people, and as we shall endeavour to relate here, they have some features which we have found even more striking than anything in the three great powers [i.e. the US, the UK, and France, note by present author].[11]

This passage was written as part of a general survey of Belgium, the first small country the mission visited after touring through the US, the UK and France. In other words, the first impression the mission got of a "small nation", was that given by Belgium. In a later chapter, "A Record of the Journey by Rail through Western Prussia", the size of Belgium was compared to Rhineland Province in Prussia: "[...] this large province is almost the size of Belgium."[12] Expressed in concrete numerical data, Belgium measured 10,382 square miles with 5,087,105 inhabitants as compared to Rhineland's 10,352 square miles and 3,578,964 inhabitants. Making abstraction of the populations, their sizes were similar.

The sentence "they may both be compared with the island of Tsukushi [i.e. Kyushu]" is an appreciation marked by a personal feeling of Kume, who hailed from Saga in Kyushu. In fact, covering an area of around 30,000 square kilometres, Belgium was considerably smaller in surface area than the seven Kyushu prefectures, which total 42,149 square kilometres.[13] Therefore, although Belgium was in numerical terms closer to the Rhineland, we might say that Kume's actual feeling was expressed in the comparison with his native Kyushu. A reference to "the island of Tsukushi" appears in another passage, in chapter 52, "A General Survey of Holland": "We had already seen how the Belgians strive for autonomy in a land of plains comparable [in size] with the island of Tsukushi, and now, on our arrival in Holland, we were once again greatly impressed by observing how a nation with the same number of people as the four Kyushu provinces of Chikuzen, Chikugo, Hizen and Higo has contrived to build a wealthy and populous nation from a land wallowing in mud."[14]

This bespeaks an unusually emotional sense of a Kyushu identity. This sense of Kyushu identity is apparent in his description in various places. While pretending to be a "Japanese" abroad, his true Kyushu identity pops up accidentally. To put it differently, keeping his native Kyushu in mind, he saw small western countries such as the Netherlands, Denmark and Switzerland against the backdrop of his own native Kyushu.[15]

After Belgium, the mission entered the Netherlands, "a small country among the European Powers" measuring 160 miles in length to 100 miles in breadth, and the mission's awareness that this was "a small country" grew even stronger. Their "small nation" concept was significantly refined not by Belgium, which had thus far virtually been unknown to the Japanese, but through the special mediation of the Netherlands, which had represented the West during the period of national seclusion. The closeness of the two countries, "Belgium and Holland being sibling nations" and "Belgium and Holland both being marshland",[16] is also relevant. In other words, "unknown" Belgium provided the first impression of a Western "small nation", and the "already known" Netherlands confirmed it. Needless to say, the Netherlands was a major colonial power, and a great maritime power, to the point that "the Dutch may be called the foremost in Europe in their commercial skills."[17] Hence, while being based on territorial scale, the "small nation" concept also considered the substance of "national strength". In that respect, there was obviously also substance involved in viewing Belgium as a small nation. "Belgians contend that if there are too few people who are [economically] self-sufficient, the country will grow weak and become difficult to preserve."[18]

This is a clear statement about how an independent government system rests on an independent people, and, in addition, about how in Belgium's case this strength had been shaped in recent years (thus demonstrating that it could be achieved by effort).

When Kume turns his gaze to industry, he makes the following appraisal:

* The thriving state of railway construction here stands foremost among the countries on the continent of Europe. This is due to Belgium's situation on a plain at the heart of traffic arteries stretching in all directions, together with an abundance of iron and coal.[19]
* now this country has the most prosperous iron-manufacturing on the continent of Europe.[20]
* Belgium is a country which has grown wealthy from its mineral resources. In the industrial arts, also, it must stand at the forefront of countries of the [European] plains.[21]

This appraisal of the infrastructure and equipment was substantiated by observation on the spot, since during the short stay of merely a week a great proportion of the official agenda was reserved for visits to factories. Various plant tours were scheduled, including visits to the De Hemptinne cotton spinning and weaving factory, to *La Lys* linen weaving mill (19 February), the Val-Saint-Lambert glassworks and the Cockerill ironworks (21 February), the Courcelles sheet-glass factory, and to Brussels-based manufacturing companies (22 February). The only visits not to factories were to the Royal Palace on 18 February, the batteries of Boechout on 20 February, and the battlefield of Waterloo on 23 February. Having visited Britain, "the workshop of the world", the mission was genuinely surprised at the high level of Belgian industry.[22] They could not help but gain an ever more favourable opinion of "small nations". Thus, having inspected Belgium and the Netherlands successively, their "small-nation" concept gained in depth, to include characterizations such as that "the Belgians are a martial people, [...] whereas the Dutch are a people of letters [...]".[23] This stance enabled them to likewise include Denmark and Switzerland, which they visited later, in their "small-nation" perspective.

One might say that the mission's awareness of small nations was thus raised in a mere fortnight's time from 17 February to 7 March, when it had Belgium and the Netherlands in its itinerary.

It goes without saying that this "small nation" perspective came about against the backdrop of "great powers" like the US, the UK, and France, but it is noteworthy that Kume, when developing his view of the Netherlands as a small nation, compares it with China, on which he was very knowledgeable from reading: "I have heard that if one sails to China and reaches the mouth of the Yangtze River, vast expanses of mud banks appear along the coast."[24] As a result, he concludes with the following perspective: "If people with the spirit of the Dutch were to live on the plains of China, who knows how many hundred Hollands could be born in the East. In terms of diligence, can the Japanese be compared with the Dutch [...]?"[25] Measuring the scale of those countries from his personal sensibility as a Kyushu islander, and with his background in Chinese classics as a permanent stock-in-trade, he set his objective for the newly emerging "Japan". The Iwakura embassy was indeed on a mission carrying the Japan of the future.

Godai Tomoatsu's View of Small Nations

Thus far we have dealt with the "small nation" concept as developed in *A True Account*, but this kind of awareness was not particularly characteristic of Kume or other mission members. Rather, it seems to have been a trend in the late Edo to early Meiji period. This may be illustrated by the figures of Godai Tomoatsu 五代友厚 (1835-85), who travelled to Europe in 1865 (Keiō 慶応 1), as leader of a group of students from the domain of Satsuma, and Sufu Kōhei 周布公平, who wrote *An Account on the Country of Belgium* (*Berugī-koku shi* 白耳義国志) based on his experiences as a student abroad. Godai left a record of his visit to Europe in his autographical *Diary of the Toured Countries* (*Kaikoku nikki* 廻国日記; vol. 4 of *Godai Tomoatsu denki shiryō* 五代友厚伝記資料).[26] According to this diary, his itinerary started on 14 September 1865 (Keiō 1.7.25), when he left London, entering Belgium the following day via Ostend. After visits to Brussels, Waterloo, and Liège, he entered Prussia via Cologne, reaching Berlin on 25 October (Keiō 1.9.6). He then returned to Cologne, entering the Netherlands on 28 October (Keiō 1.9.9), making a stop at Amsterdam and Rotterdam, and on 1 November (Keiō 1.9.13) he re-entered Belgium. He continued his itinerary via the cities of Antwerp, Ghent, Brussels, Liège, Namur, arriving in Paris, his last stop, on 12 November (Keiō 1.9.24). His diary subsequently describes his stay in Paris, and it concludes with his return to London on 20 December (Keiō 1.11.3). Thus, over about two months, he made a four-country tour of Belgium, the Netherlands, Germany, and France. Needless to say, his itinerary coincided to a large extent with

that followed a few years later by Kume and his party. However, during his continental visit Godai entered into negotiations with the count of Montblanc, a Frenchman; on 15 September (Keiō 1.7.26) he was welcomed by Montblanc in Ostend, and they met frequently in Paris in connection with the projected participation of the Satsuma domain in the impending 1867 Universal Exposition. On 24 September (Keiō 1.8.5), while in Brussels, Godai exchanged a covenant with Montblanc with a view to the eventual conclusion of a treaty of peace and amity with Belgium. A sizable part of Godai's international tour was devoted to Belgium. Apart from France, where he stayed for over a month, he spent most of his time in Belgium, while he stayed for a mere three days in Germany, and only 5 days in the Netherlands. It was only in Belgium that he made guided tours of institutions like the Mint, the Cockerill ironworks, sugar refineries, museums, hospitals, and prisons, while in the other places he observed "the local manners and customs". In that sense, while being on a tour of various countries on the continent, it was inevitable that there was a sense of one-sidedness in his observations.

Having arrived in Paris, Godai first turned his attention to Britain and France, as may be inferred from a letter he wrote on 29 November (Keiō 1.10.12) to his friend Katsura Hisatake 桂久武, in which he notes: "The size of this city is about one third compared to London" and "In Europe, France stands unchallenged as country where academic studies are most advanced." Next he notes "Among European countries, the United Kingdom has the most just and benevolent government, followed by Belgium in second position. However, he makes almost no reference to other countries such as Germany and the Netherlands. This in contrast to his companion Niiro Gyōbu 新納刑部, who favourably commented on Dutch flood defences, saying: "On this occasion we took a look at the Netherlands. This country really lies as I had been told at sea level, and has constructed dykes all around to protect it from the surrounding sea."

However, as a matter of fact, Godai's interest in Belgium was even more passionate than suggested by his letter to Katsura. Let us cull some relevant passages from *Diary of the Toured Countries*, listing dates and destinations:

29 September (Keiō 1.8.1): Brussels: visiting museums and the botanical garden.

* Compared to Britain, France, and other countries, Belgium is very small, but nonetheless the country is

very wealthy, and both museums here are much grander than one would expect from a small country.

1 October (Keiō 1.8.12): Brussels: visit of a hospital, poorhouse, and reformatory.

* Of a grandeur and beauty one would not expect from a small country.

3 November (Keiō 1.9.15): An inspection tour of Antwerp.

* These forts are laid out on a grand scale, such as one would not expect from a small country.

3 November (Keiō 1.9.15): Ghent: An inspection tour of the prison, women's section, and botanical garden.

* Belgium may be a small country, its state administration is excellent and leaves nothing to be desired. Admirable!

Godai too gives Belgium a place within the power equation of Western European societies, thus elaborating a vision on small nations. Moreover, he uses this notion exclusively for Belgium, never applying it to the neighbouring Netherlands. In this respect, Godai's perspective is much narrower than that of Kume and the Iwakura mission, in terms of the number of countries visited, the breadth of his vision, and the degree of elaboration of his views on "small nations", as compared to Kume's *A True Account*.

Sufu Kōhei's *An Account of the Country of Belgium*

In 1877 (Meiji 10), around the time *A True Account* appeared, the three-volume *An Account of the Country of Belgium* authored by Sufu Kōhei (1850-1921) was published.[27] As for the bibliographical data, copyright was granted on 29 July 1877, the first volume was issued on 29 September, followed by the 2nd and 3rd volumes on 19 October. The title page mentions that the printing blocks are owned by Seiyō Shorō 静養書楼. Judging from the colophon, "Seiyō" presumably refers to Sufu's pen name. It was a joint publication by ten booksellers, the most prominent of whom were Kishida Ginkō 岸田吟香 of Rakuzendō 楽善堂 at Ginza 銀座 2 Chōme (Tokyo), Murakami Kanbē 村上勘兵衛 who was based at Nishikyō Higashinotōin-dōri Sanjō Noboru 西京東洞院通三条上ル in Kyoto, Kumagai Kyūbē 熊谷久兵衛 of Kyūkyodō 鳩居堂 at the corner of Kamigyō Teramachi Anegakōji 上京寺町姉小路, likewise in Kyoto, and Yanagihara Kihē 柳原喜兵衛 from Minami Kyūhōji-machi 南久宝寺町,

Shinsaibashi 心斎橋, Ōsaka 大坂. On the inside cover, a calligraphic inscription reading *Ryōsai yūhō* 亮采有邦 (taken from the Chinese Classic *The Book of Documents*: "those who clarify matters will have their countries") is written in the hand of Sanjō Sanetomi 三条実美 (1837-1892), chancellor of the realm. It is followed by prefaces by Kido Takayoshi 木戸孝允 (1833-77) and Itō Hirobumi 伊藤博文 (1841-1909), and finally by Sufu Kōhei's own foreword and explanatory notes, before entering the text proper. The final volume contains epilogues by Shishido Tamaki 宍戸璣 (1829-1901) and Yamada Akiyoshi 山田顕義 (1844-1892). All four of them hailed from Chōshū Domain, as indeed did Sufu. The text proper in volume I extends over 86 sheets, in volume II 84 sheets, and in volume III 94 sheets. Volume I contains an insert with a map of Belgium. Freely translated the opening sentence in Kido's preface reads as follows: "One day, Sufu Kōhei, son of my late friend Asada Kōsuke [i.e. Sufu Masanosuke 周布政之助 (1823-64), a Chōshū Domain leader during the Bakumatsu period, author's note], who had studied in Belgium, brought me a visit carrying this book and requested me to write a preface. I exclaimed: 'Belgium is the smallest country in Europe with no long political history, but it has managed to maintain its independence among the great powers, not because of its territorial or military strength, but because of the aptitude of its institutions and prosperity of its products of civilization [...]!'"

Incidentally, Kido suddenly passed away on 26 May and never saw the publication of this book. Thereupon, Sufu asked Sugi Magoshichirō 杉孫七郎 to finish the preface: "As HE Kido, adviser to the cabinet, passed away before the completion of his manuscript, Kōhei asked me to finish it." The sentence "Belgium is the smallest country in Europe with no long political history, but it has managed to maintain its independence among the great powers" is without doubt revealing of Kido's view of "small nations". It was based on his own first-hand observation when he visited Belgium as deputy-ambassador of the Iwakura mission. In contrast, the author's own foreword reads:

Of late, when Japanese discuss the politics and customs of Western countries, they mainly focus on the United Kingdom, or France, or Prussia, or even Russia or the United States, but they almost never discuss countries like Belgium. I made a study tour to Belgium, and I got to know the country by observing its politics, regulations, regions, products of civilization and so on. A country like Belgium, existing as it does among great powers such as Britain and France, is of course no match for having very limited territory and little influence, but its population is intelligent and resourceful [...] When we realize that the level of civilization of a country has nothing to do with the extent of its territory, and that the intelligence of a man has no relation to his stature, we see that it should likewise not yield to great powers such as Britain and France in its possibilities to assist our country in the modernization effort.[28]

Here again we unmistakably come across a case of "small-nation" concept, which resonates with that of *A True Account*. In a way Belgium is the medium through which the "small-nation" concept resonates between Kume, Kido, and Sufu.

Let us take a closer look at the structure of *An Account of the Country of Belgium*:

Vol. 1: geography, climate, ethnic groups, religion, languages, manners and customs, weights and measures, currency, national debt, products, exports and imports, transportation, power grid, provinces (Brabant, East Flanders, West Flanders, Hainaut, Namur, Luxembourg, Liège, Limburg, Antwerp), brief history.

Vol. 2: system of government, monarch, demography, people's status and rights, legislative power: Chapter 1: outline of the legislative power; Chapter 2: parliament, provincial councils

Vol. 3: executive power (Ch. 1-13), judicial power (Ch. 1-6), finances (Ch. 1-4), military system (Ch. 1-4)

Appendix: retirement costs, Savings Bureau

To say a few words about its contents, in the chapter on geography the text says that "Belgium is one of the small countries in Europe", that its size is 29,456 square kilometres, that it has a population of 5,253,821 people, and that its density ranks first among European countries. The chapter "Manners and customs" says: "Their character is loyal and they have a zest for work. When meeting Belgians, you experience how very kind and hospitable they are," and it goes on to state that they are very patriotic, and are a music-loving nation. The north-western part of the country turns out agricultural products such as grain, hemp, tobacco, *houblon* (hops), and *betteraves* (sugar beets), whereas the south-eastern part produces mineral resources such as iron, lead, zinc,

and coal. Sufu also mentions the steam-powered production of glassware, woollen goods, cotton yarn, and hemp threads, but when comparing this information with the descriptions in *A True Account*, which vividly describes the situation using text and copperplates, it is not entirely satisfactory. However, one passage – "Nowadays a railway network criss-crosses the country in all directions like a cobweb; whether they want to go to the capital or to rural areas, no matter how far they want to travel, people rely on its services. Indeed, there is virtually no great European power whose national railroad infrastructure is better" – bears a close resemblance to an observation in *A True Account*: "The thriving state of railway construction here stands foremost among the countries on the continent of Europe". This represents Belgium as the railroad kingdom.

Another remarkable aspect of volume 1 is the sections discussing the several provinces. The section on the Province of Brabant includes an explanation about the capital, Brussels, while the section on the arrondissement of Leuven, also deals with the Catholic University of Leuven. Much space is allotted to geographical descriptions – in the section on the Province of Liège, for example, the Cockerill ironworks is depicted, stating that it currently employs about 9,000 workers, that the total sum of salaries and wages amounted to 8 million francs, and that the turnover was between 25 and 30 million francs. It is thus understandable that the book presents itself in the format of *Landeskunde*.

The central part of Sufu's *An Account of the Country of Belgium* comprises volumes 2 and 3, which include topics on the legislature, the executive, and the judiciary. Here Sufu introduces the various provisions of the constitution that was enacted in February 1831, starting with the position of the king, following with the rights of the people, and then discussing the Parliament, the provincial councils (vol. 2), the administrative power, the judicial power, finances, and the military system (vol. 3). *An Account of the Country of Belgium* can be defined as a book on the Belgian political and legal system, and in this respect its tenor differs markedly from *A True Account*. It can also be ranked among the earliest works introducing the Belgian constitution.[29]

Since Sufu claimed in his foreword that his book was the result of his personal study abroad, let us now investigate Sufu's studies abroad. Although his career has been discussed in a number of encyclopaedias, they remain vague on his studies abroad. "Following the Meiji Restoration, he left for a study stay abroad, and in 1876 (Meiji 9) he became fourth assistant (*gonshōjō* 権少丞) to the minister of justice."[30] "Following the Restoration, he went to study in France, and upon his return to Japan, he became the chief secretary of the cabinet (*naikaku shoki kanchō* 内閣書記官長)".[31] These are not very instructive passages. Among such sources, *Kaigai tokō jinmei nenkan* 海外渡航人名年鑑 is the only one to give a relatively detailed account:

– Position at the time of departure: student, key member of the institution's staff.
– Destination: France and Belgium.
– Period abroad: 1871-1885, time returning home: 1876-1885.
– Activities while abroad: foreign study at public expense, group inspections at public expense,
– Overseas study destinations etc.: (Second) International Commercial Law Conference.

According to this source, he had studied in France as a foreign student from 1871-1876, but according to his own foreword in *An Account of the Country of Belgium*, he must indeed have studied in Belgium. The publication of *Berugī-koku shi* was taken up in the 10 October 1877 *Tōkyō Nichi Nichi Shinbun* 東京日日新聞 newspaper and the 14 October *Chōya Shinbun* 朝野新聞 newspaper. The *Chōya Shinbun* wrote "Mr Sufu Kōhei who studied in Europe for a long time", hinting at his long-term study abroad, but the *Kōbunroku* 公文録 ("Compiled Records of the Grand Council of State") or the *Dajō ruiten* 太政類典 ("Great State Classified Codes") do not specify from which Japanese institution he had been dispatched, or to what location in Belgium he had been sent.

However, *Dajō ruiten* does mention that Sufu participated as Japanese committee member in the Second International Commercial Law Conference, which was held in Brussels from 30 September to 6 October 1888 (Meiji 21). It is possible that the year 1885 mentioned in *Kaigai tokō jinmei nenkan* refers to this event. His position then was councillor of the Japanese legation in Italy. In his debriefing report, Sufu declared: "During my stay in Belgium, I met with hospitable treatment by the Belgian government, and I received a kind reception by the citizens of Brussels, and during the Commercial Law Conference, I was officially selected as one of the chief secretaries of the conference."[33] For Sufu, this was his first visit to Belgium in more than a decade.

Sufu Kōhei and the Iwakura Mission

As is well known, Kido, who wrote a preface for Sufu's *An Account of the Country of Belgium*, was deputy-ambassador to the mission led by Ambassador Extraordinary & Plenipotentiary Iwakura. He was therefore naturally in Belgium in February 1873 (Meiji 6). At the same time Sufu was also staying in the country, and the two men indeed had contact with one another. As deputy-ambassador, Kido recorded the mission's itinerary in his diary, and it contains references to Sufu:[34]

17 February: Fukuchi 福地 has arrived from Turkey in the Indian Region together with Mokurai 黙雷. Komatsu has arrived in Austria.
18 February: Return to my hotel at 6 o'clock, Sufu, Kanazuchi 金槌, and Kōno Kōtarō 河野光太郎 pay me a visit.
21 February: Kōno, Sufu, Ogura 小倉, and Mitsuda 光田 visit me for a talk.
22 February: Return to my hotel, Ogura and Sufu visit me for a talk.
23 February: Guided by Ogura and Sufu, Ōkubo 大久保, Sugiura 杉浦, Tanaka 田中, Kume 久米 and myself went to Waterloo.

The mission had arrived on 17 February in Brussels, and almost every day from the 18th onward, Kido had meetings with Sufu and other Japanese students studying in Belgium. It may be recalled that guidance and supervision of Japanese students in the United States and Europe was one of the tasks of the mission.[35] This is borne out by many entries in Kido's diary. Indeed, from 21 December 1871 (Meiji 4) onwards, he had continual meetings with Japanese students living in the United States and the United Kingdom, as well as with those based in France, Belgium, the Netherlands, and Prussia. They include the likes of Mori Arinori 森有礼, Sugiura Kōzō 杉浦弘蔵, Tsuda Umeko 津田梅子 in the US, Aoki Shūzō 青木周蔵, Yuri Kimimasa 由利公正, and Terashima Munenori 寺島宗則 in the UK, and Shimaji Mokurai 島地黙雷 in France. The contacts between Kido and Sufu are to be seen in that light. They both hailed from Chōshū, moreover, Kōhei's father, Sufu Masanosuke, used to be a retainer of Chōshū Domain. We might say that they were very close. It can be easily imagined that they exchanged views on various issues as they travelled together to various places in Belgium.

Very interesting in this regard is the visit to Waterloo on 23 February. This event is also included in *A True Account*, where the entry begins with the words: "We left by carriage at nine o'clock this morning and headed west [south] for twelve miles before arriving in the village of Waterloo."[36] Then follows an explanation of the war and a description of the old battlefield, to conclude with the words: "Snow had fallen today and the fields were covered with patches of slush; what with the overcast sky and the damp air, the whole scene felt wretched and bleak."[37] It is a fine piece of prose which beautifully describes winter in Belgium, but it does not mention with whom the mission members made the trip to Waterloo.

Since the preface with explanatory notes of *A True Account* states that in each country they toured, they enjoyed privileged treatment from monarchs and queens, invitations, receptions and banquets from governments, escorts, mayors and aldermen, factories, and aristocracy, it is fair to assume that they went to Waterloo under the guidance of a local Belgian government official. However, in the original manuscript of *A True Account* (*Jikki sokō* 実記素稿), which is reproduced in *Kume Kunitake monjo* 久米邦武文書 3 (2001), we find the following passage in the entry for 23 February:

"As 23 [February] was a Sunday we had a day off. Today was a holiday; the townspeople covered their faces with a white cloth, some people wore masks and gathered in various places and performed dances. They said it was the annual fair of this place. It was clouded today and the wind blew snow."

The information that it snowed is the same, but according to the manuscript (*sokō*), the company watched a festival in Brussels, and did not go to Waterloo as the entry in *A True Account* would have it. This discrepancy is solved when we consider the following. The *sokō* was written focusing on the official agenda, but as there were no official events on Sunday 23 February, the entry was simply limited to a festival in Brussels, the place of their sojourn. However, as already mentioned,

Kido's diary, which was from the outset a personal diary, noted that they went on a day's outing to Waterloo guided by Japanese students including Sufu. Kume Kunitake also joined the company. Considering those data in combination, we may conclude that it was the Japanese who had taken the initiative for the trip to Waterloo on 23 February without any involvement from prominent Belgian government officials. It is conceivable that Kume, in the process of writing *A True Account*, added the Japanese-only private Sunday outing to Waterloo.

Waterloo was already then a famous place in Europe.[38] And as illustrated by Godai Tomoatsu's visit there, it was a place of interest for the Japanese too. In his *Kaikoku nikki*, Godai noted: "Thursday, 3rd day of 8th month: Leaving early in the morning, we went to have a look at the old battlefield of Waterloo, just 4 *ri* [c.16 km] from this city. [...] They say, people from various European countries come in throngs to visit it [...]. Toward the evening, we returned to our hotel."

In *Edo no Naporeon densetsu* 江戸のナポレオン伝説 (1999), Iwashita Tetsunori 岩下哲典 has demonstrated that information about Napoleon, which was first introduced in Japan through the Nagasaki interpreters around 1813 (Bunka 文化 10), was anachronistic and lagged far behind European contemporary events. It can be categorized in two strands: one is that of "biographical research within the larger perspective of the deliberate study of Western history," which was passed on between generations of Dutch-language interpreters and scholars of Dutch studies (e.g. Koseki San'ei 小関三英, Mitsukuri Genbo 箕作阮甫, and Ōtsuki Bankei 大槻磐渓); the other is the "literary reading," which started with Rai San'yō's 頼山陽 *Furansu ōka* 仏郎王歌, and was carried on by Sakuma Shōzan 佐久間象山, Yoshida Shōin 吉田松陰, and Saigō Takamori 西郷隆盛. Both Godai and Kume, as well as Sufu can be placed in the pedigree of the latter literary and patriotic reading. In other words, we may read the Sunday outing of the mission to the battlefield of Waterloo, site of Napoleon's most fateful battle, as an act of resonance with the noble-minded patriots who had lived through the political upheaval of the Bakumatsu and early Meiji periods. That kind of interpretation is warranted in the case of *A True Account*, which for the itinerary of that single day includes no fewer than four copperplate prints: the village of Waterloo; The church in Waterloo, which served as

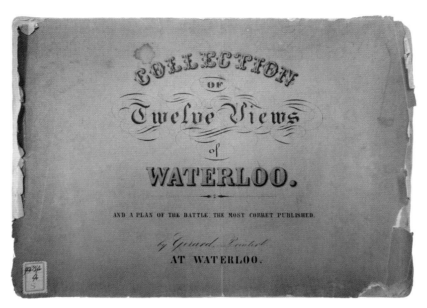

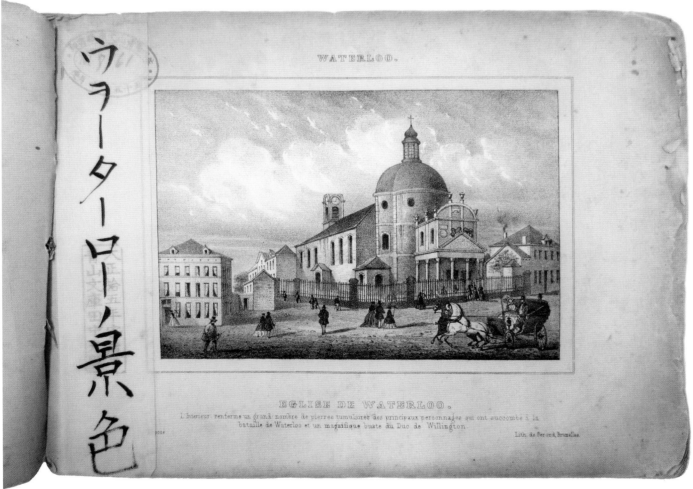

Cover of the Waterloo album entitled *Collection of Twelve Views of Waterloo and a Plan of the Battle, the Most Corret* [sic] *Published*. By Gerard, Printers at Waterloo.
Collection Seizan bunko 青山文庫 in Sagawa-chō 佐川町,
Takaoka-gun 髙岡郡 in Kōchi prefecture, Japan.
Photograph by Yutaka Yabuta.

Engraving showing the church at Waterloo with Japanese inscription reading
"Sights of Waterloo." From *Collection of Twelve Views of Waterloo and a Plan of the Battle,
the Most Corret* [sic] *Published*. By Gerard, Printers at Waterloo.
Collection Seizan bunko. Photograph by Yutaka Yabuta.

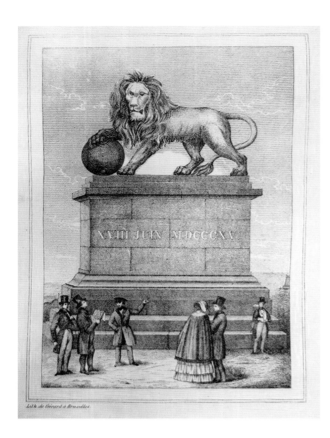

Wellington's headquarters; the great mound [Butte du Lion] at Waterloo, and the site of the British general's command post.

Incidentally, in his preface to *A True Account* Kume notes: "Many of the originals were purchased on our travels and I had them reproduced. Among them are re-worked reprints of copperplate etchings."[39] Consequently, these four prints too were reproductions of copperplate engravings they had purchased on site. However, since the prints in *A True Account* were partially cropped, and since no source was clearly specified, it is unclear which copperplate prints served as models. Fortunately, however, in the case of the Waterloo prints, there was one member of the mission who had procured an identical set for himself. This was Tanaka Mitsuaki 田中光顕 (1843-1939) who joined the mission as a commissioner from Tosa.[40]

The title on the Nile-blue cover of the set of copperplate prints purchased by Tanaka during the trip reads *Collection of Twelve Views of Waterloo and a Plan of the Battle, the Most Corret* [sic] *Published*. Inside the album a paper strip has been inserted on which a Japanese phrase is written in Indian ink: "sights of Waterloo." The church that Wellington used as his headquarters is the first of twelve prints, and bears the

title *Église de Waterloo*. Each of the prints has a French title, for example *Ferme de la belle Alliance* (prints 11 and 12), corresponding to the village of Waterloo in *A True Account*, and *Montagne du lion* (print 7) for the great mound [Butte du Lion] at Waterloo. However, since there is no print corresponding to "the site of the British general's command post," there must have existed another set of copperplates at the time. This set of prints further includes two depictions of the interior of the dome of the church that served as Wellington's headquarters, as well as a panorama of the 1815 Waterloo battlefield, a depiction of the lion statue on top of the mound, and a map of the formations of both armies on the field, none of which was included in *A True Account*. Since an inscription in the margin reads: "donated by Tanaka Mitsuaki to the *Seizan bunko* Library 青山文庫, in Taishō 15" [1926], we know that it belonged to Tanaka. This collection is very valuable, in the sense that it tells us about one of the sources of the copperplate material used in Kume's *A True Account*. Tanaka Mitsuaki, as one of the noble-minded patriots who lived through the Bakumatsu and early Meiji periods, must also have been deeply moved by Napoleon's fate.

Conclusion

Lining up Godai Tomoatsu, Kume Kunitake, Kido Takayoshi, and Sufu Kōhei around the Iwakura mission's *A True Account*, we have come to the conclusion that a "small nation" like Belgium was far from being thought little of by the Japanese. However, although it concluded a Treaty of Amity, Commerce and Navigation with Japan in the 1860s, to Japan Belgium was a "newcomer". How many Japanese were aware of Belgium's existence? Moreover, it was a "young" nation, a little over 40 years since it had been founded by gaining independence from the Netherlands. Seen in this light, the fact that the Japanese who set foot in this country showed such keen interest in and had such a high opinion of Belgium may be called "an event".

There was an objective background to this. According to *Shōkoku: Rekishi ni miru rinen to genjitsu* 小国―歴史 に見る理念と現実 by Momose Hiroshi 百瀬宏,[41] the Congress of Vienna (1814), which was held to settle the situation after the Napoleonic wars, was the first international congress to make a deliberate distinction between "great powers" and other nations on the

Rather free and naive depiction of the cast iron statue of the Lion of Waterloo. The Dutch name of the month June (juni) has been replaced by its French translation, and both the posture and the mane are rather awkward. From *Collection of Twelve Views of Waterloo and a Plan of the Battle, the Most Corret* [sic] *Published*. By Gerard, Printers at Waterloo. Collection Seizan bunko. Photograph by Yutaka Yabuta.

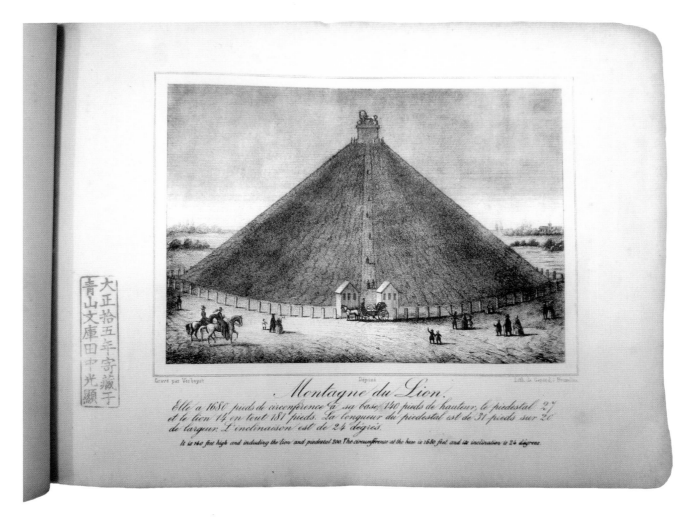

European continent. The "great powers" were Austria, Prussia, Russia, and Britain, which had played leading roles in the Napoleonic wars. The balance of power among those nations brought about the permanent neutrality of Switzerland, a country comprised of 22 cantons. Thus emerged the "small nation" whose national policy was grounded in "traditional neutrality".

Following the Swiss example was Belgium, whose permanent neutrality was guaranteed in 1839. The sphere of application of this notion gradually spread to Eastern and Northern Europe, where between the 1860s and the 1870s the number of "small nations" pursuing a "traditionally neutral" line steadily increased. The fact that the Franco-Prussian War, which erupted in 1870, was fought without implicating Belgium, enhanced on the international political level the value of "small nations" that adopted a policy of "traditional neutrality". People like Godai Tomoatsu, Kume Kunitake, Kido Takayoshi, and Sufu Kōhei happened to be in Western Europe at that moment. Meanwhile "Great Powers" such as France were reinforcing themselves by institutional reorganization, thus ushering in an era of intense confrontation and dispute. At that time, while the rights of "small nations" were guaranteed under international law, events erupted which existentially threatened these "small nations". Accordingly, while some aspects of the "small-nation" concept resonated with them, they simultaneously took note of how Prussia had developed from a "small nation" into a "Great Power". The mission did not forget to pay attention to the international environment, where "International law, too, is concerned only with a country's strength or weakness, for it is the small nations which remain neutral and are protected solely by this law, whereas great powers must use their might to claim their rights."[42]

Now, particularly in the case of Belgium, we have to touch upon an issue in which Sufu and the others had no particular interest, but which would eventually become the most serious problem for Belgium: the "language question".

The great mound at Waterloo, the Montagne du Lion (Butte du Lion), with the seal of the Seizan bunko giving the name of the donor Tanaka Mitsuaki. From *Collection of Twelve Views of Waterloo and a Plan of the Battle, the Most Corret* [sic] *Published*. By Gerard, Printers at Waterloo.
Collection Seizan bunko. Photograph by Yutaka Yabuta.

Since 1993, Belgium has officially been a federal state comprising language communities, but the antagonism between the Dutch and French languages originated already at the time when the country was founded. Consequently, Kume, as well as Sufu, like Kido and Godai, must have seen and heard about that reality. In *A True Account*, the following comment is inserted: "Three languages are spoken in Belgium. The people of mainly Belgian stock inhabiting the lands from the French borders to the central provinces use French, and today the government, administration and schools all employ French as the national language. There are some 1,800,000 people in the southern districts towards Luxembourg who speak Walloon, and about 2,400,000 people in the eastern [northern] districts around Antwerp who use Flemish, a language resembling Dutch but apparently pronounced more like French."[43]

They refer to the fact that multiple languages exist in one modern state, but they would never have expected that this would become a serious problem that even today shakes the framework of the Belgian state.

NOTE: The present article in English is the revised version of an article originally in Japanese that was included in the research report "2000－2001 nendo Kokusai Kōryūjoseikikin ni yoru Kansai Daigaku to kyōtei kōkan no kyōdō kenkyū seika hōkokusho '19 seiki no Nihon to Berugī: Kindaika to kokusai kankyō'" 2000－2001 年度国際交流助成基金による関西大学と協定校間の共同研究成果報告書『19世紀の日本とベルギー―近代化と国際環境―』

(research project representative: Prof. Asaji Keizō 朝治啓三, 2002).

(translated by David De Cooman and W.F. Vande Walle)

REFERENCES

Bakumatsu Ishin jinmei jiten
Bakumatsu Ishin jinmei jiten 幕末維新人名事典. Tokyo: Shin Jinbutsu Ōraisha 新人物往来社, 1994.

Ishizaka 1993
Ishizaka Akio 石坂昭雄. "Iwakura shisetsudan to Berugī" 岩倉使節団とベルギー. In Bei-Ō kairan jikki *no gakusaiteki kenkyū* 「米欧回覧実記」の学際的研究, ed. Tanaka Akira 田中彰 and Takada Seiji 高田誠二. Hokkaidō Daigaku Shuppankai 北海道大学出版会, 1993.

Ishizuki 1972
Ishizuki Minoru 石附実. *Kindai Nihon no kaigairyūgaku-shi* 近代日本の海外留学史. Tokyo: Mineruva Shobō ミネルヴァ書房, 1972.

Isomi et al. 1989
Isomi Tatsunori 磯見辰典 et al. *Nihon Berugī kankei-shi* 日本・ベルギー関係史. Tokyo: Hakusuisha 白水社, 1989.

Kido nikki
Kido Takayoshi 木戸孝允. *Kido Takayoshi nikki* 木戸孝允日記, 3 vols. Tokyo: Tōkyō Daigaku Shuppankai 東京大学出版会, 1967.

Kokusaijin jiten: Bakumatsu, Ishin
Kokusaijin jiten: Bakumatsu, Ishin 国際人事典:幕末・維新. Tokyo: Mainichi Komyunikēshonzu 毎日コミュニケーションズ, 1991.

Kume 1878
Kume Kunitake 久米邦武. *Tokumei zenken taishi Bei-Ō kairan jikki* 特命全権大使米欧回覧実記. 5 vols. Tokyo: Hakubunsha 博聞社, 1878.

Kume 1977–82
Kume Kunitake 久米邦武. *Bei-Ō kairan jikki* 米欧回覧実記. 5 vols. Iwanami bunko series 岩波文庫. Tokyo: Iwanami Shoten 岩波書店, 1977–82.

Kume 2002a
Kume Kunitake. *The Iwakura Embassy, 1871-1873: A True Account of the Ambassador Extraordinary & Plenipotentiary's Journey of Observation through the United States of America and Europe*. Vol. 1: *The United States of America*, trans. Martin Collcutt. Chiba: The Japan Documents, 2002

Kume 2002b
Kume Kunitake. *The Iwakura Embassy, 1871-1873: A True Account of the Ambassador Extraordinary & Plenipotentiary's Journey of Observation through the United States of America and Europe*. Vol. 2: *Britain*, trans. Martin Collcutt. Chiba: The Japan Documents, 2002

Kume 2002c
Kume Kunitake. *The Iwakura Embassy, 1871-1873: A True Account of the Ambassador Extraordinary & Plenipotentiary's Journey of Observation through the United States of America and Europe*. Vol. 3: *Continental Europe 1*, trans. Andrew Cobbing. Chiba: The Japan Documents, 2002

Kume 2002d
Kume Kunitake. *The Iwakura Embassy, 1871-1873: A True Account of the Ambassador Extraordinary & Plenipotentiary's Journey of Observation through the United States of America and Europe*. Vol. 4: *Continental Europe 2*, trans. P.F. Kornicki. Chiba: The Japan Documents, 2002

Kume 2002e
Kume Kunitake. *The Iwakura Embassy, 1871-1873: A True Account of the Ambassador Extraordinary & Plenipotentiary's Journey of Observation through the United States of America and Europe*. Vol. 5: *Continental Europe 3 and the Voyage Home*, trans. Graham Healey, Eugene Soviak, and Chushichi Tsuzuki. Chiba: The Japan Documents, 2002.

Momose 2011
Momose Hiroshi 百瀬宏. *Shōkoku: Rekishi ni miru rinen to genjitsu* 小国―歴史にみる理念と現実. Tokyo: Iwanami Shoten 岩波書店, 2011.

Nihon jinmei daijiten
Nihon jinmei daijiten 日本人名大事典. Tokyo: Heibonsha 平凡社, 1979.

Sufu 1877
Sufu Kōhei 周布公平. *Berugī-koku shi* 白耳義国志 [An Account on the Country of Belgium] 3 vols. Seiyō Shorō 静養書楼, 1877.

Tanaka 1999
Tanaka Akira 田中彰. *Shōkokushugi: Nihon no kindai o yominaosu* 小国主義・日本の近代をよみなおす. Tokyo: Iwanami Shinsho 岩波新書, 1999.

Vande Walle 1996
Willy Vande Walle. "Count de Montblanc and the 1865 Satsuma Mission to Europe." *Orientalia Lovaniensia Periodica* 27 (1996), pp. 151-176.

Vande Walle et al. 2004
Willy Vande Walle, F.G. Notehelfer, Igor R. Saveliev. "Review article: An Extraordinary Odyssey – The Iwakura Embassy Translated." *Monumenta Nipponica* 59:1 (Spring 2004), pp. 83-119.

Yabuta 2005
Yabuta Yutaka 藪田貫. "Meiji shonen no 'Nihongo' ronsō" 明治初年の「日本語」論争. In *Nihon kinseishi no kanōsei* 日本近世史の可能性, ed. Yabuta 藪田. Tokyo: Azekura Shobō 校倉書房, 2005.

A TRUE ACCOUNT OF A JOURNEY OF OBSERVATION THROUGH THE UNITED STATES OF AMERICA AND EUROPE AND *AN ACCOUNT OF THE STATE OF BELGIUM*: RESONANCES OF THE SMALL NATION CONCEPT

NOTES

1 See Kume 1878.

2 I have dealt with Kume's career and educational background in comparison with that of Mori Arinori 森有礼 and Baba Tatsui 馬場辰猪 in Yabuta 2005.

3 *The Iwakura Embassy 1871-73*, Vols. I-V, The Japan Documents, 2002. A review of this publication by W. Vande Walle and others appeared in Vande Walle 2004.

4 Tanaka 1999.

5 Kume 1977–82, vol. 1, p. 408.

6 Ch. 46, "A Record of the City of Paris", in Kume 1977–82, vol. 3, p. 133; Kume 2002c, p. 123.

7 Ch. 45, "A Record of the City of Paris", in Kume 1977–82, vol. 3, p. 117; Kume 2002c, p. 105.

8 Ch. 67, "A Record of the Country of Denmark", in Kume 1977–82, vol. 4, p. 135; Kume 2002d, p. 129.

9 Ch. 89, "A General Survey of Political Practices and Customs in Europe", in Kume 1977–82, vol. 5, p. 146; Kume 2002e, pp. 146ff.

10 Kume 1977–82, vol. 3, p. 26; Kume 2002c, p. 230.

11 Ch. 49, "A General Survey of the Country of Belgium", in Kume 1977–82, vol. 3, p. 165; Kume 2002c, p. 157.

12 Kume 1977–82, vol. 3, p. 290; Kume 2002c, p. 284.

13 Present-day Belgium has a surface of 30,528 square kilometres. After the First World War, it acquired the so-called East Cantons as part of the peace settlement at the Conference of Versailles (1919). Their surface is 1051 square kilometres. Kume's figure is not far off the mark.

14 "A General Survey of Holland", in Kume 1977–82, vol. 3, p. 321; Kume 2002c, p. 214.

15 Assuming that Belgium was a small nation, Germany represented a great power. "Then in 1866 news arrived of the defeat of Austria, with accounts of Prussia's ascendant power in Europe, but it was not until three years before our visit, with the defeat of France, that the might of Prussia truly reverberated around the world, signalling its emergence as a great nation on a par with Britain and France." [Kume 1977–82, vol. 3, p. 308; Kume 2002c, p. 302], a passage making reference to the Franco-Prussian War.

16 Kume 1977–82, vol. 3 p. 252; Kume 2002c, P; 238.

17 Kume 1977–82, vol. 3, p. 227; Kume 2002c, p. 219.

18 Kume 1977–82, vol. 3, p. 167; Kume 2002c, p. 159.

19 Kume 1977–82, vol. 3, 170; Kume 2002c, p. 162.

20 Kume 1977–82, vol. 3, p. 200; Kume 2002c, p. 191.

21 Kume 1977–82, vol. 5, p. 35; Kume 2002e, p. 23.

22 Ishizaka 1993.

23 Kume 1977–82, vol. 3, p. 46; Kume 2002c, p. 238.

24 Kume 1977–82, vol. 3, p. 221; Kume 2002c, p. 214.

25 Kume 1977–82, vol. 3, p. 221; Kume 2002c, p. 214.

26 The dates given in volume 4 of *Godai Tomoatsu denki shiryō* 五代友厚伝記資料 are reconstructed dates, since the original manuscript *Kaikoku nikki* 廻国日記 does not date its entries. Every entry is simply preceded by the day of the week, but without date. In the body of the text we find six dates according to the lunar calendar and one according to the western calendar. It is possible to reconstruct the dates on the basis of these two parameters, but there is a one day variance between them. Moreover, in order to make the dates match with dates known from other sources, we have to postulate that there is a gap of twenty days in the diary. This is the hypothesis proposed by Ōkubo Toshiaki. However, Aratani Kurō has suggested an alternative chronology. For a discussion of the merits of these varying chronologies, see Vande Walle 1996, pp. 151-176. Since this chronological issue has little or no relevance to the argument developed in this article, the dates given in volume 4 of *Godai Tomoatsu denki shiryō* are kept as they are.

27 A brief introduction to this work is included in Isomi et al. 1989, qualifying it as "the only specialized introduction to Belgium in the early Meiji period." For this article, I used a copy from the Araki English Studies Library in the possession of the Dōshisha University Information Center.

28 Sufu 1877, vol. 1, p. 158.

29 Sufu also left us *Berugī-koku kenpō shitsumonroku* 白耳義国憲法質問録 and *Berugī-koku Genrōin kisoku shitsumonroku* 白耳義国元老院規則質問録, two shorthand records (both translations by the *Genrōin*, 1886) of interviews with the Belgian Senate Secretary C. Warnant セ・ワルナン (Isomi et al. 1989).

30 *Nihon jinmei daijiten*, 3.

31 *Bakumatsu Ishin jinmei jiten*.

32 *Kokusaijin jiten: Bakumatsu, Ishin*.

33 National Archives of Japan 国立公文書館, "rui" 類, 42-1291.

34 *Kido nikki*, vol. 2.

35 For detailed information on foreign students and the mission, see Ishizuki 1972.

36 Kume 1977–82, vol. 3 p. 208; Kume 2002c, p. 201.

37 Kume 1977–82, vol. 3 p. 208-213; Kume 2002c, p. 206.

38 *A True Account* states that "[...] to this very day the French never come to visit this place. In contrast, a never-ending stream of men and women from Germany and Britain arrive daily to pay their respects." [Kume 2002c, p. 206]. According to a survey of nineteenth-century European travel books and travel guidebooks carried out by the National Library of the Netherlands in The Hague, almost all publications in this period included prints, sketches and other illustrations. For instance, the following title, published immediately after the Battle of Waterloo may be mentioned: *SKETCHES in FLANDERS and HOLLAND with some account of a tour through parts of those, shortly after the battle of Waterloo, 1816*.

39 Kume 1977–82, vol. 1, p. 26; Kume 2002a, p. 19.

40 Owned by the *Seizan bunko* Library, Sakawa Town 佐川町, Takaoka District 高岡郡, Kōchi Prefecture 高知県. In addition to Waterloo, commemorative albums on Rouen (France), Stockholm, and Switzerland remain. See *Seizan bunko zuroku* 青山文庫図録, vol. 2 (1997). For the survey and publication of photographs, I am indebted to chief librarian Matsuoka Mamoru 松岡司.

41 Momose 2011.

42 Kume 1977–82, vol. 3, p. 342; Kume 2002c, p. 335.

43 Kume 1977–82, vol. 3, p. 178; Kume 2002c, p. 170.

CROWN PRINCE HIROHITO'S VISIT TO BELGIUM

David De Cooman

JAPAN & BELGIUM
An Itinerary of Mutual Inspiration

Official portrait of Crown Prince Hirohito.
Le Patriote Illustré of 12 June 1921.

CROWN PRINCE HIROHITO'S VISIT TO BELGIUM

The visit of Crown Prince Hirohito to Belgium in June 1921, as part of a European tour, was an event of no small importance in the history of Belgian-Japanese relations. By sending the heir to the throne abroad for a considerable span of time, Japanese leaders broke entirely new ground in Japan's history, and given the critical juncture in the state affairs the country was then facing, the whole gamut of arguments had been brought forward by opponents of the tour to keep it from happening. It was nevertheless vital for Japan that its future emperor, who would eventually wield the sceptre for over six decades, should be given the opportunity in the prime of his life to learn about the intricacies of state administration by touring a selection of Western European democracies. Like the European great powers included in the itinerary, Britain[1] and France, the lesser ally Belgium correctly assessed the political and diplomatic significance of the visit. The kingdom was given the honour of receiving the crown prince of a monarchy with which it had enjoyed friendly relations for over half a century, since the conclusion of the 1866 Treaty of Amity, Commerce and Navigation. Accordingly, Belgium wanted to publicly acknowledge the services rendered by Japan, one of its First World War allies. At the same time, however, it was not indifferent to critical voices from the other side of the Atlantic, which bespoke a lurking distrust of the Empire's intentions. America and Canada were indeed left out of the itinerary, which caused dismay at what was perceived as a European good-will campaign by Japan.

This article will present an analysis of the Belgian leg of Crown Prince Hirohito's trip. The English-language version of the official record[2] written by first-hand witnesses Count Futara Yoshinari and Sawada Setsuzō, two government officials affiliated respectively with the then Imperial Household Ministry and the Foreign Ministry, served as an authoritative source in reconstructing the itinerary. In order to appreciate the mission's significance against its historical background, I have supplemented the deferential prose of the official account with sources[3] and observations discussing the deeper issues that were at stake.

Preparations

Following the death of Emperor Meiji (30 July 1912), Japanese policymakers faced a challenge fundamentally concerned with the Court. The main issue was the health of the new Emperor Taishō (reigned 1912-1926), who unlike his iconic predecessor was unable to play a significant political role. Having contracted meningitis shortly after birth, the physically and mentally challenged emperor increasingly showed signs of erratic behaviour. Although deemed competent to perform state ceremonies in 1912, by the early 1920s his condition had deteriorated to such an extent that Prime Minister Hara and three elder statesmen or *genrō* thought fit to launch a serious debate on the establishment of a regency, with Prince Hirohito (installed as crown prince in 1916) at its head. Eventually, two other closely connected court-related issues dominated the final years of "commoner" Hara Takashi's premiership (September 1918 to November 1921): the intrigues trying to annul the crown prince's betrothal to Princess Nagako and the matter of his tour in the West. For the sake of the nation's stability, the continuation of the modernization process, and the further development of Japan as a global power, it was Hara's ambition to settle these matters as soon as possible. As a first step, Hara consulted with three *genrō* as to whether the programme designed to groom the crown prince for the Regency could be expedited, in case the emperor's condition should further deteriorate. He was particularly in favour of crowning the curriculum with an opportunity such as a royal tour that would acquaint the crown prince with state affairs in the West. Moreover, the visit of a senior member of the imperial family to the Western countries would help to strengthen the ties of friendship and cooperation with Japan's allies abroad. For the UK in particular, it would underscore Japan's interest in extending the Anglo-Japanese Alliance. Consequently, in November 1919, Hara took up the matter with the *genrō*, who remained the key players behind the scenes in the policy-adopting process. His suggestion of launching a princely tour met with approval from Yamagata Aritomo, Matsukata Masayoshi and Saionji Kinmochi, who had all travelled to Europe early in their careers. The fact that the Great War had radically altered the face of Europe strengthened their conviction that the future emperor of Japan should observe the new reality with his own eyes.[4] In making a plea for the foreign trip, Prime Minister Hara was perhaps prompted by the initiative of the British Court in 1920 to send the Prince of Wales on a mission to the East (India) and Oceania (Australia and New Zealand). Considering a princely mission an instrument to forge stronger ties with allied Britain, Hara's determination, so his diary entry of June 1920 suggests,[5] may also have been inspired by the royal visits made by the Romanian Crown Prince Carol to Japan that year (the first European crown prince to visit Japan)[6] and by King Vajiravudh of Thailand. Four months later, in October, the project was once again put on the agenda. This time, the ministers agreed to break the news to the press, causing unexpectedly instant and massive coverage by Japan's major newspapers. Imperial sanction of the European tour was finally granted on 16 January 1921, following the audience between the Taishō Emperor and Matsukata, lord keeper of the privy seal. As a result, cabinet ministers, court officials and elder statesmen began discussing the further details of the itinerary in earnest.

The move for an overseas tour, however, was contested by several pressure groups. To begin with, it failed to gain wide support from conservative court officials. Hirohito's private tutor and ethics specialist Sugiura Shigetake 杉浦 重剛 (1855-1924), who headed the *Tōgū ongakumonsho* 東宮御学問所 (institute established for grooming the heir-apparent) from 1914 onward, by and large preferred a traditional curriculum, focusing on courses discussing Chinese classics and Japanese moral training. He was sceptical whether an overseas tour would contribute to a better training for the crown prince. His attitude bespoke a thorough distrust of grooming the soon-to-be emperor into an international monarch influenced by foreign notions. His concern was shared not only by his confidante Empress Sadako, but also by notorious nationalistic organizations led by Tōyama Mitsuru 頭山 満 and Uchida Ryōhei 内田良平, who joined forces in order to prevent the crown prince and his suite from leaving the country.[7] In trying to thwart the enterprise, the press was instrumentalized in introducing the reading public to an arsenal of arguments pleading against the trip to Europe. Newspapers for instance pointed out that the passage to Europe was not without risk, that security could be an issue whenever the prince

performed official duties, and that the maritime travel time precluded a swift return home if something untoward should happen to the emperor.

The opposition parties, at the same time, kept their end up and started a movement (dubbed *Kōtaishi yōkō chūshi undō* 皇太子洋行中止運動) striving, as its name literally says, for the cancellation of the crown prince's travel abroad.[8] The movement issued a petition to this effect and wanted at least the shelving of the plan.

Meanwhile, Sugiura had succeeded in arranging an engagement between Crown Prince Hirohito and Princess Nagako, eldest daughter of Prince Kuni no Miya Kuniyoshi 久邇宮邦彦 in January 1919. The betrothal however caused a rift within government circles. As she was a maternal granddaughter of Prince Shimazu Tadayoshi 島津忠義, the last daimyō of the Satsuma domain, her presence at court rekindled the rivalry between the cliques of the erstwhile domains of Satsuma and Chōshū. Above all *genrō* Yamagata was greatly dismayed by the choice, which he saw as an infringement of the interests of his own Chōshū Domain clique. The conflict provoked a cabinet crisis and interfered directly with the plan of sending the prince abroad. Those in favour of the match insisted on swiftly carrying forward the nuptial preparations, whereas Yamagata's supporters wanted to place top priority on the overseas tour in an attempt to delay and hopefully ultimately thwart the betrothal.[9] This scheme, together with the government's decision to make headway with scheduling the trip, gave those in favour of the betrothal the impression that the engagement was off or at least indefinitely put on hold. They therefore appealed to the government to give priority to the intended royal wedding, even threatening to use violence or ultimately block the route between the Imperial Palace and the departure quay. Although cabinet ministers were clearly in a dilemma about how to tackle the crisis, and for reasons of personal safety had to remain under constant surveillance, they proceeded with the original plan and drew up a budget to cover the costs needed for the mission. The estimated ten million yen[10] allocated to the project represented an enormous sum given the budgetary problems Japan was facing as a result of the recession that followed the First World War. The protests against the tour culminated in an impressive mass rally in Tokyo on *Kigensetsu* 紀元節 (Empire Day, 11 February 1921). On 21 February an audience with Prime Minister Hara was arranged, but the demand that the tour be

Wedding of Crown Prince Hirohito as announced
in *The Advertiser* of 26 February 1924.

imperial sanction was given to the inclusion of Belgium in the itinerary.[11] Not surprisingly, the United Kingdom, Japan's foremost military ally, had been selected as the key destination. The mood in the United Kingdom was still profoundly imbued with the traumatic effects of a war that had ended less than three years before. During public performances and welcome ceremonies, the Japanese guests were invariably reminded of the Great War, and the importance of the mission was generally viewed against the history of a shared military cause. Anticipating this kind of welcome, the government had seen to it that the content of official speeches and the visual impression of the delegation reflected due respect to the receiving countries' military and naval tradition. Accordingly, the crown prince as well as senior officers sported full military dress whenever the occasion required it.

On 3 March 1921, the prince and his suite boarded the royal train from Tokyo Station amid tremendous public enthusiasm, and upon arriving in Yokohama the full complement boarded the lead battleship *Katori* 香取 and its escort the *Kashima* 鹿島. A keen observer could construe the selection of these cruisers as a tribute to the UK, the main destination of the Japanese delegation, and incidentally the country which had overseen the construction of both vessels in the mid-1900s. Before arriving in London, the outbound voyage was marked by a sequence of courtesy calls to British Crown Colonies, including Hong Kong, Singapore, Ceylon and Malta. Although Crown Prince Hirohito's outings assumed a low profile, he was each time met with a full salute and invited to sumptuous luncheons laid on by official instances. His first more solemn observance on foreign soil was performed during his disembarkation at Malta, home base to the Japanese special service squadron that had supported the Allies during anti-submarine operations in the Mediterranean. On 25 April he participated in a wreath-laying ceremony at Kalkara Naval Cemetery, commemorating the seventy-seven casualties that had fallen to Axis forces. They included the sixty-eight crew members aboard the destroyer *Sakaki* 榊, which had been heavily damaged following an Austro-Hungarian torpedo attack off Corfu on 11 June 1917.[12] The ceremony could be seen as a subtle reminder to allies that Japan had contributed significantly to the war effort and that the Empire too had war victims to mourn.[13] At Gibraltar, the Japanese travellers made a final stop before reaching London. Apart from encounters with distinguished offi-

cancelled was rejected, as Hara pointed out that the plans had already passed the point of no return. After it became clear that the royal wedding would go ahead as planned, nothing stood between the crown prince and his departure for Europe.

In drawing up the official programme of the delegation, the government gave much consideration to the larger context of the First World War. It decided to include only those countries that had been allies to Japan, with the addition of the Netherlands, a neutral state with deep historical ties to Japan. On 11 May

cials from the Japanese embassy in London, including Admiral Takeshita Isamu 竹下勇 and First Secretary Yoshida Shigeru 吉田茂 — later to become Japan's first post Second World War prime minister but now commissioned to fine-tune the official programme and dress code arrangements — the prince had the opportunity of meeting Vice-Admiral Niblack, commander of US Naval Forces in European waters. The vice-admiral conveyed a salutatory message from President Harding, who hoped that the mission would travel via the US and the Panama Canal on its return voyage. Although the schedule of the homebound journey had not been decided yet, the idea was dismissed, much to the disappointment of the crown prince who really looked forward to a tour of the United States. Instead, he had to politely decline the suggestion, and vowed to visit the country at the earliest opportunity. That opportunity finally presented itself in 1975.

Visits in Europe

The formal disembarkation at Portsmouth on 9 May 1921 marked the official start of the cross-European tour. The distinguished company was first lavishly entertained by the British hosts and King George V in particular, who wished to offer his Japanese guests and the home public a splendid display of pomp; practically the first such instance since the conclusion of the war.[14] The Japanese delegation assisted at a great variety of official, military, ceremonial and cultural events. During his stay in the United Kingdom, the crown prince was initially entertained as guest of the sovereign and afterwards received the status of guest of the government. On 30 May, the prince entered France for the first time and worked his way through a programme largely dominated by official and military functions. On 10 June, the prince and his retinue, accompanied by a French escort, boarded a special train leaving France for Belgium. Shortly before 4 p.m., the Japanese party arrived at Mons railway station. There they were joined by a Belgian welcoming party and took their leave of the French officials. It had previously been arranged between both governments that the crown prince and his retinue would enter Belgium in their official capacity, implying a full ceremonial dress code for the entire company. The Belgian welcoming delegation was headed by Maurice Damoiseaux, Governor of the Province of Hainault, and included Burgomaster Lescarts and municipal

representatives of the city of Mons, as well as the Japanese envoy Dr. Adachi Mineichirō 安達峰一郎, who had just been promoted to ambassador, following the upgrading of the Japanese legation to the level of embassy on 31 May.[15] The party then travelled to Brussels, where they arrived around 5 in the afternoon. At Brussels North railway station they were personally welcomed by King Albert I and the duke of Brabant.

Arrival of Crown Prince Hirohito in Belgium as reported in *La Dernière Heure* of 10 June 1921.

Crown Prince Hirohito and King Albert. Photograph in *La Dernière Heure* of 11 June 1921.

Concluding a ceremonial inspection the of the guard of honour in front of the station, and despite the heavy rain, the royal company was driven in an open carriage to the Royal Palace, amidst the acclaim of thousands of well-wishers lining the streets. Before briefly retiring to their private chambers at the palace, the crown prince, his great-uncle Prince Kan'in no Miya Kotohito 閑院宮載仁 and some of their attendants had an audience with the queen and members of the court. The rest of the Japanese delegation was put up at the Hotel Astoria.[16] At eight in the evening, the Venice Chamber at the palace was the scene of a sumptuous banquet where about 180 invitees dined in honour of the Japanese visitors. Towards the end of the banquet, speeches were delivered by the king, his prime minister, Henry Carton de Wiart, and Crown Prince Hirohito. In his address, the king referred to Japan as a loyal wartime ally, saying that its army and navy "had played, both in Asia and in Europe, a brilliant role."[17] He admired the people of Japan for their marvellous qualities of adaptation, which made that country rank among the great modern nations under the aegis of monarchs and statesmen to whom no revelation of progress whatsoever was foreign. In direct reference to his guest of honour, the king commended the crown prince's keenness to prepare himself for his high mission by making this educational trip in Europe, giving close consideration to the institutions and to the activities of the people in all fields. The king believed that this attitude bespoke the crown prince's laudable will to learn about the world and to discriminate by personal observation between the advantages and drawbacks of ideas and institutions in different countries. Dwelling on the hardships and ravages sustained by Belgium during the wartime fighting and occupation, the king thanked the crown prince for the expression of sympathy demonstrated by his very visit to Belgium. Albert I further wished that Hirohito would take to heart the many aspects presented by the Belgian cities and countryside, the devastation and the battlefields, and that he would be convinced that the Belgians, who applied themselves entirely to the tasks dictated to them by their honour and duties, had courageously resumed work and devoted themselves with their traditional tenacity to restoring the intellectual, artistic and economic vitality to the country.[18] In concluding the royal toast, the king expressed the hope that Belgium would re-establish and expand its economic relations with the Empire of Japan, which had existed in the past,

and wished the crown prince, his great-uncle Prince Kan'in, and the other distinguished guests happy memories of their trip to Belgium.

In his reply Hirohito declared himself deeply recognizant of the very cordial reception by the royal couple, and very moved at the enthusiastic reception by the Belgian people. He took the opportunity to remind the hosts that it was a Belgian[19] who as Japan's first representative in all Europe had at the beginning of the Meiji era opened the first pages of the diplomatic history of Japanese–European relations. Ever since, the number of Japanese who came to Belgium to instruct themselves in the fields of law, the arts, and the economic, military, and financial sciences had been growing. This observation prompted the prince to conclude that anything, however little it may be, that Japan could contribute to the progress of world civilization, was due, not in the least part, to Belgium, which served as a model. Running briefly through Belgium's history, he confessed to being struck by the beauty of the periods preceding the establishment of the Belgian monarchy, and he expressly paid tribute to King Leopold II, under whose reign impressive feats had been realized. He remarked that a large number of Belgians had, thanks to their admirable accomplishments in all disciplines of human activity, put the Belgian people in the forefront of the most civilized nations. Without going into specific details, the crown prince further remarked that from the perspective of study, which he had set as an objective of his voyage, he had benefitted very greatly from the achievements of Belgians.[20] One paragraph of his speech was naturally devoted to the topic of the Great War. He commended King Albert for his feats during the war, together with the bravery of the Belgian people in the cause of justice and freedom. He remarked that it had elicited unbounded admiration in Japan and attracted the most profound sympathy of his people. He followed this observation by the phrase that "for 25 centuries, the Japanese nation was solidly impregnated by the ideals of duty, honour and patriotism;" wordings which caused a little sensation in the Belgian press. Nevertheless, in concluding he regretted not finding words strong enough to convey his feelings and made a toast to the prosperity of Belgium and the friendship between Belgium and Japan. After the banquet, the Japanese dignitaries were invited to a reception.

Futara Yoshinori, one of the two diarists who accompanied the trip, recorded that ladies were included among the notables the crown prince had conversations with,[21] a fact which may have been unconventional in the eyes of Japanese court officials at the time. Another surprise was the dress of the Belgian army officers attending. Futara noticed that the only thing that transformed an ordinary uniform into full dress was a change of shoulder straps. He surmised that there was perhaps a purpose behind these plain uniforms: they symbolized the patriotism and valour of the Belgian people. The next day, 11 June, the crown prince visited the Royal Crypt in the Church of Our Lady of Laeken and paid a floral tribute to Albert's dynastic predecessors.[22] Later that day, the Royal Greenhouses of Laeken were the setting for the luncheon offered by the royal couple. It was Queen Elisabeth herself who performed the guided tour along the various exotic flowers and shrubs. The event was concluded by a viewing of the panorama of the Battle of the Yser, in which the allied forces had successfully checked the enemy invasion. A visit to the Museum of the Belgian Congo – as the Royal Museum for Central Africa was then known – figured prominently on the afternoon programme. Next on the schedule was a banquet at the official residence of Prime Minister Carton de Wiart. And finally, at ten in the evening, a sumptuous reception attended by members of the diplomatic corps and ministers was held at the City Hall of Brussels.[23] The evening's official programme was followed by a ball attended by hundreds of ladies and gentlemen. At the end of the party, the crown prince presented Mayor Adolph Max with a donation of 5,000 francs for the relief of the poor.[24]

At nine the next morning, 12 June, Hirohito visited the Palace of Justice and then headed for Waterloo to inspect the historic battlefield. Acting as his guide was Lieutenant-General Aloïs Biebuyck, the king's aide-de-camp. After the short trip, he partook of a private luncheon hosted by the king and queen and then at 2 o'clock joined them in an afternoon visit to the Cinquantenaire Park, where they watched a horse race.[25] Later that day, Ambassador Adachi Mineichirō and his wife invited the crown prince and some thirty prominent Belgians from political, military, scientific and cultural backgrounds to a splendid dinner party in the magnificent salons of their official residence[26] in honour of Crown Prince Leopold, Duke of Brabant, who was also in attendance. The banquet was followed by a grand reception with around 300 invitees. This *soirée* marked the final stage of Hirohito's state engagements in the

country, and the prince and his entourage took up their lodgings at the Hotel Astoria.

The next morning, the agenda brought the crown prince to the province of West Flanders. He checked out at 7.30 and headed for the coastal city of Ostend. Next on the itinerary were the battlefields of Ypres and neighbouring villages. Apart from inspecting the battleground, he showed respect to the fallen soldiers by dedicating a wreath of flowers at their grave site. For the visit he was strongly indebted to Britain's King George V, who, during a conversation at Buckingham Palace, had advised him to visit this particular site. In acknowledgement, he despatched a telegram in which he conveyed his extreme awe for the scene he had experienced.[27] The king replied with a telegram, expressing his appreciation and gladness that the crown prince had been able to visit that part of Belgium. Following his excursion to the front line north of Ypres, he boarded a train and headed for Brussels.

The morning schedule of 14 June was dominated by a visit to the port city of Antwerp. Mayor Jan De Vos extended a word of welcome to the distinguished guests in Antwerp Town Hall, and the company then proceeded on a guided tour around the municipal buildings, while the city guides introduced the visitors to the mythical past, modern history and local culture of the city. The crown prince and his entourage then boarded a small steamer and embarked upon a sightseeing tour of

Crown Prince Hirohito at the church at Laeken.
Photograph in *La Dernière Heure* of 12 June 1921.

Crown Prince Hirohito (third from left) and Crown Prince Leopold (second from left)
on the steps of the Court of Justice (Palais de Justice) in Brussels.
Photograph courtesy of the Royal Museum of the Armed Forces and Military History, Brussels (ref. B1.111.112 28454).

Crown Prince Hirohito laying a wreath at the Lettenburg Cemetery.
Photograph courtesy of the Royal Museum of the Armed Forces and Military History, Brussels (ref. B1.111.113 28464).

Antwerp harbour. In the afternoon, the guests bade farewell to Antwerp, and from Antwerp Central Station took the train for Brussels. Their next appointment was a reception organized by the Belgo-Japanese Society, which had also invited a delegation of the Belgian Scouting movement.[28] As it was his last day before leaving Belgium, the crown prince took his leave of the Belgian royal family, and to end the day was entertained by Ambassador Adachi at a banquet, attended by some hundred people of standing.

Second Visit

To a grand send-off by King Albert and Crown Prince Leopold, the Japanese delegation left Brussels North Station on the morning of 15 June to begin their visit to the Netherlands. This however was not their last appearance on Belgian soil. On 20 June, the day he departed from the Netherlands, the crown prince once again directed his course to Belgium. As head of the Belgian Reception Committee, which also included Lieutenant General Biebuyck, General Major Pontus and Consul Bastin,[29] Ambassador Adachi relieved the Dutch escort at the border railway station of Essen and boarded the royal train to accompany his fellow countrymen to Leuven. Halfway through the trip, they made a short stop at Mechelen Station to allow Cardinal Mercier, Primate of Belgium, to join the cortège. The visit to Leuven could be qualified as the most poignant episode of the prince's passage through Belgium. The scars of the war were still remarkably visible in this city, dressed for the occasion with Belgian and Japanese national colours, and the havoc caused to the university's buildings and collections featured prominently during the guided tour through the city. Under the sponsorship of Prince Saionji Kinmochi and Baron Hozumi Nobushige 穂積陳重, a Japanese committee in Tokyo meanwhile investigated Japan's contribution to the restoration of the university library, and the princely visit to the city cannot be seen otherwise than as a commitment from Japan to help restore the university library to its pre-war condition. The local reception committee consisted of Burgomaster Leo Colins, Minister of State Joris Helleputte, and Baron Pierre de Dieudonné, commissioner of the arrondissement of Leuven.[30] A large crowd had assembled on the square outside Leuven railway station, and enthusiastically acclaimed the foreign visitors, who immediately

Crown Prince Hirohito, guided by Cardinal Mercier, visiting the ruins of the library of the University of Louvain/Leuven on the side of the Oude Markt.

Lithograph showing the interior of the University Hall before the fire of 1914.

Crown Prince Hirohito visiting the ruins of the library of the University of Louvain/Leuven.
Photograph courtesy of the Royal Museum of the Armed Forces and Military History, Brussels (ref.B1 111 113 28512).

Crown Prince Hirohito visiting the ruins of the University of Louvain/Leuven.
Photograph courtesy of the Royal Museum of the Armed Forces and Military History, Brussels (ref.B1 111 113 28515).

Le Patriote Illustré of 19 June 1921.

Le Patriote Illustré of 26 June 1921.

Le Patriote Illustré of 19 June 1921.

La libre Belgique of 21 June 1921.

proceeded to the ruins of the burnt-out university library. It was Cardinal Mercier who against the backdrop of the scorched library walls recounted to the prince the events leading up to the Great Fire of Leuven.[31] The crown prince, Prince Kan'in and Commander Yamamoto Shinjirō 山本信次郎, who had participated in the Versailles Peace Conference, were equally welcomed by Rector Ladeuze, whose words purportedly struck a responsive chord with the eminent visitors. An emblematic eye-catcher during the tour of the ruins was the banner along the nave of the charred library reading room, spelling out *ICI FINIT LA CULTURE ALLEMANDE*, a theme that was echoed in the address by rector Ladeuze.[33] Almost three years after the end of the Great War, unvarnished references to "Teutonic barbarity" were still rife in the public sphere and official speeches. Quite in contrast to the subdued character of the official speeches and inspections were the enthusiastic demonstrations of sympathy, shown by a mixed audience of local citizens and residing students to the procession that was heading towards the station. In particular the frantic cheers of the students must have put those present in an awkward position, considering the solemn mood surrounding the commemoration of the war atrocities shortly before. Chronicler Futara for one made an explicit comment on this issue, qualifying those cheers at such a location as somewhat pathetic.[34]

Shortly before noon, the prince and his suite once again boarded the train, this time heading for Ans Station, one stop before Liège, where they transferred to

vehicles taking them to the fort of Loncin, one of a ring of forts around Liège, about 45 km from the former German frontier. The fort had been destroyed by shelling, with a direct hit on the powder magazine, and the bleak ruins, the final resting-place of hundreds of Belgian defenders, occupied a prominent place in the collective memory. The final act of the Japanese goodwill campaign in Belgium was a visit to the city centre of Liège. From the balcony of the town hall Crown Prince Hirohito greeted the assembled public, who returned this gesture with enthusiastic acclaim. Taking leave of the burgomaster, the Japanese guests concluded their second tour in Belgium and proceeded once again to the French capital. On 18 July the crown prince embarked at Naples for his voyage home and he arrived in Tokyo on 3 September, exactly half a year after the start of the mission. Amidst an ovational welcome fit for a hero, he headed for the imperial palace, where he began preparing for his future career as head of state. Just a few months later he took the helm of the state as prince regent and five years later he succeeded as the 124th emperor of Japan.

Crown Prince Hirohito (wearing bowler hat) visiting the fortress of Loncin.
Photograph courtesy of the Royal Museum of the Armed Forces and Military History, Brussels (ref. B1.111.113 28510). The officer wearing glasses who is pointing out something to the Crown Prince is Victor Naessens, who later styled himself Victor Naessens de Loncin.

Signed studio photograph of Crown Prince Hirohito.
Photograph courtesy of Kenniscentrum, In Flanders Fields Museum, Ypres.

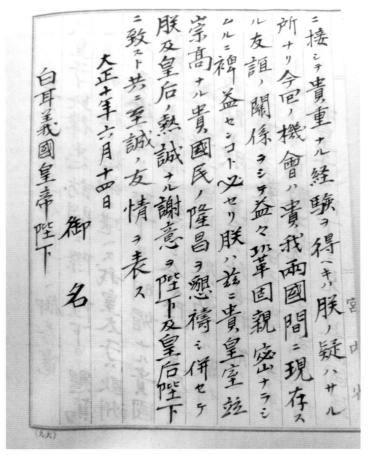

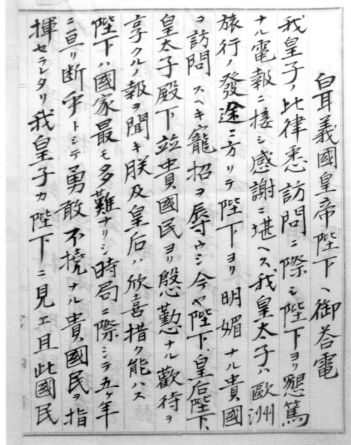

In hindsight, the epoch-making tour was generally perceived in Japan to have been a significant success. Several tour members, among them Admiral Kobayashi Masami 小林仁, supported this claim by issuing favourable reports to government ministries.[35] The official report by Grand Chamberlain Count Chinda Sutemi 珍田捨巳, presented to Prime Minister Hara on 20 September 1921, equally conveyed a satisfactory impression. When it comes to the contribution of Belgium to this success, a whole spectrum of fields and subfields should be taken into consideration, ranging from the mission's commercial, political and diplomatic achievements over its military, cultural or academic relevance to the impact on the crown prince's personal development. Little is known about the Japanese-Belgian commercial exchanges during the mission. Although no tradesmen joined the delegation, the commercial aspect was not irrelevant, as was indicated by the publication of commercial supplements in some major European newspapers.[36] Also, a considerable part of the official funding had been earmarked for promoting Japan.[37]

Moreover, the crown prince had the opportunity of meeting some Belgian captains of industry during the numerous banquets and receptions. In discussing the significance of the tour, the official diarists Futara and Sawada added a short paragraph claiming that the visit was not a political one, but that "one of the leading motives [...] was this ideal of national solidarity, and an ardent wish to uphold the tradition of personal service in the interest of the Empire and its people."[38] Our information indicates that no political negotiations between Japan and Belgium were scheduled in the programme.

The most visible effects of the mission were to be found at the level of diplomacy and goodwill between both nations. The Japanese delegation was highly pleased with the official and unofficial reception it had been given by members of the royal family and high government officials.[39] The crown prince's visit to Belgium accordingly strengthened the bonds between the ruling families of both countries. Due to the tension between Japan and its neighbours in the following years,

Telegram from the Taishō emperor to King Albert thanking the Belgian monarch for the invitation extended to the Crown Prince to visit Belgium, dated 14 June 1921. Gaikō shiryōkan 外交資料館, Kōtaishi gotoō 皇太子御渡欧, Hakkoku gohōmon no bu 白国御訪問之部.
Photograph by W.F. Vande Walle.

however, these personal contacts unfortunately became strained and Crown Prince Leopold's visit to Japan, planned for the spring of 1932, had to be cancelled.

The good impression that the Belgian hosts had made on their guests, but particularly the reception and interaction during the Leuven visit, can directly be linked to Japan's renewed diplomatic interest in Belgium. As early as December 1921, Commander Yamamoto led the initiative to create a National Committee in order to prepare a donation of old manuscripts and reproductions of pictures to the University Library, and to launch a fund-raising campaign. This project was largely indebted to Ambassador Adachi's interventions by way of a lively written correspondence with University Rector Ladeuze elaborating on the desirability of such a donation.[40]

While it is difficult to gauge the extent to which the tour changed the crown prince personally, the trip must have been an eye-opener as to how royal (or presidential), political and public affairs were conducted in the various Western countries. To the outside world, the crown prince came across as quite diligent, dutiful and interested, and his public appearances were given a good press. Without doubt, the contacts he had struck up with the leading politicians of his time were a valuable experience as emperor-to-be. An experience which may be summarized as "happy," judging by the press meeting in Nasu 那須 on 16 September 1970,[41] in which he confessed that he lived the life of a caged bird before the tour, and that abroad he was able to experience freedom.

REFERENCES

Behr 1989
Edward Behr. *Hirohito: Behind the Myth*. London: Hamish Hamilton, 1989.

Carton de Wiart 1981
Henry Carton de Wiart. *Souvenirs politiques*. Bruxelles: La Renaissance du livre, 1981.

Dickinson 2013
Frederick R. Dickinson. *World War I and the Triumph of a New Japan, 1919-1930*. Cambridge University Press, 2013.

Futara and Sawada 1924
Futara Yoshinari 二荒芳徳 and Sawada Setsuzō 澤田節藏. *Kōtaishi denka gogaiyū-ki* 皇太子殿下御外遊記. Ōsaka: Ōsaka Mainichi Shinbunsha 大阪毎日新聞社, 1924.

Futara and Sawada 1925
Futara Yoshinori and Sawada Setsuzō, revised by Harold E. Palmer. *The Crown Prince's European Tour*. Ōsaka: The Osaka Mainichi Publishing Company, 1925.

Hara 1950-51
Hara Takashi 原敬. *Hara Takashi nikki* 原敬日記, vols. 1-9. Kangensha 乾元社, 1950-51.

Hara 1965-67
Hara Takashi 原敬. *Hara Takashi nikki* 原敬日記, vols. 1-5. Fukumura Shuppan 福村出版, 1965-67.

Hatano 1998
Hatano Masaru 波多野勝. *Hirohito kōtaishi Yōroppa gaiyūki* 裕仁皇太子ヨーロッパ外遊記. Tokyo: Sōshisha 草思社, 1998.

Iwao 1978
Iwao Seiichi, ed. *Biographical Dictionary of Japanese History*. Tokyo: International Society for Educational Information, 1978.

Japan Magazine
Japan Magazine: A Representative Monthly of Things Japanese 12 (1921), p. 42.

Kojima 1981
Kojima Noboru 児島襄. *Tennō* 天皇. Vol. 1. Tokyo: Bungeishunjūsha 文藝春秋社, 1981.

Mitrasca 2002
Marcel Mitrasca. *Moldova: A Romanian Province under Russian Rule: Diplomatic History from the Archives of the Great Powers*. Algora Publishing, 2002.

Mosley 1966
Leonard Mosley. *Hirohito: Emperor of Japan*. London: Weidenfeld and Nicolson, 1966.

Nish 1997
Ian Nish. "Crown Prince Hirohito in Britain, May 1921." In *Britain & Japan Biographical Portraits*, vol. 2, ed. Ian Nish, pp. 205-215. Richmond, Surrey: Curzon Press/Japan Library, 1997.

O'Hara et al. 2013
Vincent P. O'Hara, W. David Dickson, and Richard Worth, eds. *To Crown the Waves: The Great Navies of the First World War*. Annapolis, MD: Naval Institute Press, 2013.

Shōwa tennō jitsuroku
Kunaichō 宮内庁. *Shōwa tennō jitsuroku* 昭和天皇実録. Vol. 3. Tokyo: Tōkyō Shoseki 東京書籍, 2015.

Thys 1999
Marianne Thys. *Belgian Cinema*. "Aankomst van de Japanse prins Hiro Hito." Brussels: Cinémathèque Royale du Belgique, 1999, p. 91.

Vande Walle and Servais 2001
Willy Vande Walle, and Paul Servais, eds. *Orientalia: Oosterse studies en bibliotheken te Leuven en Louvain-la-Neuve*. Symbolae Facultatis litterarum Lovaniensis B, vol. 20. Leuven: Leuven University Press, 2001.

Heraldic animal (an amalgam of a *komainu* [guardian lion-dog] and dragon)
representing Japan as one of the victor nations of the Great War on the ledge
of the newly-constructed central library of the University of Louvain/Leuven, completed in 1928.
Photograph by W.F. Vande Walle.

NOTES

1 For an in-depth discussion of the crown prince's visit to England and Scotland, see Nish 1997.

2 See Futara and Sawada 1925.

3 Most notably the book-length study by Hatano Masaru (1998), which in turn was based on the diary of Lieutenant-general Nara Takeji 奈良武次, aide-de-camp and senior army officer to accompany Crown Prince Hirohito during the 1921 princely mission. Other sources covering the trip in various degrees of detail include *Shōwa tennō jitsuroku*, Mosley 1966, and Behr 1989.

4 Nish 1997, p. 206.

5 Nish 1997, p. 206.

6 Mitrasca 2007, p. 272.

7 S.v. "Sugiura" in Iwao 1978.

8 Nish 1997, p. 206.

9 Nish 1997, p. 206.

10 Kojima 1981, p. 135.

11 *Shōwa tennō jitsuroku*, p. 290.

12 O'Hara et al. 2013, p. 313.

13 Nish 1997, p. 209.

14 Nish 1997, p. 210.

15 *Shōwa tennō jitsuroku*, p. 290.

16 Futara and Sawada 1925, p. 108.

17 Quoting and paraphrasing the original French-language address mentioned in Futara and Sawada 1925, p. 109.

18 Futara and Sawada 1925, p. 110.

19 Without mentioning him by name, the crown prince here referred to the count of Montblanc and baron of Ingelmunster, who had actually held French citizenship.

20 Futara and Sawada 1925, p. 112.

21 Futara and Sawada 1925, p. 112.

22 *De Tijd: godsdienstig-staatkundig dagblad*, 11 Jun 1921.

23 *De Telegraaf*, 13 June 1921.

24 *De Telegraaf*, 13 June 1921.

25 Futara and Sawada 1925, p. 115.

26 *De Telegraaf*, 13 June 1921.

27 Futara and Sawada 1925, p. 116.

28 Futara and Sawada 1925, p. 118.

29 *La libre Belgique*, 21 June 1921.

30 *La libre Belgique*, 21 June 1921.

31 Futara and Sawada 1925, p. 127.

32 Futara and Sawada 1925, p. 127.

33 *La libre Belgique*, 21 June 1921.

34 Futara and Sawada 1925, p. 127.

35 Nish 1997, p. 214.

36 Nish 1997, p. 214.

37 Nish 1997, p. 214.

38 Futara and Sawada 1925, pp. 9-10.

39 Futara and Sawada 1925, p. 114.

40 Vande Walle and Servais 2001, p. 67.

41 Hatano 1998, p. 7.

SECOND
PART

JAPAN'S
INSTITUTIONAL
MODERNIZATION:
SOME BELGIAN
SOURCES

LEUVEN CENTRAL PRISON: A MODEL FOR THE MODERN PENAL SYSTEM IN MEIJI JAPAN

Keiji Shibai and Dimitri Vanoverbeke

JAPAN & BELGIUM

An Itinerary of Mutual Inspiration

Miyagi Shūjikan, Meiji era (1868-1912).

Cellular prison of Leuven Central Prison.
Photograph courtesy of Stadsarchief Leuven.

LEUVEN CENTRAL PRISON: A MODEL FOR THE MODERN PENAL SYSTEM IN MEIJI JAPAN

Introduction

In the aftermath of the civil war of 1877 and in the wake of mounting political unrest at the time, Miyagi Prison (*Miyagi Shūjikan* 宮城集治監), a correctional facility for political offenders, was completed in August 1879. It was the first western-style modern prison in Meiji Japan and it heralded a new era in thecountry's penal history. The shape of the prison was typical of correctional architecture. In the centre was a hexagonal observatory from which six two-storey wings containing the cells radiated outwards. This arrangement allowed the covert observation of the prisoners by the warders in the central rotunda. This prison in Miyagi was modelled after the *panopticon* prison, which was first described by Jeremy Bentham in 1791.[1] This architectural style of prison is mainly known from Michel Foucault's analysis, which refers to this architecture as a metaphor for social change in the process of modernization. Miyagi Prison was built after one of the most innovative *panopticon* prisons worldwide: Leuven Central Prison. This prison was erected in the city of Leuven in Belgium and started its operations in 1860. At its opening it was welcomed as the ultimate realization in its field, ushering in a new era when a better control over the prisoner would make it possible to rehabilitate him/her into society. The idea behind the prison came from Édouard Antoine Ducpétiaux (1804-1868) who, until 1861, had for more than 30 years been the Inspector-General of Prisons in Belgium. He engaged in prison administration, was the architect of the reform of prison policy and the driving force behind the central prisons in Ghent and Leuven. Ducpétiaux was convinced that prisons like Leuven Central responded best to the triple purpose of incarceration: suppression, prevention and amendment, and most importantly, that the system most effectively replaced the death penalty. Ducpétiaux was vehemently opposed to the death penalty and believed that a prison system focused on the improvement of the prisoner was the only way to create the necessary context for the abolition of the death penalty.[2] This "total institution"[3] was the main reason why Leuven Central Prison was at a leading edge in modernity.[4]

It was this prison that caught the attention of the early Meiji leaders as one of the models to follow for the modernization of their penal institutions. Admiration for the prison system as it existed in Belgium in the nineteenth century can be read in the preface to the 1888 Japanese translation of the Belgian Prison Rules of 1857: "It can be said that nowadays among the Western nations Belgium has the most advanced prison system".[5] Admiration for the prison system and the penitentiary policy of Belgium existed before and after the construction of the Miyagi Prison, but its construction in 1879 was important because it marked a turning point in the history of penal institutions and policy in modern Japan.

Missions Visiting Prisons in France and Belgium in the Early Meiji Period

The earliest initiative that would influence the 1879 building of Miyagi Prison on the model of Leuven Central Prison can be traced back to Narushima Ryūhoku's 成島柳北 (1837-1884) study tour to Europe in 1872. Narushima was a scholar of Confucianism in the service of the shogunate, as well as an officer in the shogun's cavalry. The cavalry was drilled by French advisors, inspiring in Narushima an interest in France. After the Meiji Restoration he proved an important asset to the new leadership. He was sent on a study tour of Europe sponsored by the Honganji temple. His party sailed from Yokohama for Paris together with another study-tour mission sent by the Ministry of Justice. The eight officials from the Ministry of Justice included Inoue Kowashi, who would become one of the main architects of the Meiji constitution, and Kawaji Toshiyoshi, who would also play an important role as the architect of the institution of the police in Meiji Japan. According to Narushima's diary, his delegation visited the Santé prison in Paris on 22 February 1873.[6] They were also joined by some members of the Iwakura mission. Narushima was deeply impressed by the prison, writing about its excellent hygiene and its ingenious architecture, which included individual cells, a courtyard, workshops for prison labour, and even a classroom, a hospital, a visitors' area, etc. He also admired the fact that "the prison is constructed in the shape of a hexagon, with in the centre a central observatory, enabling the guards to see in one glance all six wings."[7] The French government was eager to show the Santé prison with its six radial wings and one central observatory because it viewed the institution as a symbol of modernity and civilization. Narushima highly praised the system and organization of the Santé prison, writing: "It is both extremely strict and extremely clement. I cannot sufficiently express my admiration [for this prison]."[8] About ten days after his visit to the Santé prison, Narushima met Ōkura Kihachirō in Paris on 3 February 1872.[9] They had been acquainted for several years and their friendship would grow even stronger after they returned to Japan. Narushima would also relate to Ōkura Kihachirō his impressions of the prisons he visited. Later, in 1876 when the Freedom and People's Rights Movement (*Jiyū Minken Undō* 自由民権運動) voiced criticism and mounted actions against the Meiji government, many of its leaders were arrested. One of them was Narushima, who had become a critical journalist after returning to Japan from his journey to the West. He was convicted to four months in prison for defamation of a government official and experienced the poor state of Japan's prisons first hand.[10] This experience, together with the impressions of his voyage in France and his acquaintance with the future builder of Miyagi Prison, Ōkura Kihachirō, was important for the future shape of this first modern prison in Meiji Japan.

According to *Bei-Ō kairan jikki*, Kume Kunitake's account of the Iwakura mission, examined in detail in the first part of this book, the mission visited six prisons during their journey: the prisons of Philadelphia, Manchester, Ghent, Berlin and Geneva, as well as the Santé prison of Paris.[11] After the inspection of the prison in Berlin, Kume noted, "We have seen many prisons since the visit in Philadelphia, and they are all well equipped and praiseworthy."[12] He also mentions that in Geneva a book on prison architecture was offered to the delegation by the author.

The eight civil servants from the Ministry of Justice, referred to above, were in Paris around the same time.

LOUVAIN. — La Prison

LOUVAIN   La prison cellulaire

They visited Belgium in the first months of 1873, while the Iwakura mission and Narushima were there. As already mentioned, Kawaji Toshiyoshi, Numa Morikazu and Inoue Kowashi were members of this Ministry of Justice mission. They would later become prominent actors in the modernization of Japan's institutions.[13] The first Japanese who actually visited Leuven Central Prison was Kawaji Toshiyoshi 川路利良 (1834-1879).[14] The mission visited France, Belgium and some other nations, but Kawaji focused mainly on the French and Belgian police system. He would write extensively on the police system, and use his insights to develop the police system in Meiji Japan. He did not, however, limit his attention to the institution of the police, as he also visited Leuven

Entrance to Leuven Central Prison.
Photograph courtesy of Stadsarchief Leuven.

Cellular prison of Leuven Central Prison.
Photograph courtesy of Stadsarchief Leuven.

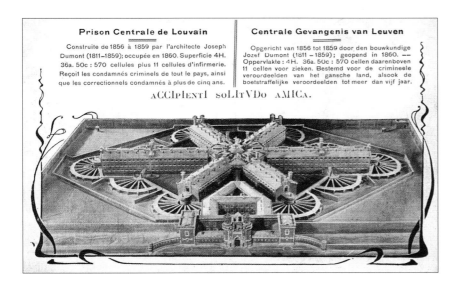

Central Prison in 1873. Although he did not leave a detailed record of his visit, his insights are said to have been the main reason that Leuven was chosen as the model for Miyagi Prison.

The dynamics for prison reform were not only set in motion by the study tours of Japanese students abroad, but also came from within Japan. Daniel Botsman points out, for example, that John Cutting Berry (1847-1936), a medical doctor, was shocked at seeing the terribly unhygienic situation in a prison in Kōbe, where he had been asked to treat patients for beriberi. Berry visited the prisons of Osaka, Kyoto and Hyōgo, and wrote a report "Notes for the Reform of the Prisons" (*Kangoku kaikakusho* 監獄改革書), which was translated and presented to Ōkubo Toshimichi in August 1876 and distributed to officials all over Japan. The main result was that officials started to take the issue of prison reform seriously.[15]

Blueprint for a Modern Penal System

In the wake of the Seinan Rebellion in 1877 and the surging Freedom and People's Rights Movement, the need for space to incarcerate the rebels was keenly felt. It was not just a problem of space but also of the different type of criminal, namely the political offender. Ōkubo consulted with national police superintendent Kawaji Toshiyoshi on the need to build a prison to confine those who had been implicated in the 1877 Seinan Rebellion.

Ishizawa Seikichi, the first governor of Miyagi Prison, recalled in his diary that "between the start of the Meiji era and the Seinan Rebellion there were more than 3,000 political offenders. They were all talented people and would become important resources for the nation after their release [...]. The person who realized this best was Ōkubo Toshimichi. He summoned Kawaji Toshiyoshi and said, 'If we treat these apprehended people well, political offenders can become valuable citizens for the nation. We should find the appropriate resources to do this.'"[16] One of the prisoners incarcerated for three years in Miyagi was Mutsu Munemitsu 陸奥宗光, the future minister of Foreign Affairs, who played an important role in the Russo-Japanese War in 1904-1905.[17] Ōkubo proved right in his assessment of the situation at the end of the 1870s and in connecting this to the need to reform the prison system. More than an issue of quantity, it was a problem of the quality of the prisons that was crucial in the new policy that Ōkubo set in motion.

Kawaji immediately followed up on Ōkubo's suggestion, and entrusted a civil servant of the Office of Home Affairs, Onoda Motohiro 小野田元熙 (1848-1919), with supervising the construction of a new prison. Onoda was to be assisted by his colleague Ishizawa Kingo 石澤謹吾 (1830-1917). Soon, however, on 9 January 1879, Onoda was ordered to leave the supervision of the construction of Miyagi Prison to Ishizawa, and to embark upon a study tour of prisons in Europe with Kawaji.[18] Ishizawa was not only able to have the prison finished in time but also within the budget. He used only 96,000 yen out of the 156,000 yen that had been allocated for the construction. The remainder of the budget would be used to finance the prison's first year of operation. Having successfully completed the construction of the prison, Ishizawa Kingo went on to become the first director of Miyagi Prison for three years, before being appointed director of Tokyo Prison for fourteen years, and subsequently director of Hokkaido Prison for six years. He is justly called the father of Japan's prisons.[19]

Why Belgium as a Model for Prison Reform?

How could Belgium contribute to Meiji Japan's new institutions and its development into a modern nation-state? Shigematsu Kazuyoshi points out that, quite apart from Ōkubo's ambition to build a prison of a different

Aerial view of Leuven Central Prison.
Photograph courtesy of Stadsarchief Leuven.

type where political offenders could be re-educated, the prison reform was just one aspect of the wider-ranging reform of the legal system, whose ultimate purpose was to induce the Western powers to renegotiate the unequal treaties.[20] This would be the only way to secure the revocation of the most disturbing clause in the unequal treaties, namely the extraterritoriality clause, which took away Japan's sovereignty on matters of justice. Foreign criminals could not be tried in Japanese courts, only in consular courts, and once convicted there was no way they would be incarcerated in Japanese prisons. To remove the label of backwardness from justice and prisons in Japan, rapid modernization was mandatory. Belgium became a cherished example for scholars and policymakers alike.

In January 1879, one of the supervisors of the construction of Miyagi Prison, Onoda Motohiro, accompanied Kawaji Toshiyoshi on a tour of prisons in Europe.[21] Kawaji elaborates on the importance of this journey, stating that "in the first place it is related to the policy of striving to obtain equal rights [...]. In anticipation of the day that we succeed in signing equal treaties, and for the sake of the police officers, we should be ready to accommodate foreigners who differ from us in manners and customs."[22] A report on the visit to the prison in Leuven can be found in the diary of one of the members of the mission, Sawa Tadashi 佐和正. He writes that after seeing off Kawaji, who due to illness embarked for Japan in Marseille on 24 August (he died the same year), they entered Belgium on 1 September, and that there, as in France, they visited penal institutions.[23] According to Takahashi Yūsai "it was well known at the time that the Belgian prisons were the most advanced in the world and therefore they visited many prisons in Belgium."[24] Leuven Central Prison, visited on 5 September 1879, made an especially deep impression, as Sawa Tadashi devoted a long entry in his diary to this visit:

> On a cloudy morning, at 9.50 a.m., we boarded the train at the Gare du Nord to visit the central prison of Leuven and arrived there at 10.25 a.m. We rented a horse carriage and after no time arrived at the prison. The governor kindly welcomed us and guided us through the prison [...]. It is clean and spacious and was newly built in 1860. The guards are carefully selected and they often talk to and instruct the inmates [...]. Several times a week, the priests will give sermons to the inmates, who can also go to the religious celebration every Sunday. [...] The inmates work diligently and with the money they earn they can buy wine, soap and other commodities [...]. Each inmate has his own cell (*isshū ichibō* 一囚一房) and they are all assigned a task tailored to their skills. When it is time to eat, they bring their plates and afterwards collect them from the other inmates using a small cart. [...] The inmates work in factories as blacksmiths or carpenters and are forbidden to talk. [...] There are washing facilities in each cell and to the ill inmates beef and eggs are served. There is a dark room for punishment but this is only used about once every year. This is achieved because it is not prohibited to smoke and there is space foreseen for leisure and to plant flowers and trees. The inmates are allowed to tend to their plants and to collect the seeds. The inmates can do what they deem appropriate and they can decide what they want to learn while in prison. The prison is kept clean and tended by warders who are different from armed soldiers [...].[25]

Inside one of the wings of Leuven Central Prison, 1920s.
Photograph courtesy of Stadsarchief Leuven.

Ōkura Kihachirō and the Construction of Miyagi Prison

The actual construction of Miyagi Prison to the north east of Tokyo was undertaken in 1878-1879 under the supervision of the wealthy merchant and businessman Ōkura Kihachirō 大倉喜八郎 (1837-1928), at the direct request of Ōkubo Toshimichi, who was in charge of the Home Office at the time and was arguably the most powerful member of the Meiji government. Ōkura signed a contract with the government, worked hard, and in a short time completed the construction in close cooperation with Ishizawa.

Ōkura Kihachirō was a self-made man and started as a small-scale trader of dried fish before seizing the opportunities at the end of the Tokugawa era and turning into a successful firearms dealer, choosing to provide arms to the domains that would topple the Tokugawa regime. He made a fortune in this turbulent period and as soon as the Meiji regime was in place, he became involved in foreign trade and construction works, among other activities that furthered the dynamics of modernization. He always remained close to the regime, which was grateful for his support in the early hours of their rebellion against the Tokugawa leaders. He would be rewarded with lucrative contracts and new opportunities. One of these opportunities for developing his business by learning — but also by what we would call "networking" — was an invitation to join the Iwakura mission. On July 1872, eight months after the Iwakura mission had sailed off, Ōkura left Japan for Europe and America to catch up with it.

A conversation in a hotel in Paris about the feasibility of the domestic production of wool cloth, in early 1872, was the first encounter between the wealthy merchant Ōkura and the powerful oligarch Ōkubo. Soon after returning to Japan, Ōkubo asked Ōkura to provide essential goods to the Japanese army in view of its dispatch to Taiwan in 1874. Ōkura became the main army supplier and extended his activities in view of a new role as a major partner for government procurement alongside some other merchant families such as Mitsui. Many of these privileged merchant families would become the pillars of Japan's economic take-off in the form of what is now known as zaibatsu or industrial conglomerates.

In May 1878, while Ōkura was building Miyagi Prison, Ōkubo was assassinated. The lucrative cooperation with the Meiji government, however, did not end there. Itō Hirobumi, the new Secretary of the Home Office, asked Ōkura to supervise the construction of Kabato Central Prison (Kabato shūjikan 樺戸集治監), likewise a penal institution for political offenders (completed in 1881) on the northern island of Hokkaido. The success of these constructions paid off and Ōkura was commissioned to build various prestigious symbols of Meiji Japan, such as the Rokumeikan Building (1883, designed by Josiah Conder), the Imperial Palace (1887), and the Imperial Hotel (1890, the first Western-style hotel in Tokyo, designed by Frank Lloyd Wright). The construction of Miyagi Prison may justly be said to be one of the first major works of the largest constructor in modern Japan: the Ōkura Group.

Leuven Prison and the Penal System after Miyagi Prison

After the completion of Miyagi Prison, penal policy continued to gain importance on the Meiji government's political agenda. The government urgently needed to restore order in the country and was eager to prove to foreign nations that it had modernized enough to renegotiate the international treaties that included a clause on extraterritoriality.

Ishizawa Kingo writes that "the new prison regulations (kangokusoku 監獄則) which were adopted on 20 September 1881 were radically different from the previous prison regulations of 1872. The reform was instigated by Onoda Motohiro, whose opinion had been formed during the studytour in Europe ordered by Police Superintendent Kawaji Toshiyoshi. It is said that France and Belgium became the model for the new prison regulations."[26]

According to Ohara Junsai, the regulations before 1881 had been based upon the English model as implemented in Hong Kong and Singapore. The regulations were reformed after the French and Belgian examples and would remain in place until 1908, when Germany would become the model for the new prison regulations.[27]

More study tours to Leuven followed. Important was the study tour of 1892 under the supervision of Kiyoura Keigo 清浦奎吾 (1850-1942), who also had an interview with the director-general of the Public Safety Bureau in the Ministry of Justice in Belgium. Kiyoura was an important politician who would take on various government positions in cabinets during the Meiji and Taishō eras, before becoming prime minister in 1924, in what is known as the high-water mark of the Taishō democracy. An extensive report of the Belgian prison system was published after Kiyoura's visit.[28]

Another important visit to Leuven Prison was the one paid by a high-level civil servant of the Office of Home Affairs, Ogawa Shigejirō 小河滋次郎 (1864-1924) in November 1897. He published a report of his findings entitled *Notes of my Observations of Leuven Prison in Belgium* (*Berugī "Rūban" kangoku (shūjikan) sankanki* 白耳義「ルーバン」監獄（集治監）参観記).[29] His observations on Leuven Prison were to influence him when he became the main architect of the prisons for juvenile delinquents in the early twentieth century. The study visits to Belgian prisons ended in 1908, when Japan decided to revise its prison regulations once more, and this time took the German example as its main model.

Conclusion

The Belgian penal system in general and Leuven Central Prison in particular attracted the attention of the Meiji rulers, who felt the need to modernize Japan's penal system in order more efficiently to accommodate political offenders, who were totally different — so Ōkubo Toshimichi said — from common criminals. He expected that these inmates, after leaving prison, would be needed to aid in the development of the new Meiji institutions. In addition to this domestic factor, modern legal institutions were considered essential for the impending negotiations with the foreign powers, who were reluctant to abandon the discriminatory clause of extraterritoriality as long as Japan's legal system was considered below the standards of modern civilization.

The prison in Leuven became a specific example for the architecture of the first modern penal institution that had to meet the changing needs. Ōkubo Toshimichi and

Kawaji Toshiyoshi were the key figures in the Meiji government who were eager to model the Miyagi Prison on the Belgian example, but many others contributed to the gradually growing influence of the Belgian prison system in general and Leuven Central Prison in particular on the development of the Japanese prison system between 1878 and 1908.

REFERENCES

Bentham 1791
Jeremy Bentham. *Panopticon or the Inspection House.* Vol. 2. 1791.

Bentham 1995
Jeremy Bentham. *The Panopticon Writings.* London: Verso, 1995.

Berugī-koku gokusei shōyaku
Keishichō kangoku Ishikawajima bunsho 警視庁監獄石川島分署, trans. *Berugī-koku gokusei shōyaku* 白耳義國獄制抄譯. 1888.

Botsman 2005
Daniel V. Botsman. *Punishment and Power in the Making of Modern Japan.* Princeton University Press, 2005.

Delierneux and Crawford 1931
A. Delierneux and William Rex Crawford. "Evolution of the Prison System in Belgium." *The Annals of the American Academy of Political and Social Science* 157 (1931), pp. 180-196.

Fujita 1976
Fujita Tadashi 藤田正. "Meiji gonen no shihōshō shisatsudan" 明治五年の司法省視察団 ["The Mission of the Ministry of Justice in 1872"]. *Shisō* 史叢 37 (1976), pp. 45-61.

Kawaji 1976
Kawaji Toshiyoshi 川路利良. "Daisanbu: Kawaji daikeishi no *Taisei kenbunshi*" 大三部・川路大警視の「泰西見聞誌」 ["Part Three: Superintendent Kawaji's *Report on Europe*"]. In *Meiji nendai no keisatsubuchō* 明治年代の警察部長 ["The Police Superintendents in the Meiji Era"], ed. Takahashi Yūsai 高橋雄豺, pp. 211-336. Tokyo: Ryōsho Fukyūkai 良書普及会, 1976.

Kobayashi s.a.
Kobayashi Kaoru 小林薫. *Ryū-ō yōkō kaikei-roku / kaidai* 柳翁洋行会計録・解題 ["Explaining the Records of the Accounts of Narushima Ryūboku's *Journey in the West*"].

Leuven Central Prison at the time of its inauguration in 1860. The outer appearance of its façade has remained unchanged to this day.
Photograph courtesy of Stadsarchief Leuven.

Kume 1878
Kume Kunitake 久米邦武. *Tokumei zenken taishi Bei-Ō kairan jikki* 特命全権大使米欧回覧実記. 5 vols. Tokyo: Hakubunsha 博聞社, 1878.

Nagai 1973
Nagai Seikichi 永井誠吉. "Nihon chigoku no chichi no hokori" 日本治獄の父の誇り ["Police Personalities from Shinshū (6), The Pride of the Father of Japan's Correctional Facilities"]. *Asahi no Tomo* 旭の友 27:6/321 (1973), pp. 58-60.

Nagai 1977
Nagai Seikichi 永井誠吉. *Nagano kenkei hyakunen no rekishi* 長野県警百年の歴史 ["The History of One Century of the Prefectural Police in Nagano"]. Sankei Newspaper Publishers, 1977

Naganuma 2010a
Naganuma Tomoe 長沼友兄. "Yōroppa kangoku jijō no shōkaisha: Onoda Motohiro (zen): Keishichō jidai o chūshin toshite" ヨーロッパ監獄事情の紹介者・小野田元熙（前）―警視庁時代を中心として ["Introducer of the prison situation in Europe: Motohiro Onoda (first half) Focusing on the days at the Tokyo Metropolitan Police Department"]. *Keisei* 刑政 121:10 (2010), pp. 52-59.

Naganuma 2010b
Naganuma Tomoe 長沼友兄. "Yōroppa kangoku jijō no shōkaisha: Onoda Motohiro (go): Keishichō jidai o chūshin toshite" ヨーロッパ監獄事情の紹介者・小野田元熙(後)警視庁時代を中心として ["Introducer of the prison situation in Europe: Motohiro Onoda (latter half) Focusing on the days at the Tokyo Metropolitan Police Department"]. *Keisei* 刑政 121:11 (2010), pp. 48-57

Narushima 1872
Narushima Ryūboku 成島柳北. *Kōsei nichijō* 航西日乗 ["Voyage to the West"], 1872.

Ogawa 1901
Ogawa Shigejirō 小河滋次郎. *Gokujidan* 獄事談 ["Stories of the Prison"]. Tokyo: Tōkyō Shoin 東京書院, 1901.

Police Association 1892a
Police Association. "Sōkai itteki: Berugī-koku shihōshō keihokyokuchō mondō" 蒼海一滴・白耳義国司法省警保局長問答 ["A Drop in the Ocean: Questions and Answers with the Director-General of the Public Safety Bureau in the Ministry of Justice in Belgium"] *Keisatsu kangokugaku zasshi* 警察監獄学雑誌 3:8 (1892), pp. 17-21.

Police Association 1892b
Police Association. "Sōkai itteki: Berugī-koku shihōshō keihokyokuchō mondō" 蒼海一滴・白耳義国司法省警保局長問答 ["A Drop in the Ocean: Questions and Answers with the Director-General of the Public Safety Bureau in the Ministry of Justice in Belgium"] *Keisatsu kangokugaku zasshi* 警察監獄学雑誌 3:9 (1892), pp. 21-25.

Police Penitentiary Association 1892
Police Penitentiary Association. "Sōkai itteki: Berugī-koku gokusei ni kansuru torishirabe jikō" 蒼海一滴・白耳義国獄制に関する取り調べ事項 ["A Drop in the Ocean: Elements of Investigation of the Penitentiary System in Belgium"]. *Keisatsu kangokugaku zasshi* 警察監獄学雑誌 3:10 (1892), pp. 29-34.

Sawa 1884a
Sawa Tadashi 佐和正. *Kōsei nichijō* 航西日乗 ["Voyage to the West"]. Vol. 1. 1884. 61 pp.

Sawa 1884b
Sawa Tadashi 佐和正. *Kōsei nichijō* 航西日乗 ["Voyage to the West"]. Vol. 2. 1884. 47 pp.

Sawa 1884c
Sawa Tadashi 佐和正. *Kōsei nichijō* 航西日乗 ["Voyage to the West"]. Vol. 3. 1884. 53 pp.

Semple 1993
Janet Semple. *Bentham's Prison: A Study of the Panopticon Penitentiary*. Oxford: Clarendon Press, 1993.

Shigematsu 1985
Shigematsu Kazuyoshi 重松一義. *Zukan Nihon no kangokushi* 図鑑日本の監獄史. Yūzankaku Shuppan 雄山閣出版, 1985.

Takahashi 1969a
Takahashi Yūsai 高橋雄豺. "Meiji nendai no keihokyokuchō (5): Onoda Motohiro" 明治年代の警保局長 (5) 小野田基熙 ["The Directors of the Home Ministry Police Affairs Bureau in the Meiji era (5): Onoda Motohiro"]. *Keisatsugaku ronshū* 警察学論集 22:10 (Sep 1969), pp. 161-176.

Takahashi 1969b
Takahashi Yūsai 高橋雄豺. "Meiji nendai no keihokyokuchō (6): Onoda Motohiro" 明治年代の警保局長 (6) 小野田基熙 ["The Directors of the Home Ministry Police Affairs Bureau in the Meiji era (6): Onoda Motohiro"]. *Keisatsugaku ronshū* 警察学論集 22:11 (Sep 1969), pp. 114-128.

Vanhulle 2010
Bert Vanhulle. "Dreaming about the Prison: Édouard Ducpétiaux and Prison Reform in Belgium (1830-1848)." *Crime, Histoire & Sociétés / Crime, History & Societies* (2010), pp. 107-130.

NOTES

1 Bentham 1791; see also: Semple 1993; Bentham 1995.

2 Vanhulle 2010, p. 113.

3 Vanhulle 2010, p. 119.

4 Delierneux and Crawford 1931.

5 *Berugī-koku gokusei shōyaku*. 今時欧米諸州に在て良獄制の名ある者蓋し白耳義國を以て最とすと云ふ.

6 Narushima 1872.

7 獄舎は六角に造り中央に警吏の臨監する処ありて、一目に六方を見渡すなり. Narushima 1872.

8 厳は厳を極め慈は慈を尽くす。まことに感嘆に堪えざるなり。

9 Narushima 1872.

10 Kobayashi s.a., pp. 28-33.

11 Kume 1878.

12 米国費拉特費府以来、牢獄を見しこと甚だ多し、皆各国にて、最も周備したる名誉の牢獄なり。

13 Fujita 1976.

14 Kawaji 1976.

15 Botsman 2005, pp. 171-172.

16 Quoted in: Nagai 1973, p. 59.

17 Nagai 1973, p. 59.

18 Takahashi 1969.

19 Nagai 1973, p. 59.

20 Shigematsu 1985.

21 Nagai 1977, p. 226; Naganuma 2010a; Naganuma 2010b.

22 第一着に条約改正に着手して対等の権利を得る事に努めざるべからず （。）対等条約成功の日に方って行政上警察官は其衝に当たるの先鋒隊となり監獄は又風俗習慣を異にする外国人を収容するの設置なかるべからず。

23 Sawa 1884a; Sawa 1884b; Sawa 1884c.

24 Takahashi 1969a, p. 170; see also: Takahashi 1969b.

25 Sawa 1884a, pp. 42-44.

26 Takahashi 1969a, p. 176.

27 Takahashi 1969a, p. 176.

28 Police Association 1892a; Police Association 1892b; Police Penitentiary Association 1892.

29 Ogawa 1901, pp. 575-590.

JAPAN AND THE BELGIAN CONSTITUTION: THE INFLUENCE OF A NEW SMALL NATION STATE ON MEIJI JAPAN

Dimitri Vanoverbeke

JAPAN AND THE BELGIAN CONSTITUTION: THE INFLUENCE OF A NEW SMALL NATION STATE ON MEIJI JAPAN

Introduction

Constitutions aim at fostering a legitimate legal order entailing the promotion of the wellbeing of people through the implementation of *inter alia* the principles of the rule of law, a separation of powers, the protection of fundamental rights, and democracy.[1] A constitution brings predictability and stability to the people of a nation. Nitobe Inazō (1862-1933), a respected Japanese diplomat and pedagogue, wrote that, "any document called a constitution"[2] is "something enumerating the rights and duties of the rulers and the ruled"[3] [...] "it's only natural that for the most part the constitution of any single country is going to resemble that of the others and not be some strange and completely different beast."[4] [...] "A society in which the observance of law is not assured, nor the separation of powers defined, has no constitution at all."[5] His observations go back to the beginning of twentieth-century Japan. Nitobe asserted that constitutionalism is not about national values but about an efficient organization of the relationship between the citizens and the state. In that sense constitutions include an "attitude, a frame of mind, the philosophy of striving towards some form of political legitimacy, typified by respect for a constitution."[6]

Japan is the nation in East Asia with the longest record with regard to constitutionalism. After Japan's turn to the West in the second half of the nineteenth century, it rapidly embarked upon a quest for the most appropriate constitution, ultimately resulting in the constitution of the Empire of Japan of 1889 (hereafter: the Meiji constitution).[7] One of the models for a constitution that played an important role in the construction of Meiji Japan's identity as a modern nation state was the Belgian constitution of 1831. In this chapter we will briefly outline how and why Japan was influenced by constitutionalism — the process of development of policy related to the constitution — and by the constitution of Belgium. We will demonstrate that modern Japan's architects were concerned not only with becoming a big nation state able to compete with the world's most prominent imperialist nation states but also with the construction of a national identity as a new nation and protecting the sovereignty as a small nation in a world where imperialism was rife. In that context, Belgium played an important role in the constitutional history of Japan. The Belgian constitution was an important example for the leaders of early Meiji Japan of the legal framework necessary to construct a national identity and domestic and international stability as a new, small nation that had constantly to keep the pressure of the imperialistic great powers at bay.[8]

Japan's Long Path towards a Constitution

The first specific introduction of constitutionalism in Japan was through the work of Aochi Rinsō 青地林宗 as early as in 1810. However, his introduction of the constitution is limited to a very summary explanation of what a parliament does and is still very remote from explaining the significance of constitutionalism. It is probably more accurate to situate the beginning of the introduction of constitutionalism with Takahashi Kageyasu 高橋景保 in 1825 when he published his *Angeriajin seijō shi* 諳厄利亜人性情志 ["Account of the Nature of the British People"], marking the shift of interest by the Japanese authorities from the institutions of the Netherlands to those of England. In this important publication, which marks a turning point in Japanese history, he explains that the "legal codes are binding upon all the people, the King being no exception."[9] Surprisingly for his times, Takahashi understood the core idea of constitutionalism as a restriction on the ruler. In the wake of the turbulent times in the twilight of Tokugawa rule a new understanding of constitutionalism can be observed. Ienaga Saburō, for example, points to a publication by the powerful ruler of the Echizen domain, Matsudaira Shungaku, stating that in "the Japanese system the individual rights are controlled by the government that decides arbitrarily on punishments while when we look back at the history of the European nations, we see that in the Parliament and in the House of Commons the political affairs of the entire nation are put forward for public discussion leading to a decision. The King (ō 王) of England and the Emperor of France are not free from these matters. In the current dynasty a reform should be carried out and the Parliament as well as the House of Commons that should be established in Edo. The Parliament should be composed of the highest administrators of the central government while the House of Commons should be composed of the most important representatives of the domains. In this House, farmers and other citizens should be added and no prince or general should be allowed to make any changes."[10]

The fact that examples of constitutionalism were discussed among the feudal leaders anxious to find a solution to the instability of the Tokugawa regime shows that although constitutionalism in Japan has mostly been discussed as a development following the Meiji Restoration, and with the sole purpose of paving the way for negotiating more favourable treaties, discussion of the adoption of constitutional rule had its origins in a wish for domestic stability already before the Meiji Restoration. Constitutionalism after 1868 remained geared towards the double purpose of domestic stability

and international respect. In the first decade of the Meiji regime, the four former Tokugawa domains that led the coup against the shogunate needed to secure cooperation from the other domains (around 280 in total) and construct a new unifying identity as a nation state. The idea of a constitution to provide the legal framework to guarantee this cooperation developed soon after the restoration. Intellectuals started translating modern law in general and constitutions in particular of nations that could become an example for Japan, or they were sent abroad to research the topic and inform the government about how constitutionalism could contribute to the stability of the new nation state.[11] Fukuzawa Yukichi, Tsuda Mamichi, Katō Hiroyuki and Nishi Amane[12] were just some of the intellectuals in early Meiji Japan who profoundly understood constitutionalism.[13] Yet many lesser-known students contributed to a better understanding of law and constitutionalism in the period around the Meiji Restoration. The most famous translator of French law was Mitsukuri Rinshō, but many other translators such as Shiota Saburō, Sufu Kōhei or Kuga Minoru, to name only three, contributed to a better understanding of law in French and often also to a better understanding of Belgian law.[14]

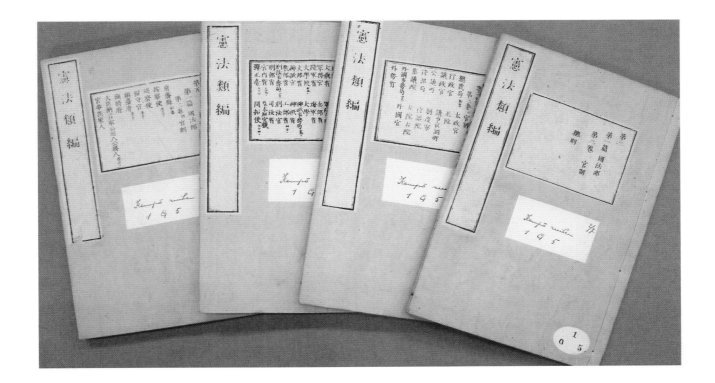

Kenpō ruihen 憲法類編, a collection of texts on constitutional issues, compiled by Etō Shinpei 江藤新平 (1834-1874) and Fukuoka Takachika 福岡孝弟 (1835-1919) and others from the School for Legal Education in the Ministry of Justice (*Meihōryō* 明法寮), published in Kyoto/Tokyo, 1873.
Fonds japonais, Réserve précieuse des bibliothèques de l'Université catholique de Louvain.

Aside from the important concern of the Meiji leaders for domestic stability and unity, constitutionalism as it developed in the Meiji period had to serve an international purpose too. The revision of the international treaties (the treaty signed between Belgium and Japan in 1866 was one of them) had to be served by the future constitution. Kido Takayoshi, one of the central statesmen in the early Meiji government, accompanied Iwakura Tomomi during his "mission" to the US and Europe from 1871 to 1873. He was convinced that a constitution was necessary in order to gain the respect of the major world powers and to start negotiations for a revision of the international treaties that were unfavourable to Japan. Ōkubo Toshimichi, who was more influential than Kido and known as a realist, stated that the time was not ripe to change the polity so drastically that "rule could be shared between Emperor and Citizen".[15] Ōkubo, however, like his fellow statesmen, favoured continuing research into the constitutions of the world. When the time became ripe, translations and understanding of the constitutions that might be models for the Japanese nation state would be ready.

So, what were the main characteristics of the Belgian constitution and how was it perceived in Meiji Japan?

The Belgian Constitution and its Perception in Meiji Japan

In 1830, Belgian legislators drafted a very liberal constitution, which nevertheless established a balance between the power of parliament and the power of the king. This balance made the Belgian constitution attractive to other nations involved in the transformations of modernization but reluctant to dispense entirely with traditional power. The Belgian constitution that came into force in 1831 was a carefully selected amalgam of aspects of existing constitutions completed with new ideas which made the Belgian constitution a unique document. John Gilissen argued that it was original in the sense that "it was the Belgian constitution of 1831 that created a type of parliamentary monarchy which restricted royal power and accorded a decisive role to the parliament not only with regard to legislation but mainly with regard to the choice of government. Parliamentary rule is the major acquisition of 1830."[16] The constitution of Belgium was an innovative

contribution to constitutional history in Europe and even led to what Hawgood called "the model state of Belgium."[17]

Some of the countries that took the Belgian constitution as the main example when drafting their own were Spain in 1837, Greece in 1844, the Netherlands in 1848, Luxembourg in 1848, Prussia in 1850, and Romania in 1864. Belgium was not only to be a model for Europe. The Iwakura mission (which toured the US and Europe from November 1871 to September 1873) upon its return issued a report that among much else indicated the necessity of establishing a constitutional system in Japan and pointed to Belgium as a possible example. Kume Kunitake, the report's author, was impressed by the liberal character of the Belgian state and even wrote that, "the politics of this constitutional monarchy differ greatly from other monarchies and empires in deportment. In autonomy for the people, it surpasses even the republics."[18] Kume Kunitake did not entirely approve of this popular aspect of the Belgian constitution.

Leadership of the Meiji government, however, started to be more concerned with peace, order and identity of the new nation-state. Inoue Kowashi, a middle-rank administrator in the Ministry of Justice at the time of the Iwakura mission and a protégé of Itō Hirobumi, was more positively impressed. In 1875 he translated the Prussian and Belgian constitutions in *The Constitution of Monarchies* (*Ōkoku kenkokuhō* 王国建国法) published by the School for Legal Education of the Ministry of Justice (*Meihōryō* 明法寮). This translation was based on E. Laferrière's *Constitutions d'Europe et d'Amérique* (Paris: Cotillon, Librairie du Conseil d'Etat, 1869). Laferrière's compilation included many more constitutions but Inoue selected only the Belgian and the Prussian. The reason why he chose the Belgian constitution was, as stated above, that he was curious as to how a new and small nation would draft a constitution. In Inoue's view, Japan faced a comparable problem and could learn from the Belgian example how a new small country could deal with constructing a nation able to be respected by the major powers in the world. Mainly thanks to Inoue's translation, Belgium and its constitution were widely known among those people in Japan interested in the development of constitutionalism. The first translator of the Belgian constitution into Japanese, Inoue Kowashi, and later architect (together with Itō Hirobumi) of the Meiji constitution wrote in February 1875 about the Belgian constitution:

> Belgium is the newest of the European nations. It is a small nation that is well organized. It is remarkable because it can do great things thanks to unity. The reason why this is possible is the constitution that according to its observers is an example of perfection. Despite the fact that Belgium is only composed of eight provinces and has not more than five million inhabitants, it has a sound political system and does not find unity in a common religion but in liberty for its people. Moreover, it does not strive for hegemony, as it is located between the Great Powers. Yet it is successful in maintaining independence and not surprisingly as indicated in its national flag it is a nation strong in unity.[19]

Inoue was almost lyrical about Belgium and saw this new small nation as an important inspiration for the construction of Meiji Japan.[20]

A more detailed outline of Belgium, its legal system and its constitution was published two years later by Sufu Kōhei 周布公平 (1851-1921) who was born in the Chōshū Domain. Soon after the Meiji Restoration, on the advice of Itō Hirobumi, he became a student of French with the famous translator Mitsukuri Rinshō.[21] Sufu's father was a close friend of one of the main leaders of the Meiji regime, Kido Takayoshi. After his friend passed away, even before he could see the Meiji era, Kido kept an eye on Sufu and helped him to arrange a journey to France to deepen his knowledge. Sufu Kōhei left in February 1871 for America to make a stop before he was supposed to continue his journey to France. There, so he recalls in an interview on his memories of Kido, he met with Itō Hirobumi, who happened to be there for research on the banking system. Itō advised Sufu Kōhei to change his destination and to "study in Belgium because in the aftermath of the Franco-Prussian War, Prussian soldiers are still stationed in Paris."[22] The Belgian consul was supportive of the demand by the Japanese delegation to grant Sufu Kōhei permission to stay in Belgium. Sufu stayed in Belgium from 1871 until 1874. From 1874 until 1876 he resided in England.[23] As a result of this stay in Belgium, where he studied at the Athénée Royal in Brussels, Sufu Kōhei published the first extensive explanation of the state system in Belgium ranging from general information on Belgium to a detailed outline of the political system, including the head of state, the rights of the people, the three powers, finances, and the military, because:

> Belgium is indeed a small nation but its material and immaterial civilization is not less developed than that of the Great Nations like England, France, Germany, etc. There are even many aspects that excel and therefore I am convinced that the institutions of this small civilized nation will be more appropriate as a guide [temoto 手本] for Japan than the Great Nations.[24]

This work rich in information was published in 1877 and widened a window on Belgium that had first been opened two years earlier by Inoue Kowashi's translation of the Belgian constitution. Sufu Kōhei's exposition on Belgium was much more detailed and embedded in the political context of the times. It was the basic document that would be used in later years by policymakers and by the opposition to underscore plans for a modern state system.

Inoue Kowashi's interest in the Belgian constitution did not end with his translation of 1875. He continued his investigations into the development of constitutionalism and the practice of the constitution in later years when he was drafting the Meiji constitution. At that time — in the 1880s — he was no longer a middle-ranking civil servant but the right hand of the Prime Minister Itō Hirobumi and the actual architect of the Meiji constitution. Inoue's source for knowledge on the Belgian constitution was mainly the publication *La Constitution belge annotée* written by Jean-Joseph Thonissen, a famous professor in the Law Faculty of the Catholic University of Leuven and at the time an important politician.[25]

The Senate's (*Genrōin*) Proposal

Soon after Inoue Kowashi's translation of the Belgian and Prussian constitutions was published, the Senate (*Genrōin* 元老院), newly established in September 1876, authored the first official constitutional draft in modern Japan. Preparations were mainly done by people such as Yanagihara Sakimitsu, as members of the Research Commission on the National Constitution (*Genrōin kokken torishirabe kyoku* 元老院国憲取調局), which was situated within the Senate. The *Genrōin* submitted three proposals, the first in October 1876, the second in July 1878, and the last in July 1880. The *Genrōin* stated that they would refer to the British, American and French constitutional systems as to the intent and that they would take specific articles out of the Prussian, Austrian, Dutch, Belgian, Italian, Spanish, and Portuguese constitutions. There seems to have been a genuine wish on the part of the members of the senate to draft a constitution which tried to establish a form of rule that was shared between the citizen and the emperor. The first draft of the *Genrōin* in 1876 closely resembled what was common to the English bill of rights and the Belgian constitution of that time. The emperor was "sacred and inviolable", possessing the "power of administration". At the same time, it stipulated that the emperor had to swear loyalty to the constitution before the two houses. Moreover, legislative power was divided between the emperor and parliament. Further it was stated that the ministers were appointed and dismissed by the emperor, but that they had to take an oath of loyalty to the constitution and could be impeached by the senate. The lower house was to have the sole right of approving the budget. The content of these proposals was too liberal for Itō and Iwakura, who were irritated by a result which in their view "did not at all take into account the specific Japanese context and was a mere copy of the European constitutions." They feared that such a constitution would have no stabilizing effect on Japan and rejected it at once. The Research Commission on the National Constitution within the Senate was abolished in 1881.

Miyazawa Toshiyoshi, however, in 1941 closely analysed the constitutional drafts of the *Genrōin* and concluded that "rather than following the British model, one should say that it followed the Belgian model or the Prussian model."[26] He asserts that in nineteenth-century Europe, referring to examples in surrounding countries was common practice when drafting a new constitution. It is therefore very difficult to draw a clear line between the various constitutions. Miyazawa states, for example, that the German constitution was made by closely referring to the Belgian constitution, but that for the Belgian constitution itself the British constitution was an important example. Therefore Miyazawa writes that even if the draft proposal by the Senate was "rather influenced by the Belgian constitution or the Prussian constitution, there must undoubtedly have been British characteristics included too."[27]

Private Constitutional Proposals

At the same time several groups involved in the civil rights movements produced their own drafts. Some of those groups and individuals were inspired by the French and Belgian constitutions, among them the *Risshisha* 立志社, "an association that functioned both as a self-help society for former samurai and as a vehicle for promoting liberal political thought." Ueki Emori was the central figure in the *Risshisha*. He drafted the "Constitutional Proposal for Japan" (*Nihon kuniguni ken'an* 日本国々憲案).[28] Ueki was born in Tosa, a region known for its activism related to the rights of the people and democracy. Ueki wrote his proposal based on Inoue Kowashi's translation of the Belgian constitution.[29] Kino Kazue points out that "the structure of Inoue Kowashi's translation of the Belgian constitution and Ueki Emori's draft 'Constitutional Proposal for Japan' show some differences as to the chapters and the parts but as to the content of the crucial articles we can say that they are very much alike."[30]

Ueki's private draft was published in August 1881 and included clear limits to the power of the monarch, as well as universal suffrage and the protection of human rights. Ueki's draft also established a federal system and judicial review, which gave it a uniquely progressive content. One example of the influence of the Belgian constitution lies in the provisions concerning the imperial enthronement. Article 100 of Ueki's draft states that "the Emperor's enthronement has to be performed before the members of parliament." This reflects one part of Article 80 in the Belgian constitution. It is apparent from his writings that Ueki Emori had a very detailed knowledge of the Belgian constitution. Even closer to the content of the Belgian constitution is Article 50, which states that the "enthronement ceremony must take place before parliament and has to be performed by the speaker of the parliament", and in the next article that "the Emperor shall respect the constitution and pledge to the people to protect order in the nation." This draft article was indeed very similar to Article 80 of the Belgian constitution.[31]

The Meiji Constitution of 1889

Pressure on the government mounted, and to prevent upheaval and stagnation in the country the process of drafting a constitution could not go on indefinitely.[32] Itō Hirobumi, Itō Miyoji and Saionji Kinmochi departed for Germany and Austria on 14 March 1882 to conduct final research on the constitution. While Itō was in Germany and Austria, Inoue remained in Japan and also prepared the constitution by receiving instruction on constitutional law from Hermann Roesler, a German scholar from the University of Rostock who lived in Japan from 1878 until 1893.[33] The constitutional drafting committee was created in the autumn of 1886 and consisted of long-time allies of Itō Hirobumi, namely Itō Miyoji and Kaneko Kentarō. German constitutional scholars Hermann Roesler and Albert Mosse were special advisors to this committee and wielded considerable influence on the final shape of the constitution. Inoue Kowashi presented two drafts while Roesler presented one draft to Itō in May 1887. Reflection upon these drafts by the three members of the committee resulted in the so-called Natsujima proposal of August 1887. Several more proposals were drafted until a final proposal was presented to the emperor in April 1888. This proposal was discussed in the Privy Council (*Sūmitsuin* 枢密院) and it was accepted with some amendments in February 1889. The Meiji constitution was promulgated on 11 February 1889, after the emperor handed it to Prime Minister Kuroda Kiyotaka. Historians have emphasized that Germany was the main example for the Meiji constitution and that the influence of the new small nations disappeared. There is, however, a remarkable source that remains on the origin of each article of the Meiji constitution. This source was drafted by Inoue Kowashi who arguably was the actual architect — in the shadow of Itō Hirobumi — of this important legal code. He notes for each article of the constitution which

constitution was taken as model (*Kenpō sanshō* 憲法参照).[34] The Prussian constitution of 1850 was most important but the final content of the Meiji constitution was informed to a greater or lesser degree by many others, such as, respectively, the 1848 Dutch and 1867 Austrian constitutions as well as various French ones, and the 1826 Portuguese and 1848 Italian constitutions.[35] The impression from Inoue's sources is that he very carefully checked many constitutions in the world before drafting an article and that it cannot be asserted which constitution was the main source for the Meiji constitution. In total there are seventy-six articles in the Meiji constitution. Inoue's notes on the sources for each article indicate that forty draft articles to some extent drew on the Belgian constitution.[36]

The Belgian Constitution and Meiji Japan

Leading constitutional scholars of the past, such as Shimizu Tōru in 1906, Miyazawa Toshiyoshi in 1941, and Kiyomiya Shirō in 1954, confirm that the influence of the Belgian constitution on Japanese constitutionalism in the Meiji period was important. What kind of influence do these important scholars discern? On the one hand, there was a direct influence as stated previously — forty out of seventy-six articles in the Meiji constitution were based on constitutions including the Belgian. On the other hand, however, there was also a more indirect influence that appeared in the process of drafting the constitution. It was the idea of creating a new nation with strong unity, identity, domestic stability and order that was the main legacy of Belgian constitutionalism in Japan. Despite the fact that the Belgian influence was hidden in the framework of the "grand" legal policies as designed mainly by Itō Hirobumi and Inoue Kowashi, historical sources show that there was another concern for the Meiji leaders entrusted with drafting the first modern constitution of Japan. This concern was best expressed by Itō Hirobumi when he addressed the Privy Council Committee for the Establishment of a Constitution (*Sūmitsuin kenpō seitei kaigi* 枢密院憲法制定会議) on 18 June 1888. He presented the draft Meiji constitution to the institution that would grant final approval before the constitution would be promulgated on 11 February 1889. Itō started by pointing out that "Constitutional politics have played no role in the history of East Asian nations and therefore

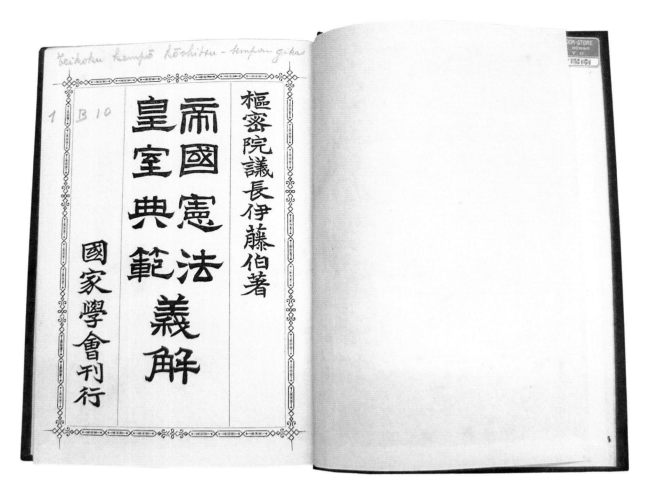

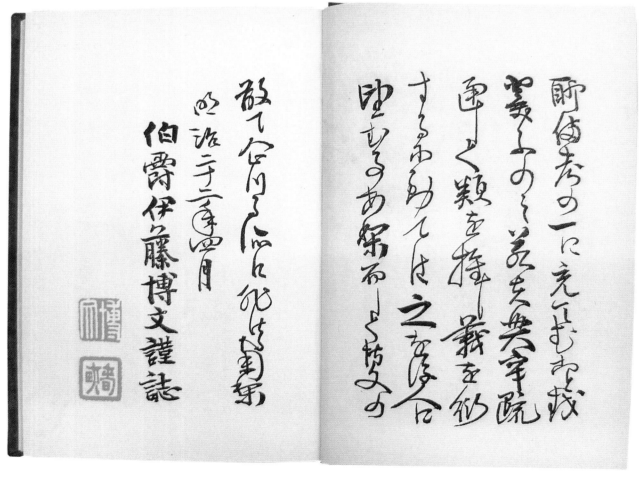

Japan will be embarking on a totally new path, of which it is unclear whether it will be beneficial for our nation."[39] Itō refers to Europe to contrast the constitutions restricting the power of the monarch with the draft Meiji constitution that did not impose any restriction on the power of the emperor: "in Europe until this century, no constitutional politics existed. Yet, it germinated in history unlike Japan, where [constitutionalism] is a totally new thing."[40] Itō continues by explaining that "today, in view of establishing a constitution, first we have to establish a main axis [kijiku 機軸], without which politics would be entrusted to the arbitrariness of the people, resulting in a loss of the unifying power of politics in a nation worthy of that name."[41] According to Itō, the central axis of the European nations as reflected in their constitutions can be found in "religion as the central axis that unifies the minds of the people. In Japan the power of religion is weak and cannot be considered an axis of the nation. Buddhism has brought prosperity to all the people by connecting them, but this is weaker than the Shintoism entrusted to us by our ancestors. Therefore, the only possible unifying axis in Japan is the emperor. Because of this, the main significance of the draft [Meiji] constitution is that it is made out of respect for the monarch..."[42]

It is here that the potential of the Belgian constitution for Japan is revealed. Japan and Belgium shared the characteristic of being new nations in search of a unifying axis (kijiku 機軸) around which the nation state could revolve and that should be reflected in the constitution. The Belgian constitution had faced the challenges in 1830 that Japan was facing in the 1880s. Belgium's constitution was the foremost answer to meet this challenge and was therefore an important example for the Meiji constitution.

Conclusion

Why can we affirm and concur with some of the most prominent Japanese constitutional scholars that the constitution of Belgium was an important source for the Meiji constitution? This was in the first place caused by the idea that Japan like Belgium was a new small nation that had to modernize the state structure to maintain its independence vis-à-vis the outside world. Another, mostly neglected, idea that lived in Meiji Japan amongst prominent leaders was that Japan, like Belgium, was not only new on the international scene but also that it had never previously existed as a unified country. Belgium, as Inoue Kowashi said, consisted of a unity of eight provinces, Japan developed out of the union of more than 280 domains. How were they to stabilize and formalize unity? The Belgian constitution offered an answer to this existential question spearheaded by Itō Hirobumi.

The Inoue translation and the more detailed explanation by Sufu Kōhei at an early stage gave ready access to the content of one of the most innovative constitutions of nineteenth-century Europe. The Belgian constitution of 1831 had proven to be efficient in diverting the threat of loss of independence and in gaining recognition from the surrounding Great Powers, and was therefore of the highest importance to the leaders of the new Meiji regime. Moreover, in view of the influence that the Belgian constitution of 1831 had exercised on the burgeoning movement towards constitutionalism in Europe from 1840 onwards, it could be expected that Meiji leaders would be interested in the Belgian constitution. It resulted in a direct influence in the form of a careful analysis of the Belgian constitution, evidenced by the fact that Inoue Kowashi was inspired by the Belgian constitution for forty out of seventy-six articles of the Meiji constitution. It also resulted in an indirect influence through receiving inspiration from the process of constitutionalism in the context of the construction of Belgium as a new nation under pressure from the imperialist powers of the world.

Itō Hirobumi 伊藤博文. *Teikoku kenpō kōshitsu tenpan gikai* 帝国憲法皇室典範義解 ("Commentaries on the Imperial Constitution and on the Law on the Imperial Household"). 5th ed. Tokyo: Maruzen 丸善, 1889. Blocks in possession of *Kokka gakkai* 国家学会.
Fonds japonais, Réserve précieuse des bibliothèques de l'Université catholique de Louvain.

Preface by Itō Hirobumi 伊藤博文 to *Teikoku kenpō kōshitsu tenpan gikai* 帝国憲法皇室典範義解 ("Commentaries on the Imperial Constitution and on the Law on the Imperial Household"). 5th ed. Tokyo: Maruzen 丸善, 1889. Blocks in possession of *Kokka gakkai* 国家学会.
Fonds japonais, Réserve précieuse des bibliothèques de l'Université catholique de Louvain.

REFERENCES

Beckmann 1957
George M. Beckmann. *The Making of the Meiji Constitution: The Oligarchs and the Constitutional Development of Japan, 1868-1891*. Lawrence, KS: University of Kansas Press, 1957.

Beer and Maki 2002
Lawrence Ward Beer and John McGilvrey Maki. *From Imperial Myth to Democracy: Japan's Two Constitutions, 1889-2002*. Boulder, CO: University Press of Colorado, 2002.

Gilissen 1968
John Gilissen. "La Constitution belge de 1831: Ses sources, son influence." *Res Publica* (1968), pp. 107-141.

Gluck 1985
Carol Gluck. *Japan's Modern Myths: Ideology in the Late Meiji Period*. Princeton, NJ: Princeton University Press, 1985.

Havens 2015
Thomas RH Havens. *Nishi Amane and Modern Japanese Thought*. Princeton, NJ: Princeton University Press, 2015.

Hawgood 1939
J.A. Hawgood. *Modern Constitutions since 1787*. London: Macmillan and Co., 1939.

Howland 2001
Douglas Howland. "Translating Liberty in Nineteenth-century Japan." *Journal of the History of Ideas* 62:1 (2001), pp. 161-181.

Ienaga 1967
Ienaga Saburō 家永三郎. *Nihon kindai kenpō shisōshi kenkyū* 日本近代憲法思想史研究 ["Research on the History of Constitutionalism in Modern Japan"]. Tokyo: Iwanami shoten 岩波書店, 1967.

Ienaga et al. 2005
Ienaga Saburō 家永三郎, Matsunaga Shōzō 松永昌三, and Emura Eiichi 江村栄一, eds. *Meiji zenki no kenpō kōsō* 明治前期の憲法構想 ["The Constitutional Concepts in Early Meiji Japan"]. Tokyo: Fukumura Shuppan 福村出版, 2005.

Inada 1960
Inada Masatsugi 稲田正次. *Meiji kenpō seiritsushi* 明治憲法成立史. Vol. 1. Tokyo: Yūhikaku 有斐閣, 1960.

Inoue 1875
Inoue Kowashi 井上 毅, trans. *Ōkoku kenkokuhō* 王国建国法 ["The Constitutions of Monarchies"], vol. 2 (no. 2). Tokyo: Meihōryō 明法寮, 1875. Translation of E. Laferrière, *Constitutions d'Europe et d'Amérique* (Paris: Cotillon, Librairie du Conseil d'Etat, 1869).

Inoue 1934
Inoue Kowashi 井上毅. "Kenpō gige / mikan shokō" 憲法義解・未完初稿 ["Understanding the Constitution" (unfinished manuscript)]. In *Kenpō shiryō / chūkan* 憲法資料・中巻 ["Documents on the Constitution, second volume"], ed. Itō Hirobumi 伊藤博文, pp. 53-206. Kenpō shiryō kankōkai 憲法資料刊行会, 1934.

Inoue 1966
Inoue Kowashi denki hensan iinkai 井上毅伝記編纂委員会. *Inoue den shiryōhen* 井上伝資料編. Vol. 1. Tokyo: Kokugakuin Daigaku Toshokan 国学院大学図書館, 1966.

Inoue 1969
Inoue Kowashi denki hensan iinkai 井上毅伝記編纂委員会. *Inoue den shiryōhen* 井上伝資料編. Vol. 3. Tokyo: Kokugakuin Daigaku Toshokan 国学院大学図書館, 1969.

Itō 1888
Itō Hirobumi, address to the Privy Council Committee for the Establishment of a Constitution (*Sūmitsuin kenpō seitei kaigi* 枢密院憲法制定会議) on 18 June 1888, National Archives of Japan (*Kokuritsu Kōbunshokan* 国立公文書館), Government, Documents of the Privy Council, Draft of the Meiji Constitution, documents from 18 June to 13 July 1888 (reference code A03033488000), available on-line: http://www.jacar.go.jp/ (last accessed 13 July 2016).

Ishii 1958
Ishii Ryōsuke. *Japanese Legislation in the Meiji Era*, trans. William Chambliss. Tokyo: Pan-Pacific Press, 1958.

Kawaguchi 1998
Kawaguchi Yoshihiko 川口由彦. *Nihon kindai hōseishi* 日本近代法制史. Tokyo: Shinseisha 新世社, 1998.

Kino 1997
Kino Kazue 木野主計. "Ueki Emori to Inoue Kowashi" 植木枝盛と井上毅 (Gakujutsu shinpojiumu "Meiji kokka to Jiyū Minken Undō" 学術シンポジウム「明治国家と自由民権運動」) [Academic symposium "The Meiji State and the Freedom and People's Rights Movement"]. *Kokugakuin hōgaku* 国学院法学 34:3 (February 1997), pp. 119-128.

Kiyomiya 1956
Kiyomiya Shirō 清宮四郎. *Berugī-koku kenpō, kenpō seibun shirīzu* ベルギー国憲法、憲法正文シリーズ. Vol. 3. Tokyo: Yūhikaku 有斐閣, 1956.

Klabbers 2009
Jan Klabbers. "Setting the Scene." In *The Constitutionalization of International Law*, ed. Jan Klabbers, Anne Peters and Geir Ulfstein, pp. 1-44. Oxford: OUP, 2009.

Kume 1996
Kume Kunitake 久米邦武, ed. *Tokumei zenken taishi Bei-Ō kairan jikki* 特命全権大使欧米欧回覧実記 ["A True Account of the Tour through America and Europe of the Ambassador Plenipotentiary"]. Vol. 3. Orig. pub. 1878. Iwanami bunko 770. Tokyo: Iwanami shoten 岩波書店, 1996 [1878].

Minear 1970
Richard H. Minear. *Japanese Tradition and Western Law: Emperor, State, and Law in the Thought of Hozumi Yatsuka*. Vol. 48. Cambridge, MA: Harvard University Press, 1970.

Miyazawa 1941
Miyazawa Toshiyoshi 宮沢俊由. "Genrō-in no kenpōsōan ni tsuite" 元老院の憲法草案について. *Kokka Gakkai Zasshi* 国家学会雑誌 ["The Journal of the Association of Political and Social Science"] 55:3 (March 1941), pp. 435-467

Mizubayashi et al. 2001
Mizubayashi Takeshi 水林彪, Ōtsu Tōru 大津透, Nitta Ichirō 新田一郎, and Ōtō Osamu 大藤修, eds. *Hōshakaishi, Shintaikei Nihonshi* 法社会史、新体系日本史. Tokyo: Yamakawa shuppansha 山川出版社, 2001.

Ono 2015
Ono Hiroshi 小野博司. "19 seiki kōhan ni okeru *Maguna Karuta* no keiju" １９世紀後半日本におけるマグナ・カルタの継受 ["The Reception by Japan in the 19th Century of the *Magna Carta*"]. In *Proceedings of the 67th plenary symposium: "800 years of the Magna Carta: Beyond the Discourse of the Myth of the Magna Carta"*, ed. Japan Legal History Association (Hōseishi gakkai 法制史学会), pp. 67-78. 2015.

Ono 2016
Ono Hiroshi 小野博司. "Kindaihō no hon'yakushatachi (2): Seido torishirabekyoku goyōgakari no kenkyū" 近代法の翻訳者たち (2) −制度取調局御用掛の研究 ["The Translators of Modern Law (2): Research on the Officers of the Office for the Investigation on Institutions"]. In *Hōseisaku kenkyū* 法政策研究 17, ed. Sensui Fumio 泉水文雄 and Kadomatsu Narufumi 角松生史, pp. 19-44. Tokyo: Shinzansha 信山社, 2016.

Peters 2015
Anne Peters. "Global Constitutionalism." In *The Encyclopedia of Political Thought*, ed. Michael T. Gibbons. First Edition. John Wiley & Sons, Ltd., 2015.

Shimizu 1906
Shimizu Tōru 清水澄. "Wagakuni kenpō to Fu, Haku kenpō to no hikaku" 我国憲法ト普、白憲法トノ比較. *Hōgaku shinpō* 法学新報 16-1:3 (1906).

Shōyū Kurabu and Matsuda 2015
Shōyū Kurabu 尚友倶楽部 and Matsuda Yoshifumi 松田好史. *Sufu Kōhei kankei bunsho* 周布公平関係文書 ["Documents Related to Sufu Kōhei"]. Tokyo: Fuyōshobō 芙蓉書房, 2015.

Steven 1977
R. P. G. Steven. "Hybrid Constitutionalism in Prewar Japan." *Journal of Japanese Studies* 3:1 (1977), pp. 99-133.

Takayanagi 1963
Takayanagi Kenzo. "A Century of Innovation: The Development of Japanese Law, 1868-1961." *Law in Japan* 5 (1963), pp. 5-40.

Takii and Noble 2007
Kazuhiro Takii and David Noble. *The Meiji Constitution: The Japanese Experience of the West and the Shaping of the Modern State*. No. 21. International House of Japan, 2007.

Thonissen 1879
Jean-Joseph Thonissen. *La constitution belge annotée, offrant, sous chaque article, l'état de la doctrine, de la jurisprudence et de la législation*. 3d ed. Brussels: Bruyland-Christophe, 1879.

Tsumaki 1935
Tsumaki Chūta 妻木忠太. *Shijitsu sanshō Kido Shōgiku-kō itsuwa* 史実参照木戸松菊公逸話 ["Kido Shōgiku's stories about historical facts"]. Tsukuba: Yūhōdō Shoten 友朋堂書店, 1935.

Vlastos 1989
Stephen Vlastos. "Opposition Movements in Early Meiji, 1868-1885." *The Nineteenth Century*, vol. 5 of *The Cambridge History of Japan*, ed. Marius B. Jansen. New York: Cambridge University Press, 1989.

NOTES

1 Peters 2015.

2 Quoted in Takii and Noble 2007, p. XII.

3 Quoted in Takii and Noble 2007, p. XII.

4 Quoted in Takii and Noble 2007, p. X.

5 Quoted in Takii and Noble 2007, p. X.

6 Klabbers 2009, p. 10.

7 Mizubayashi et al. 2001; see also: Kawaguchi 1998; Ishii 1958.

8 On the making of Japan's two constitutions, see also: Beer and Maki 2002; Beckmann 1957; Gluck 1985; Minear 1970; Steven 1977; Takayanagi 1963; Takii and Noble 2007.

9 政刑法典皆一国の議り立つる所にして、王も背く能はず. Cited in Ienaga 1967, p. 19.

10 *Kohyō henkaku bikō* 虎豹変革備考, quoted in Ienaga 1967, p. 20.

11 Ono 2016.

12 Havens 2015.

13 See also: Howland 2001.

14 Ono 2016, pp. 31-34.

15 Kawaguchi 1998, p. 136.

16 Gilissen 1968.

17 Hawgood 1939.

18 Kume 1996.

19 This quote can be found on the final two pages of Inoue 1875. For the digital version see: http://dl.ndl.go.jp/info:ndljp/pid/788895 (accessed 17 July 2016).

20 Inoue 1966; Inoue 1969.

21 Ono 2016, p. 32.

22 Quoted in Ono 2016, p. 32. Original source: Tsumaki 1935, p. 395. In this source, Sufu Kōhei talks about his relationship with Kido Takayoshi (p. 391). Sufu Kōhei returned to Japan in 1876 where he briefly became an employee of the Ministry of Justice.

23 Quoted in Shōyū Kurabu and Matsuda 2015, pp. 147-172.

24 Quoted in Shōyū Kurabu and Matsuda 2015, pp. 147-172.

25 Thonissen 1879.

26 Miyazawa 1941.

27 Miyazawa 1941.

28 Ienaga et al. 2005, pp. 385-397.

29 Kino 1997.

30 Kino 1997, p. 121.

31 Ienaga et al. 2005, pp. 72-75.

32 Vlastos 1989.

33 Inada 1960.

34 Inoue 1934.

35 Ono 2015.

36 Calculated from Inoue 1934.

37 Shimizu 1906; Kiyomiya 1956.

38 Itō 1888.

39 Itō 1888.

40 Itō 1888.

41 Itō 1888.

42 Itō 1888.

THIRD
PART

PERCEPTIONS AND FIGURES

THE PICTORIAL SOURCES OF KUME KUNITAKE'S WATERLOO ILLUSTRATIONS

W.F. Vande Walle

JAPAN & BELGIUM
An Itinerary of Mutual Inspiration

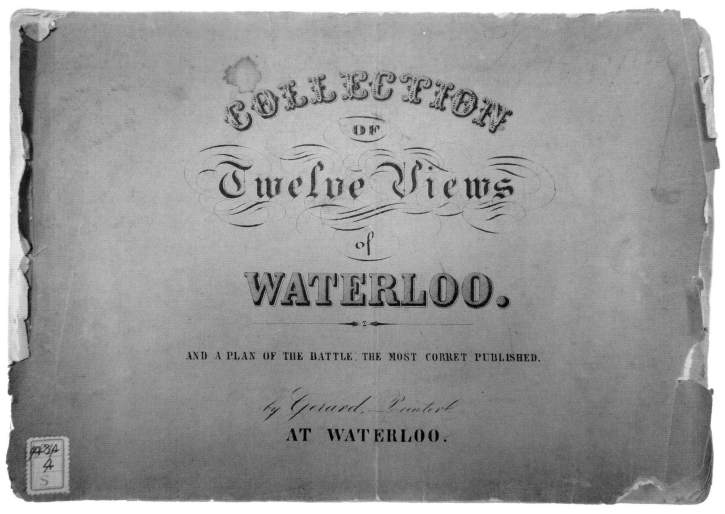

Fig. 1
*Collection of Twelve Views of Waterloo and a Plan of the Battle, the Most Corret [sic]
Published*. By Gerard, Printers at Waterloo.
Royal Museum of the Armed Forces and Military History, Brussels.
Photograph by Digitaal Labo KU Leuven.

Fig. 2
Album with Twelve Views of Waterloo.
Collection Seizan bunko 青山文庫 in Sagawa-chō 佐川町,
Takaoka-gun 高岡郡 in Kōchi prefecture, Japan.
Photograph by Yutaka Yabuta

THE PICTORIAL SOURCES OF KUME KUNITAKE'S WATERLOO ILLUSTRATIONS

The *Bei-Ō kairan jikki*,[1] the official record of the Iwakura mission to the United States and Europe (1871-1873), contains numerous engraved illustrations of the various places that the envoys visited. The sources of many of the illustrations are unknown but it has been possible to identify some of them, such as four engravings showing the battlefield at Waterloo and its environs that were included in the report of the emissaries' stay in Belgium. Some members of the mission visited Waterloo on Sunday, 23 February 1873.[2] The sources for the engravings are four lithographs published by H. Gérard, who at least for some of his professional life was based at the "Rue de la Bergère N° 6, près du Marché aux Bois" in Brussels.

H. (Henri or Hubert) Gérard designed an unspecified number of lithographs featuring views of the battlefield of Waterloo. He made it a practice to combine twelve views in an album, and this became a regular format, but the selection of views varied, and some of the engravings were produced by artists other than himself. The albums had a wide circulation and were eagerly bought as souvenirs by tourists visiting the battlefield, but of those that remaining hardly two are absolutely identical. The albums came in a French version (*Collection de Douze Vues de Waterloo. Bruxelles, chez Gérard, lithographe, éditeur, Rue de la Bergère N° 6, près du Marché aux Bois, déposé*) and an English one (*Collection of Twelve Views of Waterloo and a Plan of the Battle, the Most Corret [sic] Published. By Gerard, Printers at Waterloo*), but this difference was only a matter of adapting the title on the cover and the title page. Irrespective of the language of the cover and title page, the prints inside have either French captions or English or bilingual ones and the French, the English and the bilingual were apparently used in both versions. Not only is there a great variety in the selection of the twelve views, there is also a great variety in the execution, angle and details among engravings of the same view or subject. The human figures as well as the landscape and architectural features differ from print to print.

According to the *Répertoire des lithographes actifs en Belgique sous la période hollandaise et le règne de Léopold Ier (1816-1865)*, compiled by Marie-Christine Claes for Belgium's Royal Institute for Cultural Heritage,[3] H. Gérard (active between 1835 and 1861) was a lithographer, then publisher and dealer in prints and geographical maps. In 1845 he printed *Souvenirs de 1815. Atlas portatif pour servir à l'explorateur des champs de bataille de Waterloo et de Ligny. Orné de cartes et plans.* He is also known as the publisher of *Souvenirs de la Belgique. Album contenant douze vues des plus beaux monuments du pays et un plan de la ville de Bruxelles, Chez Gérard, lithographe, Rue de la Bergère, n° 6 à Bruxelles* (1850), a collection of thirteen lithographs, comprising twelve views and one map. Twelve views and a map was this publisher's preferred format.

The Royal Museum of the Armed Forces in Brussels owns three copies of the *Twelve Views of Waterloo* album: two identical French ones and an English one. There follows a short description of the two versions.

The French Version

The album's bluish green printed paper wrap (oblong quarto c.22 × 28 cm) bears the title *Collection de Douze Vues de Waterloo. Bruxelles, chez Gérard, lithographe, éditeur, Rue de la Bergère N° 6, près du Marché aux Bois, déposé.*

The title page bears the text: *Album Contenant un Plan de la Bataille de Waterloo. Dressé par le Général Baron de Jomini, et douze vues des environs du dit Champ de Bataille. Publié par H. Gérard, Rue de la Bergère, 6, à Bruxelles.*

No date of publication is given, but at the bottom of some of the prints we find the text "Déposée à la Direction, le 1er Septembre 1842." This does not mean however that the particular album in the Royal Museum of the Armed Forces was printed in that year, it may be a later reprint or later edition. Sets are known that bear the date 1840, which appears to be the first edition. This set will hereafter be referred to as the French version.

The twelve prints in this set are numbered. Their sequence is as follows:

N°1: Church at Waterloo*
N°2: Establishment including several interesting and Curious Souvenirs of the battle of Waterloo, fought on the 18ᵗʰ of June 1815+
N°3: Tombeau du Major Ed. Stables à Waterloo+
N°4: Monument du Major Arthur Rowley Leyland*
N°5: Ferme de Mont St. Jean+
N°6:Vue Générale du Champ de Bataille de Waterloo 18 Juin 1815*
N°7: Ferme de la Haye Sainte*
N°8: La Montagne du Lion*
[N°9]: Lion de Waterloo (not numbered)*
N°10: Monument des Prussiens à Planchenoit*
N°11: Ferme de la belle Alliance*
N°12: Restes de la Ferme et du Château d'Hougoumont*

These twelve prints are followed by the map of the battlefield.

The twelve prints listed above do not seem to constitute one identical run, for some of them bear the word "déposé" while others do not. They are at least consecutively numbered except for the print featuring the Lion of Waterloo, which is not numbered.

The Bluish Green Cover of the English Version Bears the Title:

Collection of Twelve Views of Waterloo and a Plan of the Battle, the Most Corret [sic] *Published. By Gerard, Printers at Waterloo.* (Fig. 1).

This version will be referred to below as the English version.

This copy has no title page other than the cover. Some of the prints included in this album have subjects different from the French version, most of the prints have similar subjects but in different executions, as can be seen in the composition and some details. The prints in this version are not numbered and since the stitching holding the prints has come loose they have probably been jumbled

up. Although there are twelve prints, there are only eleven different views since two of them are identical. In the list of views below, those marked with an asterisk have a counterpart in the French version:

– Eglise de Waterloo,* but different angle and altered composition.
– Monument du Major Arthur Rowley Leyland,* but altered composition and human figures.
– Vue Générale du Champ de Bataille de Waterloo 18 Juin 1815*: slightly altered composition and groups of human figures.
– Ferme de la Haye Sainte (two versions)*: different composition.
– Montagne du Lion* (no definite article "la"): different human figures and landscape background.
– Lion de Waterloo*: identical
– Monument des Prussiens à Planchenoit*: identical angle but altered groups of human figures.
– Ferme de la belle Alliance*: different view and altered composition.
– Restes de la Ferme et du Château d'Hougoumont*: different composition.
– Ferme du Caillou+
– Château de Frischemont+

The items that correspond with a view in the other version are marked with an asterisk, those that do not are marked with a cross sign. The maps in the French and the English version are also different.

The Version in the Seizan Bunko Collection

The Seizan bunko 青山文庫 in Sagawa-chō 佐川町, Takaoka-gun 高岡郡 in Kōchi prefecture has a similar album of twelve views of Waterloo, but yet again it is a different selection: sometimes the views are different, sometimes the views may be the same but the execution is slightly different. (Fig. 2).

Two views are similar but not identical to their counterparts in the French version:
– Establishment including several interesting and Curious Souvenirs of the battle of Waterloo, fought on the 18ᵗʰ of June 1815.
– Monument des Prussiens à Planchenoit.

The print in Seizan bunko has "Plancenoit" in the caption instead of "Planchenoit". Spellings vary.

Five views in the Seizan bunko are identical to counterparts in the English version:
– Eglise de Waterloo.
– Ferme de la Haye Sainte.
– Montagne du Lion.
– Ferme de la belle Alliance.
– Restes de la Ferme du Château d'Hougoumont.

One view is slightly different, namely that captioned "Vue Générale du Champ de Bataille de Waterloo 18 Juin 1815."

Seizan bunko was established by Tanaka Mitsuaki 田中光顕 (1843-1939), a major figure in the politics of the Meiji period, and a member of the Iwakura mission. It is not hard to imagine that he bought a set of the Gérard prints when the mission passed through Belgium. Some of the prints in the Aoyama bunko set bear a seal with the words "donated to the Seizan bunko in the fifteenth year of Taishō by Tanaka Mitsuaki."

This set in the Seizan bunko was "discovered" by Yutaka Yabuta,[4] emeritus professor at Kansai University, although he may have been preceded by Izumi Saburō.[5]

The four views reproduced in *Bei-Ō kairan jikki* correspond to four prints in the English version:

– Ferme de la belle Alliance (Fig. 3), captioned by Kume as "the village of Waterloo in Belgium" (Fig. 4).
– Eglise de Waterloo (Fig. 5), captioned by Kume as "church which served as the headquarters of the abovementioned English general Wellington" (Fig. 6).
– Montagne du Lion (Fig. 7), captioned by Kume as "the high mound of Waterloo in Belgium" (Fig. 8).
– Château de Frischemont (Fig. 9), captioned by Kume as "site of the post where the abovementioned English general stood his ground" (Fig. 10).

Kume's caption to the fourth print is rather queer, since according to the caption on the original Gérard lithograph, Frischemont is the site where Prussian troops under the command of General Bülow entered the battlefield, admittedly a decisive moment in the battle, but not one that involved Wellington.

Kume most probably had the Château de Hougoumont in mind, equally a fortified farm, whose defenders against all odds held out all day against successive French attacks. Wellington later declared that the successful defence of this post had played a decisive role in the final outcome of the battle. The Château de Frischemont lithograph does not figure in the Seizan bunko set. Kume's set was clearly yet a different one, not surprisingly given the great variety in the selection of the twelve views.

On the other hand, the caption to the Ferme de la belle Alliance, as "the village of Waterloo in Belgium" is also somewhat erroneous, because it was in actual fact a "cabaret" (an inn or tavern). Although the building did not play any role in the battle, it happened to be located in the centre of the French front line. Moreover, it was the place where Wellington and Blücher allegedly met at the end of the battle. Blücher wanted to adopt the felicitous hint in the name of the cabaret to name the battle, in view of the fact that it had been won by a coalition or alliance.[6] In Germany, and in particular in Prussia, the battle was known as "Belle-Alliance Sieg." One of the old plazas in Berlin, the Rondell Platz, was renamed "Belle-Alliance Platz" in 1815 in commemoration of the victory. Notwithstanding this, the name did not stick, and Waterloo became the universally accepted name.

In general, the prints in the *Bei-Ō kairan jikki* are narrowed versions of the originals. They had to conform to the format of the book, where the illustrations are almost square. Because the originals were oblong, the graphic designer had to slightly compress them, and traces of this shortening are visible in the centre of the pictures. This is notably visible in the clouds and the gable of the Château de Frischemont, and the gate to the left, which has fewer bars than the gate in the original print.

FERME DE LA BELLE-ALLIANCE.

PRES DE WATERLOO

Lith.de Gerard, Bruxelles

Fig. 3
Ferme de la belle-Alliance. From *Collection of Twelve Views of Waterloo and a Plan of the Battle, the Most Corret* [sic] *Published.* By Gerard, Printers at Waterloo.
Royal Museum of the Armed Forces and Military History, Brussels. Photograph by Digitaal Labo KU Leuven.

> **Fig. 4**
Engraving captioned by Kume as "The Village of Waterloo in Belgium." Kume 1878, vol. 3.
Photograph by Digitaal Labo KU Leuven.

REFERENCES

Izumi 2001
Izumi Saburō 泉三郎. *Shashin, ezu de yomigaeru dōdōtaru Nihonjin: Kono kuni no katachi o tsukutta Iwakura shisetsudan* Bei-Ō kairan *no tabi* 写真・絵図で甦る堂々たる日本人 この国のかたちを創った岩倉使節団「米欧回覧」の旅. Tokyo: Shōdensha 祥伝社, 2001.

Kume 1878
Kume Kunitake 久米邦武. *Tokumei zenken taishi Bei-Ō kairan jikki* 特命全権大使米欧回覧実記. 5 vols. Tokyo: Hakubunsha 博聞社, 1878.

Kume 1977–82
Kume Kunitake 久米邦武. *Bei-Ō kairan jikki* 米欧回覧実記. 5 vols. Iwanami bunko series 岩波文庫. Tokyo: Iwanami Shoten 岩波書店, 1977–82.

Logie 2003
Jacques Logie. *Waterloo: la campagne de 1815*. Bruxelles: Éditions Racine, 2003.

NOTES

1 Kume 1878.

2 For more background information, see Yutaka Yabuta's article in this book "*A True Account of a Journey of Observation through the United States of America and Europe* and *An Account of the State of Belgium*: Resonances of the Small Nation Concept."

3 See http://balat.kikirpa.be/lithographes/fiches/Gerard_H.htm (accessed 28 July 2016).

4 See Yutaka Yabuta's article in this book "*A True Account of a Journey of Observation through the United States of America and Europe* and *An Account of the State of Belgium*: Resonances of the Small Nation Concept."

5 Izumi 2001, p. 101 contains a reproduction of two prints from the Tanaka Mitsuaki album.

6 Logie 2003, pp. 69, 140, 142.

Fig. 5
Eglise de Waterloo. From *Collection of Twelve Views of Waterloo and a Plan of the Battle, the Most Corret* [sic] *Published*. By Gerard, Printers at Waterloo.
Royal Museum of the Armed Forces and Military History, Brussels.
Photograph by Digitaal Labo KU Leuven.

> Fig. 6
Engraving captioned by Kume as "Church Which Served as the Headquarters of the Abovementioned English General Wellington." Kume 1878, vol. 3.
Photograph by Digitaal Labo KU Leuven.

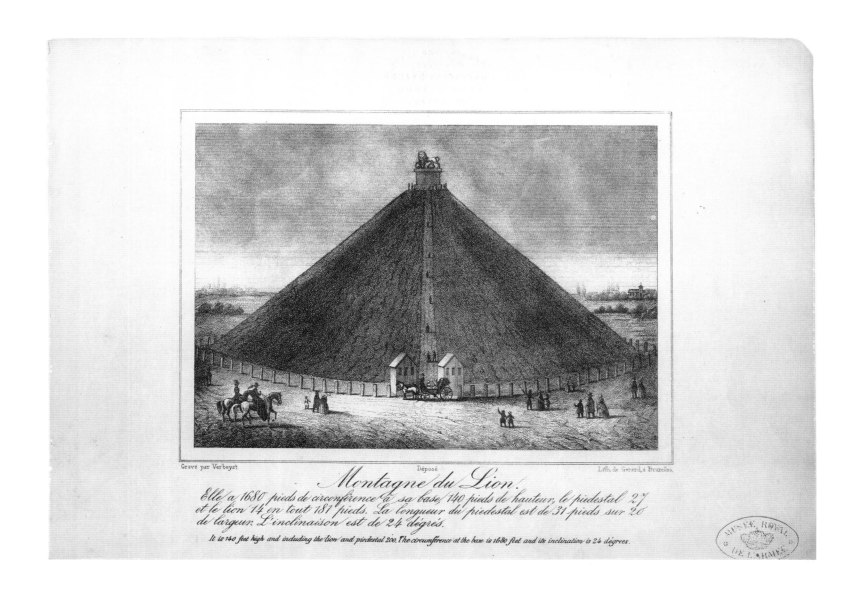

Fig. 7
Montagne du Lion. From *Collection of Twelve Views of Waterloo and a Plan of the Battle, the Most Corret* [sic] *Published*. By Gerard, Printers at Waterloo.
Royal Museum of the Armed Forces and Military History, Brussels.
Photograph by Digitaal Labo KU Leuven.

> Fig. 8
Engraving captioned by Kume as "The High Mound of Waterloo in Belgium."
Kume 1878, vol. 3.
Photograph by Digitaal Labo KU Leuven.

WATERLOO.

CHÂTEAU DE FRISCHEMONT.

Arrivée du 4me Corps de l'armée Prussienne d'un escadron de cavalerie et une Battie d'Artillerie, commandés par le Général Bulow.

Deposé   Lith de Gerard, Bruxelles.

Fig. 9
Château de Frischemont. From *Collection of Twelve Views of Waterloo and a Plan of the Battle, the Most Corret* [sic] *Published*. By Gerard, Printers at Waterloo.
Royal Museum of the Armed Forces and Military History. Brussels.
Photograph by Digitaal Labo KU Leuven.

> **Fig. 10**
Engraving captioned by Kume as "Site of the Post Where Wellington Stood His Ground." Kume 1878, vol. 3.
Photograph by Digitaal Labo KU Leuven.

JAPANESE PERCEPTIONS OF BELGIUM IN THE MEIJI AND TAISHŌ PERIODS

Fumitaka Kurosawa

特命全権大使　安達峯一郎

大正１０年５月３１日　　（大使館しよう格）

31. 5. 1921

JAPANESE PERCEPTIONS OF BELGIUM
IN THE MEIJI AND TAISHŌ PERIODS

Introduction

Relations between Japan and Belgium date from 1588, when a single Jesuit priest set foot on Japanese soil.[1] Of course, what we now consider Belgium was at that time the Southern Netherlands, one of many territories subject to the Spanish monarchy. In 1587, however, the year prior to this first visit, Toyotomi Hideyoshi's edicts against Christianity had been issued and the policies of the succeeding Tokugawa shogunate, which restricted and greatly curtailed Japan's external relations, saw the suspension of relations between the peoples of both nations. Relations between the two countries began anew on 1 August 1866, in the dying phase of the Tokugawa shogunate, through the conclusion of a treaty of amity, commerce and navigation. This was the ninth such treaty the shogunate had signed with North American and European nations, beginning with the 1858 US-Japan Treaty of Amity and Commerce, which was one of those collectively known as the "Ansei Five-Power Treaties", having been signed in the 1854-1860 Ansei period.

Thereafter, Japanese–Belgian relations proceeded in an orderly fashion focusing mostly on economic and cultural aspects, albeit with a hiatus (1941-1952) following the outbreak of the Pacific War, and continue thus to this day. Further, on the occasion of the Shōwa emperor's first post-war visit to Europe in 1971, the intimacy between the respective imperial and royal families became well known, as evidenced by the invitation extended by the King of the Belgians.

What can be seen in the consistent undercurrent of good mutual relations, is the good will and sense of affection that the respective peoples hold for each other. Needless to say, one could hardly omit mentioning the historical reality of an almost total lack of any serious points of dispute between the two nations. Indeed, in the case of the Nine-Power Pact meeting, held at the outbreak of the Sino-Japanese War, any negative impact on Japanese-Belgian relations was avoided due to the skilful leadership of the Belgian chairman.[2] Even where

political disputes took place, we must not forget that there were statesmen in both nations who strove to ensure that relations did not suffer as a result. How did these key figures in mutual relations, and through them the populations of both nations, perceive each other? How were images formed? The core concern of this chapter is to consider this issue from the Japanese perspective of the Meiji and Taishō periods (1868-1925).

Belgium in Early Meiji Publications

In the Meiji period, when Western nations were seen as "models" in the construction of a modern nation state,[3] a great number of observational accounts of foreign countries made their way into print. Some were records of government-sponsored observers, but others were derived from more personal travels; either way, they reflected, from a variety of viewpoints, their respective authors' images of the "model nation". What follows is a representative sample of works that are considered likely to have influenced the formation of Japanese perceptions of Belgium.

The first to consider is Sufu Kōhei's 周布公平 *Berugī-koku shi* 白耳義国志 ["A Record of Belgium"], which was published in 1877. With its title characters penned by Sanjō Sanetomi 三条実美, who occupied the senior post of minister of the Right in the new Council of State, and prefaced with introductions by Kido Takayoshi 木戸孝允 and Itō Hirobumi 伊藤博文, this work was by far the earliest specialist introduction to Belgium in the Meiji period. Sufu himself was a native of the south-western domain of Chōshū, a leading force in the overthrow of the Tokugawa and, after a period of study in Belgium, he returned to Japan to take up a career as a government official. He subsequently entered the House of Peers and served as a privy councillor.

By way of outline, he argued that in recent times Japanese, when discussing the political customs of western nations, had tended to focus on Great Britain, France, Prussia, Russia and the United States, with barely any attention being given to Belgium. Certainly, in comparison to great powers such as France and Britain, Belgium was incredibly small and lacked the capacity to challenge these powerful nations. However, it was also a country, "whose people are clever and resourceful, whose equals one might scarcely find in any of its neighbours." Moreover, he adds that "any who would seek to evaluate the world's manufactures and industries cannot but nominate Belgium for the perfection of its political and legal systems." Through this text, then, the reader was to be equipped with an awareness of Belgium's "good governance and the foundations of its people's customs." Sufu further states that if one could accept "that the range of a nation's borders, whether great or limited, bears no relation to either the extent of its civilization or the wisdom of its people," then the study of Belgium was in no way inferior to one of the larger European nations and "can be of value in aiding our own national enlightenment."[4] In this way, Sufu identifies Belgium, one of the smaller European nations, as a "model nation" for Japan, a small Far Eastern nation, in its own efforts to promote modernization.

Let us now consider *A True Account of the Ambassador Extraordinary & Plenipotentiary's Journey of Observation through the United States of America and Europe* (*Tokumei zenken taishi Bei-Ō kairan jikki*), which is by far the most important record of any tour of observation abroad in the early years of Meiji. Published by the Council of State's Record Department in 1878, Kume Kunitake's 久米邦武 edited official account of the Iwakura Mission to Europe and the United States (1871-1873) was commercially distributed and found a large readership.[5] *A True Account* states that the Big Three, that is to say the United States, "a land of European settlement," Great Britain, "the international hub of trade," and France, "Europe's greatest market," were "impressive nations which covered vast territories, boasted large populations and wielded an economic might that could affect the entire world." On the other hand, with regard to Belgium and the Netherlands, "if one were to speak of the size of national territory or their numbers of people, we might as well compare them to our own island of Tsukushi [modern-day

Kyushu]. Their land is boggy and of poor quality, [yet] located as they are amidst the great powers they have done well to maintain their autonomy and the strength of their commercial pursuits exceeds that of far larger nations, and they have influence on trade, not only within Europe, but globally." *A True Account* goes on to credit this to their being "diligent and co-operative peoples." For that reason, "their influence upon us could well be felt more keenly than that of the Big Three." How was it then that Belgium was able to maintain its independence and preserve its neutrality in the midst of European dog-eat-dog international politics? Further, how was it that Belgium could enjoy "commercial strength" and "national vigour" surpassing even the "great powers"?

One answer to the first question was that the maintenance of autonomy and neutrality was not merely the result of superficial military strength, but rather of the people's spirit of self-reliance and independence, which was integral to their overall strength. It was this very strength of spirit that underlay Belgium's ability to produce soldiers of such "extraordinary strength".

As to the second question, "the people of Belgium say that if a nation is lacking a self-reliant people, then that nation's strength will also be limited and it will be hard to preserve. Belgium has resolved that its form of government and its laws have as their object the nurturing of self-reliance. With high and low linking their hearts in a framework of mutual support, all could cultivate the fine quality of independence…" The Iwakura mission saw this spirit of "self-reliance" as being at the basis of the Belgian ability to eclipse the "great powers" in many ways. In this context, when referring to the Mission's visit to the Vienna World Exposition (Wiener Weltausstellung) of 1873, Kume stated that the inferiority of the products of the "great powers" of Russia and Austria was "due to the poor spirit of self-reliance amongst their respective peoples."

The mission makes meticulous note of the "self-reliant spirit" of the Belgians and states that a "nation's vigour, wealth and might is bound up in the spirit of its people." One can say that this was the most keenly felt "impression" of Belgium brought back by the Iwakura mission. Particular attention should be paid to the mission's observations on the connection between politics and the Belgian people's "spirit of self-reliance":

> This country's governance through a legally established monarchy is quite different in character compared to other imperial monarchies. In terms of the people's sense of self-reliance they excel even republics. Of all the European states, Belgium's elected monarchy, the Swiss republican government, and the former kingdom of Saxony, while all possessing considerably differing political teachings and customs, were most prosperous and wealthy nations with civilizations of the highest level. Moreover, a nation's prosperity is not merely under the influence of its politics, but rather the harmony and co-operation of its people. As the saying has it, "government is the reflection of the people."

As we have briefly seen above, the Belgian people were brimming with a "spirit of self-reliance" and, as a "top-rank" member of European civilization, were very highly evaluated by the Iwakura mission. For Japan, being unable to modernize at a single stroke in the manner of great powers on the scale of France or Britain, it was necessary to have a "model nation" for gradual modernization as a second-best plan. In this sense, the "small nation" of Belgium was recognized as being one such "model nation" for a small Far Eastern power such as Japan.

Moreover, in this context we should not forget Inoue Kowashi 井上毅, the constitutional bureaucrat who took part in drafting the Meiji Constitution and the Imperial Rescript on Education. In his 1875 translation of the Prussian and Belgian constitutions, *Ōkoku kenkokuhō* 王国建国法 ["Monarchical Constitutions"], Inoue very positively appraised Belgium for being "thoroughly good and virtuous" amongst the European states, even though it was "one of the newest."[6] He took the view that "little" Belgium was a "moral country" and a "righteous country," and recognized that it was for these very reasons that Belgium was able to maintain its national independence amongst the great powers.

The third text to consider is Yano Ryūkei's 矢野龍溪 *Shūyū zakki* 周遊雑記 ["Miscellaneous Records of a Tour"].[7] Yano was close to Ōkuma Shigenobu 大隈重信 and Fukuzawa Yukichi 福沢諭吉, participated in the formation of the Constitutional Reform Party and also

became president of the Yūbin Hōchi publishing house 郵便報知新聞社. He held Belgian industrial prosperity in high regard and considered "constitutional government" as one of the key factors behind it. Further, in *Miscellaneous Records*, Yano suggests that countries with "parliamentary [and] liberal forms of government" can exercise a positive influence even upon countries with more "autocratic forms of government," and that in Asia only Japan would in the near future be able to "gain honour in the world by applying this system."

The fourth and final text for consideration here is Yorimitsu Hōsei's 依光方成 *San'en gojissen sekai shūyū jikki* 三円五十銭世界周遊実記 ["A True Account of a Trip around the World on Three-and-a-Half Yen"], published in 1891.[8] Yorimitsu was born in the former domain of Tosa, along Shikoku's southern coast, and maintained friendly relations with activists in the popular rights movement, which accounts for the fact that three members of the newly inaugurated House of Representatives, namely, Ueki Emori 植木枝盛, Kurihara Ryōichi 栗原亮一 and Shimada Saburō 島田三郎, all contributed prefaces to his book. Yorimitsu also heaped praise on a number of features of Belgium, including its industries, foreign trade and constitutional government, in addition to the struts he saw as supporting them, such as the people's general character, education and its professional, that is, volunteer-based, military forces. In the Belgian section of his book, Yorimitsu further speculates as to how Belgium, located as it is between stronger powers, was able to maintain its independence. According to Yorimitsu, this feat should be credited to the people's "propensity for standing on their own two feet," and he surmises that two factors led to this national disposition. Firstly, there was the European balance of power, and secondly, the "power of universal education." That is to say, it was precisely because the people worked diligently at their employment that their daily lives were stable, they were able to pass their lives with a certain peace of mind, and thus were of a strong inclination to preserve their national independence. At the root of this lay the "power of universal education." Consequently, in order to maintain independence and to foster a strong passion for autonomy, the "most important and essential path" lay not in "bolstering the state's military power," but in "the education of the people." Such were Yorimitsu's overall conclusions as he sought an underlying explanation for the continued independence of Belgium.

As briefly outlined above, some of the common denominators in Japanese images of Belgium, as seen in the publications of early- to mid-Meiji, are: a small country, a civilized nation, the preservation of independence despite being wedged between much larger states, a "diligent and harmonious" people rich in a spirit of self-reliance, industrial development, constitutional monarchy, a moral nation, and a land of education. Finally, it should also be mentioned that for the most part, the areas most visited by the Japanese were Brussels, Antwerp, Liège, and the battlefield of Waterloo.

The Japanese Army and Belgium

Initially, the Meiji government's establishment and training of a modern military followed the French model, but from the latter part of the 1880s they adopted, in the main, the German model. However, attention was also paid to other European and North American military systems and technologies, and so military knowledge and information from nations other than France and Germany were also eagerly sought. In this respect, we should also consider how Belgium was viewed by the Japanese army in the Meiji period, and with what particular significance for Japan.

Japanese Army Officers and Study Tours of Belgium

Over the course of 1869 and 1870, army vice-minister Yamagata Aritomo 山県有朋 (who later served as army minister, prime minister, and *genrō*, i.e. elder statesman), directly studied the various military systems of Europe. Upon returning to Japan, on 2 February 1872, he submitted his report, co-authored with Kawamura Sumiyoshi 川村純義 (assistant to the army vice-minister) and Saigō Tsugumichi 西郷従道, entitled *Gunbi ikensho* 軍備意見書 ["A Memorandum on Armament"]. In this report, Yamagata had the following to say regarding Belgium:[9]

> Holland and Belgium are very small and situated between larger countries. They hope to avoid being dismissed and viewed with contempt by them through constant vigilance, day and night. Even though their territory and population would be no more than one third of our own imperial land, they nonetheless do well to maintain no fewer than

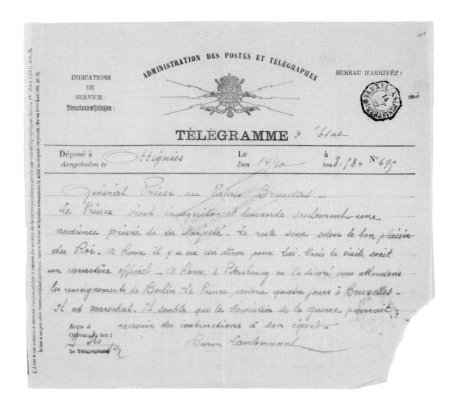

forty to fifty thousand men in a state of military preparedness. When we consider the position of our empire, the Dutch and Belgians seem as though they focus their efforts on military affairs at the expense of other matters.

That is to say, the Netherlands and Belgium were small nations hemmed in by larger powers. With their respective populations and territories amounting to no more than a third of Japan's, they attempted to avoid the threat of invasion and being viewed with indifference by devoting their efforts to maintaining a high level of military preparedness and national defence, even at the cost of neglecting other matters. In this manner, from Yamagata's point of view, Belgium was more a land of military endeavour than manufacture. Moreover, around the same time, Major Ōyama Iwao 大山巌 (later, army minister and chief of general staff) also visited Belgium on his tour of Europe to observe the Franco-Prussian War.

A little after these two visits, in March 1872, Major General Yamada Akiyoshi 山田顕義, in his capacity as a member of the Iwakura Mission, undertook a fact-finding mission to Belgium, Holland and Switzerland from his base in Paris, in order to investigate their respective military systems. Unfortunately, his report on Belgium has not survived.

Telegram from Baron Lambermont to General Brisse dated 14 October 1882 concerning the visit of Prince Arisugawa.
Archives of the Royal Palace, Brussels. Photograph by Hans Coppens.

> Letter from T. Sakurada of the Japanese Legation in Brussels to Baron Lambermont, dated 17 October 1882, concerning the visit of Prince Arisugawa to Brussels, recto.
Archives of the Royal Palace, Brussels. Photograph by Hans Coppens.

La Haye le 17 Octobre 1882

Légation du Japon
à Bruxelles
—————

Excellence,

J'ai l'honneur d'accuser la réception du télégramme de Votre Excellence m'informant qu'il plaira à Sa Majesté le Roi des Belges de recevoir en audience Son Altesse Impériale le Prince Arisugawa, oncle de Sa Majesté l'Empereur du Japon, après le retour de Sa Majesté le Roi du Château de Ciergnon.

En remerciant Votre Excellence de cette communication j'ai l'honneur d'informer Votre Excellence

Son Excellence
Monsieur le Baron A. Lambermont
Secrétaire Général du Ministère des
Affaires Etrangères de S. M. le Roi des Belges.

193

que Son Altesse Impériale a
décidé de partir d'ici pour
Berlin vu l'absence de
Bruxelles de Sa Majesté le
Roi. J'informerai Votre
Excellence à temps du voyage
de Son Altesse Impériale de
Berlin à Bruxelles et serai
personnellement à Bruxelles
2 jours avant Son Altesse.

Je profite de cette
occasion pour offrir à Votre
Excellence mes remerciments
des peines qu'Elle a bien
voulu se donner à ce sujet
et Lui renouveler l'assurance
de ma très-haute considération.

N. Sakurada

194

The next military figure to visit Belgium was Prince Arisugawa no Miya Taruhito 有栖川宮熾仁, a general in the army, who made a tour of Europe and North America after attending the coronation ceremony of Tsar Alexander III. He visited Belgium in October 1882 and inspected cannon emplacements at Antwerp, the steel mills at Liège and various military barracks and facilities. His account of his travels can be found in *Ō-Bei jun'yū nikki* 欧米巡遊日記 ["Diary of Travels in Europe and America"] , which was published in 1883.[10]

Thereafter, Major General Nozu Michitsura 野津道貫, accompanying Army minister Ōyama Iwao to Europe to study military reforms, visited Belgium in July 1884. Nozu observed military camps, the fortress at Antwerp, arsenals, munitions and armaments factories at Liège and elsewhere. He also went on to consider military budgets, troop numbers and organization, conscription laws, laws for mustering horses, mobilization plans, officers' pay, charts showing the composition of military forces in wartime and so forth. His record of his visit, including the aforementioned detailed study of the Belgian military establishment, was published in 1886 as *Ō-Bei junkai nisshi*.[11] According to this work, "the Belgian military was formed so as to provide for national defence and to protect neutrality" and at its root lay the law of conscription, which by an ordinance of 18 September 1873, "provides for the enlistment of volunteers and conscripts, it being the case that substitution is also permitted under the [conscription] law."

When Nozu inspected the Antwerp fortress, his guide, Major Hellebaut of the artillery corps, explained Belgium's national defence policy as follows:

> Antwerp is Belgium's military strongpoint and the key fortress of the nation. At the time of mobilization, troops from all over the nation are to be concentrated here in the environs of the city (there are assembly points in five localities), and should enemy forces invade, our soldiers will stand here against them. If our strength should not suffice, our soldiers are to retreat to Antwerp and fight to the death. Depending upon the circumstances, we would request assistance of Great Britain.

Nozu recorded his impressions of this explanation:

> When we observe this region today, we can see a concentration of fortifications and arsenals. Since it is impossible for Belgium to fully resist great powers on the scale of France or Germany, it has but the choice of concentrating its soldiers here in this region and to put all of its efforts into a defensive battle. Still, Belgium is a small country with a population of merely 5,500,000, or less than 1/7 of Japan, but this is not its only defensive tool. Through annual national military expenditure on the grand scale of ¥8,914,720, Belgium maintains a standing army of 46,272 men, and spends a further ¥698,320 on a force of gendarmes. In wartime they can expect to raise a further 103,683 men. All of this is due to the fact that Belgium is a small country wedged between the larger nations of France and Germany. The people know well that military strength is the means by which the nation can be held and one can well imagine the people's sentiments, powerfully drawn as they are, to their national defence.

In short, from his observations, Nozu saw in Belgium the image of a small nation situated between the larger powers of Germany and France, making fervent efforts in the spirit of national unity to defend its territory. In this way, his impression is along the lines of that earlier introduced by Yamagata.

It is worth noting that the principal sites visited by Japanese army officers tended to be places such as the Antwerp fortress, the Liège steel mills, and artillery and engineering facilities. It should also be observed that prior to the outbreak of the 1894-1895 Sino-Japanese War, a number of officers with backgrounds in artillery and engineering visited Belgium. Amongst these were artillery corps lieutenants Satō Tadayoshi 佐藤忠義 and Hijikata Hisaaki 土方久明 (both of whom had travelled with Army minister Ōyama in 1884), who began their study tour of Belgium in 1890. In the following year, four more officers commenced their studies in Belgium: artillery corps captains Amano Tomitarō 天野富太郎, Aoki Norizumi 青木宣純, Shimakawa Bunpachirō 島川文八郎 (later director of the Itabashi gunpowder plant 板橋火薬製造, attached to the Tokyo Artillery Corps; head of the artillery division, Army Bureau of Military Affairs; and director of the Weapons Bureau, Army

‹ Letter from T. Sakurada of the Japanese Legation in Brussels to Baron Lambermont, dated 17 October 1882, concerning the visit of Prince Arisugawa to Brussels, verso.
Archives of the Royal Palace, Brussels. Photograph by Hans Coppens.

Ministry); and engineering corps captain Fukuhara Shinzō 福原信蔵 (later head of the Engineering Division, Army Bureau of Military Affairs; head of the Army Artillery School; and chief of Fortress Construction, Army HQ).

Shimakawa, who was an instructor at the army's artillery school, went to Belgium particularly to conduct research on smokeless gunpowder. Incidentally, the Itabashi gunpowder plant of which he was director, was originally an outcome of research conducted into gunpowder manufacture in Belgium by Sawa Tarōzaemon 沢太郎左衛門, who had been sent to the Netherlands by the Tokugawa shogunate (he had returned to Japan in 1867). He soon discovered that due to military secrecy it was most difficult to carry out research of this kind, and so secured work as a manual labourer over the years 1865-1866 in the Belgian gunpowder factory Poudrerie Royale de Wetteren Cooppal & Cie. Here Sawa not only mastered the relevant techniques but was also successful in procuring some machinery for gunpowder manufacture. These machines were later installed by the new Meiji government and were the first to produce up-to-date black gunpowder in Japan.[12]

Belgium in Army-related Periodicals

Continuing the army theme, it is also important to consider the content of army-related periodicals published during the Meiji period and to review what sort of articles they carried pertaining to Belgian.

First, there is *Getsuyōkai kiji* 月曜会記事. The Getsuyōkai was founded in 1881 as an independent military research group of army officers with a remit to consider military affairs. It was disbanded in February 1889 on the orders of Army minister Ōyama Iwao and was thereafter absorbed into the Kaikōsha 偕行社. The *Getsuyōkai kiji* was first published in July 1885 and was issued monthly thereafter until the group was disbanded four years later. Not all issues remain to this day, but we have been able to identify translations of writings penned by two Belgian army officers, published in five issues. The Belgian officers were an artillery corps lieutenant colonel, whose name was transcribed in Japanese as "Pī Anrāru" [P. Henrart?], and an engineering corps colonel, whose name was transcribed as "Asshu

Ukuēruman" [H.?]. The articles appeared under the Japanese title of "Berugī gunji ichiran bassui" 伯耳義軍事一覧抜萃 ("Excerpts from a Survey of Belgian Military Affairs") and were carried in issues 12-16 (June-October 1886) of *Getsuyōka kiji*.

For the most part, the content of the articles dealt with the theme of "mobilization", which attracted much attention at the time of the Franco-Prussian War. The Japanese army officers who read these articles must surely have had an image of Belgium's position and of the range of military forces deployed to counter the menace of France and Germany burned into their minds. Analysing trends in the selection of *Getsuyōkai kiji* articles, we see that articles related to foreign nations account for 55.5%, with France and Germany representing 19.2% and 18.2% respectively, Russia 5.1%, Belgium 4.4%, Italy 3%, and Great Britain 2.2%. We can see that despite being a small nation, the degree to which Belgium attracted attention was relatively high.

The next periodical for consideration is *Kaikōsha kiji* 偕行社記事. The Kaikōsha was founded in 1877 as an organization to promote friendship, mutual aid and scholarly research among army officers, and was the only such army-related group to remain following the demise of the Getsuyōkai. The *Kaikōsha kiji* was published monthly from July 1888 on. Our current knowledge allows us to state that Belgium-related articles in the *Kaikōsha kiji*, most of which were translations, appeared in 28 issues out of the 485 published between July 1888 and December 1911. Two things are particularly noteworthy. The first of these is the publication in the second issue (August 1888) of *Kaikōsha kiji* of an original article on "Belgium's National Defence Strategy" ("Berugī kokubō ryaku" 白耳義国防略) written by a Japanese army officer stationed in Germany. The overwhelming majority of articles in this journal were translations, reflecting the fact that in the Meiji period the Japanese army was still modernizing. Further, at that time the Japanese army did not routinely station military attachés in Belgium. Under such conditions, this piece of original writing shows us a high-level interest in Belgium's national defence.

The following quotations are somewhat lengthy, but nonetheless make a useful introduction. First is the matter of Belgium's military composition and conscription policies:[13]

> The standing army represents a mixture of obligatory and voluntary military service. By the law on obligatory service, once a Belgian male reaches the age of 19, he must register for conscription and then a lottery is drawn until the requisite number of men needed for current service is met. No man between the ages of nineteen and thirty is permitted to marry unless he has fulfilled his military service obligations or is legally exempted from doing so. Moreover, Belgium still permits substitute military service, a corrupt custom which has yet to be reformed [...] the sons of good families and the intelligentsia find military service not to their liking, whereas jobless and dissolute fellows get readily caught up in the military and disturb military discipline on the slightest pretext.

The author goes on to make some observations on the relationship between conscription and the effectiveness of the Belgian military:[14]

> Even though the budget provides for the recruitment of 130,000 men, when one investigates the actual strength of the army, there are in effect fewer than 110,000 men under arms. Further, as this old custom of substitute service remains, it considerably affects army morale, which thus tragically falls short of a gallant and well-trained soldiery. For this reason, men of quality are particularly anxious about their country's situation and are keen to prick the parliamentarians' reveries so as to rectify the situation and to solidly establish a more effective strength in matters of national defence.

In 1888, just as this article appeared, Japan's own conscription law was undergoing full-scale revision to better approximate the principle of "all [male] citizens as soldiers". It would be reasonable to suppose that notice had been paid to Belgium's conscription system, which still recognized the principle of "substitute service".

Another matter raised by the army officer was Belgium's national defence plan and its shortcomings, which is as follows:[15]

> For the past few years Belgium's national defence planning, in the case of invasion by Germany or France, holds that two divisions of crack troops will offer resistance. In case they are outnumbered and overwhelmed, they are to fortify themselves in Antwerp, expend their full energies in their defence and request British assistance in keeping the sea-lanes clear. The objective of this plan is to gain time and wait for a change in the war situation. However, there are weaknesses to this plan, namely that firstly the capital and, secondly, three quarters of the nation will be surrendered to enemy hands.

The article goes on to point out that being thus exposed to the French and German threat, the "situation for the smaller European nations is a deplorable one": the international situation for Belgium was indeed troublesome. However, Belgium "holding on to its tiny slip of land does not yield and, paying heed to the conditions of surrounding nations, adapts its plans accordingly, concentrating on managing the nation with unswerving objectives." In this manner, Belgium continued to apply its strength to national defence in accordance with the international situation. The army officer goes on to state that this approach "indeed truly merits respect" and that "rightly all those with a patriotic spirit and loyalty to the sovereign, and who would maintain their national independence, should be as this."[16]

In drawing his conclusions, the officer stated:[17]

> Upon making a thorough investigation of German and French military strength, it is evident that they are both archrivals, which expend their full national strengths and intellectual capacities so as not to be outdone by the other. It is not easy to tell which is the superior of the two. Even though Belgium may be a small country, it has over 100,000 fine soldiers, possesses great wealth, the finest railway facilities in Europe and solid fortresses. Should either Germany or France declare themselves an enemy of Belgium, it would upset the balance of power between the two. Both are deeply aware of the high stakes, which is why I believe neither will readily violate Belgian neutrality. However, if Belgium were bereft of its

armed forces it would be easily trampled upon by its powerful neighbours: maintaining neutrality would be impossible, as indeed would be independence. So, even though it is a small country whose principal means of managing the affairs of the state is through commerce and trade, it has had to prioritize the nurturing of its real strength, as must any state that would further expand its national influence.

In other words, Belgian independence was maintained by the balance of power between the larger nations and by Belgium's own military preparedness and national defence efforts. Consequently, "the need for the state to assess in detail its own and its neighbours' true capabilities in order to maintain independence holds true for all, whether that be in Europe or Asia."[18]

As we have seen above, the article "Belgium's National Defence Strategy" discussed the military and national defence of tiny Belgium wedged in between two larger states. In addition, it also explained the necessity for Japan, a tiny country confronted by threats from the larger nations of the Far East, including China and Russia, to ensure full military preparedness as in the manner of Belgium. Incidentally, the latter half of the 1880s was also the period leading up to the 1894-1895 Sino-Japanese War, where calls for the need to improve armaments were loud and widely canvassed.

The second point to make about the articles carried in *Kaikōsha kiji* is the overwhelming preponderance of pieces concentrating either on cavalry or, especially, on artillery. As stated above, the origins of the Japanese-Belgian military relationship began with the introduction of Belgian technology and machinery in the late Tokugawa period, and with the manufacture of modern gunpowder. Following on from that, in the early years of Meiji two Belgians, Philippe Joris and Pironez, were employed by the Japanese military establishment to assist with small arms production and machine assembly. Slightly later, when Japanese officers conducted tours of Belgium, the main destinations included the fortresses of Antwerp and the factories at Liège. Meanwhile in the period prior to the outbreak of the 1894-1895 Sino-Japanese War, those Japanese dispatched to Belgium for military purposes focused on engineering and, as mentioned previously, particularly upon artillery.

While the Japanese Army's strong interest in the Belgian military establishment predominantly focused upon artillery and engineering, from the mid-Meiji onwards there was increasing Japanese interest in the Belgian cavalry. This is shown by the translation and publication of three articles by staff of the Japanese Army Equestrian School: "Horse Training at the Belgian National Equestrian School" ("Berugīkoku jōba gakkō chōjōsaku sagyō" 白耳義国乗馬学校調場索作業, 1891), "A Report on Horse Training for the Belgian Military" ("Berugīkoku taiba chōkyō sho" 白耳義国隊馬調教書, 1892), and "The Belgian Cavalry Manual" ("Berugīkoku kihei sōten" 白耳義国騎兵操典, 1892, 1893).

The Japanese Army's interest in Belgium during the Meiji period can therefore be boiled down to the two following points. The first was Belgium's national defence efforts in relation to its position in international politics as a small country wedged between larger and more powerful nations. The significance here lay in the potential comparison with Japan and its position at the time. The second was the attention paid to artillery, engineering and cavalry, with particular regard for artillery given Belgium's advanced industrial techniques. This latter point in turn reflects the fact that even non-military students sent by the Japanese government to study in Belgium concentrated largely on engineering and machine technology. For the Japanese Army in the Meiji period, Belgium was viewed as a country of considerable interest and significance.

Perceptions of Belgium in the Late Meiji Period

Changes in Japanese Interest in Belgium

A considerable number of records and observations of foreign trips were published in the Meiji period. A compilation of the main publications deposited in the Japanese National Diet Library and the Japanese National Archives Cabinet Library can be found in Asakura Haruhiko's *Meiji Ō-Bei kenbunroku shūsei*,[19] which provides clues as to what trends are observable as Japanese interest in Belgium changed over time.

A list of these materials of interest in order of publication date is as follows (those which make reference to Belgium are indicated with an asterisk):

1) Murata Fumio 村田文夫, *Seiyō kenbunroku* 西洋見聞録, April 1869 *

2) Prince Arisugawa 有栖川二品親王, *Ō-Bei jun'yū nikki* 欧米巡遊日記, May 1883 *

3) Morooka Kuni 師岡国, *Itagaki-kun Ō-Bei man'yū nikki* 板垣君欧米漫遊日記, June 1883

4) Shimizu Masujirō 清水益次郎, *Itagaki-kun Ō-Bei man'yūroku* 板垣君欧米漫遊録, July 1883

5) Yamashita Yūtarō 山下雄太郎, *Kaigai kenbunroku* 海外見聞録, March 1886 *

6) Yano Ryūkei 矢野龍溪, *Shūyū zakki* 周遊雑記, April 1886 *

7) Nozu Michitsura 野津道貫, *Ō-Bei junkai nisshi* 欧米巡回日誌, June 1886 *

8) Kuroda Kiyotaka 黒田清隆, *Kan'yū nikki* 環遊日記, Nov. 1887 *

9) Ministry of Agriculture and Commerce (Nōshōmushō 農商務省), *Ō-Bei junkai torishirabesho* 欧米巡回取調書, 7 vols., Feb. 1888 *

10) Torio Koyata 鳥尾小弥太, *Yōkō nikki* 洋行日記, Sept. 1888

11) Ishii Kendō 石井研堂, *Tōkakan sekai isshū* 十日間世界一周, July 1889 *

12) Inoue Enryō 井上円了, *Ō-Bei kakkoku seikyō nikki* 欧米各国政教日記, Nov. 1889 *

13) Nagayama Takeshirō 永山武四郎, *Shūyū nikki* 周遊日記, 1889 *

14) Yamabe Gonrokurō 山辺権六郎, *Gaikō kenbunshi* 外航見聞誌, July 1890

15) Yorimitsu Hōsei 依光方成, *San'en gojissen sekai shūyū jikki* 三円五十銭世界周遊実記, Jan. 1891 *

16) Takada Zenjirō 高田善治郎, *Shutsuyō nikki* 出洋日記, March 1891

17) Suehiro Tetchō 末広鉄腸, *A no ryokō* 啞之旅行, 1891

18) Watanabe Kumashirō 渡辺熊四郎, *Ō-Bei ryokō nikki* 欧米旅行日記, March 1894 *

19) Kamata Eikichi 鎌田栄吉, *Ō-Bei man'yū zakki* 欧米漫遊雑記, June 1899 *

20) Ōtani Kahē 大谷嘉兵衛, *Ō-Bei man'yū nisshi* 欧米漫遊日誌, Sept. 1900 *

21) Nakakōji Kiyoshi 仲小路廉, (Hasegawa Tomojirō 長谷川友次郎 ed.) *Ō-Bei jun'yū zakki* 欧米巡遊雑記, Sept. 1900

22) Ōhashi Otowa 大橋乙羽, *Ō-Bei shōkan* 欧米小観, July 1901 *

23) Ōoka Kenkai (Ikuzō) 大岡硯海 (育造), *Ō-Bei kanken* 欧米管見, Oct. 1901 *

24) Nagata Shūtō 長田秋濤, *Yōkō kidan shin akamōfu* 洋行奇談新赤毛布, May 1902

25) Takebe Tongo 建部遯吾, *Seiyū manpitsu* 西遊漫筆, Jan. 1903

26) Shibusawa Eiichi 渋沢栄一, *Ō-Bei kikō* 欧米紀行, June 1903 *

27) Mori Jitarō 森次太郎, *Ō-Bei shosei ryokō* 欧米書生旅行, Oct. 1906

28) Haseba Junkō 長谷場純孝, *Ō-Bei rekiyū nisshi* 欧米歴遊日誌, Feb. 1907

29) Hagino Mannosuke 萩野萬之助, *Gaiyū sannen* 外遊三年, April 1907

30) Togawa Shūkotsu 戸川秋骨, *Ō-Bei kiyū niman sanzenri* 欧米記遊二萬三千哩, March 1908

31) Ishikawa Shūkō 石川周行, *Sekai isshūgahō* 世界一周画報, Sept. 1908

32) Iwaya Sazanami 巌谷小波, *Shin'yōkō miyage* 新洋行土産 (first volume) April 1910

33) Nakamura Kichizō 中村吉蔵, *Ō-Bei inshōki* 欧米印象記, June 1910

34) Iwaya Sazanami 巌谷小波, *Shin'yōkō miyage* 新洋行土産, (final volume) Sept. 1910

35) Kuroita Katsumi 黒板勝美, *Seiyū ninen Ō-Bei bunmeiki* 西遊二年欧米文明記, Sept. 1911 *

36) Nakajima Rikizō 中島力造, *Ō-Bei kansōroku* 欧米感想録, Nov. 1911

As can be seen from this list, the authors included a real variety of people, among them politicians, journalists, economists, civil officials, scholars, and military figures. Of course, it is not as if all made reference to Belgium, but if one were to include only those accounts that did, of the fourteen volumes published between 1869 and 1890, ten sources, or 71%, do refer to Belgium.

In that particular period, Japan enacted its Imperial Constitution in 1889 and opened the Imperial Diet in 1890. However imperfectly, this was a time when Japan transformed itself into a modern nation with western nations as the model. Belgium, which issued its declaration of independence in 1830, was a relatively new nation within Europe, with many of its laws derived from reference to good practice as observed in a variety of nations. Because of this, Japan was able to refer to the fruits of Belgian learning through its own process of

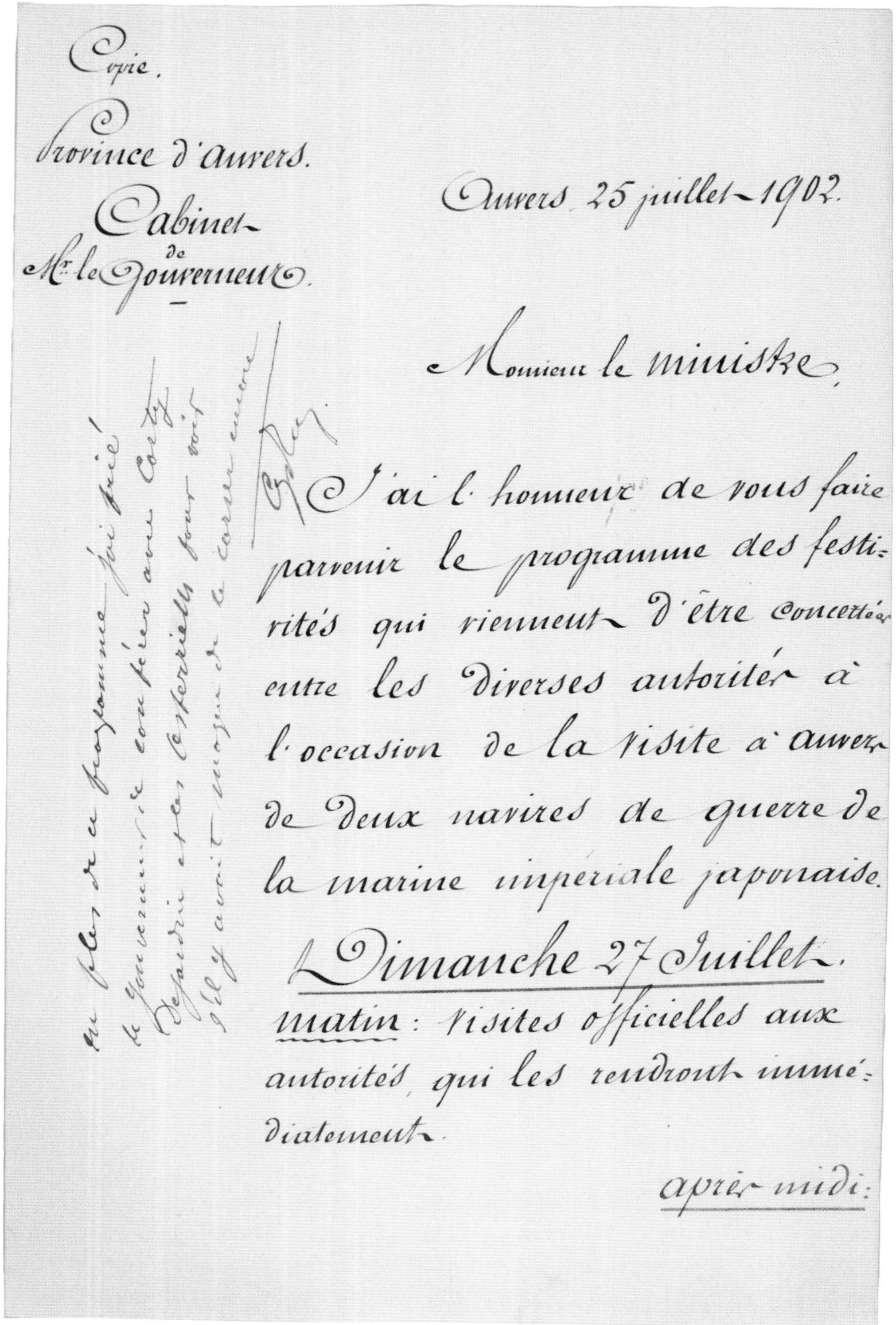

Province d'Anvers.

Cabinet
de
Mr. le Gouverneur.

Anvers, 25 juillet 1902.

(note marginale à gauche)
Au plan de ce programme j'ai prié
le Gouverneur de conférer avec Cortz
depuis et les Esperiells pour voir
s'il y avait moyen de le communiquer

Monsieur le ministre,

J'ai l'honneur de vous faire
parvenir le programme des festi-
rités qui viennent d'être concertées
entre les diverses autorités à
l'occasion de la visite à Anvers
de deux navires de guerre de
la marine impériale japonaise.

Dimanche 27 Juillet

<u>Matin</u>: visites officielles aux
autorités, qui les rendront immé-
diatement.

<u>après-midi</u>:

(colonne de droite — fragment)

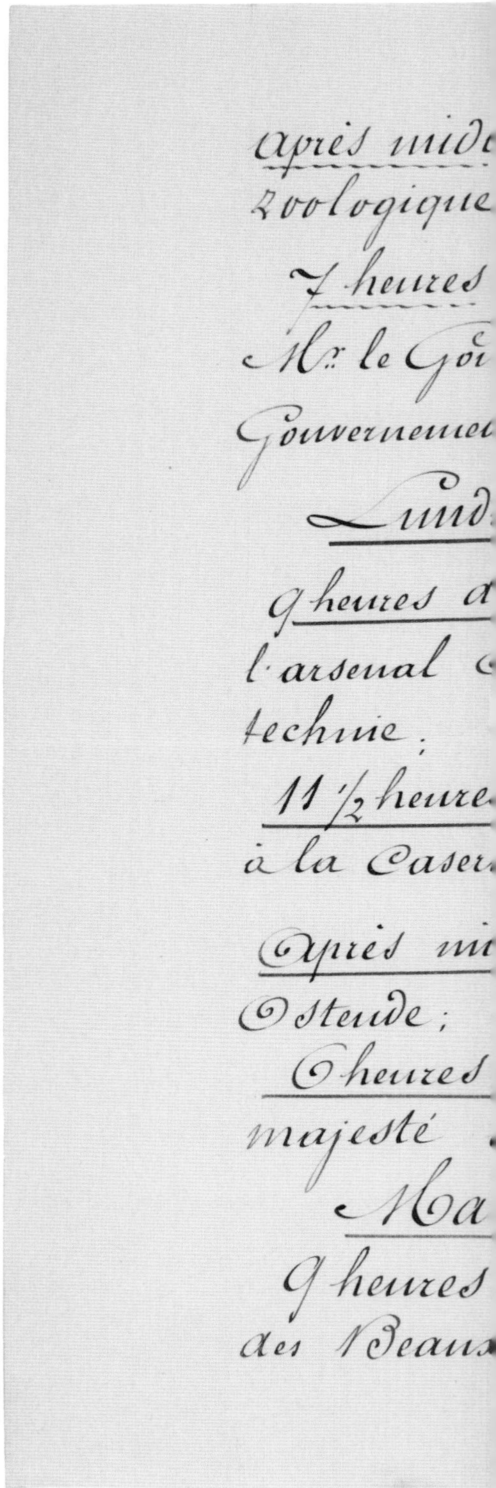

après midi
zoologique

7 heures
Mr le Gou
Gouvernement

<u>Lundi</u>

9 heures à
l'arsenal
technie;

11 ½ heures
à la Caser

<u>Après mi</u>
Ostende;

6 heures
majesté

<u>Ma</u>

9 heures
des Beaux

du jardin
ois heures,
t offert par
à l'hôtel du
incial.
uillet.
visite de
et de la pyro=
ion des marins
7me de ligne
Spécial pour
ion par Sa
i.
Juillet.
des musées
Plantin, la
Cathédrale,

Cathédrale, etc.

12 ½ heures: déjeuner à l'hôtel de ville;

de 3 à 5 heures: visite des installations maritimes;

le Soir: banquet offert par le lieutenant-général Ninitte.

Quant au Mercredi, ne sachant pas la date et l'heure exactes du départ, il a été impossible de fixer un programme. Je tiens cependant à vous faire connaître que les projets ne manquaient pas pour utiliser cette journée.

Agréez, monsieur le ministre, l'expression de mes sentiments très distingués. Le Gouverneur.

Correspondence between the governor of Antwerp and the Minister of the King concerning the visit of two Japanese battleships to Antwerp in 1902.
Archives of the Royal Palace, Brussels. Photograph by Hans Coppens.

studying the principles of law in Britain, France, Prussia and elsewhere. This fact holds great import in considering the manner of Japanese modernization.

For example, the Bank of Japan was established with Belgium's National Bank as the template. Further, in constitutional matters, the Japanese Chamber of Elder Statesmen's *Nippon kokken'an* 日本国憲按 ["Inquiry on an Imperial Constitution"], the *shigikenpō* 私擬憲法 ["Privately Drafted Constitution"], and the steps leading to the drafting of the Imperial Constitution, all show the influence of the Belgian constitution (the very same can be said for the Prussian constitution, but it was the Belgian constitution which was the model).[20]

In this manner, for Japan in the Meiji period, Belgium had considerable significance as a "model nation", and one can consider that this is the one thing in the background of most of the texts mentioned above. Indeed, if one were to include the specialist works or translations of Sufu Kōhei and Inoue Kowashi referred to earlier, the number of authors writing on matters related to Belgium counts for a substantial percentage. Incidentally, if we broaden the publication period under consideration from 1869 to 1903, we can observe that of the twenty-six publications, seventeen (65%) touch on Belgium.

However, with Japan's victory in the 1904-1905 Russo-Japanese War, Japan attained a ranking on a par with the European and North American great powers. If we were to look at accounts of tours of observation from around that period, say 1901 to 1911, there is a marked decrease in the number of authors who refer to Belgium, from fifteen volumes to four. In the years between 1901 and 1903, three of five sources refer to Belgium, but if we look at the period from 1906 to 1911, in the aftermath of the war with Russia, only a single text out of ten does. Moreover, this solitary source was published only in 1911.

One might well say that Japanese interest in Belgium declined rapidly in the wake of the Russo-Japanese War of 1904-1905. There is need for further investigation on this point, but, for example, in 1908, when the newspaper *Asahi shinbun* planned a tour around the world, it included on its list of nations to visit: the United States, Great Britain, France, Italy, Switzerland, Germany

and Russia, but not Belgium.[21] There is no detail given to as to why Belgium was omitted, but perhaps one can infer a waning of interest in that nation.

Perceptions of Belgium in the Late Meiji Period

In the years between 1901 and 1911, four sources with observations of Belgium were published: Ōhashi Otowa 大橋乙羽, *Ō-Bei shōkan* 欧米小観 ["A Brief Description of Europe and America"][22] and Ōoka Ikuzō 大岡育造, *Ō-Bei kanken* 欧米管見 ["Personal Views on Europe and America"][23] both in 1901; Shibusawa Eiichi 渋沢栄一, *Ō-Bei kikō* 欧米紀行 ["An Account of Travels in Europe and America"] in 1903;[24] and Kuroita Katsumi 黒板勝美, *Seiyū ninen Ō-Bei bunmeiki* 西遊二年欧米文明記 ["A Record of Two Years of Adventures in American and European Civilisation"] in 1911.[25]

By way of a brief introduction to their contents, Ōhashi provides a detailed guide to the Waterloo battlefield; Ōoka, a politician, mentions electoral audits for general elections to the Belgian national parliament and the use of government buildings in Brussels as places for conducting occasions such as civil weddings ("it is a matter of course that those city inhabitants who bear the tax burden obtain such a benefit"). "An Account of Travels in Europe and America" is a record of Shibusawa's travels through the US, Britain, Germany, France, Belgium and Italy as a representative of the Japan National Federation of Chambers of Commerce. With regard to Belgium, he recounts official visits to the Brussels and Antwerp Chambers of Commerce, and trips to the port of Antwerp, steel mills in Liège, and plate-glass factories.

"A Record of Two Years of Excursions Through American and European Civilisation" written by the historian Kuroita Katsumi, who "even on excursion through America and Europe keenly sensed that there was much more to be learnt from [the West]" and "believed that there were still many more typical elements to be adapted from the West, while at the same time preserving and strengthening the quintessential essence of our nation." From this point of view he argued "that the civilization we have imported over the past few decades is for the most part biased towards the material, which has led to us obtaining no more than its superficial aspects, and that, in travelling through Europe and America, we should henceforth pay more attention to the spiritual." He introduced his readers to Western art galleries, museums, libraries as well as to nature and ancient ruins, in addition including numerous illustrations. Concerning Belgium, beginning with a comparison of Belgium as a "miniature France" and the Netherlands as a "miniature Britain", he gave detailed introductions to the painters Rubens and Rembrandt as representing their two respective countries.

In this manner, articles on observations of Belgium in this period can be increasingly seen to be interest pieces specific to certain types of concerns. In this they are somewhat different in angle from earlier publications, which provided introductions to Belgium on a broad range of themes. In view of the basic knowledge about Belgium that had been accumulated to a considerable extent, the need for a general introduction declined. We can perhaps see this as reflecting a lessening of the general interest in Belgium, but on the flip side a heightening of interest in more specific topics.

Perceptions of Belgium and the First World War

As has been seen above, the period of interest in pursuing Belgium as a "model nation" entered into relative decline with the Russo-Japanese War. With the outbreak of the First World War, however, interest in Belgium again increased.[26] On 4 August 1914, Germany, which had already declared war on Russia, invaded Belgium. Liège was occupied on 7 August, and the capital, Brussels, on 20 August. Large numbers of refugees escaped to neighbouring countries, including the Netherlands, France, and Britain. King Albert I continued to direct resistance from a small village near Veurne on the French border, while the government had no choice but to flee to Le Havre, France.

Aid to Belgium during the Great War

Battlefield reports on the "Great European War" were published in Japanese newspapers on a daily basis, and there were many articles on combat conditions in Belgium and the privations of life under German

military occupation. For example: "The Belgian King at the Head of his Army" ("Jintō ni okoru Hakukoku kōtei" 陣頭に起る白国皇帝, *Hōchi shinbun* 報知新聞, 8 August 1914); "Belgian Army Evacuates Capital" ("Hakugun shufu tettai" 白軍首府撤退) and "German Army Enters Belgian Capital" ("Dokugun Hakukoku shufu ni iru" 独軍白国首府に入る, *Tokyo Asahi shinbun* 東京朝日新聞, 23 August); "Belgian Government into Exile" ("Hakukoku seifu ichō" 白国政府移庁) and "Belgian Women Abused – Appalling Brutality of German Army" ("Shiitagerareshi Hakukoku fujin, dokugun no bōjō hanahadashi" 虐げられし白国婦人、独軍の暴状甚し, *Tokyo Asahi shinbun*, 15 October).

The Japanese people were generally sympathetic to Belgium's plight and both the Tokyo and the Osaka *Asahi shinbun* planned the presentation of a Japanese sword to the Belgian king as a means to encourage the people who were continuing their brave resistance. On 15 November, a proposal was submitted to the government-in-exile that the sword could be presented, along with a congratulatory address, on the occasion of the king's birthday. On 30 January 1915, special correspondent Sugimura Sojinkan (Kōtarō) 杉村楚人冠, who had been selected as envoy, had an audience with the king and was finally able to present the sword. A correspondent of *The Times* who had accompanied Sugimura picked up the story and reported it world wide, which did not fail to arouse positive feelings towards the Japanese among the Belgians.

Upon returning to Japan, Sugimura published a book, *Tatakai ni tsukaishite* 戦に使して ["Dispatched to War"] which focused mainly on the circumstances of this event. In response to a message of thanks from the king of Belgium for the presentation of the sword, the *Asahi shinbun* planned a magic lantern show telling of Belgium's suffering and launched a campaign to collect funds for Belgium. For example, over 10-11 February 1915, the *Osaka Asahi shinbun* published an article entitled "Our Sympathies Lie with the People of Belgium" ("Berugī kokumin ni dōjō seyo" 白耳義国民に同情せよ), which read:

> When war first broke out, the Belgian nation was trampled upon without any just reason whatsoever. They have now reached the point whereby there is nothing for it but to fight and gamble with the future of their nation. Belgium, with its successful

commerce and industry has, in an instant, come to face the danger of being kicked and trampled over by the savage German army. However, the entire nation's full might and strenuous efforts plague the mighty German army and even as they have lost a full half of their national territory they do not surrender. Even cowards with no sense of honour are standing up to fight bravely for their nation.

Labelling Belgium's ferocious struggle in these terms, the newspaper went on to appeal to the sympathies of the Japanese people for Belgium by adding that "the Belgians were the first to feel the sword of this [German] demon, and so the first to brandish the sword of righteousness against it is also Belgium."

In addition, the Belgian consul in Japan, Georges della Faille, appealed for further Japanese donations in an article sent to the *Jiji shinpō* 時事新報 (8 October 1915) entitled "An Appeal to the Righteous Spirits of the Japanese to Support the People of Belgium" ("Berugī kokumin no sanjō ni tsuki Nihon kokumin no gishin ni uttau" 白耳義国民の惨状に付き日本国民の義心に訴ふ).

Perceptions of Belgium in Japanese Wartime Publications

Aside from newspaper articles, there were many other publications related to Belgium issued during the First World War. This shows the height of Japanese interest in Belgium following the German invasion, and this interest can in turn be broadly divided into two themes: those pertaining to the German violation of Belgium's permanent neutrality; and secondly, those written by Belgians to spread knowledge of their plight and to provide aid through arousing public sympathy.

Examples of the first type include: Nagaoka Shun'ichi 長岡春一, a councillor in the Ministry of Foreign Affairs, publishing *Berugī oyobi Berugījin* 白耳義及白耳義人 ["Belgium and the Belgians"] (Fuzanbō Jijisōsho 冨山房時事叢書, 1914) immediately after the outbreak of war; Tachi Sakutarō 立作太郎, a scholar of international law, producing an article entitled "Berugī no chūritsu" 白耳義ノ中立 ["The Neutrality of Belgium"], published in *Hozumi sensei kanreki shukuga ronbunshū* 穂積先生還暦祝賀論文集 (Yūhikaku 有斐閣, 1915); Yoshino Sakuzō, a

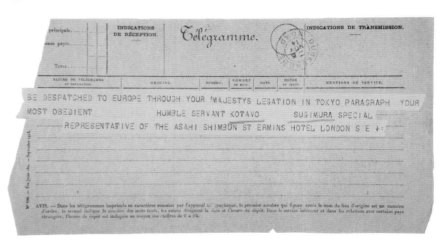

Telegram from Sugimura Kōtarō, London representative of the newspaper *Asahi shinbun*, notifying his newspaper company's wish to present a sword to King Albert I.
Archives of the Royal Palace, Brussels. Photograph by Hans Coppens.

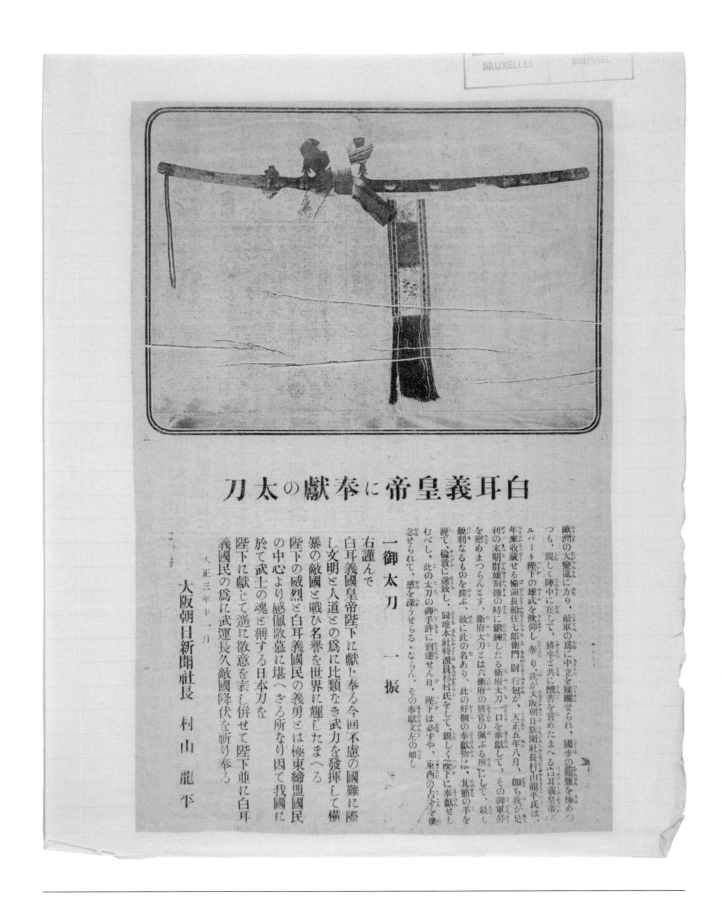

Newspaper clipping from the newspaper *Asahi shinbun* featuring the article about the presentation of a ceremonial sword, reproduced in the photograph, to King Albert I by Murayama Ryōhei (Ryūhei), president of the Osaka *Asahi shinbun* newspaper. The left half of the article is a verbatim reproduction of the letter of presentation, observing the convention of beginning a new line whenever reference is made to the monarch.

Archives of the Royal Palace, Brussels. Photograph by Hans Coppens.

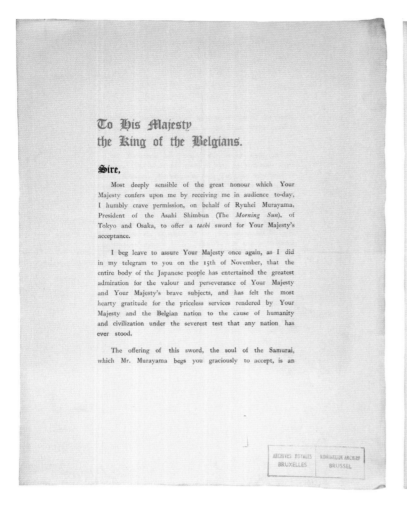

To His Majesty the King of the Belgians.

Sire,

Most deeply sensible of the great honour which Your Majesty confers upon me by receiving me in audience to-day, I humbly crave permission, on behalf of Ryuhei Murayama, President of the Asahi Shinbun (The *Morning Sun*), of Tokyo and Osaka, to offer a *tachi* sword for Your Majesty's acceptance.

I beg leave to assure Your Majesty once again, as I did in my telegram to you on the 15th of November, that the entire body of the Japanese people has entertained the greatest admiration for the valour and perseverance of Your Majesty and Your Majesty's brave subjects, and has felt the most hearty gratitude for the priceless services rendered by Your Majesty and the Belgian nation to the cause of humanity and civilization under the severest test that any nation has ever stood.

The offering of this sword, the soul of the Samurai, which Mr. Murayama begs you graciously to accept, is an

endeavour to express the very high appreciation of the people of Japan for the brave nation of the West, whose heroism has been recognized throughout the world.

Mr. Murayama has chosen this sword from his art collection. The blade was made in 1577 by a famous smith named Nakagawa Shichiroyemon-no-jo Yukikane, who lived at Osafuné, in the province of Bizen, in Western Japan, and died in 1588. Bizen is celebrated for having produced good sword-blade makers in ancient times.

I again most respectfully beg leave, Sire, to tender to Your Majesty the expression of my profound thanks for your gracious condescension in accepting the gift and in receiving me in personal audience to-day.

KOTARO SUGIMURA,
Special Representative of the
ASAHI.

January , 1915.

---

political scientist and theorist on democracy, writing *Ōshū dōran shiron* 欧州動乱史論 ["A Historical Theory of European Upheavals"] (Keiseisha 警醒社, 1915); the series edited by Naitō Minji 内藤民治, *Sekai jikkan* 世界実観 ["A True View of the World"] including a section on "Belgium – Holland" (Nihon fūzoku zue kankōkai 日本風俗図絵刊行会, 1916). For the most part, these publications held that Belgium's permanent neutrality was less a declaration made out of national concern than one rooted in the balance and interests among the great powers in the context of European international relations. For that reason, Belgian permanent neutrality was from the beginning of limited effectiveness. Interest in Belgium's permanent neutrality from this perspective was not readily observable amongst the Japanese of the Meiji period and so is a step forward on the hitherto prevailing perspectives of Belgium as wedged between larger nations and a nation that put great efforts into its national defence. There was a

definite growth in awareness of Belgium as a "buffer state", a crucial axis in European international politics.

As to the second strand of writing, those pieces produced by Belgians, one could consider the following (translated) texts as representative: Charles Basten, the Belgian consul in Yokohama, wrote "Berugījin no mitaru Ōshū sensō" 白耳義人の観たる欧州戦争 ["The Belgians' View of the European War"], Waseda Daigaku Shuppanbu, July 1915; Pierre Nothomb produced "Senketsu no Berugī" 鮮血の白耳義 ["The Blood of Belgium"] (Yokohama Berugī Sōryōjikan 横浜ベルギー総領事館, July 1915), based upon reports by a committee established in response to a call by the Belgian minister of Justice to investigate German Army atrocities; the Belgian consul, Della Faille, contributed "Berugī to Yōroppa senran" 白耳義と欧羅巴戦乱 ["Belgium and the Battles of Europe"] (Berugī kōshikan ベルギー公使館, November 1915); Eugene Baron Beyens, Belgian minister of foreign affairs and

---

Official letter presented by Sugimura Kōtarō, representative of the newspaper *Asahi shinbun* to King Albert I, on the occasion of his being received in audience, to mark the presentation of the ceremonial sword to the king by Murayama Ryōhei (Ryūhei), president of the Osaka *Asahi shinbun* newspaper.
Archives of the Royal Palace, Brussels. Photograph by Hans Coppens.

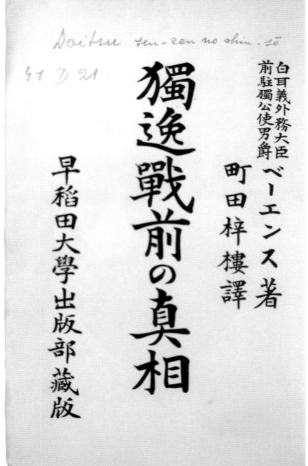

former Belgian ambassador to Germany, wrote *Doitsu senzen no shinsō* 独逸戦前の真相 ["The Truth about Pre-War Germany"] (Waseda Daigaku Shuppanbu, June 1916) and *Hakukoku no gisen* 白国の義戦 ["Belgium's Righteous War"] (Teimi Shuppansha 丁未出版社, 1918).

The last of these, "Belgium's Righteous War", was originally compiled by Camille Baron Buffin, an officer in the Belgian Royal Army, under the title *Récits de combattants* and "met with great acclaim among the reading public of Europe." The Japanese-language version was prepared by Machida Shirō 町田梓楼, a translator working at the Belgian Consulate in Yokohama. For reasons of space, I shall put aside the introductions written by the ambassadors and ministers of Britain, Russia, Italy, the United States, France, Thailand, Brazil, China and Belgium. Instead, the focus will rest on the contributions by some prominent Japanese, including former Prime Minister Ōkuma Shigenobu 大隈重信, minister of Foreign Affairs Uchida Yasuya 内田康哉, Navy minister Katō Tomosaburō 加藤友三郎, Army minister Tanaka Giichi 田中義一, former minister of Foreign Affairs Gotō Shinpei 後藤新平, Director of Navy Headquarters Shimamura Hayao 島村速雄, Shibusawa Eiichi 渋沢栄一, Deputy to the House of Representatives Shimada Saburō 島田三郎, and Army Colonel Sakurai Tadayoshi 桜井忠温, author of *Nikudan* 肉弾 ["The Human Bullet"].

Firstly, the translator, Machida Shirō, wrote the following on his purpose in preparing the translation:

> I do not intend that this book should inspire the martial spirit of the Japanese. I do not imagine that the spirits of our people have reached a point of being so depressed as to require inspiration by the heroic deeds of foreign soldiers. I would like to publish this book because the way chosen by the Belgian people at this time of crisis in the survival of their state is one of a noble national spirit transcending the material.

However, this view was not limited to Machida alone and was in fact a rather typical image of Belgium shared by

Cover of Eugène Baron Beyens. *The Truth about Prewar Germany* (Bēensu. *Doitsu senzen no shinsō* ベーエンス著独逸戦前の真相. Waseda Daigaku Shuppanbu, June 1916). Translation by Machida Shirō 町田梓楼 of Baron Eugène Beyens's *Deux années à Berlin 1912-1914* (2 vols., Brussels, 1931).
Fonds japonais, Réserve précieuse des bibliothèques de l'Université catholique de Louvain. Photograph by W.F. Vande Walle.

Title page of Eugène Baron Beyens. *The Truth about Prewar Germany*.
Fonds japonais, Réserve précieuse des bibliothèques de l'Université catholique de Louvain. Photograph by W.F. Vande Walle.

the Japanese intelligentsia of the time. For example, the perceptions of Belgium are as follows in the contributions by Shimada Saburō, Uchida Yasuya, Katō Tomosaburō, Tanaka Giichi, Gotō Shinpei, Shimamura Hayao and Shibusawa Eiichi.

Shimada's "Dokujin no bōrei to Hakujin no gifun" 独人 の暴戻と白人の義噴 ["German Atrocities and Belgian Righteous Anger"] portrayed wicked Germany versus good Belgium and in that frame a number of others commented on the "noble national spirit." Uchida Yasuya wrote:

> Oh, what a heroic tale is that of the bravery and patriotism of the Belgians, who chose noble death rather than slavish dishonour when their small nation faced a mighty enemy. Their story crowns the history of recent time. In addition, this book provides us with abundant information of interest regarding the bravery of His Majesty, the king of the Belgians, and of his Royal Army. This translation has moved me, as one who did not have accurate knowledge earlier, and it will be most appropriate to inspire our people with the moral principles, the courage and the patriotic spirit of the Belgians.

Katō Tomosaburō commented that "perusing this translation as well as the original will reveal to the readers the Belgians' loyalty, bravery, justice and fury, in addition to their high spirit when facing hardships, never disgracing their forefathers," while Tanaka Giichi observed that:

> against German brutality which ignored justice and violated the neutrality of Belgium, the Belgian military has fought bravely, although its troops are far fewer in number than their counterparts, and after a noble effort willingly faced death for justice. All Japanese citizens cannot help but admire their spirit.

Gotō Shinpei remarked that, "all over the world, people are supporting Belgium which has risen in anger for its honour and justice. I am convinced that this translation will provide a clear understanding and complete knowledge of the Belgian citizens' courageous nature and fervent patriotism." Shimamura Hayao added:

> facing an unprecedented national hardship, all the citizens along with the king have been unified in

rising against a fearsome enemy whose cruelty and outrages are beyond words. The Belgian royal family, introduced in this work, represents grandeur of spirit responding to the citizens while showing its fierceness with dauntless perseverance, as well as valour rising above any defeats, and its willingness to protect the nation. Readers will be excited to learn of their fortitude.

Shibusawa Eiichi stated:
> it is in the true spirit of *bushidō* that the Belgians roused themselves and took arms for justice even while they probably anticipated defeat. I believe their war should not be evaluated in the light of victory or defeat since they fought for honour and fidelity. The determination of Belgium shares the idealism of Kusunoki Masashige [at the Battle of Minatogawa, 1336], although their times are far removed from each other. There is nothing in their struggle that is shameful before earth or heaven.

Further, Machida Shirō himself asserted that: "Although the decision of Belgium to resist was thrilling, the fate of the nation was extremely grievous. However, their future must be bright for the sublime spirit of sacrifice which Belgians showed during the struggle for the nation's destiny aroused sympathy from all over the world and appealed to the spirit of international justice."

In summary, the contributors confirmed the Belgians' spirit of sacrifice in dying for justice, bravery and patriotism, and the unity between the king (the royal family) and the citizens at the time of a national crisis in which they anticipated defeat. Japan at that time was experiencing the so-called "Taishō Democracy" and we see how in the context of the instability of imperial rule brought on by the Taishō emperor's illness, and the uncertainty of national values, the contributors projected the national values of Japan onto the image of the brave fight of the Belgians, superposing the two countries in view of both of them being monarchies. The following extract by Ōkuma Shigenobu makes clear this particular point of view:
> It is no coincidence that the Belgian people are so loyal to obligations, especially their international duties, and faithful in the preservation of treaties, freedom and honour as well as to the future unity of the human race. They are men of honour,

respect, liberty, glory, have sustained their independence and have shown perseverance in the face of hardship. Their characteristics have been handed down to them from over hundreds of years: a respectful and genuine blood has been passed on to the Belgians of today. In accordance with the ideas of self-determination, the current generation of Belgians must also devote themselves to their nation to the very last drop of blood. How heroic, how praiseworthy! We need to pay special attention to the fact that they have had wise and benevolent rulers, for example in the former king, Leopold II. Leopold led the nation while encouraging charity, discovery and exploration. He also provided liberty to the people and in turn earned the love and respect of his citizens, being known as the "father of the nation". The king's virtue has extended to the people. Also, the current King Albert has taken the initiative in this just war, trusts his people and serves them. The queen often visits the soldiers and shares in the hardships of the people. Such a noble mind in leaders guides citizens to nobility. We should admire the unity of the monarch and the people, and the splendid spirit of devotion to the nation. When their efforts finally earn the fruits of virtue and they reach the divinely ordained victory, as we expect them to, we will joyfully celebrate, and indeed that time is now approaching.

Thus it may be said that the Japanese perception of Belgium was partly condensed into, and represented by, the title of the work, *Belgium's Righteous War*. With this attention to the ideal of unity of sovereign and people as expressed in the form of King Albert's cooperative bond with his people, a biography of the king was later published in Japan. *Berugī kōtei* 白耳義皇帝 ["The King of the Belgians"] (Kaihatsusha 開発社, 1919) was edited by Yaguchi Tatsu 矢口達, a lecturer at Waseda University and was based upon an earlier work, *Berugī kōtei Arubēru heika no denki* 白耳義皇帝アルベール陛下の伝記 ["Biography of His Majesty King Albert of Belgium"], written by an Englishman, John Crucy MacDonell.

As the above shows, the bulk of the Japanese people sympathized with the noble national spirit of the Belgians and the unity of sovereign and people in this time of national crisis. In turn this sympathy was a motive for a still greater amount of Japanese interest in Belgium. Many Japanese politicians and intellectuals also wished to see in Belgium in the midst of the Great War a reassertion of the ideals they held vital to their own nation.

Conclusion

In this study we have tried to clarify some of the perceptions of Belgium as embraced by the Japanese from the early Meiji to the early Taishō periods. Put simply, they resonated with the process of the establishment of the modern Japanese state and reflect the times, as well as the individual viewpoints and areas of interest. They shine a light on how people thought and what their concerns were. Their thoughts regarding Belgium serve as a mirror of their own concerns regarding Japan. This is often the case with the way people view other nations and their achievements. However, the sharpness with which people applied their observations of Belgium to their own immediate surroundings, or explicitly drew out the meaning they held for Japan, and how important they were in the context of Japan's relations with other nations, would vary. In that sense, it can be said that the existence of the Belgian state from early Meiji to late Taishō was one which, if we exclude the period of the Russo-Japanese War, attracted the interest of many Japanese, served as a point of reference and elicited a feeling of closeness.

By way of conclusion, I would like briefly to consider the matter of the raising of the status of Belgian-Japanese diplomatic relations from the consular to the ambassadorial rank, as Belgium recovered domestically and forged new diplomatic relations upon regaining independence following the First World War.[27] The intention to raise the status of the official Belgian representative to Japan from consul to ambassador was communicated to the Japanese consul, Adachi Mineichirō, by King Albert I on 23 July 1919. At a banquet hosted by Albert with the French president as guest of honour to commemorate the transition of French representation from consul to ambassador, the king announced that, "As with France, we must send ambassadors to all of the great nations and it is my hope that Japan shall be among them."

Upon learning of this Belgian intention, the cabinet of Prime Minister Hara Takashi (Kei) 原敬, in its meeting of 28 October, decided to raise the status of Japan's diplomatic representative in Belgium to the rank of ambassador. In 1916, Britain, France and Russia had declared their intention to grant aid to restore Belgium to its former condition, and to include it in the peace talks. Japan and Italy were also in agreement on these points. Of these five great allied powers, all but Japan had previously attained ambassadorial status in their relations with Belgium, and so it was considered necessary to likewise raise Japan's diplomatic status to ambassadorial level to maintain the balance with the other powers. This decision was immediately communicated to the Belgian government and King Albert expressed great pleasure at this outcome.

Many of the allied nations justified their participation in the Great War by the need to provide succour to Belgium from a sense of sympathy and righteousness. Consequently, after peace had returned, to have one's diplomatic status raised to permit the dispatch of an ambassador to Belgium was a means of showing respect to the country. Furthermore, proposing to send an ambassador from those great powers was straightforwardly a matter of international respect for the Belgian king, who had become an object of global admiration. Indeed, exchanging ambassadors was viewed as showing a special kind of respect and diplomatic intimacy to the rulers of both the dispatching and the receiving nations. In addition, post-war Belgium, developing globally and acting as one through the bonds of king and people, was regarded as being among the first rank of nations in terms of culture. Consequently, from the perspective of Belgium's international standing and from the position of Japan as one of the five Great Powers, the dispatch of a Japanese ambassador to Belgium could be considered "a most natural step."

Having said that, in actual fact the proposal to exchange ambassadors showed little progress in terms of providing the necessary budgetary support. However, by good fortune, Crown Prince Hirohito planned to visit Belgium in June 1921, and in preparation Japan's consul was upgraded to the status of ambassador on 31 May 1921, the incumbent consul Adachi Mineichirō remaining at his post under the new title. On the other hand, the order to appoint Albert de Bassompierre as ambassador to

Japan was issued on 11 June of the same year, but due to some problems over the exchange of credentials the change in diplomatic status was delayed until September, after Crown Prince Hirohito's return to Japan. Either way, relations between both nations were marked by the higher status of exchanging ambassadors, and the ties between the two were thus ever deeper. Incidentally, Albert de Bassompierre later headed the diplomatic corps in Japan, and even in the difficult times of early Shōwa never ceased to demonstrate empathy and affection for Japan.[28]

Ambassador de Bassompierre (second from left) with the officers of the Belgian Canon-Legrand mission (1923). The mission, including industrialists and military and led by Louis Canon-Legrand, visited China and Japan in 1923.
Reproduced by courtesy of the heirs of Baron de Bassompierre.
Photograph by Maxime Darge.

The Belgian industrial mission with their Japanese hosts at the Kōrakuen arsenal, April 1923.
First row third from left: Mrs de Bassompierre; second row fourth from left,
behind Mr. de Bassompierre, Ambassador de Bassompierre.
Reproduced by courtesy of the heirs of Baron de Bassompierre. Photograph by Maxime Darge.

Ambassador and Mrs Albert de Bassompierre in formal attire (1924).
Reproduced by courtesy of the heirs of Baron de Bassompierre. Photograph by Maxime Darge.

REFERENCES

Asakura 1987-89
Asakura Haruhiko 朝倉治彦, ed. *Meiji Ō-Bei kenbunroku shūsei* 明治欧米見聞録集成, 36 vols. Yumani Shobō ゆまに書房, 1987-89.

"Berugī kokubōryaku"
"Berugī kokubōryaku" 白耳義国防略. *Kaikōsha kiji* 偕行社記事 2 (August 1888), pp. 175-183.

Inoue 1969
Inoue Kowashi 井上毅. "Ōkoku kenkokuhō" 王国建国法. In *Inoue Kowashi-den, shiryōhen* 井上毅伝　史料篇, vol. 3, ed. Inoue Kowashi denki hensan iinkai 井上毅伝記編纂委員会, pp. 463-464. Kokugakuin University Library 国学院大学図書館, 1969.

Ishikawa 1989
Ishikawa Shūkō 石川周行. "Sekai isshū gahō" 世界一周画報. In *Meiji Ō-Bei kenbunroku shūsei* 明治欧米見聞録集成, vol. 30. Yumani Shobō ゆまに書房, 1989.

Isomi 1967
Isomi Tatsunori 磯見辰典, trans. *Bassonpiēru taishi kaisōroku: Zainichi jūhachi nen* バッソンピエール大使回想録　在日十八年. Kashima Shuppankai 鹿島出版会, 1967.

Isomi et al. 1989
Isomi Tatsunori 磯見辰典, Kurosawa Fumitaka 黒沢文貴 and Sakurai Ryōju 櫻井良樹. *Nihon Berugī kankei-shi* 日本・ベルギー関係史. Tokyo: Hakusuisha 白水社, 1989.

Kume 1979
Kume Kunitake 久米邦武, ed. *Tokumei zenken taishi Bei-Ō kairan jikki* 特命全権大使米欧回覧実記, vol. 3. Tokyo: Iwanami Bunko 岩波文庫, 1979.

Mōri 1985
Mōri Toshihiko 毛利敏彦. "Iwakura shisetsudan no bunmei-kan" 岩倉使節団の文明観. *Nihonshi kenkyū* 日本史研究 274 (1985).

Ōyama 1966
Ōyama Azusa 大山梓, ed. *Yamagata Aritomo ikensho* 山県有朋意見書. Tokyo: Hara Shobō 原書房, 1966.

Sufu 1877
Sufu Kōhei 周布公平. *Berugī-koku shi*. Seiyō Shorō 静養書楼, 1877.

Yamamuro 1984
Yamamuro Shin'ichi 山室信一. *Hōsei kanryō no jidai* 法制官僚の時代. Bokutakusha 木鐸社, 1984.

NOTES

1 Isomi et al. 1989, p. 17. The present piece draws upon many of the themes raised in this publication.

2 Isomi et al. 1989, p. 384.

3 On the concept of "model nations", see Yamamuro 1984, *passim*.

4 Sufu 1877, author's preface, pp. 1-12.

5 This piece mainly cites Kume 1979. On Belgium, see also vols. 4 and 5. On the Iwakura mission's high evaluation of Belgium, see also Mōri 1985.

6 Inoue 1969, pp. 463-464.

7 Asakura 1987-1989, vol. 2.

8 Asakura 1987-1989, vol. 18.

9 Ōyama 1966, p. 44.

10 Asakura 1987-1989, vol. 2.

11 Asakura 1987-1989, vol. 4.

12 Isomi et al. 1989, pp. 84-85.

13 "Berugī kokubōryaku", pp. 175-176.

14 "Berugī kokubōryaku", p. 180.

15 "Berugī kokubōryaku", p. 183.

16 "Berugī kokubōryaku", pp. 189-190.

17 "Berugī kokubōryaku", p. 190.

18 "Berugī kokubōryaku", pp. 191-192.

19 Asakura 1987-89.

20 Isomi 1989, pp. 157-172.

21 Ishikawa 1989.

22 Asakura 1987-1989, vol. 23.

23 Asakura 1987-1989, vol. 24.

24 Asakura 1987-1989, vol. 26.

25 Asakura 1987-1989, vols. 34-35.

26 Isomi et al. 1989, pp. 275-299.

27 Isomi et al. 1989, pp. 331-343.

28 Isomi 1967.

The Belgian industrial mission in Yokohama, with Ambassador de Bassompierre
(fourth from the right), June 1923. The tall man with the huge beard roughly in the middle
of the second row is the mission's leader Louis Canon-Legrand.

Reproduced by courtesy of the heirs of Baron de Bassompierre. Photograph by Maxime Darge.

A QUANTITATIVE ANALYSIS OF THE BELGIAN POPULATION IN JAPAN FROM 1876 TO 1938

Ryōju Sakurai

JAPAN & BELGIUM

An Itinerary of Mutual Inspiration

Légation

DE S. M. LE ROI DES BELGES

AU

JAPON.

Yokohama 8th May 1875 — 001

His Excellency Mr Kuroda
Governor of Yesso, Kaitakushi, Shiba

Dear Sir,

I should feel obliged to Your Excellency
to fix me a moment where I could call
on you, to present you my respects and
thank you for the kindness you showed
me lately.

I am, with respect and consideration
of Your Excellency, the very truly,

de Groote —

A QUANTITATIVE ANALYSIS OF THE BELGIAN POPULATION IN JAPAN FROM 1876 TO 1938[1]

Introduction

A number of years ago, together with Isomi Tatsunori and Kurosawa Fumitaka, I published a book entitled *Nihon Berugī kankei-shi* ("The History of the Relationship between Japan and Belgium") that comprehensively discussed the relationship between the two countries in modern times, depicting a wide range of human and material exchanges.[2] It served as the basis for my contributions to a book published in English in 2005 entitled *Japan and Belgium: Four Centuries of Exchange*.[3] In the present paper, I shall mainly use statistical materials to deepen the study of the relationship between the two countries. Above all, this study is the first to approach the question using human statistics.[4]

Belgium's Position in the Eyes of Japan

Diplomatic Relations

Diplomatic relations between Japan and Belgium were established in 1866, toward the closing days of the Tokugawa Shogunate. Belgium was the ninth country to establish diplomatic relations with Japan, following the United States, Great Britain, Russia, the Netherlands (all of these in 1854), France (1858), Portugal (1860), Prussia (1861), and Switzerland (1864), in that order. It was in 1870, after the collapse of the Tokugawa Shogunate and the Restoration of Meiji, that A. t'Kint de Roodenbeek, who had negotiated the establishment of diplomatic relations as the first envoy to Japan, arrived at his post as minister Plenipotentiary.

The first legation seems to have been located around Shinagawa in present-day Tokyo, but in 1874, it was situated at lot 59 in the Yamate Settlement (Yamate kyoryūchi 山手居留地) in Yokohama. In November 1893, however, immediately after Albert d'Anethan, the fourth envoy, arrived at his post, the legation was transferred to Tokyo, where it was located at No. 3 Sanbanchō 三番町,

Kōjimachi Ward 麹町区, on the site where the residence of Ōkubo Toshimichi 大久保利通 had once stood. Subsequently, in 1929, it was moved to No. 5 Nibanchō 二番町, Kōjimachi Ward 麹町区 (present-day Chiyoda Ward), where the former residence of Katō Takaaki had been purchased, and it remains there to this day.

Meanwhile, a Japanese legate was accredited to Belgium in 1873, but he served also as the legate for the Netherlands, France and Germany. Only in 1898 was a legation exclusively accredited to Belgium. After ambassadors had been exchanged between Japan and other major powers in the wake of the Russo-Japanese War, the legation in Belgium was eventually raised to the status of embassy in June 1921. Belgium was the eighth country to receive a Japanese resident ambassador, following Great Britain (in 1905), the United States, Germany, France (all of these in 1906), Italy, Austria (1907), and Russia (1908). After Belgium followed Brazil (1923), Turkey (1925), Manchukuo (1932), China (1935), Poland (1937), Argentina (1940), and Thailand (1941). Since the countries where the legations had been raised to embassies before the 1914-1918 war were major European powers, and the countries with which ambassadors had been exchanged after the war were, in most cases, considered to be important to Japan, the exchange of ambassadors with Belgium appears to indicate its political importance to Japan.

Belgium established several consulates at various locations in Japan. Belgian consulates, as will be described below, were established in accordance with the needs of the Belgian population in Japan, and what I have gathered so far is that consulates were established in Yokohama (1867-1942), Tokyo (1868-1907), Nagasaki (1869-1936; an honorary consulate from 1929), Kōbe (1872-?; an honorary consulate from 1926) and Osaka (1879-1911; reopened as an honorary consulate from 1927), as well as in Seoul and Dalian.

< Letter from Charles de Groote, minister (from 1873 to 1879), and minister Extraordinary and Plenipotentiary (from 1879 to 1884), to Kuroda Kiyotaka, director of the Hokkaido Development Commission, dated Yokohama, 8 May 1875. Diplomatic Archives of the Ministry of Foreign Affairs of Japan. Photograph by Dirk De Ruyver. From 1 January 1874, the Belgian legation was in Shinagawa. See Gaimushō kiroku sōmokuroku sen-

zenki 外務省記録総目録戦前期, vol. 1, Meiji Taishō 明治大正 6:1:3:1. *Zaihonpō kakkoku kōshikan setchi iten kankei ikken* 在本邦各国公使館設置移転関係一件. Keiō 2 – Meiji 4. "Zaihonpō Berugī-koku kōshikan kasetsu tsūchi no ken" 在本邦白耳義国公使館仮説通知之件. Yokohama, 28 December 1873 (copy). Correspondence from De Groote to Foreign minister Terashima, concerning the rent of a house owned by Enoye Massaru Esq. (Inoue Masaru) in Shinagawa, with a view to installing the Belgian legation there (as of 1 Januari 1874).

Originally, diplomatic relations between Japan and Belgium were established as a result of strong action on the Belgian side, not from the desire of the Japanese side (the Shogunate). Belgium expected much from Japan. A. t'Kint de Roodenbeek, who was dispatched to Japan to establish diplomatic relations and subsequently became Belgium's first resident envoy there, reported in his "Rapport sur Yokohama 1864-1865."[5]

> Nowadays Japan presents an important and increasingly rich market to Belgian commerce, and Belgian trade with Japan, like that with China, does not lag behind that of any other country. Therefore Belgium can compete from the same advantage as any other country. [...] Thanks to the detailed information provided by Mr. Lejeune, the merchants and industrialists can now identify the major resources of the Yokohama market. As a result, the consulates[6] established in Yokohama and Nagasaki will continue to provide Belgian trade with practical and detailed information available only to experts. However, considering the importance of the Yokohama market, which is already a reality, Japan's bright foreign-trade future, and above all its advantage as a virgin soil where trade volume continues to increase, [...] it is desirable to establish a state-owned trade company in Yokohama. Its excellent organization will be the key to success.

Although Belgium was the ninth country to establish diplomatic relations with Japan, the Japanese market had only just been opened to the world. So, from the Belgian perspective, Japan must have looked like a market where newcomers could still compete, and which left enough room for expansion. Regarding Belgium's need to enter into trade with Japan immediately, an Antwerp entrepreneur called Van Montenaecken is said to have warned, "It will be too late to enter the Japanese market one year from now, while in China the situation one year on will remain more or less the same."[7]

Trade Relations

Was Belgium able to enter the Japanese market as it had initially intended? Tables 1 and 2 and Graph 1 show the value of the trade between the two countries during the pre-war period.[8] In 1911 the Bureau of Commerce and Industry of the Ministry of Agriculture and Commerce analysed the trade between the two countries.[9] The analysis shows a clear trade imbalance in Belgium's favour: imports from Belgium far exceeded exports from Japan, with the exports about one third of the imports. On average, from 1909 through 1911, Japan's imports from Belgium and Japan's exports to Belgium accounted for about 1/250th of Belgium's total imports and exports. Japan ranked as the nineteenth country in Belgium's total imports and the twenty-first country in Belgium's total exports. These figures are based on Belgian trade statistics.

TABLE 1 : JAPAN'S EXPORTS/IMPORTS TO/FROM BELGIUM (THOUSAND YEN)

year	export	import
1877	0	63,474
1882	793	128,932
1887	23,816	322,196
1892	50,125	951,538
1897	109,312	3,173,218
1902	600,497	6,977,656
1907	2,054,397	13,398,299
1912	3,080,150	9,087,488
1917	0	12,897
1922	1,889,694	14,844,959
1927	2,205,865	14,318,582
1932	4,160,845	6,133,198
1937	20,650,000	41,058,000

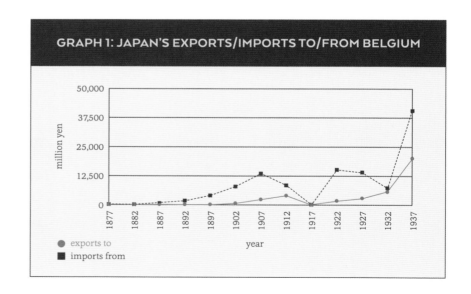

GRAPH 1: JAPAN'S EXPORTS/IMPORTS TO/FROM BELGIUM

The following is a survey of the share that bilateral trade between Japan and Belgium occupied in the whole of their respective trade, based on figures from the *Nihon bōeki seiran* 日本貿易精覧 ["Japan's Trade Review"]. As shown in the statistics for five separate years, Japan's exports to Belgium accounted for only 0.65% of Japan's total exports and 2.7% of Japan's total imports at the most. Japan's exports to Belgium ranked thirteenth in 1881 (following China, India, Great Britain, France, Germany, Italy, Russia, Austria, the Netherlands, Spain, the United States, Australia, in that order), sixteenth in 1911 (behind China, Hong Kong, Singapore, Indonesia, the Philippines, Great Britain, France, Germany, Italy, Russia, the United States, Canada, Australia, and Hawaii) and eighteenth in 1931. Japan's imports from Belgium ranked seventh in 1881 (following China, India, Great Britain, France, Germany, and the United States), ninth in 1911 (behind China, India, Indonesia, Indochina, Great Britain, Germany, the United States, and Australia) and twenty-first in 1931. As pointed out by the Bureau of Commerce and Industry, the trade balance was unfavourable to Japan, since Japan's imports from Belgium always ranked higher than its exports to Belgium. Moreover, the fact that both the exports to and the imports from Belgium gradually ranked lower from the Meiji era onward to the Shōwa era, indicates a decrease in the relative importance of the trade relations between Japan and Belgium. However, Japanese statistics from that period do not give the full picture, because they do not reflect imports from and exports to Belgium via third countries.

What type of articles were imported from and exported to Belgium? According to a document from 1911[10] the main goods exported to Belgium were zinc, rapeseed, cotton yarn waste, copper ingots and locks, vegetable oils, and dyes, while the main goods imported from Belgium were iron and steel, plate glass, paper, woollen textiles, machinery and dynamite. It points out in particular that, as far as plate glass for windows and thick plate glass for mirrors were concerned, Belgian products accounted for 99% and 45% of the total imports, respectively, given the fact that these products were hardly produced in Japan. Other articles exported to Belgium included ceramics, lacquer ware, folding screens, and *habutae* silks in the first half of the Meiji era, rice, fish oil, whale oil, and timber in the second half of the said period, and fish oil, whale oil, rapeseed oil, palm oil, timber, peanuts, floss silk, and braids in the Taishō era. There were no noteworthy articles in the pre-war Shōwa period. Articles imported from Belgium included printing paper, paper from pulp, candles, woolen cloth, window panes, iron cables, iron nails and electric wire, iron utensils, and zinc plates in the first half of the Meiji era, printing paper, woollen cloth, dyes, window panes, plate iron, iron wire and pipes, rails, electric wire, and zinc plates in the second half of this era, wool, dyes, morphine, thick sheet glass, iron, and jewellery in the Taishō era, and woollen yarn, iron, and aluminium in the pre-war Shōwa period. In short, the goods exported from Japan were agricultural products and lightly processed goods, while the imported goods were industrial goods, in other words, the typical trade structure between a developed

TABLE 2: JAPAN'S IMPORT AND EXPORT

	Japan's import and export (%, 1912=100)		Japan's total import and export (%, 1912=100)		compared to Japan's total trade amount (%)	
year	to Belgium	from Belgium	to Belgium	from Belgium	export	import
1877	—	0.7	—	0.231	4.4	4.4
1882	0.0	1.4	0.002	0.438	7.2	4.8
1887	0.8	3.5	0.045	0.727	9.9	7.2
1892	1.6	10.5	0.055	1.334	17.3	11.5
1897	3.5	34.9	0.067	1.447	31.0	35.4
1902	19.5	76.8	0.232	2.568	49.0	43.9
1907	66.7	147.1	0.475	2.710	82.1	79.9
1912	100.0	100.0	0.585	1.468	100.0	100.0
1917	—	0.1	—	0.001	304.2	167.3
1922	61.4	163.4	0.115	0.785	310.7	305.4
1927	71.6	157.6	0.111	0.057	378.1	352.0
1932	135.1	67.5	0.295	0.428	267.6	231.3
1937	670.4	451.8	0.650	1.085	602.6	611.2

Western-style building in Kōjimachi Ward, Tokyo, seen from the street side.
Archives of the Royal Palace, Brussels. Photograph by Hans Coppens.
The residence and garden were once the property of the Meiji statesman Ōkubo Toshimichi.
The building, remodelled by the British architect Josiah Condor, served as Belgian legation
and embassy from 1893 until 1928.

Western-style building in Kōjimachi Ward, Tokyo, seen from the garden.
Archives of the Royal Palace, Brussels. Photograph by Hans Coppens
The residence and garden were once the property of the Meiji statesman Ōkubo Toshimichi.
The building, remodelled by the British architect Josiah Condor, served as Belgian legation
and embassy from 1893 until 1928.

country, Belgium, and a developing country, Japan, was maintained throughout the pre-war period, even after Japan had become an industrialized country.

Quantitative Overview of the Belgian Population in Japan

Yearly Changes and Rankings by Country

Table 3 and Graph 2 show the total number of Belgians in Japan based on the *Nippon teikoku tōkei nenkan* 日本帝国統計年鑑 ("Statistical Yearbook of the Empire of Japan"; the figures for 1912, 1914 and 1925, otherwise lacking, are supplied from the *Naimushō tōkei hōkoku* 内務省統計報告 ["Statistical Report of the Ministry of Home Affairs"]). We include also the tables on the staff of the legation (embassy) and the consulates quoted in the Yearbook. When the consular jurisdiction was abolished in 1899, the listing method in the tables also changed. That is, before 1899, the population was classified into "staff of legation and consulates," "public servants," "private servants," "residents of settlements," or "businessmen, etc.," but from that year on only the total number of people was given (legation and consular staff were shown in an annexed table). However, since no significant fluctuations are observed in the figures before

TABLE 3: NUMBER OF BELGIANS IN JAPAN

year	number	legation staffs	year	number	legation staffs	year	number	legation staffs
1876	6	5	1897	26	7	1918	36	7
1877	18	5	1898	25	7	1919	38	3
1878	9	4	1899	20	6	1920	35	5
1879	5	3	1900	22	8	1921	34	6
1880	17	5	1901	23	7	1922	22	8
1881	11	3	1902	24	8	1923	26	7
1882	8	5	1903	33	6	1924	21	7
1883	9	5	1904	24	6	1925	28	7
1884	6	2	1905	13	5	1926	35	10
1885	6	2	1906	12	3	1927	26	
1886	9	4	1907	31	6	1928	16	11
1887	24	4	1908	16	7	1929	31	10
1888	32	5	1909	25	7	1930	27	9
1889	31	5	1910	22	7	1931	38	10
1890	26	6	1911	19	7	1932	39	6
1891	20	4	1912	23	6	1933	39	8
1892	20	3	1913	19	8	1934	45	12
1893	22	5	1914	18	8	1935	46	9
1894	20	4	1915	17	8	1936	45	8
1895	27	8	1916	23	7	1937	53	7
1896	25	7	1917	25	6	1938	43	8

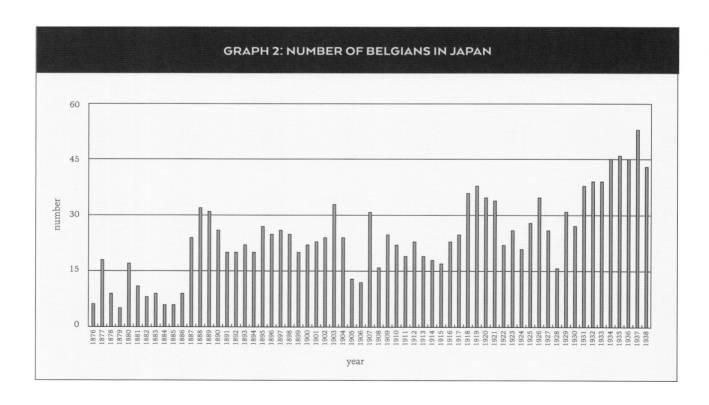

GRAPH 2: NUMBER OF BELGIANS IN JAPAN

and after 1898, we believe that there was continuity in the evolution. Also, there might have been Belgians who did not report themselves as Belgians, but this also applies to other foreigners, so this possibility was ignored.

As can be seen at a glance, the Belgian population in Japan in the pre-war period peaked at fifty-three in 1937, with its lowest point at five in 1879. Before 1887 there were fewer than eleven belgians in Japan, excluding the years 1877 and 1880, and fluctuated widely. Between 1887 and 1904, the Belgian population slightly increased to about twenty or thirty (thirty-three at most). During the period from 1905 through 1917, it again decreased to somewhere between ten and thirty, excluding the year 1907. Above all, the decrease during the Russo-Japanese War was conspicuous. From 1918 (after the end of the First World War), the Belgian population again increased to twenty or thirty, excluding the year 1928. And from 1931 on, it sharply increased from less than forty to around fifty.

Was this population figure large or small? The largest group of foreigners resident in Japan throughout the pre-war period was Chinese, taken to include subjects of the Qing dynasty, and citizens of the Republic of China and Manchukuo. The Koreans are not included in the analysis because they became Japanese citizens in 1910, but before 1910 there were periods in which large numbers of Koreans were registered as resident foreigners in Japan. Foreigners from Great Britain, the U.S.A., Germany and France accounted for most of the Westerners, followed by those from the Netherlands, Portugal, Russia and Switzerland. The Russian population, including White Russians and those left stateless after the Russian Revolution, increased considerably after 1917. Foreigners from Spain, Denmark, Italy, Austria, Sweden, etc. constituted the third group of Western nationals in Japan in that order of population volume, and Belgium also belonged to this group. The order of countries listed here is based on the statistics for 1880, when the precise number of foreign residents in Japan by country was as follows: 3,739 from Qing China, 933 from Great Britain, 414 from the U.S.A., 307 from Germany, 181 from France, 71 from the Netherlands, 57 from Portugal, 35 from Russia, 32 from Switzerland, 30 from Spain, 23 from Denmark, 22 from Italy, 19 from Austria, 14 from Sweden, and 12 from Belgium.

Belgium ranked fifteenth, with an extremely small population in absolute numbers, accounting proportionately for about 0.2% of the total number of foreign residents. The Belgian population in Japan, as observed at intervals of about ten years, dropped from fourteenth place in 1891, to nineteenth place in 1901 and to eighteenth place in 1910. In 1910 the precise number of foreigners in Japan from each country was as follows: 8,420 from Qing China, 2,430 from Great Britain, 1,633 from the U.S.A., 782 from Germany, 534 from France, 216 from Portugal, 117 from Russia, 113 from Switzerland, 95 from Canada, 85 from Austria, 85 from the Netherlands, 76 from Denmark, 67 from Italy, 62 from Spain, 52 from India, 28 from Turkey, 24 from Sweden, and 22 from Belgium. In 1910 the number of Belgians accounted for about 0.15% of the total number of foreign residents.

While the Belgian population in Japan again ranked eighteenth in 1921 and nineteenth in 1931, in 1938 it dropped to the twenty-fifth place, marking a sharp fall. That is, the weight of the Belgian presence in Japan tended to diminish over the long term. Incidentally, the demographic ranking is analogous to that of trade shown above. Belgium was the ninth country with which Japan established diplomatic relations and the eighth country with which Japan exchanged ambassadors, however it did not rank very high in terms of trade relations or the number of Belgian residents in Japan.

Where Did They Live?

Table 4 shows the number of Belgians living in the various prefectures of Japan. For the period from 1880 to 1883, the figures in the Statistical Yearbook of the Empire of Japan were used, and for 1902 and from 1913 onwards, the figures in the Statistical Report of the Ministry of Home Affairs (the years for which no data were available were simply omitted). The table shows that Belgians lived only in Kanagawa (Yokohama) and Nagasaki Prefectures from 1880 through 1883, and from 1902 on they lived in Tokyo, Kanagawa, Osaka, Nagasaki and Kumamoto Prefectures. There were formerly foreign settlements in all of these prefectures, except Kumamoto Prefecture. Belgians tended to live in the places which had formerly been home to foreign settlements, even after their abolition, and showed little tendency to move out to other areas of Japan. Although there had also been a foreign settlement in Osaka, there was only one Belgian (male) registered as living there from 1913 to 1917 and from 1928 to 1934.

Even so, some Belgians stayed for longer than one year in some of the other prefectures: Okayama (one male from 1917 to 1918), Fukuoka (one male from 1928 to 1929), Miyazaki (one male from 1931 to 1932), Aichi (one male and one female from 1932 to 1935), Ōita (one male from 1933 to 1936), Hiroshima (two females from 1935 to 1936), Iwate (six females in 1936 and 1942), Kyoto (one male in 1917) and Toyama (one male and two females from 1919-1920). Detailed investigation may reveal more background data for each of these cases.

Since there is a possibility that they have been omitted in the Statistical Report of the Ministry of Home Affairs, I have shown in Table 5 the statistics for Tokyo, Kanagawa and Hyōgo Prefectures. It shows as a general tendency that the number of Belgians in Kanagawa Prefecture was high in the first half of the Meiji era, and then gradually decreased, while the number of Belgians in Hyōgo and Tokyo Prefectures gradually increased. The reasons for this trend are presumed to be the relocation of the legation from Yokohama to Tokyo and the effect of the Great Kantō Earthquake of 1923. The number of Belgians resident in Kanagawa Prefecture at the end of 1923 and in 1924 was found to be zero. Although Tokyo should also have been affected by the earthquake, no sharp decrease in the number of Belgians resident in Tokyo was observed from the statistics. If we compare the statistics of Tokyo City, Yokohama City and Kōbe City shown in Table 5, we may infer that the effects of the earthquake were less severe in Tokyo than in Yokohama, since people living in the Tokyo area had by that time already moved to live in the suburbs.

Although the data are fragmentary and scarce, the locations of Belgians resident in Tokyo can be specified in considerable detail. The statistics for Tokyo Prefecture show that in 1901, seven Belgians lived in Kyōbashi Ward, in 1903 five lived in Kyōbashi Ward, two in Kōjimachi Ward and one in Kanda Ward, and in 1907, two in Kyōbashi Ward and one in Azabu Ward. Kyōbashi Ward was the area where formerly the foreign settlement of Tsukiji was located. The statistics show that in 1926,

three years after the earthquake, eleven Belgians lived in Kōjimachi Ward, two in Shiba Ward, one in Koishikawa Ward and two in Toyotama District. Kōjimachi Ward was where the Embassy of Belgium was located. In this time bracket, Westerners as a whole were moving from Kyōbashi to Azabu Ward, Shiba Ward and Ebara District. What we see is that Belgians likewise were moving to the suburbs, where they found better surroundings.

What Were the Occupations of Belgians Living in Japan?

For what purposes did Belgians stay in Japan? Various statistical compilations provide data about the occupation of the foreign residents. First, according to the Statistical Report of the Ministry of Home Affairs, in 1902 there were twenty-five Belgian residents in Japan, including one government official, one public servant, one missionary, three students, one grocer, one engineer, one servant, two clerks and nine persons without occupation.

TABLE 4: NUMBER OF BELGIANS BY PREFECTURES

year	Tokyo	Kanagawa	Osaka	Hyōgo	Nagasaki	Kumamoto
1880	0	11	0	0	1	0
1881	0	10	0	0	1	0
1882	0	7	0	0	1	0
1883	0	8	0	0	1	0
1902	4	9	0	4	1	6
1913	3	3	1	10	2	0
1914	2	7	1	6	1	1
1915	2	5	1	7	1	1
1916	3	5	1	5	1	1
1917	4	6	1	11	1	1
1918	4	11	0	10	9	1
1919	14	11	0	7	2	1
1920	12	9	0	6	3	2
1922	6	3	0	9	0	2
1923	12	0	0	10	2	2
1924	9	0	0	8	2	2
1925	12	5	0	8	2	1
1927	10	3	0	10	2	1
1928	4	3	1	5	1	1
1929	12	3	1	12	1	1
1930	18	3	1	3	1	1
1931	19	3	1	11	1	1
1932	15	3	1	11	1	5
1933	15	8	1	9	1	2
1934	13	8	1	17	1	2
1935	11	10	0	17	1	2
1936	13	9	0	10	2	2
1941	10	5	0	10	2	1
1942	—	—	—	8	2	1

TABLE 5: NUMBER OF BELGIANS IN THE PREFECTURES OF TOKYO, KANAGAWA, HYŌGO AND IN THE CITIES OF TOKYO, YOKOHAMA AND KŌBE

year	P. of Tokyo	C. of Tokyo	P. of Kanagawa	C. of Yokohama	P. of Hyōgo	C. of Kōbe
1871						2
1872						
1873					0	
1874						
1875						
1876						
1877	1					
1878					1	1
1879					1	1
1880			11		1	1
1881			10		1	1
1882			8		0	
1883			7		0	
1884			2		0	
1885			1		0	
1886	1		1		0	
1887	5		9		0	
1888	6		14		1	
1889	5		12		2	2
1890	1		13		2	2
1891	5		6		1	1
1892	4		7		1	1
1893	8		4		1	1
1894	7		2		2	2
1895	7		2		5	3
1896	8		3		4	
1897	4		7		0	
1898	4		7		0	
1899	2	3	7		4	
1900		4	8		4	
1901	7	7	9	7	4	4
1902	3	3	9	8	4	4
1903	8	8	4	9	6	6
1904	5	5	3	9	5	5
1905	3	3	4	8	0	0
1906	1	1	4	9	0	0
1907	3	3	20	11	1	0
1908	4	4	2	11	1	0
1909			4	8	15	7
1910			3	7	14	14
1911			5	7	13	9
1912			3	7	13	8
1913			3	7	10	8
1914			7	6	6	5
1915	2	3	5	5	7	6
1916	3	1	11	11	5	4
1917	4	1	10	6	11	10
1918	4	1	11	9	10	8
1919	14	1	11	10	7	5
1920	12	0	9		6	5
1921	8	1	10		10	9
1922	7	1	—		9	8
1923	14	2	0		10	7
1924	9	3	0	2	8	5
1925	12	3	5	5	8	5
1926	16	12	3	3	13	7
1927	10	11	3	0	10	8
1928	4	4	3	3	5	14
1929	12	9	3	3	12	11
1930	18	17	3	3	3	2
1931	19	19	3	3	11	11
1932	15		3	3	11	11
1933	15		8	3	9	11
1934	13		8	8	10	17
1935	11		10	10	17	20
1936	13		9	9	10	8
1937	15		6	6	11	15
1938	14		7	0	8	8
1939	10		4		14	9
1940					13	
1941					10	

In 1911 there were nineteen Belgian residents (thirteen males and six females), consisting of five businessmen, one missionary, two trading merchants, two government officials, two hotel proprietors, one person engaging in miscellaneous affairs, and three persons without occupation. In 1915 there were seventeen Belgian residents (twelve males and five females), comprising one businessman, two missionaries, two teachers, one trading merchant, one engineer, two government officials and eight persons without occupation. We have only data for late Meiji to the early Taishō periods, but they give us an idea about the general trend: they were businessmen, teachers, missionaries, students, engineers, and the like.

Were there any regional peculiarities? Let us examine Tokyo, Kanagawa and Hyōgo Prefectures. For Tokyo, only the data for two years are available. In 1903, there were eight Belgian residents in Tokyo, comprising one government official, one person employed by the Japanese government, two missionaries, one trader and three persons without occupation. In 1904 there were five Belgian residents in Tokyo, comprising one teacher, one missionary, one dressmaker and two persons without occupation.

For Kanagawa and Hyōgo Prefectures, data are available starting with the late Meiji era. Table 6 shows the data at intervals of about five years. Since both Yokohama and Kōbe have been representative trade ports, the two show similar tendencies. Persons entered as "government officials" or "people in the service of government officials" were probably consular staff. People entered as "managers, merchants, businessmen, traders and company employees" were no doubt engaged in trade. The persons with occupations of a "different nature" were those engaged in religious work in Kanagawa Prefecture and the missionaries in Hyōgo Prefecture. Since some Belgian missionaries were also included in the statistics for Tokyo, we may assume that Belgian missionaries represented an important section of Belgian residents. A peculiarity of Belgian residents in Hyōgo Prefecture was that some of them were working in industrial crafts such as glasswork, celluloid production and metalwork. One example is the Belgian engineers and glassworkers who were employed at the glassworks of Asahi Glass Co., Ltd. in Amagasaki for the transfer of flat glass technology. From the above, the occupations of Belgian private citizens living in Japan can roughly be reconstructed.

Servants of diplomats, teachers, missionaries (priests), monks (nuns), traders, and artists and musicians who visited Japan as travellers, generally made up the bulk of the Belgian residents in Japan throughout the whole pre-war period.

Conclusion

In this contribution we have made an overview of the activities of Belgians in pre-war Japan. The Belgian presence was not felt strongly because the trade relations and human exchanges between the two countries remained limited. However, Japan and Belgium established diplomatic relations and exchanged ambassadors at a relatively early stage. In other words, the salient characteristic of the relationship between the two countries was that the diplomatic stature was higher than the actual relationship warranted. The fact that both minister Albert d'Anethan and Ambassador Albert de Bassompierre stayed in Japan for a long time and served as doyens of the diplomatic corps in Japan may have had something to do with this relatively high profile.

Furthermore, even allowing for the active lobbying of Adachi Mineichirō, an influential diplomat, the promotion of the Legation to the status of Embassy after the First World War would not have been realized had

TABLE 6: OCCUPATIONS OF BELGIANS RESIDENT IN KANAGAWA AND HYŌGO PREFECTURES

year	number of persons	occupation
1) Kanagawa Prefecture		
1911	5	government official: 1; manager: 1; others: 2; without occupation: 1
1916	11 (male: 5; female: 6)	merchant: 1; government official: 1; businessman: 1; without occupation: 8
1921	10 (male: 5; female: 5)	food/beverage manufacturer: 1; merchant: 1; religious worker: 1; without occupation: 7
1928	3 (male: 2; female: 1)	servant of public official: 1; without occupation: 2
1933	8 (male: 4; female: 4)	shipping agent: 1; servant of public official 1; without occupation: 6
1938	7 (male: 4; female: 3)	merchant: 1; servant of public official: 1; without occupation: 5
2) Hyōgo Prefecture		
1909	15 (male: 11; female: 4)	government official: 1; merchant clerk: 3; trading merchant: 1; glasswork engineer: 7 family members: 3
1912	13 (male: 9; female: 4)	government official: 1; merchant clerk: 2; trading merchant: 1; engineer: 1; celluloid engineer: 1; smithery: 1; wool comber: 1; miscellaneous: 1; without occupation: 4
1918	10 (male: 8; female: 2)	government official: 1; businessman: 3, engineer: 2, miscellaneous: 1; family members: 3
1923	10 (male: 4; female: 6)	trading merchant: 2; missionary: 2, businessman: 1, family members: 5
1928	5 (male: 1; female: 4)	trading merchant: 1; family members: 4
1933	9 (male: 4; female: 5)	trading merchant: 1; miscellaneous: 1; family members: 7
1938	8 (male: 4; female: 4)	businessman: 4, trading merchant: 1; family members: 3

Japan not placed great importance on Belgium. That Japan attached much importance to Belgium, can also be inferred from the fact that on his European tour of 1921 the Crown Prince of Japan not only visited Great Britain, France, the Netherlands and Italy, but also included Belgium in his itinerary.[11] However, why did Japan exchange ambassadors with Belgium while ignoring the Netherlands? The relationship between Japan and the Netherlands, which had existed since the Edo period, had been closer than that with Belgium. Moreover, the Netherlands ranked higher than Belgium in terms of trade volume and the number of residents in Japan. This observation compels us to consider the special position of Belgium. One possible reason is the fact that Belgium was an ally of Japan in the First World War, both countries fighting against Germany, while the Netherlands remained neutral. Note that the other major allies had also begun to exchange ambassadors with Belgium. Another possible reason is that Belgium had a special geopolitical significance in that it was located between the great powers in Europe, in other words because Belgium occupied a key position on the European continent. The fact that the EU is based in Brussels is indicative of this same geographical position. Accordingly, Belgium had to play a neutral and mediating role among European countries, and the Japanese government may have attached great importance to this unique trait, and perhaps expected it to be useful in some way or other. In fact, prior to the Second World War, the foreign ministers of Belgium were important players in the international political arena in chairing various meetings. The third possible reason is that Belgium had a certain interest and influence elsewhere in Asia (above all in China). This, however, is a topic that requires further exploration.

REFERENCES

Isomi et al. 1989
Isomi Tatsunori 磯見辰典, Kurosawa Fumitaka 黒沢文貴 and Sakurai Ryōju 櫻井良樹. *Nihon Berugī kankei-shi* 日本・ベルギー関係史. Tokyo: Hakusuisha 白水社, 1989.

Kajita 2005
Kajita Akihiro 梶田明宏. "Taishō jūnen kōtaishi gogaiyū ni okeru hōmonkoku kettei no ikisatsu ni tsuite" 大正十年皇太子御外遊における訪問国決定の経緯について. *Shoryōbu kiyō* 書陵部紀要 57 (2005).

Vande Walle 2005
W.F. Vande Walle, ed. *Japan and Belgium: Four Centuries of Exchange*. Brussels: The General Secretariat of the Government of Belgium at the Aichi Expo 2005, Japan, 2005.

NOTES

1 This contribution is an adaptation of the paper "An Integrated Comparative Study of Japan and Belgium from the Perspective of Regional Studies", read at the workshop held at Leuven University, Belgium, on 29 and 30 August 2006. A detailed account of the activities of the Belgians residing in Japan was omitted in this paper.

2 Isomi et al. 1989.

3 Vande Walle 2005. My contributions to this book comprise: "Prewar Economic and Trade Relations", "Belgium's Contribution to the Development of the Glass Industry in Japan," "The Visit of Tokugawa Akitake to Belgium", "Japan and Belgium during the First World War", and "Relations between Japan and Belgium during the 1930s."

4 The statistical compilations used in this paper were all annual reports of *Nippon teikoku tōkei nenkan* 日本帝国統計年鑑, *Naimushō tōkei hōkoku* 内務省統計報告, *Tōkyō-fu tōkeisho* 東京府統計書, *Kanagawa-ken tōkeisho* 神奈川県統計書, *Hyōgo-ken tōkeisho* 兵庫県統計書, *Tōkyō-shi tōkei nenpyō* 東京市統計年表, *Kōbe-shi tōkeisho* 神戸市統計書, *Yokohama-shi tōkeisho* 横浜市統計書, and *Kōbe kaikō sanjūnen-shi gekan* 神戸開港三十年史下巻.

5 Archives du Ministère des Affaires étrangères, No. 2865. Isomi et al. 1989, pp. 58-59.

6 It is unclear whether t'Kint here means the consulates of other European nations.

7 Isomi et al. 1989, p. 61.

8 Graph 1 was published previously in "Japan and Belgium in Prewar Times". *The Japan-Belgium Society Bulletin* 69 (2005).

9 Bureau of Commerce and Industry, the Ministry of Agriculture and Commerce. *An Outlook of the Trade Between Japan and Belgium in 1911*. 1913.

10 A letter from Komura Jutarō 小村寿太郎 to Nabeshima Keijirō 鍋島桂次郎, dated 18 April 1911. (A Matter on the Revision of the Commercial Treaty between Japan and Belgium. Record of the Foreign Ministry. 2-5-1-90).

11 Recently, Kajita 2005 discussed the decision as to which countries the crown prince should visit.

WILLEM A. GROOTAERS

Linguist and Ethnographer[1]

W.F. Vande Walle

WILLEM A. GROOTAERS

Background and Training

"De rode en de zwarte aalbes en hun semantisch verband" ("The red and the black currant and their semantic relation"), published in 1937, was the scientific debut of a dialectologist who was destined for the Far East. Willem Grootaers (born in St. Servais, now part of the city of Namur, in 1911) was so to speak a born dialectologist. His father was the academic Ludovicus Grootaers (1885-1956),[2] a well-known specialist in Flemish and Dutch dialects and compiler of numerous dictionaries. His mother, Alice Anciaux[3], was a Walloon and so the young Willem received a perfectly bilingual education. At home the study of dialects was daily fare. At an early age he witnessed the process of dialect cartography in his father's study. In 1930 he joined the Society of Jesus, but in 1932 he transferred to the congregation of Scheut and began to study Chinese.[4]

Between 1935 and 1939 he studied Chinese at the Seminary of Scheut in Leuven under the guidance of Father Jozef Mullie, erstwhile missionary in Eastern Mongolia and well-known specialist in Chinese linguistics, while also working at the Centre for Dutch Dialectology founded by his father, where he learned the trade of dialectologist and became thoroughly familiar with the methodology of linguistic geography. Linguistic geography as a sub-discipline of linguistics had been founded by Jules Gilliéron (1854-1926), whose method spawned a school with a following throughout Europe and beyond. In 1938 Grootaers was ordained a priest.[5]

Parental home of Willem Grootaers, at Naamsesteenweg 162, Heverlee.
Photograph courtesy of Prof. Inoue Fumio.

Professor Ludovicus Grootaers, father of Willem, photograph taken in 1950.
Photograph courtesy of Prof. Inoue Fumio.

‹ Grootaers on his bicycle.
Photograph courtesy of Prof. Inoue Fumio.

To the China Mission

In October 1939 he left Europe to do missionary work in China. He was first sent to Beijing for further study of the Chinese language, and then, in 1941, to the village of Xi-ce-tian cun 西册田村 in Datong 大同 Prefecture, some fifty kilometres southeast of Datong, to become head of a local primary school. This village, together with thirty-six neighbouring villages, all located close to the Great Wall (about 250-260 km west of Beijing) constituted his parish. In one of his autobiographical writings in Japanese, he reminisces about this time:

> In October 1939 I started learning Chinese conversation at the Scheut language school in Beijing named Pu ai tang 普爱堂. We were twenty-two students. The other twenty-one ended their course in June of the following year and were sent out to their diocese in Northern China. I alone was allowed to stay on for another year and secured permission to receive instruction from Professor Zhou Dianfu 周殿福, who in his early years was an authority on phonetics. [...] In June 1941, at my own request, I was sent out to Scheut's only diocese south of the Great Wall. It was the area of Datong, once the capital of the Northern Wei Dynasty (386-550). West of Datong lie the famous caves of Yungang (460s). The local population had been living here for at least fifteen hundred years, therefore from a linguist's point of view, it was a significant and important area. However, the so-called Pekinese I had learned in Beijing, was not understood at all in this region. Consequently, the study of the dialect of Datong became an urgent task. So I started studying the dialect like a madman. In the dialect of this region I noticed a characteristic that was lacking in Pekinese. This was the fact that the pronunciation of some word endings was accompanied by a glottal stop (*seitai heisa* 声带閉鎖).[6]

Here he is referring to the glottal stop that typifies the fifth tone, which had long disappeared from the Pekinese vernacular, but was apparently still alive in this northern dialect of old ancestry.

In March 1943 the Japanese forces of occupation sent him to an internment camp in the Wei 维 Prefecture in Shandong Province. The inmates of the camp numbered 1,800 persons, and included 300 Catholic missionaries

and 400 sisters. In August of that year the missionaries and sisters were transferred to Beijing, where they were put in lenient confinement in the vacated language school for missionaries under the supervision of a French Jesuit, until the end of the Sino-Japanese War in 1945.[7]

His confinement was so loosely enforced that he was able to establish contacts with the then still little known French palaeontologist Pierre Teilhard de Chardin SJ (1888-1955), a controversial thinker who was on bad terms both with Rome and his Society. Grootaers was captivated by the Jesuit's worldview and vision of the future. It is said that Flemish Scheutists in Beijing supported Teilhard financially and morally. Grootaers later declared that meeting the French Jesuit scholar had had a decisive influence on his orientation in life, in

Willem Grootaers (in cassock, with beard) with his parents and siblings. Willem is standing fourth from the left. Photograph taken in 1938.
Photograph by courtesy of Prof. Inoue Fumio.

Willem Grootaers with his parents, a sister and his younger brother Jan, and two other priests. Photograph taken in 1939 shortly before his departure for China.
Photograph by courtesy of Prof. Inoue Fumio.

particular on his positive commitment to combine the life of a scholar with that of a priest. In his congregation, as indeed generally in the Church, the view of scholarly pursuits was that they had value as long as they were undertaken with the intention of serving God. In other words, scholarship in itself did not have any intrinsic value, but only in as much as it was undertaken in the service of God. This view constituted a serious trammel on the scholarly ambition of the young missionary Grootaers. Teilhard however took an entirely different approach to the issue. Far from seeing a possible conflict between the two vocations, he asserted that scholarship was essentially a contribution to the expansion of the Kingdom of God. Spiritual progress was by definition a progress towards God.[8] As is well known, Teilhard was a proponent of *orthogenesis*, the idea that evolution unfolds in a directional, goal-driven way, a notion also known as convergent evolution. Thus Grootaers embraced what he later aptly called the hyphenated life of priest and linguist.[9] He once explained this at considerable length in a round-table discussion entitled "Why do I study dialects?," organized as part of the programme of the Twentieth Congress of Japanese Dialectology (1975). Noting that all scientific research contributes to the expansion of the spiritual realm, he is convinced that the Christian who is active in "worldly sciences" is in his mind and his heart placed between "what strives upward" (towards God) and "what strives forward" (towards the future of mankind). He feels this dual dimension not as a contradiction but as a wonderful harmony. Thus he can claim that his study of dialects is one of his religious exercises.[10]

During his internment in Japanese-occupied Beijing, Grootaers, in collaboration with his confrères Fathers Paul Serruys and Henri Van Boven, taught a course in Chinese history to three different missionary communities. After the end of his confinement he taught the same course twice at the Catholic University of Peking. In collaboration with Father Serruys he prepared the course text for publication as a *Handbook of Chinese History*, which was to include two parts, the first being an outline of Chinese history, the second a bio-bibliographical list of 8,000 famous Chinese persons. The tome was scheduled for publication by Scheut Editions in Beijing, and would have run to about five hundred pages,[11] but in the end it never saw the light of day. The archives of the congregation do, however, hold a typewritten history of China in Dutch.[12]

At the request of his superiors he also wrote a couple of studies on Chinese religions,[13] intended to be read by his confrères. His study of Buddhism he condensed into a lecture, delivered to an audience of Protestants, as well as to an assembly of two hundred officers of the American Executive Headquarters in China.[14]

Before his internment Grootaers had carried out field surveys and had published several reports on the dialect distribution in the Central Plain, exemplifying what is called the microscopic approach.[15] In doing so he became the first to apply the methods of linguistic geography in China. His first findings were published during his internment in the learned journal *Monumenta Serica*, published by the Catholic University of Beijing (Fu Jen Daxue 辅仁大学). This university, run by the German SVD congregation, had been allowed to carry on its activities under the Japanese occupation. After the conclusion of the Sino-Japanese War, Grootaers was appointed research fellow of dialect geography, founding the university's Bureau of Linguistic Geography in 1947.

Grootaers also wasted no time in resuming his field research in collaboration with a handful of young Chinese scholars. In 1947 he conducted a dialect and ethnographical survey of Wanquan 万全 Prefecture in the Province of Chahar 察哈尔, and the following year a similar survey in Xuanhua 宣化 Prefecture[16] in the same province.

In those days dialectal differences in the Chinese language were mainly discussed in terms of phonological and tonal changes that went back to the stage of Karlgren's Ancient Chinese (Old Chinese 上古汉语). The main objective of this research was the macroscopic classification of dialects. There was little if any interest in microscopic dialectal differences between settlements within a given area. Most Chinese scholars did not see the relevance of this kind of approach.[17] Against this background it was Grootaers's ambition one day to see the realization of a nation-wide survey carried out on the basis of the methodology of linguistic geography.[18] But as a contemporary reviewer noted, with the civil war between the Communists and the Nationalists plunging China into chaos, his efforts were "a mere pailful as compared with the ocean of effort to be expended and results to be tabulated."[19] Carrying out such a long-term and large-scale project would require the training of considerable numbers of personnel, and funding on a scale that was simply not available at the time. Worse still, in 1948 Grootaers was forced to return to Europe together with the other missionaries. None too soon, for after the Communists had taken power in 1949, Western missionaries were no longer welcome in the country.

During his ten-year stay in China, he had conducted rigorous research into a few language variants and the folklore in a specific area in northern China. He had studied temple inscriptions and popular traditions in more than 300 villages along the Great Wall. In his efforts to determine dialect boundaries, he had discovered that many of them were traceable to the Ming period. These numerous forays into the field later resulted in the publication of a host of scientific contributions on Chinese linguistics, folklore, epigraphy and iconography, which now have become all the more invaluable since the sweeping changes China has gone through in the latter half of the twentieth century, have obliterated many of the linguistic features and traditional practices he was then studying. Expelled from China, he returned to Belgium with a wealth of dialectological and ethnographic material in his luggage. Only parts of these materials would he be able to process and see through the press in some fifteen articles. A large part was doomed to gather dust in drawers, but fortunately would eventually see publication towards the end of his life.

With Grootaers's project shelved indefinitely after his departure from China, Chinese linguistic studies remained by and large confined to the two traditional objectives: reconstructing ancient Chinese phonology, and classifying its "dialects" and demarcating their respective areas of distribution.[20] It is fair to say that after 1948 linguistic geography in China all but ceased to exist.

The study of ancient Chinese phonology with a view to its reconstruction has a venerable pedigree. During the Qing period eminent philologists made laudable efforts to reconstruct the sound system of the language of the Zhou Period (1020-249 BC), which they called "old sounds" (*guyun* 古韵). Their achievements have been compared to those of comparative linguistics in the West, which as it happened were developed at about the same time. However, the Qing philologists, with few exceptions, were not familiar with the method of reconstructing proto-languages from modern living languages. They only referred to dialectal evidence in so far as they were dealing with questions of etymology. They relied on the rhyming dictionary *Qieyun* 切韵 (edited by Lu Fayan 陆法言 in 601 CE) as the source of

phonological data. These data, reflecting the sounds of the fifth and sixth centuries, they called "modern sounds" (*jinyun* 今韵).[21]

On to Japan

After his return to Belgium, Grootaers for a while taught phonetics at the Scheut Seminary in Leuven. However, already in 1950 we see him once again heading to the Far East, this time to Japan, since after the Communist takeover it was impossible for missionaries to get a visa for entry into China. He opted for Japan because in his own words, "he could use Chinese characters there".[22] His first station was the city of Himeji, where he was sent with a view to learning Japanese. In June 1951, judging he had mastered enough of the language, his congregation assigned him to the town of Toyooka in Hyōgo Prefecture, to do pastoral work there. In the fall of 1955 he was posted to Tokyo, where he was to remain attached to the parish of Matsubara until his death in 1999.[23]

In that period the *Kokuritsu kokugo kenkyūjo* 国立国語研究所 (*Institut national de linguistique japonaise, National Institute for Japanese Language and Linguistics*, founded in 1948), had just begun work on the preparation of a Linguistic Atlas of Japan: *Nihon gengo chizu* 日本言語地図 (*Atlas Linguistique du Japon*). The leadership of the project was in the hands of Shibata Takeshi. As early as October 1955, Grootaers accompanied him on a preliminary field study to Izumo, Okayama and Kōchi.[24] The project's aim was to find explanations for two problems on the basis of a limited questionnaire (285 items): a) the formation of the modern Japanese standard language and b) the dialectal differences in Japan and their history. The method was based on personal interviews. Thus 2,400 localities were surveyed, spread throughout the Japanese territory. This yielded a total of 540,000 index cards, which were then processed. The findings were subsequently projected onto distributional maps by the team of Shibata, including Grootaers. The result, a monumental atlas containing 300 maps in 6 volumes, was published between 1966 and 1975.

At about the same time as this nationally sponsored project, Grootaers, together with Shibata and Tokugawa Munemasa, later reinforced by Mase Yoshio, embarked on a private project: the linguistic atlas of the region of

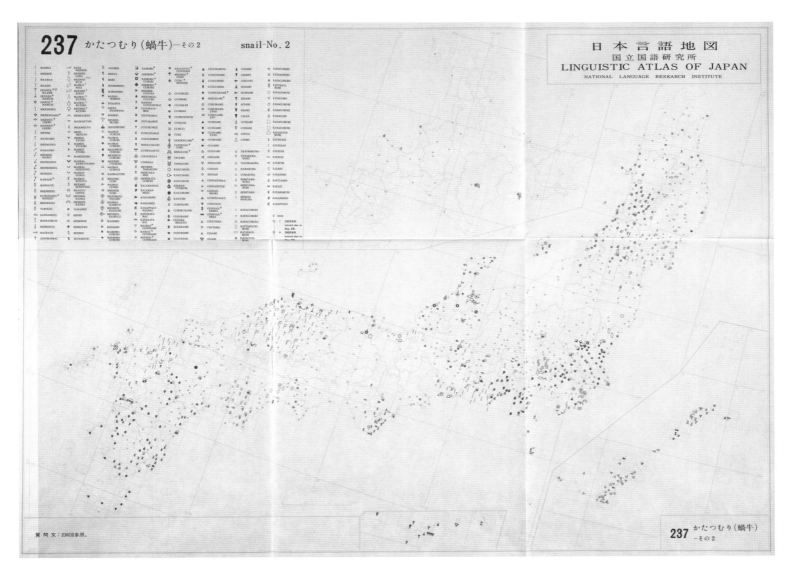

Itoigawa (Niigata Prefecture). It was the first time in the history of Japanese dialect research that a geolinguistic interpretation was applied to the vocabulary of the Japanese language. In total, between 1958 and 1987, the researchers devoted no fewer than 122 articles to the fruits of their research. Their efforts culminated in the publication of *The Linguistic Atlas of Itoigawa Niigata Prefecture Japan*, in three volumes, the first of which saw the light in 1988. The Itoigawa study was innovative in several respects and gave impetus to similar studies on the dialects of Shinpi, Sado, Shimokita and Setonaikai.

Vicariously Reconnecting with China

After his departure from China Grootaers refrained from corresponding with his former students and colleagues for fear that his letters might put his addressees in an awkward position. After the Reform and Liberation Policy of China, he was at last able to resume contact with them.[25] In 1994, he received the visit in Tokyo of his two erstwhile ethnographic collaborators Li Shiyu 李世瑜, then aged seventy-two, and the sixty-five-year-old Wang Fushi 王辅世.[26] Resumption of contact did not mean that Grootaers was in a position to contemplate the possibility of resuming his microscopic field research on Chinese dialects. Fortunately, Japanese scholars in Chinese linguistics centring around Dr. Iwata Rei (Ray), took up the enterprise where Grootaers had left it off, and embarked on a series of projects which embodied much of his erstwhile ideal to carry out a comprehensive survey of all Chinese dialects. Realizing the value of his early works,[27] they translated his papers into Japanese[28] and subsequently also into Chinese.[29]

They also undertook joint research with Chinese colleagues on Chinese dialectology and compiled an

Dialect map showing the various dialectical variants for the standard word *katatsumuri* ("snail"). Map drawn by Willem Grootaers. Map donated by Prof. Inoue Fumio.
Photograph by Digitaal Labo KU Leuven©.
Note the multitude of symbols representing the various variants.

except for a few pioneers such as Yanagita Kunio (1875-1962), Tōjō Misao (1884-1966) and Umegaki Minoru (1901-1976). It was only around the time that Grootaers joined a small group of prominent Japanese dialectologists, including Hirayama Teruo (1909-2005), Fujiwara Yoichi (1909-2007), Kindaichi Haruhiko (1913-2004) and Shibata Takeshi (1918-2007), that linguistic geography was finally taking off in earnest. His know-how and skills in drawing up dialect maps, as well as his personality gave added impetus to the project as it was being launched. Their fieldwork came to first fruition in the compilation and publication of a *Linguistic Atlas of Japan* (1966-1974).[34] Especially noteworthy is his collaboration with the great dialectologist and sociolinguist Shibata Takeshi, his life-long *compagnon de route* in linguistic geography, and translator into Japanese of many of his writings.

Shibata described Grootaers's approach very nicely: "In his linguistic vision, language is one of the human activities. In such vision dialect geography fits perfectly: as the science that studies language in relation to the place where man lives (geography), the community he has built (village, hamlet), human consciousness (introspection and folk etymology) and the tools man makes."[35] Small wonder that his dialectal surveys went hand in hand with ethnographical activities. Indeed, they are closely related.

"To me dialect is not just a lively form of expression," says Grootaers, "Man lives in his natural environment, according to ancestral traditions, sometimes victorious over nature, sometimes defeated by nature, he leads his life. From these experiences man draws a practical, sober wisdom, which is reflected and takes shape in the unique world of the dialects."[36]

In 1976 Shibata reminisced about his collaboration with Grootaers. He succinctly summed up what Grootaers had taught the Japanese: the use of a code to specify the situation when recording the dialectal form; how to draw up a blank map; the system of numbering localities with a unique number at a national level; the use of colour-coded stamps; the system of using stamps of differing shapes; in addition, the use of synthetic maps; the mapping of non-linguistic data; drawing historical deductions from the shapes mapped out.[37]

Not only was he involved in surveys and research, but he also passed on his know-how to the next generation. From October 1957 onwards he for many years taught Japanese linguistics and dialectology at Tokyo

atlas based on the oldest dialect dictionary in the world, *Fangyan* 方言 by Yang Xiong 扬雄 (53 BCE-18 CE).[30] Besides, they published an atlas of Chinese dialects using computational techniques.[31] Its focus on the distribution of individual lexical items clearly set it apart from the general tendency of Chinese dialectology, which was still mostly concerned with phonology or tone. In that sense the atlas is a continuation of the geolinguistic approach advocated and introduced by Grootaers in China in the 1940s.[32] Although the current international trend in geolinguistics is to map, analyse and assess dialect resources by means of computer-based GIS (Geographic Information Systems), researchers such as Iwata still consider the use of the classical method of linguistic geography, as proposed by Grootaers in the 1940s, as valuable and indispensable.[33]

The methodology of linguistic geography was already known in Japan before Grootaers's arrival there. A few publications by the founding fathers of linguistic geography had even been translated into Japanese, most notably the work of Dauzat (Dauzat 1922), translated by Matsubara and Yokoyama (1958). However, although known, it was hardly being applied in actual practice,

Metropolitan University (*Tōkyō Toritsu Daigaku* 東京都
立大学) in the Japanese capital, thus contributing to the
formation of a new generation of Japanese linguists.

Epigraphic and Iconographic Surveys

While doing surveys in the area where he was stationed
in Datong Prefecture, he had arrived at the hypothesis
that it straddled a dialect boundary that went back to the
fourteenth century. To substantiate this claim, he
embarked on the study of the steles in temples, the
history of these temples, the cultic practices in these
temples, as well as their iconography, using a systematic
procedure, similar to the geographical method he had
developed for the dialect surveys. As already noted above
he combined dialectal surveys with ethnographical ones.
In his surveys of cult practices, he managed to cover
three areas, before his final departure from China in
1948. First, the region south-east of Datong comprising
140 villages, 401 shrines (cultic edifices) and 605 cultic
units (units of worship).[38] Second, the area of Wanquan
bounded by the bend of the Great Wall in the north and
the district of Xuanhua in the south, in total 93 villages,
602 cultic edifices and 857 cultic units.[39] Finally, the area
of Xuanhua. Of this latter survey, he managed to publish
the results of about 115 satellite villages of the city, but
not of the city of Xuanhua itself. In these 115
surrounding villages he inventoried 361 cultic edifices
and 637 cultic units.[40] The data he and his team had
collected about the city of Xuanhua itself remained

unpublished for half a century. In the end they were
published in Japanese,[41] and eventually in English under
the title *The Sanctuaries in a North-China City. A
Complete Survey of the Cultic Buildings in the City of
Hsüan-hua (Chahar)*.[42]

In her review of the English edition, Françoise Aubin
writes that Grootaers had "réalisé ici le rêve de tout
ethnographe: publier une enquête exhaustive, menée sur
une situation maintenant irrémédiablement éteinte,
dans un lieu étroitement localisé, en un temps
clairement fixé du passé."[43] The first section of the book
(up to page 121) is an inventory of all the temples and
"cult units" as found by Grootaers and his collaborators
in August 1948 in Xuanhua, 140 km northwest of Beijing
and a few kilometres south-east of Kalgan and the Great
Wall.[44] The inventory was written up in 1949 while
staying in Belgium.

During the month of August 1948, Grootaers and his
two collaborators, Li Shiyu and Wang Fushi, had combed
the city street by street, and recorded with extreme
precision the name of each building, its location, its state
of conservation (some buildings had disappeared, but
were identified on the basis of epigraphic evidence), the
iconography and the accessories that were present, the
deities that were worshipped and the inscriptions that
were found. Although Françoise Aubin praises the
edition by the Institut Belge des Études Chinoises, as of a
flawless clarity,[45] honesty compels me to admit that there
are a number of places where the editorial process was
not flawless.

The book is descriptive and microscopic, which seems
to be the approach that Grootaers always favoured. The
most salient notion he proposes in the book is that of
"cultic unit." He needs to bring this analytical notion into
his description, because one shrine often contains
various distinct cults.

Besides part one and part two, the book also contains
an appendix and a long supplement (pages 124-170),
dedicated to a detailed study of one of the most popular
deities in China, Zhen-wu 真武 (known as Xuan-wu 玄武
until the turn of the first millennium). It is a verbatim
reproduction of the original version the author
published in *Folklore Studies* 11.[46] Aubin calls it the
classic reference on the subject.[47] It deals with the
representations of the deity in the literature until the
fourteenth century, the content of novels devoted to him
after that time, and the references to him in the 169
temples dedicated to him within the three areas explored

Grootaers posing near a stele among Chinese children.
Photograph courtesy of Prof. Inoue Fumio.

by the author.[48] This study is followed by a collection (pages 171-234) of the photographs Grootaers took in 1948 of some of these cultic units, and their images. They are a valuable testimony to a popular art almost completely obliterated since.

Assessment of Grootaers's Scientific Contributions

In Japan, eminent sinologists such as Ogawa Tamaki 小川環樹 had a great esteem for Grootaers's achievements in China. Ogawa, one of his first academic contacts in Japan, with whom he could converse in Chinese, introduced Grootaers to eminent Japanese dialectologists.[49] Iwata Rei, himself an internationally acclaimed specialist of Chinese dialects, collected a number of Grootaers's treatises, and in collaboration with Ms Hashizume Masako 橋爪正子, and with the advice of Grootaers himself, produced a careful and well-annotated Japanese translation, also including a bibliography.[50] The translation consists of four chapters and related documentation on Grootaers's Chinese dialect research. The original articles were published between 1945 and 1958. The reason for publishing them half a century *post factum* was mainly because many of Grootaers's aims and claims had lost nothing of their relevance and urgency for the study of Chinese dialects.

When Grootaers was sent to China in 1939, in spite of the chaos caused by the Sino-Japanese War, some scholars were timidly groping their way towards genuine modernization. In the field of linguistics, scholars and students were beginning to shed the trammels of antiquated philology and ushering in a new era. They were working at the establishment of historical linguistics based on the models of biology and geology.[51] In the West, some scholars had opened up new avenues of research into historical phonology, among them Bernhard Karlgren (1889-1978), who asserted himself as an exponent of this modernization process.[52] He had been trained in the tradition of comparative linguistics. His innovation consisted in taking "modern sounds" (which he called "ancient Chinese") as a reference point for the study of the entire history of the Chinese language. He reconstructed the "old sounds" (his "archaic Chinese") on the basis of Ancient Chinese. In this regard his approach was not much different from that of the Qing Philologists, but where he made a radical departure

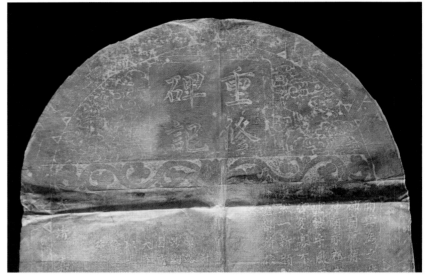

from his Chinese precursors was in his effort to explain the phonetic forms of modern dialects as reflections of Ancient Chinese. In his groundbreaking study, *Études sur la phonologie chinoise* (1915-1926), he reconstructed the sound system of Ancient Chinese, on the basis of his own survey of twenty-four dialects. In other words he adopted the comparative method and applied it to Chinese.[53]

Karlgren studied primarily the static forms of the language and leaned heavily upon the comparative method, while acknowledging the need to use material drawn from the modern dialects. Modern Chinese linguists such as Zhao Yuanren 赵元任, Li Fanggui 李方桂, and Luo Changpei 罗常培 were deeply influenced by him. Grootaers, while recognizing Karlgren's merits, levelled some fundamental criticism at the methodology

Rubbing taken by Willem Grootaers of an inscription on a stele commemorating the reconstruction of the Chinese temple Qiu-an-si.
Photograph by W.F. Vande Walle.

Rubbing taken by Willem Grootaers of an inscription on a stele commemorating the reconstruction of a Chinese temple.
Photograph by W.F. Vande Walle.

adopted by the Swedish sinologist. Especially his long article "La géographie linguistique en Chine: Nécessité d'une nouvelle méthode pour l'étude linguistique du chinois. Première partie: La méthode de la géographie linguistique"[54] stands as one of his most innovative writings. Criticizing Karlgren as Grootaers did was a courageous thing to do then. In this sense he was ahead of his time, but probably because of this, his assertions and the methodology he championed were almost completely ignored in subsequent Chinese dialect research. The acceptance of a certain methodology (which of necessity reflects a certain view on language) is predicated on cultural, social and political conditions prevailing in the receiving country. In recent years dialect studies in China have made remarkable progress, and at long last the objective conditions for examining the specific problematic brought forward by Grootaers are present. Grootaers was one of the first to point out that "The most peculiar aspect in researching Chinese dialects, is the fact that the peculiarity of the Chinese language is overstressed."[55]

The comparative method and comparative linguistics in general are based on the assumption that "sound laws have no exceptions", a theory especially championed by the Neogrammarians. Critics of the Neogrammarians, including Grootaers, take the opposite position, stressing that "each word has its own history" and denying by the same token the existence of the mechanical application of a set of rules. The main theatre for the clash between these rival theories was Europe, but China formed a kind of subsidiary theatre, where the respective protagonists were Karlgren and Grootaers. Grootaers was not the inventor of a new theory or method *per se*, but the transmitter, not unlike the Jesuits who were transmitters of European science, technics and arts in the seventeenth and eighteenth centuries. Still, there is an innovative side to his design. In a country where such great stock is set by the written word, in which the written language and learning enjoy so much prestige, only a westerner could have proposed conducting a survey of Chinese as actually spoken by the mass of the people, that is to say, by the illiterate.

After 1949, under the PRC regime, Chinese dialectology's mission was to promote a standard language, *Putonghua*. Nevertheless, the descriptive study of language lingered on for another decade, as exemplified by the model case survey carried out by the Academy of Social Sciences in Changli County, Hebei

Province (Chinese Academy of Social Sciences, 1960). Thereafter, descriptive studies were only revived in 1979. Once again the Academy's mission was to classify and demarcate the dialects. This led to the publication of the *Language Atlas of China*, published in 1987, comprising eighteen maps of the Chinese (Han) dialects and seventeen maps of the minority languages.[56]

Unlike in former days, recent trends in Chinese dialectology are widely diversified. While the mainstream still seems to emphasize classification and demarcation, new methodological and theoretical trends such as "lexical diffusion" and "comparative dialectal grammar" have gained recognition. In the comparative field, Jerry Norman and his students have long endeavoured to reconstruct the regional proto X dialects by comparing purely colloquial vernaculars in a bottom-up fashion. This would mean, in effect, the abandonment of Karlgren's dogma, which set Ancient Chinese as the reference point in the historical study of Chinese.[57]

Chūgoku no hōgen chirigaku no tame ni 中国の方言地理学のために,[58] was retranslated into Chinese by Professor Shi Rujie 石汝杰 and Iwata Rei 岩田礼 as *Hanyu fangyan dilixue* 汉语方言地理学 ["Contributions to Chinese Dialect Geography"],[59] thus bringing Grootaers's linguistic geography back to its initial field of activity. Two publications explicitly mentioning "dialect geography" in their titles have appeared in recent years: Xiang Mengbing 项梦冰 and Cao Hui 曹晖. *Hanyu fangyan dilixue – Rumen yu Shixian* 汉语方言地理学—入门与实践[58] ["Chinese Dialect Geography: Introduction and Practice"] and Simmons et al. *Jianghuai guanhua yu Wuyu bianjie de fangyan dilixue yanjiu* 江淮官话与吴语边界的方言地理学研究 ["Chinese Dialect Geography: Distinguishing Mandarin and Wu in Their Boundary Region"].[60] Both studies were based on detailed surveys and contained abundant phonetic data, yet they were still mainly concerned with the issues of isoglosses and dialect boundaries.[61]

The *Linguistic Atlas of Chinese Dialects* 汉语方言地图集, edited by Cao Zhiyun 曹志耘, published by Beijing Language and Culture University,[62] is item-based, comprising 205 phonetic maps, 203 lexical maps and 102 morphological and syntactic maps, compiled using a GIS-based computer system. Cao and his colleagues surveyed 930 localities all over the Han Chinese speaking area. The surveyors avoided big cities or county seats, deliberately selecting small villages or towns, and chose as informants mostly males born during the years from

1931 to 1945. These are all survey criteria already codified and applied by Grootaers in his surveys of Chinese dialects.[63]

A Predilection for Time-honoured Conveyances

In his memoirs Grootaers relates with relish the little adventures he had with the conveyances at his disposal. In the pre-communist China of the 1930s and 1940s the customary means of transport in rural areas were the mule, the donkey or the horse. In his parish in Xi-ce-tian, Grootaers, assistant priest, had a mule at his disposal, while the head priest of the parish rode a Mongolian horse. The latter animal, while trustworthy, had a peculiar habit. Besides hay and kaoliang stalks, it required beans as fodder. When on a trip the horse all of a sudden stumbled and fell, this was clear sign that it had not had its indispensable beans and it followed from there that the boy who was in charge of feeding the horse had presumably misappropriated the beans. There was a clear causal link between the boy's act and the horse's behaviour. The mule, nicknamed "whitey" for obvious reasons, on the other hand was happy and content with nothing but kaoliang stalks, but had its own bad habit: it hated the bit and the saddle and was prone to kicking. On his rounds, Grootaers would borrow the trousers of a local fellow to put over the head of the mule, and tie its two front legs together, before putting on the saddle and loading the luggage on its back. Once he had mounted the animal, it became meek and submissive. It had yet another peculiar habit, which was a fear of turning wheels. When it saw the turning wheels of a bicycle or a horse cart, even in the distance, it was frightened out of its wits and threw its rider off in the fields. Hence Grootaers was always on the alert lest a turning wheel might appear on the horizon.

To illustrate the environment where he was living, the following anecdote is telling. North of Grootaers's mission station ran the river Sangganhe 桑乾河. Across the river hung a suspension bridge about thirty metres long, made of logs tied together with leather straps. It was very narrow, merely five centimetres wider than the axle width of a two-wheel horse cart, he claims, and it had no railing. Moreover, it was steeply inclined, its northern end being high and its southern end low. It divided, he declared, all living creatures into two categories: those living north of the bridge and those

living south of it. The people who lived north of the bridge had a hard time when crossing the bridge. As they neared the middle of the bridge, below them they saw a gaping abyss, forty metres deep, which gave many vertigo. When he first travelled to his mission station in early June 1943, he too had to cross the bridge from north to south. Fortunately the villagers taught him a good technique to cross it. One had to keep the reins very short and walk close to the head of the mule. The mule, belonging to the category of the creatures living south of the bridge, had the knack to cross it without difficulty. It used to cross the bridge some ten times a day.

Crossing the bridge with a two wheel horse cart was an art in its own right. The farmers first unloaded the cart, and carried the goods across the bridge to the other side. Next, they drew the mule across the bridge. Then, one of the farmers, taking the place of the mule, would grab the shaft of the cart. At the rear two more farmers held a rope that was attached to the back of the cart. Standing on the rocks at the northern end, the two farmers at the rear, slowly slackened the rope, as the man in front slowly, step by step, descended the slope of the bridge. A little miracle, a feat of great dexterity, Grootaers noted.[65]

Grootaers on Whitey.
Photograph courtesy of Prof. Inoue Fumio.

In the highly motorized Japan of the post-war period there was no room for horses or mules, but Grootaers developed a great fondness for the bicycle, at a time when cycling was far less fashionable than it is now. From 1952 onwards he developed a passion for cycling in the Japanese countryside. This was the beginning of a habit that he would carry on for thirthy-six years until the age of seventy-seven. In his own testimony there is no prefecture he has not crossed on his bicycle and there is a host of places he has visited several times, each year plotting different courses. These bicycle trips gave him the opportunity of seeing and meeting the variety of Japan's landscapes and people. Every year during the summer vacation he would make a major trip of two weeks. In addition he made smaller excursions during the Golden Week, the first week of May. And every Wednesday, his weekly day off, he made short trips. He even gained some public renown in Japan as the "cycling father".

When Ishihara Shintarō 石原慎太郎 became chief of the Environment Agency (*Kankyōchō* 環境庁) he set up a deliberative panel consisting of citizens, and Grootaers was selected as one of its members. Most of the members drove cars, so generally their remarks were made from a motorist's perspective. Grootaers appeared to be the only one on the panel who genuinely represented the viewpoint of the pedestrian and the cyclist.

It was not unusual for him to cover more than 100 kilometres a day on his cycling tours. This required some eight hours of pedalling a day. One day, he made a stop at the church of a small parish north of Hiroshima, hoping to be given a bed and a warm meal. He had hardly slept the night before, and was starving. The caretaker priest happened to be the elderly Johannes Laurès SJ, professor at Sophia University and a well-known specialist of the history of Christianity in Japan. Dr. Laurès, seeing his tired, sun-tanned, sweaty and dusty appearance, assumed that he was a vagrant. Grootaers overheard Laurès making a call in another room to the head church in Hiroshima to ask what he should do with this "vagrant who had just presented himself claiming that he was a priest". Grootaers had to take out his passport and show it to the suspicious Laurès to convince him that he was indeed the person he claimed to be. At last he could enjoy the warm meal he had been longing for.

Willem Grootaers was the eldest of six siblings. His brothers and sisters had a total of twenty-five children

Grootaers with fellow missionaries and children on the suspension bridge.
Photograph courtesy of Prof. Inoue Fumio.

General view of the suspension bridge.
Photograph courtesy of Prof. Inoue Fumio.

Grootaers crouching on the suspension bridge.
Photograph courtesy of Prof. Inoue Fumio.

between them. In addition there was a host of cousins and aunts. All these family members apparently craved for some news from their missionary relative in Japan. Since he could not send letters to all of them, he had decided to send none, until in 1957 one of his brothers suggested making sixty copies of the letters he would send in order to distribute them among all interested relatives. It was agreed that he would send a letter every other month. One day he made a trip from Shimokita Peninsula via Lake Towada to Morioka, from where he took the train back to Tokyo. After his return he took the trouble of writing a report of his adventures during the trip and sent the little travelogue to his family in Belgium. A couple of weeks later, one Belgian lady, whom he did not know but who had presumably read his report, sent him a letter to comfort him. She expressed her sympathy for the suffering he must have endured on the bicycle in the northern part of Japan. Anticipating that before long the American Army would construct a railway in those parts, she assured him that he would not have to suffer on his bicycle much longer.[66]

A Touch of Mischievousness

Everyone who knew him, remembers him as a man who loved humour and was fond of innocent pranks and good stories. His autobiography abounds with amusing anecdotes, which I cannot repeat here, but I will mention one just to give a taste of his keen observation. In 1984, on the *Bunka no hi* ("Culture Day", 3 November), Grootaers was awarded the Order of the Sacred Treasure, 3rd Class. On that day he felt that he had finally become a real Japanese, a wish he had expressed many years before in a book titled *Watashi wa Nihonjin ni naritai* ("I want to become a Japanese"). On that day all recipients of a decoration gathered in the Ministry of Foreign Affairs to receive it from the hands of Foreign minister Abe Shintarō 安倍晋太郎. They had to present themselves thirty minutes before the ceremony, so as to have time to rehearse the ceremony. The recipients and their spouses were placed in a neat row. Grootaers being a priest had no spouse. Instead he proposed his younger brother, then Head Librarian of the Royal Library of Belgium, who had come all the way to Japan to attend the ceremony. However, this replacement was not allowed by the officials in charge of the ceremony, since his brother did not qualify as spouse. After the awarding ceremony,

champagne was offered to all those present. When the champagne had been poured out, the minister's secretary unobtrusively replaced his boss's champagne glass with a glass filled with water. The minister then proposed a toast lifting his water-filled glass. From the Ministry a bus took him and his fellow recipients to the Imperial Palace, where they were lined up in three rows. Here too his younger brother was excluded from joining the party, and had to wait in the bus. One of the other recipients was a Japanese lady, who had been teaching calligraphy in San Francisco for thirty years. She was accompanied by her son, who had American nationality, but looking like an ordinary Japanese as he did, he had no difficulty joining the party.

After the audience with the Emperor the party returned to the Foreign Ministry, where each of the award recipients was given a present from the Emperor. When a final souvenir photograph had to be taken, his brother was at last allowed to stand next to him. After the ceremony, on the way home, he opened the wrapping of the imperial present. Inside he found a package of fifty cigarettes decorated with the imperial crest, and red and white coloured steamed bean-jam buns. On a bench in the station they downed the imperial buns. Grootaers liked to tell this anecdote to his Japanese friends, explaining that in his home, unlike most Japanese, he had no Shinto altar to which he could have offered the buns, and so he had enjoyed them together with his brother in the station. He concludes this anecdote with typical irony: "when I tell this to my Japanese friends they make a funny face and burst out in laughter. Why would that be?"

Photograph of the Grootaers family taken inside their home.
Photograph taken around 1949 after his expulsion from China.
Photograph courtesy of Prof. Inoue Fumio.

In 1988 Grootaers received a decoration from the Belgian Government (Knight in the Order of Leopold). In his autobiography the ever-playful Father remarked that the box which contained the Belgian decoration was a small, rather unbecoming one, with an ill-fitting lid, a stark contrast with the beautiful lacquer box, featuring old-style calligraphy, containing his Japanese decoration.[67]

Legacy

Shibata Takeshi, his friend and fellow dialectologist, once said of Grootaers that he had three home countries. One was Belgium where he was born and raised, one was Japan where he worked for more than 40 years, and another was China. He lived in China for only a decade, but in that limited span of time he managed to publish some 10 treatises on dialect geography. Although his work in Japan had seen many brilliant results, his treatises on Chinese dialect geography since 1943

exerted no influence whatsoever on the Chinese academic world. Reasons for this lack of influence were the fact that China was war-torn, that he stayed only a decade, and, as is emphasized in his book *Chūgoku no hōgen chirigaku no tame ni*,[68] the "unfortunate" tradition of Chinese dialectology founded by Karlgren.

Living in Japan, and with time passing, he had resigned himself to the fact that his Chinese dialect research had become something of the past. However, his work was picked up by Japanese scholars of Chinese linguistics, and translated in its entirety by Iwata Rei. This translation gave a new impetus to Chinese linguists, and was eventually translated into Chinese. Iwata Rei and his collaborators took the relay of Grootaers in the endeavour to propagate dialect geography in China. Thus Grootaers's dream was coming full circle after all, in spite of his earlier despondency and resignation. While in Japan he teamed up with scholars who were fellow-dialectologists and therefore his colleagues and fellow travellers rather than disciples or students, in China he was incontestably a pioneer of the discipline, training young Chinese in its theories and methodologies. It is therefore ironic that his efforts bore less fruit in China than they did in Japan, where he found an academic structure already in place for the realization of the projects he had had in mind for China.

In 1981 Grootaers was awarded an honorary doctorate from the Catholic University of Leuven, in recognition of his contributions to linguistics and ethnography. The Japanese emperor conferred on him the Order of the Sacred Treasure, 3rd Class (1984) and the Belgian king made him a Knight in the Order of Leopold (1988). Contemporary studies on languages, religions and cultures in China abound with references to Grootaers's work. He was an eminent representative of a generation of Flemish Scheutists that made seminal contributions to the study of Chinese and Japanese culture: he ranks with Fathers Joseph Mullie, Desmedt, Antoine Mostaert, Schramm, Dries Van Coillie, and others, as missionaries whose "intellectual apostolate" left a deep and lasting imprint. This was a new tendency in the institutional culture of the congregation.

Father Legrand was one of the proponents of this approach, which had had a precursor in the Jesuit missionary method in the seventeenth and eighteenth centuries. Father Legrand published his ideas in a long essay "Apostolat intellectuel en Chine" in the *Collectanea Commissionis Synodalis*.[69] Some priests of an intellectual

---

Official photograph of Willem and his younger brother Jan, taken on the occasion of his being awarded the Order of the Sacred Treasure in 1984.
Photograph courtesy of Prof. Inoue Fumio.

inclination championed this "ideology" as a means of proselytizing. Although not all in the congregation were favourable to the idea, intellectual argument was indispensable if they wanted to reach the intellectual elite. Moreover, as Father Dries Van Coillie remarked in his report, already quoted above, "thanks to their intellectual actions the Protestants have many prominent figures in China's administration." In the light of the competition with the Protestant mission, intellectual apostolate had become a must. "If only we Catholics do not arrive late," Van Coillie sighed.[70] With a view to consolidating this ideology, proposals for the establishment of a Verbiest Academy were formulated and submitted to the general chapter of the congregation. This academy was subsequently founded in "The Half Acre Garden", Pan-Mou Yüan 半亩园, a former residence of a Manchu prince in Beijing. Grootaers contributed to the establishment of linguistic geography in two ways: directly through his personal influence and indirectly through influential collaborators and colleagues. Prof. Inoue Fumio, one of his former students, has noted that this is not unlike the method missionaries in China and Japan used in disseminating Christianity.[71] In a letter dated 30 June 2014, he also wrote: "As I have written before the National Institute of Japanese Language and Linguistics is eager to disseminate its research results worldwide. The dedication of Dr. W. Grootaers was great in those days, and the cost-performance of his contribution to the dissemination of research results was also excellent because the institute did not have to pay any amount to invite this great scholar to Japan. Dr. W. Grootaers should be re-evaluated from this new point of view." Tōjō Misao, the founder of modern dialectology in Japan, has described Grootaers as the "Chamberlain of the Shōwa era." The British scholar Basil H. Chamberlain (1850-1935) was the first professor of linguistics at the University of Tokyo, appointed to the position in 1886. Even allowing for the rhetorical flourish of this statement, it does indicate that Grootaers has made a noteworthy contribution to the scientific study of Japanese.

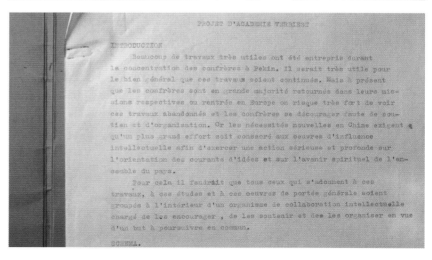

Grootaers and fellow linguists. Grootaers is sitting in the middle, flanked by Shibata Takeshi and his wife. Standing behind them are a few other collaborators from the National Institute for Japanese Language and Linguistics, including Tokugawa Munemasa (first from left) and Mase Yoshio (second from left).
Photograph courtesy of Prof. Inoue Fumio.

Grootaers sitting in his study in Matsubara, Tokyo, in 1995.
Photograph courtesy of Prof. Inoue Fumio.

Initial paragraph of a draft by Father Legrand making a case for the establishment of a Verbiest Academy in Peking as a means of strengthening intellectual apostolate.
Documentatie- en Onderzoekscentrum voor Religie, Cultuur en Samenleving KADOC, Schodts family archive. 1947-1999. Photograph by W.F. Vande Walle.

REFERENCES

A. PUBLICATIONS BY WILLEM A. GROOTAERS

NOTE: this list includes all relevant publications authored or co-authored by W. Grootaers.

Grootaers 1937
"De rode en de zwarte aalbes en hun semantisch verband." *Handelingen van de Koninklijke Commissie voor Toponymie en Dialectologie* (Brussel) 11, pp. 241-291. 3 maps.

Grootaers 1938
"Construction d'un appareil pour la mesure de la hauteur musicale." *Leuvensche Bijdragen* 30:3/4, pp. 125-139. 4 figs.

Grootaers and Van Coillie 1939
and Dries Van Coillie. *Proeve eener bibliographie van de missionarissen van Scheut (Congregatio Immaculati Cordis Mariæ)*. Brussel: Priestermissiebond, 1939.

Grootaers 1941a
"De Oblationibus confucio factis. Responsa ad questiones." *Tatung* 3:4, pp. 254-269.

Grootaers 1941b
Aanvullingen en verbeteringen op de proeve eener bibliographie van de Missionarissen van Scheut. Peking: Imprimerie des Lazaristes.

Grootaers 1943
"La géographie linguistique en Chine, Nécessité d'une nouvelle méthode pour l'étude linguistique du chinois, Première Partie: La méthode de la géographie linguistique." *Monumenta Serica* 8 (1943), pp. 103-166. 4 maps, 2 figs.

Grootaers 1944a
"Textes et traduction des stèles du Nan-t'ang." *Le Bulletin catholique de Pékin* 31:376, pp. 586-599. 1 fig.

Grootaers and Serruys 1944b
Kort overzicht der Geschiedenis van het Chineesche Keizerrijk door de P.P. Grootaers – P. Serruys C.I.C.M. 1944 – Peking. Volgens handschrift ex Typis Taip'ingts'ang, Peking.

Grootaers 1945a
Fragments Bouddhiques. Première Série: Apologétique et dévotion. Pékin: Imprimerie des Lazaristes 8+127 pp.

Grootaers 1945b
"La géographie linguistique en Chine, Nécessité d'une nouvelle méthode pour l'étude linguistique du chinois, Seconde Partie: Une frontière dialectale dans le Nord-est du Chansi." *Monumenta Serica* 10 (1945), pp. 389-426. 4 maps, 4 figs.

Grootaers 1945c
"Les temples villageois de la région au sud-est de Ta-t'ong (Chansi Nord): Leurs inscriptions et leur histoire." *Folklore Studies* 4 (Catholic University of Peking), pp. 161- 212. 1 map, 8 figs.

Grootaers 1945d
"Une stèle chinoise de l'époque mongole au sud-est de Ta-t'ong (Chansi-Nord)." *Monumenta Serica* 10, pp. 91-116. 1 map, 5 figs.

Grootaers 1946a
"Dialectes chinois et alphabétisation: À propos de la Romanisation inter-dialectique." *Bulletin de l'Université l'Aurore* 3:7/2 (Shanghai), pp. 207-235.

Grootaers 1946b
"Differences phonétiques dans les dialectes chinois: Un exemple d'évolution linguistique locale dans les parlers de Ta-t'ong (Chansi-Nord)." *Monumenta Serica* 11 (Peiping: Catholic University Press), pp. 207-232. 2 maps.

Grootaers 1946c
Programma voor de studies van het Chineesch in de Congregatie van Scheut. Peking.

Grootaers 1946d
Questionnaire for the Exploration of Village Temples, Questionnaire pour une enquête sur les temples villageois. Peiping: Ethnological Museum of the Catholic University. 8 pp.

Grootaers 嵗賀登 1946e
"Une société secrète moderne I-Koan-Tao: Bibliographie annotée." *Folklore Studies* 5 (1 January 1946), pp. 316-352. Peking: Catholic University of Peking.

Grootaers 1947a
"Catholic University Expedition to Wan-ch'üan (South Chahar): Preliminary Report." *Monumenta Serica* 12 (Peiping: Catholic university), pp. 236-242. 1 map.

Grootaers 1947b
and Zhōu Diànfú 周殿福.*Vier-jarige cursus in de geschreven nationale taal*. Peking-Brussel, 1947-1950, Deel I, 135 pp.; Deel II, 160 pp.

Grootaers 1948a
"La méthode géographique en linguistique et en folklore." *Bulletin de l'Université l'Aurore* 5 (Shanghai), pp. 221-233. 4 maps.

Grootaers 1948b
"Problems of a Linguistic Atlas of China". *Leuvense bijdragen* 38, pp. 52-72. 1 map, 1 fig.

Grootaers 1948c
and Lǐ Shìyú 李世瑜, and Zhāng Jìwén 張冀文. "Temples and History of Wan-ch'üan (Chahar): The Geographical Method Applied to Folklore." *Monumenta Serica* (Peiping Catholic University) 13:1, pp. 209-316. 8 maps, 20 photographs.

Grootaers 1948d
"The Hutu God of Wan-ch'üan (Chahar): A Problem of Method in Folklore." *Studia Serica* 7 (Ch'engtu / Peiping Catholic University), pp. 41-53. 1 map.

Grootaers 1948e
Běipíng nántáng liǎng bēi zhī yìwén 北平南堂兩碑之譯文. Vol. 3, 5th ed. Beijing: *Shàngzhì biānyìguǎnkān* 上智編訳館刊, pp. 189-191.

Grootaers 1948f
trans. Chén Dìngmín 陳定民. "Zhōngguó yǔyán xué jí mínzú xué zhī dìlǐ de yánjiū"中國語言學及民族學之地理的研究. *Yànjīng xuébào* 燕京学報 35, pp. 1-27. 6 maps.

Grootaers 1948g
"Catholic University Expedition to Hsüanhua (South Chahar) 'Preliminary Report'." *Folklore Studies* 7 (1 January 1948), pp. 135–138.

Grootaers 1949a
Analyse du communisme chinois. Sl: sn.

Grootaers 1949b
"Twintig jaar Chinese linguistiek." In *Handelingen van het 18e Vlaamse Filologencongres*, 19-21 april 1949, pp. 67-72. Leuven, 1949.

Grootaers 1949c
trans. Féng Zànzhāng 馮贊璋. "Zhōngguó mínjiān chuántǒng zōngjiào zhī yánjiū" 中國民間傳統宗教之研究. *Wénzǎo yuèkān* 文藻月刊 2:1/2, pp. 18-20.

Grootaers in 1998.
Photograph courtesy of Prof. Inoue Fumio.

Grootaers 1949d
"Pejelidikan Geografi Bahasa di Tiongkok." *Pembina Bahasa Indonesia* (Djakarta) II, pp. 129-136.

Grootaers 1950a
La Chine communiste connaîtra-t-elle des déviations Titistes? Sl: Casterman.

Grootaers 1950b
"Les deux stèles de l'église du Nan-t'ang à Pékin." *Neue Zeitschrift für Missionswissenschaft* (Seminar Schöneck/Beckenried, Schweiz) 6:4, pp. 246-255.

Grootaers 1950c
"Une courte exploration linguistique dans le Chahar (Chine du Nord), avec un projet de questionnaire dialectal." *Bulletin de la Société Linguistique de Paris* (Paris: Klincksieck) 46:1, pp. 123-143. 3 maps.

Grootaers 1951a
"Une séance de spiritisme dans une religion secrète à Pékin en 1948." *Mélanges chinois et bouddhiques* 9 (Bruxelles: Sainte-Catherine), pp. 92-98. 6 photographs.

Grootaers 1951b
"Further Materials on the Hutu god of Chahar." *Studia Serica* 10 (Ch'engtu). 1 map, 5 photographs.

Grootaers et al. 1951c
and Lǐ Shìyú 李世瑜, and Wáng Fǔshì 王輔世. "Rural Temples around Hsüan-Hua (South Chahar), Their Iconography and Their History." *Folklore Studies* 10:1 (1 January 1951), pp. 1–116. 72 photographs, 8 maps.

Grootaers 1952a
"Chinese Dialectology (1948-1951): On non-Chinese Languages of China." *Orbis* (Louvain: Centre international de dialectologie générale) 1:1, pp. 210-218.

Grootaers 1952b
"Language Behavior of an Individual during One Day, Japan." *Orbis* (Louvain: Centre international de dialectologie générale) 1:1, pp. 126-129.

Grootaers 1952c
"Notes on Japanese Dialectology: 1949-1951." *Orbis* (Louvain: Centre international de dialectologie générale) 1:2, pp. 517-531.

Grootaers 1952d
"Quelques remarques concernant le langage des femmes; Différences entre langage masculin et féminin; Quelques tabous linguistiques." *Orbis* (Louvain: Centre international de dialectologie générale) 1:1, pp. 82-86.

Grootaers 1952e
"The Hagiography of the Chinese God Chen-Wu: The Transmission of Rural Traditions in Chahar." *Folklore Studies* 11:2 (Tokyo, 1 January 1952), pp. 139-181. 1 map, 7 photographs.

Grootaers 1952f
"Tōjō Misao's Influence on Japanese Dialectology." *Orbis* (Louvain: Centre international de dialectologie générale) 1:2, pp. 566-569. 1 photograph.

Grootaers 1952g
"Shina no nōson ni okeru bunka shoyōso no kankei no ichirei" 支那の農村に於ける文化諸要素の関係の一例. *Natura et Cultura / Shizenshi gakkai* 自然史学会 (Kyoto 京都) 2, pp. 59-69. 2 figs., 1 map.

Grootaers 1953a
"Initial 'pə' in a Shansi Dialect: A Problem of Grammar." *T'oung-Pao* 42:1/2 (Leiden), pp. 36-39.

Grootaers 1953b
"Language Study in China (1951-1952)." *Orbis* (Louvain: Centre international de dialectologie générale) 2:1, pp. 165-175.

Grootaers (under the pen name of Jacques Nédon) 1953c
"Une amitié chinoise." *La revue nouvelle* 17:2, pp. 150-155; 17:3, pp. 240-250; 17:4, pp. 390-397; 17:5, pp. 479-490; 17:6, pp. 599-606 (Bruxelles).

Grootaers 1953d
trans. Nomoto Kikuo 野元菊雄 and Shibata Takeshi 柴田武. "Gaikokujin no mita Nihongo" 外国人の見た日本語. *Gengo seikatsu* 言語生活 21:6, pp. 34-42.

Grootaers 1954a
Chao Yüan-jen (Yuen Ren Chao), China's leading dialectologist. Louvain: Centre international de dialectologie générale.

Grootaers 1955
trans. Katayama Seiichi 片山清一. "Nihongo wa muzukashii deshō ka" 日本語はむずかしいでしょうか. *Kokugoka Chūgaku kyōiku gijutsu* 国語科・中学教育技術 4:12 (1955), pp. 36-42. 1 photograph.

Grootaers 1956a
Japon: Bibliothèque du son, société de radiodiffusion japonaise, Tokyo (1951). Louvain: Commission d'enquête linguistique.

Grootaers 1956b
"Phonogram Archives in China." *Instituts de Phonétique* (Louvain), pp. 97-98. 1 map.

Grootaers 1956c
trans. Shibata Takeshi 柴田武. "Berugījin no gengo seikatsu" ベルギー人の言語生活. *Gengo seikatsu* 言語生活 56:5, pp. 54-63. 1 map.

Grootaers 1956d
trans. Shibata Takeshi 柴田武. "Nihongo no chōsho to tansho" 日本語の長所と短所. In *Sekai no kotoba, Nihon no kotoba* 世界のことば、日本のことば, pp. 267-277 Tokyo: Sōgensha 創元社.

Grootaers 1957a
Linguistic Geography of the Hsüan-hua Region (Chahar Province). Taibei: Academia Sinica, 1957; repr. from *The Bulletin of the Institute of History and Philology, Academia Sinica* 29, Studies presented to Yuen Ren Chao on his sixty-fifth birthday. Taipei, Taiwan, China, November 1957.

Grootaers 1957b
"Japanese Linguistic Atlas: End of the Preliminary Work." *Orbis* (Louvain: Centre international de dialectologie générale) 6:1, pp. 68-85. 1 map, 1 photograph.

Grootaers 1957c
trans. Ogawa Tamaki 小川環樹. "Chūgokugo no hōgen" 中国語の方言. In *Chūgoku gogaku jiten* 中国語学辞典, vol. 1, pp. 64-73. Kōnan shoin 江南書院.

Grootaers 1957d
trans. Ogawa Tamaki 小川環樹. "Yōroppa no Chūgokugo kenkyū" ヨーロッパの中国語研究. In *Chūgoku gogaku jiten* 中国語学辞典, vol. 3, pp. 20-27 Kōnan shoin 江南書院.

Grootaers 1957e
and Hashimoto Mantarō 橋本萬太郎. "Gengogaku no jutsugo taishōhyō" 言語学の述語対照表. In *Chūgoku gogaku jiten* 中国語学辞典, vol. 7, pp. 27-30. Kōnan shoin 江南書院.

Grootaers 1957f
"Les débuts de la géographie linguistique au Japon." *Orbis* (Louvain: Centre international de dialectologie générale) 6:2, pp. 342-352. 1 photograph, 1 map.

Grootaers 1957g
"Fujiwara Yo'ichi, a Dialect-geographical Study of the Japanese Dialects." *Orbis* (Louvain: Centre international de dialectologie générale) 6:2, pp. 534-540. 2 maps.

Grootaers 1958a
Linguistic Geography of the 宣化 *Hsuan-Hua Region* (蔡哈爾 *Chahar Province*). Studies Presented to Yuan Ren Chao 中央研究院歷史語言研究所集刊、29 上 (Taipei, Taiwan), pp. 59-86. 10 maps.

Grootaers 1958b
"H. Frei-shi no pə no bunseki" H. Frei 氏のpəの分析. *Chūgoku gogaku* 中国語学 75:3-8, p. 16.

Grootaers 1958c
"Report on the Linguistic Institutes of China, until 1957." *Orbis* (Louvain: Centre international de dialectologie générale) 7:1, pp. 205-211.

Grootaers and Ogawa 1958d
and Ogawa Tamaki 小川環樹. "Chūgokugo no hōgen; Yōroppa no Chūgokugo kenkyū" 中国語の方言；ヨーロッパの中国語研究. In *Chūgoku gogaku jiten* 中国語学 辞典. Kōnan shoin 江南書院, pp. 64-73; 312-319. [Chinese translation：王立達『漢語研究小史』北京・商務印書館、1959, 124-131, 欧州の漢語研究 （pp. 318-319 were deleted "on the ground that the viewpoint was incorrect and in some cases even reality was distorted"）.

Grootaers 1958e
"A Dialect-Geographical Study of the Japanese Accents in Chiba Prefecture." *Monumenta Nipponica* 14:3/4 (1 October 1958), pp. 247–276. 25 maps.

Grootaers 1958f
Premier répertoire des instituts et sociétés linguistiques de la Chine et du Japon. Leuven, pp. 85-86; 173-179. 1 photograph.

Grootaers 1958g
"Two New Approaches in the Field of Japanese Dialectology." *International Congress of Orientalists in Japan* 3, pp. 71-74.

Grootaers 1958h
"Etymology through Maps: A Dialect Geographical Study of the Names of the Sty in Itoigawa (Niigata Prefecture)." *Folklore Studies* (Tokyo) 17, pp. 187-198, 2 maps.

Grootaers 1959a
"Origin and Nature of the Subjective Boundaries of Dialects." *Orbis* (Louvain: Centre international de dialectologie générale) 8 (1959), pp. 355-384.

Grootaers 1959b
"Six Hundred Mistranslations in *The Nun's Story.*" *Missionary Bulletin* (Tokyo) 4, pp. 173-176.

Grootaers 1959c
trans. Shibata Takeshi 柴田武. "*Chiba-ken akusento no gengo chirigakuteki kenkyū*" 千葉県アクセントの言語地理学的研究. *Kokugogaku* 国語学 37, pp. 1-34. 25 maps.

Grootaers 1959d
"Graham Greene's Translations in Japanese." *Saito's Commemorative Volume.* Fukui University, pp. 123-134.

Grootaers 1959e

"Origin and Nature of the Subjective Boundaries of Dialects." *Orbis* (Louvain: Centre international de dialectologie générale) 8:2, pp. 355-384. 8 maps.

Grootaers 1959f

and J.L. Van Hecken. "The Half Acre Garden, Pan-Mou Yüän" 半畝園. *Monumenta Serica* (Nagoya) 18, pp. 360-387. 16 photographs, 1 map.

Grootaers 1961

Hommage à la mémoire de Sever Pop. Gembloux: Duculot.

Grootaers 1962a

trans. Tokugawa Munemasa 德川宗賢. "Hōgen kukaku-ron" 方言区画論. *Kokubungaku kaishaku to kanshō* 国文学・解釈と鑑賞 27:2, pp. 16-24.

Grootaers 1962b

trans. Shibata Takeshi 柴田武. "Hōgen chizu no kakikata to yomikata" 方言地図の書き方と読み方. In *Hōgengaku gaisetsu* 方言学概説, pp. 344-373. Musashino Shoin 武蔵野書院. 4 maps.

Grootaers 1963

"Les premiers pas à la recherche des unités dialectales." *Orbis* (Louvain: Centre international de dialectologie générale) 12:2, pp. 361-380. 8 maps.

Grootaers 1964a

trans. editorial board. "Gaikokujin no mita Nihon no kokugomondai" 外国人の見た日本の国語問題. *Gengo seikatsu* 言語生活 149:2, pp. 57-62.

Grootaers 1964b

trans. Shibata Takeshi 柴田武. *Watashi wa Nihonjin ni naritai.* Tokyo: Chikuma Shobō 筑摩書房. 238 pp. [2nd ed., 1966; 3rd ed. 1969].

Grootaers 1964c

"Une nouvelle méthode pour déterminer la chronologie des aires dialectales." *Actes du Premier Congrès de Dialectologie*, pp. 60-64. 3 maps.

Grootaers 1964d

trans. Shibata Takeshi 柴田武. "Kagyū-kō no furusato" 蝸牛考のふるさと. *Yanagita Kunio-shū geppō* 柳田国男集月報 34:10, pp. 267-268.

Grootaers 1964e

trans. Shibata Takeshi 柴田武. "Hōgen kukaku e no shuppatsu. Itoigawa no hōgen chirigaku chōsa o riyō shite" 方言区画への出発・糸魚川の方言地理学調査を利用して. In *Nihon hōgen kukaku* 日本方言区画. Tōkyōdō 東京堂.

Grootaers 1964f

"In Memoriam K. Kagami, 1909-1963." *Orbis* (Louvain: Centre international de dialectologie générale) 13:1, pp. 337-342. 2 maps.

Grootaers 1964g

"La discussion autour des frontières dialectales subjectives." *Orbis* (Louvain: Centre international de dialectologie générale) 13:2, pp. 380-398. 2 maps.

Grootaers 1964h

trans. Shibata Takeshi 柴田武. "Itoigawa chihō ni okeru hyōjungo to onaji goi taikei no keisei ni tsuite." 糸魚川地方における標準語と同じ語彙体系の形成について. *Kokugogaku* 国語学 59:12, pp. 1-10. 3 maps.

Grootaers 1964i

trans. Shibata Takeshi 柴田武. "Kōzō gengo chirigaku no shin hōhō" 構造言語地理学の新方法. *Hiroshima hōgen kenkyū nenpō* 広島方言研究年報 7, pp. 45-56. 5 maps.

Grootaers 1965a

"Yōroppa no gengo sensō" ヨーロッパの言語戦争. *Gengo seikatsu* 言語生活 161:2, pp. 28-33. 1 map.

Grootaers 1965b

trans. Ōkubo Tadatoshi 大久保忠利. "Mogura no shippo – Gengochirigaku no ikkōyō" モグラのしっぽ―言語地理学の一効用. *Nihongo* 日本語 4, pp. 21-25. 3 maps.

Grootaers et al. 1966-75

with Uemura Yukio 上村幸雄, Nomoto Kikuo 野元菊雄, Tokugawa Munemasa 德川宗賢, Katō Masanobu 加藤正信, Hondō Hiroshi 本堂寛, Satō Ryōichi 佐藤亮一, and Takada Makoto 高田誠. *Nihon gengo chizu* 日本言語地図, vols. 1-6. Tokyo: Kokuritsu Kokugo Kenkyūjo 国立国語研究所. Maps 1-300. Kaisetsusho 解説書 1-6.

Grootaers 1966b

"Rekishi to chiri no kōsaten ni aru hōgen. Gengogaku no atarashii kanten" 歴史と地理の交差点にある方言。言語学の新しい観点. *Nihongo* 日本語 6, pp. 2-10. 3 maps.

Grootaers 1966c

"Gaijin kara mita Nihongo no keigo" 外人から見た日本語の敬語. *Kokubungaku* 国文学 11:8, pp. 167-172.

Grootaers 1966d

"Kagyū-kō saikō – Chūkan hōkoku" 蝸牛考再考―中間報告. *Nihon hōgen kenkyūkai happyō genkōshū* 日本方言研究会発表原稿集 34, pp. 50-59.

Grootaers 1966e

trans. Mita Minoru 美田稔. "L'atlas du Centre japonais, et un problème lexical." *Orbis* (Louvain: Centre international de dialectologie générale) 15:2, pp. 397-403. 4 maps.

Grootaers and Shibata 1967a

with Shibata Takeshi 柴田武. *Goyaku: hon'yaku bunkaron. Mistranslations: How One Culture Is Presented to Another.* 5th pr. Tokyo: Sanseidō, 1967.

Grootaers 1967b

trans. Shibata Takeshi 柴田武. "Goyaku sareta Sarutoru to Maruseru: Gengo ni okeru yosoku dekiru koto to yobunna mono" 誤訳されたサルトルとマルセル：言語における予測できることと余分なもの. *Sekai* 世界 254, pp. 238-248.

Grootaers 1967c

interviewed by Ozaki Moriteru 尾崎盛光. "Nihongo no mirai to gaikokugo" 日本語の未来と外国語. *Kotoba no uchū* ことばの宇宙 2:4, pp. 52-60.

Grootaers 1967d

trans. Tokugawa Munemasa 德川宗賢. "Fushigina hōgen chizu: Nihon gengo chizu no igi" 不思議な方言地図：日本言語地図の意義. *Gengo seikatsu* 言語生活 187, pp. 66-71. 3 maps.

Grootaers 1967e

"Japanese Dialectology." In *Current Trends in Linguistics.* The Hague: Mouton. Vol. 2, pp. 585-607.

Grootaers 1967f

trans. Shibata Takeshi 柴田武. *Gogaku hon'yaku bunkaron* 誤訳・ほんやく文化論. Sanseidō 三省堂, 1st ed., 210 pp. [14th ed., 1974].

Grootaers 1968a

"Nihon bungaku wa okurete iru ka" 日本文学は遅れているか. *Mita bungaku* 三田文学 4, pp. 72-77

Grootaers 1968b

"Interprétation des isoglosses au moyen de la connaissance active et passive." Verhandlungen des *Zweiten Internationales Dialektologenkongress, 1965.* Marburg, pp. 283-287. 4 maps.

Grootaers 1969a

trans. Hashimoto Mantarō 橋本萬太郎. "Hōgen chizu" 方言地図; "Hōgen chōsa" 方言調査. In *Chūgoku gogaku Shinjiten* 中国語学新辞典, pp. 180-183. Kōseikan 光生館. 2 maps.

Grootaers 1969b

"Gilliéron Redivivus: Thaumaturgie Linguistique au Japon." *Cahiers Ferdinand de Saussure* 25:1 (January 1969), pp. 133–142. 5 maps.

Grootaers 1969c

"Watashi to hōgen chirigaku" 私と方言地理学. *Shinshū Daigaku gakuseibu gakujutsu bunka kōenshū* 信州大学、学生部学術文化講演集 4, pp. 1-6. 2 maps.

Grootaers 1969d

"Saikin no Ō-Bei ni okeru hōgen kenkyū" 最近の欧米における方言研究. *Kokubungaku kaishaku to kanshō* 国文学・解釈と鑑賞 34:18 (July 1969 extra issue), pp. 101-109.

Grootaers 1969e

trans. Hashimoto Mantarō 橋本萬太郎. "Hōgen chizu; hōgen chōsa" 方言地図；方言調査. In *Chūgoku gogaku shinjiten* 中国語学新辞典, pp. 180-183; 311-315. Tokyo: Kōseikan 光生館.

Grootaers 1970a

with Tokugawa Munemasa 德川宗賢. "Gengo chirigaku ni okeru kaishaku towa nani ka" 言語地理学における解釈とは何か. *Nihon hōgen kenkyūkai kenkyū happyō genkōshū* 日本方言研究会研究発表原稿集 7, pp. 43-61. 12 maps.

Grootaers 1970b

trans. Tokugawa Munemasa 德川宗賢. "Chōkanteki kōiki gengo chizu to bisai gengo chizu" 鳥瞰的広域言語地図と微細言語地図. *Hōgen kenkyū no mondaiten* 方言研究の問題点. Meiji Shoin 明治書院, pp. 683-707 6 maps.

Grootaers 1970b

"Nouvelles méthodes et nouveaux problèmes. Le nouvel atlas linguistique du Japon." *Xme Congrès international des linguistes, Bucharest 1967*, vol. 2, pp. 113-118. 2 maps.

Grootaers 1971a

trans. Yoshida Toyokazu 吉田豊一. "Kahoku no Senka / Banzen ryōken ni okeru HUTU shinkō" 華北の宣化・万全両県におけるＨＵＴＵ信仰. *Dōkyō kenkyū* 道教研究 4, pp. 195-224. 2 maps, 9 photographs.

Grootaers 1971b – 1974

trans. with Shibata Takeshi 柴田武. "G. Haruto gengo chirigaku no tame ni. Sono gyōseki, hōhō, tenbō" Ｇ・ハルト言語地理学のためにその業績・方法・展望. *Nihon hōgen kenkyūkai happyō genkōshū* 日本方言研究会発表原稿集. No. 13 (1)-(29), 9 maps; no. 14, (30)-(39), 3 maps; no. 15, (40)-(63), 3 maps; no. 16, (64)-(80), 2 maps; no. 17 (81)-(95), 2 maps; no. 18, (96)-(112), 1 map; no. 19, (113)-(118).

Grootaers 1973a

"The Sixty-four Wutao-temples of Hsüan-hua City." *Fujen Studies* (Taipei, Taiwan), pp. 29-38. 1 map, 2 photographs.

Grootaers 1973b

trans. Shibata Takeshi 柴田武. "Hōgen: Berugī to Nihon no baai" 方言―ベルギーと日本の場合. *Hōsō bunka* 放送文化.

Grootaers 1973c

trans. Mita Minoru 美田稔. "Gengo ni yoru sokubaku, gengo ni yoru kaihō" 言語による束縛、言語による解放. *Hiroba* ひろば (Spring issue), pp. 57-61.

Grootaers 1973d
trans. Tokugawa Munemasa 德川宗賢. "Watashi to *Nihon gengo chizu*" 私と『日本言語地図』. *Seiki* 世紀 4, pp. 42-45, 1 map.

Grootaers 1973e
"Nihon no hon'yakukai" 日本の翻訳界. *Kikan hon'yaku* 季刊翻訳 1, pp. 118-119.

Grootaers 1973f
"Suisu, Berugī, Oranda ni okeru hōgen kenkyū" スイス・ベルギー・オランダにおける方言研究. In *Hōgen kenkyū sōsho* 方言研究叢書, vol. 2, pp. 95-107 Tokyo: Miyai Shoten 三弥井書店.

Grootaers 1973g
"Hon'yakuron no genjō to kadai" 翻訳論の現状と課題. *Kikan hon'yaku* 季刊翻訳 3, pp. 177-183.

Grootaers 1973h
"Fifty Years with the Dialects: Personal Musings." *Studies on Japanese Culture* 2 (P. E. N. Club, Tokyo), pp. 416-421. 2 maps.

Grootaers 1973-1974
Awa-gun gengo chōsahyō daiikkai 安房郡言語調査票・第一回. Vols. 1-2. Jōchi Daigaku Gengogaku Daigakuin Kenkyūshitsu 上智大学言語学大学院研究室.

Grootaers 1974a
trans. Izumi Kunihisa 泉邦寿. "Gengo to shakai" 言語と社会. In *NHK hōsō daigaku gengo to shikō* NHK放送大学・言語と思考, vol. 1, pp. 57-64. Tokyo: Nihon hōsō shuppan kyōkai 日本放送出版協会. 5 maps.

Grootaers 1974b
trans. Kawamoto Takashi 川本喬. "Hōgen to tomo ni gojū nen" 方言とともに五十年. *Gekkan gengo* 月刊言語 3:7, pp. 36-41.

Grootaers 1975a
Awa-gun gengo chōsahyō dainikai 安房郡言語調査票・第二回. Jōchi Daigaku Gengogaku Daigakuin Kenkyūshitsu 上智大学言語学大学院研究室, 14 pp.

Grootaers 1975b
trans. Mitsuishi Yasuko 三石泰子. "Gengo chirigaku no tenbō" 言語地理学の展望 *Gengoseikatsu* 言語生活 284, pp. 16-22.

Grootaers 1975c
trans. Shibata Takeshi 柴田武. "Hōgengaku to shinpu no tanima" 方言学と神父の谷間. *Nihon hōgen kenkyūkai kenkyū happyō genkōshū* 日本方言研究会研究発表原稿集 20, pp. 64-68. 1 map.

Grootaers 1975d
"Gengo to chiiki shakai" 言語と地域社会. In *Gengo to ningen to bunka* 言語と人間と文化, pp. 141-167 Nihon hōsō shuppan kyōkai 日本放送出版協会. 8 maps.

Grootaers 1975e
and Shibata Takeshi 柴田武. "Seisho nimo goyaku ga aru ka – Gengogaku no me kara" 聖書にも誤訳があるか—言語学の目から. *Seisho to kyōkai* 聖書と教会 9, pp. 15-19.

Grootaers 1975f
and Shibata Takeshi. "What Is Wrong with the Japanese Bible Translations?" *Missionary Bulletin* (Tokyo) 29:11, pp. 595-608.

Grootaers 1975g
"Kyōdōyaku seisho no shomondai" 共同訳聖書の諸問題. *Hon no hiroba* 本のひろば 210:12, pp. 8-14.

Grootaers 1975h
"Hōgen ni miru chihō no seikatsu to bunka" 方言にみる地方の生活と文化. *Hito to kokudo* 人と国土 1:3, pp. 79-85. 1 map.

Grootaers 1975i
trans. Shibata Takeshi 柴田武. *Nihon bunka no omote to ura* 日本文化のオモテとウラ. Ushiku-shi 牛久市: Tsukuba Shorin 筑波書林, 246 pp.

Grootaers 1975j
and Mori Yōko 森洋子. "*Buryūgeru zenhanga* (Iwanami Shoten) no kitai to shitsubō – bijutsushika to gengogakusha no tachiba kara" 『ブリューゲル全版画』（岩波書店）の期待と失望—美術史家と言語学者の立場から. *Hon'yaku* 翻訳 7, pp. 42-60, 2 fig.

Grootaers 1976a
interviewed by Mitsuishi Yasuko 三石泰子. "Semai chiiki no kuwashii gengo chizu – Itoigawa gengo chizu" 狭い地域の詳しい言語地図・糸魚川言語地図. *Kōshiji* 高志路 240:2, pp. 6-9. 1 map.

Grootaers 1976b
"Hōgen to chihō bunka" 方言と地方文化. *Kokusai kōryū* 国際交流 9 (Spring issue 1976), pp. 23-34. 7 maps.

Grootaers 1976c
Nippon bunka-kō – sono ta にっぽん文化考・その他. Tokyo: Daiyamondo-sha ダイヤモンド社, 217 pp.

Grootaers 1976d
Awa-gun gengo chōsahyō daisankai 安房郡言語調査票・第三回. Jōchi Daigaku Gengogaku Daigakuin Kenkyūshitsu 上智大学言語学大学院研究室, 16 pp.

Grootaers 1976e
trans. Kawamoto Shigeo 川本茂雄. "Nihongo no goi no tokushoku" 日本語の語彙の特色. In *Nihongo kōza* 日本語講座, vol. 1, p. 10. Tokyo: Taishūkan Shoten 大修館書店.

Grootaers 1976f
trans. Iso Yurie 磯由利江. "Hōgen no henka to ningen no shakai" 方言の変化と人間の社会. In *Nihon no kotoba to bunka – shakai* 日本のことばと文化・社会, vol. 2. Chōbunsha 汐文社. 12 maps.

Grootaers 1976g
co-ed. Tokugawa Munemasa 德川宗賢. *Hōgen chirigaku zushū* 方言地理学図集. Tokyo: Akiyama Shoten 秋山書店, 180 pp.

Grootaers 1976h
Nihon no Hōgen chirigaku no tame ni 日本の方言地理学のために ["Etudes de géographie linguistique japonaise"]. Tokyo: Heibonsha 平凡社, 1976.

Grootaers 1977
"Senka shinai no Shinbu-byō (1948-nen genzai)" 宣化市内の真武廟（1948年現在）. In *Yoshioka hakase kanreki kinen: dōkyō kenkyū ronshū – dōkyō no shisō to bunka* – 吉岡博士還暦記念・道教研究論集—道教の思想と文化—, pp. 753-765.

Grootaers and Tokugawa 1980
and Tokugawa Munemasa. *Hōgen chirigaku zushū / Dialectgeographical maps: teaching manual*. 4th ed. Tokyo: Akiyama.

Grootaers 1981
Curriculum: Prof. Willem Grootaers, dialektoloog. BRT Dienst Kunstzaken: Brussel.

Grootaers 1983a
Fifty years hyphenated life: Priest – linguist. Sl: Scheut.

Grootaers and Hirohama 1983b
Grootaers, W.A. and F. Hirohama, eds. *Nara-ken to Mie-ken no kyōkai chitai hōgen chizu, A Word Geography of the Boundary Area of Nara and Mie*. Tokyo: Tenri Press, 1983.

Grootaers and Sasaki 1984
and Sasaki Hideki. *Jōchi daigaku: Daigakuin gengogaku kenkyūshitsu / A Word Geography of Tateyama City and Awa District (South Chiba Prefecture)*. Tokyo: Sophia University.

Grootaers 1990
trans. Sasaki Hideki 佐々木英樹. "Jikken onseigaku to watashi" 実験音声学と私. In *1990-nen Nihon onsei gakkai zenkoku taikai kenkyū happyō ronshū* 1990年日本音声学会全国大会研究発表論集, pp. 3-11.

Grootaers 1991
"Ōdo kōgen o ayunde: Chūgoku Kahoku de no hōgen chōsa" 黄土高原を歩んで：中国華北での方言調査. *Sinica* しにか (July 1991), pp. 76-81.

Grootaers 1993a
Chūgoku no chihō toshi ni okeru shinkō no jittai: Senka-shi no shūkyō kenzōbutsu zenchōsa 中国の地方都市における信仰の実態——宣化市の宗教建造物全調査 ["A real picture of beliefs in China's countryside towns – a complete survey of religious buildings in Xuanhua City"]. Tokyo: Gogatsu Shobō 五月書房, 200 pp. 65 photographs.

Grootaers 1993b
Chūgoku no chihō toshi ni miru Shūkyō no jittai. Senka chihō no shiramitsubushi chōsa 中国の地方都市に見る宗教の実態・宣化地方のしらみつぶし調査 ["Religious practice as seen in a regional Chinese town: a microscopic survey of the region of Chahar"]. Tokyo: Gogatsu shobō 五月書房, 1993.

Grootaers 1994a
The Religious and Cultic Buildings in a North China City: The Results of a Complete Survey of Hsüan-hua (Chahar), August 1948. Leuven: Peeters. 250 pp. 65 photographs (English version of Grootaers 1993b).

Grootaers 1994b
trans. Iwata Rei 岩田礼, and Hashizume Masako 橋爪正子. *Chūgoku no hōgen chirigaku no tame ni* 中国の方言地理学のために ["Contributions to Chinese Dialect Geography"]. Tokyo: Kōbun Press 好文出版, 1994.

Grootaers 1995
The Sanctuaries in a North-China City. A Complete Survey of the Cultic Buildings in the City of Hsüan-hua (Chahar), by the Survey team Fujen University, August 1948, W.A. Grootaers, Li Shih-yü, Wang Fu-shih. Bruxelles: Institut belge des Hautes Etudes chinoises, 1995, XVIII + 245 p. (64 planches photographiques, illustr., caractères chinois, index) (Mélanges chinois et bouddhiques, volume XXVI).

Grootaers 1999
Soredemo yappari Nihonjin ni naritai それでもやっぱり日本人になりたい ["I still want to be a Japanese"]. Tokyo: Gogatsu shobō 五月書房, 1999.

Grootaers 2003
trans. Shi Rujie 石汝杰 and Iwata Rei 岩田礼. *Hanyu fangyan dilixue* 汉语方言地理学 ["Contributions to Chinese Dialect Geography"]. Shanghai: Shanghai Jiaoyu Press 上海教育出版社, 2003.

B. PUBLICATIONS BY OTHER AUTHORS

Akitani 2003
Akitani Hiroyuki 秋谷裕幸. *Wuyu Chuqu fangyan (xibei pian) guyin gouni* 吴语处衢方言(西北片) 古音构拟 ["A reconstruction of the proto Chu-Qu dialect (northeast sub-group) of Wu"]. Tokyo: Kobun Press 好文出版, 2003.

Aubin 1996
"The Sanctuaries in a North-China City. A Complete Survey of the Cultic Buildings in the City of Hsüan-hua (Chahar) by Willem A. Grootaers." Review by: Françoise Aubin. *Archives de sciences sociales des religions* 41:96 (Oct. – Dec. 1996), pp. 91-92.

Bielenstein 1979
Hans Bielenstein. "Bernhard Karlgren (1889-1978)." *Journal of the American Oriental Society* 99:3 (Jul-Sep 1979), p. 553.

Cao 2008
Cao Zhiyun 曹志耘. "'Hanyu fangyan detu ji' jianjie"《漢語方言地図集》簡介. In *Linguistic Atlas of Chinese Dialects*, ed. Iwata Rei 岩田礼, pp. 5-14. Beijing: Shangwuyin Press 商务印, 2008.

Changli fangyan zhi
Chinese Academy of Social Sciences, ed. *Changli fangyan zhi* 昌黎方言志 ["Research report on the Changli dialect"]. Beijing: Kexue Press 科学出版, 1960.

Chao 1928
Chao Yuenren. *Studies in the Modern Wu-Dialects*. Tsing hua college research institute Peking, 1928.

Chao 1978
Chao Yuenren. *Further Problems in Chinese-English-Chinese Lexicography*. Taipei: Academia Sinica, 1978.

Chen 1982
Chen Chengsiang 陳正祥. *Chūgoku rekishi bunka chiri zusatsu* 中国歴史文化地理図冊 ["A Historical and Cultural Atlas of China"]. Tokyo: Hara Shobō 原書房, 1982.

Chiu 1937
Chiu Bienming. *A Quoyu Pronouncing Dictionary and Cipher Code*. Amoy: University of Amoy, 1937.

Dauzat 1922
Albert Dauzat. *La géographie linguistique*. Paris: Librairie Ernest Flammarion, 1922. [Japanese translation by Matsubara Hideji 松原秀治 and Yokoyama Kiiko 横山紀伊子. *Furansu gengo chirigaku* フランス言語地理学. Tokyo: Daigaku Shorin 大学書林, 1958].

DeFrancis 1984
John DeFrancis. *The Chinese Language Fact and Fantasy*. Honolulu Hawaii: University of Hawaii press, 1984.

DeFrancis 1996
John DeFrancis, ed. *ABC (Alphabetically Based Computerized) Chinese-English Dictionary*. London: Curzon, 1996.

Denlinger 1961
Paul B. Denlinger. "Chinese Historical Linguistics: The Road Ahead." *Journal of the American Oriental Society* 81:1 (1 January 1961), pp. 1–7.

Eder 1950
Matthias Eder. "Gedanken zur Methode der Chinesischen Volkskundeforschung." *Folklore Studies* 9 (1 January 1950), pp. 207–212.

Ellen et al. 1990
Roy Ellen, Bettina Lerner, Murray L. Wax, Barrie Reynolds, Alexander Schulenburg, and Willem A. Grootaers. "Letters." *Anthropology Today* 6:3 (1 June 1990), pp. 21–22.

Francis 1977
W. Nelson Francis. "International Colloquium on Automatic Dialect Mapping: A Report." *Computers and the Humanities* 11:6 (1 November 1977), pp. 339–340.

Fu 1928
Fu Sinian 傅斯年. *Zhongyang yanjiuyuan lishi yuyan yanjiusuo gongzuo zhi zhiqu* 中央研究院歷史語言研究所工作之旨趣 ["The Objective and Interests of the Task of the Institute of History and Philology"]. Academia Sinica, 1928.

Gilliéron and Roques 1912
Jules Gilliéron and Mario Roques. *Etudes du géographie linguistique d'apres l'Atlas Linguistique de la France*. Paris: Librairie Honoré Champion, 1912. [Japanese translation by Y. Ōkawa 大川, W Grootaers グロータース, and H. Sasaki 佐々木 (1991-1997). "ALF ni yoru gengo chirigaku teki kenkyū" ALFによる言語地理学的研究. *Proceedings of Dialectological Circle of Japan* 日本方言研究会予稿集 52-57, pp. 61-64].

Handel 2003
Zev Handel. "Northern Min Tone Values and the Reconstruction of 'Softened Initials.'" *Language and Linguistics* 4:1 (Institute of Linguistics, Academia Sinica, 2003), pp. 47-84.

Hashimoto 1978
Hashimoto Mantarō 橋本萬太郎. *Gengo ruikei chiri ron* 言語類型地理論 ["Typo-geographical Linguistics"]. Tokyo: Kōbundō Shuppan 弘文堂出版, 1978.

Hayashi 2005
Hayashi Tomo 林智. "Introduction to the PHD System." *Progressive Report* 1, Grant-in-Aid for Scientific Research (B), 2004-2006, Director: Ray Iwata, Linguistic Geography of Chinese Dialects by Use of a Newly Developed Computer System "PHD", pp. 8-24.

Inoue 1983a
Inoue Fumio. "A Note on Recent Changes of Dialect near Tokyo." *Area and Culture Studies* 33 (1983).

Inoue 1983b
Inoue Fumio. "New Dialect and Linguistic Change — An Age-area Survey near Tokyo —" *Proceedings of the XIIIth International Congress of Linguists*, 1983.

Inoue 2011
Inoue Fumio. "Willem A. GROOTAERS (1911-1999)." *Dialectologia* 7 (2011), pp. 167-174.

Iwata 1988
Iwata Rei 岩田礼. "Kōso Anki ryōshō ni okeru shinzoku shōi keishiki no chiriteki bunpu to koshōi taikei no saikō" 江蘇·安徽両省における親族称謂形式の地理的分布と古称謂体系の再構 ["The Geographical Distribution of Kinship Terms in Jiangsu and Anhui Provinces – A Reconstruction of the Proto Kinship System"]. In *Kango-shi no shomondai* 漢語史の諸問題, ed. Y. Ozaki and S. Hirata, pp. 207-272. Kyoto: Institute for Research in Humanities, Kyoto University 京都大学人文科学研究 所共同研究報告, 1988.

Iwata 1992
Iwata Rei 岩田礼. "Kango shohōgen no gengo chirigakuteki kenkyū: PHD (Project on Han Dialects) no gaiyō to kekka" 漢語諸方言の言語地理学的研究 PHD (Project on Han Dialects) の概要と結果. In *Nihon hōgen kenkyūkai dai 55 kai kenkyū happyōkai yokōshū* 日本方言研究会第55 回研究発表会予稿集, pp. 27-36.

Iwata 1995a
Iwata Ray. "Linguistic Geography of Chinese Dialects – Project on Han Dialects (PHD)." *Cahiers de Linguistique Asie Orientale* 24:2 (1995) [Paris, EHESS-CRLAO], pp. 195-227.

Iwata 1995b
Iwata Rei 岩田礼. "Kango hōgen-shi no furenzokusei: Chūgokugo gengo chirigaku josetsu" 漢語方言史の不連続性一中国語言語地理学序説. *Jinbun ronshū* 人文論集 45:2 (Shizuoka Daigaku Jinbun Gakubu 静岡大学人文学部), pp. 43-77

Iwata 1995c
Iwata Rei 岩田礼. "Hanyu fangyan "zufu" "waizufu" chengwei di dili fenbu – fangyan dili xue zai lishi yuyan xue yanjiu shang de zuoyong 漢語方言"祖父""外祖父"称謂的地理分布一方言地理学在歴史語言学研究上的作用. *Zhongguo yuwen* 中国語文 3 (1995), pp. 203-210.

Iwata 1996
Iwata Rei 岩田礼. "Du 'Shandong fangyan zhi' liu zhong" 読《山東方言志》六種. *Zhongguo yuwen* 中国語文 3 (1996), pp. 236-240.

Iwata 2000a
Iwata Ray. "The Jianghuai Area as a Core of Linguistic Innovation and Diffusion: A Case of the Kinship Term 'ye' 爺." *In Memory of Professor Li Fang-Kuei: Essays of Linguistic Change and the Chinese Dialects*, pp. 179-196. University of Washington: Academia Sinica, 2000.

Iwata 2000b
Iwata Rei 岩田礼. "Gendai Kango hōgen no chiriteki bunpu to sono tsūjiteki keisei" 現代漢語方言の地理的分布とその通時的形成. In *Chūgoku ni okeru gengo chiri to jinbun – shizen chiri (7): Gengo ruikei chiriron shinpojiumu ronbunshū* 中国における言語地理と人文・自然地理(7): 言語類型地理論シンポジウム論文集 (Kakenhi kenkyū seika hōkokusho, kenkyūdaihyōsha 科研費研究成果報告書、研究代表者: Endō Mitsuaki 遠藤光暁), pp. 5-49.

Iwata 2002
Iwata Rei 岩田礼. "Sekai no hōgen chirigaku: Chūgoku" 世界の方言地理学：中国. In *Hōgen chirigaku no kadai* 方言地理学の課題, ed. Mase Yoshio 馬瀬良雄, Satō Ryōichi 佐藤亮一 et al., pp. 117-126. Meiji Shoin 明治書院, 2002.

Iwata 2005
Iwata Ray. "Linguistic Geography of Chinese Dialects by Use of a Newly Developed Computer System 'PHD' – History, Aim and Some Controversial Issues –", *Progressive Report* 1, Grant-in-Aid for Scientific Research (B), 2004-2006.

Iwata 2006
Iwata Ray. "Homonymic and Synonymic Collisions in the Northeastern Jiangsu Dialect – On the Formation of Geographically Complementary Distributions." In *Linguistic Studies in Chinese and Its Neighboring Languages: Festschrift in Honor of Professor Pang-hsin Ting on His Seventieth Birthday*, pp. 1035-1058. Institute of Linguistics, Academia Sinica, 2006.

Iwata 2007a
Iwata Rei 岩田礼. "Fangyan jiechu ji hunxiao xingshi de chansheng – Lun Hanyu fangyan 'xigai' yici de lishi yanbian" 方言接觸及混淆形式的産生－論漢語方言"膝蓋"一詞的歷史演變 ["Dialect Contact and the Production of Contaminated Forms – A Reconstruction of the History of Chinese Words for 'Knee'"]. *Chūgoku gengogaku shūkan / Bulletin of Chinese Linguistics* 中国言語学集刊 1:2 (2007), pp. 117-146.

Iwata 2007b
Iwata Rei 岩田礼. "Hanyu fangyan 'mingtian', 'zuotian' deng shijian-ci de yuyan dilixue yanjiu" 漢語 方言〈明天〉、〈昨天〉等時間詞的語言地理學研究 ["Geo-linguistic Study of Time Words, Such as 'Tomorrow' and 'Yesterday'"]. *Chūgoku Gogaku* 中国語学: *Bulletin of the Chinese Linguistic Society of Japan* 254 (2007), pp. 1-28.

Iwata 2007c
Iwata Rei 岩田礼, Ōta Itsuku 太田斎, eds. *Fangyan detu ji qi jieshi (Zhongwen ban)* 方言地図及其解釈(中文版). Heisei 16-18 nendo kagaku kenkyūhi kibankenkyū (B) kenkyū seika hōkokusho "Chūgokugo hōgen no gengo chirigakuteki kenkyū – Shin shisutemu ni yoru *Kango hōgen chizushū* no sakusei" daisan bunsatsu. 平成16-18 年度科学研究費基盤研究(B)研究成果報告書"中国語方言の言語地理学的研究新システムによる『漢語方言地図集』の作成" 第3分冊.

Iwata 2008
Iwata Rei 岩田礼, ed. *Kokusai shinpojiumu: Nitchū ryōkoku no hōgen no kako, genzai, mirai* 『国際シンポジウム：日中両国の方言の過去、現在、未来. Kanazawa Daigaku Nitchū mukei bunka isan purojekuto hōkokusho dainishū 金沢大学日中無形文化遺産プロジェクト報告書第2 集, Kanazawa Daigaku Bungakubu 金沢大学文学部. (authors: Cao Zhiyun 曹志耘、Ōnishi Takuichirō 大西拓一郎 et al.).

Iwata 2009
Iwata Ray. *The Interpretative Maps of Chinese Dialects.* Tokyo: Hakuteisha, 2009.

Iwata 2010
Iwata Ray. "Chinese Geolinguistics: History, Current Trend and Theoretical Issues." *Dialectologia* 1 (Special issue, 2010), pp. 97-121.

Karlgren 1926
Bernhard Karlgren. *Études sur la phonologie chinoise.* Archives d'études Orientales 15. K.W. Appelberg, 1926

Language Atlas of China
Chinese Academy of Social Sciences and Australian Academy of Humanities, ed. *Language Atlas of China.* Hong Kong: Longman, 1987.

Li 1985
Li Rong 李荣. "Hanyu fangyan fenqu de jige wenti" 漢語方言分区的幾個問題. *Fangyan* 方言 2 (1985), pp. 81-88.

Linguistic Atlas of Japan
NLRI (National Language Research Institute). *Linguistic Atlas of Japan*, vols. 1-6. Ōkurashō Insatsukyoku, 1966-1974.

Liu 1969
Liu Shih-hong. *Chinese Characters and Their Impact on Other Languages of East Asia.* Taipei: Eurasia Book Company, 1969.

Mase 1992
Mase Yoshio 馬瀬良雄. *Gengo chirigaku kenkyū* 言語地理学研究 ["Studies in Linguistic Geography"]. Tokyo: The Ōfū Press 桜楓社, 1992.

Mase 1996
Mase Yoshio. "Professor Takesi Sibata's Accomplishments in the Field of Linguistic Geography." *American Speech* 71:2 (1 July 1996), pp. 162–170.

Matsue 2006
Matsue Takashi 松江崇. "Han-dai fangyan zhong de tongyan-xianshu – ye tan genju 'Fangyan' de fangyan quhua-lun" 汉代方言中的同言线束－也谈根据《方言》的方言区划论— ["Isoglosses in the Han Era – With Discussing the Dialect Demarcation According to 'Fangyan'"]. In *Yangxiong Fangyan jiaoshi huizheng* 扬雄方言校释汇证, ed. Hua Xuecheng 华学诚, pp. 1509-1533. Beijing: Zhonghua Press 中华书局, 2006.

Norman 1973
Jerry Norman. "Tonal Development in Min." *Journal of Chinese Linguistics* 1:2 (1973), pp. 222-238.

Norman 1988
Jerry Norman. *Chinese.* Cambridge: Cambridge University Press, 1988.

Norman 1989
Jerry Norman. "What is a Kejia Dialect." In *Proceedings of the Second International Conference on Sinology (Section on Linguistics and Paleography)*, pp. 323-344. Taipei: Academia Sinica, 1989.

Pop and Grootaers 1960
Sever Pop and Willem A. Grootaers. *Willem A. Grootaers: Notice biographique et bibliographique et Résumés de ses conférences : Quelques réflexions sur les méthodes en usage dans la géographie linguistique et Un atlas régional en préparation au Japon.* Louvain: Centre international de dialectologie générale, 1960.

Preston 1999
Dennis Preston, ed. *Handbook of Perceptual Dialectology*, vol. I. Amsterdam, Philadelphia: John Benjamins, 1999.

Sanada 2010
Sanada Shinji. "The 'Glottogram': A Geolinguistic Tool Developed in Japan". *Dialectologia* 1 (Special issue, 2010).

Serruys 1960
Paul L.-M. Serruys. *Five Word Studies on Fang Yen.* Sankt Augustin: Institut Monumenta Serica-1960.

Shibata 1969
Shibata Takeshi 柴田武. *Gengo chirigaku no hōhō* 言語地理学の方法 ["Method in Linguistic Geography"]. Tokyo: Chikuma Shobō 筑摩書房, 1969.

Shibata 1988-95
Shibata Takeshi 柴田武. *Linguistic Atlas of Itoigawa* 糸魚川言語地図, 3 vols. Akiyama shoten 秋山書店, 1988, 1990, 1995.

Shibata 1998
Sibata Takeshi. *Sociolinguistics in Japanese Contexts*, ed. Tetsuya Kunihiro, Fumio Inoue & Daniel Long. Berlin, New York: Mouton de Gruyter, 1998.

Simmons et al. 2006
Richard Simmons, Shi Rujie 石汝杰 and Gu Qian 顾黔. *Jianghuai guanhua yu Wuyu bianjie de fangyan dilixue yanjiu* 江淮官话与吴语边界的方言地理学研究 ["Chinese Dialect Geography: Distinguishing Mandarin and Wu in Their Boundary Region"]. Shanghai: Shanghai Education Press 上 海教育出版社, 2006. 338 pp.

Van Hecken and Grootaers 1986
Jozef Leonard Van Hecken and Willem A. Grootaers. *The Half Acre Garden, Pan-Mou Yüan.* Steyler Verlag, 1986.

Van Nieuwenborgh 1999
Marcel Van Nieuwenborgh. "Taalkundige Willem Grootaers overleden – De laatste Vlaamse mandarijn." *De Standaard* (Wednesday 11 August 1999).

Ware 1949
James R. Ware. Review of "La géographie linguistique en Chine: Nécessité d'une nouvelle méthode pour l'étude linguistique du chinois," by Willem A. Grootaers. *Language* 25:1 (Jan-Mar 1949), pp. 80-83.

Xiang and Cao 2005
Xiang Mengbing 項夢氷 and Cao Hui 曹暉. *Hanyu fangyan dilixue – Rumen yu Shixian* 汉语方言地理学.入门与实践 ["Chinese Dialect Geography: Primer and Practices"]. Beijing: China Wenshi Press 中国文史出版社, 2005.

Yang 1967
Paul Fu-mien Yang. *Elements of Hakka Dialectology.* Sankt Augustin: Institut Monumenta Serica, 1967.

Zavyalova 1983
Olyga Zavyalova. "A Linguistic Boundary within the Guanhua Area." *Computational Analyses of Asian & African Languages* [Tokyo: Institute of Asian & African languages & Culture] 21 (1983), pp. 149-159.

Zavjalova and Astrakhan 1998
Olyga Zavyalova and E. Astrakhan. "The Linguistic Geography of China." *Progressive Report* 1 (1998), Grant-in-Aid for Scientific Research (A), 1997-1999, Director: Mitsuaki Endō, Linguistic Geography & Cultural-Natural Geography in China.

Zhao 1928
Zhao Yuanren 赵元任. *Xiandai Wuyu de yanjiu* 现代吴语的研究 ["Studies in the modern Wu dialects"]. Monograph no. 4. Beijing: Tsing hua College of Research Institute 清华学校研究院, 1928.

Zhao et al. 1948
Zhao Yuanren 赵元任, Ding Shengshu 丁声树, Yang Shifeng 杨时逢, Wu Zongji 吴宗济 and Dong Tonghe 董同龢. *Hubei fangyan diaocha baogao* 湖北方言调查报告 ["Report on a survey of the dialects of Hupeh"]. Shanghai: Shangwuyin Press 商务印, 1948.

NOTES

1 Most of the photographs reproduced here were graciously provided to the author by Prof. Inoue Fumio 井上史雄, Professor of Sociolinguistics, Meikai University, Urayasu, Japan, and visiting professor of the National Institute of Japanese Language and Linguistics.

2 Ludovic Jean Joseph Grootaers, born on 9 August 1885 at Tongeren, died on 12 October 1956 at Leuven, Belgium.

3 Alice Anciaux, born on 10 February 1886 at Nivelles, died on 3 January 1974 at Leuven.

4 He testifies about this move in his last book, his autobiography. During his novitiate with the Jesuits he had displayed a great gift for languages. To his horror this ability led his superior to adumbrate a possible assignment as teacher of Latin and Greek in one of the Jesuit colleges in Belgium. Since his high school days he had made up his mind to become a missionary in Africa. Consequently, he quit the Society and applied for entry into the missionary society of *Les Pères blancs*, whose official name is *Missionnaires d'Afrique* [M.Afr.]. Being told that they did not accept someone from another order or congregation he applied to the congregation of Scheut. Although he was accepted at once, he could not be posted in Africa due his medical history. However, China, their oldest mission field, being much colder presented less of a health hazard, and so he was assigned to the China mission (Grootaers 1999, pp. 41-44). His transfer to Scheut was not inspired by any motive of linguistic adherence in the Belgian context, although it is a fact that the congregation of Scheut was the most "Flemish" of all congregations, in contrast to the Society of Jesus, where the "corporate culture" was much more geared to francophone culture. As a matter of fact, the Flemish province of the Jesuit Society was founded as late as 1935.

5 Grootaers 1976h, p. 282.

6 Grootaers 1999, p. 45.

7 Grootaers 1976h, p. 282, and Grootaers 1999, pp. 63-70.

8 Grootaers 1999, pp. 80-88.

9 Grootaers 1983a.

10 Grootaers 1976h, p. vi.

11 Report by Father Dries van Coillie, dated Peiping 19 April 1947, in KADOC Documentatie- en Onderzoekscentrum voor Religie, Cultuur en Samenleving – KADOC. BE/942855/1405: Archief familie Schodts.

12 Titled "Kort overzicht der Geschiedenis van het Chineesche Keizerrijk door de PP. Grootaers-P. Serruys C.I.C.M. 1944 – Peking. Volgens handschrift ex Typis Taip'ingts'ang, Peking."

13 Grootaers 1945a and Grootaers 1946e.

14 Report by Father Dries van Coillie, dated Peiping 19 April 1947, in KADOC Documentatie- en Onderzoekscentrum voor Religie, Cultuur en Samenleving – KADOC. BE/942855/1405: Archief familie Schodts.

15 Inoue 2011, p. 168.

16 Grootaers 1976h, p. 282.

17 Inoue 2011, pp. 168-169.

18 Grootaers 1943, 1945b, 1957a.

19 Ware 1949, p. 81.

20 Iwata 2010, p. 98.

21 Iwata 2010, p. 99.

22 Grootaers 1999, p. 78.

23 Grootaers 1976h, p. 282.

24 Grootaers 1976h, p. 282.

25 Inoue 2011, p. 172.

26 Photograph in Grootaers 1995, p. 235.

27 Iwata 2010.

28 Grootaers 1994b.

29 Grootaers 2003; Inoue 2011, pp. 172-173.

30 Inoue 2011, p. 173.

31 Iwata 2009.

32 Inoue 2011, p. 173.

33 Grootaers 1943, Grootaers 1945b, Iwata 2010, p. 98.

34 Iwata 2010, p. 98.

35 Shibata's epilogue in Grootaers 1976h, p. 286.

36 Grootaers 1984, p. 198.

37 Postface by Shibata in Grootaers 1976h, p. 285.

38 Grootaers 1945c.

39 Grootaers 1948c.

40 Grootaers et al. 1951c.

41 Grootaers 1993b.

42 Grootaers 1995; see also Aubin 1996.

43 Aubin 1996, p. 91.

44 The walled city of Xuanhua, with 25,000 inhabitants, contained at least 180 shrines. Aubin 1996, p. 92, notes that Grootaers 1995, p. XIII, mentions 182 shrines; Grootaers 1995, p. 1, has 274 shrines, while in a previous publication in Japanese *Sinica* II, No. 7, 1991, p. 80, the author gives 189 shrines, and in a private letter he mentioned 246.

45 Aubin 1996, p. 92.

46 *Folklore Studies* 11:2, pp. 139-182; Grootaers 1952e.

47 Aubin 1996, p. 92.

48 Examples of iconography: Grootaers 1995, pp. 167-169; map of locations: Grootaers 1995, p. 170.

49 Preface to Grootaers 1976h.

50 Grootaers 1994b.

51 Fu 1928.

52 Bielenstein 1979, p. 553.

53 Iwata 2010, p. 99.

54 Grootaers 1943.

55 Grootaers 1994b, p. 35.

56 Iwata 2010, p. 100.

57 Iwata 2010, p. 100; Norman 1973 & 1988; Handel 2003; Akitani 2003.

58 Grootaers 1994b.

59 Grootaers 2003.

60 Xiang and Cao 2005.

61 Simmons et al. 2006.

62 Iwata 2010, p. 100.

63 Cao 2008.

64 Grootaers 1957a; Iwata 2010, pp. 100-101.

65 Grootaers 1999, p. 47-48; p. 57-58.

66 Grootaers 1999, pp. 129-139.

67 Grootaers 1999, pp. 217-221.

68 Grootaers 1994b.

69 First part: *Collectanea Commissionis Synodalis* 1944: May-December issue, pp. 269-304; 2nd part: *Collectanea Commissionis Synodalis* 1955: January-June issue, pp. 22-67.

70 Report by Father Dries van Coillie, dated Peiping 19 April 1947, in KADOC Documentatie- en Onderzoekscentrum voor Religie, Cultuur en Samenleving – KADOC. BE/942855/1405: Archief familie Schodts.

71 Inoue 2011, p. 169.

FOURTH
PART

LITERARY
CROSSROADS

THE FIRST JAPANESE ESSAY ON BELGIAN LITERATURE

Ueda Bin

JAPAN & BELGIUM
An Itinerary of Mutual Inspiration

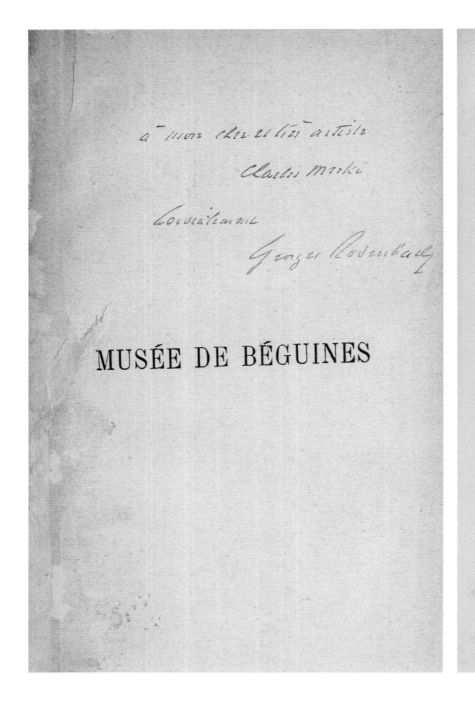

à mon cher et très artiste

Charles Morke

Cordialement

Georges Rodenbach

MUSÉE DE BÉGUINES

À Monsieur le représentant Coomans

Hommage affectueux de l'auteur —

Georges Rodenbach

LA MER ÉLÉGANTE.

THE FIRST JAPANESE ESSAY ON BELGIAN LITERATURE

By way of introduction to the section on Literature, we include here a translation of the article on Belgian literature that Ueda Bin wrote in 1895 under the pseudonym Bi Yūshi 微幽子. The title of the article is "Berugī bungaku" 白耳義文学, and it appeared in *Teikoku bungaku* 帝国文学 1 (Jan 1895), pp. 13-19. The style is high-flown and pedantic, but it is worth quoting in full as the first Japanese critical essay on the topic.

Belgian Literature

In Belgium's literary world there is a school, now in the ascendant, that is trying to make headway into the literary world of neighbouring France. It is called *La Jeune Belgique*. When Maeterlinck, one of the leaders of this movement, recently moved to Paris, taking with him a new theatrical play, he gradually made a name for himself among literary critics, reaping all sorts of accolades. In his melancholy he was said to be more profound than the writer of *Hamlet*, his evocation of feelings and his depiction of love was hailed as superior to the play of *Romeo*. No sooner was it brought on stage than it seemed as if the Republic of Letters had suddenly taken to a new fashion. Whereas two or three months earlier critics had likened him to Shakespeare and hailed him as the master of the modern age, he was now branded as a country cousin from the North, as a "Teutonic" imposter. They put him down as a mediocre "Flemish" writer, who may have been writing in French but who was still Flemish in his thinking. The critic Pessart[1] lamented: "After Tolstoy followed Ibsen, after Ibsen there was Strindberg, and after Strindberg came Maeterlinck."[2] The fact that prominent figures such as Coppée,[3] Lemaître,[4] Theuriet,[5] and Francisque Sarcey[6] mustered all their power to stem the invasion of the Northerners,[7] amply demonstrates that this new school was gaining a high stature in the literary world. I have learnt recently that Georges Rodenbach, a writer belonging to this school, succeeded in staging his new play *Le voile* at the Comedie-Française. It should therefore not necessarily be useless to give here a survey of this new literature, thus clarifying an aspect of modern trends in Europe. The innovative movement in Belgian literature was brought into the limelight by a lecture about trends in Flemish literature delivered by Henri Conscience at the Royal Academy around 1880.[8] In it he made a plea for the establishment of a national literature, echoing the patriotism sung more than forty years earlier: "We are neither Flemings nor Walloons, Belgian should henceforth be our name."[9] In that song, he said, we tuned our strings and sang in unison for the sake of our homeland, the same fatherland for Walloons and Flemings. Indeed, it turned out that the momentum of revolutionary change had matured unnoticed, thus laying firm foundations for a Belgian literature. Théodore Hannon's sonnets saw the light as early as 1876.[10] The brimming and untrammelled spirit flares up from the sentences, the mood of pessimism and world-weariness slumbers in each poem in a remarkable way. It is neither a banal Byronic *Weltschmerz*, nor the cool pessimism that hailed from Germany. There is an effusion of feelings, and the imagination is rich. It threw the lacklustre and pallid scene of Belgian poetry into disarray, just like the French Parnassians did back in 1866. Both movements struck out in a new direction on the contemporary literary scene, aspiring to tap from the source of poetry. Their motto was: "quietly retiring into the recesses of the great temple, we want to keep aloof from the madding crowd, venerate exquisite beauty, and forever devote ourselves to the religion called arts."

When reading poems by *La Jeune Belgique*, echoes of Baudelaire linger between the lines, they pile up his adjectives of colour, conjuring up mysterious beauty. When thus their tone exudes elegance and profundity, it is truly an apt reflection of modern ideas. Hannon's *Rîmes de Joie* is not a work singing the praises of worldly trivial joy. "Joy" as it is called here, specifically refers to the unfathomable charm of an attractive woman, the natural beauty of a courtesan, as in the poem by Laforgue, which exclaimed, 'Woman, woman, thou art the one who unhinges the world of man.'[11]

> *Amour, Amour, on t'a bien dit*
> *Un contact couteux d'épidermes*

This verse by Hannon is said to be on everybody's lips in Belgium. Following in Hannon's footsteps is Iwan Gilkin, who wrote: "Come, how joyful is the world of man, come handsome lads. By your lover's kiss, I will lead you through the fragrant fields, to the celebration of joy."

Surnaturelle, calme et puissante Beauté
Fontaine de santé, miroir d'étrangeté

Or again,

O bonté de la vie! O santé du soleil.

When hearing these verses, it is as if one's soul is transported to the refined and subdued realm of ancient Greece, passing through the wildflower meadows where Alcyone abides, tapping the rich source of life, and bathing in Apollo's warm light of grace; it is truly as if one is within Theocritus' *Bucolics*. But as one moves on to read his poems on women, suddenly the dark tides and wild billows of the end of the nineteenth century rear their heads, darkening the meadows and mountains, withering the grasses, washing away the flowers; suddenly one beholds a rueful sight. When I read those verses, I see the women who gather in merry theatres and assemble at banquets during sumptuous evening parties, and I discern beyond their rosy features and shiny faces the shapes of ferocious wild animals. Reading back and forth I am surprised at how hard it is to grasp the essence of this poet. On the one hand, he appears to be singing the pleasures of society, and extolling the pathos of love and women, and when one considers how at times he describes the lofty feminine ideal, and pays homage to it, he resembles Goethe in his veneration for what the latter called *Das Ewig-Weibliche*. But turning to his other, dark side, everyone is bound to be aghast at his morbidities. When looking at women, he associates pleasures of the world with their fragrant hair, and singing songs and raising cups he praises the beauty of their bodies, while on the other hand a kind of gloomy and bleak wave of pessimism surges up, pushing him to branding women as the white cats, the crazy dogs and the wild boars of the world. That all these wild billows are a major force that human power can hardly resist, we can prove by examples from French literature, ranging from Balzac's *Don Juan*,[12] where the mood of fluttering appears for the first time, to Flaubert's *La Tentation de Saint Antoine*, which shows the effects of torment without precedent. In reading the moving verses of Alfred de Musset and in perusing the strange poems of

Verlaine, it is as if in the shade of beautiful flowers even more beautiful little snakes lie curled, and when Baudelaire's poems *Les Fleurs du Mal* appeared, it reflected the mind-set of his age. It was unavoidable that those with an innovative spirit in Belgium's literary world would eventually join this new trend. After the storm, a blue sky; likewise the flowers of timeless art, after the rain has stopped and the wind has abated, in due course put forth a new scent.

More than a decade has passed since the foundation of the new society *La Jeune Belgique*. A prolific writer like Georges Eekhoud, who has steadily improved his style, published the year before last *La Nouvelle Carthage* [1893]. It is a work in which he probes with incisive and stern spirit the depraved morals of Antwerp, and the Royal Academy eventually awarded him a prize to the value of 5,000 francs. In addition, Camille Lemonnier, whose recent work differs from the writings of his prime, is remarkable for his placid and aloof style. In contrast Edmond Picard[13] shifted to a more exuberant and sensual style. In his account of his career as a diplomatic representative he goes into full details. That his book entitled *El Moghreb al Aksa* has lost the smooth style of his earlier works, adds rather to its appeal.[14] Maeterlinck produced three puppet plays ["trois petits drames pour marionnettes"], namely *Alladine et Palomides*, *Intérieur* and *La Mort de Tintagiles*. Rodenbach wrote the poems of the *Musée de Béguines* [1894], which, I hear, portray Belgian life and manners. Among the young poets who have made their debut, we cannot leave unmentioned G. De Mey, Noterdaeme, and others. Furthermore, it is interesting that Guido Gezelle's poetry uses the West Flemish dialect. Hélène Swarth's poems strike an elegant tone and exude a rich imagination, so that we must say that this poetess is a promising talent.

In the world of prose too there is exceptionally beautiful work, notably a collection of short stories written by the female author Virginie Loveling, and entitled *Een vonkje van genie* ("A spark of genius"). It is stylishly and elegantly written, yet has a certain robustness running throughout the entire work, it is said. The young novelist Cyriel Buysse has written *Het recht van den sterkste* ("Might makes Right"). Dealing mainly with the lives of outcasts and thieves, it is a harrowing tale that portrays the dark side of Flemish society. In this book the reader may now and then hear Zolaesque echoes, but his work seems to have a special robust characteristic, and since it is difficult to predict when the mustard seed will grow into a tree, we should anyway wish this man a bright future. Which brings us to the end of Belgian literature. The promising vigour of *La Jeune Belgique* is still not spent, and when it once again amazes the European literary scene with its unconventional poetry and prose, we will not fail to report on it.

(translated by David De Cooman and W.F. Vande Walle)

REFERENCES

Conscience 1881
H. Conscience. "Histoire et tendances de la littérature flamande". Redevoering uitgesproken in de Kon. Academie v. België. Brussel. Havermans. 1881. In *Bulletin de l Académie Royale* 50:3 (1881), pp. 709-724.

Cuisinier 1925
Jeanne Cuisinier. *Jules Laforgue*. Paris: Albert Messein, 1925.

Lemaître 1920
Jules Lemaître. "Maeterlinck: Bouffes-Parisiens: Pelléas et Mélisande, drame en cinq actes de M. Maurice Maeterlinck. 21 mai 1893." In *Impressions de théâtre: onzième série*. Paris: Boivin & Cie, 1920.

Nachtergaele 2003
Vic Nachtergaele. "Les dessous parisiens d'un flirt franco-flamand." *Septentrion* 32 (2003), pp. 78-85.

Picard 1893
Edmond Picard. *El Moghreb al Aksa: Une Mission Belge au Maroc*. Brussels: Paul Lacomblez, 1893.

NOTES

1 Nachtergaele 2003, pp. 78-85.

2 "Après Tolstoï, Ibsen; après Ibsen, Strindberg; après Strindberg, Maeterlinck."

3 François Coppée, born Paris, 26 January 1842; died Paris, 23 May 1908.

4 Jules Lemaître, born Vennecy, 27 April 1853; died Tavers, 5 August 1914.

5 André Theuriet, born Marly-le-Roi, 8 October 1833; died Bourg-la-Reine, 23 April 1907.

6 Born Dourdan, 8 October 1827; died Paris 16 May 1899.

7 Lemaître wrote: "Nous pouvons le dire, maintenant qu'ils ne sont plus là, les jeunes gens farouches qui, l'autre jour, surveillaient les boulevardiers frivoles: Pelléas et Mélisande, ce n'est pas du Shakespeare, car Shakespeare est toute la vie; ce n'est pas du Musset, car Musset est tout l'amour; ce n'est pas de l'Edgar Poe, car Edgar Poe est toute la peur. Mais c'est une charmante amusette de décadence, un bizarre joyau de simplicité artificielle, un doux et baroque petit poème de balbutiement concerté, d'un vague et d'un inachevé très précieux." See Lemaître 1920.

8 The lecture "Histoire et tendances de la littérature flamande", delivered to the Royal Academy of Science, Letters and Fine Arts of Belgium.

9 Antoine Clesse (30 May 1816 – 9 March 1889): "Soyons unis !... Flamands, Wallons, Ce ne sont là que des prénoms, Belge est notre nom de famille!" [passage from the poem "Flamands, Wallons" (1849)].

10 *Les vingt-quatre coups de sonnet*, printed in Brussels by Félix Callewaert senior.

11 "O femme, femme! Toi qui fais l'humanité monomane." Cuisinier 1925, p. 53.

12 Balzac's variation on the Don Juan story was published under the title *L'Élixir de longue vie* (1846).

13 Born Brussels, 15 December 1836; died Dave, 19 February 1924.

14 Picard 1893.

TRANSFUSION
OF A BELGIAN NOVEL IN JAPAN:
THE RIVER SUMIDA
AND
BRUGES-LA-MORTE

Sadafumi Muramatsu

Photograph of Georges Rodenbach sporting a fur coat on the dedication
page ("homage à M. Francis Magnard") of *Bruges-la-Morte*,
second edition of 1910.

TRANSFUSION OF A BELGIAN NOVEL IN JAPAN: *THE RIVER SUMIDA* AND *BRUGES-LA-MORTE*

Introduction — Reception of Rodenbach in Japan

In any discussion of French–Belgian literature in the nineteenth century, we cannot fail to mention the poet and novelist Georges Rodenbach (1855-1898). His most remarkable collections of verse, *La Jeunesse blanche* (1886), *Le Règne du silence* (1891) and *Le miroir du ciel natal* (1898) were published in Paris. He actually started composing verse with regret and nostalgia for his native land, Flanders. He arrived at Symbolist poetry through the technique of allusion and analogy. His first novel was *L'Art en exil* (1889). *Le Carillonneur* (1897) was a long novel, and his last novel was *L'Arbre* (1898). He also left us short stories such as *Musée de béguines* (1894), *Le Rouet des brumes* (1901). *Le Voile* (1894) and *Le Mirage* (1901) also deserve our appreciation. The former gained renown after its performance at the Comédie-Française. The latter was a dramatization in four acts of *Bruges-la-Morte* (1892).

However, it is fair to say that it was *Bruges-la-Morte* more than any novel that decided Rodenbach's fame. The background of this nostalgic novel is the ancient city of Bruges, Flanders. The writer describes the melancholy of a widower, Hugues Viane, who is obsessed with the memory of his dead wife, and the frantic love he feels for a look-alike of his wife, Jane Scott. Finally, in the epilogue, Jane is strangled by Hugues because of her blasphemy of his dead wife. While Rodenbach represented the imaginative pictures in Hugues's mind throughout the story, it is quite obvious that the main character of this story was the town of Bruges itself. He explained that his aim was to evoke the town as a living being. In the preface to the novel, he writes:

> *Dans cette étude passionnelle, nous avons voulu aussi et principalement évoquer une Ville, la Ville comme un personnage essentiel, associé aux états d'âme, qui conseille, dissuade, détermine à agir. Ainsi, dans la réalité, cette Bruges, qu'il nous a plu d'élire, apparaît presque humaine... Un ascendant*

s'établit d'elle sur ceux qui y séjournent. Elle les façonne selon ses sites et ses cloches. Voilà ce que nous avons souhaité de suggérer : la Ville orientant une action ; ses paysages urbains, non plus seulement comme des toiles de fond, comme des thèmes descriptifs un peu arbitrairement choisis, mais liés à l'événement même du livre. C'est pourquoi il importe, puisque ces décors de Bruges collaborent aux péripéties, de les reproduire également ici, intercalés entre les pages : quais, rues désertes, vieilles demeures, canaux, béguinage, églises, orfèvrerie du culte, beffroi, afin que ceux qui nous liront subissent aussi la présence et l'influence de la Ville, éprouvent la contagion des eaux mieux voisines, sentent à leur tour l'ombre des hautes tours allongée sur le texte.

Bruges-la-Morte first appeared as a ten-part series in *Le Figaro* in February 1892. Later in June, it was published by Marpon and Flammarion. When publishing his novel in book form, Rodenbach added a preface and two chapters with thirty-five black-and-white photographs of the old town of Bruges interspersed throughout the text. The novel has been widely recognized in France and Belgium as a masterpiece, and it has also been translated into several languages. The Opera *Die tote Stadt*, composed by Erich Wolfgang Korngold and performed in 1920, deserves special mention because it was greatly inspired by Rodenbach's *Bruges-la-Morte*. Naturally enough, when Rodenbach described Bruges as a dead city, its citizens were displeased. Nowadays, however, one room of the Bruges City Hall has been named "Georges Rodenbach", and a street in his hometown Tournai has been named after him.

How then was Rodenbach's work received in Japan? It is said that the works of Rodenbach have been read in Japan for more than a century. We can find the first appearance of his name in a magazine issued in 1895, which carried an introductory article by Ueda Bin 上田敏 (1874-1916) about *Le Voile*. Ten years later, in 1905, Ueda translated one poem of *Le règne du silence* titled "Twilight" (*Tasogare* 黄昏 in Japanese). The poem "Twilight" was included in *Kaichōon* 海潮音 ("The Sound of the Tide", 1905), an anthology of poems translated into Japanese. Ueda's translation was superb and is particularly worthy of admiration for the lyrical vividness of the Japanese wording. It was through Ueda's excellent translation that Rodenbach became a well-

... Il traversait la ville, les ponts centenaires, les quais mortuaires.

View of Bruges, "similigravure" included in *Bruges-la-Morte*, second edition of 1910, p. 40. Rodenbach interspersed his text with dozens of black-and-white photographs of views of Bruges. It is believed to be the first work of fiction illustrated with photographs (See James Gardner. "Incarnating the World Within." *Wall Street Journal* (10 December 2011)).

Portrait of Rodenbach, as reproduced in photogravure frontispiece in *Bunshō sekai* 文章世界 (October issue of 1909).

> View of the Rozenhoedkaai. "Similigravure" from *Bruges-la-Morte*, second edition of 1910, p. 41.

known poet among Japanese devotees of literature. As a matter of fact, there was an increasing number of enthusiastic admirers of Rodenbach from that time on. One of these enthusiasts was Yano Hōjin 矢野峰人, who claimed that Ueda's translation was vastly superior to the original.

It is not exaggerating to say that we really owed a sudden rise in the number of Japanese lovers of Rodenbach to Ueda Bin, but we are equally indebted to Nagai Kafū 永井荷風 (1879-1959). Nagai Kafū lived in France from 1907 to 1908, and on his return to Japan he confessed that he was fascinated by Rodenbach's works. We sense his deep infatuation with Rodenbach in his many essays as well as in the preface to the fifth edition of *Sumidagawa* すみだ川 ("The River Sumida", 1909), in which he implies that he wrote it using *Bruges-la-Morte* as a model. It was not until the Shōwa era (1926-1989) that the modern public could read a Japanese translation of *Bruges-la-Morte*. The first translation was by Ema Toshio 江間俊雄 (1933, 1940), and the second by Kuroda Kenji 黒田憲治 and Tada Michitarō 多田道太郎 (1949). Other translators were Kubota Han'ya 窪田般彌 (1976; 1988), Tanabe Tamotsu 田辺保 (1984) and Takahashi Yōichi 高橋洋一 (2005); in total we have six different versions today.

It seldom happens that in only half a century as many as six translations of one nineteenth-century Western novel should be published. How could this book strike such a sympathetic cord in its Japanese readership? Why did it exert such an extraordinary fascination? In the postscript to his translation Tanabe Tamotsu reveals his long-cherished worship of *Bruges-la-Morte*, noting, "I was reluctant to translate this work, but I couldn't help expressing my secret ardent love of Rodenbach by offering my translation for my own satisfaction." Nearly all translators must have cherished similar feelings for this work. Every one of them was entirely moved by this novel, and desired to identify himself with the author by presenting a translation in his own words. Why on earth did *Bruges-la-Morte* continue to appeal to the Japanese for than a century? Proceeding chronologically, I will explore the reasons why.

Nagai Kafū and Rodenbach

The Poet and His Sadness

Though nothing is left to tell us when and where Kafū acquired an original copy of *Bruges-la-Morte*, we know that immediately after he returned from America and France the name of Rodenbach appears again and again in his writings. First, he partly translated a poem by Rodenbach in his short story *Hana yori ame ni* 花より雨に ("From the Flowery to the Rainy Season", 1909), in which he quotes some lines from "La pluie", a poem in the collection *La Jeunesse blanche*. He quotes two passages about winter rain. He states that winter rain distresses him and calls forth a response. In another article, *Reishō* 冷笑 ("A Cold Smile", 1910), Kafū writes that in Rodenbach's "regional novel" Bruges figures as a character, and that *Bruges-la-Morte* is a representative model for "regional literature". Two years later, in the travel sketch *Kaiyō no tabi* 海洋の旅 ("Ocean Journey", 1911), he notes that he only wished he could sing like Rodenbach of a piece of furniture in a study, a church bell, a nun, a water bird and the water in the canals of a ruined city.

Kafū, after his return from France, endeavoured to absorb a certain Western literary trend, and his fondness of Rodenbach's poetic world and literary style must be interpreted in that light. Which of Rodenbach's books had he read? In his essay *Bungei yomu ga mama* 文芸読むがま〻 ("In Reading Literature", 1912), we find reference to two of Rodenbach's poem collections: *Le miroir du ciel natal* and *Le règne du silence*. The sequel to this essay deals with poetical melancholy and metaphorical versification in detail, and summarizes the plot of *Bruges-la-Morte*, giving it as Japanese title: *Haishi no kane* 廢市の鐘 ("Bells of a Ruined City"). Kafū also picks up several main elements: the sad procession of nuns, the water in the dead canal, a bell calling to prayer, all the things in a medieval ruined town that act like a living person. He emphasizes that the town itself is the main figure. In fact, he even confesses having had the intention of writing a novel modelled on *Bruges-la-Morte*, but in the end he gave up the idea, because imitating was too contemptible a thing to do.

Kafū's sojourn in France took place fifteen years after the publication of *Bruges-la-Morte* in 1892, and twenty years later, its plot was introduced by him in Japan. The outline is more or less correct, although there are some differences with the original. This may however precisely be the reason why Japanese devotees of literature wished to read the original. Perhaps we should first pay attention to a letter that has some relevance to Kafū's idea of writing a similar novel set in the ancient capital of Nara instead of Bruges. It is a letter addressed to Kafū by Ueda Bin, who sent it from Nara in 1910. Two years later, Kafū confessed he had considered writing an imitation of Rodenbach's novel. Ueda was traveling with his wife and daughter in Nara. In his letter Ueda wrote the ancient capital of Nara somehow reminded him of Bruges. The dead city of Nara or *Nara-la-Morte* was not evoked by the sound of a carillon but by a mournful temple bell.

Kafū had already become acquainted with Ueda Bin in Paris, Kyoto and Tokyo. He respected Ueda, who was five years older. Reference to Nara as *Nara-la-Morte* is not simply a word play on *Bruges-la-Morte*, but reflects the fact that the ancient city of Nara did indeed conjure up the image of the ancient city of Bruges. Why would Ueda refer to this mental association in a letter to Kafū, unless both were familiar with *Bruges-la-Morte*? In the eighth century, Nara was the location of the court of Yamato, and as an ancient town harboured the remains of palaces and castles. Bruges on the other hand is a medieval city which prospered from the thirteenth to the fourteenth century on account of its role in international trade. Although the two cities prospered in different ages, both had religious architecture, historic spots and a local village-like atmosphere in common. They were very much alike.

Now we can make two assumptions. The first is that this phrase in Ueda's letter gave Kafū the idea of writing a novel, and the second is that Kafū had previously planned an imitation of Rodenbach's work. Bin and Kafū may have been talking about the title "Bruges-la-Morte" and related topics before. Two years later, Kafū confessed his intention of writing an imitation. In any case, he never wrote a *Nara-la-Morte*, and the literary fancy of superposing Nara on Bruges must have been a pleasure only entertained by two sophisticated Japanese writers in private conversation.

Cities as Dramatis Personae

It is certain that Kafū never wrote a novel evoking an atmosphere of antiquity with Nara as backdrop. Yet, *Bruges-la-Morte* did contribute to Kafū's literary imagination in subtler ways. He wrote *Sumidagawa* inspired by *Bruges-la-Morte*. He published it in 1909, one year after returning from abroad. The novel vividly describes old Tokyo at the end of the nineteenth century. *Sumidagawa* evokes the nostalgic atmosphere of life along the riverside in the 1890s. The old towns of Japan began to be destroyed by the surprisingly rapid Westernization.

Chōkichi 長吉, the main character of *Sumidagawa*, is an eighteen-year-old student. His mother Otoyo お豊 teaches *tokiwazu* 常磐津, traditional dramatic recitation sung to the accompaniment of kabuki. Otoyo wants her son to become a wealthy man, but Chōkichi aspires to become an actor or an entertainer because he belongs to an older world that is on the verge of disappearing. He wanders around his beloved streets in the districts of Imado 今戸 and Asakusa 浅草. His childhood friend Oito お糸 leaves him because she is destined to become a geisha girl. In spite of their friendship they are doomed to become strangers. Chōkichi's heart is filled with disconsolate and gloomy feelings about his future. After a flood he desperately wanders through the streets, and develops typhoid fever. He lacks the courage to kill himself, but would be glad if he could die of it. He has an uncle named Ragetsu 蘿月, a professional *haikai* poet. He knows a lot about worldly affairs but he feels dishonoured in his pretensions of being a man of the world. Ragetsu recalls his own youth, takes pity on Chōkichi, and decides to assist him to be an actor and marry Oito.

The novel was published along with some other short stories by the publisher Momiyama Shoten 籾山書店 in 1911. In the preface to the fifth edition, Kafū revealed his true intention in creating this work. When he returned to Tokyo, he felt disappointed: "Tokyo was no longer a pleasant place to walk for people who want to enjoy composing poetry, it had turned into a veritable shambles." This is the exact reason why he intended to recreate a landscape of the past, with which he had been familiar from his childhood on, overlooking the banks of the River Sumida.

The preface to the fifth edition of *Sumidagawa* is quite significant. Kafū stated that this novel had a naturalistic slant and described an imaginary vision by which he was attracted. The landscapes in the novel should be considered as more important than the characters. We come across the same idea in the preface of *Bruges-la-Morte*:

> In this impassioned study it has been my primary ambition to evoke in the form of an intangible personality the spirit of a town, endowing it not merely with the power of entering into all the fluctuating conditions of the soul, but causing it further to be an agency in guiding, counselling and determining the whole scope of human action.
>
> (translated by Thomas Duncan, published by Swan Sonnenscein & Co., Lim., 1903)

This similarity of perspective between Rodenbach and Kafū is no coincidence. Kafū was fascinated not only by situations and atmospheres, but also by writing methods. In 1920 he wrote about his method of creating fiction in the twenty-ninth issue of *Shōsetsu sahō* 小説作法 ("The Method of Writing Novels"). This article, ten years after the publication of *Sumidagawa*, confirms that he used the technique of depicting a city as a persona.

Conformity of Structure

It is not by chance that two novels of the East and the West employ a similar method to deal with the changing times. In *Bruges-la-Morte* the story develops from November to the following May, i.e. spanning half a year. *Sumidagawa* also starts in early autumn and ends in the early summer. Both these novels are not long, are condensed, and move slowly with the cycle of the seasons. The stories mainly progress in winter. Scenes of winter days are suitable for the evocation of the heroes' melancholic, sentimental feelings. These two novels are similar in three respects: the hankering for the past, the powerful use of proper nouns, and a play within a play. While describing a real city, *Sumidagawa* revives memories of past days. This technique is exactly the same as the one employed in *Bruges-la-Morte*. In order to make the Middle Ages real and alive, Rodenbach described scenes of the nineteenth-century town. Kafū in his turn wrote an elegy of the past, a reminiscence of the Edo era. Thus their writing techniques are similar to all

intent and purpose. Both novels represent a graphic illusion of decay from the writer's point of view. Moriyasu Masafumi 森安理文, a scholar and critic, comments that *Sumidagawa* is a requiem for a moribund Sumida (*Nagai Kafū: Hikage no Bungaku* 永井荷風—ひかげの文学, 1981). The same comment can be applied to *Bruges-la-Morte*.

The backgrounds of the two stories consist of places of childhood memories, evoking nostalgia, even though they were not the places where the authors were born. Approximately twenty spots are depicted in *Bruges-la-Morte*, and seventy spots in *Sumidagawa*: the waterside, bridges, alleys, historic sites, religious buildings, and so on. The proper nouns in particular lend this fiction an enormous impact. They not only enhance reality, but also imply origin and history. Proper nouns furthermore evoke religious events and private remembrances. For instance, Hugues frequently visits the Church of Our Lady. It is a magnificent example of Gothic architecture constructed in the thirteenth century. It contains the celebrated tombs of Charles the Bold and his daughter, Mary of Burgundy. In the fifteenth century, she governed Flanders and died young. The sweet princess, who is lying supine, reminds Hugues of his dead wife. The princess has her hands delicately joined and her head rested upon a cushion. One day when Hugues leaves church, he encounters the dancer Jane Scott for the first time. She is the spitting image of his wife. The church must be no other than the Church of Our Lady because this church symbolizes Bruges' prosperous years in the medieval period, and it was here that Mary of Burgundy reminded him of his dead wife. The *Minnewater* (The Lake of Love), the St Ursula Shrine, and so on, everything and every place is suggestive of ancient Bruges and pangs of love.

In *Sumidagawa*, it is the Imado Bridge (where the San'yabori 山谷堀 Canal joins the River Sumida) that Chōkichi crosses time and again. On this bridge in the moonlit night, he sees off his childhood friend, Oito. Ever since, even when he sees the moon on the backdrop of a stage, he cannot stop recalling the moon of that night. A moonlit night on the Imado Bridge is the subject of a painting by Kobayashi Kiyochika 小林清親 (1847-1915), the famous woodblock-print artist. It is one of the most picturesque landscapes near the River Sumida. Chōkichi's uncle, Ragetsu, usually visits his younger sister Otoyo, Chōkichi's mother, in the Imado district by going across the River Sumida on a ferryboat, and crossing this bridge, too. As dramatis persona, the Imado Bridge is indispensable to this story. Moreover, place names such as streets, shrines and temples all allude to the background and history. Above all, as places of poetical association they lend body and suggestion to the story. In addition, the insertion of a theatre scene is another element similar to *Bruges-la-Morte*. In Chapters 6 and 7 of *Sumidagawa*, Chōkichi goes to a playhouse, the Miyato Theatre 宮戸座. *Ume yanagi naka no yoizuki* 梅柳中宵月 ("The Evening Moon amidst the Plum and Willow Tree") is being performed. This tragic love story overlaps with Chōkichi's disconsolate love for Oito. It is after his visit to the theatre that he decides to leave school and become an actor.

On the other hand, in Chapter 3 of *Bruges-la-Morte*, Hugues follows a woman into the theatre, and there he realizes that the woman is a dancer on the stage. She is playing a nun in Meyerbeer's *Robert le Diable*. The dancer is Jane Scott from Lille. She plays an immoral abbess who seems to be a devil in disguise. The plot in each story is different, however, the play within a play controls the way of thinking and acting of the main character. There is no doubt that Kafū's *Sumidagawa* is based on *Bruges-la-Morte*. Needless to say, Kafū does not try to imitate Rodenbach, but rather learnt from Rodenbach the technique of composing a novel, the technique of dramaturgy.

A Poet and *flâneur*

Certainly, what Rodenbach and Kafū have in common is their natural talent for writing. Rodenbach could be considered as a wandering poet. His collection of short stories, *Le Rouet des brumes*, includes "Le chasseur des villes", a story about a man who shadows a woman on the street and conquers her as if he were a hunter. Many *flâneurs* make their appearance in the works of Rodenbach. *Bruges-la-Morte*, so to speak, is a story of perambulations around the town. Hugues Viane strolls from canal-side to canal-side and visits scenic spots and places of historic interest. By depicting the characteristics of a *flâneur* and through the power of the frequently used place names, nostalgia for a lost, bygone town is vividly evoked in the background.

Soon after returning from France, Kafū published *Furansu monogatari* ふらんす物語 ("French Stories", 1909). The stories have similar characteristics. Kafū would stroll freely around the streets in Lyon. Eventually many of Kafū's perambulations in the city led him to create short stories, sketches and essays. While walking along the riverside, crossing bridges and visiting churches in the city, he could identify buildings, places, and streets and described them under those circumstances. Kafū's writing method, i.e. to stroll, to observe, and to describe a view and finally to put it into a work, did not change after his return to Japan. He completed *Fukagawa no uta* 深川の唄 ("A Song of Fukagawa", 1909) and *Sumidagawa* in this way. He took to strolling and sketching, so he spent most of his time wandering the old streets and scribbling down whatever came to his mind. The description of the district along the River Sumida and his favourite surroundings there makes us feel nostalgic for the old town. Kafū did not have to assimilate Rodenbach's method, because he was already a perambulator by nature. We can say that Rodenbach and Kafū are truly wandering writers. As for *French Stories*, written after Kafū's return from France, some illustrations of the Parisian landscape were supposed to be inserted in the publication, but the sale was prohibited just before its first release, so neither cover nor book binding are left to us. In this book, Kafū actually planned to show the picture postcards that he had brought back from Paris. Using the method of reproducing land- and cityscapes by illustrations to produce a visual effect, he tried to join a tradition started by Rodenbach in *Bruges-la-Morte*.

Floating Coffin on the Water

Incidentally, Kitahara Hakushū 北原白秋, a well-known Japanese poet, was likewise a devotee of Rodenbach. In his verse, he depicted his decaying hometown in words and images, using the unique techniques proper to Rodenbach. Kitahara felt nostalgia for his dying hometown, Yanagawa. He also associated Yanagawa with Bruges. Yanagawa as he remembered it evoked a "ruined town" or a "floating coffin on the water." Kitahara used the word "ruined town" one year before Kafū used it in reference to *Bruges-la-Morte*. Kitahara probably learnt it through Mori Ōgai's 森鴎外 translation (1902) of *Improvisatoren* (1835) by Hans Christian Andersen

(1805-1875). At the end of this novel Venice is called a "dead town" and a gondola a "floating coffin on the water." During the last years of the Meiji era, quite a few writers strongly inclined toward adoration for Rodenbach, in particular for *Bruges-la-Morte*. In the background of this tendency, there was an increasing nostalgia for the lost world. It was the time when Japan's good old things languished because of the modernization. After Japan's victory in the Russo-Japanese War (1904-1905), Tokyo developed into a Westernized city in which modern department stores were constructed and tramways built. After a five-year-life abroad, Kafū returned to Japan and took offense at Japan's radical modernization and progress. He seemed to detest the ugliness of the burgeoning city, which prompted him to haunt the neighbourhood of the River Sumida, where people maintained the old Edo era atmosphere. This was the area where he used to spend a lot of time before going abroad.

Cover of Japanese translation of *Bruges-la-Morte* by Ema Toshio 江間俊雄, published by Shun'yōdō (1933).
Reproduced from Muramatsu 2014.

Cover of Japanese translation of *Bruges-la-Morte* by Ema Toshio 江間俊雄, published by Shun'yōdō (1940).
Reproduced from Muramatsu 2014.

Cover of the Japanese translation of *Bruges-la-Morte* by Kuroda Kenji 黒田憲治 and Tada Michitarō 多田道太郎, published by Shisakusha (1949).
Reproduced from Muramatsu 2014.

Survey of Translations

In the late Meiji era, the decadent image of the "dead town" or "town in decay" increasingly gained popularity among writers and artists. With the advent of the Shōwa era, several translations of *Bruges-la-Morte* appeared in Japanese, notably:

1) A translation by Ema Toshio, 1933, 1940, published by Shun'yōdō 春陽堂.
This rendering was the first translation of the novel, a soft-covered book included in the *World Masterpieces Series*. Seven years later, it was republished in book form. According to the postscript, the translator had visited Bruges and referred to the writings of Ueda Bin and Nagai Kafū introducing Rodenbach. This translation made the number of readers expand considerably.

2) A translation by Kuroda Kenji and Tada Michitarō, 1949, published by Shisakusha 思索社.
This joint translation adopted a natural style, and included three other short stories by Rodenbach.

3) A translation by Kubota Han'ya, 1976, published by Meisōsha 明窓社.

4) A translation by Kubota Han'ya, 1988, published by Iwanami Shoten 岩波書店.
Twenty-seven years after the second translated version, the third version of 1976 included thirty-four photographs. Scenes of Bruges were reprinted from the

original edition of *Bruges-la-Morte*. In 1988 Kubota entirely revised his first translation and republished it as part of a paperback series published by Iwanami Shoten.

5) A Translation by Tanabe Tamotsu, 1984, published by Kokusho Kankōkai 国書刊行会 as one of the volumes in the *Fin-de-siècle French Literature Series*. The volume also

Portrait of Georges Rodenbach (c.1895).
Pastel by Lucien Lévy-Dhurmer, 36 × 55 cm.
First exhibited in 1896, purchased by the Musée du Luxembourg in 1899, now in the Cabinet des dessins, Musée d'Orsay, Paris.
Reproduced from Muramatsu 2014.

dream-like world of *Bruges-la-Morte*, in which dream and reality coalesce, is epitomized in this single pastel rendering. The painter shows a portrait expressing grief and melancholy, so any reader of *Bruges-la-Morte* knows that Rodenbach's portrait refers to the book's protagonist, Hugues Viane. The detailed description and the dreamy traditional fascination form a harmonious whole.

One may safely say that *Portrait of Georges Rodenbach* is another work that made Rodenbach famous in Japan, because the Japanese are absolutely moved by this portrait full of limpid clarity. Therefore, Rodenbach is a novelist who has been read, and will continue to be read by generation after generation of Japanese readers, because of his peculiar elaboration of the symbolic refinement of atmosphere.

(Adapted by W.F. Vande Walle from *"The River Sumida* and *Bruges-la-Morte"* in Muramatsu Sadafumi 村松定史. *Joruju Rōdenbakku kenkyū* ジョルジュ・ローデンバック研究. Tokyo: Kōgakusha 弘学社, 2014, pp. 191-199).

includes a translation of *Le Rouet des brumes*, as well as nineteen photographs of Bruges and notes.
6) Translation by Takahashi Yōichi, 2005, published by Chikuma Shobō 筑摩書房.
The newest translation in paperback also contains a translation of *Le Rouet des brumes* and several other translated fragments.

Why do we have as many as six translations of *Bruges-la-Morte* in Japanese?

Since the Meiji era the Japanese have had a great appetite for cultural assimilation from the West. *Bruges-la-Morte* can be seen as a symbolic example. It is one of the most popular Belgian novels in Japan. Why do the Japanese enjoy reading *Bruges-la-Morte*? In particular Japanese writers of the aesthetic school such as Mishima Yukio 三島由紀夫, Fukunaga Takehiko 福永武彦, Mori Mari 森茉莉, etc. love Rodenbach. We can find a reason for the popularity of Rodenbach's world in *Portrait of Georges Rodenbach* (1895) by the French painter Lucien Lévy-Dhurmer (1865-1953). The painter shows Rodenbach's face against a background vaguely evoking the canal city. The Gothic church spire, roofs, and gables are placed in the background, while his face is drawn realistically like in a photograph. Rodenbach's shoulders seem to fade completely into the canal behind him. The

REFERENCES

Rodenbach 1894
Georges Rodenbach. *Musée de béguines*. Paris: Bibliothèque-Charpentier, 1894.

Maeterlinck 1909
Maurice Maeterlinck. *L'oiseau bleu: Féerie en six actes et douze tableaux*. Paris: Fasquelle éditeurs, 1909.

Maeterlinck 1910
Maurice Maeterlinck. *L'oiseau bleu: Féerie en cinq actes et dix tableaux*. Paris: Librairie Charpentier et Fasquelle, 1910.

Rodenbach s.a.
Georges Rodenbach. *Bruges-la-Morte*. Ill. by Marin Baldo. Paris: Ernest Flammarion, s.a.

Tentoonstelling Georges Rodenbach
Tentoonstelling Georges Rodenbach. 100 jaar Bruges-la-Morte. Brugge: Centrale Openbare Bibliotheek De Biekorf, 8 mei – 27 juni 1992.

Muramatsu 2014
Muramatsu Sadafumi 村松定史. *Joruju Rōdenbakku kenkyū* ジョルジュ・ローデンバック研究. Tokyo: Kōgakusha 弘学社, 2014.

Monument to Georges Rodenbach by George Minne in Ghent, Oud Begijnhof Sint-Elizabeth (inaugurated in 1903).
Photograph by Muramatsu Sadafumi.

Tomb of Georges Rodenbach in Père Lachaise Cemetery, Paris. Sculpture by Charlotte Besnard.
Photograph by Muramatsu Sadafumi.

MAETERLINCK IN JAPAN: A HOSPITABLE HABITAT FOR *THE BLUE BIRD*

W.F. Vande Walle

JAPAN & BELGIUM

An Itinerary of Mutual Inspiration

Title page of *Aoi tori no oshie* (detail).
Collection of Jidō bunka kenkyū sentā 児童文化研究センター,
Shirayuri University 白百合女子大学, Tokyo.

MAETERLINCK IN JAPAN
A HOSPITABLE HABITAT FOR
THE BLUE BIRD

One day I asked my students whether they knew Maurice Maeterlinck, and for many, to my great surprise, his name did not immediately seem to ring a bell. It is true, literature does not excite the majority of the young generation, and certainly not when it deals with themes such as boredom, languor, waiting, the "soul of the night", sultry greenhouses, weariness of life, and unawakened things,[1] as in so many of Maeterlinck's poems and plays. In today's Flanders, most people are familiar with Hollywood blockbusters, but Maeterlinck does not belong to the "canon" of Flemish youth. As the only Belgian author ever awarded the Nobel Prize in Literature, the Ghent-born writer nonetheless continues to feature in anthologies of Nobel Prize winners, in series of modern classics, and in … Japan.

Along with the tragedy *Pelléas and Mélisande*, adapted as an opera of the same name and set to music by the composer Claude Debussy, *The Blue Bird* represents Maeterlinck's strongest claim to literary immortality. Japan in particular has turned out to be quite a hospitable habitat for *The Blue Bird*. Its remarkable and enduring career in that country has undoubtedly at least in part to do with the fact that there is a lot in it that appeals to the Japanese outlook on life, if one can make a generalization of that kind. The "blue bird" of the title is the symbol of the quest for happiness and truth of two children under the guidance of a fairy. The play, conceived as an allegorical fantasy, features in the lead roles Mytyl and Tyltyl, the children of a poor woodcutter. In their bedroom hangs a cage with a little bird. Falling asleep after a Christmas without presents, they dream that the fairy Bérylune sends them off in search of "the bird that is blue". She gives them a diamond that makes the souls of the objects that surround them visible. The children visit the Land of Memory, the Garden of Happiness, and the Kingdom of the Future, before returning home and being awakened by their mother. When their neighbour Berlingot (the fairy Bérylune) begs Tyltyl to give her his little bird for her dying child, Tyltyl notices that the bird is blue. The neighbour's child

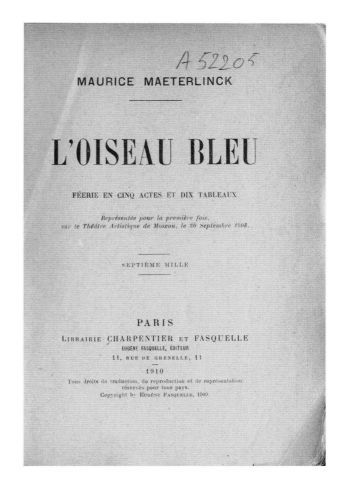

happily recovers, but the bird escapes. The children then turn to the audience and ask them to join in their quest for the bird.

The Blue Bird was completed as a play in 1908 and its world première took place the same year at the Moscow Art Theatre under the direction of Konstantin Stanislavsky. The play had an almost one-year run in Moscow. It was produced at the Haymarket Theatre in London in 1909, opened in New York in October 1910, and was staged at the Théâtre Réjane in Paris in 1911. In 1940, a screen version under the English title *Blue Bird* and directed by Walter Lange appeared, starring Shirley Temple, Spring Byington, Nigel Bruce, Eddie Collins, and Gale Sondergaard. The 1976 remake by George Cukor, starring such celebrities as Elisabeth Taylor, Jane Fonda, and Ava Gardner, was a Russian-American co-production, intended as a gesture of friendship and a symbol of entente between East and West.

Cover of *L'oiseau bleu, Féerie en cinq actes et dix tableaux.*
Paris: Librairie Charpentier et Fasquelle, 1910.

Japan's Acquaintance with Maeterlinck

The gifted scholar Ueda Bin (1874-1916) was the first to introduce Maeterlinck to a Japanese readership. "Readership" may be a misnomer, as it probably concerned a small group of intellectuals, taking interest in the most recent developments in Western literature. In a time when virtually no Japanese read French, he made considerable contributions to a better knowledge and understanding of French literature in his country. What is even more remarkable is his apparent interest in the work of Belgian authors. In the first issue of *Teikoku bungaku* 帝国大学 (January 1895), a learned journal published by the University of Tokyo, he published an article on "Belgian literature" under the pen name Biyūshi 微幽子 ("the secretive one").[2] This article is generally considered to be the first introduction in Japan of Symbolist literature, or even in a broader sense, of *fin de siècle* literature. In it Ueda mentions among others Maeterlinck, Georges Rodenbach, Iwan Gilkin, and Théodore Hannon. He claims that Baudelaire's influence can be seen in their verse, for instance in the use of colour adjectives to suggest mood or atmosphere.[3]

Ueda obtained his information for the greater part from an article by William Sharp, entitled "La Jeune Belgique" and published in the September 1893 issue of *The Nineteenth Century*. Although indebted to Sharp, in his analysis of the literary merits he uses an abundance of terms from classical Chinese and classical Japanese literary criticism, since the Japanese language still lacked standard terms corresponding to the terminology of Western literary criticism. At the time Ueda was still a student at Tokyo University. He graduated in the summer of 1897. He was enrolled in the English department, and his professor Lafcadio Hearn, the renowned interpreter of the Japanese tradition, once said about him that he was the only Japanese out of ten thousand people able to communicate properly in English. Ueda had an amazing gift for languages. Although specialized in English he also acquired a high level of proficiency in French, Italian, German, Spanish, Greek, and Latin. Later on, he would reveal himself particularly as an authority on French literature, and he was one of the founders of the academic study of literature in Japan.

His essay was not really an in-depth study of the topic; that could hardly be expected of a first introduction to the new trends in Belgian literature. Its main merits were that it had been written at all, that it made mention of the latest publications in Belgium, and that it acquainted the Japanese public with Belgian Symbolism.[4] Even more exceptional for that time is the fact that he also mentions in passing the Dutch-language (Flemish) literature in Belgium. This is perhaps the first reference to Flemish literature in the Japanese academic press. He more specifically refers to a lecture on Flemish literature delivered by Henri [sic] Conscience to the Royal Academy of Belgium. He mentions Guido Gezelle, "who writes in the West Flemish patois" and Cyriel Buysse who authored *Het recht van den sterkste* ("The Law of the Jungle"). It is unclear which source he used for this bit of information, since William Sharp made no reference to Flemish literature in his article.

Ueda describes how Maeterlinck had left for Paris with a newly written play a few years before, and how he had been hailed as a new Shakespeare.[5] When his play was put on the stage, however, he was showered with an avalanche of criticism, and was run into the ground for being an uncouth northerner, a Teutonic, someone who, to be sure, made use of French, but who had remained a mean Fleming in spirit. It is not clear which critics Ueda is referring to here, but it is a fact that Maeterlinck's work elicited a polemic in Paris during the 1890s.

At the end of the nineteenth century, many Belgian writers and artists were living in Paris, a considerable proportion among them coming from Flanders and having excellent chances in literature or the arts. Certain critics discerned in this Belgian or Flemish provenance a meaningful common characteristic, something that defined their art and made it special. It was believed to be redolent of the earthiness of Flemish clay, the uncanniness of scudding low-lying clouds, the mystery of the Middle Ages conjured up by stepped gables, Gothic gargoyles, Bruegel, and Flemish mysticism. Although this was for the most part a construct sprung from the imagination of the critics, the notion caught on, and turned into a cliché or commonplace in French criticism that tended to frame all Belgian literature and art. Japanese academics and writers dealing with French literature adopted this framing and have largely maintained the tendency to view Belgian writers in that

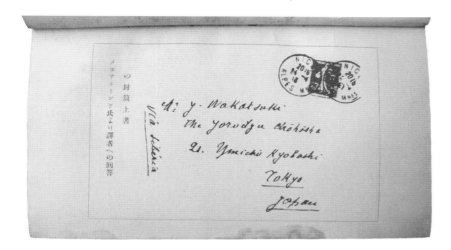

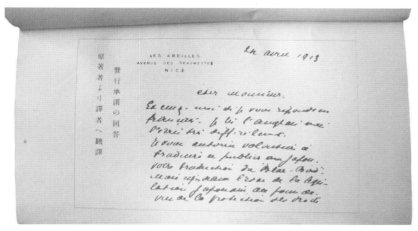

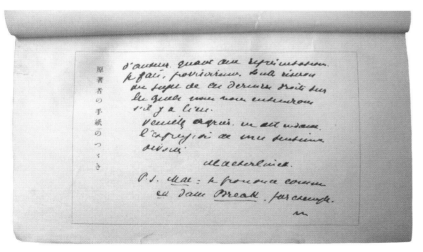

Envelope of a letter addressed by Maeterlinck to Japanese translator Wakatsuki Shiran, dated Nice, 24 April 1913. Reproduced in *Aoi tori* 青い鳥, translated by Wakatsuki Shiran 若月紫蘭. Tokyo: Gendaisha 現代社, 1913. (Kindai kyakuhon sōsho 近代脚本叢書 10 & 11).
Courtesy of Kabinet Maeterlinck, Ghent.

Letter from Maeterlinck to Wakatsuki Shiran, giving him permission to publish his Japanese translation in Japan, but reserving the author's rights with regard to the staging of the play. Reproduced in *Aoi tori* 青い鳥, translated by Wakatsuki Shiran 若月紫蘭. Tokyo: Gendaisha 現代社, 1913. (Kindai kyakuhon sōsho 近代脚本叢書 10 & 11).
Courtesy of Kabinet Maeterlinck, Ghent.

light. The poet and novelist Kaneko Mitsuharu (1898-1975) for instance, who on two occasions resided in Belgium for a considerable period of time, certainly embraced a similar view of Flemish art.

In 1905 Ueda published an anthology of Symbolist poetry.[6] It comprised translations of Verhaeren, Verlaine, Rimbaud, Mallarmé, Puvis de Chavannes, Sully Prud'homme, among others, but Maeterlinck was not included. In the introduction he does briefly touch upon Maeterlinck, but in the following year he devoted an article to him in the well-known literary magazine *Myōjō*.[7] His posthumously published collection of translations *Bokuyōshin* 牧羊神 ("The goat god / Pan") contains some seven of Maeterlinck's most famous poems in a Japanese version.[8]

Takagi Toshio 高木敏雄 (1876-1922), was actually the first to devote a feature article to Maeterlinck. It appeared in two instalments in the aforementioned *Teikoku bungaku* (November and December 1902). This article is not very thorough, and remained virtually unnoticed. Afterwards, Takagi applied himself to the comparative study of mythologies, and he became one of the founders of folklore studies and ethnology in Japan. This perhaps explains why his article went unnoticed among literary critics.

Japanese Translations

The first Japanese translation of *The Blue Bird* (*Aoi tori* 青い鳥) was by Shimada Motomaro 島田元麿 and Higashi Sōsui 東草水 and published by the publishing house Jitsugyō no Nihonsha 実業の日本社 in 1911. In their introduction, the translators state that their work is a simplified and condensed version of the original, intended as a reader for children. They had even given the two children in the play Japanese names: "Chikao" (for the boy) and "Michiko" (for the girl). In 1913 Wakatsuki Shiran 若月紫蘭 (1879-1962) published a full Japanese translation on the basis of the English version. In his foreword he notes that he had received permission for the translation directly from the author himself, and even reproduces the letter from Maeterlinck to support his claim. In 1915 Shiran published a revised translation based on both the English version and the French original.

Even so, it was not until 1920 that *The Blue Bird* was first staged in Japan, notably by the theatrical company *Minshū-za* 民衆座 ("The People's Theatre") under the direction of Hatanaka Ryōha 畑中蓼坡 (1877-1959). The preparations took a considerable time; the rehearsals alone took four months, or according to some sources even five months. This version premièred on Thursday, 11 February 1920. It ran for seven days, with performances beginning at 5 p.m., plus Saturday and Sunday matinees at noon.[9] In March 1920, *Minshū-za* also staged performances in Kōbe for one week. The play consisted of seven acts and ten scenes. Much care had been devoted to the props and the settings. Hatanaka had spared no expense, and this had been made possible by a grant from a Japanese whom he had met in America, the son of a certain Tanaka, a wealthy person from Yokohama, but further information about him is lacking.[10] The cast was impressive: more than eighty actors made their appearance on the stage in the course of the play. Most of them were impersonations of things and phenomena, such as the night, sugar, stars, a cold, and so forth.[11]

According to the testimony of actress Mizutani Yaeko 水谷八重子, who played Tyltyl (the boy character), the play was a huge success. The newspapers were enthralled, and Osanai Kaoru 小山内薫 (1881-1928), the godfather of Japanese theatre in those days and one of the founding fathers of Japanese realistic theatre in the Western style (*shingeki* 新劇), praised it as one of the best theatrical performances he had lately seen, although he also in a somewhat *blasé* tone pointed out all sorts of shortcomings.[12] *The Blue Bird* was indeed staged in the style of the *shingeki*. This is a Western-style theatre, characterized by what would to our eyes seem overacting: heavy make-up, theatrical gestures, melodramatic expression, and uncomfortable kissing. *Shingeki* still exists as a theatrical genre today, played by such troupes as the *Shiki gekidan* 四季劇団 ("The Four Seasons Theatre"). This dramatic company incidentally has often staged performances of *The Blue Bird*. Osanai had seen the performance in Russia and also in the *Deutsches Theater* in Berlin under the direction of Max Reinhardt. He was the senior expert in Japan and was able to compare the Japanese performance with the normative productions of Moscow and Berlin.[13]

Everything seems to indicate that the staging in Japan was largely influenced by the Russian mise-en-scène.

Shimada too apparently had seen the play, and his Japanese translation was based on the Russian rendering, whereas, as has already been mentioned, Wakatsuki Shiran's more famous translation was based on the English translation. This production of *The Blue Bird* was a milestone in Japan's theatrical history. According to the late Professor Tomita Hiroyuki 冨田博之, an authority on youth theatre in Japan, the première of *The Blue Bird* marked the true beginning of serious youth theatre in his country. This historical significance was the reason for Tomita taking a lifelong interest in *The Blue Bird*.

The script for the production of the Japanese première, however, was based neither on Shimada's translation nor on Shiran's, but on that of Kusuyama Masao 楠山正雄 (1884-1950), who had published his version especially for the stage in 1919. In point of fact there is not much difference between the translations of Shiran and Kusuyama. Both translators happened to be journalists. Shiran was a graduate of the English Department of Tokyo University, while Kusuyama was a graduate of the English Department of Waseda University. Generally speaking, subsequent stage productions tended to rely more often on Kusuyama's version than on Shiran's. Since then, the popularity of Maeterlinck's play has been virtually unabated in Japan. Roughly 170 different publications bearing the title *Aoi tori* ("The Blue Bird") have been inventoried. Although this figure includes all formats and categories, it is impressive by any standard.

There was even a board game featuring the characters of *The Blue Bird*, distributed on 1 January 1921 as an inset in the magazine *Manabi no tomo* 学びの友. The first square was the room of the children Tyltyl and Mytyl, and players had to cover the entire track of the children in order to finally rejoin the blue bird at home.[14]

From Theatre to Narrative (*monogatari*), from Narrative to Fairy Tale

Maeterlinck wrote predominantly for the theatre, but in Japan a number of his plays were adapted into stories, although generally the reverse is the more common practice. A first example in this regard was *Māterurinku monogatari* マアテルリンク物語 by the great poet Masamune Hakuchō 正宗白鳥 (1903). His adaptation was inspired by the example of Charles Lamb, who had

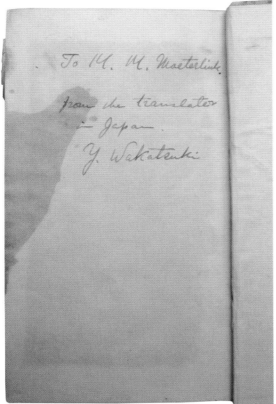

compiled *Tales from Shakespeare*. Hakuchō adapted a number of plays into narratives. Accordingly, the title of his work should be translated as *Tales from Maeterlinck*. It was an anthology comprising the following dramas: *Princess Maleine*, *Pelléas and Mélisande*, *The Intruder*, *The Blind*.[15]

A distinction should be made between the real narratives and the adaptations. Most of the publications in Japan are so-called "recountings" in simple Japanese, understandable to a young readership. Wakatsuki Shiran's version went on to serve as the basis of many adaptations into a story for children. Subsequent adaptations were increasingly simplified and enriched with illustrations, thus further deviating from the original narrative. *The Blue Bird* quickly took on the stature of a classic of youth literature, and still today is firmly entrenched in that category, although Maeterlinck presumably did not intend this. In some cases the name of Maeterlinck even disappeared from the credits, as in the case of the adaptation by the Nobel Prize-winning author Kawabata Yasunari. Here the story is presented as if written by Kawabata himself.

After the Second World War, as manga and anime became all-pervasive, it was natural for *The Blue Bird* also to be adapted to these new formats of popular culture. In 1980 *Blue Bird: Tyltyl and Mytyl's Adventurous Journey* was aired on Fuji Television as a 26-episode anime series. It was directed by Sasagawa Hiroshi, with character designs drawn by Matsumoto Leiji (Reiji), a giant in the Japanese world of manga. It was a musical anime, broadcast in stereo although at that time only a small part of the viewership was able to receive in stereo. This in turn gave rise to *anime ehon*, illustrated books based on anime, and manga versions, usually adopting the same style for their characters. Thus in 1985 an *anime ehon* appeared, scripted by Hirata Shōgo 平田昭吾 and illustrated by Ōno Yutaka 大野豊, as number 13 in the Popura Publishers series *Sekai meisaku fantajī* ("World masterpieces of fantasy"). In 2010 the book was reprinted.

During the 1970s, Japan witnessed a boom of anime adaptations of classic Western children's stories. Famous examples include *A Dog of Flanders*, *The Rose of Versailles*, and *Heidi, Girl of the Alps*. These adaptations fitted the story to European settings and put European

Cover of *Aoi tori* 青い鳥, translated by Wakatsuki Shiran 若月紫蘭. Tokyo: Gendaisha 現代社, 1913. (Kindai kyakuhon sōsho 近代脚本叢書 10 & 11).
Courtesy of Kabinet Maeterlinck, Ghent. The cover design, a clear reference to classical antiquity, suggests that in the early years *Aoi tori* was considered a "serious" play targeted at an adult audience. In contrast, later editions of this translation and later translations usually feature the two children in the cover illustration.

Dedication from Y(asuharu) Wakatsuki to Maeterlinck. Flyleaf of *Aoi tori* 青い鳥, translated by Wakatsuki Shiran 若月紫蘭. Tokyo: Gendaisha 現代社, 1913. (Kindai kyakuhon sōsho 近代脚本叢書 10 & 11).
Courtesy of Kabinet Maeterlinck, Ghent. "Yasuharu" was Wakatsuki's real name, "Shiran" was his penname.

No. 10 Nisikatamati, Hongo,
Tokyo, Japan,
Jan. 9, 1919.

The most respected
M. M. Maeterlinck:—

I have an honour to write you again. A few years ago you have greatly honoured me by giving a privilege to translate your renowned drama "The Blue Bird" into Japanese.

I sent the Japanese translation soon after, and I think you received it.

Now I hear that you have written another new drama "The Betrothal" as the sequel of "the Blue Bird,"

...and that it has been produced with great success in America.

Would you kindly give me another honour of privilege to translate "The Betrothal" into Japanese and to publish it in Japan?

But I regret that I must confess you that I, as another men of letters in Japan, am as poor as ever that I can not forward you any reward except some copies of the translation when published.

Thanking you in anticipation for your kind and respectful answer, and hoping that your Madame, you and your beloved country will as ever be blessed!

I am yours most faithfully,
Yasuharu Wakatuky.

---

characters on the stage: in some cases concrete and recognisable, in other cases the décor is a kind of potpourri of European set elements hand-picked from diverse countries, cities, and landscape types. The story unfolds somewhere in an ageless Europe, "Ruritania", a utopian world, exemplifying the Japanese counterpart to Western orientalism. This trend undoubtedly had to do with the economic boom in Japan during the 1970s. The Japanese identified their own country with progress and industrialization, and they created a fictional rural and idyllic Europe. It is a utopian, static continent that transcends history, as it were. This responds to Maeterlinck's original intention, to the extent that his *féerie* also constituted a quest through another world.[16]

Under the Spell of the "Blue Bird"

No matter how successful the theatrical performance was, what really made *The Blue Bird* a shared point of reference for Japanese children was the publication and reading of the many recountings and illustrated versions, so much so that the expression "blue bird" gradually became a widespread metaphor. Incidentally, during his lifetime the abovementioned Professor Tomita Hiroyuki collected everything relating directly or indirectly to *The Blue Bird* in Japan, including books dealing with other works by Maeterlinck. As soon as something about Maeterlinck or the "blue bird" had appeared in a book, an article, or in any other format, he added it to his collection. He even went so far as to incorporate a work like Ogawa Hideki's 小川秀樹, *Berugī:*

Copy of English language letter from Yasuharu Wakatsuki [Shiran] [Wakatsuky in his own spelling] to Maeterlinck, dated 9 January 1919, asking permission to translate into Japanese *The Betrothal* (staged in New York in 1918, published in 1922 under the title *Les Fiançailles*, as a sequel to *L'oiseau bleu*).
Courtesy of Archief Maeterlinck, Stadsarchief Gent.

Yōroppa ga mieru kuni ベルギー ヨーロッパが見える国 ("Belgium, a country where you can see Europe") in his collection, a book which otherwise has nothing to do with Maeterlinck. In the process he succeeded in building up a unique *The Blue Bird* library (292 volumes all told), which is now housed in the institute he was formally affiliated to, Shirayuri University, Tokyo.[17] During the seventies, a Japanese carmaker launched a model called *Bluebird*. Newspaper ads for this model equally found their way into Tomita's collection. Still, his collection is largely limited to publications in the Japanese language. As for Maeterlinck, he only included a few original French editions as well as a number of English translations. Maeterlinck was indeed first introduced in Japan by way of English translations, and only afterwards also through direct translations from the French. Tomita's collection represents a documentary monument to the history of *The Blue Bird*'s reception in Japan.

A Metaphor

The diversity of documents in Tomita's collection, both in terms of format and of content, is a reflection of how widespread the expression "blue bird" had become as a metaphor for "happiness close at hand" or "a modest utopia". In 1949, the Japanese socialist politician Katayama Tetsu, Japan's prime minister for some time shortly after the Second World War, participated in the Conference of the Moral Re-Armament Association, an international pacifist movement, held in Switzerland. Reporting about his journey to Europe, the Conference and his meetings with personalities from the world of politics and labour unions, he published an account he entitled *In Search of the Blue Bird*. The title was meant to convey to the Japanse reader the aspiration to a peaceful world, which the participants hoped to build through moral re-armament.

Yet the "blue bird" is an ambivalent metaphor. It also represents the feverish pursuit of happiness in faraway places beyond one's reach, the failure to see that happiness is within reach and commonplace. This particular meaning of the metaphor is reflected in the expression *aoi tori shōkōgun* ("bluebird syndrome"). At the end of the 1970s, when Japan started to reap the fruits of its economic prosperity, the new generation

---

Aoi tori. Adaptation by Kawabata Yasunari 川端康成. Drawings by Takei Takeo 武井武雄. Tokyo: Akane bunko あかね文庫, 1949. Sekai meisaku monogatari sensho 世界名作物語選書 no. 1.
Collection Jidō bunka kenkyū sentā 児童文化研究センター, Shirayuri University 白百合女子大学, Tokyo.

Mēterurinku Aoi tori. Adaptation by Wakatsuki Shiran. Illustrations by Kawashima Haruyo. Tokyo: Kōdansha, 1951.
Collection Jidō bunka kenkyū sentā 児童文化研究センター, Shirayuri University 白百合女子大学, Tokyo.

became increasingly picky about jobs. While formerly most people were happy to have a job, and were content to stay in that job for the rest of their working life, now, more and more university graduates took to job-hopping, displaying choosiness about the content of the job. Many graduates believed they belonged to the elite, and thought that their current job offered too few possibilities for self-realization. Thus they went looking for another job, just to find out that this one too was below their level or potential. Thus many continued their quest for the ideal job, time and again ending in disappointment. For many people the continued frustration resulted in despair and depression. The psychotherapist Shimizu Masayuki labelled this unrelenting search for a better job, with the ensuing frustration and despair, the "bluebird syndrome". He first identified this problem in a column written for the newspaper *Sankei shinbun* in 1980. He ascribed the phenomenon to the exaggeratedly high expectations cherished by young adults when they entered the job market, and he blamed the education system for its obsession with school achievements and the acquisition of access to elite education. The media took up the issue, and it became for some time the subject of social debate.[18]

In 1991, the Women's Association for a Better Aging Society (*Kōreika shakai o yokusuru josei no kai* 高齢化社会をよくする女性の会) organized a symposium on the problems of aging, entitled "In Search of the Blue Bird of Old Age".[19]

The Secret of the Blue Bird's Success?

The million-dollar question is of course: what do the Japanese find so attractive about *The Blue Bird*? What did they read into it? And what are they still reading into it? In my opinion, it has to do with the moral dimension. The story appeals to popular values. Maeterlinck called it a *féerie*, but the Japanese made it into a kind of morality. Maeterlinck may have intended his play as philosophical reflection, but there is only a thin line between that and a moralizing fable. After all, the play contains a number of ingredients that can easily be deflected towards a moral and even moralizing perspective. The main characters are children, which makes identification for a youthful audience easy. It was a matter of course that it would be

adapted for children. Since the characters are children, the play easily lapses into a sentimental tone. Spectators allegedly used to shed profuse tears during the performance, but then again Japanese audiences relish tear-jerkers. Moreover, traditionally the majority of the theatre audience are women.

It is to be doubted whether Maeterlinck himself considered *The Blue Bird* one of his masterpieces, or thought of it as more than a lighthearted interlude between his more serious works. His preceding plays had more ambition, and described tragic human relations. They were fatalistic and pessimistic. Some have alleged he had become more optimistic under the influence of his life partner Georgette Leblanc (1875-1941), and that *The Blue Bird* may have been a manifestation of this new-found optimism.

Maeterlinck's *féerie* was about the quest for happiness, but if seen as a fable, the drift of the message is ambivalent. On the one hand, it seems to convey the message that one should be happy with what one has, but then again, the blue bird escapes at the end of the play and everyone is called upon to come and help to find it.

When the play premièred in Japan, the country was undergoing a process of rapid urbanization. Many young people wanted to say goodbye to the tough and dull country life, and try their luck in the city, where hopefully a better life was waiting, but where there also lurked many dangers such as material ruin and temptations to moral decay. This was the Taishō era (1912-1926), a period of increasing democracy and frantic pursuit of more freedom. The new trends provoked social tensions. For powers trying to maintain or strengthen the moral, social or political status quo, a story like *The Blue Bird* was just what was needed. Do not aspire to impracticable dreams, be content with what you have, was the message many liked to read into the story. Educators with a mission to shore up the social status quo saw in it a useful wisdom. It is from this connotation that the expression "blue bird" has secured currency in the Japanese language and has become an elegant synonym for simple happiness within one's reach, happiness that one should find in one's daily life. It is not difficult to imagine why Japanese educators in the first decades of the twentieth century found the message of

The Blue Bird so suitable. They certainly had a hand in the popularity of the story, and none more so than Miyazaki Saishō 宮崎最勝, whose activity I will highlight in the following paragraph. It was the play's moralizing quality that appealed to them. It is not without irony to note that the same metaphor turned into a syndrome during the early 1980s, and that education was held to be responsible for this.

The famous model of car, already mentioned above, presents a striking instance of the use of "blue bird" symbolism. During the 1970s, Nissan launched a model that was dubbed Bluebird. The carmaker probably opted for the English variation because of the fact that cars were then still associated with America, and the choice may even have been inspired by analogy with the American Thunderbird. According to Tomita Hiroyuki, the message underlying the name was that the new model was the result of the harmonious collaboration between the management and the workers. Accordingly, the term "blue bird" implied an ideological connotation: not the Marxist model of conflict but the obvious and traditional, and somewhat paternalistic, relationship between management and labour would bring happiness within the reach of both.[20] I personally doubt whether the "blue bird" is used here as a metaphor for social harmony. It would seem more obvious to me that the car embodies happiness within reach.

Miyazaki Saishō, Man with a Mission

In 1918, ten years after the stage première, the American film company Artcraft Pictures Corporation released a silent film version of *The Blue Bird*, a fantasy film directed by Maurice Tourneur (2 February 1876 – 4 August 1961) and produced by Adolph Zukor. Maurice Tourneur was a noted French film director and screenwriter, at the time active in the United States. In recent times several of his films have been deemed "culturally, historically, or aesthetically significant" by the United States Library of Congress and selected for preservation in its National Film Registry, among them *The Blue Bird*, allegedly the first family film ever made.

This film premièred in Japan in 1920. It was shown on 29 and 30 April in Tokyo's Imperial Theatre (*Teikoku gekijō* 帝国劇場). However, as the film had been imported into

Japan through a special route, it could not be shown in other regular movie theatres. A merchant by the name of Omita Takamichi 小美田隆道, a relative of Miyazaki on his mother's side, was staying in New York when a party was thrown to celebrate the launching of the film. Maeterlinck and his spouse Renée Dahon were present at the party. Omita Takamichi requested a meeting with the couple, and secured their permission to introduce the film in Japan. But this permission had been granted on the strict condition that the film should not be screened for commercial reasons, but solely for "cultural purposes", a rather vague distinction, but one that probably carried some weight in those days, since films were not generally considered serious "art" or "culture" but entertainment. For that reason the film was not shown in commercial cinemas. This rather unusual procedure of circumventing the film company and securing permission directly from the author may have been motivated by the hope to avoid paying high royalties. Still it remains rather puzzling that the scheme succeeded. The fact is that a copy was imported to Japan and shown on 29 and 30 April.

Title page of Miyazaki Saishō's *Aoi tori no oshie*.
Collection Jidō bunka kenkyū sentā 児童文化研究センター, Shirayuri University 白百合女子大学, Tokyo.

Since the commercial circuit could not be used, a special "Blue Bird Society" (*Seichōkai* 青鳥会) was founded on 2 June 1920, the main objective of which was to screen the film in Japan. The society teamed up with the Railway Youth Organization (*Tetsudō seinen-kai* 鉄道青年会), to organize screenings in all major cities throughout the country. By the early Shōwa period (the early 1930s) the film had allegedly been viewed by approximately four million people.[21] A prominent member of the Blue Bird Society was Miyazaki Saishō. He played a pivotal role in the screening campaign, acting as *benshi* 弁士, narrator, at the screenings. Actually, to call him a narrator does not do him full justice, for a *benshi* did much more than simply provide live narration for silent films. A *benshi* would stand to the side of the movie screen, introduce the story to the audience, read the intertitles, voice all on-screen characters, at times add his own commentary, explaining what was happening in a shot or what had happened in a confusing transition. Some *benshi* were even known to interpret and add to a script. The *benshi* therefore was an important part of the silent film experience in Japan. His style of delivery was theurgic and theatrical, a carry-over from the traditional Japanese theatre. Miyazaki also compiled a kind of companion to the film, a booklet entitled *Aoi tori no oshie* 青い鳥のをしへ ("The Teachings of the Blue Bird").[22]

The film was lost during the Second World War, but after the war Miyazaki, who now went by his real name Hirose Tomohisa 広瀬友久, discovered a copy at the American Film Library, and imported a new print to Japan in 1972. Once again he started screening the film, acting as *benshi* for another ten years. To carry on spreading the message of the "blue bird" in a by now antiquated medium may seem futile, but it is certainly a testimony to Miyazaki/ Hirose's commitment, zeal, and sense of mission.

Let us take a closer look at the Blue Bird Society. Its prospectus begins with the grandiloquent statement that Japan is a spiritual country, close to being the concrete embodiment of the dignity of spirituality and the absolute and unquestioning subservience to it. This is the essence of Japan's body politic, the very reason why Japan is the most eminent country in the world. Maeterlinck is portrayed as someone who emphasized the value of spirit over matter, taught the immortality of the soul and eternal life, and strongly advocated the notion that true happiness lies in clarifying one's own spirituality and finding contentment in one's duties.

The text then continues:

> We consider the ideas of Maeterlinck as the harbinger of the ideological world that will expel the dangerous materialism of today. This is the basis on which the unity of the ideological worlds of East and West must be promoted; that we do not doubt. Only thoughts can oppose received thoughts.

In other words, the views and ideas of Maeterlinck were harnessed for the moral armament or rearmament of Japan, and by extension of the world. Strangely enough, as has already been mentioned, after the Second World War, Katayama Tetsu, having attended the moral rearmament conference, would write a report entitled "In Search of the Blue Bird".

Article 2 of the Rules of the society states: "Our society venerates the imperial family, studies and spreads Western ideas which are in accord with Japan's body politic and beliefs. It sets as its goal to enrich the spiritual life of the Japanese people and aspires to harmonize the ideas of East and West." Further on, the rules specify the kind of activities the society will undertake to achieve its goal. They include translation and publication of the works of Maeterlinck, film screenings, talks and lectures, but in actual practice its activities never went beyond the screening of the film.

The society had two secretaries (*kanji* 幹事): Kurihara Kojō 栗原古城 and Omita Takamichi, all other members were called *dōjin* 同人. The original member list featured twenty-five names and included luminaries from the literary world, such as the abovementioned Osanai Kaoru 小山内薫, leader of the theatre *Tsukiji shōgekijō* 築地小劇場, who was also actively involved in the screening of the film, writers such as Baba Kochō 馬場孤蝶, Shimazaki Tōson 島崎藤村, Taketomo Sōfū 竹友藻風, Toki Aika 土岐哀果 etc. Furthermore, we also see such names as the translator Wakatsuki Shiran 若月紫蘭, Kusuyama Masao 楠山正雄, Yamada Kōsaku 山田耕筰, and Nagao Yutaka 長尾豊. Needless to say, the list also included the name of Miyazaki Saishō, also known as Hirose Tomohisa. At the time he was twenty-four years old, and had just joined the commercial company Kuhara Shōji 久原商事.

Thus the Blue Bird Society, in conjunction with the Railway Youth Organization, set out organizing screenings of the film in all the major cities of Japan. Miyazaki himself received instruction from Osanai Kaoru to become a *benshi*, and started touring the country. In December 1921 he published his booklet *Aoi tori no oshie* 青い鳥のをしへ. Hatanaka reports having seen a copy of the book whose colophon mentioned a sixty-fourth impression, dated 3 November 1925. In the span of a mere four years the book had gone through sixty-four printings. This figure suggests how many occasions the Blue Bird Society had created for screening, and how popular the story had become. We may assume that every screening was the occasion to promote sales of the booklet as well.

Perhaps it is now time to take a look at the booklet itself. It begins with the following epigraph:

Erinnerung

Willst du immer weiter schweifen?
Sieh, das Gute liegt so nah.
Lerne nur das Glück ergreifen,
Denn das Glück ist immer da.

This poem by Johann Wolfgang von Goethe (1749-1832), the full title of which is *Gedichte – Erinnerung an Charlotte von Stein*, is perfectly in tune with the notion that happiness is close at hand. In the preface to what is basically a digest of *L'Oiseau bleu*, the editor Kurihara Kojō 栗原古城 waxes lyrical about the way wise men open the eyes of us common mortals, conveying as they do deep wisdom by way of simple imagery. He then goes on stating that Maeterlinck's *L'Oiseau bleu* is a case in point. That book does not stop at satisfying the immediate, but has the power to enter deep into our hearts and convert unhappiness into happiness. He even ranks it among the "holy books of civilization" (*bunmei no seisho* 文明の聖書). Although there are a couple of translations, as well as adaptations into the format of fairy tale or digest, it still remains an abstruse book. Therefore Miyazaki has written this "interpretation" under the title *Aoi tori no oshie* 青い鳥のをしへ, supplemented with, to quote the writer of the preface, "close commentaries" by himself. It purports to contain

the gist of Maeterlinck's work. Just as Nature's teachings are boundless, so each reader will be able to draw all kinds of lessons from this work.

Aoi tori no oshie contains six short chapters, summarizing the original chapters of Maeterlinck's work, each of them followed by a commentary. Hatanaka has demonstrated that this booklet *Aoi tori no oshie* 青い鳥のをしへ actually distorts the intent and drift of the original work. This is clear at once from the fact that the writer of the preface elevates what is an allegorical fantasy to the status of holy book of civilization, a boundless source of teachings *kyōkun* 教訓. The simple family life, thrifty but diligent and happy, fits perfectly the family image portrayed in contemporary handbooks of *shūshin* 修身 ("moral education").

Hatanaka also argues that the booklet *The Teachings of the Blue Bird* interpreted the message of *L'Oiseau bleu*, if there was one intended in the original, in the perspective of values which were embodied in the Japanese paedagogical ethics *shūshin*. This was an approach to ethics that had been introduced into Japanese education in the middle of the Meiji period, an ideology that inculcated a set of Confucian-inspired values, such as filial piety, loyalty, obedience, and so forth, all values that are conducive to giving priority to the community over the individual. After the war the occupying forces led by the Americans judged that this *shūshin* had been one of the ideological underpinnings of the authoritarian political system and abolished it.

A few examples will show the ways in which Miyazaki adapted the original intent. In the final clause of his work, for example, he writes that the message is that everyone has to look for the "blue bird" in his own family, but that is not what is written in the original. In the original, Tyltyl calls on the audience to look for the blue bird and to return it to him if they find it. That is quite another slant.

Hatanaka Keiichi has convincingly argued that the activities of Miyazaki Saishō were instrumental in popularizing the "blue bird" in Japan. He toured the country with the film as a *benshi*. This gave him ample opportunity to twist the *serifu* 台詞 ("script") in a sense he found appropriate and desirable. Since he had received training from Osanai Kaoru as a *benshi*, and since he was always narrating the same film, we may assume that he had reached a high professional level. One can easily imagine him pulling out all the stops of his art to deeply stir the hearts of his young audience.

Incidentally, this Seichōkai or "Blue Bird Society", based in Tokyo, must not be confused with various namesakes, which were founded after the Second World War, such as the *Zaidan hōjin seichō-kai* 財団法人青鳥会, a charity founded in Tokyo in 1950 by the *Nihon kyōshokuin kumiai* 日本教職員組合, which administered the Helen Keller Prize (disbanded in 2013), nor with the *Shakai fukushi hōjin Aoi tori-kai* 社会福祉法人青い鳥会, a private foundation established in 1959 and based in Hikone, nor the *Shakai fukushi hōjin Seichō-kai* 社会福祉法人青鳥会, established in Kagoshima by the gynaecologist Maki Misumaro 牧美須磨 (first chairman / *shodai rijichō* 初代理事長) in 1966. There appear to be many non-profit organizations, private foundations and charities which carry the name "blue bird". As a rule they are all dedicated in one way or another to the care and rehabilitation of mentally or physically handicapped persons. The reference to the "blue bird" is obviously intended to suggest that their goal is to secure a happy and comfortable life for the handicapped.[23]

Echoes from Japanese Myths, Legends and Stories

Although our analysis of the activities of the Blue Bird Society may have revealed a major socio-cultural factor in the popularity of the "blue bird", the question why it struck a responsive chord with the Japanese public has not been fundamentally answered. The focus of the question has simply been redirected to another level, for Miyazaki's campaign can only have caught on because there was a cultural environment that was receptive to his interpretation of the story. It reverberated with the collective subconscious of the Japanese audiences.

Indeed we find a number of mythical or legendary narratives both in traditional Japanese high culture, and in popular folklore, which display structural similarities with the story as viewed by Miyazaki. The most widely known narrative, one which belongs to the tradition of high culture, is the story of *The Land of Peach Blossom Spring* (Tōgenkyō 桃源郷, also called Buryōtōgen 武陵桃

源), which is Chinese in origin but has gained wide currency among the educated strata of Japanese society. It is a fairyland outside the world we live in. Although it may be tempting to compare it with the Western notion of utopia, it is quite dissimilar, probably even fundamentally different.[24]

The story is codified in a poetic text by the ancient Chinese poet Táo Yuānmíng 陶淵明 (365-427), entitled *Táohuāyuán jì* 桃花源記 ("The Peach Blossom Spring"). It relates the adventures of a fisherman who hits by chance upon a mysterious grotto lying deep in a blooming peach orchard. When he penetrates its recesses he all of a sudden emerges above ground at the other end of the cave in a bucolic land, inhabited by good and generous people. After staying for some time with his hospitable guests, he makes his way back home, taking note of the places he passes. He is received by the governor of his region and tells him about this paradise. The governor sends a messenger equipped with the fisherman's description to locate the paradise, but he loses his way. *Liú Zǐjì* 劉子驥, a lofty gentleman from the region of Nanyang, likewise hears of the paradise and makes plans to go and search for it, but, unfortunately dies of a disease before he realizes his plan. The grotto remains forever elusive. Revisiting the Peach Blossom Spring is indeed impossible, and it is, at least according to Itō Naoya 伊藤直哉, a prominent researcher on Táo Yuānmíng, exactly in this impossibility that the essence of the narrative lies. It was a place that could not be found if one intentionally went searching for it, whether their aims were mundane, as one might expect of commoners or officials, or the more lofty and noble intentions of wise men.[25]

Although written some 1600 years ago, the story of *The Peach Blossom Spring* is still well known in Japan today. Through the centuries it has come to symbolize the moral message that this land of happiness does not exist in the outside world, but has to be found in one's heart. The fact that the fisherman could not revisit it, or that Liú Zǐjì 劉子驥 was unable to visit it, was because they sought it outside themselves. If one intentionally looked for it somewhere on earth, it would forever elude one.[26]

Itō Naoya points out that Thomas More's *Utopia* and all its derivatives reflect the deliberative aspiration to build an ideal society. Although depicted as a far-off island nation, both in geographical and societal terms, it is not a completely unattainable dreamland. *The Peach Blossom Spring* on the other hand rather teaches us to abandon our aspiration to build an ideal society. During periods of turmoil in Chinese history, when people tried to escape from the reality of suffering and deprivation, poetry about mystical excursions (*yūsenshi* 遊仙詩, that is, poems about traveling to the realm of the immortals) was popular among the class of literati.[27] Although Táo Yuānmíng's work resembles in subject matter this mystical excursion poetry, in Itō's view its philosophy is essentially different.[28] Táo never believed in the fairyland, denied its real existence, and set much value on everyday life.[29] Itō argues that utopian thought as embodied in Thomas More's classic gave rise to totalitarian experiments which, quite opposite to their ideal, ended in disaster, whereas the quietist, unreal fable of *The Peach Blossom Spring* actually was able to give substantial spiritual comfort to people. Itō Naoya quotes the lyrics from the theme song of the film *Spirited Away* as a good commentary on the philosophy of *The Peach Blossom Spring*:

> No need to search the land, nor sail across the sea 'Cause it's here shining inside me, it's right here deep inside me Thanks to you I've found the light, and it's always with me.[30]

Although the wording is less bombastic, in essence this view strikes me as an echo of Miyazaki Saishō's reading of *The Blue Bird*.

In China, the story of *The Peach Blossom Spring*, which was located deep in a grove of peach trees, in later centuries became suffused with Daoist thought, particularly with the notion of the immortal. Legends about getting lost in the mountains and meeting an immortal, about eating the magical peach to become an immortal, and about the peach of immortality in the legend of the Queen Mother of the West were amalgamated with the story of *The Peach Blossom Spring*, which thus became the land where immortals resided. Sū Shì 蘇軾 the great *literatus* of the Northern Sòng Dynasty (960-1127), had his doubts about its being the abode of immortals, stating: "if it was the abode of the immortals, why would they kill chickens to feast a fisherman?" The Táng poet Lǐ Bó 李白 seems to have believed that *The Peach Blossom Spring* was synonymous with the abode of immortals (*senkyō* 仙境), whereas Sū

Shì and Wáng Ānshí 王安石, poet and statesman of the Northern Sòng Dynasty, considered it essentially to be a human society free of exploitation and war.

Although it may be debatable whether Itō Naoya's interpretation of the Chinese fable *The Peach Blossom Spring* truly reflects the intention of its author in all its details, it does show a remarkable similarity with Miyazaki's interpretation of the narrative of *The Blue Bird*. Incidentally, in contemporary Japan the name *Tōgenkyō* is found in a diluted sense as the name for blossom viewing locations, gardens or orchards in several places, including the blossom viewing park (Hanami-yama 花見山) in the City of Fukushima, and the city of Minami-Alps (Yamanashi Prefecture), where tourists can visit the vast orchard known as *Shirane Tōgenkyō*.

On a popular level, in the native folklore of Japan, we equally find legends that are analogous to the Chinese story. People in ancient Japan believed in the Land of Eternity (*Toyo no kuni*), a land supposedly located beyond the seas. It was conceived of as a kind of utopia, associated with immortality, eternal youth and permanence. This mythological other world view can be found in the ancient scriptures, notably *Kojiki* (712), *Nihon Shoki* 日本書紀 (720), *Man'yōshū* 万葉集 (760), some of the *Fudoki* 風土記, and some other texts. It is cognate with the other world view of Okinawa, known as *Nirai kanai*. The god Sukunabikona descended from the heavens together with Okuninushi to create the land and after the job was done he returned to the Land of Eternity.

The *Man'yōshū* contains a poem (Poem no. 1740, vol. 9) authored by Takahashi no Mushimaro, that deals with the story of Urashimako. According to that poem, Urashimako sets out to fish but after seven days he does not return and rows his boat over the sea to the World of Eternity, to go and live in the palace of the deity Watatsumi no kami together with the daughter of that deity. In that palace he neither ages nor dies. Although he can live there forever, Urashimako decides to return home. When he realizes that his own home no longer exists, he opens a box which he should not have opened. The land of Eternity depicted in this *chōka* is an immortal world ruled by a deity of the sea, where the chronological dimension is fundamentally different from that in the earthly world. The alternative name for

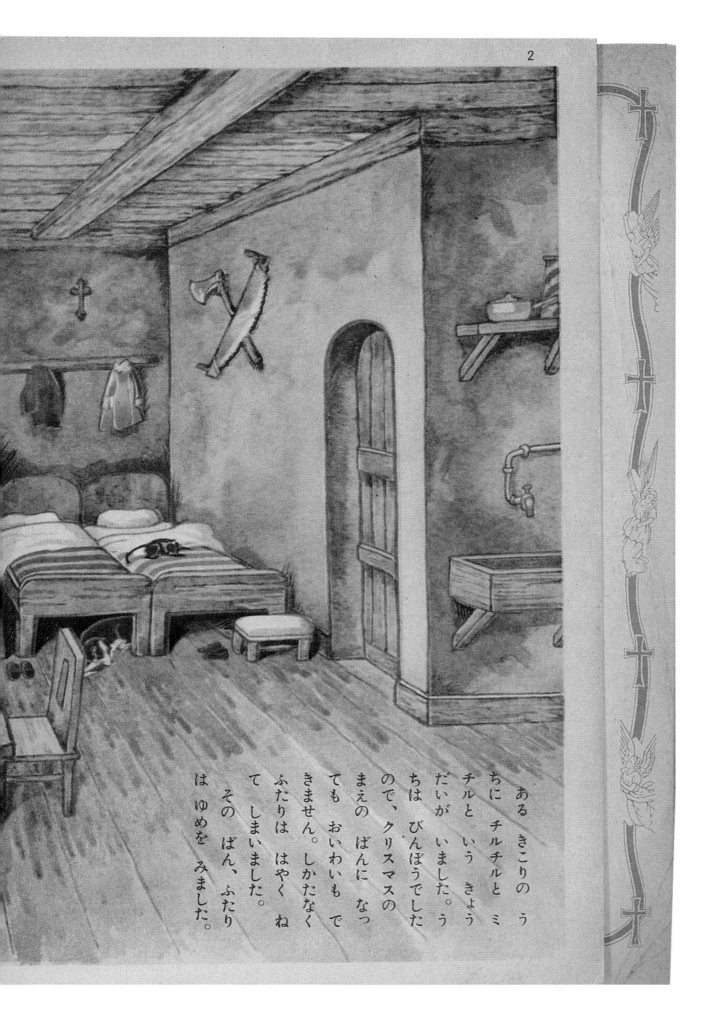

あるきこりのうちにチルチルとミチルというきょうだいがいました。うちはびんぼうでしたので、クリスマスのまえのばんになってもおいわいもできません。しかたなくふたりははやくねてしまいました。そのばん、ふたりはゆめをみました。

the land beyond the seas is Hōraizan 蓬莱山, a notion derived from Chinese and meaning the land of the immortals. In order to make the crossing to the land of Eternity, one needs to cross the seas. The palace of the sea god Watatsumi no kami is equally located in that world, suggesting that in ancient Japan the Land of Eternity and the seas are closely intertwined with one another. In the *Man'yōshū* there is a stock phrase, *Toyo no nami no shikinami no yosuru kuni* 常世の浪の重浪寄する国, which equally suggests that the waves washing the beach are directly connected to the other world of Eternity. Moreover, this land of Eternity does not just mean the land beyond the seas; it also implies various other connotations such as the afterlife, the world of the dead, or the world of the immortals.

Another notion in Japanese folklore and legends is that of *kakurezato* ("the hidden hamlet"). It is believed to be located in the deep recesses of the mountains or beyond the other end of a cave. Hunters get lost deep in the mountains and incidentally hit upon a peculiar land, or they hear the sound of a weaving loom or of rice being pounded in the mountains. In various places in Japan there are legends about people finding chopsticks and rice bowls floating down the river. The inhabitants of this different world do not know any strife and live a peaceful life in a mild climate and on a fertile soil. They receive alien visitors kindly and offer them a pleasant stay, but when the visitor later wants to revisit the place he cannot find it. According to some, these stories of *kakurezato* are the residual reflection of the existence of places where the remnants of the Taira clan sought refuge, and in point of fact there are hamlets that are referred to as Taira valleys or the hidden abode of the Taira clan. In addition, it is believed that mountain worship and notions of utopian locales, pre-existent to Buddhist Pure Land thought had an influence on this notion of *kakurezato*. *Kakurezato* is a different world hidden deep in the mountains or in the midst of a cave or on the upper reaches of a river or in the folds of a dell. In these *kakurezato* there is no distress or sorrow, only peace, while time proceeds at a different pace than it does in the human world. Common mortals cannot go there but virtuous people sometimes get the chance to cast a glimpse of that world.

Tōno monogatari ("The Legends of Tōno") contain an interesting example. The wife of a poor family sets out to

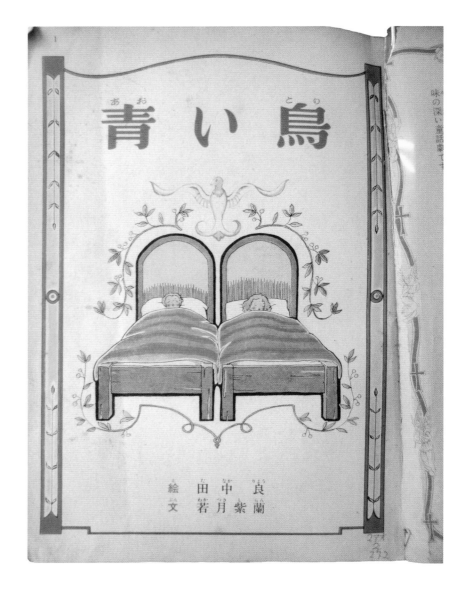

collect butterbur (*fuki* 蕗, homonymous with *fuki* 富貴 "riches and prestige") along a small river, but she loses her way and wanders off into the deep recesses of a valley, where she hits upon a splendid house, with a large garden full of red and white flowers in bloom and many hens running about. In the back of the garden there are sheds with many cows and a stable with many horses. Inside the house she notices many red and black serving trays and bowls, a charcoal brazier and a tea kettle filled with briskly boiling water. There is no trace of a person and, overcome with fear, she runs off and returns home. She tells the people about her discovery, but no one believes her.

Frontispiece of *Aoi tori*, text by Wakatsuki Shiran, illustrations by Tanaka Ryō. Tokyo: Kōdansha, 1952.

Collection Jidō bunka kenkyū sentā 児童文化研究センター, Shirayuri University 白百合女子大学, Tokyo.

「まあ、きれい」。チルチルとミチルは、むかいの金もちの家のクリスマス・ツリーを見て、さけびました。

Illustration from *Aoi tori*, text by Wakatsuki Shiran, illustrations by Tanaka Ryō. Tokyo: Kōdansha; 1952.

Collection Jidō bunka kenkyū sentā 児童文化研究センター, Shirayuri University 白百合女子大学, Tokyo.

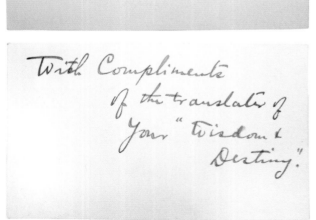

Another day, when she is washing things in front of her house, a red bowl comes floating down from upstream. She hides the beautiful bowl in the grain box. When she uses the bowl to measure the grain, it turns out that the stock never decreases. From that point on the family fortunes begin to flourish and they become the richest family in the village. In this story the woman is slightly simple-minded and without greed. That is why the bowl came floating in her direction and brought richness to her family.[31]

Maeterlinck after the Blue Bird

It is perhaps time to return to our author. In the meantime Maeterlinck had moved on and so had the world. When the First World War broke out, there was little room left for fantasies. Maeterlinck made lecture tours for the Allied cause in Europe and in the United States; notably in Italy, where both the cabinet and the public opinion remained divided about whose side to choose, and which eventually entered the war on the Allied side in May 1915, nearly a year after the outbreak of hostilities.

During that time his relationship with Georgette Leblanc came to an end, and in 1919 he married Renée Dahon, who had acted in one of the performances of *L'Oiseau bleu*. The couple made their home outside Paris at the Château de Médan and spent their winters at a villa near Nice, named "Les Abeilles". Maeterlinck's interest now gradually shifted from fantasies toward naturalistic and psychological topics and themes.

During the interwar period, he wrote essays and plays, among others *La Vie des Termites* (1926), in which he examined totalitarian systems in the light of the ethology of the termite. In 1932 he was made a count by King Albert I. On the eve of the Second World War he travelled to Portugal, where he enjoyed the protection of the prime minister, António Salazar, and from where he fled to the United States. During these years he fell on hard times because his writings had lost much of their appeal and he was in no position to collect royalties from the sales of his books in Europe. In 1947 he returned to his home in Nice. Maeterlinck died of a heart attack on 6 May 1949. In accordance with his agnostic worldview, he was buried

---

Title page of *Chie to unmei* 知恵と運命. Translation of Maeterlinck's *La sagesse et la destinée* (1898) by Ōtani Jōseki 大谷繞石 (real name Masanobu 正信). Tokyo: Nanbokusha 南北社, 1913.
Courtesy of Kabinet Maeterlinck, Ghent.

Calling card of Ōtani Jōseki 大谷繞石 (Masanobu) with compliments to Maeterlinck, inserted in *Chie to unmei* 知恵と運命. Translation of Maeterlinck's *La sagesse et la destinée* (1898) by Ōtani Jōseki 大谷繞石 (Masanobu 正信). Tokyo: Nanbokusha 南北社, 1913.
Courtesy of Kabinet Maeterlinck, Ghent.

without religious rites. His last book, *Bulles Bleues*, a collection of happy reminiscences, appeared in 1948.

In the past Japanese publicists have often introduced Maeterlinck as "Belgium's national writer" (*Berugī no kokumin sakka* ベルギーの国民作家). This is a misconception, the product of a projection from their own cultural background. The assumption is clearly that a nation's only winner of the Nobel Prize for Literature, who in addition wrote works with a universal appeal, cannot but be a generally acclaimed author in his own country. It is, unfortunately, a false assumption, and bespeaks a lack of knowledge about Belgium's literary landscape and literary history.

Although he lived until 1949, he very much remained a man of the preceding age, that of the nineteenth century. In 1918 the Dutch writer and critic Jan Greshoff slighted him as "den philosooph voor het jonge-meisjes-pensionaat" (the philosopher of the young girls' boarding school), a statement that for all its succinct injustice suggests that he was no longer considered a modern writer by the new generation. His fame rested on a small number of works written during the nineteenth and early twentieth centuries, and most of all on *La Princesse Maleine*, a play that had not even needed to be performed to make him famous. Parisian literature pundit Octave Mirbeau's wildly enthusiastic review, published in *Le Figaro* of 24 August 1890, was sufficient to catapult him to the Elysian fields of fame. He earned his Nobel Prize relatively early in his career, and unlike many other laureates, he could enjoy it for a long period in his lifetime. He was quite unconventional for his time in ethical matters, yet in photographs he emerges as a privileged bourgeois, hardly adventurous and leading an indolent and comfortable life. He always had domestic staff at his disposal, and apparently had few financial worries, except during the war, when he was cut off from the income of royalties. How else to explain the string of stately homes he lived in? Most notable of these was the Villa Orlamonde, where he died, although it seemed to be a source of great (financial) concern to him at the end of his life.

Due to illness Maeterlinck was unable to travel to Stockholm to receive the Nobel Prize at the hands of the Swedish king. At the ceremonial banquet at the Grand Hôtel, Stockholm, on 10 December 1911, the acceptance speech was delivered by Mr Charles C. M. A. Wauters, minister of Belgium. Mr Wauters evoked the Flemish plains:

> strewn with monuments in stone whose façades recall the lacework that Flemish peasant women do on their lace pillows, sitting on the thresholds of their houses. Often one hears, in the calm of the countryside, strong, deep voices singing slow and dreamy chants. And in the old towns of Flanders with their winding and picturesque streets, the silence of night is interrupted at regular intervals by the clear sound of bells which, silvery and poetic, impart a sense of medieval times, of centuries of glory, heroism, and prosperity.[32]

If this dreamy, rural and "medieval" Flanders is indeed at the heart of Maeterlinck's literary genius, it is perhaps also one of the reasons why he can no longer capture a wide readership in the highly industrialized and urbanized region Flanders has become since his day.

In 1914 Maeterlinck's collected works (*opera omnia*) were listed on the Roman *Index Librorum Prohibitorum* (Index of Prohibited Books). He incurred the ban on account of the publication of *La Mort* (1913). Although the author interpreted this as an excommunication, according to André Capiteyn, the prohibition was limited to works dealing with religion and ethics.[33] The Index was "abolished" as a binding rule for Catholics in 1966. Still, when in 1962 a Dutch translation of a selection from Maeterlinck's oeuvre was published under the title *Maurice Maeterlinck: gedichten / toneel en proza, met een inleiding over auteur en werk door Prof. Dr. Mathieu Rutten*, as part of a series *Pantheon der winnaars van de Nobelprijs voor literatuur* (Pantheon of Laureates of the Nobel Prize in Literature), presenting selections from the works of all the laureates of the Nobel Prize in Literature, the publishing house, the Hasselt-based Uitgeverij Heideland, found it necessary to include the following disclaimer:

> By decree of 26 January 1914, Maeterlinck's works (*opera omnia*) were listed on the Index. The selection of works included in this Pantheon edition is not subject to this prohibition. According to the explanation of competent canonists (e.g. Wagnon, Onclin, Brys), the strict interpretation, attributed by the 1940 Index to the formula *opera omnia*, has no retroactive force.

Applied to authors who were banned between 1900 and 1940, this proviso only concerns the *books* proper by these authors (and not necessarily *all* their books), and consequently not their lesser publications, pamphlets etc., except when these latter publications fall within the purview of the general rules of the ban on reading.[34]

Should we conclude from this disclaimer that the Pantheon edition only included lesser publications, or did it mean that a selection made by an editor could not be construed as a book by the author? Whatever the purport, it is indicative of the sway the *Index* once held and perhaps even held in 1962. It is undeniable that Maeterlinck's inclusion in the *Index* contributed to his lack of popularity in Flanders. The ban, whatever its extent, must surely have made Catholic educators wary of including any part of his oeuvre in the French literature curriculum of secondary education at Flemish Catholic schools, which trained the overwhelming majority of Flemish youth.

The better part of Maeterlinck's works have been translated into Japanese. Already in the 1920s, his collected works were published in eight volumes. As early as 1922, a so-called critical biography (*hyōden* 評伝) appeared, written by Yoshie Kogan 吉江孤雁 and published by the publishing house Tōkasha 冬夏社. In Japan Maeterlinck did indeed enjoy the stature of a great writer. One would have been hard put to find a country that had provided a more favourable habitat for the "blue bird" than Japan. One can imagine the blow when, after the Second World War, the writer, out of anger at Japan's role in the war, had it put down in his will that his stage plays were no longer to be performed in Japan. This left all lovers of the "blue bird" in the cold. Fortunately a Japanese puppet theatre company, Pūku (Puck), in 1957 persuaded his widow, Renée Dahon, countess Maeterlinck, to lift the ban. Since then, the play has been staged countless times.

NOTE: the author expresses his gratitude to the staff of Jidō bunka kenkyū sentā 児童文化研究センター (Centre for research on children's culture) of Shirayuri University, Tokyo: Prof. Ishii Naoto, director, Prof. Sasaki Yuriko, and her collaborators Hara Hisano, Fukuchi Ai and Yatsushiro Hanako, for their assistance and advice when he consulted the Tomita collection.

Theatre entrance with billboard announcing the performance of *Aoi tori* by the assembled schools of Tamagawa gakuen 玉川学園 on 15 February 1959.
Collection Jidō bunka kenkyū sentā 児童文化研究センター, Shirayuri University 白百合女子大学, Tokyo. Photograph by W.F. Vande Walle

REFERENCES

———

While not laying any claim to completeness, this list of references does include most monographs and studies, mainly in Japanese, germane to one or more topics touched upon in this article.

Actes Sud et Labor 1989
Actes Sud et Labor. "Principales mises en scène de *L'oiseau bleu*" (Mai 1989), pp. 149-151.

Anon. 1902a
Anon. "Kaigai sōdan: Mōrisu Māterurinku (I)" 海外騒壇―モオリス、マアテルリンク（上）. *Teikoku Bungaku* 帝國文學 8:11 (Nov 1902), pp. 1324-1332.

Anon. 1902b
Anon. "Kaigai sōdan: Mōrisu Māterurinku (II)" 海外騒壇―モオリス、マアテルリンク（下）. *Teikoku Bungaku* 帝國文學 8:12 (Dec 1902), pp. 1458-1462.

Anzai 1982
Anzai Chiaki 安齋千秋. "*Aoi tori* no ezoterisumu – Giji inishieishon geki" 『青い鳥』のエゾテリスム―擬似イニシエイション劇. *Furansu bungei* 仏蘭西文芸 7 (Dec 1982), pp. 49-64.

Aotori
Aotori 青鳥 1 (1 July 1935). Tokyo: Aotorikai Insatsubu 青鳥会印刷部, 1935.

Asahi shinbun 1989
Asahi shinbun 朝日新聞. "Aoi tori ni, naritai" 青い鳥に、なりたい. 16 Jan 1989.

Bi 1895
Bi Yūshi 微幽子 [=Ueda Bin 上田敏]. "Berugī bungaku" 白耳義文學. *Teikoku Bungaku* 帝國文學 1 (Jan 1895), pp. 13-19.

Brucher 1972
Roger Brucher. *Maurice Maeterlinck. L'oeuvre et son audience. Essai de bibliographie 1883-1960.* Bruxelles, Palais des académies, 1972.

Capiteyn 2008
André Capiteyn. *Maeterlinck. Een Nobelprijs voor Gent.* Gent: Uitgeverij Snoeck, 2008.

Chihōshi Kenkyū Kyōgikai 1990
Chihōshi Kenkyū Kyōgikai 地方史研究協議会, ed. *Rekishi shiryō hozon kikan sōran "Higashi Nihon"* 歴史資料保存機関総覧〈東日本〉. Tokyo: Yamakawa Shuppansha 山川出版社, 1990.

Donnell s.a.
Dorothy Donnell. *The Blue Bird / Aoi tori* 青い鳥. Kyoto: Aoi Tori Kōfukukai 青い鳥幸福会, s.a.

Fujita 1962
Fujita Tamao 藤田圭雄. "Māterurinku seitan hyakunen o mukaete" マーテルリンク生誕百年を迎えて. *Mainichi shinbun* 毎日新聞 (24 Aug 1962).

Gotō 1914a
Gotō Kanpei 五島寛平. "Mēteruringu to sono sakuhin – Jō" メーテルリングと其作品（上）. *Shinbun shūsei Taishō-hen nenshi* 新聞集成 大正編年史 (Mar 1914), pp. 445-446.

Gotō 1914b
Gotō Kanpei 五島寛平. "Mēteruringu to sono sakuhin – Ge" メーテルリングと其作品（下）. *Shinbun shūsei Taishō-hen nenshi* 新聞集成 大正編年史 (Apr 1914), p. 478.

Hanse & Vivier 1962
Joseph Hanse & Robert Vivier, eds. *Maurice Maeterlinck, 1862-1962.* Bruxelles: La Renaissance du livre, 1962.

Hatanaka 1999
Hatanaka Keiichi 畑中圭一. "Miyazaki Saishō to *Aoi tori no oshie*" 宮崎最勝と『青い鳥のをしへ』. *Mēteruringu* Aoi tori *juyōshi kō* メーテルリング「青い鳥」受容史考 *Nagoya Meitoku Tankidaigaku Kiyō* 名古屋明徳短期大学紀要 14 (1999), pp. 319-350.

Hirose 1972
Hirose Tomohisa 広瀬友久. "Niwaka benshi no 'aoi tori' angya" にわか弁士の「青い鳥」行脚. *Nihon keizai shinbun* 日本経済新聞 (20 Dec 1972), p. 24.

Horiguchi 1920
Horiguchi Daigaku 堀口大学, trans. *Yōdō satsuriku* 幼童殺戮. Tokyo: Tōkasha 冬夏社, 1920.

Ichiyanagi 2001
Ichiyanagi Hirotaka 一柳廣孝. "Mushanokōji Saneatsu: Mēterurinku juyō no hikari to kage" 武者小路実篤―メーテルリンク受容の光と影. *Kokubungaku* 國文學 46:11 (Sep 2001), pp. 44-49.

Itō 2010
Itō Naoya 伊藤直哉. *Tōgenkyō to yūtopia – Tō Enmei no bungaku* 桃源郷とユートピア―陶淵明の文学. Shunpūsha 春風社, 2010.

Iwamoto 1920
Iwamoto Kiyoko 巖本清子. "Muetarinku o mukaete – Ge" ムエタリンクを迎へて（下）. *Shinbun shūsei Taishō-hen nenshi* 新聞集成 大正編年史 (Feb 1920), p. 505.

Katayama 1950
Katayama Tetsu 片山哲. "Aoi tori" 青い鳥. *Bungei shunjū* 文芸春秋 special issue (June 1950), pp. 9-10.

Katayama 1952
Katayama Toshihiko 片山敏彦, trans. *Hinja no takara* 貧者の宝. Tokyo: Shinchōsha 新潮社, 1952.

Kōreikashakai o yokusuru josei no kai 1992
Kōreikashakai o yokusuru josei no kai 高齢化社会をよくする女性の会, ed. *Oi no aoi tori o motomete: Daijikkai josei ni yoru kōreikashakai shinpojiumu no kiroku* 老いの青い鳥を求めて―第10回女性による高齢化社会シンポジウムの記録. Tokyo: Minerva Shobō ミネルヴァ書房, 1992.

Kurihara 1919
Kurihara Kojō 栗原古城, trans. *Reichi to unmei* 霊智と運命. Tokyo: Genkōsha 玄黄社, 1919; Tokyo: Sanbunsha 山文社, 1954.

Kusuyama 1920
Kusuyama Masao 楠山正雄, trans. "Aoi tori" 青い鳥. In *Kindaigeki senshū (I)* 近代劇選集（一）. Tokyo: Shinchōsha 新潮社, 1920.

Kyōshinbun 1957
"Nihon no kodomo e *Aoi tori* – Mēterurinku mibōjin kara sengo hatsu no jōen kyoka" 日本の子供へ『青い鳥』・メーテルリンク未亡人から戦後初の上演許可. *Kyōshinbun* 京新聞 (15 Mar 1957), p. 4.

Maeterlinck 1948
Maurice Maeterlinck. *Bulles bleues: Souvenirs heureux.* Monaco: Ed. du Rocher, 1948.

Mainichi shinbun 1977
"Rōjō tsuzuku 'Aoi tori'" ろう城続く「青い鳥」. *Mainichi shinbun* 毎日新聞 (3 Aug 1977).

"Mēterurinku hen" 2007
S.v. "Mēterurinku hen" メーテルリンク編. In *Zusetsu jidō bungaku hon'yaku daijiten* 図説児童文学翻訳大事典, ed. Jidō bungaku hon'yaku daijiten henshū iinkai 児童文学翻訳大事典編集委員会, vol. 3, pp. 789-812. Tokyo: Ōzorasha Nada Shuppan Sentā 大空社ナダ出版センター, 2007.

"Mēterurinku hen" 2009
S.v. "Mēterurinku hen" メーテルリンク編. In *Zusetsu hon'yaku bungaku eawase jiten* 図説・翻訳文学絵合事典, vol. 4, pp. 1005-1008. Tokyo: Nada Shuppan Sentā ナダ出版センター, 2009.

Miyauchi 2004
Miyauchi Junko 宮内淳子. "Shajitsu e no teikō: Mēterurinku 'Tantajīru no shi' jōen o megutte" 写実への抵抗―メーテルリンク「タンタジールの死」上演をめぐって. *Kokugakuin Zasshi* 國學院雑誌 105:11 (Nov 2004), pp. 395-411.

Miyazaki 1920
Miyazaki Saishō 宮崎最勝. *Aoi tori no oshie* 青い鳥のをしへ. Tokyo: Sanseisha 三星社, 1920.

Miyazaki 1921
Miyazaki Saishō 宮崎最勝. *Aoi tori no oshie* 青い鳥のをしへ. Tokyo: Seichō-kai Shuppanbu 青鳥会出版部, 1921.

Mori s.a.
Mori Ryō 森亮. "*Kaichōon* kōtei oboegaki: Hanrei o kanete" 『海潮音』校訂覚え書―凡例を兼ねて, pp. 607-610.

Mori s.a.
Mori Ryō 森亮. "*Kaichōon* henchū" 『海潮音』編注, pp. 611-617

Mori 1910a
Mori Hono'o 森ほのほ. "Mēterurinku no *Aoi tori* no kōgai" メーテルリンクの『青い鳥』の梗概. *Kabuki* 歌舞伎 124 (1 Oct 1910), pp. 56-63.

Mori 1910b
Mori Hono'o 森ほのほ. "Buryū bādo Mēterurinku no *Aoi tori* no kōgai (II)" ブリュー・バードメーテルリンクの『青い鳥』の梗概（二）. *Kabuki* 歌舞伎 125 (1 Nov 1910), pp. ?

Mori 1910c
Mori Hono'o 森ほのほ. "Mēterurinku no *Aoi tori* no kōgai (III)" メーテルリンクの『青い鳥』の梗概（三）. *Kabuki* 歌舞伎 126 (1 Dec 1910), pp. 63-78.

Murakami 1917
Murakami Shizuto 村上静人, trans. *Mēterurinku kessakushū* メエテルリンク傑作集. Tokyo: Satō Shuppanbu 佐藤出版部, 1917. [Contains *Shinnyūsha* 侵入者, *Aguravēnu to Serisetto* アクラエ゛エヌとセリセツト, *Aoi tori* 青い鳥, *Monna Vanna* モンナワ゛ンナ, *Shitsunai* 室内 and *Gunmō* 群盲].

Nihon Jidōbungaku Daijiten
S.v. "Ogawa Mimei" 小川未明. In: *Nihon Jidōbungaku Daijiten* 日本児童文学大事典, Tsuzukihashi Tatsuo 続橋達雄, ed. Ōsaka kokusai jidōbungakukan 大阪国際児童文学館, vol. 1, pp. 161-164. Tokyo: Dainippon Tosho 大日本図書, 1993.

Nihon Jidōbungaku Daijiten
S.v. "Akai Tori Sha" 赤い鳥社. In: *Nihon Jidōbungaku Daijiten* 日本児童文学大事典, ed. Ōsaka kokusai jidōbungakukan 大阪国際児童文学館, vol. 2, p. 319. Tokyo: Dainippon Tosho 大日本図書, 1993.

Nihon Jidōbungaku Daijiten
S.v. "Seichōkai" 青鳥会. In: *Nihon Jidōbungaku Daijiten* 日本児童文学大事典, ed. Ōsaka kokusai jidōbungakukan 大阪国際児童文学館, vol. 2, pp. 423-424. Tokyo: Dainippon Tosho 大日本図書, 1993.

Odanaka 1993
Odanaka Akihiro 小田中章浩. "Engeki to kaigasei: Mēteruranku no *Mōjintachi* ni tsuite" 演劇と絵画性―メーテルランクの『盲人たち』について. *Engekigaku* 演劇學 34 (1993), pp. 1-11.

Okamoto 1913
Okamoto Seiitsu 岡本清逸, trans. *Mitsubachi no seikatsu* 蜜蜂の生活. Tokyo: Tōadō Shobō東亜堂書房, 1913.

Osanai 1909
Osanai Kaoru 小山内薫. "Māteruringu no *Aoi tori*" マアテルリングの『青い鳥』. *Shumi* 趣味 4:4 (1909), pp. 16-21.

Ozaki 1981
Ozaki Kazuo 尾崎和郎, trans. *Shiroari no seikatsu* 白蟻の生活. Tokyo: Kōsakusha 工作舎, 1981.

Rutten 1962
Mathieu Rutten. "Maurice Maeterlinck." In *Maurice Maeterlinck: gedichten/toneel en proza, met een inleiding over auteur en werk door Prof. Dr. Mathieu Rutten*. Pantheon der Winnaars van de Nobelprijs voor Literatuur. Hasselt: Uitgeverij Heideland, 1962.

Sakakibara 2003
Sakakibara Takanori 榊原貴教. "Mēterurinku hon'yaku sakuhin nenpyō: Meiji 35 nen – Shōwa 17 nen" メーテルリンク翻訳作品年表―明治３５年～昭和１７年. *Hon'yaku to Rekishi* 翻訳と歴史 16 (Jul 2003).

Shimamura 1913
Shimamura Hōgetsu 島村抱月, trans. *Monna Vanna* モンナ・ヴンナ. Tokyo: Nanbokusha 南北社, 1913.

Shimazaki 1920
Shimazaki Tōson 島崎藤村. "*Aoi tori* o butai no ue ni mite"『青い鳥』を舞台の上に見て. Shinbun shūsei Taishō-hen nenshi 新聞集成 大正編年史 (Feb 1920), p. 569.

Shimizu 1983
Shimizu Masayuki 清水將之. *Aoi tori shōkōgun hensachi erīto no matsuro* 青い鳥症候群 偏差値エリートの末路. Tokyo: Kōbundō 弘文堂, 1983.

Shoshi Kenkyū Konwakai 1979a
Shoshi Kenkyū Konwakai 書誌研究懇話会, ed. *Zenkoku Toshokan Annai* (I) 全国図書館案内 (上) Tokyo: San'ichi Shobō 三一書房, 1979.

Shoshi Kenkyū Konwakai 1979b
Shoshi Kenkyū Konwakai 書誌研究懇話会, ed. *Zenkoku Toshokan Annai (II)* 全国図書館案内 (下). Tokyo: San'ichi Shobō 三一書房, 1979.

Shūkan Asahi 1957
"*Aoi tori* maimodoru – Nihon e no nikushimi toku?"『青い鳥』舞い戻る一日本への憎しみ解く？ *Shūkan Asahi* 週刊朝日 (7 Apr 1957).

Staden 2010
Cobus van Staden. "Heidi in Japan: What Do Anime's Dreams of Europe Mean for Non-Europeans?" In *The Asiascape Collection v. 1: Essays in the Exploration of CyberAsia*, ed. Christopher Goto-Jones, pp. 29-32. Leiden: Asiascape.net and Modern East Asia Research Centre, 2010.

Suematsu 2002
Suematsu Himiko 末松氷海子. "*Aoi tori* no fushigi"『青い鳥』のふしぎ. In *Zusetsu kodomo no hon hon'yaku no ayumi jiten* 図説 子どもの本・翻訳の歩み事典, ed. Kodomo no hon hon'yaku no ayumi Kenkyūkai 子どもの本・翻訳の歩み研究会, pp. 70-71. Tokyo: Kashiwa Shobō 柏書房, 2002.

Suezaki s.a.
Suezaki Noriko 末崎教子. *Jidōbunkashi no naka no Kusuyama Masao* 児童文化史の中の楠山正雄. S.a., s.l., pp. 13-42.

Sugimoto 1985
Sugimoto Hidetarō 杉本秀太郎, trans. *Onshitsu: Shishū* 温室：詩集. Tokyo: Sekkasha 雪華社, 1985.

Sugimoto 1988
Sugimoto Hidetarō 杉本秀太郎, trans. *Taiyaku Pereasu to Merizando* 対訳ペレアスとメリザンド. Iwanami Bunko red 岩波文庫赤 (32)-583-1. Tokyo: Iwanami Shoten 岩波書店, 1988.

Sugimoto 2003
Sugimoto Sonoko 杉本苑子. "Mēterurinku *Aoi tori*" メーテルリンク「青い鳥」. *Bungei Shunjū* 文藝春秋 79:8 (Aug 2001), pp. 305-307

Tanaka 1981
Tanaka Yoshihiro 田中義廣, trans. *Ari no seikatsu* 蟻の生活. Tokyo: Kōsakusha 工作舎, 1981.

Teihon Ueda Bin Zenshū **1978**
Teihon Ueda Bin Zenshū 定本上田敏全集, ed. Ueda Bin Zenshū Kankōkai 上田敏全集刊行会, vol. 1. Tokyo: Kyōiku Shuppan Sentā 教育出版センター, 1978.

Tezuka 1990
Tezuka Osamu 手塚治虫. *The Line of Winged Species / Chōjin taikei* 鳥人大系. Tokyo: Daitosha 大都社, 1990.

Tomita s.a.
Tomita Hiroyuki 冨田博之. "*Aoi tori* ninki no fushigi"「青い鳥」人気のふしぎ. pp. 8-12.

Tomita 1976
Tomita Hiroyuki 冨田博之. "*Aoi tori* no shoen"「青い鳥」の初演. In *Nihon jidōengekishi* 日本児童演劇史, ed. Tomita Hiroyuki, pp. 113-122. Tokyo: Tōkyō Shoseki 東京書籍, 1976.

Tomita 1986
Tomita Hiroyuki 冨田博之. "*Aoi tori* kotohajime"「青い鳥」事始. Gekkan hyakka 月刊百科 (Jul 1986), pp. 39-43.

Tomita 1988
Tomita Hiroyuki 冨田博之. *Aoi tori* no sashie「青い鳥」の挿絵. Hōsho Gekkan 彷書月刊 1 (1988), pp. 20-22.

Tomita 1989
Tomita Hiroyuki 冨田博之. "Nihon no *Aoi tori* josetsu" 日本の「青い鳥」序説. *Shirayuri Joshi Daigaku Jidō Bunka Gakkai* 白百合女子大学児童文化学会 (Sep 1989), pp. 134-141.

Tōyama 1990
Tōyama Hiroo. *La Fin de siècle en Flandre*. Tokyo: Librairie Geirin-Shobo, 1990.

Tōyama 2010
Tōyama Hiroo 遠山博雄. "Shōchōshugi inyū no shomondai (jō)" 象徴主義移入の諸問題(上), *Komazawa University Journal of the Faculty of Arts and Sciences / Komazawa Daigaku Sōgōkyōiku Kenkyūbu Kiyō* 駒澤大学総合教育研究部紀要 4 (Mar 2010), pp. 363-385.

Uchida 2006
Uchida Tomohide 内田智秀. "Nihon no *Aoi tori* juyō ni tsuite no ikkōsatsu" 日本の『青い鳥』受容についての一考察. *Nihon Furansugo Furansu bungakkai chūbu shibu kenkyū hōkokushū* 日本フランス語フランス文学会中部支部研究報告集 30 (Mar 2006), pp. 77-98.

Ueda 1901
Ueda Bin 上田敏. "Berugī bungaku" 白耳義文学. *Bungei ronshū* 文芸論集 (Dec 1901), pp. 274-286.

Ueda 1904
Verhaeren, trans. Ueda Bin 上田敏. "Sagi no uta" 鷺の歌. *Myōjō* 明星 (Jan 1904), p. 104.

Ueda 1905
Ueda Bin 上田敏, trans. *Kaichōon* 海潮音. Tokyo: Hongō Shoin 本郷書院, 1905; repr. Nihon Kindai Bungakukan 日本近代文学館, 1981, pp. 5-6.

Ueda 1906
Ueda Bin 上田敏. "Māterurinku" マアテルリンク. *Myōjō* 明星 6 (Jun 1906), pp. 1-9.

Ueda Bin Zenshū Kankōkai 1978
Ueda Bin Zenshū Kankōkai 上田敏全集刊行会. "Danutan danshakufujin no shōsetsu" ダヌタン男爵夫人の小説. In *Ueda Bin Zenshū* 上田敏全集, vol. 3, pp. 479-480. Tokyo: Kyōiku Shuppan Sentā 教育出版センター, 1978.

Ueda Bin Zenshū Kankōkai 1980
Ueda Bin Zenshū Kankōkai 上田敏全集刊行会. "Māterurinku" マアテルリンク. In *Ueda Bin Zenshū* 上田敏全集, vol. 7, pp. 140-150. Tokyo: Kyōiku Shuppan Sentā 教育出版センター, 1980.

Wakatsuki 1950
Wakatsuki Shiran 若月紫蘭, trans. *Aoi tori* 青い鳥. Tokyo: Iwanami Shoten 岩波書店, 1950.

Wake 1921
Wake Ritsujirō 和気律次郎, trans. *Magudara no Maria* マグダラのマリア. Tokyo: Genbunsha 玄文社, 1921.

Washio 1920a
Washio Hiroshi 鷲尾浩, trans. *Māterurinku zenshū* マーテルリンク全集 I. Hinja no takara 貧者の宝, Nofarisu ノフアリス, Emāsun エマースン, Chie to unmei 智慧と運命. Tokyo: Tōkasha 冬夏社, 1920.

Washio 1920b
Washio Hiroshi 鷲尾浩, trans. *Māterurinku zenshū* マーテルリンク全集 II. Yamamichi 山道, Shigo no seikatsu 死後の生活, Mitsubachi no seikatsu 蜜蜂の生活. Tokyo: Tōkasha 冬夏社, 1920.

Washio 1920c
Washio Hiroshi 鷲尾浩, trans. *Māterurinku zenshū* マーテルリンク全集 III. Uzumoretaru dendō 埋れたる殿堂, Nijū no sono 二重の園, Jinsei to hana 人生と花. Tokyo: Tōkasha 冬夏社, 1920.

Washio 1921a
Washio Hiroshi 鷲尾浩, trans. *Māterurinku zenshū* マーテルリンク全集 IV. Marēnu hime マレエヌ姫, Agurabeinu to Serisetto アグラベイヌとセリセット, Pearesu to Merisando ペアレスとメリサンド, Gunmō 群盲, Shichiōjo 七王女, Tantajīru no shi タンタヂイルの死, Beatorīsu ni ベアトリース尼. Tokyo: Tōkasha 冬夏社, 1921.

Washio 1921b
Washio Hiroshi 鷲尾浩, trans. *Māterurinku zenshū* マーテルリンク全集 V. Magudara no Mariya マグダラのマリヤ, Chinnyūsha 闖入者, Aoi tori 青い鳥, Arajin to Paromīdo アラヂンとパロミイド, Naibu 内部, Seito Antoniyusu no kiseki 聖徒アントニユスの奇蹟, Kon'yaku 婚約. Tokyo: Tōkasha 冬夏社, 1921.

Washio 1922a
Washio Hiroshi 鷲尾浩, trans. *Māterurinku zenshū* マーテルリンク全集 VI. Michi no hinkaku 未知の賓客, Shōni gyakusatsu 小児虐殺, Higan no shi 彼岸の死. Tokyo: Tōkasha 冬夏社, 1922.

Washio 1922b
Washio Hiroshi 鷲尾浩, trans. *Māterurinku zenshū* マーテルリンク全集 VII. Monna Vanna モンナ・ヴンナ, Joaizeru ジョアイゼル, Suchirumondo shichō スチルモンド市長, Ruisuburō ルイスブロー. Tokyo: Tōkasha 冬夏社, 1922.

Yamamura 1922
Yamamura Takashi 山村巍, trans. *Suchirumondo no shichō* スチルモンドの市長, *Arujian to Bābu buryū* アルジアンとバーブ・ブリュー, *Ichimei munashiki kaihō* 一名空しき解放, *Chinnyūsha* 闖入者, *Beatorīsu ni* ベアトリース尼. Tokyo: Bunsendō Shoten 文泉堂書店, 1922.

Yamanouchi 1925
Yamanouchi Yoshio 山内義雄, trans. "Marēnu hime" マレエヌ姫. In *Taisei gikyoku senshū* 泰西戯曲選集, vol. 14. Tokyo: Shinchōsha 新潮社, 1925.

Yamashita 1990
Yamashita Mayumi 山下真由美. "Takahama Kyoshi no shinsakunō to Mēterurinku" 高浜虚子の新作能とメーテルリンク. *Hikaku Bungaku Kenkyū* 比較文學研究 57 (Jun 1990), pp. 206-215.

Yanagita 1910
Yanagita Kunio 柳田國男. *Tōno monogatari* 遠野物語. Tokyo: Shūseidō 聚精堂, 1910.

Yanagita 1975
Yanagita Kunio, trans., with an introduction by Ronald A. Morse. *The Legends of Tōno*. Tokyo: the Japan Foundation, 1975.

Yasuda 1978
Yasuda Yasuo 安田保雄. "*Bokuyōshin* henchū" 『牧羊神』編注. In *Teihon Ueda Bin Zenshū* 定本上田敏全集, ed. Ueda Bin Zenshū Kankōkai 上田敏全集刊行会, vol. 1, pp. 631-659. Tokyo: Kyōiku Shuppan Sentā 教育出版センター, 1978.

NOTES

1 Rutten 1962, p. 29.

2 That he was still writing under an archaic pen name probably had to do with the fact that as a student he could or would not profile himself too much among the other authors publishing in the magazine. Some of them were authorities, like the famous professors Inoue Tetsujirō and Ueda Mannen. He could have been blamed for having had the nerve to rank himself among these greats. The selection of the characters *bi* and *yū* ("vague, indistinct, mysterious, secretive") for his pen name perhaps also relates to what Ueda considered to be typical of Symbolism.

3 Tōyama 2010, p. 364.

4 In an article discussing Paul Verlaine, published in the March 1896 issue of *Teikoku bungaku*, he coined *shōchōshugi* as the Japanese equivalent for "Symbolism".

5 It was apparently the play *Princess Maleine* which earned him the epithet the new Shakespeare. Rutten 1962, p. 10.

6 Ueda 1905.

7 Ueda 1906.

8 *Teihon Ueda Bin Zenshū* 1978, pp. 271-295, and Yasuda 1978, pp. 631-659.

9 Tomita 1976, p. 117.

10 Tomita 1976, p. 116.

11 Tomita 1976, pp. 116-118.

12 The performance happened at a time when the *Geijutsu-za* was disbanded and the theatre movement *Tsukiji shōgekijō* still had to be launched. Tomita 1976, p. 118.

13 Tomita 1976, p. 119.

14 Tomita 1976, p. 120.

15 Hanse & Vivier 1962, p. 97.

16 See Staden 2010.

17 The Tomita collection is incorporated in the *Jidō bunka kenkyū sentā* 児童文化研究センター (Research Centre for Children's Culture).

18 Shimizu 1983.

19 Kōreikashakai o yokusuru josei no kai 1992.

20 Tomita 1986.

21 Hatanaka 1999, p. 329.

22 Miyazaki 1921, 64 pp.

23 This paragraph is largely based on the one article I know of that is dedicated to this topic: Hatanaka 1999.

24 Itō 2010, pp. 153-154.

25 Itō 2010, p. 169.

26 Itō 2010, pp. 177-178.

27 Itō 2010, pp. 155-156.

28 Itō 2010, p. 81.

29 Itō 2010, pp. 84-91.

30 Itō 2010, p. 179.

31 "The mysterious *mayoiga*", story no. 63 in Yanagita 1975, pp. 45-46; Yanagita 1910, pp. 48-50.

32 "The Nobel Prize in Literature 1911 Maurice Maeterlinck Banquet Speech." Posted on The Official Web Site of the Nobel Prize, http://www.nobelprize.org/nobel_prizes/literature/laureates/1911/maeterlinck-speech.html. Accessed 23 Oct 2016.

33 Capiteyn 2008, p. 79.

34 Rutten 1962, p. 73.

FIFTH
PART

ARTISTIC
INSPIRATION

ART NOUVEAU IN BELGIUM IN THE LIGHT OF CROSS-CULTURALISM: THE CASE OF *KATAGAMI*, JAPANESE STENCILS

Yōko Takagi

ART NOUVEAU IN BELGIUM IN THE LIGHT OF CROSS-CULTURALISM: THE CASE OF *KATAGAMI*, JAPANESE STENCILS [1]

At the juncture often referred to as *fin-de-siècle*, Japanese art and design was a powerful source of inspiration for the Belgian decorative style known as Art Nouveau. This was a movement imbued with an avant-garde spirit akin to Neo-Impressionist and Symbolist aesthetics and that aspired to make the most of art in everyday life. The term "Art Nouveau" originated from the name of a gallery of decorative art, founded in Paris in 1895 by Siegfried Bing, a dealer in Japanese art. In fact, Bing was inspired by the exhibitions of *La Maison d'Art*, a gallery opened in Brussels a year earlier by Edmond Picard, in which the objects were exhibited in several rooms as if decorating a bourgeois home interior. To open his gallery, Bing also appointed a number of Belgian designers. Henry Van de Velde was entrusted with the interior design of three showrooms. Georges Lemmen did the design of the letterhead and the invitation to the opening. Victor Horta, who had constructed the first building in Art Nouveau style, the Hôtel Tassel (1893) in the Belgian capital, prepared plans for the façade of Bing's gallery, but in the end they were not retained.

The principal actors of Art Nouveau, Van de Velde, Lemmen, Horta, Gustave Serrurier-Bovy, Gisbert Combaz, Adolphe Crespin and Paul Hankar, were all devoted to fine art and applied arts from Japan. They studied and found inspiration in ukiyo-e woodblock prints, books in woodcut printing technique, porcelains, netsuke, woodwork, metalwork and *tsuba*.[2]

Katagami 型紙 (stencil paper for a dye-resistant technique in textile printing), one of the newest and latest items of nineteenth-century Japonism, was introduced to Europe in around 1890. Industrial art museums collected these linear ornamental designs in great quantity. There are about 4,000 in the Victoria and Albert Museum in London, and about 15,000 in the Kunstgewerbemuseum, Dresden.

This essay will try to demonstrate how a tool of the textile manual workshop in Japan had a considerable impact on the decorative arts and architecture of Belgium, while also contributing to the more general revival of crafts. We will first survey the background of the birth of Belgian Art Nouveau and describe how Japanese art and design was introduced and was related to the movement. Further focusing on *katagami*, we will see how three principal Art Nouveau artists – Van de Velde, Horta and Serrurier-Bovy – applied *katagami*. Through the case of Van de Velde, who was interested in both Japanese *katagami* and Javanese batik design, we will examine the complex cross-cultural impact of non-European design.

The Development of Decorative Arts and the Birth of Art Nouveau in Belgium

> There was a remarkable amalgamation of old customs and very modern ideas, of the blackest ultramontanism and the most refined industrialism, of the spirit of a bourgeois aristocracy and of revolutionary Socialism.[3]

This is the modern art critic Julius Meier-Graefe's comment, in his *Entwicklungsgeschichte der modernen Kunst* (1904), on late nineteenth-century Belgium as a crucible that spawned new forms and ideas through its fusion of tradition and revolution, capitalism and socialism. It is in this atmosphere of "remarkable amalgamation" in Brussels that Art Nouveau appeared.

Having won its independence from the Kingdom of the Netherlands in 1830, Belgium was endowed with a very advanced constitution for its time, including equality of all citizens, freedom of thought, and the separation of Church and State. Following where Britain had led, it was also the first nation on the European continent to become fully industrialized.

The decline of decorative arts had been evident at the Great Exhibition in London in 1851, and was also undeniable in Belgium. In the fields of glasswork,

---

‹ Fig. 6
Decorative design with fans and tendrils on trellis background:
Le Japon Artistique 6, pl. FC.
Collection Central Library KU Leuven, East-Asian Library.
Photograph by W.F. Vande Walle.

ceramics, porcelain, furniture and metalwork, larger industrial companies absorbed the smaller ones and under pressure from mechanization and the industrial division of labour, any former craftsmanship tended to be forgotten. Lower pricing and utility took precedence over aesthetic value. The easy solution for decoration came to be a remake of the forms and motifs of French Rococo, as well as Flemish Gothic and Renaissance styles. The fine arts and the applied arts had now definitely gone separate ways.[4]

To confront this crisis in industrial applied arts, the British government created an exhibition place, originally the South Kensington Museum, now the Victoria and Albert Museum, a year after the Great Exhibition of 1851. This Museum was to specialize in decorative and industrial arts and its mission also included educating craftsmen who made decorative objects, as well as their customers, in aesthetics. Similar museums or institutions were established in the 1860s in Germany, Austria and France.[5]

The education system was also adapted, with, for instance, the establishment of schools attached to the museums of decorative arts. This was only one of the actions taken by the governments of the various countries to foster industrial development. Belgium equally adopted a similar policy leading to the creation of the Museum for Decorative and Industrial Arts in Brussels in 1889, now known as the Royal Museums of Art and History. Before that, the School for Decorative Arts was founded in 1886, close to the Academy of Fine Arts in Brussels. At that time, a different movement developed which reconsidered the position of decorative arts in the field of fine arts. Closely linked to the birth of Art Nouveau, this movement first developed as an artistic group created in 1883 which organized exhibitions: Les XX. Another association, La Libre Esthétique, replaced this group in 1894. Led by Octave Maus, Les XX organized its annual salon in February presenting the most recent artworks from Belgium and elsewhere. This event was a true forum for avant-garde art in Europe. Without taking a position on style, the group exhibited, from 1891 onwards, decorative art alongside paintings and sculpture, at a location where it attempted to provide a global view of the artistic domains through concerts, conferences and other media. Les XX also made the English Arts and Crafts movement

known on the continent. All the efforts of this group to promote decorative arts were closely linked to the relations with a radical political movement to change society. The growing importance of industry in the applied arts and its need for productivity affected not only aesthetics: it also created a significant social problem, namely the unemployment of former artisans and the resulting demoralization of the previously employed. The main vehicle of Les XX was the monthly magazine *l'Art Moderne Revue critique des Arts et de la Littérature*. Its editors, Edmond Picard, Octave Maus, and the symbolist poet Emile Verhaeren, were all outspoken advocates of liberal-socialist political ideas.

Already in the first issue of *l'Art Moderne* in 1881, it was stated that art should have its place in the home, in furniture, and in all aspects of daily life.[6] When the prices of industrial products dropped significantly in 1884, the whole of Europe went into a crisis, with Belgium no exception, giving rise to a series of riots. In the meantime, the Liberal Party, which had implemented the liberal economic reforms that led to the crisis, was replaced in power by the Catholic Party. It is in this context that the Belgian Workers Party was founded in 1885, bringing together radicals, socialists, and the working class. The Workers Party established an arts section in its organizational structure and asked Les XX to provide conferences as part of their programme of artistic development.

For these artists, to engage in the decorative arts was to oppose the traditional hierarchy of arts and demonstrate their willing participation in the reform of society. This was the spirit in which Les XX, in February 1891, exhibited posters by Jules Chéret, albums by Walter Crane, ceramics by Paul Gauguin and W. Finch. In 1892, posters by Henri de Toulouse-Lautrec, as well as ceramics by Auguste Delaherche and a tapestry project by Van de Velde, "Faneuses", were presented to the public. In 1893, Les XX devoted two rooms to decorative arts. From 1894 onwards, the emphasis on decorative arts grew even stronger and Les XX was dissolved and supplanted by the artistic society La Libre Esthétique. Despite their radicalism, their artistic creations were in general supported by the bourgeoisie and each opening reception was considered an important social event.

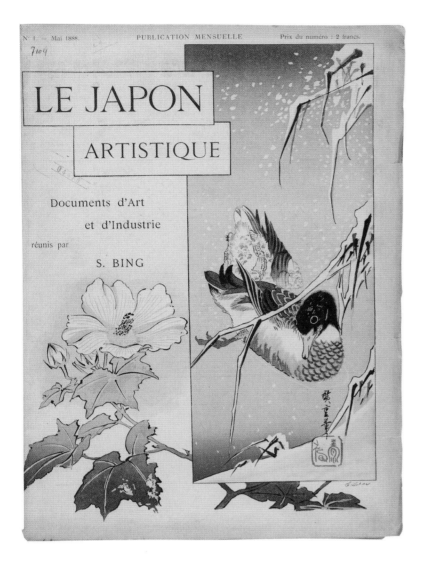

Perfectly illustrating the "remarkable amalgamation" mentioned by Meier-Graefe, the salons organized by Les XX became a space of cross-pollination for art works with a socialist agenda, to be appreciated by the rising urban bourgeoisie, which had only recently acquired financial power in industry and commerce and which was, crucially, not constrained by tradition.

Japanese Art as a Reference for a Synthesis between Art and Daily Life

Artists who wanted to break away from tradition and a public similarly unbound to the past were both in search of new forms of art which would not simply be an expression or an echo of the past splendour of Flanders. It was at precisely that moment that the encounter with

Japanese art occurred. The enthusiasm for things Japanese known as *Japonisme* reached its apex with the opening of the World Exposition in Paris in 1878. Simultaneously it reached Belgium, so close to French culture and in part sharing the same language. Belgian artists frequently visited Paris to see its museums and exhibitions or to serve apprenticeships in the studios of its masters. From the autumn of 1884 until early 1885, for instance, Van de Velde studied with Jules Bastien-Lepage and Emile Auguste Carolus-Duran. Victor Horta similarly trained with the architect and decorator Jules Debuysson from 1877 to 1880. While staying in Paris, they most probably came into contact with some form of Japanese art and Japonism.

At the beginning of the 1880s, it became fashionable for the Belgian bourgeoisie to embellish their apartments, previously mostly decorated in an older style, with vases, fans, bronzes or folding screens made in Japan. These objects were no longer exclusively reserved to true enthusiasts thanks to a sudden increase in shops selling Japanese paraphernalia. *La Compagnie Japonaise*, created in 1880, opened a shop on the Rue Royale, a fashionable district in Brussels, representing the trading company Mitsui Bussan in Belgium. According to the memories of Van de Velde, the members of Les XX were literally stunned in their admiration in front of the shop window, when, before 1891, *La Compagnie Japonaise* was selling both Japanese objects and contemporary objects made in the United Kingdom.[7] So-called Japanese Art, so much in demand in Brussels, included decorative objects, furniture and utensils with both a practical and an artistic dimension. As may be read in the first number of *l'Art Moderne*, Japanese art was a reference providing a synthesis between art and daily life. It should be noted that in England decorative art had already undergone a "Japanization", even generating an Anglo-Japanese style. This explains why *La Compagnie Japonaise* put Japanese objects alongside products of British Japonism in its window display.

It was, however, only with the exhibition organized by Siegfried Bing in 1889 in the rooms of *Le Cercle Artistique et Littéraire* that Japanese paintings and woodcuts were presented in the Belgian capital on a large scale. It was the first exhibition devoted to three aspects of Japanese art in three different rooms: painted scrolls (*kakemono*), ukiyo-e style woodblock prints, and illustrated albums.

Fig. 1
Cover of *Le Japon Artistique*, issue of May 1888.
Collection Central Library KU Leuven, East-Asian Library.
Photograph by Hans Coppens.

Fig. 2
Cover of *Le Japon Artistique*, issue of July 1888.
Collection Central Library KU Leuven, East-Asian Library.
Photograph by Hans Coppens.

Fig. 3
Cover of *Le Japon Artistique*, issue of May 1890.
Collection Central Library KU Leuven, East-Asian Library.
Photograph by Hans Coppens.

articles in art journals such as *The Studio*, information on these *katagami* travelled fast and they quickly became one of the favourites of lovers of Japanese art.[9]

Katagami applied by Gustave Serrurier-Bovy, Henry Van de Velde and Victor Horta

The architect and furniture designer Gustave Serrurier-Bovy (1858-1910) owned a boutique in Liège, selling English decorative motifs (starting with textiles from Liberty and wallpaper from Essex and Co.) as well as Japanese imports.[10] After beginning to sell his own creations, he soon opened a boutique in Paris. With respect to furniture design, Serrurier-Bovy's originality resided in the simplicity of highlighted wood texture and surface decoration, which was seemingly the result of the use of *katagami*, initially used in dyeing techniques.

The "Cabinet de Travail" (Fig. 7; Fig. 8) presented by Serrurier-Bovy at the first exhibition of La Libre Esthétique in 1894 provides a good example of applying Japanese stencil plates to Belgian decorative arts. Reluctant to exhibit his furniture in isolation, the decorator created a veritable scene of daily life in one of the rooms of the Royal Museum. It was, in fact, a visionary way of displaying objects. Other galleries quickly followed suit: Edmond Picard's Maison d'Art in December 1894, Bing's Art Nouveau in December 1895,

The principal reference work in Belgium on Japanese art at that time was *Le Japon Artistique*, a monthly magazine published by Bing. This periodical appeared in three languages, French, English and German, over a period of three years starting in 1888. In essays and through illustrations, it revealed a Japanese culture in which art was an integral part of daily life. *Le Japon Artistique*, carrying the sub-title "*A Monthly Illustrated Journal of Arts & Industries*", aimed at suggesting practical ideas for craftsmen and manufacturers of decorative arts. The periodical was available at the Royal Library of Belgium and we know that Victor Horta owned the complete series. (Fig. 1-6).

Among its illustrations, a *katagami* design was published for the first time. The *katagami* were represented under different names: industrial models, industrial motifs, decorative motifs, and decorative models. If a work by Andrew W. Tuer published in 1892 is to be believed,[8] most people had not yet identified these *katagami* as stencil plates of a dye-resisting technique for the textile industry. However, because of the increasing number of

"UN CABINET DE TRAVAIL"   DESIGNED BY G. SERRURIER
(From a Photograph by Alexandre. See Brussels Studio-Talk)

"UN CABINET DE TRAVAIL"   DESIGNED BY G. SERRURIER
(From a Photograph by Alexandre. See Brussels Studio-Talk)

and Meier-Graefe's La Maison Moderne in 1899. Serrurier-Bovy's "Cabinet de travail" contained basic furniture in a rustic style. The walls were clad with an original English paper depicting large fantastic flowers in a Japanese style.[11] The decoration of this painted paper frieze, showing wild poppies, was certainly made with the *katagami* technique, which had started to be known in Europe.

At the following year's La Libre Esthétique salon, in 1895, Serrurier-Bovy adopted the same formula in his "Chambre d'Artisan" (Fig. 9). The carnation motif on the wall frieze of this room was also made with a *katagami* technique, explained by the decorator as "of relatively modest price since directly applied on paper."[12] In short, Serrurier-Bovy encouraged the use of Japanese stencil plates for decorating wallpapers, allowing the wider population of the working class and artisans to add some art to their lives without too much cost. While it was most likely for economic reasons that the decorator used *katagami* techniques, the motifs of Japanese stencil plates were soon recognized as fashionable. This is evidenced by the interior decoration of the restaurant Le Pavillon Bleu, built for the Paris World Exposition of 1900, and in the Silex furniture collection, chosen for the Château de La Cheyrelle (*Katagami* 2007, cat. no. 173).

Serrurier-Bovy had been admitted to the salon of La Libre Esthétique in 1894 on the recommendation of Henry Van de Velde (1863-1957).[13] After having cultivated Realism, followed by Neo-Impressionism in painting, Van de Velde became a member of Les XX in 1888. In 1892 he abandoned his paintbrushes to devote himself to decorative arts. At the exhibition of Les XX in 1893, he exhibited an embroidered tapestry, *La veillée des anges*, marking a landmark turn in his career. His wife Maria, who supported him very strongly and whom he had only recently married, was a student of painter Theo Van Rysselberghe:

> She (Maria) had all the skills to adapt the abstract, linear and dynamographic motifs of the kind that adorned the poetry collections of my dear friend Max Elskamp (*Katagami* 2007, cat. no. 165, 167) and the recent periodical of my friend Auguste Vermeylen (*Katagami* 2007, cat. no. 168, 169, 170), to wallpaper techniques, various printed textiles or stencil plate.[14]

Fig. 7 + 8
Gustave Serrurier-Bovy. "Un cabinet de travail" exhibited at *La Libre Esthétique*, 1894. Illustration from *The Studio, An Illustrated Magazine of Fine and Applied Art* (London) 8 (July 1896), p. 118.

Shortly after starting to work in the field of decorative arts, Van de Velde began using *katagami*. A text he wrote in this period shows how he appreciated the anonymous character of Japanese works, which according to him were the ideal of art in society.[15] This anonymous character put forward the artwork itself regardless of the historical context in which it had been conceived. When depicting Japan as an ideal society where art and daily life objects were at the same level, Van de Velde probably had the *katagami* in mind.

According to Van de Velde, the hierarchy of arts, with the so-called fine arts at the top, had to be abolished to rehabilitate the minor arts, secondary arts, decorative arts, industrial arts and applied arts, in short, all the arts considered inferior, and also to integrate them in everyday life.[16] This theory was to be put into practice by Van de Velde in 1895-1896, when building his home, Bloemenwerf, in Uccle, a suburb of Brussels: he designed furniture, chinaware and wallpapers. Undoubtedly, he had to select motifs and forms carefully, the best to reflect his aesthetic conception for his family haven, where life and art were to be at one.

In 1898, Meier-Graefe founded the decorative and functional arts journal *L'Art Décoratif* in Paris. As indicated by the subtitle, *Revue Internationale d'Art Industriel et de Décoration*, the magazine covered the latest trends in modern art and the art movements that involved industry and decoration occurring in all areas of Europe. The inaugural issue, published in October 1898, included a feature article on Henry Van de Velde.

One of the illustrations of the magazine showed the central hall of Bloemenwerf. To decorate the left side of the door opening, Van de Velde chose a *katagami* representing carps swimming up a waterfall.[17] While the stencil plates in Japan were simple tools used by artisans and industry, Van de Velde displayed this one framed in a white background to indicate that it was appreciated as a work of art. From a western perspective, the publication of these illustrations in the contemporary art magazine *L'Art Décoratif: Revue Mensuelle d'Art Contemporain* transformed *katagami* into art.

The same *katagami* is also shown in a photograph in his workshop on the ground floor of Villa Bloemenwerf. One can notice that the unfinished panel on the working

"UNE CHAMBRE D'ARTISAN"   DESIGNED BY G. SERRURIER
(From a Photograph by Alexandre. See Brussels Studio-Talk)

table, together with the decoration of the wallpaper, reflected the beauty of this stencil plate. Convinced that the dress of the lady of the house, an essential component of a family home, also had to be aesthetic, Van de Velde started to design a dress for his wife Maria. A photograph survives in which his model can be seen in front of a *katagami* with the dress decorated with abstract motifs stitched on velvet. As mentioned earlier, one of the *katagami* that decorated the workshop and Villa Bloemenwerf showed a motif of carps swimming in a wild stream. The other one represented falcons flying in the wind. The match between the curves of the *katagami* and the dress is evident and we can imagine these stencil plates were chosen especially as a background for the picture.

As director of the School for Applied Arts (Kunstgewerbe-schule), which he created in Weimar in 1908, Van de Velde was soon to teach on the synthesis of applied arts in the period of industrialization, playing an intermediary role between Art Nouveau and Bauhaus, which in turn gave birth to the functionalist design aesthetic. He believed that decoration (i.e., artistic expression of forms) had to correspond as much as possible to its function, and that therefore it logically derives from parameters such as function and structure.

In an essay on the design and production of contemporary furniture, published in the art magazine *Pan* in 1897, Van de Velde claims to have discovered that the negative edges of the empty spaces resulting from cuttings have an aesthetic value much like positive edges usually do in setting the boundaries of an object. He also adds that of all his discoveries, this may be the most important one.[19]

Overall, thanks to its piercings and curves, the furniture can harmoniously fit the interior space of a construction. This intrinsic relation between positive and negative adds to the modelling characteristics of *katagami*, using the alternative white-brown flat representation. Other particularities of Japanese stencil plates may be noted, such as the tendency to stylize to abstraction motifs originally modelled on nature, their expression through dynamic curves deployed in waves, the continuity of these motifs, and the essential condition of applying them on textile without interrupting the balance.

For Van de Velde, who in designing textiles and wallpapers often employed one continuous motif, all these characteristics surely made *katagami* the ideal model. One of the places where we can find examples of the application of these Japanese stencil plates is a book cover designed for a collection of poems by his childhood friend Max Elskamp (*Katagami* 2007, cat. no.165), and for a Flemish literary magazine *Van Nu en Straks* (*Katagami* 2007, cat. no.168). In any event, the abstraction and vigorous rhythm of curves and lines in S-form, the continuity of motif and its spread (*Katagami* 2007, cat. no. 169 and 170), are all clearly inspired by *katagami*. Soon, Van de Velde was to expand its application to other forms as well: a poster (*Katagami* 2007, cat. no. 156, 157), a table set (*Katagami* 2007, cat. no.171) (Fig. 10), and a carpet (*Katagami* 2007, cat. no.177) (Fig. 11) (Fig. 12).

As an artist however, Van de Velde was also a passionate student of decoration in its own right, examining issues such as the dynamism of lines.

In his essay *Die Linie* in 1910, Van de Velde explains to the reader how much of a revelation the lines in Japanese art were for him:

> This account would be incomplete if we were not to mention that, just as the neo-impressionists showed us the new line at a moment when no sign of it was to be found in architecture or in ornamental design, the sudden revelation of Japanese art aroused in us the sense of line. [...] The wonders born of a well-judged balance between the subordination that can be demanded of line and the freedom that must be granted to it came to us as an overwhelming revelation: it was like a sudden blaze of sunlight emerging from a thick cloud. The Japanese line brought salvation.[18]

He does not write in this essay about the medium that conveyed this sense of Japanese lines. However, as seen in the photographs of the interior decoration in his home, it is possible that *katagami* provided this inspiration.

Van de Velde moved to Germany in 1900. Much like the enthusiasm for Japanese design in the 1890s, a recent study by Maria Wronka-Friend shows he also developed an interest in Javanese batik and played a leading role as practitioner of batik-inspired design and as an educator during his time in Weimar between 1902 and 1917. After the Netherlands, Germany also became interested in this technique. Friedrich Deneken, director of the Kaiser Wilhelm Museum in Krefeld, organized an exhibition of

Fig. 10
Henry Van de Velde. Dish and Sauce boat "Peitschenhieb," 1903/04, porcelain and glaze. Dish, 5 × 37.5 cm; sauce boat, 12 × 29.5 × 13 cm.
Courtesy of Design Museum Ghent.

art from the Dutch East Indies in 1907, with sixty-seven batiks on show. As a result, the status of Indonesian works shifted from that of exotic curiosities to works of art, in a way quite similar to what had happened with Japanese art in the late nineteenth century. Van de Velde himself did not apply the technique, but the motif spread to industrial imitations printed in the Netherlands, the United Kingdom, and Switzerland at the beginning of the twentieth century. Using this large production system, he supplied Javanese-style batik to the increasing demand in German society.[20]

Fig. 11
Henry Van de Velde. Carpet, c.1902-1903, wool, 166 × 166 cm.
Courtesy of Design Museum Ghent, 76/245.

H. VAN DE VELDE À BRUXELLES   CABINET DE TRAVAIL (EXPOSÉ AU SALON DE LA SÉCESSION À MUNICH)

Batik is a dye-resistant technique, the development of which was centred in Java, then part of the Dutch East Indies (now the Republic of Indonesia). The design is executed by drawing with wax or with copper stamps or with a copper reservoir called a *tjanting*. Both *katagami* and batik avoid realistic representations or illusionistic effects, instead sharing a flat, two-dimensional ornamentation with a repeating motif. Linearity and abstraction were the major points. According to a recent study of the influence of batik in the Weimar school, the impact of Japanese design was limited to the end of the 1890s, after which Van de Velde's interest changed to batik. His linear ornaments in the 1890s are irregular and capricious, while from around 1896 his lines become less feverish and agitated but more regular and rhythmical.

Such a clear-cut explanation seems rather hazardous. The regular and rhythmical lines are precisely characteristic of *katagami*. Moreover, an artistic inspiration is rarely singular and is usually associated with others in an intricate and complicated way, with which it shares many formal elements. It was Johan Thorn Prikker (1868-1932) who introduced Van de Velde to batik in 1894 as an exotic element in Dutch Arts and Crafts and Art Nouveau. Motifs from the Dutch colony mixed with Japonism reached Holland after 1890 and mixed with a curvilinear Art-Nouveau style from Belgium and France. The influence of *katagami* design in the Netherlands lies hidden in this multi-cultural

design context.[21] Van de Velde's practices were a good example of that cross-culturalism.

At the time of the building of the Hôtel Tassel, the architect Victor Horta (1861-1947) had a fierce rivalry with Van de Velde.[22] Horta, who studied in Ghent and at the Academy of Fine Arts in Brussels, had been initiated into Neo-Classicism by the architect Alphonse Balat. Becoming his assistant at the Free University of Brussels, he was able to meet with Emile Tassel, a professor of the university, and Eugène Autrique, who were both very open to truly innovative plans in the architectural domain. Horta was part of a society of artists and architects with a socialist vision of the modern world, as can be seen from the request made by the Belgian Labour Party to build their headquarters, a house for the working class named "Maison du people," from the exhibition of a set of furniture for the Hôtel Solvay at the salon of La Libre Esthétique in 1897, as well as from the plans drawn up in 1902 for a prominent member of the Labour Party, the lawyer Max Hallet.

In the 1890s, the works of Horta in urban housing — for instance in the city of Brussels, the Hôtel Tassel (1893), the Hôtel Van Eetvelde (1895), the Hôtel Solvay (1895), and the Maison & Atelier Horta (1898), registered since 2000 on the UNESCO World Heritage List — are characterized by the architect's ability to set off all constraints imposed by the location of the building through innovative open structures and the use of metal and glass. Before this, narrow strips and plots of land on which city dwellings were aligned next to each other were the norm, much like the *nagaya*, traditional homes of the lower-class Japanese. With his approach Horta achieved a synthesis between the building itself and its environment by combining several materials with strong curves.

Among the works mentioned above, the Hôtel Tassel, considered the first Art Nouveau architecture, comes closest to the expression of Japanese aesthetics. For instance, in the hallway of the staircase, the dynamic curves of roots and bulbs from which vegetation emerges transcend the different materials used, to continue on the wall paintings and mosaic floors, and grow up along the staircase to finally open up on the ceiling frescoes and the capitals of the metal columns. It would seem that some of the forms and motifs chosen by Horta for the

Fig. 12
Henry Van de Velde. "Cabinet de travail (exposé au salon de la Sécession à Munich)." *L'Art Décoratif* 1 (October 1898).
Collection Central Library KU Leuven. Photograph by Digitaal Labo KU Leuven©.

Hôtel Tassel originated from ukiyo-e woodblock prints.[23] We will see that a comparison with *katagami* is also relevant.

In 1898, Horta started the design of his house and workshop (now the Hortamuseum, Rue Américaine/ Amerikastraat 25, 1060 Brussels), where he could freely express his design ideas. On the orange walls of the staircase, illuminated by a ceiling light, he drew a continuous motif of a plant in cream tones, vigorously growing from the floor into flowers with a large corolla. This motif repeats itself on the handrail and glass window. The handrail in wrought iron, a combination of empty and filled spaces, as well as the stained glass window with motifs combining metal and glass through which the light penetrates, fundamentally have the same structure as a *katagami*. The expression of Japanese stencil plates which had started to bloom in the staircase of the Hôtel Tassel, is perfectly assimilated in the house of Horta to become the symbol of Art Nouveau in all its splendour.

Katagami as the Ideal Lexicon for Belgian Architects and Designers

Katagami was one of the last items of nineteenth-century Japonism introduced to Europe. In Japan, it was neither an artwork nor a final product but a tool for the dye industry. As it was used inside craftsmen's workshops and factories, the Japanese generally did not appreciate its aesthetic. The possible existence of a Japanese promoter is also unknown. One may assume that westerners discovered its aesthetic character and decided to collect it. Thus the means of its application became dissociated from its original purpose and spread to the surface design of various materials.

Ukiyo-e had an enormous influence on Western painting during the second half of the nineteenth century. Since these prints were in fact, first of all, a kind of painting, tapping into their exotic iconography for inspiration for the European decorative arts could only occur with a certain transposition. *Katagami*, on the other hand, although taking its themes from flora, personal objects or natural phenomena like clouds, thunder, and hail, are stylized through a linear expression, excluding any volume, texture or colour. This stylization sometimes leads to abstraction, where it becomes impossible to distinguish the origin of one or the other motif. From this, possibilities for anti-naturalist and symbolist artistic expressions arise, attracting attention for their originality. More practically, *katagami* are thus a medium which are easy to use in architecture and decorative arts, since they are inspired by nature, take a distance from it towards abstraction, and are set free from any foreign cultural context. They certainly represented the ideal lexicon for Belgian architects and designers yearning for the beauty of the line *an sich*.

Katagami simultaneously answered a question debated across nineteenth-century Europe: how to improve artistic quality without affecting the return on investment required by industry? From 1893 on, Van de Velde, Serrurier-Bovy and Horta started to elaborate on the decorative motifs inspired by *katagami*. This was not because they felt compelled by the policies of the time to boost industry: for them, art was a means of expressing their opposition to traditional values. Through a happy coincidence, *katagami* started to become known thanks to publications by Tuer and to art magazines just at the time when artists, strongly linked to political movements and seeking to create a better society through art, were truly engaging with the field of decorative arts. This media was probably first integrated in the socialist thoughts of avant-garde artists as it was a method that embodied an artistic dimension at a low cost. At the dawn of the twentieth century, it had become a means of modern aesthetics, where one could already feel the coming birth of Art Deco.

REFERENCES

"Arts et Industrie"
"Arts et Industrie, les arts décoratifs en Belgique au XIXe siècle". In *Actes du colloque, 23-24 octobre 2003*. Brussels: Musées royaux d'Art et d'Histoire.

Aubry 2005
Françoise Aubry. *Horta ou la passion de l'architecture*. Antwerp: Ludion, 2005.

Britt 1992
David Britt, trans. *Japonisme in Western Painting from Whistler to Matisse*, ed. Klaus Berger. Cambridge University Press, 1992.

Dulière 1985
Cécil Dulière. *Victor Horta, Mémoires*. Brussels: Ministère de la Communauté française, 1985.

Groot 2012
Marjan Groot. "Katagami and Japonisme in the Netherland". In Exh. cat. (English version) *Katagami Style*, pp. 66-68 [pp. 306-309 in the Japanese original version]. Tokyo: Mitsubishi Ichigokan Museum; Kyoto: The National Museum of Modern Art; Mie: Prefectural Art Museum, 2012.

Katagami 2007
Katagami: Les pochoirs japonais et le japonisme, exhibition held at the Maison de la culture du Japon à Paris, 19 October 2006 – 20 January 2007 (see Takagi 2007).

Meier-Graefe 1904
Julius Meier-Graefe. *Entwicklungsgeschichte der Moderne Kunst*, vol. 2. Stuttgart: Jul. Hoffmann, 1904.

Meier-Graefe 1968
Julius Meier-Graefe, trans. Florence Simmonds and George W. Chrystal. *Modern Art: Being a Contribution to a New System of Aesthetics*. New York: Arne Press, 1968.

"Notre Programme"
"Notre Programme". *L'Art Moderne* (6 March 1881).

Takagi 2002
Takagi Yoko. *Japonisme in Fin de Siècle Art in Belgium*. Antwerp: Pandora, 2002.

Takagi 2007
Takagi Yoko. "Les *katagami* et l'Art Nouveau en Belgique". In *Katagami: Les pochoirs japonais et le japonisme*, pp. 32-29. Maison de la culture du Japon à Paris, 19 October 2006 – 20 January 2007.

Van de Velde 1894
Henry Van de Velde. "Première prédication d'art". *L'Art Moderne* (21 January 1894), p. 21.

Van de Velde 1895
Henry Van de Velde. *Aperçus en vue d'une synthèse d'art*. Brussels: Vve Monnom, 1895.

Van de Velde 1897
Henry Van de Velde. "Ein Kapitel über Entwurf und Bau Moderner Möbel". *Pan* 3 (1897), p. 261.

Van de Velde 1955
Henry Van de Velde. "Die Linie". In *Zum Neuen Stil*. Munich: R. Piper & Co. Verlag, 1955 [1910].

Van Loo 1992
Anne Van Loo, ed. *Henry Van de Velde: Récit de ma vie, Anvers-Bruxelles-Paris-Berlin. I, 1863-1900*. Bruxelles: Versa, 1992.

Watelet 2000
Jacques-Grégoire Watelet. *L'œuvre d'une vie: Georges Serrurier-Bovy, Architecte et décorateur liégeois 1858-1910*. Alleur-Liège: Éditions du Perron, 2000.

Wronska-Friend 2014
M. Wronska-Friend. "Henry van de Velde and Javanese Batik". In *Henry van de Velde. Interior Design and Decorative Arts: A Catalogue Raisonné in Six Volumes. Vol. 2: Textiles*, ed. Thomas Föhl and Antje Neumann. Leipzig: Seemann Henschel, c.2014.

NOTES

1 This essay is based on the author's contribution to the Workshop "An Integrated Comparative Study of Japan and Belgium from the Perspective of Regional Studies" (29-31 August 2006, University of Leuven), and was published in the exhibition catalogue of the exhibition *Katagami: Les pochoirs japonais et le japonisme*, held at the Maison de la culture du Japon à Paris, 19 October 2006 – 20 January 2007 (see Takagi 2007). All the references (Cat. no., Fig., Photo) correspond to the illustrations of that catalogue. The version published here incorporates all revisions emanating from recent research results on this subject. This work was supported by JSPS KAKENHI Grant Number 26370177.

2 Takagi 2002.

3 Meier-Graefe 1904, p. 666; Meier-Graefe 1968, p. 290.

4 For more details on the difficulties encountered in the decorative arts in Belgium at the end of the nineteenth century, reference can be made to "Arts et Industrie".

5 Museums on decorative arts and industry opened one after the other in Vienna and Lyon in 1864, Karlsruhe in 1865, and Berlin in 1867. *L'Union Centrale des Arts Décoratifs* was founded in Paris in 1864.

6 "Nos monuments, nos maisons, nos meubles, nos vêtements, les moindres objets dont chaque jour nous nous servons, sont repris sans cesse, transformés par l'Art, qui se mêle ainsi à toutes choses et refait constamment notre vie entière pour la rendre plus élégante, plus digne, plus riante et plus sociale." In "Notre Programme".

7 Van Loo 1992, pp. 161-163.

8 *The Book of Delightful and Strange Designs Being One Hundred Facsimile Illustrations of the Art of the Japanese Stencil-Cutter to which the Gentle Reader is Introduced by One Andrew W. Tuer, F.S.A. Who Knows Nothing at All about it.* Its playfully archaisizing French title is *Le Livre de desseins charmants et étranges, contenant cent spécimens fac-similé de l'art du Graveur sur papier japonais, présenté au doulx lecteur par un certain Andrew W. Tuer, lequel n'y connoit pas grand'chose.*

9 The Royal Museums of Art and History acquired the Japanese collection of Edmond Michotte in 1905. This collection includes 44 *katagami* (M1640-1655, M1657-1670, M1672-1673, M1675-1686).

10 *La Wallonie* (1886), nos. 2, 3, 4, 5, 6.

11 "Sur les murs, on a tendu un papier anglais original avec de grandes fleurs fantastiques à la façon japonaise." *L'Express* (20 February 1894).

12 Watelet 2000, p. 64.

13 Watelet 2000, p. 161.

14 "Elle (Maria) disposait de tous les moyens pour adapter les motifs abstraits, linéaires et dynamographiques de la même famille que ceux qui décoraient les recueils de poèmes de mon fraternel ami, Max Elskamp et la jeune revue de mon ami Auguste Vermeylen, aux techniques du papier peint, des divers tissus imprimés ou exécutés au pochoir." Archives et Musée de la Littérature, FSX47.

15 "Je pose en fait que si les œuvres d'art eussent été anonymes, l'art n'en serait pas arrivé à l'état de déconsidération où il est tombé aujourd'hui. Au Japon – et l'étude de l'art japonais nous a révélé une formule du rôle et de la condition de l'artiste dans la société, qu'il faudra bien accepter comme la seule vraie, parce qu'elle est la seule vraiment respectueuse de l'art et capable de le régénérer – s'inquiète-t-on de l'auteur d'une œuvre d'art?

"À une récente réunion de la *Japan Society* un jeune Japonais, insistant sur ce fait qu'en son pays les œuvres attiraient plutôt l'attention que leur créateur, déclarait: 'Chez vous, quand vous avez besoin d'objet d'art, les « Royal académiciens » les dessinent. Aussitôt leurs dessins sont reproduits dans vos revues et généralement, à cette occasion, il en est beaucoup parlé dans les journaux. Au Japon – encore aujourd'hui – quand il nous est donné de voir un nouvel objet d'art, nous l'examinons, l'admirons s'il est beau, mais nous ne demandons jamais QUI l'a produit.'" Van de Velde 1894, p. 21.

16 Henry Van de Velde 1895.

17 *L'Art Décoratif* 1 (October 1898), p. 16.

18 Van de Velde 1955, p. 191; translated by David Britt in Britt 1992, pp. 275-276.

19 Van de Velde 1897.

20 Wronska-Friend 2014, p. 397.

21 Groot 2012.

22 Horta wrote of Van de Velde, commissioned to deliver the textile from Liberty and ceramics from A. W. Finch for the interior decoration of the Hôtel Tassel, as a "decorator and salesman of textiles", which bespeaks his low esteem for Van de Velde. Dulière 1985.

23 According to Françoise Aubry, Tassel was a great collector of Japanese art, and must have been delighted to distinguish the influence of the "floating world" (ukiyo-e) in his house. Aubry 2005, pp. 37; 46-49.

THE KING'S DREAM:
THE MUSEUMS OF THE FAR EAST
AND THEIR COLLECTIONS

Nathalie Vandeperre

JAPAN & BELGIUM
An Itinerary of Mutual Inspiration

THE KING'S DREAM:
THE MUSEUMS OF THE FAR EAST AND THEIR COLLECTIONS

When approaching Brussels from the north, the visitor's eye is drawn by a Japanese pagoda, dominating the skyline of this part of the capital. Quite unexpectedly, this odd sight is matched by a golden Chinese-style pavilion, just across the road. This exotic site, known today as the Museums of the Far East, is one of the departments of the Royal Museums of Art and History and hosts part of their Far Eastern collections. (Fig. 1 + 2)

M. Henri de Mayrena, secrétaire général.   LE TOUR DU MONDE   M. Alexandre Marcel, architecte.

The history of the site dates back to 1900, year of the *Exposition universelle et internationale* in Paris. Leopold II (1835-1909), King of the Belgians, was among the 50 million visitors to the exhibition. He showed particular interest in a panorama called *le Tour du Monde* ("Around the world"), designed by the French architect Alexandre Marcel (1860-1928) and financed by the Compagnie des Messageries Maritimes. This building, well located next to the Eiffel Tower, took its visitors on a journey around the world by mixing architectural styles, thus combining a Portuguese and an Indian tower with composite facades containing Chinese and Arabo-Moorish elements and, last but not least, a Japanese porch flanked by a pagoda (Fig. 3).

Leopold II, who had never before shown any particular interest in the arts of China or Japan, nevertheless saw the economic opportunities both countries could offer to a small, industrious country like Belgium. Even before ascending the throne in 1865, he had made several proposals to the senate to enhance relations between Belgium and the Far Eastern nations. On the other hand, he had since the 1860s had very ambitious plans for the urban development of Brussels. One of the topics in his programme was to encircle Brussels with a ring of tree-lined boulevards, parks, and prestigious buildings. After visiting the *Tour du Monde*, he saw the potential of creating an exotic complex on the north of the city, on the edge of his estate in Laeken, in a part of the city that at the time was still rural. The architecture would attract visitors and promote Laeken as an international cultural centre.

In 1901, Leopold II personally commissioned the Parisian architect Alexandre Marcel to build the Japanese Tower and Chinese Pavilion. The building of the Japanese Tower in Brussels started right after the

< Fig. 1
The Japanese Tower. In the foreground, the garden kiosk that stands in front of the Chinese Pavilion.

Fig. 2
The Chinese Pavilion.

Fig. 3
Le Tour du Monde, designed by Alexandre Marcel for the 1900 Paris World Exposition. The pavilion included, among other attractions, a panorama that illustrated the principal ports of the Compagnie des Messageries maritimes liners serving the Far East. The Japanese entrance porch would later be rebuilt in Brussels.

Fig. a
Detail of the entrance porch to the Japanese Tower.
Photograph by W.F. Vande Walle.

Fig. b
Base of one of the engaged pillars on the front of the entrance porch to the Japanese Tower, with the signature of the carpenter Komatsu Mitsushige.
Photograph by W.F. Vande Walle.

Fig. c
Signature of Komatsu Mitsushige on the lower left panel in the door to the entrance porch of the Japanese Tower.
Photograph by W.F. Vande Walle.

exhibition, in 1901. Contrary to common belief, the pagoda is not a replica of the one in Paris, and is certainly not a replica of a real Japanese pagoda. In fact, the entrance porch to the Japanese Tower in Brussels is that from the *Tour du Monde*, which was moved to Brussels after the *Exposition universelle et internationale*. It is the only genuinely Japanese part of the building, made and signed by a Tokyo carpenter, Komatsu Mitsushige 小松光重 (Fig. a, b, c). The rest of the construction was built by Belgian carpenters and decorated by French craftsmen. They produced the painted canvas decorations in the staircase, with designs taken directly from Japanese woodblock prints, the stained glass windows with battle scenes illustrating the Wars between the Minamoto and Taira clans (Genpei 源平 Wars ,1180-1185) (Fig. 4), the ceiling decoration and the impressive lotus chandeliers. To add an authentically Japanese look, the architect had thousands of gilded metal plaques and sculpted wooden panels sent from Yokohama, which were used to decorate the building inside and out. Other orders included ceilings to be installed in some of the upper storeys, exterior lanterns, furniture, decorative objects and textiles.

Architecturally, the building is composed of three parts. Beside the entrance porch, Alexandre Marcel designed a gallery with large windows, covering a monumental staircase (Fig. 5 and Fig. g) leading some twenty metres up from the porch to the five-storey pagoda, which is sixty-two metres high. Even though at first glance it looks like a faithful reproduction of a real Japanese pagoda, there are some essential differences from the traditional Buddhist architecture: this one has six levels under its five roofs, instead of the regular five. Also, while in Japan only the single ground floor is useful, the upper levels of this tower are converted to storeys accessible by a semi-projecting staircase. Lastly, the tower and the rest of the building were equipped from the very beginning with the most modern western comforts, such as telephone, electricity, heating and elevators. The construction of the Japanese Tower was completed in November 1904.

Except for some private invitations and a public opening during a royal garden party on 6 May 1905, the intended use of the Tower remained uncertain until 1909, when Leopold II decreed that the Belgian state should use it as a commercial museum. The Ministry of Foreign Affairs (responsible for the new museum) officially undertook

Fig. 4
Detail of one of the stained glass windows in the Japanese Tower, by the French decorator Jac Galland.

Fig. 5
Monumental staircase of the Japanese Tower, decorated with carved wooden panels and gilded metal plaques, ordered directly from Japan, bronze chandeliers by A. Rollet, stained glass windows and paintings after ukiyo-e prints by Jac Galland.

Fig. g
Exterior view of (part of the) monumental staircase linking porch to pagoda.
Photograph by W.F. Vande Walle.

Fig. 7
Lacquer box for documents (*fumibako*), attributed to Kawanobe Itchō
川之辺一朝 (1830-1910). It is decorated with flowers and plants of the four
seasons using *takamakie*, *hiramakie* and *heidatsu* techniques, c.1905-
1910. Gift of the Meiji emperor, 1911. 45 × 36 × 17.8 cm.
Inv. TJ.3b.

> **Fig. 6**
Vase in white porcelain with under-glaze blue peony decoration, made
by Miyazawa Kōzan 宮川香山 (also known as Makuzu Kōzan 眞葛香山,
1842-1916). The vase is signed Makuzu Kōzan-*sei* 眞葛香山製 and was
made c.1910. Gift of Meiji emperor, 1911. H. 52.5 cm.
Inv. TJ.3a.

Fig. 9
A pair of large vases in cloisonné enamel on a copper ground. The decoration continues from one vase to the other, with on the right vase three
geese in a marsh under the full moon, and two other geese landing to join
them on the left vase, *c.*1910. Gift of the Japanese Ministry of Industry
and Foreign Trade, 1910. H. 45 cm.
Inv. TJ 51

Fig. 10
Stoneware vase with two polar bears, Makuzu mark (Miyagawa Kōzan) in under-glaze blue on the base, c.1910. Gift of the Japanese Ministry of Industry and Foreign Trade, 1910. H. 33.5 cm.
Inv. TJ.5.

Fig. 11
Vase in Kutani porcelain with aubergine mark. Kutani yaki Taniguchi sei 九谷焼谷口製 on the base, c.1910. Gift of the Japanese Ministry of Industry and Foreign Trade, 1910. H. 42.8 cm.
Inv. TJ.44

the management and decided to install substantial documentation and collections of various products with the aim of improving trade relations between Belgium and Japan. This view was also shared by Japan, which sent a sizeable official participation. The Japanese Ministry of Industry and Foreign Commerce was responsible for choosing and sending useful Far Eastern products. On the Belgian side, however, the initiative was left entirely to private companies. In the end, the museum finally fulfilled a dream that Leopold II had first had in 1858: opening up Belgian industry to the rest of the world and vice versa. Leopold, however, would never see it come to fruition, as he died at the end of that same year and it was his successor, King Albert I, who finally opened the first exhibition, under the name "Permanent Belgo-Japanese exhibition", in June 1911. The venture was encouraged by the Meiji emperor himself, who sent a personal gift to celebrate the opening of the exhibition. The emperor selected a porcelain vase by Miyazawa Kōzan 宮川 香山 (Fig. 6) and a lacquer box (Fig. 7). Both were first exhibited in a specially made showcase that still exists today (Fig. 8). Other Japanese artefacts in the exhibition that would escape later war damage include a pair of large vases in cloisonné enamel on a copper ground, decorated with geese on a moonlit pale blue ground (Fig. 9), an intriguing vase created by Miyagawa Kōzan, in the shape of a cave with stalactites and two polar bears (Fig. 10) and a large Kutani yaki 九谷 焼 vase by Taniguchi Kichijirō 谷口吉次郎, with a decoration of water and cherry blossoms painted in enamel over the glaze and gold (Fig. 11). Today, they are among the few surviving souvenirs of this successful event. The outbreak of the First World War put an abrupt end to the exhibition, which had attracted over 202,500 visitors in 38 months. The subsequent years would prove to be extremely detrimental to the Tower.

Meanwhile, the project of the Chinese Pavilion was running behind schedule. Unlike the Japanese Tower, the building of the pavilion only started in 1903. The king never saw the completion of the work, since it was finished early in 1910, shortly after his death. Part of the reason why the building work dragged on for seven years is that Alexandre Marcel, in his concern to give the pavilion an authentic Chinese appearance, commissioned some of the external decorations in China: the pair of stone lions that mark the entrance, glazed roof tiles and, most importantly, all the sculpted woodwork for the

façades and for the small garden kiosk. It took several years for all the orders to arrive in Brussels. Besides the Chinese decoration, Alexandre Marcel commissioned most of the decorative elements from Parisian craftsmen and artists, such as J. Galland for the painted glass and tiles in glass paste that covered the facades and E. Muller for glazed stoneware decorations to cover the brick walls and decorate the curved roof ends.

For the interior, Marcel decided to create a magical, festive atmosphere in the style of rococo *chinoiserie*. The ground floor (Fig. 12 + 13), decorated with a profusion of Chinese figures, dragons, and paintings of exotic landscapes and colourful birds, are reminiscent of the work of eighteenth-century French artists such as Watteau, Pillement and Huet (Fig. 14). This is the main reception room in the restaurant, and the mirrors, marble and gilded stucco would have made it a perfect setting for receptions and elegant banquets. On the first floor, smaller rooms, each with a distinct European, Chinese, Japanese or even Indian-style decoration, were designed for private meetings (Fig. 15). However, the Pavilion was never used as a restaurant. The Belgian government, which by the end of the construction works had taken over financial responsibility for the project – until then funded personally by Leopold II – decided that it should house a commercial museum. From then on, it was run by the Belgian Foreign Ministry. In 1913, it would open to the public as a part of the "Permanent Far-Eastern commercial exhibition", together with the Japanese Tower (Fig. 16 + 17).

Fig. 8
The gifts of the Meiji emperor in the permanent Belgian-Japanese exhibition in the Japanese Tower, 1911.

Fig. 12 + 13
The main reception room on the ground floor of the Chinese Pavilion.

Fig. 14
Detail of the ceiling of the Saxony Salon, with *singeries* (satirical scenes in which monkeys ape human behaviour), which were a staple of eighteenth-century French interior decoration.

Fig. 15
The so-called "salon hindou" on the first floor of the Chinese Pavilion, 1910. With French copies of Indian cashmere wall decoration and stucco relief inspired by Cambodian temples.

Bruxelles. — EXPOSITION COMMERCIALE PERMANENTE DE LAEKEN
2 Le Pavillon Chinois de Laeken édifié d'après les plans de M. Marcel. architecte sous le règne du Roi Léopold II, est consacré à l'Exposition de produits pouvant faire l'objet d'échanges commerciaux entre la Chine et la Belgique.
Edit. DESAIX, Brux. — Rep. int.

Bruxelles. — EXPOSITION COMMERCIALE PERMANENTE DE LAEKEN
7 Le mobilier japonais exposé dans la grande salle du 1er étage du Pavillon Chinois.
Edit. DESAIX, Brux. — Rep. int..

Fig. 16
The commercial exhibition on the ground floor
of the Chinese Pavilion, 1913.

Fig. 17
The commercial exhibition in the Japanese room
on the first floor of the Chinese Pavilion, 1913.

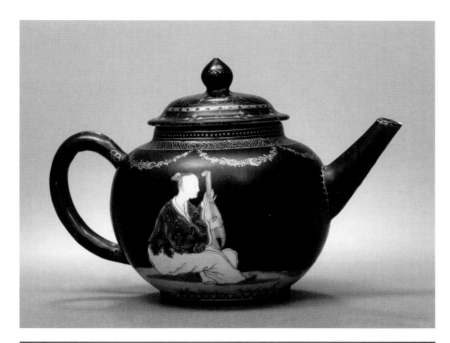

Fig. 18
Teapot decorated in black, gold and various enamels over the glaze.
Decoration in the style of European *chinoiserie* designs. On one side a
woman in a semi-Chinese dress playing the lute, on the other side a
dancing Chinese boy. The black enamel ground was probably applied
in Europe, *c.*1740. Purchased in 1844. H. 12 cm.
Inv. 4596

Fig. 19
Large dish in blue and white porcelain and gold, 1740. Purchased in 1844.
Diam. 50.5 cm. The decoration is one of the well-known designs that the
Dutch artist Cornelis Pronk did for the Vereenigde Oostindische Compagnie (The Dutch East India Company). It is his fourth design for the VOC,
called "Het Prieel" (The Arbour). The dish is rare on account of its size and
colours, since "The Arbour" was more commonly executed in polychrome
enamels over the glaze.
Inv. 4621

In front of the large dish, a pair of vases, decorated in various enamels
over the glaze with a design by Cornelis Pronk known as "De vier doc-
toren" (The four doctors), 1738. Purchased in 1844. H. 18.5 cm.
Inv. 4588

But unfortunately, the promising future of the
Chinese Pavilion, just like that of the Japanese Tower,
would soon be cut short by the outbreak of the First
World War.

From 1921 on, the Royal Museums of Art and History
were entrusted with the responsibility for the buildings
on the site and gave them a second lease of life. Even
without a proper collection, both buildings were
extremely popular with visitors, until they were again
closed during the Second World War.

However, a few years later, the Chinese Pavilion was to
achieve its own identity. In 1944, the Belgian government
received an important donation from Henry Verhaeghe
de Nayer (1864-1943). It consisted of some 2,000 objects,
mostly export porcelain from China and Japan, and was
the legacy of three generations of passionate collectors.
The Chinese Pavilion, with its hybrid, exotic architecture,
seemed the perfect setting for these objects that had been
made in the Far East to satisfy the taste of Western
connoisseurs. In June 1946, the exhibition opened to the
public. The future of the Chinese Pavilion was thus
secured. Over the years, all the Chinese and Japanese
export porcelain that was owned by the Royal Museums
of Art and History would be added to the Verhaeghe de
Naeyer collection and make the Chinese Pavilion what it
is today: a museum dedicated to Chinese export
porcelain.

As is the case in many European museums, the
collection was not brought together on purpose, but in its
current composition is formed by several gifts and
bequests. It consists mainly of polychrome, enamelled
pieces, and there is a conspicuous absence, for instance,
of early eighteenth-century under-glaze blue porcelain.
It is remarkable to note how early some of the pieces
were acquired: they entered the museum's collection as
early as 1844 (Fig. 18 + 19) and as such are some of the
earliest acquisitions to what are now the immense
collections of the Royal Museums of Art and History.

Among the collections that were transferred to the
Chinese Pavilion in the 1970s and added to the
Verhaeghe De Naeyer donation were the Chinese export
porcelain from the large bequests by G. Vermeersch
(acquired by the Royal Museums of Art and History in
1911), H. and I. Godtschalk (acquired in 1915) and E.

Lohest (acquired in 1910), to name but a few. All of these collections reflect the personal taste of their previous owners, and therefore do not represent a complete overview of export porcelain production in China.

The Verhaeghe De Nayer collection is remarkable as much for its quantity as for its diversity, covering Chinese export production from the 1680s to the end of the Qianlong reign (1736-1795). It is exceptionally rich in high quality *famille verte* porcelain. One of the undoubted masterpieces in this category is the tall, square vase with a different flower decoration on each side: chrysanthemums, lotuses, cherry blossoms and peonies. It bears an under-glaze blue Chenghua 成化 mark on the base, but should be dated as late-seventeenth or early-eighteenth century (Fig. 20). A large dish with overall decoration in *famille verte* with over-glaze blue enamel, showing figures in a landscape, competes with another dish combining *famille verte* enamels and powder blue, depicting a couple on horsebacks, followed by their servant and a dog in a mountainous landscape (Fig. 21).

The pear-shaped coffee pot on a foot, decorated in early *famille rose* enamels is a rather rare model. The curved spout ends in a monster or dragon head, whereas the handle sprouts from an animal's beak. The domed lid is topped by a knob in the shape of what is known as a *fo*-dog (known in Japanese as a *komainu* 狛犬). The decoration on either side shows an interior scene with a European couple with a servant – often called the "Dutch couple" – and a hunting scene with two Europeans, one riding a fabulous animal and shooting a bird. (Fig. 22)

The Vermeersch bequest (1911), totalling almost 3,000 objects of European furniture, sculptures, tapestries and ceramics was also a major contributor to the collections of the Chinese Pavilion. Of particular interest among the 600 pieces of Chinese and Japanese ceramics are the refined small dish with a kingfisher, plum blossom and camellias (Fig. 23). Its plain white background and asymmetric composition reflects the Chinese taste more than that of the European connoisseurs of the time, but it is nevertheless accounted one of the finest examples of *famille rose* in the collection. For contrast we include two examples that typify Western taste, one from the Vermeersch bequest and one from the Lohest bequest (Fig. 24 + 25).

Fig. 23
Small dish with a kingfisher design in enamels over the glaze of the *famille rose* type, c.1730-1740. Vermeersch bequest, 1911. Diam. 20.5 cm.
Inv. V.1484

Fig. 24
Teapot decorated in blue under the glaze and various enamels over the glaze. The spout, handle and decorative pattern on the body are modelled as ropes. The silver-gilt mount with Amor on the knob is probably contemporary Dutch, c.1680-1700. Vermeersch bequest, 1911. H. 14.5 cm.
Inv. V.1232

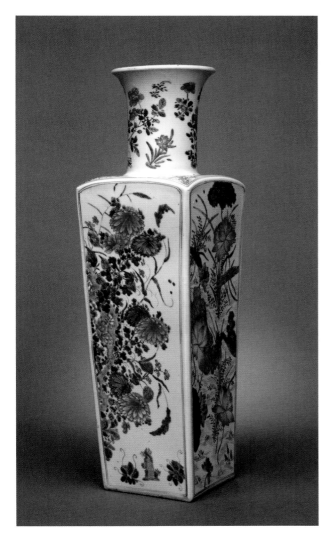

Fig. 20
Large square porcelain vase with over-glaze decoration of the *famille verte* type, bearing a Ming *Chenghua* mark on the base but obviously dating from the Kangxi period (1662-1722). Verhaeghe de Naeyer bequest, 1946, H. 51 cm.
Inv. VDN.76.

Fig. 22
Early *famille rose* coffee pot featuring a Dutch couple and a third figure greeting them, *c.*1720-1730. Verhaeghe de Naeyer bequest, 1946.
H. 34.5 cm.
Inv. VDN.171.

Fig. 21
Large porcelain dishes decorated in *famille verte* enamels, early 18th century; the one on the left bears a Kangxi mark on the base. Verhaeghe de Naeyer bequest, 1946. Diam. 41 cm and 38 cm.
Inv.VDN.14 and VDN.56.

While the Chinese Pavilion was experiencing continuing success, not only as a museum but even more as a tourist attraction, a favourite of the citizens of Brussels, the Japanese Tower, had to remain closed between 1947 and 1989, due to lack of staff. The building was restored, and it was reopened to the public – at least up to the first floor of the pagoda – on the occasion of *Europalia Japan*, a comprehensive festival of Japanese arts, both classical and modern, staged in numerous Belgian cities and towns in 1989.

Today, it is dedicated to Japanese artistic production for the western world. Again, the eclectic interior turned out to be the perfect background for the display of the kind of artefacts Japan shipped to the West from the seventeenth century onwards. A huge showcase with an impressive array of brocade Imari 伊万里 ware suggests the way these large dishes, vases and ornaments were shown in the palaces and residences of the first privileged collectors (Fig. 26 + 27).

But most of the displays in the Japanese Tower consists of the artefacts Europeans discovered more recently, during the last decades of the nineteenth century, after Japan had reopened to the West after two centuries of deliberate isolation. Belgian collectors were no exception to the "Japanese craze" that enraptured the Western artistic scene when these objects first appeared on the market. The Japanese government was not blind to this development and actively promoted Japanese arts and crafts by participating in World Fairs, sending its first official representation to the Paris World Exposition of 1867. The objects they put on show were often created for the West, that is, with the express aim of catering to the exotic tastes of European buyers. Part of the selection Japan sent to the exposition in Liège (Belgium) in 1905 was purchased by the Museum (Fig. 28-31), including technical masterpieces like the large bowl in cloisonné enamel on a stamped silver ground (*tsuiki-jippō* 槌起七宝), created by Ogasawara Takikirō, or the small vase in wireless cloisonné enamel (*musen* 無線) on a copper

---

Fig. 26
Selection of the Japanese *imari kinrande* 伊万里金襴手 porcelain collection as displayed in the Japanese Tower today.

Fig. 25
Cup and saucer, decorated in various enamels over the glaze and Indian ink, with a gilded design of
three monkeys opening a cage with two birds, c.1730-1735. Lohest bequest, 1910. H. 3.3 cm (cup),
diam. 11.3 cm (saucer). In European iconography the monkey traditionally has a sexual connotation,
whereas the caged bird alludes to chastity.
Inv. LH.451.

Fig. 27
Large plate, set of three covered jars and in front, a cup for hot chocolate with saucer and lid
with silver mount, Japanese Imari porcelain, c.1690-1720 for the plate and early 18th century for the others.
Diam. 54.9 cm (plate), H. 27.4 cm (jars) and H. 11.5 cm (cup), diam. 16 cm (saucer).
Inv. 6201, V 1596, 4660.

Fig. 30
Vase in the shape of a crane, cloisonné enamel with silver ground and silver wire, c.1900-1905. Purchased after the Liège World Exposition (1905). H. 20.7 cm.
Inv. J.343

Fig. 28
Large bowl in cloisonné enamel on a stamped silver ground (*tsuiki jippō* 槌起七宝), created by Ogasawara Takikirō, c.1900-1905. Purchased after the Liège World Exposition (1905). H. 21.5 cm, diam. 36 cm.
Inv. J.308

Fig. 29
Small vase in wireless cloisonné enamel (*musen* 無線) with its original box, Andō manufactures, c.1900-1905. Purchased after the Liège World Exposition (1905). H. 11.5 cm.
Inv. J.309

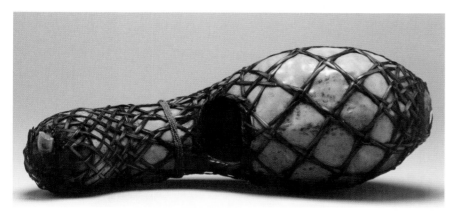

ground, decorated with white cranes against a pale bluish background, produced by the Andō 安藤 Manufacture.

This European passion for all things Japanese from the late 1860s onwards became known as *Japonisme*, a term originally coined by the French journalist and art critic Philippe Burty in 1872. The museum owns two glazed earthenware sake bottles that once belonged to Philippe Burty (Fig. 32). The calabash-form and decoration illustrate the very close relationship the Japanese arts have always had with nature, an empathy that caused a sensation in Europe. It was a revelation to artists of every discipline, and prompted them to explore new, uncharted horizons and inspired the naturalist aesthetics of Art Nouveau. The Art Nouveau style is reflected in many decorative elements of the Japanese Tower, which underscores how fitting this environment is for housing Japanese export art collections. One could say that the collections relate to Japanese culture to the same degree as the tower relates to Japanese architecture: both reflect the European knowledge and passion for Japan at the beginning of the twentieth century.

A third building on the site, that has not been mentioned so far, only came into the picture during recent decades. It is the modest, discreet outbuilding that lies just behind the Chinese Pavilion, hidden from the road (Fig. 33). It was intended by Alexandre Marcel as the garage for the carriages and automobiles of the guests dining at the Chinese restaurant. Archives indicate that the installation was commissioned in November 1906, after the layout of the park, in other words well before the main building was finished. Since the Chinese Pavilion

never became a restaurant, the outbuilding was never used until the 1990s, when the museum decided to turn it into a Museum of Japanese Art. The sobriety of the architecture – especially compared to the overwhelming decor of the main building – made it a particularly appropriate showcase for the Japanese collections of the Royal Museums of Art and History. Its ground plan is arranged symmetrically around a huge central area, originally intended for parking vehicles, with an upper part for unharnessed horse-drawn carriages and a lower part for motor vehicles, then still quite rare. The rooms on either side on both levels were to be used as stables, saddle rooms, haylofts, and restrooms for coachmen and chauffeurs. Since 2006, these rooms have housed small, rotating presentations of the collections, according to eight major themes: armour, swords and sword ornaments, painting, textiles, *inrō* and *netsuke*, Buddhist art, ceramics and ukiyo-e prints. (Fig. 34)

Fig. 32
Vase in the shape of a calabash, Bizen stoneware, 19th century. Acquired in 1891, former collection of Philippe Burty. H. 26.5 cm.
Inv. J.499.

Fig. 31
Vase in the shape of a gourd, stoneware with green glaze and bamboo, c.1900-1905. Purchased after the Liège World Exposition (1905). L. 33.5 cm.
Inv. J.305.

Unlike the pieces manufactured for export, exhibited in the Japanese Tower and the Chinese Pavilion, the objects on display here were produced for the domestic Japanese market, and nearly all of them date from the Edo period. The history of these Japanese collections is examined in an article, "Collecting the Far East", in the special 250th edition of *Arts of Asia* (2012).

In conclusion, it is important to note that the restoration of the Japanese Tower is a work in progress. Due to their state of conservation, the upper floors of the Tower, still in their original state, are not yet open to the public. A multidisciplinary workshop of conservators and art historians met in 2011 to discuss the preliminary report of a scientific study focusing on the upper floors of the tower to determine the origin of the materials and the techniques used in the construction. They could be either Japanese or European or a mixture of both. The final outcome of their research will be a challenge for the museum in the years to come.

NOTE: all photographs are copyright of the Royal Museums of Art and History, Brussels, unless otherwise stated.

Fig. 33
The Chinese Pavilion seen from the rear. On this side of the Pavilion is the smaller building originally designed as a garage for automobiles and carriages (c.1910) since 2006 the Museum of Japanese Art.

Fig. 34
The Museum of Japanese Art's rotating display of objects from the
Japanese collection of the Royal Museums of Art and History, since 2006.

TINTIN IN JAPAN

Kazuko Iwamoto

JAPAN & BELGIUM

An Itinerary of Mutual Inspiration

TINTIN IN JAPAN

Who is the most famous Belgian in Japan? Tintin certainly must be one of the top candidates for the distinction. No "bande dessinée" or "BD" (the French for a comic book) is as well known to the general public in Japan as the *Tintin* series is. In this essay we would like to examine how this Belgian BD has been received in Japan.

Reception of Tintin in Japan

Les Aventures de Tintin ("The Adventures of Tintin"),[1] a BD by Hergé (the pen name of Georges Remi, derived from the French pronunciation of his reversed initials R.G.), was originally published in serial form in newspapers and magazines. Publications in book format followed and have retained their popularity for more than 50 years, not only in Belgium and in France but all over the world. Moreover, many animated cartoons and live action movies have been produced. The total number of copies of the 24 albums published in the world now exceeds 350 million.[2]

The BD is an important part of Belgian culture. The historical background to this high status was a desire to establish the identity of Belgian literature independently from Paris, the dominant centre of francophone literature, and to promote what in Paris was considered a marginal literary genre. The status of the BD in Belgium as an important form of art can, for example, be seen in the magnificent "Centre belge de la bande dessinée", the comic books museum located in the heart of Brussels. The centre welcomes visitors with a large statue of Tintin and a bright red and white moon rocket. Its building is a historical monument in art-nouveau style. In Belgium, BD is considered the really important "Ninth Art". We may incidentally note that, in 2009, an exhibition of Japanese manga was held there to celebrate twenty years of explosive popularity of the genre in Europe, showing many manga as "high quality art", ranging from *Akira* and works of Miyazaki to those of the latest authors. We can also refer to the Hergé Museum (Musée Hergé) which opened some years ago in the university town of Louvain-la-Neuve south of Brussels.

The reception of *Tintin* in Japan began in 1968 with the publication of three albums, titled *Bōken Tantan*

ぼうけんタンタン ("Tintin's Adventures", translated by Sakata Hiroo 阪田寛夫), by the publishing company Shufunotomosha 主婦の友社.[3] The albums were targeted at a public of parents wanting to push their children to read books. Tintin was thus considered as an instructive story and was regarded as being very different from manga, which in those days were becoming more and more popular and had the reputation of representing an "anti-educational" culture. These three albums remained almost unknown. Fifteen years later, in 1983, Fukuinkan Shoten 福音館書店 (a publisher of religious books) published all twenty-four albums, in a translation by Kawaguchi Keiko 川口恵子 under the title *Tantan no bōken ryokō* タンタンの冒険旅行 ("The Adventurous Travels of Tintin"), which gained popularity. In 2011, the same publishing house issued a new edition with a slight change of title, *Tantan no bōken* タンタンの冒険 ("The Adventures of Tintin").[4] The total number of copies sold in the form of albums in Japan is now estimated at about 1,100,000.[5] In the same year, owing to the release of the American 3D film *The Adventures of Tintin, The Secret of the Unicorn*, directed by Steven Spielberg, a paperback version of the Japanese translation was published, of which 260,000 copies have now been sold. Since then, the popularity of Tintin in Japan has become more general and it is now well established.

As to television, *Tintin's Adventures*, a black-and-white animated cartoon, was broadcast by Fuji TV Station every evening at 6 o'clock from November 1964 to July 1965.[6] This five-minute serial work had originally been co-produced by Bellevision Studio of Brussels and Télé Hachette of Paris, and was imported to Japan through the United States. The pronunciation of Tintin was "tintin" as in English (the original French pronunciation has no equivalent in English or Japanese phonetics). The broadcast was limited to the Kantō and Chūbu areas and *Tintin* did not at that time attract a wide audience. A Canadian-French animated cartoon, *The Adventures of Tintin*, produced in 1991-1992, was broadcast in 1998 — save for three episodes about the Soviets, the Congo and Alph-Art — on the channel of NHK Satellite Station 2 and boosted the popularity of Tintin in Japan.

Two live-action movies were made in 1960 and 1964 but did not attract much attention in Japan. Cinephiles had to wait until the successful Spielberg movie, mentioned above, which was however received as an American work.

The reception of *Tintin* in Japan can be characterized by the fact that it circulated as illustrated books or children's books, not as BD or manga. The first translation issued by Shufunotomosha was mainly targeted at housewife readers and the next publisher, Fukuinkan Shoten, specialized in Bibles, educational books for the young, illustrated books, and so forth. This may have determined the orientation of the readership. This also led to *Tintin* being distinguished from manga and escaping concerns about uncultured and anti-educational materials, just like in Belgium and in France. In fact many of *Tintin*'s fans in Japan will talk about their childhood memories of joyful reading and learning about European culture thanks to Tintin, recommended by their enthusiastic and education-minded parents. Tintin also carries messages about universal human love and friendship, rather than about love between man and woman. And Snowy ("Milou" in the French original), Tintin's faithful canine partner, is immensely popular and loved for his nature: coward, naughty but reliable in an emergency.

Even if the Japanese are not particularly well acquainted with the Tintin stories or their historical and social background, they have ample sympathy with the various characters and their images. This may be a phenomenon not unlike the popularity of the image of the Little Prince, the attractive illustration of Saint-Exupéry's novel. Chiba Bank is now using the image of Tintin as its poster boy. In the spring of 2015 Uniqlo put on sale several kinds of T-shirts bearing images of *Tintin* characters and attracted many young buyers. There are Tintin Shops in Tokyo, Kyoto and other big cities which sell spin-off merchandise based on the cartoon. We can also find on the internet Japanese sites selling character goods. Tintin thus seems to have widespread name recognition in Japan.

Japan(ese) in Hergé's Work

As remarked above, even though the images of the *Tintin* characters are widely popular in Japan, very few fans know the episodes in detail. We will now examine the relationship between Hergé himself and Japan, that is, how he understood and showed Japan and what sort of influences he received from Japan.

Japan comes up in the story *Le Lotus bleu* (*The Blue Lotus*),[7] serialized in *Le Petit Vingtième* in 1934-1935. Hergé set the story in the China of 1931. He tells the story of a friendship between Tintin and Tchang, a brave Chinese boy. The episode is based on the Mukden Incident of 18 September 1931, an explosion on the tracks of the South Manchuria Railway. The historical facts are that, in the wake of this incident in Manchuria and the Shanghai Incident, Japan, having been seriously criticized by the Lytton Commission, decided to leave the League of Nations. *The Blue Lotus* adopts these facts and mixes them with imaginary places and persons, adding a good dose of exaggeration and stereotyping. For example, the Japanese army invading China is painted in the role of the absolute villain. A Japanese businessman named Mitsuhirato, a perpetrator of the explosion, is presented as an ugly and stereotyped Japanese with protruding teeth and thick glasses. Moreover, he eventually commits hara-kiri. The name of "Mitsuhirato" is in itself mysterious and fictional, the first name and the family name being impossible to distinguish.

At the same time in real life, Hergé became friends with a Chinese student at the Fine Arts Academy in Brussels. Through his friendship with this kind and intelligent Asian he developed a knowledge of Chinese civilization, religion, arts, poetry, and so forth.[8] The information about Japan that he could access was comparatively limited and did not go beyond the stereotypes prevailing in Europe in those days. However, in a later story, *Le Crabe aux pinces d'or* (*The Crab with the Golden Claws*) (1940), Hergé again introduced a Japanese character. Named Bunji Kuraki (a realistic name this time)[9] he was a protector of Tintin. Was there any change in Hergé's feelings about Japan? It is difficult to say, because the latter story was serialized in *Le Soir*, a journal censored under German occupation, and Japan was then allied with Germany. We can also remark that the concierge of Tintin's apartment cannot distinguish a Japanese from a Chinese: she describes Kuraki to the police as "a Japanese or a Chinese". In the next scene she completely mixes up the two nationalities, or rather she does not pay much attention: "three men suddenly attacked the Chinese [...] and they shoved the Japanese in their car [...]" (p. 8). This scene might mock the Europeans' limited knowledge of Asia. In a further story, *Tintin au Tibet* (*Tintin in Tibet*) (1950), Tintin has another adventure with Tchang, his Chinese friend.[10] This Chinese boy is described again as an excellent and talented person.

Did Japan influence the drawing technique and the art of Hergé? In his study "Japanese Inspiration in Hergé's Work" on the influence of Japonism in *Tintin*, Philippe Goddein points out the influence on Hergé of ukiyo-e (the Japanese prints of the Edo period).[11] Goddein claims that, since Hergé was asked to illustrate Japanese poems in the Brussels journal *Le Vingtième Siècle*, he very probably sought inspiration from ukiyo-e prints. Goddein also shows the connection between the clarity of line (*ligne claire*) in *Tintin* and in ukiyo-e, as well as between the daring composition in both. He highlights, for example, the resemblance between the scene of Tintin in a boat on a stormy sea (a frame from the black and white version of *Les Cigares du pharaon* [*Cigars of the Pharaoh*]) and Hokusai's "Wave with a distant view of Mount Fuji": "[...] observant readers would find countless fleeting encounters with Japanese art in the albums Hergé produced at the height of his powers, whether in whirling snow, in the folds of a garment or the forms of a landscape, in the posture of a bird on a branch or the expression on a face."[12] Were these examples really inspired directly by ukiyo-e? It would be necessary to find more positive proof to support this claim.

We must remember that clarity of line has its origin in American comics. It was Tintin which introduced this technique in European BDs, at the same time as the use of speech balloons to enclose dialogues or narrations.[13] Until then captions (*légendes*) had been used, separated from the pictures and usually placed in the lower part of their frames. After their introduction by Hergé, the techniques of clarity of line and speech balloons became increasingly prevalent in French and Belgian BDs, together with the development of other techniques. The 1960s and 1970s have been called a time of "BD revolution", when an enormous quantity of high-quality work was created and when BD gained recognition as the Ninth Art. We can now classify BD into three main styles: first the clarity of line represented by *Tintin* or in the French series *Astérix*, second the realistic style represented by Enki Birals or Mœbius, and last the

opened line (*ligne ouverte*), an unclear and trembling line often used in caricatures. Some Japanese cartoonists already discovered the BD in this early period and began to undergo its influence. The influence of Mœbius upon Ōtomo Katsuhiro's 大友克洋 Akira is a famous example, and another interesting one is that of Uderzo's *Astérix* on Tezuka Osamu 手塚治虫.[14] Yanase Takashi やなせたかし, author of the famous *Anpan-man*, admired *Tintin* and drew much inspiration from it. These early cases of influence were truly precursory because at that time most Japanese readers still only knew American comics. However, going further back in history, the American cartoonist Winsor MacCay (1869-1934), who is regarded as one of the originators of clarity of line, is said to have been himself influenced by Art Nouveau. And the Art Nouveau style, under the influence of Japonism in the second half of the nineteenth century, was a Europeanized variation on the Japanese ukiyo-e style. Which suggests that the characteristic style of the Belgian BD would not have existed without the ukiyo-e art...[15] BD and Japanese manga have thus been connected with regard to the essential characteristics of their technique, from long before American comics and, later, francophone BD started to be introduced and translated in Japan.

The "Belgianness" of Tintin

There seems to be another important aspect of *Tintin* which facilitated its reception in the world and in Japan. It is related to the story's concept and its universality. At the same time and paradoxically, these aspects also reveal the Belgian identity, or in another word the "Belgianness" of Hergé's work. In this section we are going to examine this point.

Let us repeat that the author of *Tintin*, a major representative of the francophone BD, was Belgian. The fact that very many important BD works are "made in Belgium" is unknown even to French-speaking readers. To give some examples besides *Tintin*, we may mention *Spirou, Lucky Luke, Bob & Mortimer, Bessy, Boule & Bill, Cédric, Largo Winch, Thorgal, XIII,* and *The Smurfs*. This wealth can be explained by the conjunction of several causes: a literature nourished with great Flemish paintings and visual art, the development of illustrated tales, the early introduction of clarity of line, etc. These are contextual and technical factors. The publication environment also played a role. The Belgian publishing industry tried to adopt an original and independent approach in the face of France and its massive cultural power in the francophone world. It deliberately emphasized the publication of religious books, juvenile books and BDs. The inflow of American comics into post-war France provoked an opposition arguing that they had a harmful effect upon youngsters and were an incitement to crime. A French law of 16 July 1949 imposed strict censorship on material printed for young readers. Belgian BD magazines like *Tintin* or *Spirou* were quick to seize the opportunity and to publish "demonstratively educational" BDs — historical stories or adventures — for the sake of setting right the prejudice of censors and educators against the BD. Especially toward the end of the 1950s, Belgian publishers tried decisively to penetrate the French market.[16]

The serial publication of Tintin began in January 1929 across facing pages of *Le Petit Vingtième*, the children's supplement of the major Belgian Catholic daily newspaper *Le Vingtième*. This was *Tintin au pays des Soviets* (*Tintin in the Land of the Soviets*), a story about the Soviets of the time. We can already identify in this first story a difference in the publication environment between France and Belgium. In comparison with the French Republic, which stands for the strict principle of separation of political and religious affairs, the Kingdom of Belgium and its system of constitutional monarchy under a Catholic King often tended to favour, especially before and during the War, a "wholesomeness" in line with the thought of Catholicism. Hergé himself had been a boy scout in his childhood, and basing himself on the scouts' spirit of wholesomeness he developed the idea of young journalist Tintin's adventures in the world.

The second serial, *Tintin au Congo* (*Tintin in the Congo*), was published in 1930 and compiled into a book the following year. After the Second World War, in 1946, a revised colour version was issued. This became an established method: 1) newspaper serial, 2) publication in monochrome book form, 3) publication in revised colour edition. During the War the space available to *Tintin* in the newspaper was gradually reduced because of a shortage of ink and paper under the Nazi occupation. Eventually the serial had to be moved to *Le Soir*, the newspaper that stood at the time under the supervision of the Nazis. An important point to note is that both pictures and stories were considerably changed during revision for publication in a colour version. The

main modifications were the modernization and the simplification of the content and pictures, to help a new generation to understand the scripts more easily. There were also numerous deletions of expressions of ideological prejudice such as imperialism and racism, which may have been more or less inevitable during the War, and of the more conspicuously Belgian elements. When the market expanded internationally with translations into more than 80 languages, many requests poured in for changing details in a way that suited the situation of each country or region, which Hergé generally tried to accommodate. We shall cite some examples.

The first work, *Tintin in the Land of the Soviets*, was not compiled as a book nor published again for a long time because of its excessive prejudice and hostility towards the Soviets. As a consequence the facsimile of the original edition published in 1983 became a very valuable document. A Japanese translation has since become available as well. In the first frames of the album, Tintin is presented as a young journalist of *Le Petit Vingtième*, who is sent to report about the then unknown Soviets.[17] Readers are told about Tintin's Belgian nationality in a scene set in Berlin, where Tintin is interrogated about his job and address (p. 7), and in another scene in the train that brings him back home (p. 137).

The second album, *Tintin in the Congo*, is an adventure story taking place in what is now the Democratic Republic of the Congo, which in 1930 was a Belgian colony. It was significantly modified in the revised colour version published after the War, probably because of its evident imperialism and racial prejudice. We can compare the two versions on the website dedicated to the life and work of Hergé, set up by Daniel Bellier (bellier.org), which carries a full facsimile of *Le Petit Vingtième*.[18] Let us examine some differences between the original version and the later versions. When Tintin stands in for a missionary teaching in a local elementary school, this is what he tells the schoolboys in the original edition: "Hello everybody, I'm going to tell you today about your fatherland: Belgium!"[19] In the revised colour edition the scene is changed to that of an arithmetic class, where Tintin says "Let's start with addition [...] two and two make...?"[20] — which was not necessarily much better, as the fact that nobody in the class can answer this simple question still suggested a deep-rooted imperialistic or paternalist prejudice against the Congolese. In the last scene of the 1930 edition, showing Tintin leaving Congo in an airplane, the pilot tells him "I'll bring you to Belgium". In the colour edition the text was changed into: "I'll bring you to Europe". The pilot also says "Good-bye Congo" in the first edition, and "Good-bye Africa" in the second. Almost all occurrences of the word "Belgium" were changed into "Europe" in the revised edition.[21]

The third album, *Tintin en Amérique* (*Tintin in America*), was revised in depth three times. For the 1973 edition Hergé acceded to the requests of his American publisher and deleted three scenes featuring Blacks, whose presence alongside Whites was felt to be undesirable for a young public.[22] In the revised colour edition of *The Broken Ear* the scenes featuring radio news about the Italian-Ethiopian War and Mussolini were cut, and Tintin only hears the following news item about a robbery in an ethnographic museum (pp. 1-2). When *The Black Island*, set in Scotland, was retained for publication in English, the London-based publisher pointed out 131 errors in the album's depiction of Britain. Hergé was asked to correct them in line with the "actual" situation,[23] and accepted all these requests. The scene showing Palestinian and Jewish terrorist groups under British rule was, for example, changed to a fictional story in some unidentified Arab county.[24] We can find countless further examples of this sort.

Titles are also remarkable. After three early albums set in the Soviet Union, the Congo and America, geographical proper nouns disappeared from the titles (except for Tibet and Sydney in the latest series). The fifth album, *The Blue Lotus*, still dealt with real affairs in China and Japan, the Mukden Incident and the Sino-Japanese War. But the places of Tintin's adventures became more and more fictional over time. Countries were fictional but looked like they could quite possibly exist somewhere. For example "Syldavia" is not entirely unlike Poland. And a South American country in the middle of a coup d'état could of course also have existed in the real world of the time. Tintin's trip to the moon did not anticipate by much the first real moon landing. Hergé's fictional world was always "quite probable", because many current issues were reflected and on the basis of photographs or models astonishingly accurate scenes were depicted of landscapes and buildings that really existed somewhere, or of cars, trains, ships, planes or even rockets that resembled those being developed at the time. The Brussels scenery was sometimes used, even though Hergé tried to avoid explicit references to Belgium. For example the Cinquantenaire Park (Jubelpark),[25] the Avenue Louise, where Tintin lives,[26] the Avenue de la Toison d'Or,[27] and a flea market in the Jeu de Balle,[28] are among the Brussels locations depicted realistically without disclosing where they are actually located. The Royal Palace in Brussels is painted as that of a fictional country.[29] Tintin and the characters move around against these real-fictional backgrounds, without ever aging. This may appear as a rather "improbable" world. The world of *Tintin*'s stories, despite its reliance on details of a reality that was familiar to Belgian readers, shows a kind of statelessness and universality. This might be one of the reasons why *Tintin* has been so well received all over the world.

We should also pay attention to the characters' names, which cause important problems of translation. First, Tintin himself. He seems to have no family nor background. We do not know why, young as he is, he is already a journalist from the very beginning of his adventures, or how he acquired the skills to drive a car and pilot an airplane ... He has the intelligence and the athletic ability of an adult, even though he never grows older. He seems to be, so to speak, a "symbol" or an empty "vessel" without an individual identity.[30] His name itself — only a first name, without a family name — differs in the northern part of Belgium, for in Dutch he is called "Kuifje". The dog, Tintin's best friend, is called "Snowy" in the Japanese version, a direct import from the English version. In the original French text his name is "Milou", and in Dutch "Bobbie". "Professor Beaker (Bīkā)" is a name used only in the Japanese version; the Professor's French name is "Tryphon Tournesol", in English he is "Cuthbert Calculus" and in German "Balduin Bienlein".[31] The two detectives, "Dyupon & Dyubon" in Japanese, are named "Dupond et Dupont" in their original French appearance, two words that have the same pronunciation. The similarity of pronunciation is also achieved in Dutch ("Jansen en Janssen") and in English ("Thomson and Thompson"). Conversely, Hergé himself occasionally played with quite free modifications of his characters' names. A case in point is Haddock. In the French version Tintin usually calls him simply "Capitaine," while Madame Castafiore calls him one name after another, for example, Kodak, Kabock, Bulldog, Hammock, Medoc, Panic, etc.

An ambiguous identity, a transit point without a "centre", the statelessness of a hero who is constantly running and escaping. These distinctive features in the *Tintin* series correspond with what we call "Belgianness", a phenomenon that we have long studied through Belgian literature in the French language. Hergé himself seemed to have been quite conscious of this Belgian characteristic, especially in contrast to France. He therefore added, intentionally maybe, a layer of universality and flexibility to his original works whenever he had a chance to revise the *Tintin* series for distribution in France or in translations for other foreign markets. This explains why he could very flexibly modify not only the names of his characters but also the locations and contents of his stories, in a process of adjustment to the evolution of the times and to the situation of each individual country.

Conclusion – Accessibility and Universality

As stated above, *Tintin*'s language and context have been intentionally adjusted and adapted by the author with a view to facilitating reception of his work outside Belgium. The clarity of line, adopted in Europe by Hergé before many others, helped to shape very simple contours and character faces and was also a helpful device in promoting his work's intelligibility and accessibility. The speech balloon technique was used for the first time in Europe in *Tintin* and later became a peculiarity of the BD form. This technique was particularly suitable for translation of the characters' words into other languages, independently of the pictures. The BD art originally stuck to the French tradition of illustrated stories, emphasizing its literary aspect and giving weight and independence to the text. Taking this tradition one step further, BD authors, especially Belgian authors following in the footsteps of *Tintin*, made use of the newly-invented balloons. Their adoption was also inspired by practical business considerations. The words spoken by the characters and placed in balloons were written on tracing paper separately from the pictures; most onomatopoeia and mimetic words similarly went into speech balloons. In this way authors did not need to remove the French text from their pictures when producing translations.[32] This global strategy of the Belgian BD industry has since also been adopted by the French BD. The typical French BD is now published in album-style books, in full colour and hard bound. This unique form of BD was established in

the early 1970s for commercial reasons.[33] It allows us at least to enjoy the beautiful coloured pictures even when we have difficulties understanding the language. Moreover, the work required for the translation of BDs of this type is much less intensive than that required for the translation of Japanese manga, for example, which are nevertheless being translated and distributed in great volume throughout the world, especially in Europe.[34] Today the francophone world publishes BD albums in abundance. A number of new trends in stories and techniques already exist which were explicitly influenced by Japanese manga, and the BD has become an art form in its own right — the Ninth Art. *Tintin* was certainly a starting point in this evolution. Reconsidering Hergé's work, including its adaptation for other media such as animation or live-action movies, from a historical and contextual viewpoint would therefore be a very worthwhile endeavour.

REFERENCES

Farre 2001
Michael Farre. *Tintin, le rêve et la réalité – L'histoire de la création des Aventures de Tintin*. Brussels: Éditions Moulinsart, 2001.

Goddein 2005
Philippe Goddein. "Japanese Inspiration in Hergé's Work." In *Japan & Belgium, Four Centuries of Exchange*, ed. W.F. Vande Walle, p. 404. Brussels: Commissioners-General of the Belgian Government at the World Exposition of Aichi 2005, Japan, 2005.

Hergé 1943
Hergé. *Les Aventures de Tintin – Le Lotus bleu*. Brussels: Casterman, 1943.

Hergé 1960
Hergé. *Les Aventures de Tintin – Tintin au Tibet*. Brussels: Casterman, 1960.

Hergé 1981a
Hergé. *Les Aventures de Tintin* (renewed). Brussels: Casterman, 1981, nos. 1-24.

Hergé 1981 [1942]
Hergé. *Les Aventures de Tintin – Le Crabe aux pinces d'or*. Brussels: Casterman, 1981 [1942].

Hergé 1981b
Hergé. *Les Aventures de Tintin – Au pays des Soviets*. Brussels: Casterman, 1981.

Hergé 1981 [1943]
Hergé. *Les Aventures de Tintin – Le Secret de la Licorne*. Brussels: Casterman, 1981 [1943].

Hergé 1981 [1946]
Hergé. *Les Aventures de Tintin – Tintin au Congo*. Brussels: Casterman, 1981 [1946].

Hergé 1981 [1947]
Hergé. *Les Aventures de Tintin – Le Sceptre d'Ottokar*. Brussels: Casterman, 1981 [1947].

Hergé 1981 [1967]
Hergé. *Les Aventures de Tintin – Coke en stock*. Brussels: Casterman, 1981 [1967].

Hergé 2011
Hergé, trans. Kawaguchi Keiko 川口恵子. *Tantan no bōken* タンタンの冒険 (renewed). Tokyo: Fukuinkan Shoten 福音館書店, 2011, nos. 1-24.

Honoré 2015
Patrick Honoré. "Bando deshine no idenshi to sono shinkaron" バンド・デシネの遺伝子とその進化論 ["Genesis and evolution of the French-Belgian comics"]. In *Nichi-Futsu manga no kōryū: Hisutorī adaputēshon kuriēshon* 日仏マンガの交流 – ヒストリー・アダプテーション・クリエーション ["Cultural exchanges between manga and *bande dessinée* comics: History, adaptation and creation"]. Kyoto: Shibunkaku Shuppan 思文閣出版, 2015.

Peeters 1990
Benoît Peeters. "Conversation avec Hergé (15 décembre 1982)." In *Le Monde d'Hergé*. Brussels: Bibliothèque de Moulinsart, Casterman, 1990.

Peeters 2003
Benoît Peeters. "1929 Naissance de Tintin – un roman de désapprentissage." In *Histoire de la littérature belge 1830-2000*, eds. Jean-Pierre Bertrand, Michel Biron, Benoit Denis and Rainier Grutman. Paris: Fayard, 2003.

Regards croisés
"Introduction." In *Regards croisés de la bande dessinée belge, publié à l'occasion de l'exposition "Les regards croisés de la bande dessinée belge", Musées royaux des Beaux-Arts de Belgique, Bruxelles, du 27 mars au 28 juin 2009*. Ghent: Snoeck, 2009.

"Tintin au Congo"
"Tintin au Congo," *Le Petit Vingtième*, Publication *Petit Vingtième* du 5 juin 1930 au 11 juin 1931 – *Petit Vingtième* 3 (15 janvier 1931), p. 64. Cf. http://www.bellier.org/PVIndex.htm.

Websites
<http://www.bellier.org/indexsuite.htm>
<http://www.bellier.org/PVIndex.htm>
Wikipedia, s.v. "タンタンの冒険," last modified November 2014, http://ja.wikipedia.org/wiki/タンタンの冒険.

NOTES

1 Hergé 1981a.

2 Wikipedia, s.v. "タンタンの冒険," last modified November 2014, http://ja.wikipedia.org/wiki/タンタンの冒険.

3 Wikipedia, s.v. "タンタンの冒険."

4 Hergé 2011.

5 Wikipedia, s.v. "タンタンの冒険."

6 Wikipedia, s.v. "タンタンの冒険."

7 Hergé 1943.

8 Peeters 1990, p. 204.

9 Hergé 1981 [1942].

10 Hergé 1960.

11 Goddein 2005, p. 404.

12 Goddein 2005, p. 404.

13 Farre 2001.

14 Honoré 2015, p. 144.

15 Honoré 2015, pp. 146-147.

16 *Regards croisés*, p. 2.

17 Hergé 1981b, p. 4.

18 See http://www.bellier.org/PVIndex.htm>, especially the page of Le Petit Vingtième: http://www.bellier.org/PVIndex.htm, created by Daniel Bellier (1949-2012), a Belgian BD fan.

19 He goes on however as follows: "Belgium is what is called…a leopard," which may be construed as an ironical take on the very idea of suggesting that Belgium is the fatherland of the Congolese.

20 Hergé 1981 [1946], p. 36.

21 Admittedly, the fact that he systematically removes explicit references to Belgium may be construed as suggesting that it is not the Belgianness that attracts the international reader.

22 Farre 2001, p. 38.

23 Farre 2001, p. 72.

24 Farre 2001, p. 129. For example an English soldier wearing a kilt is replaced by an Arab military police officer in the revised edition (*Tintin au pays de l'or noir*, p. 16).

25 Hergé 1981 [1947], p. 1.

26 Hergé 1981 [1947], p. 7.

27 Hergé 1981 [1967], p. 1.

28 Hergé 1981 [1943], pp. 1-3.

29 Hergé 1981 [1947], p. 35.

30 Peeters 2003, pp. 337-345.

31 Cf. Wikipedia, s.v. "タンタンの冒険."

32 *Regards croisés*, p. 4.

33 *Regards croisés*, p. 4.

34 Of course the unrestrained drawing style and image layout, and the abundance of onomatopoeia and mimetic words are important elements in Japanese manga. BD and manga must be read and enjoyed in different ways.

SIXTH
PART

EXCHANGE
OF KNOW-HOW

CONSTANT HUYBRECHT: FLAX CRAFTSMAN IN JAPAN

W.F. Vande Walle

JAPAN & BELGIUM
An Itinerary of Mutual Inspiration

Portrait of Constant Huybrecht.
Photographic archive of Roger Vandelanotte (grandson of Constant Huybrecht),
with thanks to Philippe Haeyaert.

CONSTANT HUYBRECHT, FLAX CRAFTSMAN IN JAPAN

vuur bij het vlas brandt wonder ras[1]

Constant Huybrecht (1851-1922), unto the Flax Born

Constant Huybrecht was born in Wevelgem on 13 February 1851 as the third child of the flax trader and innkeeper Petrus Casimirus and his wife Mathilde Sophia Deman, who kept the inn *De Gouden Leeuw* ("The Golden Lion"). His official name was Constantinus, which soon evolved into "Constant". Like many children, he was better known by a nickname, in his case "whitey" on account of his blond hair.[2] In late 1860 Constant emigrated with his parents and sister (Leonie) to Russia, together with a few other citizens from Wevelgem.[3] A few years after his father had died in Russia, the family returned to Wevelgem and took up residence in a house on the marketplace along Grooten Steenweg, at number 4. Here his mother kept another inn, known as the *Hof van Russen* ("Inn of Russians"). While living here the family had their share of setbacks. His younger brother Rudolf died on 28 April 1869, followed by his mother on 10 June 1871. By then, Constant, known as "Ko de Witte van Trussenhof" ("Whitey Ko from the Russians' Inn"), was already active in the flax industry as a flax worker.[4] On the Feast of St Nicholas in the year 1876, he married the twenty-year-old Elize Corne, daughter of Clement (horse and carriage blacksmith) and of the late Rosalie

Francisca Lahousse. They took up residence in Menenstraat 79b, and later in Menenstraat 87. The marriage was blessed with ten children, three of whom died within a few months of birth.[5]

Wevelgem was a flax-growing area. Through the village runs the River Lys, known for its excellent retting qualities. Along its banks lies the area known as the Mecca of the Belgian flax industry, with the city of Kortrijk as its commercial hub. In reference to its vital role for the prosperity of the region the River Lys was called the "Golden River", in spite of the stench that comes from the retting process. The Huybrecht family had been involved in the flax industry for many generations. Constant himself had been familiar with it from a very early age and grew up to become a technician of some repute. During the 1880s, he was brought into contact with the Japanese, who were looking for the right know-how to start up a flax and linen industry in Japan. From February 1889 to July 1890 Constant Huybrecht stayed in Sapporo 札幌 to teach how to grow and process flax.[6] According to the testimony of his grandson Roger Vandelanotte, Constant Huybrecht took the train from Wevelgem in early December 1888, with an 18-month visa (from February 1889 through July 1890).[7] He crossed Belgium, the German empire and Russia, travelling through Moscow, Gorki, Kirov, Perm and Sverdlovsk. Beyond the Urals, he took the Trans-Siberian Railway and after a journey of approximately 11,000 kilometres he reached Vladivostok.[8]

By ship he crossed the Sea of Japan, a voyage of 500 kilometres. Once arrived on the island of Hokkaido, he still had to take a train to Sapporo. Sapporo had only recently become an urban area (the seat of the Hokkaido Development Commission was transferred to Sapporo village in 1871), with streets laid out in the American style. When he arrived there the town had only 17,000 inhabitants. Since 1886 it had been the administrative capital of Hokkaido. The town had a residential area reserved for Westerners.[9]

Sapporo train station (1885).
Courtesy of the Sapporo City Board of Education, with thanks to Philippe Haeyaert.

Flax and Linen for Hokkaido

Mankind has grown flax since time immemorial, and it is believed to be the world's oldest fibre crop.[10] It is said to have originated in Asia Minor. In Ancient Egypt flax was already cultivated and linen woven around 10,000 BCE. In the tombs of Egyptian kings around 2700 BCE we find murals depicting flax cultivation, and mummies were customarily wrapped in linen shrouds.[11] Linen also features in many passages in the Bible. Linen culture was transmitted to Europe around 800 CE, and became a deeply rooted part of material culture during the Middle Ages. From here it also spread to Russia. Until the advent of cotton as a product of the Industrial Revolution, it was a common material for clothing. Linen underwear was standard in Europe until the nineteenth century. In the nineteenth century, hemp, ramie and flax still represented 35% of the total fibre consumption.[12]

In Japan, during the Asuka and the Nara periods (late sixth to late eighth centuries), ramie was a favourite material for clothing, as is attested in the *Nihon shoki* 日本書紀 (720), and during the Edo period it was still the dress for the common people. The Japanese word *asa* 麻 already appears in the *Man'yōshū* 万葉集 (759). The term is a catch-all concept. In its broad meaning it refers to about twenty varieties of the fibre crops mentioned above.[13] Traditionally the Japanese were familiar with hemp (*taima* 大麻), ramie (*karamushi* 苧麻), jute (*ōma* 黄麻), Manila hemp (*Manira-asa* マニラ麻) and China grass or ramie (*Nankin-asa* 南京麻), but not with flax (*ama* 亜麻). In Japan the plant that supplies the raw material is called *ama*, whereas the end product, linen, is called *asa*.[14] In its narrow sense until the Meiji period it meant either ramie or hemp. *Kamishimo* 裃, the ceremonial dress of the samurai during the Tokugawa period, was made of hemp, while the high quality fabrics produced in various regions as local specialties were made from ramie.[15] In present-day usage, *asa* refers to cloth made from ramie or flax/linen, but since ramie is no longer grown, in actual fact it refers to linen.[16]

It is not clear when the seed of the flax plant was first introduced into Japan. There are two different views. One is that it was imported from China during the Genroku period around the year 1690. At that time linseed for medicinal use was planted in the herb garden of Ōji in Edo.[17] Allegedly in the year 1887 the wild descendants of these plants could still be found near the place where the herb garden once grew. According to another hypothesis, linseed first came to Japan in the second half of the sixteenth century in the context of Western medicine introduced by the Portuguese. Later it continued to be imported by VOC (Dutch East India Company) ships and it was sown for the first time in Edo in the year 1780.[18] Flax did not thrive as a crop due to the humidity of the Japanese climate. It grows in the period of the rainy season and therefore rots easily. At any rate procurement of linseed never posed a serious problem. Flax always served for the production of linseed and linseed oil, which particularly found application in medical use.[19]

The first attempt to grow flax with an eye to using the fibre was made in Hokkaido in the year 1867. The Bakufu (shogunal government) had had a bale of linseed sent from Russia to Hakodate. Thence the bag was sent on to the settler Ōtomo Kametarō 大友亀太郎 in the village of Sapporo-mura, with the request that he test its growing qualities. The bale from Russia was accompanied by a booklet explaining the crop growing method in Russia, the production of fibre (retting and scutching), spinning yarn, weaving, and the processing of the residual fibres for the manufacture of paper, as well as the use of the linseed for the production of linseed oil. With the seeds the first experimental crop was grown, probably in the year 1868.[20]

At that time a Prussian merchant named R. Gartner was living in Hakodate. He had rented an extensive swath of land from the Japanese authorities in the village of Nanae-mura 七重村, where he tried out European agricultural methods, importing tools, seeds and seedlings from Europe. However his venture lasted only three years because the fledgling Meiji government pressurized him into returning the land he had leased in the eleventh month of 1870, a transaction known as the Gartner Reclamation Contract Incident (*Garutoneru kaikon jōyaku jiken* ガルトネル開墾条約事件).[21] As it happened, one of the crops sown in this experimental farm was flax. The following year, in 1871, Thomas Antisell (1817-1893), an American advisor to the Hokkaido Development Commission, made an inspection tour of the region and noted in Nanae-mura that flax was growing on the fields formerly leased to Gartner. The following year he submitted to the deputy-director of the Hokkaido Development Commission (*kaitakushi* 開拓使 Kuroda Kiyotaka 黒田清隆) the following advice:

> Some time ago you asked me to report on the findings I made in the course of my inspection tour of Hokkaido in the autumn of last year. Hereafter follow my findings. Agriculture must concentrate in the first place on the production of plants for the daily diet; in the second place it is urgent to produce plants that are in demand for trade. The best I think is using the bare fibres (*hadaito* 肌糸) of hemp and flax to make nets. To launch the cultivation of these crops I think there is an urgent need now to send farmers and settlers thither. Flax can serve for the production of oil or line fibre. If it turns out that these areas are suitable for the production of fine line, it seems preferable to me to opt for this because it turns out a higher profit than the production of oil. There are a variety of plants related to flax but much cheaper than flax, from which one can prepare oil. It would be a shame to cultivate flax solely for the purpose of producing oil.[22]

In 1873 Thomas Antisell recommended the purchase of flax machines (precursors of the flax break and the scutching wheel). He wrote:

> Some time ago I saw the flax grown by your Development Commission. Since you have expressed a desire to know the method for high quality production, I enclose two scale drawings of equipment. I recommend that you have a prototype built and have it executed in Tokyo.[23]

The Hokkaido Development Commission continued to test-grow flax on the fields Gartner had left in Nanae-mura. In 1875 it imported seeds from America, and in 1878 seeds from Russia and America, and in 1879 seeds from England, America and Russia, which it distributed to the government test fields of Nanae-mura, Sapporo and Nemuro 根室. In 1879 it not only reaped the crop, but it also conducted an experimental fibre processing of the flax grown in Nanae-mura and Sapporo: retting and scutching the flax stalks Russian-style with machines based on models Enomoto Takeaki 榎本武揚 had procured from Russia.[24] The year before, in April 1878, then-director Kuroda Kiyotaka of the Hokkaido Development Commission had given a lecture on flax at an agricultural fair organized at the government test

fields of Tokyo. He had said that fibre flax could be used for the production of sail and rigging:

> As is clear from the proposal of Antisell and the documents from Enomoto Takeaki about the experiments in Russia [Enomoto had been plenipotentiary consul in Saint Petersburg from January 1874 to October 1878], we must keep the seed and find a method to gradually increase production in subsequent years.

In this way the efforts of the Bureau for the Colonization of Hokkaido paid off and proved that Hokkaido was suitable for fibre flax cultivation.[25] The landscape in Hokkaido resembles that of north-western European countries or regions such as northern France (Normandy), Flanders and Zeeland. The soil composition is propitious for the cultivation of flax.

In 1882, the Hokkaido Development Commission was disbanded and replaced with three prefectures (*ken* 県), Hakodate, Sapporo and Nemuro, under one directorate (*kyoku* 局). During the period from 1882 to 1885 there was very little development. It was not until 1887, shortly after Hokkaido was put under the jurisdiction of a single agency (*dō* 道), that fibre flax production started in earnest, a development reinforced by the establishment of the company *Hokkaidō Seima kaisha* 北海道製麻会社 (1887). In 1888 the Hokkaido Agency requested farmers living in the neighbourhood of Sapporo to grow a mixture of home-grown seeds and seeds from Kyoto, where Nakagawa Yoshimune 中川誾宗 and other private entrepreneurs had started sowing and processing their own fibre flax.

In 1889 the Japanese consul posted in Russia, and Yoshida Kensaku 吉田健作 (1852-1892), who was at the time on a mission to France, were asked to buy and send seeds from Russia and France. The Hokkaido Agency distributed the seeds to the Agricultural School of Sapporo, the Sapporo military farm, Sapporo prison, as well as to the villages in the districts (*gun* 郡) of Sapporo, Ishikari 石狩, Sorachi 空知, and Muroran 室蘭 for crop growing. The Hokkaido Agency invited the flax craftsman Constant Huybrecht from Belgium to teach the local farmers how to grow the crop. In that year the surface of the test fields was 38.8 *chō* 町 (one *chō* being 2.451 acres), and the average yield per *tan* 反 (0.245 of an acre) was 680 pounds of flax stalks and 65 catties (*kin* 斤 1.323 lb.) of seed. In 1890, in connection with the start of operations of *Hokkaidō Seima*, the Hokkaido Agency for the first time promoted regular cultivation (not test growing) of seeds, using a mixture of seeds imported from France (200 *koku* 石, one *koku* being 278.3 litres), seeds from Russia (50 *koku*), and seeds directly imported by *Hokkaidō Seima*. The area sown at that time covered some 337.8 *chō*. This marked the real start of industrial flax growing in Hokkaido.[26]

One of the people who played a key role in the launch of flax growing as an industrial enterprise in Hokkaido was Yoshida Kensaku. He was born in Fukuoka 福岡 (Northern Kyushu) but moved to Tokyo in 1875, where he joined the department of industrial promotion of the Ministry of Home Affairs. While studying under the guidance of the herbalist Tanaka Yoshio 田中芳男 he became aware that industrial and agricultural development were an urgent challenge for the Japan of his days. In particular he had a strong interest in flax breeding and in September 1877 he filed a formal request with his superior Matsukata Masayoshi 松方正義 to send him abroad to study agricultural techniques. He had espoused the policy of the new Meiji government, which was to promote industrialization as a first priority of the new Japan (*shokusan kōgyō* 殖産興業). It has been suggested that his resolve to go and study the flax industry was inspired or at least awakened by reading an article entitled "The Theory of Flax" ("Ama no setsu" 亜麻 の説) published by Tsuda Sen 津田仙 in the *Nōgaku zasshi* 農学雑誌 of May 1876.[27] To quote a relevant passage from the said article:

> Cloth woven from its fibre is called linen, and since the Japanese have recently started using it, demand for the product has been growing by the day. People from all walks of life, from the highest nobility to the lowliest commoner, everybody is wearing it as a summer garment. As a result the demand has grown to such an extent that nowadays we are importing the product from Europe and the United States to the tune of several hundred thousand yen per annum, which translates into a staggering outflow of money and loss for our country. The cultivation of flax would constitute the only good strategy to stem this outflow of money caused by the purchase of linen.[28]

In April 1878 Yoshida travelled to Paris as a member of the Japanese delegation led by Matsukata Masayoshi to

the 1878 Paris Universal Exposition. After the closure of the exposition he stayed on in France and resided in a spinning mill in the city of Lille, where he spent three years, learning about the various processes of sowing, growing, harvesting, the production of line fibre and on through to spinning and weaving. He returned to Japan in January 1881. In July 1881 he submitted his views[29] to the Ministry of Agriculture. In his proposal he argues that Japan needs to grow flax and to launch a flax industry of its own, but he recognizes that this is not easy and will take time. Therefore he advises the government to start with building a factory to make thick yarn from hemp, a traditional crop, and then later on, when the time was ripe, to convert to linen weaving. He not only advocated this course of action, he himself engaged in a promotional campaign, travelling through the country to appeal to people with an entrepreneurial spirit. His efforts were rewarded when the *Ōmi mashi bōshoku kaisha* 近江麻糸紡織会社 Company was founded in Ōtsu 大津 in 1884, the first flax factory in Japanese history.[30]

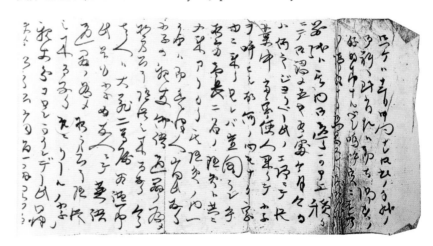

The smooth start of this company stimulated similar ventures elsewhere: in Hokkaido, where in 1887 the company *Hokkaidō Seima kaisha* was founded and in Kanuma 鹿沼 (Tochigi prefecture), where the company *Shimotsuke asa bōshoku kaisha* 下野麻紡織会社 was established. Thus the foundations for Japan's flax and linen industry were laid.[31] Yoshida, who had played a major part in the establishment of the *Hokkaidō Seima*, resigned from his government post in 1890 to become the Commissioner General of the company, but unfortunately in January 1891 he was taken ill with a pulmonary disease and became bedridden. On 5 February 1892 he died at the age of forty-one. Yoshida Kensaku may justly

Letter from Yoshida Kensaku to his family, sent from Lille and relating how, while living there, he received an unannounced visit by Matsukata Masayoshi.
Collection Yoshida Masuzō papers, Mukyūkai 無窮会, Machida.

be called the founding father of Japan's flax industry. In the city of Ōtsu there is a memorial monument commemorating his merits.[32]

The Founding of *Hokkaidō Seima*

As of 1 January 1886 the three prefectures dividing the island were disbanded and the Hokkaido Agency was established. The promotion of industrialization was a fundamental tenet of its policy. Its first director-general paid a visit to the newly established company *Ōmi mashi bōshoku kaisha* and keenly felt the need to establish a similar kind of enterprise in Hokkaido. He launched an appeal to capitalists in Tokyo and Kyoto, succeeding in collecting 800,000 yen of capital, with which *Hokkaidō Seima* was incorporated in Sapporo in 1887.[33] The technicians Yoshida Kensaku and Yokota Manjunosuke 横田万寿之助 were transferred from the Ministry of Agriculture and Commerce to the administration of the Agency in order to prepare the establishment of the company. The first assignment given them by the Agency was to travel to Europe in order to purchase machines for spinning and weaving, and to study the cultivation and manufacturing processes. At the same time the Agency administration ordered its own technicians to oversee the building of the factory, in the meantime promoting flax as raw material for the products to be manufactured in the factory.[34]

In the *Hokkaidō Seima ryakushi* 北海道製麻略史 ("A Short History of *Hokkaidō Seima*"), published in 1894, we read the following:

> For the construction of our company we worked with blueprints checked in Europe, and after consulting Doctor of Engineering Tatsuno Kingo 辰野金五,[35] we sent building engineer Sugiyama Shūkichi 杉山輯吉 to Sapporo to survey the situation on the ground. The employee Miyamura Sakuzō 宮村朔三 (formerly an employee of *Ōmi mashi bōshoku*) was put in charge on the ground. Reference was made to a wide range of theoretical expertise and experience. For the purpose of ensuring convenience and solidity, building stone, bricks, iron pillars and rafters were used. The works started in July 1887, first with the manufacture of bricks and the quarrying of stone. In July 1888 the groundwork started, and when in May 1889 the iron pillars arrived from Europe, the construction works started at once. In December of the same year more than half was completed. This may seem like a long period, but we must take into account the remoteness of this newly opened-up land, which was the cause of all kinds of inconvenience. Moreover, winter conditions were very severe, practically disabling all work from November of that year until April of the next. To make matters worse, the quality of the stones quarried in Hokkaido was too soft for the duties they had to perform in the hemp and flax softener and other vital machinery, and appropriate stones had to be hauled from faraway places such as Shōzujima 小豆島 in the province of Bitchū [now western Okayama prefecture 岡山県]. Moreover, the tiles of the roof were not of a quality that would withstand the severe cold, and therefore had to be ordered from Seikyō Daibutsu 西京大仏.[36]

Another passage from *Hokkaidō Seima ryakushi* runs as follows:

> In November 1887 the Hokkaido Agency decided to send the two technicians Yoshida and Yokota on a mission to Europe, in order to purchase machines for our company, hire foreign experts and study the various processes involved in cultivation and manufacturing. They left Japan in December 1887 and travelled to France, Germany and Belgium in order to select the most recent and best machines. They ordered the machinery from Walker, a company in Lille in northern France. These machines were custom-made, as is borne out by the fact that the name of our company was cast in each machine. The total weight of the machines ordered was 1,951.5 tonnes. They were shipped from the port of Antwerp in three shipments directly to the port of Otaru 小樽 in Hokkaido. The installation of the machines was done by various foreign experts who arrived one after another and started the installation work from July 1889 onwards. The works were completed in June 1890. A test run was done when the installation was completed and everything went according to plan. The Japanese were greatly impressed by the way the foreign experts followed the instructions of the supervisors, as well as by their expertise and diligence.[37]

Another passage in *A Short History of Hokkaidō Seima* deals with the manpower:

> Once all the machines were operational in the company the number of workers needed to operate them appeared to be more than 700 people. Even in the early days of operation when the factory was only running at half capacity, around 400 men and women were needed. It was impossible to find the necessary workforce in Hokkaido. Therefore they had to be recruited from the mainland [i.e. Honshu]. In July 1889 sixty men from Sapporo were hired, in September thirty-one women from Kyoto, in November twenty women from Sapporo, in December eighty women from Kagoshima, and thirty-eight men and sixteen women from Fukushima, in January 1890 twenty-four men and four women from Tokyo, nineteen men and five women from Shiga, and in July sixty men and forty-two women from Sapporo.[38]

Sapporo in those days numbered only 3,400 families and 21,000 people. Operations started in July 1890, but in January 1891 the workers mounted a strike to demand shorter working hours and higher pay, halting operations for two days. The factory in Sapporo generated its own electricity starting in October 1890. This was the first electricity on the entire island of Hokkaido, and it aroused much interest among the local inhabitants, who used to flock around the factory buildings when evening fell to gaze at the wonder of electric light.[39]

The Kariki Flax Mill

At the beginning of operations the Sapporo factory procured its raw materials, both hemp and flax, from the Kariki 雁木 Flax Mill (founded 1889), but the entire production of Kariki was not sufficient to feed the

The city of Sapporo, as seen from the Hokkaido Agency (1889).
Courtesy of the Sapporo City Board of Education, with thanks to Philippe Haeyaert.

Another view of the city of Sapporo as seen from the Hokkaido Agency (1889).
Courtesy of the Sapporo City Board of Education, with thanks to Philippe Haeyaert.

factory. Supplies had to be supplemented with flax from Belgium, hemp from Italy and jute from India. It was not until 1895 that Hokkaido was fully self-sufficient in the supply of the raw materials.[40] In the beginning *Hokkaidō Seima* procured its line fibre from traders who acted as intermediaries between the flax growing farmers and the company, an arrangement inspired by the situation in Western Europe. But soon it was realized that this did not work well and the company set up its own flax mill by way of experiment. Later on new flax mills were added, similarly directly dependent on the company. Both the name Kariki Flax Mill and the location were chosen by Yoshida Kensaku. In the end Hokkaido had no fewer than 85 such flax mills. This first one at Kariki was put up along the banks of the Toyohira River 豊平川, on a location which at the time served as gravel pit for the Railways Section of the Hokkaido Agency. *Hokkaidō Seima* obtained the use of the land rent-free and work was begun in August 1889 under the guidance of Constant Huybrecht. The brushwood was first cleared and then construction was begun. The mill started test operations in the same year. Thirty wheels for scutching (or: swingling, to use a word cognate with Dutch "zwingelen") flax, and six breakers for breaking hemp were installed.

Constant Huybrecht gave direct instruction to the personnel in the operation of these machines, as well as in the preceding stages of the process such as retting the hemp and flax. For the retting he adopted running water retting, the method he was used to in Belgium, where the flax was retted in the slow-running River Lys. In the same way as in the River Lys, bundles of fibre flax in weighted-down wooden crates, were immersed in the running water of the River Toyohira and fixed with ropes, in order to break down the pectin layer, which glues the fibre bundles to the stem. The water, penetrating to the central stalk portion, swells the inner cells, bursting the outermost layer, thus increasing absorption of both moisture and decay-producing bacteria. Retting time must be carefully judged; under-retting makes separation difficult, and over-retting weakens the fibre. The retting period varies from three days to a week or a little more, depending on the temperature of the water. It has now virtually disappeared in Europe but is still practiced in Egypt and China. After retting was completed, the flax stalks were spread out on the riverbanks to dry. But in September of 1889 the

Toyohira, swollen by torrential rains, burst its banks and washed away both the crates and the drying flax. In order to avoid a similar calamity from occurring again it was then decided to dig ponds near the river, fill them up with water from the river and ret the flax and the hemp in the ponds.[41]

In the autumn of 1889, its first harvest year, the Kariki Flax Mill produced 1,500,000 pounds of flax and hemp each. In addition it purchased 170,000 pounds of raw materials at a price certified by the Hokkaido Agency, applying a system of three quality levels. By March 1890 it had turned out 160,000 pounds of scutched hemp fibre, 5,000 pounds of hemp tow, 7,000 pounds of scutched line fibre (*shōsen* 正線) and 6,000 pounds of flax tow (*sosen* 粗線). The flax mill of Kariki was the first of its kind, but it was soon followed by many others, starting with Kotoni 琴似, Tōbetsu 当別, and Sapporo. In 1895 Kariki caught fire, and after reconstruction it decommissioned its equipment for breaking hemp, and increased its scutching equipment by thirty new units. The Kariki mill was eventually closed down in 1909.

Initially the surface of hemp growing was around 100 *chō*. After the founding of *Hokkaidō Seima* in 1887 it reached a peak of 500 *chō* in 1888. It maintained this output level for a few years, but in the wake of the Sino-Japanese War it reached a new peak of 1,600 *chō* in 1896. But from that point in time onwards hemp growing tapered off, while flax growing increased. In 1894 flax overtook hemp, and by 1904 hemp had practically disappeared from the fields of Hokkaido and had been entirely replaced by flax. From 1905 onwards the authorities exclusively promoted flax growing, thus finally realizing Yoshida Kensaku's dream.[42] It must be noted that linen became increasingly popular as a material for high-quality haberdashery, exemplified by the cambric handkerchief, epitome of elegance and refinement. In addition, its military use as canvas to make rope, truck canopies, tents, sails, coverings for vehicles and goods, bags, uniforms, shoes, firehoses etc., for the army expanded rapidly.[43] The Sino-Japanese War, the Russo-Japanese War, the First and Second World Wars, all required huge supplies of linen-based products. Each war boosted the industry, but when it was over, it was followed by restructuring, ushering in a period of mergers and acquisitions in the sector. Farmers were assigned acreage on which they had to cultivate flax.

At its peak, in 1945, the acreage of flax cultivation ran
to more than 40,000 hectares, processed in no fewer than
85 mills.[44] Eighteen of these mills were founded in the
Meiji period, fifty-three in the Taishō period, the heyday
of flax, and another fourteen in the early Shōwa period.[45]
When the Second World War ended, flax, which had
been protected as a vital national crop, was exposed to
competition and quickly lost ground to the rapidly
expanding synthetic fibres. In order to reduce the hard
labour involved in pulling and processing the flax, and
in an effort to reduce labour cost, the sector sought the
solution in mechanization. In 1952 the company *Teikoku
Seima kabushikigaisha* 帝国製麻株式会社 imported
small harvesters made by Depoortere N.V.[46] in Belgium,
and sought new markets for its linen products in Brazil
and the United States, but the market did not have much
appetite for natural fibre. The last of the company's (now
called *Teikoku sen'i*) plants, the Otofuke 音更 factory
closed in 1968. Cultivation had been discontinued the
year before.[47]

The Imperial Flax and Linen Company
Teikoku Seima

In 1937, when Yasuoka was writing his *Nihon no seima-
gyō* ("The Flax and Linen Industry in Japan"), he could
proudly state that *Teikoku Seima* represented seventy to
eighty per cent of all linen production in Japan. The
history of *Teikoku Seima* is therefore almost synonymous
with the history of flax and linen in Japan. This
monopolistic company was the result of various mergers
and acquisitions, incorporating a number of smaller
companies as it developed and grew. The *Ōmi mashi
bōshoku kaisha*, founded 1884 in the city of Ōtsu, the
Shimotsuke Seima established in 1887 and the *Nihon
Senshi* 日本繊絲, later renamed *Ōsaka Mashi* 大阪麻糸
founded 1895, merged into *Nihon Seima
kabushikigaisha* 日本製麻株式会社 in 1903. Out of
Nihon Seima and *Hokkaidō Seima* (established in
Sapporo in 1887), came the merger *Teikoku Seima
kabushikigaisha* 帝国製麻株式会社 ("Imperial Flax and
Linen Company") in 1907 Later on it acquired *Nihon
Mashi* (1923) and *Nihon Seima* (1927). The company
continued to go through a series of acquisitions and
mergers, and in 1941 it merged with *Taiyō Rēyon*, at
which time it was renamed *Teikoku Sen'i kabushikigaisha*
帝国繊維株式会社. The company still exists today, and is

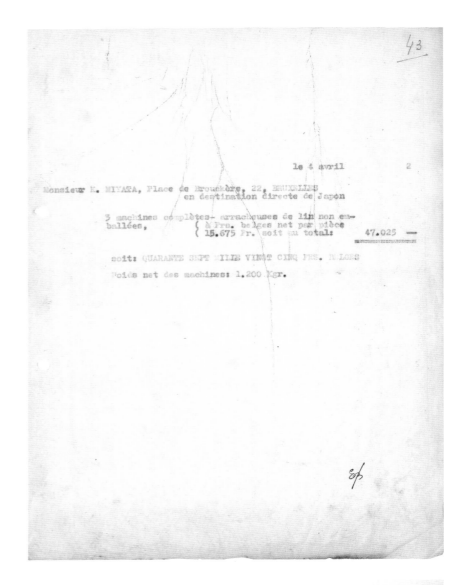

Copy of sales invoice for three flax harvesters issued by Depoortere N.V.
to K(ōzō) Miyata in 1952. The copy does not mention *Teikoku Seima*, but
that was very probably the final destination of the goods.
Courtesy of Peter Rosseel, CEO Depoortere N.V., with thanks to Geert Benoit.
Miyata Kōzō, mentioned in the next chapter (p. 373), was the founder of the first
Japanese trading company in Belgium.

Flax field in Sapporo. Photograph undated but presumably late 19th
century.
Courtesy of the Sapporo City Board of Education, with thanks to Philippe Haeyaert.

better known under the name *Teisen*, but it has since greatly diversified its business and product range.

All these companies had been founded in areas which produced traditional plants or fabrics, such as hemp or hemp cloth (*mafu*). However, although they had originally processed that local material, once they became part of *Teikoku Seima*, or even earlier than that, they had switched to the processing of flax as raw material. Therefore the location of these factories no longer had anything to do with local traditional materials.[48] Only *Hokkaido Seima* was designed from the outset to process flax, which was earmarked as an appropriate crop to boost development in the virgin lands of Hokkaido. Opening its first factory in Sapporo in 1889, it invited Constant Huybrecht to teach cultivation and processing of the product. This marked to all intents and purposes the beginning of flax cultivation in Japan.[49]

The Sapporo factory of *Teikoku Seima* in Sapporo, located on the banks of the River Sōseigawa 創成川, was pulled down in the late sixties.[50]

Constant Huybrecht, the Instructor

In 1888 Yoshida Kensaku and Yokota Manjunosuke travelled to the area of Kortrijk and Wevelgem where they met Constant Huybrecht. They invited him to come to Japan as an expert. He accepted the invitation, travelled to Japan and reached Hokkaido in March 1889. At that time *Hokkaidō Seima* had just ordered spinning equipment from France. Thus at around the same time the technicians commissioned to install the equipment also arrived in Japan: an Englishman, named Rich, for the installation of the boiler and engines, a Frenchman, whose name is unclear, for the installation of the

Girls working in spinning mill at Sapporo. Photograph undated but presumably early 20th century.
Courtesy of the Sapporo City Board of Education, with thanks to Philippe Haeyaert.

spinning machines, another Frenchman for the installation of the weaving looms, and the Belgian Desmet for the bleaching equipment.

These four foreign experts were employed by *Hokkaidō Seima*, whereas Huybrecht was hired by the Hokkaido Agency. His treatment was not particularly good. In those days the Agency employed ten foreign instructors: three teachers, two agricultural engineers, two sugar-making engineers, one hospital director, one brewer, and one harbour engineer. Their annual salaries varied between 2,000 and 4,800 yen. In contrast Constant Huybrecht only received 600 yen.

Constant Huybrecht played a major role in the foundation of the Kariki Flax Mill, but he also did much to teach the local farmers who had never seen flax before. He told them how to sow in the spring, how to grow it, how to weed, how to harvest and barn it, in short the whole process of crop growing. At Kariki Flax Mill, Constant Huybrecht had a number of disciples, among whom we have to mention Matsuo Manjirō 松尾万次郎. He was the elder son of Matsuo Yūzō 松尾友三, a pioneer colonist from the village of Abuta-mura 虻田村. He became Constant Huybrecht's pupil in 1890, and was taught the technique of flax retting.[51] In the notes taken by Matsuo we read about the double retting method: two little bundles are put top to bottom on one another, and are tied together at three points. The top and the sides of the frames are covered with planks or straw, and the whole contraption is soaked in water twice, with an interval for drying. This double-phase retting method was supplanted by the single-phase retting method after the Sino-Japanese War.[52] That same year Matsuo built a flax mill in Abutamura and started producing line fibre by means of a wooden man-driven contraption. The following year the manpower was replaced by waterpower. He thus pioneered the family-run spinning industry. He also pioneered a method of retting in a cased frame which was assembled in the ground. *Hokkaidō Seima* learned about his new method and imitated it in its own flax mills of Kotoni and Tōbetsu, where it used the cased-frame method along with the tank-retting method.

Constant Huybrecht lived in the same housing as the four technicians employed by *Hokkaidō Seima*. It was located a few houses from the north-western corner of

the Agency building and close to the Botanical Garden. He understood English but his Japanese did not go any further than *ohayō* ("good morning"). He gave his instructions by gestures. He was hardworking, and quite stern and strict in his guidance. For instance, when he was teaching the use of the scutching wheel, he would pull out one or two threads from underneath a pile of scutched line on the scutching table, and when the threads did not come out smoothly, it meant that the work had not been done properly, and he disqualified the product and overturned the whole heap of scutched line. He was an excellent technician, whether it came to sowing, or harvesting, retting, putting the wet flax straw upright, or turning it. He was also an expert in the manufacture of line and the assortment of the various qualities of the manufactured fibre. However, expert though he was, he remained a pure technician with no theoretical or scholarly background. The skills he was teaching lacked any theoretical grounding. In this respect he may have somewhat disappointed his Japanese disciples because they were eager to acquire more background knowledge. It even seems that he was slightly looked down upon by some as being someone without any culture or refinement. There are no anecdotes concerning Constant Huybrecht left in the world of the Hokkaido flax-spinning business, a fact that may suggest a lacklustre personality. Such at least is the assumption of Hara.[53]

Back in Belgium

After his stint in Hokkaido was terminated by the Hokkaido Agency in July 1890,[54] he returned to Belgium and to his family trade. Once back home, around September 1890, Huybrecht maintained an on-going contact with the Japanese company *Hokkaidō Seima* and its successor *Teikoku Seima*. He seems to have felt nostalgia for Japan and when Japanese from the flax manufacturing industry came to his area, he tried to be helpful to them in every possible way.

The first Japanese who enjoyed his generosity and hospitality were Fukuda Hisanori 福田久徳, director of the Sapporo factory, and Kanai Bunnosuke 金井文之助, head of the Tōbetsu Flax Mill, who went to Belgium in 1897. They showed him how the cultivated acreage had grown since his stint in Hokkaido and praised him for his contribution. Constant Huybrecht, while excited about the increase in planted acreage, voiced concern that rapid increase of acreage might lead to sloppy cultivation and processing practices. The two Japanese visitors, looking at the flax in the area of Wevelgem and Kortrijk, realized that flax growing and manufacturing in Japan in recent years had indeed become more haphazard, that the weight of seeds sown per acre had decreased, that the harvest season had become later, and that the various operations in the factory had become looser.[55]

In the spring of 1906 Suzuki Suzuma 鈴木鈴馬 from *Hokkaidō Seima*'s head office paid him a visit, bringing a sample of scutched line fibre from Kuriyama Flax Mill 栗山 to show to Constant Huybrecht, who judged that the retting, scutching and assorting were deficient. Thereupon Suzuki sent orders that samples from Kotoni in the three qualities (superior, intermediate, and standard) be sent over and asked Constant Huybrecht to process them according to his own method. From August to September Huybrecht ran the samples through the

double-phase retting process in the River Lys. Then the scutched line produced from the samples was sent back to the flax mill of Kotoni. When comparing the returned line sample with the equivalent line produced at Kotoni, the quality of the samples, although from the same rough material, appeared to be so much better than the local manufacture. This experiment proved that the place of growing was less important than the method of retting and scutching in determining the quality of the end product.

In the wake of the Russo-Japanese War, in the years 1909-1910 *Teikoku Seima* (*Hokkaidō Seima*'s new name since the 1907 merger), confronted with production surplus, was able to export 626,000 pounds of their scutched line to Belgium. In this export venture Constant Huybrecht acted as intermediary and he was able to sell the goods on the Wevelgem market, passing them off as Kortrijk flax.

Posthumous Honours

Constant Huybrecht indeed went on acting as a supportive adviser to the Japanese flax-spinning industry. He died on 30 October 1922, at the age of seventy-one. He had been a widower since 14 June 1894, when his wife died at the age of only thirty-eight years. When Constant Huybrecht died, the staff of *Teikoku Seima* decided to raise funds for the endowment of a monument in his memory. In his native town his grave is marked by a tombstone with epitaph, donated by *Teikoku Seima*. The initiative for this donation was taken by Santō Yoshika 山藤芳嘉 of *Teikoku Seima*, who visited Belgium in 1923. In conjunction with some Japanese who were studying at Belgian universities, including the University of Leuven, or were otherwise active in Belgium, they erected and inaugurated the monument in 1924 (with Japanese and French inscriptions).[56] It can still be visited at the back of the municipal cemetery in Wevelgem on the side of the Menenstraat, not far from the Calvary and the Josson-Delcour and Debrabandere family tomb (located diagonally across).[57]

The professional weekly *Het vlas. Orgaan van het Belgisch Vlasbazenverbond* ("The Flax. Organ of the Belgian Association of Flax Growers") of Tuesday, 15 April 1924, reports that a number of leading Japanese had set up a committee with the aim of raising funds for the building

Tomb of Constant Huybrecht.
Photograph taken at the commemoration on 5 May 2001.
Photograph courtesy of Rinzy Callewaert, Wevelgem, with thanks to Philippe Haeyaert.

of this monument. With the help of some newspapers, subscription lists were circulated among the Japanese population. The yield was such that a year and a half later the practical costs for the erection of the monument had been collected. On Sunday 27 April 1924 a ceremony was held at the municipal cemetery in Wevelgem. It was attended by the family, the community and Wevelgem notables, as well as Dr Adachi Mineichirō 安達峰一郎, Japanese ambassador in Brussels, and Leon Janssens de Bisthoven, then the governor of West Flanders. At the ceremony Constant Huybrecht was hailed as "founder" of the flax industry in Japan.[58]

In 1923 *Teikoku Seima* compiled a guide to the process of producing line fibre in thirty postures, illustrated by photographs featuring the employee Yoshikawa Yoneta 吉川米多. The album was entitled *An Illustrated Guide to Scutching* (*Mūran sagyō zukai* ムーラン作業図解). It was a tribute to Huybrecht's orthodox scutching method.

On 13 February 1951 the centenary of Huybrecht's birth was duly celebrated in Wevelgem. It was a day-long programme, including a welcome of the personalities and relatives by the local music society "De Eendracht," who played the Japanese and Belgian national anthems. Besides the family and the municipal authorities, various prominent persons attended the ceremony, including the representatives of the Algemeen Belgisch Vlasverbond (The All-Belgian Flax Association), Mr Andries Dequae, the Belgian minister of the Colonies, as well as a Japanese delegation, including among others Mr Santō Yoshika, and Yamada Torizō 山田酉蔵, then president of *Teikoku Seima*. The celebration included a Mass at the church of St Hilary, an official reception at the town hall, and an act of homage at the funerary monument. After the ceremony there was a banquet, attended by more than two hundred guests, including a large number of people from the world of the flax trade.[59] Mayor Achiel Wallays welcomed everyone and outlined the importance of the "giant work" that Constant Huybrecht had achieved in Japan. The Japanese delegation read some letters from the mayor of Sapporo, Mr Takata Tomiyo 高田富與, and from the Supreme Court of Japan.

Every year until her death in 1977, his daughter Denise Huybrecht would receive visits around the period of All Saints and All Souls from a few Japanese who came to

pay their respects at the funerary monument of Constant Huybrecht.[60]

In 2001 the town of Wevelgem celebrated the 150th anniversary of his birth. The commemoration was held on 5 May, which in Japan is children's day (*Kodomo no hi*). The programme included a visit to the National Flax Museum in Kortrijk, and naturally a visit to the tomb of Constant Huybrecht, where the Japanese ambassador and the mayor, among others, delivered a speech. Noteworthy was the exhibition held in the Municipal Public Library of Wevelgem (from 28 April to 12 May 2001). It not only highlighted the person of Constant Huybrecht and his family, but also the flax trade in his days, the funerary monument in the cemetery, the previous commemorations, and even a section presenting a profile of the city of Sapporo (both in the time of Constant Huybrecht's sojourn and today). The local history society *Wiblinga* was instrumental in the organization of the programme and the conception of the exhibition.

NOTE: the author is much indebted to Mr. Philippe Haeyaert, Wevelgem, for graciously providing some of the photographs reproduced here, as well as a copy of his two articles on Constant Huybrecht (listed in the references that follow).

> Members of the Japanese delegation in front of Huybrecht's tomb during the 1951 commemoration. The man in the middle is Santō Yoshika.
Courtesy of Philippe Haeyaert.

REFERENCES

Haeyaert 2001a
Philippe Haeyaert. "Constant Huybrecht (1851-1922) en het land van de rijzende zon." *Wibilinga* 14:1 (2001), pp. 15-19.

Haeyaert 2001b
Philippe Haeyaert. "Constant Huybrecht (1851-1922) en het land van de rijzende zon." *Wibilinga* 14:3 (2001), pp. 12-26.

Hara 1980
Hara Matsuji 原松次. *Hokkaidō ni okeru amajigyō no rekishi* 北海道における亜麻事業の歴史. Tokyo: Funkawansha 噴火湾社, 1980.

Kimura et al. 2012
Kimura Yōji 木村洋司, Tone Satomi 刀禰聡美, Shimizuike Yoshiharu 清水池義治, and Andō Seiichi 安藤清一. "Chiiki shigen toshite no ama no sen'i shokuhin nado e no katsuyō kanōsei no kenkyū: Furansu nado no ama saibai sangyō kara dairokuji sangyōka o saguru" 地域資源としての亜麻の繊維・食品などへの活用可能性の研究–フランスなどの亜麻栽培産業から第六次産業化を探る. *Nayoro shiritsu daigaku Dōhoku chiiki kenkyūjo nenpō* 名寄市立大学道北地域研究所年報 30 (2012), pp. 85-97.

Mishima 2008
Mishima Tokuzō 三島徳三. "Ima, naze ama na no ka: Seima-gyō fukkatsu e no kitai" いま、なぜ亜麻なのか 製麻業復活への期待. *Nayoro shiritsu daigaku Dōhoku chiiki kenkyūjo nenpō* 名寄市立大学道北地域研究所年報 26 (2008), pp. 1-12.

Tanabe 2010
Tanabe Yasukazu 田辺安一. *Buna no hayashi ga kataritsutaeru koto: Puroshiajin R. Garutoneru Nanaemura kaikon tenmatsu-ki* ブナの林が語り伝えること プロシア人 R・ガルトネル七重村開墾顛末記. Sapporo: Hokkaidō shuppan kikaku sentā 北海道出版企画センター, 2010.

Teikoku Seima 1959
Teikoku Seima kabushikigaisha 帝国製麻株式会社, ed. *Teikoku Seima kabushikigaisha gojūnen-shi* 帝国製麻株式会社五十年始. Tokyo: Teikoku Seima kabushikigaisha 帝国製麻株式会社, 1959.

Yasuoka 1936
Yasuoka Shirō 安岡志郎. *Nihon no seima-gyō* 日本の製麻業. Tokyo: Teikoku Seima kabushikigaisha 帝国製麻株式会社, 1936.

Yasuoka 1937
Yasuoka Shirō 安岡志郎. *Teikoku Seima kabushikigaisha sanjūnen-shi* 帝国製麻株式会社三十年始. Tokyo: Teikoku Seima kabushikigaisha 帝国製麻株式会社, 1937.

NOTES

1 Dutch proverb: Fire close to flax burns marvellously fast.

2 Haeyaert 2001a, p. 16.

3 Haeyaert 2001a, p. 16.

4 Haeyaert 2001a, p. 16.

5 Haeyaert 2001a, p. 16.

6 Haeyaert 2001a, p. 16.

7 Haeyaert 2001b, p. 13.

8 Haeyaert 2001b, p. 12.

9 Haeyaert 2001b, p. 13.

10 Kimura et al. 2012, p. 86.

11 Mishima 2008, p. 5.

12 Kimura et al. 2012, p. 86.

13 Mishima 2008, p. 4.

14 Yasuoka 1936, pp. 1-2.

15 Kimura et al. 2012, p. 86.

16 Kimura et al. 2012, p. 86.

17 Kimura et al. 2012, p. 85.

18 Hara 1980, p. 8.

19 Hara 1980, p. 9.

20 Hara 1980, p. 9; Yasuoka 1937, p. 155; Kimura et al., p. 86.

21 Described in detail in Tanabe 2010.

22 Quoted in Hara 1980, pp. 9-10.

23 Quoted by Hara 1980, p. 10.

24 Yasuoka 1937, p. 155.

25 Quoted by Hara 1980, p. 10.

26 Hara 1980, p. 11.

27 Hara 1980, p. 13.

28 Quoted by Hara 1980, p. 14.

29 *Asa bōseki kōjō setsuritsu ikensho* 麻紡績工場設立意見書.

30 Hara 1980, p. 14.

31 Teikoku Seima 1959, p. 6.

32 Hara 1980, p. 15.

33 Teikoku Seima 1959, p. 5.

34 Hara 1980, p. 17.

35 Famous Japanese architect (1854-1919), known as the designer of the Bank of Japan building (1896) and the Marunouchi building of Tokyo Station (1914).

36 Quoted by Hara 1980, p. 18.

37 Quoted by Hara 1980, pp. 18-19.

38 Quoted by Hara 1980, p. 19.

39 Hara 1980, p. 19.

40 Hara 1980, pp. 19-20.

41 Hara 1980, p. 20.

42 Hara 1980, p. 21.

43 Mishima 2008, p. 2.

44 Kimura et al. 2012, pp. 86-87.

45 Mishima 2008, pp. 10-11.

46 Mishima 2008, p. 8. The Depoortere company, based in Beveren-Leie (Waregem) was founded in 1925, and specialized in designing, manufacturing and perfecting flax harvesting machines, and all other machines for the preparation of natural fibres: processing, cleaning and packing.

47 Kimura et al. 2012, p. 87.

48 Yasuoka 1936, p. 3.

49 Yasuoka 1936, p. 4.

50 Mishima 2008, p. 1.

51 Yasuoka 1937, p. 158.

52 Hara 1980, p. 24.

53 Hara 1980, pp. 24-25.

54 Yasuoka 1937, p. 156.

55 Hara 1980, p. 25.

56 Haeyaert 2001b, p. 16.

57 Haeyaert 2001a, p. 16.

58 Haeyaert 2001b, p. 16.

59 Haeyaert 2001a, p. 16; Haeyaert 2001b, p. 19.

60 Haeyaert 2001b, p. 19.

Group photograph of prominent personalities attending the celebration
of the centenary of Huybrecht's birth in 1951. Sitting in the middle of the front row,
wearing thick rimmed glasses, is Yamada Torizō. On his right is Dries Dequae. On his left Huybrecht's son.

Photograph courtesy of Philippe Haeyaert.

Photo taken during the 1951 centenary.
Sitting alone is one of the sons of Constant Huybrecht.
Standing in the middle is Santō Yoshika.

Photograph courtesy of Philippe Haeyaert.

JUN'ICHI HOBO AND THE ART OF CHICK SEXING

W.F. Vande Walle

JAPAN & BELGIUM
An Itinerary of Mutual Inspiration

Jun'ichi Hobo with a grown brood of chickens (1952).
Photograph courtesy of Koichi Hobo.

JUN'ICHI HOBO AND THE ART OF CHICK SEXING [1]

Waregem, a town in the southern part of the province of West Flanders, is home to three generations of Hobo, not a familiar Flemish family name but a "transplant" from Japan that dates back to pre-war times. It is also the name of a restaurant and a company, Hobo C&S bvba. They are the heirs and heritage of Jun'ichi "Paul" Hobo 保母準一 (1916-2006), born in 1916 in Mizunami 瑞浪 (Gifu prefecture, Japan), a place about an hour by rail from Nagoya. He was the oldest of four siblings. Born on a farm, he was destined to succeed his father, who ran a poultry hatchery, as head of the family. The area of Nagoya was and still is known as a centre of poultry farming, to the extent that there is a breed named after the city. In the early 1880s local chickens were crossed with the Chinese Buff Cochin. The offspring with a buff colour were selected for further breeding. In 1905 the chicken was recognized as the first practical breed for poultry farming in Japan, and after some additional improvements the Nagoya breed was formally established in 1919.[2]

In the early stages breeding was on a very small scale as a side activity of farming. Chickens were bred both for eggs and for meat. During the 1920s thanks to a large-scale ten-year programme for increased production launched by the Japanese government, Japan's poultry farming went through a phase of rapid development, transforming it from an insignificant side-line of farming into one of the most important branches of agriculture. Inspecting and studying the methods that yielded record stock in North America, the Japanese breeders imported the best of the high-record bloodlines from Canada and the United States. In the government poultry-breeding farms and the departments of agriculture and education in Japan these bloodlines were multiplied and then distributed to the farmers.[3] Official records indicate an increase of 12 million head of high-productivity poultry from 1927 to 1932. Over the same period, egg production itself was raised from an average of 107.2 eggs per hen lifetime to 122.8.[4] At the time this was the highest average achieved in any country in the world, in spite of the fact that Japan's poultry population still included a considerable proportion of less productive native breeds like the Nagoya.[5] The dazzling growth of the Japanese poultry industry had the unfortunate side-effect of an enormous surplus of unwanted or unsaleable cockerels. These developments coincided with world depression in the wake of the crash of 1929. In Japan, where grain was dearer than in most other poultry-industry nations, raising a huge number of unwanted cockerels was a luxury the country could ill afford.[6] From the 1920s on the Japanese had been taking on the challenge posed by this problem and had succeeded in overcoming the obstacle.[7]

The secrets behind this success story was a new method to determine the sex of baby chicks by detecting the differences in their rudimentary reproductive organs, particularly the cloaca. The reader may ask what the connection is. As the demand for eggs grew, and poultry farming expanded to an industrial scale, the fact that hatchlings have very few external characteristics to distinguish their sex became a real problem, since industrial farms that produce eggs do not need male chicks (cockerels). The extra equipment, heat, space, labour and feed required just to rear the chickens to the age where sex can be detected entails superfluous costs. It takes a few weeks before the sexual characteristics start to show. For large commercial hatcheries it was necessary to separate female chicks or pullets from the cockerels at the earliest stage possible. There simply was no market able to absorb the staggering numbers of young cockerels that were produced.

Japanese scientists in the field of embryology and anatomy came to the rescue as they perfected their technique of sex determination. As early as 1924 Dr Masui Kiyoshi 増井清 (1887-1981) and two collaborators, Hashimoto Jūrō 橋本重郎 and Ōno Isamu 大野勇, then working at the livestock experimental station of the ministry of Agriculture and Forestry (Nōrinshō 農林省), published an article on anatomical differences they had discovered in male and female neo-natal chicks. The following year they reported on their findings to the Japan Livestock Studies Conference (Nihon chikusan gakkai 日本畜産学会).[8] Incidentally, Dr Masui was appointed professor at Tokyo Imperial University in 1935, and, after the war, became one of the founders of the Faculty of Agriculture (founded in 1951) of the University of Nagoya, and its first dean.[9] When more advanced findings were reported upon in 1927 at the

Third World's Poultry Congress held in Ottawa, Canada in a paper on "The Rudimentary Copulatory Organ of the Male Domestic Fowl with Reference to the Difference of the Sexes of Chicks,"[10] the interest of poultry breeders in the West was aroused, although insiders remained sceptical as to the method's commercial feasibility in the context of hatcheries or poultry farms.[11]

What they had developed was a method of vent sexing. It involves squeezing the faeces out of the chick, which slightly opens up the chick's anal vent (called a cloaca), allowing the chicken sexer to discern in a split second whether the chick has a small "bump", which would indicate that the chick is a male. Some pullets also have bumps, but they are rarely as large as those of cockerels. It is the tininess of the bump and the split second during which it is visible that filled the observers with scepticism.

But then practical-minded pioneering poultry breeders such as Kojima Manabu 小島学 and Sakakiyama Yūzō stepped in. Informed by Dr Masui's findings, Kojima started examining the reproductive organs of chicks of varying age, in the process gradually improving his familiarity with the organs and their differences, working his way down from chicks of sixty days to thirty days and so on, to a point where he could distinguish the sexes at a day old.[12] Further practice enabled him to sex chicks at high speed.[13] Now, breeders could buy baby chicks from hatcheries with the near certainty that they would all be pullets. The grim upshot of this method for the cockerels is however that they are eliminated within hours of hatching. That notwithstanding, the vocation of the professional chick sexer was born. In 1930 a training centre was founded under the name of Japan Chick Sexing Propagate Association (*Nihon shiyūkanbetsu fukyūkai* 日本雌雄鑑別普及会), which trained and certified sexers.[14] In the same year the first sexing contest was held, with thirty contestants taking part. The prize to the winner was a free trip to America. By 1932 expert sexers had been trained who were able to distinguish at high speed and 100 per cent accuracy.[15] Young Hobo Jun'ichi too was sent to Nagoya to train as a chick sexer, and he proved to have a talent for it. He thus joined the ranks of the burgeoning new profession. An accredited chick sexer successfully detects with the human eye under the light of a 200 watt lamp the sex of hatchlings at a rate of around 1,000 chicks per hour with an accuracy rate of 98%.[16]

In 1933 the Japan Chick Sexing Association (*Nihon shiyūkanbetsu kyōkai* 日本雌雄鑑別協会), later called All Japan Chick Sexing Association, with headquarters in Nagoya, was founded by the merger of five groups of professional sexers. It included important scientists and officials in Japan, and received strong support from the *Japan Poultry Journal*. The sexing experts themselves made up the principal rank and file membership in this professional organization.[17] One of the cores of the organization was the Japan Chick Sexing Propagate Association, the above-mentioned training centre for baby chick sexers.[18] It also ran a programme of supporting propagation activities. In that same year, the winner of the first contest, Yogo Hikosaburō 余語彦三郎, was dispatched to North America with the brief to propagate the technique, and to dispel any lingering doubts about its practical feasibility. Demonstrations were arranged for and held at the University of British Columbia, Oregon Agricultural College, the University of California, and many hatcheries in different centres on the Pacific coast.[19] The training centre for baby chick sexers (*shoseisū shiyūkanbetsushi yōseijo* 初生雛雌雄鑑別師養成所) went through various name changes, but is now a division of the Japan Livestock Technology Association (*Shadanhōjin chikusan gijutsu kyōkai* 社団法人畜産技術協会).

In 1934 sexers were dispatched to various continents, including Europe. The group that sailed to Europe had as its destinations Britain, France and Belgium. Jun'ichi Hobo, who was one of top-class sexers, trained and

Chicken sexers in action.
Photograph courtesy of Hein Vandewalle.

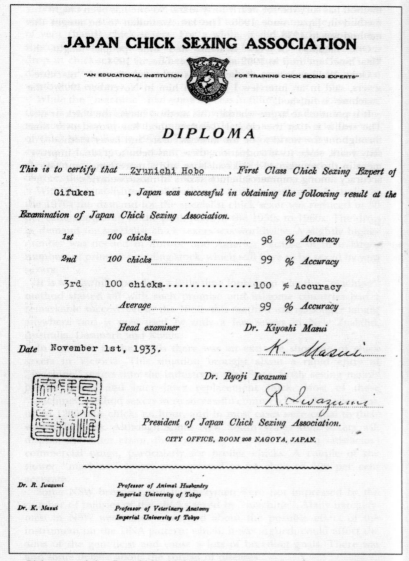

JAPAN CHICK SEXING ASSOCIATION

"AN EDUCATIONAL INSTITUTION"   FOR TRAINING CHICK SEXING EXPERTS"

DIPLOMA

This is to certify that <u>Zyunichi Hobo</u> , *First Class Chick Sexing Expert of*

<u>Gifuken</u> , *Japan was successful in obtaining the following result at the*

Examination of Japan Chick Sexing Association.

1st	100 chicks	98	%	Accuracy
2nd	100 chicks	99	%	Accuracy
3rd	100 chicks	100	%	Accuracy
	Average	99	%	Accuracy

Head examiner   Dr. Kiyoshi Masui

Date   November 1st, 1933.   *K. Masui.*

Dr. Ryoji Iwazumi

R. Iwazumi

President of Japan Chick Sexing Association.

CITY OFFICE, ROOM 208 NAGOYA, JAPAN.

Dr. R. Iwazumi   *Professor of Animal Husbandry*
Imperial University of Tokyo

Dr. K. Masui   *Professor of Veterinary Anatomy*
Imperial University of Tokyo

Diploma awarded to Zyunichi [Junichi] Hobo, November 1, 1933. (Courtesy of Takashi Hobo, Belgium)

accredited by the Japan Chick Sexing Association, was selected as a member of the five-member delegation sent to Europe. The association paid for the travel expenses, and provided a daily allowance and a salary for four months in the spring season.[20]

The group reached London aboard the ship *Yasukuni-maru* 靖国丸 in December 1934. Leaving his colleagues in the UK and France, Jun'ichi travelled on to Belgium, where he arrived at the chick hatchery of the Stepman family in Kaster (Avelgem) in January 1935. During the early months of his stay, his employer, Gaston Stepman, who saw the huge benefits of the novel technique, visited farmers and breeders in the area to promote the services of his Japanese guest. Initially he met with scepticism

and suspicion, for the down-to-earth no-nonsense West Flemish farmers simply could not believe his story, until they saw the result. Stepman introduced Jun'ichi as Mister Hobo, but the locals, not conversant in English, corrupted this "mister" to "miester," which means "master" in the local dialect. "Master Hobo" must have seemed an appropriate name for someone with his uncanny skills.[21]

Pre-industrial hatching was a seasonal activity in those years, so that the intervention of the sexers was only needed for a few months. Jun'ichi was planning to go back to Japan towards the end of the season, but Gaston, convinced that the technique of chick sexing would eventually find acceptance, suggested that he stay on to study Flemish, so that by the following year he could better communicate with the hatchers and breeders. Jun'ichi agreed to the proposal. Staying with the family he embarked upon his language course.[22] He was allegedly intent on securing integration in the local society that surrounded him. In an interview in 2001 he declared: "I learned Flemish from a teacher in Anzegem and I have been able to integrate in Flanders. As a foreigner one has no other choice, because one is a minority. I stayed on here to learn a little Flemish."[23] He seems to have gone native indeed. Other witnesses confirm that he rarely sought contact with fellow countrymen residing in Belgium. The Japanese consulate-general in Antwerp used to hold receptions for Japanese residents in Belgium on the occasion of New Year and the Emperor's Birthday. Even when he attended these receptions, Hobo would always keep a distance from the other Japanese attending. He ostensibly felt ill at ease observing the many rules governing civilized social intercourse among Japanese. This may have been connected with his rural background. Most Japanese travelling abroad had a more urbane background. He felt however admiration for Miyata Kōzō 宮田耕三, a pioneer Japanese businessman based in Antwerp and owner of the company Miyako Shōkai 都商会.[24] It has been said that this was the only Japanese to whom Hobo talked when Japanese met for a social occasion in Belgium.[25]

During the following years (1936-38), while his popularity grew among the local hatcheries, Jun'ichi travelled back to Japan each year after the busy season. The money he earned in those three or four months was more than sufficient for the whole year. He travelled by boat and later by the Trans-Siberian railway to continue on from Vladivostok by boat to Japan.[26]

Jun'ichi Hobo's diploma of First Class Chick Sexing Expert (1933).
Photograph courtesy of Koichi Hobo.

Meanwhile, Dr Masui, Dr Hashimoto and Mr Ōno had carried on their research on anatomical differences in different breeds and strains of chicks and other phases. Their findings were compiled in a book, which was translated into English and published in 1933 under the title *Sexing Baby Chicks*.[27] The work was published again as *Sexing Baby Chicks and Work of the Japanese Chick Sexing Association*, by The Japan Chick Sexing Association, Nagoya, 1936.[28] In 1937 the 6th International Poultry Conference was held in Leipzig from 24 July to 2 August. Besides the two official representatives sent out by the Japan Chick Sexing Association, the conference organizers also invited Professor Masui, as well as three expert sexers, among them Jun'ichi Hobo. The sexers' task was to demonstrate the know-how and practical sexing skill based on Prof. Masui's method. Following his scholarly lecture Masui showed his audience a film, which told the history of his research and depicted the procedures in great detail. The film had been produced by the Japan Chick Sexing Association under his supervision.[29] The presentation and demonstration met with much acclaim, earning universal recognition of the technique. Incidentally, the film went missing after the war, but it was rediscovered in 2005 in the archives of the Japan Chick Sexing Association, and is preserved now in the Nagoya University Museum.[30]

In 1939, just before the outbreak of the war, Hobo was once again on his way home, but he was refused passage to Japan, and was sent back to Kaster. Later he admitted that he was not entirely unhappy about this reversal, because he also had private reasons to return to the Stepman family...[31] In 1941, after converting to Catholicism and being christened Paul, he married Marie-Louise (1920-2013), the oldest daughter of his employer.[32] It is not hard to imagine that this was the first interracial marriage in the small village of Kaster. In an interview with the *Nihonjinkai* in 1995 (published in *Nihonjinkai kaihō* 日本人会会報 no. 152), he confided that it took him two years to secure his employer's blessing for his marriage to his daughter Marie-Louise.

By the end of the war the young family had three children: Takashi, Miyako and Miyoshi. In 1945 they moved into a new house in Waregem, where Jun'ichi soon started up the Hobo Chick Sexing company. It functioned as a clearing house for chick sexing activities in Belgium and later across Europe. It served as the home base for hundreds of Japanese chick sexers who

Jun'ichi Hobo showing hatchlings to his three children (1952).
Photograph courtesy of Koichi Hobo.

Young Jun'ichi Hobo with his son Takashi (1952).
Photograph courtesy of Koichi Hobo.

came to Europe to serve the hatching and breeding community. Jun'ichi further improved the technique and built his company into an absolute market leader in Europe, dispatching the predominantly Japanese chick sexers to destinations all over Europe. In its heyday, Hobo's company would contract up to 150 specialists per season, who would fly all over the continent at short notice to determine the sex of the chicks barely an hour after the eggs were hatched.[33] Waregem became the European foothold of the Nagoya-based All Japan Chick Sexing School. Following the latter's example, the company Hobo C&S bvba even used to organize yearly chick sexing championships until some twelve years ago. Belgium thus became the only country outside Japan organizing such championships.[34]

Although chicken sexing was and remains strongly associated with Japan, there were also Belgian sexers. One was Jozef Vandewalle from Handzame, as it happened a cousin of the present author's father, an accomplished sexer in his own right, and active from the 1950s through the 1980s, although he had never been to Japan. He had seen demonstrations of sexing in Belgium, but his mastery of the technique was largely intuitive, he was a "natural". He worked individually and reputedly made few mistakes. Since he had to be on the spot at a moment's notice, and worked at very irregular times, he slept whenever he could. For that purpose he had a driver who took him to his destination whenever he was called upon. This allowed him to sleep in the car during travel as well as in between assignments. Although a well-paid job, due to the irregular schedules, it was physically taxing. Having a chauffeur was thus no luxury, but in rural Flanders in those days, it was absolutely exceptional, almost outrageous.

Jun'ichi did not neglect timely preparations for the succession of his company. The oldest son, Takashi, who now runs the business with his son Koichi, was sent to Himeji after he had finished his studies in Belgium, to study Japanese. A good working knowledge of the language was and still is essential, given the preponderance of Japanese in the profession. Even today Japanese sexers still represent 35% of the trade, the others being mainly Koreans, but also some Indian, Turkish or European specialists.[35] Jun'ichi's other son Miyoshi runs the restaurant Hobo's in his former house. It serves a unique mix of Japanese and Belgian food. His grandson Koichi runs the stylish pub "Den Hemel" in the centre of Waregem.

Demonstration of an electric chicktester (1952).
Photograph courtesy of Koichi Hobo.

Jun'ichi Hobo.
Photograph courtesy of Hein Vandewalle

For his achievements, Jun'ichi received several awards in various European countries, but the award he was most proud of was the *Order of the Rising Sun*, which he received in November 1986 from the Japanese Prime Minister Nakasone Yasuhiro.[36] Jun'ichi died in 2006, and his wife in 2013, but their offspring carry on the Hobo legacy.

NOTE: the photographs reproduced here were graciously supplied by Takashi and Koichi Hobo, Waregem, and Hein Vandewalle, Handzame.

REFERENCES

Benoit 2016
Geert Benoit. "The Hobo Family: 80 Years of Japanese Innovative Entrepreneurship in Waregem." *Belgium Japan Association Newsletter. Trade Flows & Cultural News, the BJA quarterly newsletter* 110 (March 2016), pp. 12-13.

Gunji 1985
Gunji Sadanori 軍司貞則. *Nihon kabushikigaisha o sodateta otoko: Antowāpu no samurai shōnin* 日本株式会社を育てた男 アントワープのサムライ商人. Tokyo: Bungei shunjū 文芸春秋, 1985.

***Het Nieuwsblad* 2001**
Het Nieuwsblad. "Stukje Japan in Waregem." Interview by Jan Decock with Juni'ichi Hobo and spouse. 17 November 2001.

Hirunagi 2006
Hirunagi Kanjun 蛭薙観順. "Original film of 'Chick Sexing: On the Development and Practise of Baby Chick Sexing Method' Was Found / Eiga 'Shoseisū shiyūkanbetsuhō no hatten to sono fukyū' no orijinaru firumu no hakken" 映画（初生雛雌雄鑑別法の発展とその普及）のオリジナルフィルムの発見. *Nagoya University Museum Bulletin / Nagoya Daigaku Hakubutsukan hōkoku* 名古屋大学博物館報告 22 (2006), pp. 65-72.

Lloyd 1933
E. A. Lloyd. "Canadian Poultry." In *Sexing Baby Chicks*, ed. Kiyoshi Masui, Jurō Hashimoto, and Everton Alexander Lloyd. Vancouver, B.C.: Journal Print. Co., 1933.

Martin 1994
R.D. (Robert Dickson) Martin. *The Specialist Chick Sexer*. Melbourne: Bernal Publishing, 1994.

Nakamura 2006
Nakamura A., Kino K., Minezawa M., Noda K., and Takahashi H. "A Method for Discriminating a Japanese Chicken, the Nagoya Breed, Using Microsatellite Markers." *Poultry Science* 85:12 (2006), p. 2124.

Jozef Vandewalle at a party for people in the hatchery business and their families.
Photograph courtesy of Hein Vandewalle.

Jozef Vandewalle with two of the Hobo children.
Photograph courtesy of Hein Vandewalle.

NOTES

1 This contribution is much indebted to Geert Benoit's interview of Takashi Hobo and his son Koichi Hobo, the son and grandson of Jun'ichi Hobo, published in Benoit 2016.

2 Nakamura 2006.

3 Martin 1994, p. 6.

4 Martin 1994, p. 6.

5 Lloyd 1933.

6 Martin 1994, p. 7.

7 Martin 1994, p. 7.

8 Website of the Japan Livestock Technology Association: http://jlta.lin.gr.jp/chick/history.html.

9 Hirunagi 2006, p. 65.

10 Martin 1994, p. 4.

11 Website of the Japan Livestock Technology Association: http://jlta.lin.gr.jp/chick/history.html.

12 Martin, p. 4.

13 Lloyd 1933.

14 Martin 1994, p. 9.

15 Website of the Japan Livestock Technology Association: http://jlta.lin.gr.jp/chick/history.html.

16 Benoit 2016, pp. 12-13.

17 Lloyd 1933.

18 Website of the Japan Livestock Technology Association: http://jlta.lin.gr.jp/chick/history.html.

19 Martin 1994, p. 11.

20 Gunji 1985, p. 92.

21 Benoit 2016, pp. 12-13.

22 Benoit 2016, pp. 12-13.

23 *Het Nieuwsblad* 2001.

24 Gunji 1985, p. 93.

25 Gunji 1985, p. 113.

26 Benoit 2016, pp. 12-13.

27 Martin 1994, p. 12.

28 Lloyd 1933; Hirunagi 2006, p. 72.

29 Hirunagi 2006, p. 71.

30 Hirunagi 2006, p. 71.

31 Benoit 2016, pp. 12-13.

32 *Het Nieuwsblad* 2001.

33 Benoit 2016, pp. 12-13.

34 Benoit 2016, pp. 12-13.

35 Benoit 2016, pp. 12-13 and information supplied by Koichi Hobo.

36 Benoit 2016, pp. 12-13.

Diploma conferring the Order of the Rising Sun, fifth class gold and silver rays, on Jun'ichi Hobo (1986).

Photograph courtesy of Koichi Hobo.

POST-WAR BELGIAN-JAPANESE TRADE AND INVESTMENT RELATIONS

Henri Delanghe

JAPAN & BELGIUM
An Itinerary of Mutual Inspiration

Assembly plant for motorcycles in Honda Belgium in Aalst,
Japan's first industrial plant in Belgium, early 1960s.
Courtesy of Honda Motor Europe Logistics N.V.

Front view of the factory building of Honda Belgium in Aalst, 1963.
Courtesy of Honda Motor Europe Logistics N.V.

POST-WAR BELGIAN-JAPANESE TRADE AND INVESTMENT RELATIONS[1]

This contribution provides a brief overview of post-war economic relations between Belgium and Japan. These are two very different economies. They are far from each other in geographical terms and oriented in the first place towards their own regional economy, Belgium to the EU and Japan to East and Southeast Asia. The Belgian economy is not very large, whether looked at from a global or a European perspective, while Japan is the second economy in Asia and the third at the global level.[2] The Belgian economy is one of the world's most open economies, open to imports as well as to foreign direct investment, while the same cannot be said of Japan.

In relative quantitative terms, the bilateral economic relations of Belgium and Japan are not very important to either country. But there is an importance to Belgian companies in being active in Japan, and to Japanese companies in being active in Belgium, that the raw figures do not bring out. Being active in Japan has feedback effects for Belgian companies that benefit domestic operations and operations overseas elsewhere, while for Japanese companies being active in Belgium offers a convenient exploratory point of access to the European market where high-value-added activities can be deployed. Furthermore, since relations are rather low key and not politicized, they offer a good insight into structural dynamics.

The specific focus of this chapter is on bilateral trade and investment relations, and the institutional infrastructure supporting them. So the focus is on Belgian exports to and imports from Japan, as well as Belgian direct investment in Japan, and Japanese direct investment in Belgium. To the extent possible, we provide a comprehensive quantitative picture of the trade and investment flows between the two countries. We also try to say something about the drivers behind these flows, and discuss major trends. This means that nothing is said about, for instance, migration, and that an issue like science and technology is only discussed to the extent that it interacts with trade and investment. The emphasis is also on the second half of the post-war period. The first half of the post-war period will only be treated very briefly as this period has already been analysed in detail elsewhere.[3]

The first part of this chapter then contains a brief discussion of the first part of the post-war period. The second part focuses on the period since the late 1970s. The first section of this second part consists of a discussion of the size, composition and macro- as well as micro-drivers of Belgian-Japanese trade. This is followed by a review of Belgian-Japanese investment relations, focusing first on Belgian investment in Japan and next on Japanese investment in Belgium. In the third section, something is said about the institutional infrastructure supporting Belgian-Japanese trade and investment relations. In the third and final part of this chapter, some concluding observations are offered.

The First Half of the Post-war Period[4]

In the early post-war period, the development of Belgian exports to Japan was hampered by a lack of interest, institutional obstacles, and a lack of trade complementarity. In line with the protectionist policy inheritance from the 1930s depression era, the early post-war period was characterized by a substantial degree of state involvement in foreign trade. Like the private Belgian export community, however, the Belgian state was not very interested in developing Belgian exports to Japan, oriented as it was in the first place towards Europe and Africa. Neither was Japan interested in promoting Belgian imports, sticking as it did, with American support, to a rigidly protectionist policy until at least the 1960s.[5] Even if there had been genuine mutual interest in promoting Belgian exports to Japan, this would have been hampered by the substantial bureaucracy resulting from mutual concerns about bilaterally balanced trade, the balance of payments, and foreign exchange shortages.[6] Several false starts were made. The so-called Beltrade Memorandum that Belgium signed in August 1947 was never implemented, and the commercial agreement reached in July 1949 proved unworkable. The revised commercial agreement reached in August 1950, although renewed until 1959, was implemented in an atmosphere of profound mutual suspicion, and from 1957 onward the Japanese government considered its principle of bilaterally balanced trade a dead letter. But perhaps the main problem affecting the development of Belgian exports to Japan consisted of a lack of trade complementarity. Japan was interested mainly in importing fuels, food products and mineral resources, goods which Belgium could not easily provide.[7] The end result was that Belgium did not at an early stage establish a firm presence in the Japanese market, and was unable to capture so-called first mover advantages.

The picture differed when it came to Belgian imports from Japan. Japan was eager to develop its exports to Belgium, but Belgium was rather wary of these. The pre-war Belgian experience of competing with Japan was highly negative, especially in the field of cotton textiles, for which Japan became the world's largest exporter in the 1930s, overtaking Great Britain.[8] As cotton textiles were once more a large share of Japanese exports in the early post-war period, and the Belgian colonies started importing large quantities of them, Belgium again began to harbour the same fears. This was one of the main reasons why Belgium, while formally aligning itself with the US aim of bringing Japan into the non-communist fold, was highly reluctant, as were other European nations, to provide Japan with unrestricted GATT membership.[9] The irony was, however, that at the very

moment that Japanese cotton textile exports were everywhere being restricted, Japan was already losing competitiveness in this area and shifting to exports from heavy industries.

The result was that Belgian exports to Japan reached a rather limited 2.8 billion Belgian francs in 1968 (increasing to 6.3 billion Belgian francs in 1976), while in the same year Belgian imports from Japan reached 3.5 billion Belgian francs (increasing to 21.5 billion Belgian francs in 1976). But Belgian-Japanese trade was not in deficit from the very beginning of the post-war period. Until 1960 it is best to make a clear distinction between trade between the Belgian-Luxembourg Economic Union (BLEU) and Japan on the one hand, and trade between Congo, Rwanda and Burundi and Japan on the other. The latter was in constant deficit, centring on colonial imports of Japanese textiles. The former was in surplus until the end of 1961 (Fig. 1). In the 1950s, Belgian exports to Japan centred on raw materials. In the 1960s, a shift was noticeable from chemical products and raw materials to manufactured products, machinery and transport machinery, and diamonds. In the 1950s, Belgian imports from Japan consisted mainly of wood, canned fish and textiles, while in the 1960s food products, raw materials, and oils and fats became less important, the share of textiles remained constant, and chemical products, as well as machinery and transport machinery, increased to varying extents, smaller in the former case, greater in the latter.

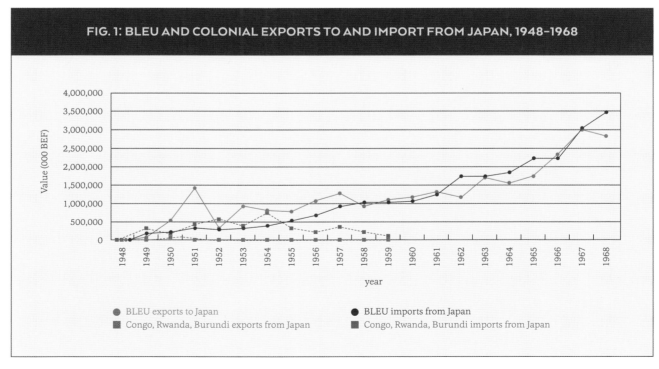

FIG. 1: BLEU AND COLONIAL EXPORTS TO AND IMPORT FROM JAPAN, 1948–1968

● BLEU exports to Japan
■ Congo, Rwanda, Burundi exports from Japan
● BLEU imports from Japan
■ Congo, Rwanda, Burundi imports from Japan

Data: Van Laer (2004)

The Second Half of the Post-war Period

Belgian-Japanese Trade Relations

Over the course of the post-war period, the importance of international trade to the world economy and to individual economies has grown significantly. In 2014, Belgium was the world's ninth most trade-intensive country, with trade in goods and services amounting to 165 per cent of GDP. Both export and import intensities are high for Belgium. In 2014, exports of goods and services amounted to 83.6 per cent of GDP, while imports of goods and services amounted to 81.7 per cent of GDP. This high trade intensity causes Belgium to account for shares of world exports and imports that are much larger than its share of the world economy. In 2014, Belgium was the world's thirteenth largest exporter and the world's twelfth largest importer.[10]

Japan is somewhat less of a trading nation. In 2013, Japan was the seventh *least* trade-intensive country in the world with trade in goods and services amounting to a mere 35 per cent of GDP. Export as well as import intensities are rather low for Japan. In 2013, exports of goods and services accounted for 16.2 per cent of GDP, while imports accounted for 19.0 per cent of GDP. In spite of this low trade intensity, Japan accounts for substantial shares of world exports and imports, and this because of the large absolute size of its economy. In 2013, Japan was the world's sixth largest exporter and the world's fourth largest importer.[11]

Bilateral trade relations are not overly important to either Belgium or Japan. In 2014, Japan was Belgium's nineteenth largest client and Belgium's twelfth largest supplier.[12] On the other hand, in 2014, Belgium was only Japan's twenty-fourth largest export market, taking 0.8 per cent of total exports, and its thirty-sixth largest supplier, providing 0.3 per cent of total imports.[13]

In spite of this relative unimportance of bilateral trade relations, a brief quantitative case study of Belgian-Japanese trade relations in the period 1988-2014 points to an interesting dynamic.

Fig. 2 shows the value of Belgian-Japanese trade over the period 1979-2014 in both Japanese Yen (1979-2014) and ECU/EUR (1988-2014). The value of the trade in Japanese Yen is plotted on the vertical axis on the left of the figure while the value of the trade in ECU/EUR is plotted on the vertical axis on the right of the figure. Showing the value of Belgian-Japanese trade in both Japanese Yen and ECU/EUR is interesting since it shows exchange rate effects clearly.

Between 1979 and 2014, the value of Belgian exports to Japan increased rather moderately in relative terms and remained rather small in absolute terms (in 2014, EUR 3.1 billion) (Fig. 2). This increase was rather gradual and sustained, with little variation around the trend.

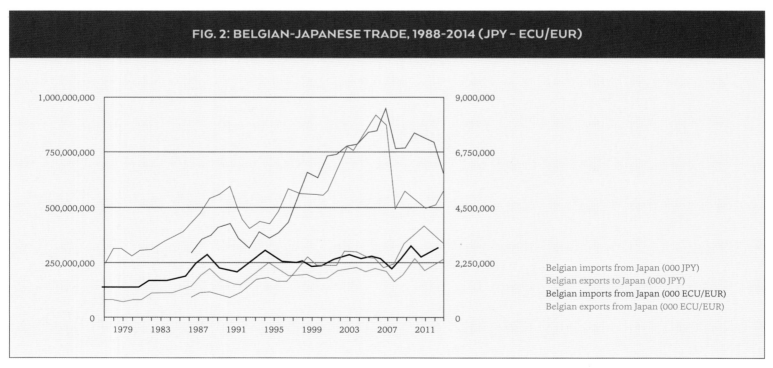

FIG. 2: BELGIAN-JAPANESE TRADE, 1988-2014 (JPY – ECU/EUR)

Belgian imports from Japan (000 JPY)
Belgian exports to Japan (000 JPY)
Belgian imports from Japan (000 ECU/EUR)
Belgian exports from Japan (000 ECU/EUR)

Data: Japanese Ministry of Finance; Belgian Foreign Trade Agency
Note: Figures in ECU/EUR: 1988-1998: Figures for Belgium and Luxembourg (BLEU), 000 ECU; 1999-2014: Figures for Belgium, 000 EUR

Since 2012, the value of exports has been decreasing somewhat.

The value of Belgian imports from Japan had reached a much higher level in absolute terms by 2014 (EUR 5.9 billion) (Fig. 2). There was also more variation around the trend, with a period of slow growth succeeded by periods of more rapid growth and significant decline.
The logical result of the fact that Belgian imports from Japan far exceed Belgian exports to Japan is that Belgium runs a trade deficit that, after increasing for a long time because of the more rapid increase in imports than in exports, is now sharply decreasing because of the more rapid decrease in imports than in exports.

The nature of Belgian-Japanese trade, and in particular that of Belgian exports to Japan, has changed considerably over time (Tables 1 and 2). In 1988, precious metals and stones (59.98%), chemicals (11.93%) and base metals (4.77%) were the top three export products, together accounting for about 77 per cent of Belgian exports to Japan. By 2014, however, the share of precious metals and stones had dropped to a mere 1.65 per cent of exports. That of chemicals had increased significantly to no less than 48.28 per cent of exports. Chemicals were

then followed by various categories of equipment and instruments (transport equipment (9.13%), machinery and equipment (8.78%) and optical instruments (8.40%)) together accounting for about 26 per cent of exports. Interesting is the case of foodstuffs, the share of which increased from 2.18 per cent in 1988 to 7.08 per cent in 2014 and the value from ECU 18.1 million to EUR 216.7 million.

Within both established and newly emerging export product categories, products that are less bulky but more knowledge-intensive are increasingly being exported. Such knowledge-intensive Belgian exports to Japan include, for instance, diagnostic kits for the detection of human enteric pathologies and respiratory diseases; reagents and kits for academic research and the pharmaceutical industry; innovative and high-performance complementary metal oxide semiconductor (CMOS) imagers characterized by large numbers of pixels, large area, high frame rates, and high dynamic range; software products and information systems for environmental monitoring and control; and vision and inspection solutions in semiconductor back-end and electronic assembly applications.[14]

TABLE 1: COMPOSITION OF BELGIAN EXPORTS TO JAPAN, 1988 (000 ECU, %)

Precious metals and stones	498,161.4	59.98%
Chemicals	99,062.0	11.93%
Base metals	39,630.3	4.77%
Transport equipment	38,267.6	4.61%
Machinery and equipment	37,859.2	4.56%
Textiles	37,420.7	4.51%
Foodstuffs	18,114.3	2.18%
Plastics	13,079.2	1.57%
Stone, plaster, cement	11,857.2	1.43%
Paper and paperboard	9,406.3	1.13%
Vegetable products	5,679.7	0.68%
Live animals	5,237.8	0.63%
Mineral products	5,170.5	0.62%
Miscellaneous manufactured articles	3,356.7	0.40%
Optical instruments	2,571.6	0.31%
Footwear, headgear, etc.	2,173.7	0.26%
Works of art	1,644.4	0.20%
Raw hides, skins, leather, etc.	1,522.7	0.18%
Arms and ammunition	244.5	0.03%
Fats and oils (animal or vegetable)	70.0	0.01%
Wood	64.9	0.01%
Non-classified articles	15.3	0.00%
	830,609.9	100.00%

TABLE 2: COMPOSITION OF BELGIAN EXPORTS TO JAPAN, 2014 (000 EUR, %)

Chemicals	1,476,990.6	48.28%
Transport equipment	279,222.0	9.13%
Machinery and equipment	268,668.9	8.78%
Optical instruments	256,853.0	8.40%
Foodstuffs	216,697.3	7.08%
Mineral products	152,134.4	4.97%
Plastics	105,048.6	3.43%
Base metals	67,203.6	2.20%
Precious metals and stones	50,540.5	1.65%
Textiles	49,123.9	1.61%
Non-classified articles	32,493.5	1.06%
Vegetable products	24,794.0	0.81%
Live animals	19,878.1	0.65%
Raw hides, skins, leather, etc.	19,830.2	0.65%
Stone, plaster, cement	15,517.0	0.51%
Wood	8,196.2	0.27%
Miscellaneous manufactured articles	6,948.6	0.23%
Paper and paperboard	3,657.8	0.12%
Footwear, headgear, etc.	3,639.2	0.12%
Works of art	1,013.3	0.03%
Fats and oils (animal or vegetable)	891.5	0.03%
Arms and ammunition	150.2	0.00%
	3,059,492.5	100.00%

Data: Belgian Foreign Trade Agency

Another major trend is the growth of Belgian exports of services to Japan, resulting in a fading of the borders between trade and investment. Two examples will illustrate this. It used to be the case that Japanese companies themselves undertook large investments in Belgium in fields such as logistics and distribution, or research and development, adding to the stock of Japanese foreign direct investment (FDI) in Belgium. Increasingly, however, Japanese companies contract these kinds of activities out to specialized Belgian companies, on a shorter or longer term basis, thus adding to Belgian exports to Japan. One example is provided by Katoen Natie taking responsibility for European logistics and distribution activities for several Japanese companies. Another example is provided by the Inter-university Micro-Electronics Centre (IMEC) collaborating with Japanese companies in the development of microelectronics, nanotechnology, and information and communication technology (ICT).[15]

The composition of Belgian imports from Japan has remained rather more stable (Tables 3 and 4). All product categories appearing in the top six in 1988 appear in the top six in 2014 as well. The top two import products, transport equipment and machinery and equipment have remained the same, though their combined share has decreased from about 80 per cent of imports in 1988 to about 64 per cent in 2014. The share of optical instruments has increased somewhat and that of base metals has decreased somewhat, while the shares of chemicals and plastics have increased significantly (both times 3.6).

A number of factors at the macro-level drive the development of Belgian-Japanese trade. Two basic preconditions for the continued existence and development of bilateral trade are the existence of some degree of complementarity — a company in country X has a product on offer which a company or consumer in country Y needs — and of some degree of international competitiveness — the company in country X can provide this product at a lower price, a higher quality, or both, than a company in country Z. Given the aforementioned bilateral trade pattern these two basic preconditions appear to have been met.

In the short term, however, the competitiveness of a country's companies and export products is often

TABLE 3: COMPOSITION OF BELGIAN IMPORTS FROM JAPAN, 1988 (000 ECU, %)

Transport equipment	1,136,952.2	43.18%
Machinery and equipment	959,335.5	36.43%
Optical instruments	124,731.2	4.74%
Chemicals	106,552.7	4.05%
Base metals	82,412.0	3.13%
Plastics	73,513.5	2.79%
Precious metals and stones	41,472.8	1.58%
Stone, plaster, cement	28,381.6	1.08%
Miscellaneous manufactured articles	24,591.3	0.93%
Textiles	20,434.4	0.78%
Paper and paperboard	16,529.6	0.63%
Foodstuffs	6,395.2	0.24%
Fats and oils (animal or vegetable)	2,518.8	0.10%
Mineral products	2,489.7	0.09%
Works of art	1,997.2	0.08%
Arms and ammunition	1,421.7	0.05%
Live animals	946.5	0.04%
Raw hides, skins, leather, etc.	763.2	0.03%
Vegetable products	760.8	0.03%
Footwear, headgear, etc.	545.6	0.02%
Wood	293.2	0.01%
Non-classified articles		
	2,633,038.5	100.00%

TABLE 4: COMPOSITION OF BELGIAN IMPORTS FROM JAPAN, 2014 (000 EUR, %)

Transport equipment	1,975,650.5	33.26%
Machinery and equipment	1,854,499.4	31.22%
Chemicals	867,261.2	14.60%
Plastics	597,082.4	10.05%
Optical instruments	336,144.7	5.66%
Base metals	108,512.8	1.83%
Stone, plaster, cement	68,157.4	1.15%
Textiles	32,945.1	0.55%
Non-classified articles	19,788.1	0.33%
Miscellaneous manufactured articles	18,402.4	0.31%
Precious metals and stones	12,514.2	0.21%
Arms and ammunition	9,763.8	0.16%
Mineral products	9,078.7	0.15%
Footwear, headgear, etc.	6,785.5	0.11%
Works of art	5,414.9	0.09%
Foodstuffs	4,927.9	0.08%
Paper and paperboard	4,516.8	0.08%
Vegetable products	4,276.6	0.07%
Live animals	2,757.8	0.05%
Fats and oils (animal or vegetable)	684.0	0.01%
Raw hides, skins, leather, etc.	332.2	0.01%
Wood	317.7	0.01%
	5,939,813.9	100.00%

Data: Belgian Foreign Trade Agency

dependent to a significant extent on the bilateral exchange rate. The normal expectation is that, other things being equal, the strengthening of a country's currency will reduce that country's exports (having a negative impact on the competitiveness of a company in one country versus a company elsewhere) and increase its imports, while the weakening of a country's currency will have the reverse effect. It cannot be denied that the bilateral exchange rate has affected Belgian-Japanese trade to a certain extent, though not always in the predicted way. The strengthening of the yen (*endaka*), for instance, does not appear to have had the hoped for positive effect on Belgian exports to Japan. Some 70 per cent of respondents to a 1995 Belgium-Japan Association and Chamber of Commerce in Belgium (BJA) business survey, for instance, reported that *endaka* had not had a positive effect on exports to Japan. The BJA itself ascribed this to the fact that highly specialized exports, which account for most of Belgian exports to Japan, are not that sensitive to changes in the bilateral exchange rate, and to the fact that any positive effect conferred by the *endaka* on Belgian exporters to Japan would effectively be neutralized by exporters from other countries enjoying the same benefit.[16]

Once the two basic preconditions are met, and making abstraction of the exchange rate, the first determinant of the long-term development of bilateral trade is *market size* (the benefits of which are multiplied the more homogenous the market is, such as is the case for Japan). The size of each market increases with the rate of growth of each economy, which is determined by the business cycle. Belgian-Japanese trade has been affected by recessions. Examples are the bursting of the Japanese bubble in the late 1980s, the Japanese recessions of the second half of the 1990s and the first half of the 2000s, and the global economic-financial crisis starting in 2008.

The second determinant of the long-term development of bilateral trade is market access. Ever since the establishment of GATT shortly after the Second World War, a number of trade liberalization rounds have been held. These have contributed to the gradual reduction of tariff barriers, thus contributing to an increase in bilateral trade. In a 1995 BJA business survey, for instance, 50.7 per cent of respondents reported having experienced obstacles in their relations with Japan; but tariffs or taxes accounted for only 6 per cent of these obstacles.[17] In a 2001 BJA business survey, 63 per cent of respondents reported experiencing any particular

obstacles when doing business with Japan. Import duties accounted for 10 per cent of these obstacles.[18] In a 2005 BJA business survey, 45.3 per cent of companies experienced problems with respect to exporting to Japan. 5.8 per cent of respondent companies pointed to customs duties, indicating some progress in this respect.[19]

Non-tariff barriers accounted for 86 per cent of the obstacles to Belgian exports to Japan identified by 50.7 per cent of the respondents to a 1995 BJA business survey. The category of non-tariff barriers covers a wide range of possible obstacles to Belgian exports to Japan including Japanese habits and language, local specifications, the local distribution system, local packaging requirements, etc. While Japanese habits and language ranked top in the BJA survey (119 out of 306 answers), local specifications and the local distribution system shared an important second place (67 and 66 answers respectively), with local packaging requirements constituting a sizeable third (32 answers).[20] These figures were largely confirmed by the aforementioned 2001 BJA business survey. In a 2005 BJA business survey, 20.1 per cent of the respondent companies pointed to language as an obstacle, 14.4 per cent to technical standards, 12.2 per cent to business customs, 11.5 per cent to culture and 10.1 per cent to regulations.[21]

The keys to Belgian companies' successes in Japan are a good product, good communication to find out the final customers' needs, and commitment to respond to those needs. A Belgian company wishing to export to Japan needs first of all to have a good quality product to offer. Sometimes the company is lucky enough to be able to export this product to Japan without having to modify it for the Japanese market, usually when it is a highly differentiated product like fashion or specialty beers.[22] Then it just has to make sure that its defect rate approaches zero as the Japanese market is very unforgiving in this regard. In the food industry, this means meeting extreme requirements in terms of visual attractiveness.[23] In both the food and pharmaceutical industries, there are strict government product safety standards to be met, often perceived as overly rigidly enforced and giving rise to long delays.[24] More often than not, adaptation is required, if not of the product itself then of its packaging in the broadest sense. In the case of coffee, for instance, this means adapting the coffee blend, in the case of pharmaceuticals, producing smaller dosages, and in the case of steel wire, producing diamond mesh instead of square mesh, or changing the wire diameter.[25] A Belgian company wishing to export to Japan will also have to meet stringent requirements in terms of before- and after-sale service, packaging, and delivery.[26]

Being active on the very demanding Japanese market, and having to meet all these stringent requirements, has important feedback effects for Belgian companies. For instance, having to approach a zero defect rate for the Japanese market, and therefore having to reorganize one's production system, but then being able to apply the lessons learnt to the production for other markets, has obvious benefits. The same goes for having to improve the quality of packaging for the Japanese market.[27] The same can also be said of being forced by Japanese customers to be able to deliver flexibly. In the case of L. De Schouwer, a seller of *witloof* (a special strain of chicory grown in Belgium), the requirements of Japanese customers forced a venture into production methods that would otherwise not have been explored.[28] Finally, there is the most generic feedback effect of being active in a regionally oriented, highly competitive "benchmark" market, and being forced to carry out R&D and upgrade products not only to increase market share but even simply to maintain it.[29] In the 1995 BJA business survey, "product development" was the by far most quoted "adaptation necessary to face Japanese competition".[30]

"Communication" with the Japanese market can be facilitated by proactive Japanese importers and distributors, always on the lookout for a new business opportunity. Casual evidence of the use of such intermediaries is often found in the testimonies of Belgian companies.[31] But the 1995 BJA business survey quoted above also offers more systematic evidence on this practice. Import/export companies are by far the most marked "intermediary to start contacts," being marked 151 times, as compared to 88 for colleagues, 32 for consultants and 31 for Japanese distributors.[32] These intermediaries offer the final customer a Japanese language counterpart, and instil trust with regard to quality and supply guarantees.[33] They also assist in carefully targeted marketing towards the right segment in a difficult and fickle market.[34] Within the context of a notoriously difficult and expensive distribution network, they help with (flexible) distribution through their own networks, but at a price.[35]

In their dealings with the Japanese market, many Belgian companies rapidly move along a learning curve.

Initially they may operate through an importer or distributor. Then they may gradually take on more responsibility by establishing their own liaison offices and organizing their own sales. Similar curves are also seen as far as production is concerned. Production may initially be organized on a joint venture basis but afterwards be taken on as a sole responsibility.[36]

But whether one works through sales or production partners or organizes sales and production by oneself, it is necessary to invest in communication. That first of all means having Belgian staff knowledgeable in Japanese. Some of the most successful Belgian companies in Japan, such as Innogenetics or Barco, have made that kind of investment. More often than not the European Commission's Executive Training Programme (ETP) plays an important role.[37] A very useful role is also played by the Japanese Ministry of Education scholarships. Belgian companies also have to be willing to provide frequent training and demonstrations to importers, distributors and final customers, as well as paying frequent visits to and hosting frequent visits from Japan, and participating in Japanese fairs.[38]

Belgian-Japanese Investment Relations

The discussion of Belgian-Japanese investment relations cannot be completely divorced from that of Belgian-Japanese trade. Trade and foreign direct investment are quite closely related to each other. Continued exports to a particular market, for instance, can eventually result in the establishment of a local sales office or production facility. In turn the establishment of a local production facility can give rise to increased imports of, for instance, specialized machinery and equipment. More complex possible links between trade and investment also exist. A good example is that of Bekaert, which started exporting to Japan as a result of an affiliate of a Japanese company in Belgium becoming familiar with its products.[39] As already described above, because of outsourcing in, for instance, the logistics and R&D fields, the borders between trade and FDI are also fading.

Before starting a more in-depth discussion of bilateral investment relations, it is important to note how different an attitude both countries have when it comes to foreign direct investment.

Belgium has always been very open to foreign direct investment. In the pre-crisis period 2005-207, Belgium

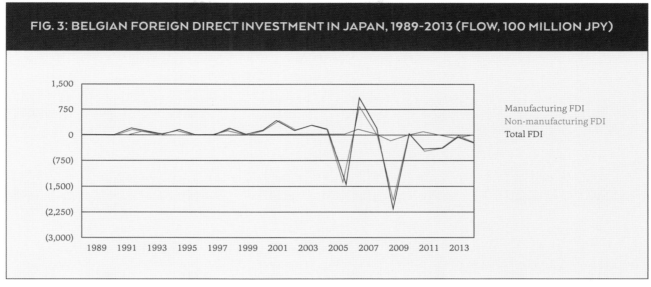

FIG. 3: BELGIAN FOREIGN DIRECT INVESTMENT IN JAPAN, 1989-2013 (FLOW, 100 MILLION JPY)

Source: Japanese Ministry of Finance

received on average US$ 62 billion of inward FDI per year, amounting to 10.5 per cent of EU inward FDI, 6.8 per cent of developed economy inward FDI, and 4.5 per cent of global inward FDI, so much more than warranted by the size of the Belgian economy. In 2014, the inward FDI stock accounted for 98.3 per cent of GDP.[40]

Japan, on the other hand, is not very open to foreign direct investment. In the pre-crisis period 2005-2007, Japan received on average US$ 6 billion of inward FDI per year, amounting to 0.7 per cent of developed economy inward FDI, and 0.4 per cent of global inward FDI, so much less than warranted by the size of the Japanese economy.[41]

Belgian Foreign Direct Investment in Japan

Belgian Foreign Direct Investment in Japan remained at a very limited scale before the year 2000, took on a certain scale in the first few years of the twenty-first century, and has fluctuated heavily since 2004 marked by a sharp investment peak in 2006 and deep disinvestment peaks in 2005 and 2008 (Fig. 3). Belgian Foreign Direct Investment in Japan has been driven mainly by non-manufacturing investment in sectors such as wholesale and retail, finance and insurance, and services. Manufacturing investment focused on sectors such as chemicals and pharmaceuticals; iron, non-ferrous, and metals; and transportation equipment.

Japanese Foreign Direct Investment in Belgium

The value of Japanese Foreign Direct Investment in Belgium has always been substantially higher than that of Belgian Foreign Direct Investment in Japan. It reached a first peak in 1994 and a higher one in 2002 but has since been marked by significant instability including substantial disinvestment in 2007-2008 and 2012-2013 (Fig. 4).

Unlike Belgian Foreign Direct Investment in Japan, Japanese Foreign Direct Investment in Belgium has not been mainly non-manufacturing. Quite the contrary, manufacturing investment has been predominant, in particular since the year 2000. Manufacturing investment has been diversified, focusing on sectors as different as food, chemicals and pharmaceuticals, general machinery, electric machinery, transportation equipment, rubber and leather, glass and ceramics, and precision machinery. Non-manufacturing investment has been more concentrated, focusing on such sectors as wholesale and retail, finance and insurance, services, and transportation.

A 2012 JETRO survey provided an interesting overview of Japanese manufacturing Foreign Direct Investment in Belgium since 1979.[42] The number of Japanese manufacturing affiliates in Belgium increased quite rapidly from 18 in 1979 to 60 in 1992, reached a peak of 63 in 1996, and then started declining to reach 43 in

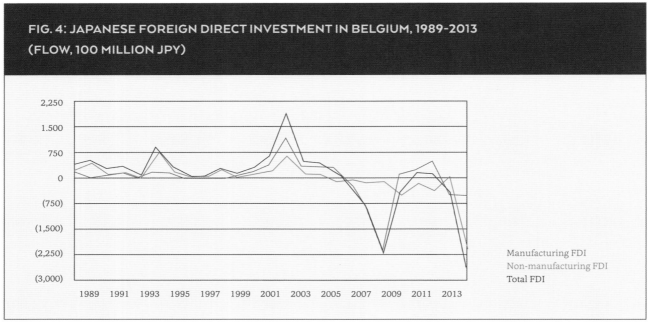

FIG. 4: JAPANESE FOREIGN DIRECT INVESTMENT IN BELGIUM, 1989-2013
(FLOW, 100 MILLION JPY)

Manufacturing FDI
Non-manufacturing FDI
Total FDI

Source: Japanese Ministry of Finance

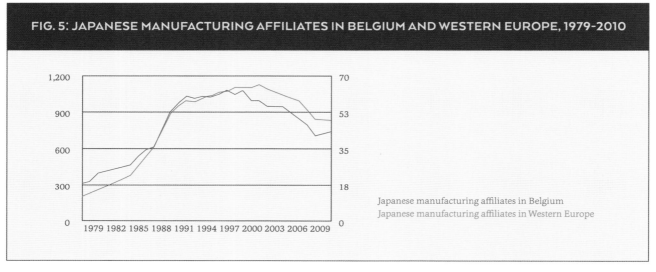

FIG. 5: JAPANESE MANUFACTURING AFFILIATES IN BELGIUM AND WESTERN EUROPE, 1979-2010

Japanese manufacturing affiliates in Belgium
Japanese manufacturing affiliates in Western Europe

Data: JETRO 2012

2010 (number of Japanese manufacturing affiliates in Belgium plotted on the vertical axis on the right of Fig. 5). While in 1979, Belgium accounted for about 10 per cent of the number of Japanese manufacturing affiliates in Western Europe, that percentage had dropped to about 5 per cent by 2010 (number of Japanese manufacturing affiliates in Western Europe plotted on the vertical axis on the left of Fig. 5). By that time, survey respondents considered China, Russia and India to be the most promising countries as production bases in the mid to long term. For Western Europe, they referred to problems such as high labour costs, exchange rate fluctuations, lower prices offered by competitors, and the European economic downturn stemming from the Euro financial crisis.

In 2010, 7 Japanese manufacturing affiliates were active in chemical/petrochemical products, 7 in plastic products, 5 in electric and electronic machinery, 4 in pharmaceutical products, 4 in transportation machinery parts (automobiles, motorcycles), 3 in ceramics, soil and stone, 3 in electric and electronic parts, 2 in food products, agricultural and fisheries product processing, 2 in rubber products, 2 in other manufacturing, 1 in paper and pulp, 1 in metal products (including plated products), 1 in general machinery (including moulds and machinery tools), and 1 in precision machinery. Belgium is significantly more important in a number of specific industries than it is in overall terms. Thus Belgium accounts for 18.4 per cent of Japanese affiliates in Western Europe in plastic products, 14.3 per cent of those in paper and pulp, 14.3 per cent of those in ceramics, soil and stone, 13.3 per cent of those in pharmaceutical products, and 13.3 per cent of those in rubber products. It is no surprise that these are areas of traditional Belgian strength. To a growing extent, Japanese companies carry out R&D in Belgium. In 2010, JETRO counted no less than twenty-five Japanese R&D/design centres in Belgium, of which ten were stand-alone centres.

Japanese companies invest in Belgium for a number of reasons.[43] Its points of attraction include its central geographical location combined with its excellent domestic infrastructure and international transport links (roads, railways, ports, airports) with the rest of Europe and globally; its strategic importance (proximity to the European institutions and Eurocontrol, NATO, EU-wide lobbying organizations, other multinationals, companies in the same sector); its easy access to international staff and high-quality professionals including legal and financial advisors, marketing and advertising experts, IT and logistics support, recruitment specialists, translation services; its relative neutrality as a small country; its political stability; and its overall economic stability and attractive business environment including EU and Eurozone membership.

The quality of the Belgian labour force is also highly appreciated, in particular the fact that it is generally well-educated and highly skilled, has a good work ethic and high productivity, has a generally open attitude, including as regards Japanese management methods such as *Kaizen* and Quality Circles, and is multilingual. The quality of Belgium's science and technology institutions is also emphasized.

Another asset is the high quality of life for Japanese expatriates, which includes, among other attractions, a multicultural environment including the common use of English, a safe environment, excellent educational and healthcare systems, excellent food and leisure opportunities, Japanese shops, restaurants and schools, good transport and telecommunication links, and relatively low real estate and rental prices.

Japanese companies also benefit from government support such as fiscal incentives, including the notional interest deduction and tax cuts for R&D personnel, direct grant support including for R&D (e.g. IWT), etc.

Points of attention include Belgium's complicated political structure, administrative burdens (e.g. time sometimes required to obtain environmental permits or work permits for Japanese staff), high labour costs (though a number of companies explicitly state that this is offset by the quality of the workforce and the logistic advantages) and high levels of taxation.

Institutional Infrastructure

Belgian-Japanese trade and investment relations have been supported by two basic kinds of mechanisms, some of an ad hoc nature and some more sustained. To start with those of an ad hoc nature, there are first of all the trade missions, many of which have taken place in the post-war period. Perhaps more eye-catching, however, are the World's Fairs. Two in particular stand out: the 1958 Brussels Expo and the Japan World Exposition at Osaka in 1970.

Other mechanisms are of a more permanent nature. Public institutions play an important role. On the Belgian side, there is a whole range of institutions. There has been quite substantial change over the past few years, especially since the gradual devolution of trade and investment policy. One agency still remains at the federal level (Agency for Foreign Trade – Belgische Dienst voor Buitenlandse Handel – Agence pour le Commerce Extérieur – AFT/ABH/ACE). The weight, however, has shifted to the regional level with its own trade and investment organizations. In Flanders, there are Export Vlaanderen for trade and the Flanders Foreign Investment Office (FFIO) for FDI, in Wallonia, the Agence Wallonne à L'Exportation (AWEX) for trade and the Office for Foreign Investors (OFI) for FDI, and in the capital, Brussels Export for trade and the Brussels Enterprise Agency for FDI. Each region's trade and FDI organizations collaborate increasingly closely with one another (or are even expected to merge). These bodies have taken an ever more pro-active approach, organizing international trade fairs, multi-industry or sector-based trade missions and promotion weeks in foreign countries, providing information, advice and training (personalized or collective), and offering financial incentives. On the Japanese side, there is JETRO. At the international level there is the European Commission with its long-term ETP programme and its shorter-term Gateway to Japan programme.[44] Private organizations include the Belgium-Japan Association & Chamber of Commerce (BJA) and the Belgian-Luxembourg Chamber of Commerce in Japan (BLCCJ). The respondents to a 1995 BJA business survey mentioned as their "main source of information concerning Japan" when starting business with Japan, the Belgian and Japanese embassies, the BJA, the Belgian federal and regional government agencies dealing with foreign trade, and the Japan External Trade Organization (JETRO).

Conclusion

Belgium and Japan are two very different economies. They are far from each other in geographical terms. They are oriented in the first place towards their own regional economy. The Belgian economy is not very large while Japan is the second economy in Asia and the third at the global level. The Belgian economy is one of the world's most trade-intensive economies and one of the world's most open economies in terms of foreign direct investment, while the same cannot be said of Japan. The bilateral economic relations between Belgium and Japan are not very important in relative terms or in terms of absolute quantity. Over the course of the post-war period, trade relations have intensified gradually – Belgian imports from Japan more so than Belgian exports to Japan – though recent years have been marked by a weakening of bilateral trade due mainly to the global economic-financial and Euro crises. The composition of Belgian exports to Japan has changed significantly over time while that of Belgian imports from Japan has remained rather stable. Japanese foreign direct investment in Belgium, which is focused mainly on manufacturing, is more substantial than Belgian foreign direct investment in Japan, which is focused mainly on non-manufacturing. Both types of investment reached peaks in the early and middle 2000s but have been marked by substantial disinvestment in recent

years, again mainly as a result of the global economic-financial and Euro crises, as well as the prospects offered by the Chinese market.

REFERENCES

BFTA 2015
Belgian Foreign Trade Agency (BFTA). *Belgium & Japan*. Brussels: Belgian Foreign Trade Agency, 2015.

BJA 1995
Belgium-Japan Association & Chamber of Commerce (BJA). *Doing Business with Japan, Presentation Made by Mr J.A. Moorkens, Vice-President of BJA and President of the Business Committee, on 8th November 1995 in the Conrad Hotel – Brussels*. Brussels: Belgium-Japan Association & Chamber of Commerce, 1995.

BJA 1997
Belgium-Japan Association & Chamber of Commerce (BJA). *Export to Japan – 20 Belgian Success Stories*. Brussels: Belgium-Japan Association & Chamber of Commerce, 1997.

BJA 2000
Belgium-Japan Association & Chamber of Commerce (BJA). *The Experience of 20 Japanese Companies in Belgium*. Brussels: Belgium-Japan Association & Chamber of Commerce, 2000.

BJA 2003
Belgium-Japan Association & Chamber of Commerce (BJA). *Export to Japan – 20 Belgian Success Stories – Part 2*. Brussels: Belgium-Japan Association & Chamber of Commerce, 2003.

BJA 2005
Belgium-Japan Association & Chamber of Commerce (BJA). *Export to Japan Survey 2005*. Brussels: Belgium-Japan Association & Chamber of Commerce, 2005.

BJA 2006
Belgium-Japan Association & Chamber of Commerce (BJA). *The Experience of 20 Japanese Companies in Belgium – 2006*. Brussels: Belgium-Japan Association & Chamber of Commerce, 2006.

BJA 2012
Belgium-Japan Association & Chamber of Commerce (BJA). *The Experience of 20 Japanese Companies in Belgium – 2012*. Brussels: Belgium-Japan Association & Chamber of Commerce, 2012.

BJA 2014
Belgium-Japan Association & Chamber of Commerce (BJA). *Belgium and its Neighbours' Business Climates Compared*. Brussels: Belgium-Japan Association & Chamber of Commerce, 2014.

Duus 1997
Peter Duus. "Introduction." In *The Twentieth Century*, vol. 6 of *The Cambridge History of Japan*, ed. Peter Duus, pp. 1-52. Cambridge/New York/Melbourne: Cambridge University Press, 1997.

Japan Ministry of Finance 2014
Japan Ministry of Finance. *Trade Statistics*. Tokyo: Japan Ministry of Finance, 2014.

JETRO 2012
Japan External Trade Organisation (JETRO). *Japanese Manufacturing Affiliates in Europe and Turkey – 2011 Survey*. Tokyo: JETRO, 2012.

Kōsai 1997
Yutaka Kōsai. "The Post-war Japanese Economy, 1945-1973." In *The Twentieth Century*, vol. 6 of *The Cambridge History of Japan*, ed. Peter Duus, pp. 494-537. Cambridge/New York/Melbourne: Cambridge University Press, 1997.

Shimizu 1986
Hiroshi Shimizu. *Anglo-Japanese Trade Rivalry in the Middle East in the Interwar Period*. London: Ithaca Press, 1986.

UNCTAD 2015
United Nations Conference on Trade and Development (UNCTAD). *World Investment Report*. Geneva: UNCTAD, 2015.

Van Laer 2004
Arthe Van Laer. "La Belgique renoue avec le Japon, 1945-1968." In *La diplomatie belge et l'Extrême-Orient. Trois études de cas (1930-1970)*, ed. Olivier Servais, Louis Tulkens and Arthe Van Laer, pp. 201-264. Louvain-la-Neuve: Academia Bruylant, 2004.

World Bank 2015
World Bank. *Online Data*. Washington: World Bank, 2015.

NOTES

[1] I would like to thank the following institutions and persons for their kind attention and co-operation in the preparation of this chapter: Prof. Dr Willy Vande Walle, the Belgian Embassy in Tokyo (Ms Séverine de Potter), the Belgian Foreign Trade Agency (Ms Christelle Charlier, Mr Dennis Gijsbrechts), the Belgian-Japan Association & Chamber of Commerce (Ms Anja Oto-Kellens), Flanders Investment & Trade (Mr Dirk De Ruyver, Ms Michèle Surinx).

[2] World Bank 2015.

[3] See, for instance, Van Laer 2004.

[4] Unless otherwise stated this section is based on Van Laer 2004.

[5] Kōsai 1997, pp. 522-524.

[6] Kōsai 1997, pp. 508-509.

[7] Kōsai 1997, p. 526.

[8] For details on Belgian-Japanese cotton textile competition between the World Wars, see, for instance, Shimizu 1986.

[9] Duus 1997, p. 28.

[10] World Bank 2015.

[11] World Bank 2015.

[12] BFTA 2015.

[13] Japan Ministry of Finance 2014.

[14] The Coris Bioconcept, Eurogentec, Fillfactory, Hemmis and ICOS Vision Systems testimonies in BJA 2003.

[15] The IMEC testimony in BJA 2003.

[16] BJA 1995.

[17] BJA 1995.

[18] BJA 2003.

[19] BJA 2005.

[20] BJA 1995.

[21] BJA 2005.

[22] Ann Demeulemeester and Duvel Moortgat testimonies in BJA 2003.

[23] L. De Schouwer & Co. testimony in BJA 1997.

[24] Innogenetics N.V., Janssen Pharmaceutica N.V., L. De Schouwer & Co. and UCB testimonies in BJA 1997 and Coris Bioconcept testimony in BJA 2003.

[25] Koffie F. Rombouts N.V., Janssen Pharmaceutica N.V. and Bekaert N.V. testimonies in BJA 1997.

[26] Callebaut N.V., Interbrew, Koffie F. Rombouts N.V. and L. De Schouwer & Co. testimonies in BJA 1997.

[27] Interbrew testimony in BJA 1997 and Duvel Moortgat testimony in BJA 2003.

[28] L. De Schouwer & Co. testimony in BJA 1997.

[29] Agena/Delsey and Fillfactory testimonies in BJA 2003.

[30] BJA 1995.

[31] Callebaut N.V., D.M.V. Comelco, Innogenetics N.V. and Interbrew testimonies in BJA 1997 and Agena/Delsey, Ann Demeulemeester, Coris Bioconcept, Duvel Moortgat, Eurogentec, Fillfactory, Frisk International, Hemmis and ICOS Vision Systems testimonies in BJA 2003.

[32] BJA 1995.

[33] D.M.V. Comelco testimony in BJA 1997.

[34] Callebaut N.V., Interbrew and Koffie F. Rombouts N.V. testimonies in BJA 1997.

[35] Callebaut N.V., Koffie F. Rombouts N.V. and L. De Schouwer & Co. testimonies in BJA 1997 and Agena/Delsey testimony in BJA 2003.

[36] Eurogentec testimony in BJA 2003.

[37] BARCO N.V., Innogenetics N.V. and LMS International N.V. testimonies in BJA 1997 and Eurogentec testimony in BJA 2003.

[38] Callebaut N.V., Interbrew and L. De Schouwer & Co. testimonies in BJA 1997 and Ann Demeulemeester testimony in BJA, 2003.

[39] Bekaert N.V. testimony in BJA 1997.

[40] UNCTAD 2015.

[41] UNCTAD 2015.

[42] JETRO 2012.

[43] See BJA 2000, 2006, 2012 and 2014.

[44] See Coris Bioconcept, Hemmis testimonies in BJA 2003.

THE AUTHORS

David De Cooman

David De Cooman is a research assistant at the Department of Japanese Studies, KU Leuven (2002-present), where he received his MA in Japanology in 1999 with a thesis on Japanese proverbs. Having spent two years as a research student at Kyushu University in Fukuoka (2000-2002), he is now involved in editing an online Japanese-Dutch wiki dictionary, and teaches courses at the KU Leuven on classical Japanese grammar, Kanbun, and modern Japanese vocabulary. His major fields of interest include lexicography, onomastics, premodern text translation and Japanese language history.

Henri Delanghe

Henri Delanghe holds Master degrees in history (University of Leuven) and international affairs (Columbia University) and a PhD in economic history (University of Leuven). He has worked at the United Nations and the University of Leuven and now works at the European Commission. He has published on EU science, technology and innovation policy, Japanese and Latin American economic history and Belgian-Japanese and Belgian-Latin American relations.

Dirk De Ruyver

Dirk De Ruyver is the Flemish Economic Representative for Japan and head of the Tokyo office of Flanders Investment & Trade. He holds a degree in Economic Sciences (*Licentiaat in de Economische Wetenschappen*, 1986) and a degree in Japanese Studies (*Licentiaat in de Japanologie*, 1990), both from Leuven University in Belgium. Having obtained a *Monbushō* scholarship from the Japanese Ministry of Education he improved his knowledge of Japan through studies and research work at Osaka University for Foreign Studies and Nanzan University in Nagoya (1990-92). In 2009, he was co-editor of a Japanese-English publication *The Belgian Legation in Yokohama (1874-1893)*.

Kazuko Iwamoto

Kazuko Iwamoto is professor at the Graduate School of Intercultural Studies of Kobe University. Holder of a doctoral degree in Literature (Kobe University), her main field of research is literature and the arts in the French speaking countries, with a special interest in the French literature of Belgium and the work of Stendhal. Her major publications include *Berugī to wa nanika: aidentiti no tasōsei* ベルギーとは何か─アイデンティティの多層性─ (in collaboration with others, Shōraisha 松籟社, 2013); *Shūen no bungaku: Berugī no furansu-go bungaku ni miru nashonarizumu no hensen* 周縁の文学─ベルギーのフランス語文学にみるナショナリズムの変遷─ (Shōraisha 松籟社, 2007); *Sutandāru to imōto Pōrīnu: sakka e no michi* スタンダールと妹ポーリーヌ─作家への道─ (Aoyama-sha 青山社, 2008).

Fumitaka Kurosawa

Fumitaka Kurosawa is professor of Japanese modern history at the Division of International Relations, Department of Global Social Sciences at Tokyo Woman's Christian University. His publications in Japanese include book-length studies including *Taisenkanki no Nihon rikugun* 大戦間期の日本陸軍 (Misuzu Shobō みすず書房, 2000); *Nihon Sekijyūjisha to Jindōenjo* 日本赤十字社と人道援助 (co-editor, Tōkyō Daigaku Shuppankai 東京大学出版会, 2009); *Rekishi to wakai* 歴史と和解 (co-editor, Tōkyō Daigaku Shuppankai 東京大学出版会, 2011); *Taisenkanki no kyūchū to seijika* 大戦間期の宮中と政治家 (Misuzu Shobō みすず書房, 2013); and *Futatsu no "kaikoku" to Nihon* 二つの「開国」と日本 (Tōkyō Daigaku Shuppankai 東京大学出版会, 2013).

Sadafumi Muramatsu

Sadafumi Muramatsu is emeritus professor of Meijo University who specialized in French and Belgian literature at Gakushuin University and Paris IV-Sorbonne. His main publications include studies such as *Tabi to bungaku* 旅と文学 / *Voyages et impressions littéraires* (2011); *Joruju Rōdenbakku kenkyū* ジョルジュ・ローデンバック研究 / L'Œuvre de Georges Rodenbach et son influence au Japon (2014); and translations of G. Rodenbach, including *Ki* 樹 (*L'Arbre*; 2009), and *Shiroi seishun* 白い青春 (*La Jeunesse blanche*; 2016).

Ryōju Sakurai
Ryōju Sakurai is professor at the Faculty of Foreign Studies, Reitaku University. He holds a doctoral degree in history (Sophia University, 1988) and specialized in modern Japanese history and in the modern history of Tokyo. His major publications include *Taishō seiji-shi no shuppatsu* 大正政治史の出発 (Yamakawa Shuppansha 山川出版社, 1997); *Shingai Kakumei to Nihon seiji no hendō* 辛亥革命と日本政治の変動 (Iwanami Shoten 岩波書店, 2009); *Katō Takaaki* 加藤高明 (Minerva Shobō ミネルヴァ書房, 2014); and *Kahoku chūton Nihongun* 華北駐屯日本軍 (Iwanami Shoten 岩波書店, 2015).

Keiji Shibai
Keiji Shibai graduated from the Faculty of Letters and Graduate School of Letters of Kyoto University and worked for three years as assistant professor at Kyoto University. From 1984 onwards he has been teaching Western History at Kansai University (Suita, Osaka, Japan). Since October 2016 he is president of Kansai University. Keiji Shibai published a series of essays about the methodology of history, the history of historiography and the 18th-century English historian Edward Gibbon and his family history: "Contemporary Studies of History and Quantitative Methods" (1981), "Robert Fogel and His Cliometrics" (1983), "Montesquieu and History"(1984), "Civilization and Barbarism of Edward Gibbon" (1991), "Grandfather Edward Gibbon and His Remitting Activities" (1997), "Bank of England Stock-Trading by Grandfather Edward Gibbon" (2003), "Two Letters of Hester Gibbon to Grandfather Edward Gibbon" (2011), "The Last Will and Testament of Captain John Saris" (2012), "Great Grandfather Matthew Gibbon in Papers of Office of Ordnance" (2014) and *New Introduction to History*, (new version, 2002).

Yōko Takagi
Yōko Takagi, is a professor in the Graduate School of Fashion and Living Environment Studies at Bunka Gakuen University, Tokyo. She earned her PhD in Art Science and Archaeology at the Free University of Brussels in 1999, and published her thesis in 2002, entitled: *Japonisme in Fin de Siècle Art in Belgium* (Antwerp: Pandora).

Her research focuses on the transboundary aspects of fashion and textiles from the end of the nineteenth century to the present day. She has contributed to numerous publications and curated several exhibitions, including "Katagami: Les Pochoirs Japonaise et le Japonisme" (Paris, 2006-2007), "6+ Antwerp Fashion" (Tokyo, 2009), "Feel and Think: A New Era of Tokyo Fashion" (Tokyo, 2011, Kobe, 2012 and Sydney, 2013) and "Katagami Style" (Tokyo, Kyoto and Mie, 2012).

Nathalie Vandeperre
Nathalie Vandeperre studied Sinology and Cultural Studies at the University of Leuven. She is presently curator of the East Asian collections (China – Korea – Japan) and of the Museums of the Far East (Chinese Pavilion – Japanese Tower – Museum of Japanese Art) at the Royal Museums of Art and History in Brussels. She has a particular interest in the exotic site of the Museums of the Far East and their export art collections. She contributed an important article about the site to the special 250th edition of *Arts of Asia* (2012) under the title *The King's Dream*. She curated the exhibition "Ukiyo-e. The finest Japanese prints" (Brussels, October 2016 – February 2017) and is editor of the catalogue.

W.F. Vande Walle
W.F. Vande Walle is emeritus professor of Japanese Studies at the University of Leuven. He was educated at the University of Ghent (PhD in Oriental Studies, 1976), Osaka University of Foreign Studies, and the State University of Kyoto. He did research at the Academy of Social Sciences, Beijing (1986), the Institute for Oriental and Occidental Studies, Kansai University, Osaka (1987 and 1996), the Faculty of Arts of the University of Pennsylvania (1992), and was a guest professor at the International Research Center for Japanese Studies, Kyoto (1993). His publications, in Dutch, English, French and Japanese cover a wide range of Japan-related topics, including Buddhism, Japanese diplomatic history, Sino-Japanese relations, societal issues, language, and art history. With regard to the history of Belgian-Japanese relations mention should be made here of *Japan & Belgium: Four Centuries of Exchange*. Brussels: Commissioners-General of the Belgian Government at the World Exposition of Aichi 2005, Japan, 2005, edited in collaboration with David De Cooman. Through the years he has collaborated on a number of exhibitions of Japanese art and, more particularly, he chaired the Scientific Committee of Europalia Japan 1989. In 2000 he was the first Belgian scholar to be awarded the prestigious Japan Foundation Special Prize, in

recognition of his contributions to the field of Japanese Studies. In 2006 he was decorated with the Order of the Rising Sun in recognition of his contributions as an educator and a scholar to a better understanding between Japan and Europe. In 2009 he was awarded an honorary doctorate by the University of Kansai (Osaka). In 2016 he was awarded the Yamagata Bantō Prize (Osaka).

Dimitri Vanoverbeke

Dimitri Vanoverbeke holds a PhD from Leuven University (KU Leuven) and is a professor of Japanese Studies at the Department of Area Studies there. He is director of Leuven University's Area Studies Research Unit and coordinator of its *Europe-Asia: Interactions and Comparisons* module in the Master of Arts programme in *European Studies: Transnational and Global Perspectives* (MAES). He is the executive director of the Double Degree EU-Japan Multidisciplinary Master (EU-JAMM) programme, which involves four Japanese and six European universities. His research deals with the history of judicial policymaking, the function of legal institutions and the relationship between law, politics and society in modern and contemporary Japan, as well as with regional cooperation in East Asia. Recent book-publications include: *Juries in the Japanese Legal System: The Continuing Struggle for Citizen Participation and Democracy* (London: Routledge [Asian Law Series], 2015); *The Changing Role of Law in Japan: Empirical Studies in Culture, Society and Policy Making* (Vanoverbeke, D., Ed., Maesschalck, J., Ed., Nelken, D., Ed, Parmentier, S., Ed.) (London: Edward Elgar Publishers, 2014); *EU-Japan Relations, 1970-2012: From Confrontation to Global Partnership* (Vanoverbeke, D., Ed., Keck, J., Ed., Waldenberger, F., Ed.) (London: Routledge, 2013).

Yutaka Yabuta

Yutaka Yabuta is emeritus professor of Kansai University (since 2015). He graduated as master of arts from Osaka University (1971), and earned a doctor of letters degree at Osaka University (1992). As a professor of Japanese history (Kansai University, 1990-2015), he has published numerous contributions on gender and social classes in premodern Japan both in Japanese and English, including a study on women in Tokugawa Japan (Harvard University, 2000). He was director of the Research Center for Studies of Cityscape and Cultural Heritage of Osaka (Kansai University, 2010-2015) and is

currently director of the Hyogo Prefectural Museum of History (since 2014) as well as member of the Subcommittee of Cultural Property, Agency for Cultural Affairs (since 2002).

(Utagawa) Gountei Sadahide (歌川)五雲亭貞秀 (1807-1879). 横浜鈍宅之図
Yokohama dontaku no zu (A free day in Yokohama). Triptych print in
ōban format, 1861.

Collection Koninklijke Bibliotheek van België/Bibliothèque royale de Belgique, Brussels.
The print depicts a typical Sunday in the Foreign Settlement of Yokohama. French,
Russians, Americans, Englishmen, and Dutch watch a brass band parading on the
quay. The word "dontaku" in the title is derived from Dutch "zondag." In Japanese its
meaning was widened to include any "free day." The print was based on a so-called
Nagasaki-print which depicted a similar parade of Dutchmen in Nagasaki.

COLOPHON

Concept
W.F. Vande Walle

Editor
W.F. Vande Walle

Assistant editor
David De Cooman

Contributions
David De Cooman
Henri Delanghe
Dirk De Ruyver
Kazuko Iwamoto
Fumitaka Kurosawa
Sadafumi Muramatsu
Ryōju Sakurai
Keiji Shibai
Yōko Takagi
Nathalie Vandeperre
W.F. Vande Walle
Dimitri Vanoverbeke
Yutaka Yabuta

Copy-editing
Paul Arblaster

Proofreading
Lee Preedy

Book design
Leen Depooter – quod. voor de vorm.

If you have any questions or remarks, please contact our editorial team: redactiekunstenstijl@lannoo.com.

© Lannoo Publishing, Tielt, 2016
D/2016/45/419 – NUR 654
ISBN: 9789401438421